STALIN

Man and Ruler

Robert H. McNeal

Professor of History
University of Massachusetts at Amherst

MACMILLAN PRESS in association with
St Antony's College, Oxford

First published 1988

Published by
THE MACMILLAN PRESS LTD
Houndmills, Basingstoke, Hampshire RG21 2XS
and London
Companies and representatives
throughout the world

Typeset by Wessex Typesetters
(Division of The Eastern Press Ltd)
Frome, Somerset

Printed and bound in Great Britain at
The Camelot Press Ltd, Southampton

British Library Cataloguing in Publication Data
McNeal, Robert H.
Stalin: man and ruler.—(St. Antony's/
Macmillan series).
1. Stalin, I.   2. Heads of state—
Soviet Union—Biography
I. Title   II. Series
947.084′2′0924   DK268.S8
ISBN 0-333-37351-0

For
Harold G. McNeal

Contents

List of Plates

Preface

Stalin was, and remains, a hard man to know. After pursuing him for about thirty-five years I still am not confident that I know him well. He was devious in life for sound political reasons, and left a legacy of repressed and concealed biographical records. Almost thirty-five years after his death we know the official file number of the Stalin papers in the Central Party Archive (*fond* 558), but that is all we know about this presumably vast store of information. Compared to his major contemporaries, such as Churchill, Hitler or Roosevelt, the available body of Staliniana is modest. But some important pieces of evidence are buried in obscure sources that previous researchers have not probed. One of the purposes of this book, then, is to ventilate a number of previously unused or under-used sources on Stalin.

Much of this material consists of legal, which is to say official, Soviet publications. Obviously this evidence must be treated with critical reserve, but there are some things to be said in its favour. First, there is a large body of material, for example party resolutions, that was published for operational, internal purposes of the regime rather than for propaganda. For this reason it merits guarded credibility. Second, it is reasonably well established that neither in Stalin's day nor afterwards did Soviet officialdom manufacture for publication any significant volume of documents. There is a well-known instance when the regime made some use of forged documents that inculpated certain Soviet military leaders, but it is not clear who initiated the forgery, which was in any case not circulated outside of high circles and still remains secret. The point is that the regime has resisted the temptation to invent documents showing, for example, Lenin's admiration or distaste for Stalin, depending on the period in which such an item might have been welcome. In attempting to exaggerate his role in leading the October Revolution, Stalin made do with a most inadequate short document that almost surely was not forged, rather than producing a more satisfactory piece of evidence. (Had the document been forged it surely would have been more useful to Stalin's case.) This is not to argue that deliberate lies have not been disseminated by the Soviet regime. They have been and often. But in matters pertaining to the present subject the lies, such as courtroom confessions or newspaper assertions, have not been buttressed with phony official records.

Nor is this to argue that the official records have not been sanitized by the removal of unwanted evidence. A particularly important case in point for the biography of Stalin is his *Works*. In using these thirteen volumes the researcher cannot always obtain writings or portions of writings that are believed to have existed but which were excluded from this compilation. In 1964, while preparing an annotated bibliography of Stalin's works, I came across an impressive example of such sanitary engineering. Unable to obtain in the West, Moscow or Leningrad any file of a provincial newspaper that presumably contained one piece by Stalin that had not appeared in his *Works*, I was gratified to have a bound volume of the newspaper delivered to me in the Rostov-na-Donu Public Library. Only to find that the page (and only that page) that I wanted had been neatly excised, surely by Stalin's long arm, which had preceded me in this remote library. But the majority of the papers of Stalin that appear in the *Works* can be checked against an earlier, published version, sometimes with interesting results. Apart from utilizing this kind of textual criticism, this book attempts to take a close look at key items in Stalin's papers, for example his speeches of March and December 1937, which in some respects probably reveal more than he intended.

Paradoxically, some of the important documentation on Stalin's career has escaped substantial investigation by scholars not because his regime suppressed it but because it was for many years in the glare of excessive, redundant publicity. This is the large body of material on the cult of Stalin, which, with some justification, was usually treated as junk by those who did not feel obliged to regard it with uncritical reverence. The point in studying this material is not, of course, to judge whether Stalin was the kindly, all-wise teacher, leader and friend of progressive humanity, as asserted. It is rather to describe a basic component of his system of rule, the image of Stalin. He ruled as much by the manipulation of images as by repression, and his handling of the civic cult of his own person was by no means static or uniform over the many years in which he was General Secretary of the Communist Party. Another purpose of this book, then, is to integrate the evidence of the Stalin cult into his biography. This is especially desirable because Stalin's successors have thoroughly dismantled the cult and have suppressed recollection of it. Even the partial restoration of his good name in the Soviet pantheon has carefully avoided resurrection of the embarrassing image of the super-hero Stalin. But it is too important a dimension of the Soviet and Communist experience to be banished from historical memory.

The management of official information on Stalin during and after his life inevitably encouraged a flourishing culture of unofficial rumour. Some of this folklore developed in Stalin's Gulag, the labour camps in which the inmates were more inclined to talk than their 'free' compatriots. Anecdotes and oral history achieved greater scope in the post-Stalin dissident sphere in the Soviet Union and its transplanted colonies in emigration. There is valuable evidence on Stalin's career in this material, but it is a culture that understandably did not attach great importance to the criticism of sources. Limited opportunities for research and seething moral indignation saw to that. Another aim of this book, therefore, is to subject some of the more important emigrant and underground sources on Stalin to such critical examination as circumstances permit. One means of evaluation is the checking of unofficial sources against official sources, where it seems likely that the latter are reliable. Another means is the consideration of internal consistency of the unofficial sources, when that is possible.

Finally, Stalin is an elusive, in a sense devious, man in another respect. If he was not actually as omnipotent and omniscient as his cult alleged, he was for many years extremely powerful. For this reason, his life, especially after about 1930, tends to dissolve into the general history of the Soviet system. While there is some justification for attributing to Stalin responsibility for a wide range of policies and events, it is possible to exaggerate his personal role or to make unwarranted assumptions about it. And the merging of the man and the system vitiates the purpose of biography. This book therefore attempts to pursue as closely as the sources permit the activities of one person. If this approach underrates some matters in which Stalin's involvement is highly probable but not documented, it is hoped that appraisal of his documented role in a wide range of matters will add something important to the understanding of this perplexing and extremely consequential life.

Leverett, Mass.   R. H. McN.

Acknowledgements

Having been involved for many years in the study of Stalin and his times, I am unable to recall all the people who have assisted me in one way or another and therefore regret that I cannot thank them appropriately. Just in the last few years, while working on the present book, I have become indebted to the following people for their help on a great many specific points: John L. Black, Bohdan Bociurkiw, Stephen F. Cohen, Peter Czap, Ralph Carter Elwood, George Enteen, Yuri Glazov, Robert Griffith, J. Arch Getty, Horst Herlemann, Robert Herrick, Dee Holisky, Jerry Hough, Robert E. Jones, Edward Kassinec, Galina and Robert Rothstein, Karl Ryavec, Boris Sapir, Louise Shelley, H. Gordon Skilling, William Taubman, Laszlo Tikos, Ilya Tabagua, Leo Van Rossum, Tova Yedlin. Abel Alves' careful proof-reading has spared this book many errors. Roy Doyon generously applied his cartographic expertise to the preparation of the map of Stalin's travels.

Note on Spelling and Dates

Russian proper names are spelled according to the English convention, except in the Bibliography and Notes, where they are spelled according to the simplified Library of Congress transliteration convention.

Dates prior to February 1918 are given in the Old Style, which is twelve days behind the New Style, or Western calendar, for the nineteenth century and thirteen days for the early twentieth century.

STALIN'S TRAVELS, JUNE 1918 - NOVEMBER 1920

1 - Defence of Tsaritsyn, June - Oct. 1918.

2 - Inspection of Eastern Front, Jan. 1919.

3 - Defence of Petrograd, May - June 1919.

4 - Organization of Western Front, July - Sept. 1919.

5 - Supervision of Southern Front, Oct. 1919 - Jan. 1920.

6 - Direction of Ukrainian affairs, Feb. - March 1920.

7 - Supervision of Southwestern Front, May - Aug. 1920.

8 - Organization of Soviet rule in North Caucasus and Azerbaijan, Oct. - Nov. 1920.

Generalized Travel Areas

POLES - Anti-Soviet Forces

1 Orthodoxy

In the rolling uplands of the valley of the Kura River, flanked on the northern horizon by the Caucasus Mountains, stands the Soviet Georgian city of Gori and in it a handsome, meticulously maintained marble building in the Moorish style, which contains, among other things, a haunted room. Or so the designers would have the visitor feel. This room, perhaps eight metres square, presents an eerie contrast of darkness and light, sunken in gloom except for its centre where spotlights focus on the golden face of a tranquil, strong man. This pool of brilliance is marked by a circle of white columns, the more suggestive of some kind of otherworldly shrine because they do not reach the ceiling and support nothing. The man whose spirit is thus conjured is Iosif Stalin.[1] His death mask was presumably the most striking image available to the contrivers of this necromantic, wordless memorial, and it is not a bad prop with which to convey the idea of apotheosis, more evocative than a corpse. An embalmed body had been tried for this purpose, Stalin in military uniform, lying beside and upstaging the austere remains of Lenin in the mausoleum on Red Square in Moscow. In 1961 Stalin was removed from the mausoleum for political, not aesthetic, reasons, but it may be argued that the embalmed corpse was too material, too mortal an artefact and that the death mask, displayed in ghostly splendour, really was the more impressive image.

The management of Stalin's image was no new enterprise. Not more than one hundred metres from the death mask stands the monument to his birth, which memorializes not only the beginning of his life but also the veritable industry of Staliniana. This structure was the work of Lavrenty Beria in 1935 when he was the head of the Communist Party of Georgia, not yet a member of the Politburo and director of the police apparatus of the Soviet Union.[2] The only available photograph of the cottage in which Stalin was born, taken at some date before it was incorporated into a civic shrine, shows a one-storey hovel of rough brick with a flimsy wooden lean-to garret.[3] To have preserved this intact would have dramatized the dizzying upward mobility achieved by Stalin but perhaps would have associated his image excessively with the spirit of poverty, even dirt. The architects of the shrine accordingly improved the raw material, slicing off the garret and rearranging the windows and doors on the front of the structure, perhaps annexing an adjacent hovel in the process. The resulting cottage was housed under a 'pavilion', a kind of neo-classical temple with four marble posts, each topped by a light-globe, giving an incongruous touch of modernity to the ensemble. A plaque on the wall of the cottage revealed that the 'beloved leader and teacher of

1

the peoples of the USSR and the international proletariat, the great
Stalin, was born here and lived with his parents Vissarion Ivanovich and
Ekaterina Georgevna from 1879 to 1883'.[4] At some point between
Khrushchev's attack on Stalin in 1956 and the year 1963 the original
plaque was replaced with one that omitted the reference to the 'beloved
leader and teacher'.[5]

Then, between April 1963 and May–December 1983, some authority
chose to remodel the shrine. The lamp posts on the roof of the pavilion
were removed and the front of the cottage made much more attractive by
refinishing the wall with white stucco and adding a porch with graceful
wooden pillars and railing. The once-impoverished hovel now assumed
the appearance of a charming example of Georgian folk-architecture.[6]
The plaque was changed once again, omitting any mention of the fact that
the young Stalin moved out in 1883. In the absence of such information
the visitor was permitted to believe that Iosif passed his boyhood in this
dwelling, implicitly enhancing its importance as a shrine. But there is no
reason to disbelieve the original version, which implies that Stalin, if he
was indeed born here on 21 December 1879 (or 9 December according to
the Julian calendar then in use in Russia) could not have been over four,
perhaps barely three, when he moved out. As an adult he probably had
little or no memory of the house, which he never visited after its
enshrinement. And where did the boy Soso (the Georgian diminutive of
Iosif) Dzhugashvili (his surname at birth) live after leaving his birthplace?
Only one place has been identified, and that vaguely, perhaps reluctantly,
for it was the home of an Orthodox priest named Charkviani. In the
absence of any alternative information, despite assiduous Soviet research,
it is fair to conclude that Soso spent the remainder of his years in Gori,
about ten in all, under the roof and probably the personal influence of a
clergyman. Soviet writings in the time of Stalin's eminence were
exceedingly reticent in discussing religion in his boyhood, so it is hard to
appraise the influence of Father Charkviani on Soso, but it may have
been considerable.[7]

Soso's parents were as obscure and impoverished as the town of Gori.
The father, Vissarion, was a cobbler by trade, a hard-drinking man who
on occasion would sell even his belt to raise the price of a bottle, probably
the firey spirits distilled from the grape that the Georgians call 'cha-cha'.[8]
He tried to make a living as an independent artisan, failed and when Soso
was five went off to Tbilisi, the major city of Georgia, about 75 km to the
east; here he found employment in the Adelkhanov shoe factory. As a
young adult, writing a political tract, the future Stalin used his father's
experience to illustrate the way in which capitalism transforms the *petit
bourgeois* artisan into a proletarian. In this version the worker, having
gone to the factory with hopes of saving money and returning to his own
business, becomes disillusioned, joins a labour union and absorbs socialist

ideas. But there is no reason to think that Vissarion's dismal career was edified by any such awakening. On the contrary he seems to have been so attracted to the life of the factory worker that he tried to impose it on his son, then a boy of about ten. Although the details of Soso's career as a factory worker remain unclarified, it seems that he worked as an odd-job hand in the Adelkhanov factory for perhaps as much as a year.[9]

That he did not spend his life as a factory worker was in large measure the achievement of his mother, Ekaterina, née Geladze, a pious and hardworking woman who had lost two previous infants and was determined that her last-born would escape the round of ignorance, poverty and toil. Her hopes were threatened by narrow escapes during Soso's childhood, smallpox, which scarred his face, and blood poisoning. The family was too poor to afford treatment by a physician and went to a folk-herbalist to deal with these illnesses. This may have resulted from another near-calamity when the lad was struck by a carriage while watching a religious festival and was carried away injured. Iosif emerged from these childhood illnesses with a permanently stiffened left arm.[10]

Ekaterina saw education, and specifically a clerical vocation, as an upward path for her son. Not that this was mere calculation on her part. Ekaterina was a devout believer, and not long before her death in 1937 she said that she wished that her son had become a priest. If, as is quite well established, Soso was a pious boy, this owed much to the influence of his devoted mother. That she was able to enrol him in the four-year elementary school that the Orthodox Church maintained in Gori probably owed something to her influence with Father Charkviani. At this time she was living in his home and probably working there as a servant, for there is ample testimony that she toiled as a house-cleaner, a laundress and seamstress. After Soso had passed the first two grades of school with great success their circumstances were slightly improved by a grant of a stipend of three roubles a month, perhaps as much as his mother earned in cash.[11] 'His mother loved him to distraction', one of his schoolmates recalled, 'Despite her meagre pay she did not stint on Soso's clothing. The boy wore good boots, a coat of sturdy broadcloth. I recall even his winter hood, which was homemade. Iosif always dressed immaculately, precisely.' This impression is confirmed by the school photograph, which shows not only a scrubbed and combed Soso but in general a group that strove for middle-class westernized cultural standards.[12] 'He studied excellently,' Ekaterina told a Soviet journalist in 1935, 'but his father, my late husband Vissarion, intended to take the boy from school in order to teach him the cobbler's trade. I objected as much as I could, even quarrelled with my husband, but it didn't help. The husband insisted on having his way.' Indeed, this was certainly not the first fight in the Dzhugashvili household. Years later Stalin told his daughter that Vissarion beat Ekaterina, and on one occasion he came to his mother's aid by throwing a knife at his father. Only by hiding with some neighbours did he escape paternal wrath.[13]

Vissarion's decision to take Soso to Tbilisi when his son was aged about ten probably accounts for the fact that this excellent student required six years to finish a four-year course, although illness may have been involved in the delay.[14] In any case it was Ekaterina who won out. 'After some time I succeeded all the same in enrolling him again in school', she recalled, and Soso's return to Gori probably marked the end of his active relationship with his father. Vissarion lived on until 1909, a tramp towards the end of his life, his death in Tbilisi perhaps the result of a stabbing in a tavern brawl.[15] Meanwhile Soso pursued his education with gratifying success, earning the highest grade on the scale, five, in sacred history, modern history, catechism, divine service, church Slavonic, Georgian, geography, handwriting and church singing. Several memoirists mention his gift as a singer, an important talent for an Orthodox priest, whose principal public role is to chant the service. On one occasion the school choir-master supposedly postponed a concert because Soso could not make the time. Only in Greek and arithmetic did he receive a grade as low as four.[16]

Consistent excellence in subjects connected with Orthodox Christianity was not mere careerism in Soso. This pupil in the Gori Ecclesiastical Seminary was a zealous believer, a point never stressed in official Soviet writing and, evidently, never mentioned by Stalin to his daughter, who believed that he 'never had any religious faith'. But the very reticence in official Staliniana concerning his boyhood piety lends credibility to the bits of evidence that escaped the inconsistent vigilance of some Soviet editors. There is, for example, the testimony of a schoolmate named Glurdzhidze, who in 1939 was asked to recall what he could of his illustrious friend and had no motive to falsify when he said that 'he was very believing [less literally, 'a firm believer'], punctually attending all the divine services, was the leader of the church choir. I remember that he not only performed the religious rites but also always reminded us of their meaning.'[17]

Another schoolmate, one Ramadze, also interviewed in 1939, concurs on this question of piety in connection with an exceptional event in 1892, a triple public hanging of three brigands from the mountains. Ramadze's recollections are all the more persuasive because they differ from the version of this event that appeared in a large-circulation volume of 1939. In that account one learns that the teachers at the seminary took the pupils to the morbid spectacle in order to terrorize them, that the boys were deeply depressed, moved to tears, that Soso was among them and was greatly agitated. Ramadze, however, tells a different story, and one cannot but wonder how, in the wake of the great terror of the later 1930s, he was thanked for his innocent recollections. As he recalls, the school authorities had nothing to do with Soso's attendance at the hanging; Dzhugashvili and four comrades simply decided to go. What they saw turned out to be not exactly a triple hanging, for the authorities commuted the sentence of one man. But they then proceeded, inadvertently, to compensate for this by hanging one victim twice, the rope having broken on the first try. Far from expressing horror or indignation, Soso watched it all with equanimity. This was not psychological aberration, merely normal adjustment to a tough society. It was on their walk home that the religious meaning of the events emerged. The boys debated the question of whether the deceased would be punished by eternal fire. 'Soso Dzhugashvili resolved our doubts: "They", he said thoughtfully, "have already borne punishment, and it would be unjust on the part of God to punish them again." ' This was not only a believer, and a leader in his circle, but a lad with firm confidence in the orthodoxy of his opinions.[18]

The church authorities in Gori displayed no doubts about their pupil's Orthodoxy when they recommended him to the seminary in Tbilisi, which he entered in September 1894. This building still stands on one of the main squares of the city, in excellent repair and open to the public as an art museum. While no architectural masterpiece, it is a respectable example of the official neo-classical style of the Russian Empire. Against the predominantly yellow stucco background a white-columned portico over the main entrance asserts pomp and power, and a white frieze seeks to lighten the impression of the two wings that extend rearward in a 'V', following two streets that radiate from the square. In its interior three high-ceilinged storeys are connected by a broad staircase with marble steps. It seems that the most spacious room, two storeys high, was the chapel, while the opposite wing, with its thirty-one large windows on each side of each floor, contained living quarters for the seminarians. Today these spacious, well-lit and ventilated rooms show no sign on the parquet floor of former partitioning into separate cubicles, so we may believe the former seminarian Gogokhia when he writes that the students lived in open dormitory chambers in groups of twenty or thirty. These were comfortable, if not private, quarters, not inferior to accommodation at many privileged private boarding-schools in Britain or America. Apart from icons and other religious decorations that have long since vanished, there is nothing religious about this edifice, but it is substantial, and in the setting of a small and impoverished provincial city it projected authority and importance. Surely these pretensions affected the young Iosif Dzhugashvili when he entered the seminary, probably helping to form his idea of a style appropriate to a powerful Empire. If the official architecture of the Soviet Union in the 1930s turned away from the stark modernism that had been associated with revolutionary style in the 1920s and returned to porticoes and friezes, this may well have reflected the impressions that Stalin had acquired in his youth.[19]

The revival of traditional pedagogy in the Soviet Union in the 1930s, following a decade of radical modernism, also may reflect Stalin's respect for the education that he had received in the seminary, which offered solid, old-fashioned classes in mathematics, Greek, Latin, Russian literature, history, Old Slavonic and theology. While the mature Stalin replaced the last-named subject with 'dialectical materialism', and added courses on the natural sciences, he evidently had no basic quarrel with the kind of education he received at the seminary. In 1931 he complained to the interviewer Emil Ludwig about the spying of the priests on the students, but not about the quality or the style of the education. Though the level of his scholarly performance declined, compared to his record at Gori, this appears to reflect his growing preoccupation with illicit extracurricular activities rather than contempt for the curriculum.[20] Because there were very few secondary schools and no universities in Russian Transcaucasia at this time, the seminary had attracted many who had no religious vocation but simply found it the best education that was accessible to them. In particular, young Georgians who were experiencing a nationalist awakening turned up there. For a number of years before Iosif's arrival there had been intermittent student protests against the administration, partly concerning the heavy-handed Russification that the curriculum imposed. For the newcomer from Gori to be drawn into the stream of Georgian nationalist dissidence in the seminary was natural enough.[21]

The unequal confrontation of Georgian and Russian national cultures was an unavoidable fact of life for any ambitious Georgian youth. Should one give up one's ethnic heritage, including a rich language, in order to gain advancement in the larger world of the Russian Empire? Many non-Russians in this multinational realm, including most members of the former ruling family of Georgia, the Bagrations, were willing to make this sacrifice. Indeed, one of the great strengths of the Russian Empire was its ability to attract many of the privileged or talented people from the diverse non-Russian cultures that made up about half the total population of the Empire. Apart from the powerful intrinsic appeal of Russian culture, the alternative of remaining resolutely Georgian (or Polish, Uzbek and so on) implied the loss of most opportunities for career advancement in one's native area, because the civil service, the schools and even, in Georgia, the Orthodox Church were in the hands of Russians and required a degree of Russification, starting with the language. Iosif Dzhugashvili had started his career in Gori by making at least the minimum compromise by beginning to learn the Russian language, probably starting with some tutoring from a neighbour before he started school.[22] His success in learning Russian is attested by his survival in a school that operated in this language, and one fellow-pupil in Gori recalls how hard Iosif worked on this, 'how absolutely flawlessly he wrote in

Russian, what clear handwriting he cultivated on his own'. That this is not mere reverence is evidenced by samples of Stalin's adult handwriting in Russian, now on display in the museum in Gori.[23] True, he retained for life a Georgian accent, hard for my non-Russian ear to follow in recorded speeches, partly because he tended to swallow his case-endings, hoping (as I have done when speaking Russian) that this would cover his uncertainties concerning the mysteries of Russian grammar. The persistence of an accent is natural, considering that he learned Russian among other Georgians and for many years spoke it with other non-Russians.

But while Iosif was learning Russian in Gori he was reading poetry and fiction in his native Georgian, specifically the nationalist writing of Rustaveli, Eristavi, Chavchavadze and Kazbegi. Their exaltation of the Georgian nation did not contradict Iosif's religious beliefs, for Orthodox Christianity, dating back to the fourth century – when the Slavs were still pagan – was an integral part of the Georgian national heritage. A Georgian patriot might feel outrage concerning the Russification that was occurring within the Orthodox Church, but this was a quarrel within eastern Christianity. For example, Prince Ilia Chavchavadze, a major figure in the rise of Georgian nationalism, merged this doctrine and Christianity in a poem entitled 'The Hermit, A Legend'.[24] Young Dzhugashvili not only read these works but also imitated their romantic nationalist style in his own maiden literary efforts, which he submitted to Chavchavadze as editor of a journal. Five of his poems appeared in this publication, a sixth in another journal, when Iosif was only fifteen.[25] This was not incredibly precocious: the Georgian nationalist intelligentsia was small, and the editors of its literary organs could not have been flooded with submissions in the mid-1890s. For that matter, the practice of publishing, without remuneration, the work of local poets in newspapers and magazines of many countries was widespread in the nineteenth century. The poems read very much like those by Chavchavadze and his contemporaries, marked by romantic effusions concerning the Georgian homeland, its natural beauties and even 'the providence of the Almighty'. That his literary gifts in his native tongue were adequate for this kind of expression is implied by a memoirist who knew him a few years later and in time came to regard him as a betrayer of his homeland and also of socialism, one David Sagirashvili. Referring to his first meeting with Iosif around 1900, he recalled, 'He spoke exceptionally pure Georgian. His diction was clear, and his conversation betrayed a lively sense of humour.'[26]

One dimension of Dzhugashvili's interest in Georgian poetry was the image of the hero, partly imbibed from *the* Georgian poem, the twelfth-century folk-epic of Shota Rustaveli, *The Knight in the Tiger's Skin*. Iosif surely read this classic in his days at elementary school, and he retained

an affection for it all his life. A meandering tale of romantic love and the
intrepid loyalty of two superman-heroes, it has spoken to all patriotic
Georgians, so it is hard to demonstrate that it made some special mark on
Stalin or inspired him to propagate his own heroic myth.[27] It might,
however, be significant that in the 1930s the eminent Georgian artist I. M.
Toidze made the two heroes of the poem into idealized clones of the two
famous sons of Soviet Georgia at that time, Stalin and Ordzhonikidze.
Did he dare do this without obtaining permission? And one might wonder
if Stalin, rereading the poem in the 1930s attached special importance to
some vivid references in it to treachery as the bane of great heroes: 'I
heard treachery planned for you . . . these men are traitors to thee', and
so on. It is at least demonstrated from manuscript materials on display in
the Stalin museum that in the late 1930s he personally edited a translation
of *The Knight* from Georgian into Russian by Sh. Nutsubidze, whose
request for permission to acknowledge Stalin's assistance was denied.[28]

But there were other cultural influences competing with Georgian
nationalism in Dzhugashvili's seminary days. Assuming that it was a
foundation for loyalty to the Empire, the authorities required the
seminarians to acquire a really good working knowledge of Russian.
Among Georgians this provided access through translations into Russian
of a wide world of literature that otherwise might have been unknown to
them. Iosif, for example, never learned western languages, except for
some self-taught German when he was in his early thirties, but by 1896 he
was caught reading in Russian translation a variety of forbidden western
books, novels by Hugo and Thackeray, general works on culture and the
social sciences.[29] The reading itself and the conflict that the possession of
these forbidden books provoked between Iosif and the cleric-teachers
soon led him to the final break with the faith of his ancestors. One cannot
place the precise time of this breach. There might even be something to
the recollections of his schoolmate in both Gori and Tbilisi, Glurdzhidze,
that Iosif read something by or about Darwin when they were still in
elementary school, but this sounds like the kind of idealized revolutionary
precocity that one would expect of propagandists in the year 1939. Much
more juvenile and credible is the same person's recollection of an
experimental test of God's powers that Iosif conducted in the Tbilisi
Seminary. And if this anecdote is true, the one about Darwin seems all
the more suspect. 'In the Seminary they [the priests] frightened us, if you
please,' recalls Glurdzhidze, 'with the story that if we took communion
unprepared [that is, without prior fasting], we would be burned by fire [at
once, not in eternity]. Once before communion Iosif proposed to me that
instead of fasting we eat "khashi" [a dish made of entrails] in order to see
if such fire would appear on us. We ate a solid meal and, of course,
nothing happened to us. "There, you see," said Iosif, "there's evidence of
the worthlessness of the priests' chatter." '[30]

A completely convinced atheist scarcely needs such experiments to 'prove' the non-existence of God, and it suggests something about the literal, rather mechanical character of Iosif's mind that he found the test necessary or convincing. It seems to suggest a dogmatic inclination that is common enough among true believers. Truth for them is indivisible and absolute. Such a person in casting off one orthodoxy seeks for a replacement, in this case one compatible with 'scientific atheism'. Such a system of belief was at hand, was received and remained Dzhugashvili's orthodoxy for life. The practical experience of politics might in time encourage in him a considerable level of cynicism concerning men, but it did not preclude a persistent adherence to his own orthodoxy, which in the course of time he called 'Marxism–Leninism'.

It is impossible to determine exactly when the seminarian transferred his allegiance to Marxism. The official version that Stalin established in an interview in 1931 is that 'I joined the revolutionary movement when 15 years old, when I became connected with underground groups of Russian Marxists then living in Transcaucasia.'[31] This might be an exaggeration of his radical precocity, but if one takes into account that he was fifteen until almost the mid-point of his second year in the seminary and that the kind of connection with revolutionaries is not specified, it does not challenge credibility. Quite possibly the first contacts with radicals were in a bookshop run by one Chelidze, a place frequented by young intellectuals, including seminarians, Dzhugashvili among them. Chelidze recalls that Iosif came there to read and occasionally joined in a sociable game of cards for small stakes. The absence of any pretentious political claims on behalf of Iosif makes this account plausible, although, incidentally, it casts doubt on assertions by others that the seminary authorities hardly ever let their charges off the premises. The idea of a gradual introduction to radicals and radicalism was suggested by Stalin himself in another interview, which he gave to an admiring American visitor, Jerome Davis, in 1926.

> It is difficult to describe the process. First one becomes convinced that existing conditions are wrong and unjust. Then one resolves to do the best one can to remedy them. Under the Tsar's regime any attempt genuinely to help the people put one outside the pale of the law; one found himself hunted and hounded as a revolutionist.[32]

In the Russian Empire the traditional starting point for any dissident political movement was the *kruzhok* or discussion circle. This had been true in the earlier part of the nineteenth century when intellectuals had attempted first to formulate a critique of the existing order, then to consider ways of leading a peasant revolt. So it was in the 1890s when Marxism first began to attract substantial support among the radicals. At this stage such informal, small groups had to devote much of their effort

simply to learn something of Marxist theory. Especially in a provincial
centre like Tbilisi there was very little pertinent reading matter at hand, a
few works of Marx and Engels in Russian translation, some publications
of Georgi Plekhanov, who resided in Switzerland, and some writings by
the new generation of Russian Marxists. Just what from this modest
assortment was available to the Tbilisi circles that Iosif joined in 1896 is
hard to know. If broad and deep learning in Marxist theory really were a
precondition for an active Marxist political movement, then the whole
enterprise never would have amounted to much in any country. At least
Iosif and his comrades must have been able to absorb the basic idea of the
struggle between oppressing capitalists and the oppressed proletariat, and
this was ample to sustain their commitment. Having made some progress
in such studies, in August 1898 Iosif joined an organization that was
attempting to move beyond mere 'circle' activity to political action among
the workers of Tbilisi, the so-called 'Third Group'. In undertaking this
activity, which exposed him to the risk of arrest, Dzhugashvili had need
of a pseudonym and chose 'Koba'. This was somewhat pretentious, for
that was the name of the hero of a well-known romantic nationalist
Georgian novel by Alexander Kazbegi, *The Patricide*. It is possible that
Soso had been called Koba as a lad in Gori, having been impressed then
by this heroic figure, but it is unlikely that he was called that in his
seminary days. A revolutionary could not conceal his identity from the
police by using his well-established nickname. 'Koba' was the first of
many cover-names which he utilized in the following years, but the only
one, apart from 'Stalin', that stuck. At least a few of his old friends still
called him 'Koba' in the years of his eminence.[33]

In connection with the Third Group he led a Marxist study circle
among the railway workers. He was only eighteen, but even partly
educated activists were few enough, and the movement was accustomed
to look for fresh talent among the seminarians, for several of its leaders
had studied there. If the seminary and police authorities had known of
this, they surely would have done something about Koba, but in fact he
was allowed to continue his studies until almost the end of his fifth year.
By this time the friction between the disaffected seminarian and the
clerical authorities reached a crisis over issues that were less serious than
active revolutionary organizing. Iosif continued to be found in possession
of forbidden, but not Marxist or overtly political, books, and he was
punished in juvenile fashion by incarceration in a detention room in the
seminary for a few hours at a time. Becoming fed up with all this, Koba
informed a visiting inspector of schools that he was 'dissatisfied with the
regime in the seminary'. This regime reciprocated the antagonism and in
May 1899 ended the career of Iosif Dzhugashvili in Orthodox Christianity
by expelling him from the school.[34]

2 Underground

That Dzhugashvili was not yet considered a political criminal when he left the seminary is implied by the first surviving document of any sort in his own handwriting. This is a neat list of temperature readings that he compiled for 2 and 12 January 1901 as an employee of the Tbilisi Physical Institute, a state agency that presumably would not hire known subversives.[1] His comrades in the Marxist movement also seem not to have considered him one of the handful of professionals, for he was not yet subsidized from their meagre resources and had to have a job. It was not demanding work and gave him time to continue his underground propagandizing of industrial workers. If one may believe one of them, Sergei Alliluev, who in 1918 became Stalin's father-in-law, young 'Soso' Dzhugashvili was the main organizer of a May Day gathering of workers in 1900.[2] This was not what one would call a demonstration, because the estimated crowd of 500 made their way in small clusters at night or early morning to a deserted place near a monastery some eight miles outside Tbilisi, chosen by the ex-seminarian for security. Here they could in privacy unfurl a red banner bearing the portraits of Marx and Engels, sing the *Marseillaise* and listen to several speakers. The last of these was Dzhugashvili, making his début as an orator. Even in 1946, well into the era of the Stalin cult, Alliluev did not note that the speech was a particular success, even though the audience, he recalled, was full of revolutionary fervour. Nevertheless it is fair to guess that the meeting helped to establish Dzhugashvili as a force in the Georgian labour movement.

It also probably helped to attract the attention of the police. On 21 March 1901 they searched his lodgings at the observatory, but did not arrest him. One week later he decided to go underground.[3] Henceforth he was a professional revolutionary, and, excepting periods as a prisoner of the regime, he presumably lived on such meagre means as the movement could provide. Dzhugashvili looks ill-nourished and impoverished in photographs from these years, dressed in a worn black coat that presumably belonged to a bourgeois suit but was never accompanied by a necktie. The moustache of later fame appears in some photographs from this time, and in others he has not shaved at all.[4]

With this deliberately scruffy appearance went personal mannerisms that were by turns good-humoured and abrasive. A Georgian whom Stalin later drove into exile recalls how, as a lad of eleven, he met 'the man they call Koba' and found in his conversation 'a lively sense of humour' and also a sense of rigid ideological commitment. Koba abruptly interrupted the conversation of the small company by rising, patting the boy on the head, saying that he 'hoped I would choose the road of common struggle for a brighter future', and walking out. Similarly the owner of a left-wing bookshop who knew the young Dzhugashvili recalled that he had 'joked a lot, telling various funny tales of seminary life', but had refused to attend the church wedding of the store-owner because even this gesture of friendship would have offended his ideological scruples. Another who knew him from his seminary days remembered the same rigidity when Iosif refused to observe the social convention of exchanging kisses with fellow-students when they met at the end of summer holidays. 'I don't want to be a pharisee', said Iosif, 'and kiss those that don't love me.'[5]

The difficult side of the youth's personality probably was involved in his departure from Tbilisi to the city of Batumi on the Black Sea in November 1901.[6] Connected with the acerbic personality was a penchant for the kind of tactics that would appeal to a dogmatic young militant, but may have appeared premature, or simply frightening, to some of his comrades. Official Soviet accounts in Stalin's day credited him with the application of aggressive tactics on May Day 1901, this time holding a demonstration in Tbilisi itself rather than some rural setting. This resulted in a number of casualties when the authorities dispersed the crowd by sending in a contingent of Cossacks. Koba was pleased with this result. Later in the year he published in the second issue of the illegal organ of the movement in Tbilisi an article extolling clashes of this sort. 'The sacrifices we make today in street demonstrations will be compensated a hundredfold. Every militant who falls in the struggle or is torn out of our ranks [by arrest] rouses hundreds of new fighters.' This, he said, is so because the combat would attract the attention of 'curious onlookers', who would feel the lash of the repressing forces, which would attack everyone in sight, 'conforming to "complete democratic equality" '. Only 'two or three years' of such 'Pyrrhic victories' would bring about a 'people's revolution', the 'death warrant' of the government.[7] Arriving in Batumi in late 1901, Koba set about putting such ideas into practice. According to a Soviet account of 1937 he successfully arranged an open confrontation between workers and troops, which led to a fusillade and the death of fourteen demonstrators. The account gains credibility because it does not attempt to show that Koba stood heroically in the ranks of the workers.[8] He survived unscathed and was arrested several weeks later, remaining in jail from April 1902 until 'autumn' 1903 when the regime decided to exile him to Siberia for three years.[9]

This was the standard term of 'internal exile', the means by which the police sought to neutralize political suspects whom they did not want to bring to trial. After being held in prison while the case was being decided, the radical would be sent to some locality, perhaps in Siberia, to live as a sort of parolee, receiving a small living allowance from the state. Koba

arrived at his place of exile, Novaia Uda, about 230 km from Irkutsk, at
that time the terminus of the Trans-Siberian Railway, on 27 November
1903 and left illegally on 5 January 1904. In an earlier attempt to escape
via Irkutsk he was forced back by frostbite. Having obtained better
clothing, he made it on the second try. His entire trip back to
Transcaucasia took five or six weeks, mainly in getting from Novaia Uda
to the railway, travelling only by night in a sledge, the driver of which
accepted payment only in vodka. Once on board a train it was possible to
get from Irkutsk to the European end of the Trans-Siberian Railway in
just over one week.[10]

Koba had been out of political action for almost two years, and in that
time there had been a fundamental change in the politics of the Russian
Empire. Since the 1860s there had been a fairly continuous revolutionary
movement but no Empire-wide political party. The first generation of
activists believed that Russia, an an overwhelmingly agrarian land, should
have a social and political revolution based on the peasant population, the
narod (literally 'the people'). Intellectuals could perhaps inspire this
upheaval by means of terrorism, and a wave of assassinations culminated
in the death of Tsar Alexander II in 1881. But this brought not revolution,
only repression and consequent depression among the radicals. In the
1890s, however, their optimism revived, partly because of the emergence
of a new generation of radical intellectuals, among them a man who came
to be known as Lenin. He, like many of his cohort, drew inspiration from
Marxism. Previously Russian radicals had admired Marx and Engels as
prophets of western European revolution against industrial capitalism,
but did not consider this directly pertinent to peasant society in Russia.
Marx and Engels themselves had shown at least some approval of the idea
that Russia could pass directly from its pre-capitalist condition to socialism
without experiencing full-blown capitalism, thanks to the collectivist values
of Russian peasant society. Adherents of this tradition organized a 'Party
of Socialist-Revolutionaries' in the early twentieth century and competed
with the Marxists until the latter crushed these 'neo-narodniks' after the
Revolution of 1917. But the other trend of Russian socialism held that the
Empire of the tsars was already becoming capitalist and in due course
would undergo a proletarian revolution. Such was the doctrine of
Plekhanov, who first embraced this doctrine in 1883, followed by Lenin
and others in the next decade. A few pockets of industrialism were indeed
growing in Russia, and the new class of workers showed much more
interest in strikes and demonstrations than the peasantry had ever
displayed.

In the mid-1890s the Russian Marxists moved beyond the traditional
organizational form of discussion circles and established committees on a
city-wide basis in such centres as St Petersburg. They succeeded in
reaching workers, organizing strikes and by the close of the decade were

determined to form an illegal Empire-wide party. The first effort to do so occurred in 1898 when Dzhugashvili was still a seminarian, but it consisted of only a few activists, most of whom were arrested soon after the 'First Congress'. The main achievement of the Congress was the adoption of a 'Manifesto', written by an important Marxist intellectual, Peter Struve. This called attention to a problem that was to plague Russian Marxism for years: 'The further east one goes in Europe, the more cowardly, mean and politically weak is the bourgeoisie, and the greater are the cultural and political tasks of the proletariat.'[11] Traditional Marxism held that 'bourgeois democracy' would prevail under capitalism, and that this was the regime that the proletariat would overthrow. But how could this come about in Russia, given the weakness of its bourgeoisie? Struve replied that the proletariat would have to play a major role in overthrowing the tsarist, 'feudal', regime. But if the proletariat succeeded in this, would it meekly hand power to the despised bourgeoisie and then retire to await a later revolution after capitalism had outlived its day? At the opening of the century none of the Russian Marxists had confronted this question. This became clear in 1903 when a Second Congress of the Social-Democratic Party convened in Brussels, finishing its work in London. The 'Programme' adopted at this assembly still regarded the coming revolution as the overthrow of 'our old pre-capitalist order', 'tsarist autocracy', leading to the establishment of a 'democratic republic', a form of capitalism ameliorated by such measures as an eight-hour day and old-age insurance.[12] Organizationally the Congress was a serious affair, consisting of fifty-seven delegates representing twenty underground and eleven emigrant groups. Its size owed much to Lenin. He had collaborated with Plekhanov and one of the younger Marxists, Yuli Martov, in publishing in emigration *Iskra (The Spark)*, which advocated the convocation of a second congress to found a united, effective party. In a seminal essay of 1902, *What Is to be Done?*, Lenin emphasized that this party should consist of professional revolutionaries who alone could give the proletariat the leadership that is needed, if it was to move beyond mere 'trade-union consciousness'.[13] This conception turned out to be divisive, splitting the party congress between Leninists, who wanted a relatively small, élite party, and adherents of Lenin's erstwhile friend Martov, who favoured the recruitment of a mass party of workers. Since Lenin narrowly won one of the votes that pitted these factions against one another, he claimed the label 'Bolshevik' (majority-ite) and consigned his opponents to the status of 'Menshevik' (minority-ite).[14]

As these labels imply, the internal politics of the Social-Democratic party was assumed to be parliamentary and democratic, a concensus that was embodied in the 'Statutes' of the new party. So far from dictatorship was this constitution that it did not even provide for any chief executive post. The practice of more or less parliamentary politics within the party occupied Lenin, and Stalin too, for many years to come. As long as the forms of parliamentary democracy retained any vitality within the party, its leaders would have to deal with some form of opposition and with the winning of votes in this or that party body. This was not an occupation that Lenin or Stalin relished, and in the long run the democratic aspects of internal party life became empty ritual. But this decline took many years and much effort. In the shorter run Lenin and his rivals struggled inconclusively to gain the upper hand in the party and in so doing managed to split it into two separate organizations with rival publications, conventicles and local underground groups. Thus from infancy the Russian Marxist movement was engaged in two struggles, externally against the regime and internally, comrade against comrade.

When Koba returned from Siberia to Transcaucasia in the winter of 1904, he spent several months touring the area in secret to appraise the situation in the movement and to decide where he would fit in. He visited Tbilisi, Batumi, Kutaisi and his native Gori. Here he stayed not with his mother, who was said to be weeping with worry 'over her Soso', but with his uncle, one Gio Geladze.[15] At first it was not clear to the local activists that the disagreements at the Second Party Congress had produced a serious split. It took time for the rival leaders to begin the production of polemics and for these to be smuggled into Russia and distributed to the outlying regions. But Koba already was a Bolshevik in the sense that he was committed to a hard, militant revolutionary line, which set him apart from most Georgian Social-Democrats, who in the long run turned out to be a major element in the Menshevik movement. One of those who became a Menshevik, and eventually a refugee from Stalin, recalled meeting him at this time:

> a young man, dry, boney, with pale brown hair, pockmarked, with a lively and shrewd gaze, animated, free-and-easy, self-sufficient. With his first words he began to point out the several defects, which, in his opinion, existed in our literature: he did not care for the insufficiently militant tone of the leaflets.

In Tbilisi Koba offended the local Marxist committee by not calling on them, no doubt regarding them as hopelessly moderate, but instead going directly to some of the activists among the ordinary industrial workers and proposing to them some kind of radical action. But he received such a poor reception that he gave it up and stalked out of the meeting. At this or a similar meeting he 'insulted everybody in the room, calling them "petit-bourgeois", then left with two or three of his followers'.[16]

As an odd man out among the less militant Marxists, it was even more certain that Koba would opt for the Bolsheviks when the time came for choosing sides. He probably knew of Lenin by this time, but one has to discount stories of much later years that depict Lenin and Stalin as veritable partners in revolution from this early period. There are, however, two letters from Koba to an *émigré* Georgian Marxist, M. Davitashvili, which place him in the Bolshevik camp in the fall of 1904. And when the Georgian Menshevik Arsenidze met Koba at the beginning of 1905 he found 'an orthodox, convinced Leninist, repeating the arguments and thoughts of his teacher with gramophone-like accuracy'. Coming from an opponent, this description, apart from the sarcastic tone, is all that Stalin's latter-day propagandists could desire to demonstrate Stalin's Leninism.[17]

Given the factional split, Koba now directed his militancy as much against the Mensheviks as the regime, no doubt reasoning that one must set the party straight before one could make a revolution.[18] This assumption seriously hampered Lenin and his followers during the real revolutionary upheaval that began in January 1905 when the tsar's soldiers shot a large number of workers who were demonstrating in St Petersburg for improved material and political conditions. In the course of that year the anti-regime activity of workers, peasants, students, soldiers, sailors and even professional people grew steadily. For some months the authorities seemed paralysed, fearing to drown in blood the demands for democratic reforms. They first promised limited measures, such as a consultative assembly, but could not pacify the public so easily. By October 1905 the capital was virtually under the control of a 'Soviet (council) of Workers' Deputies', workers were arming and the loyalty of the tsar's forces was in doubt. In desperation the tsar promised to establish a parliament (Duma) in which all classes would be represented (not necessarily equally) and to grant the people the rights of free expression and association. By this time many middle-class people were frightened by the rising social revolution, and the tsar's promises won over some of the liberals. Moreover, the regime regained a degree of self-confidence in November–December 1905 and successfully suppressed the soviets in St Petersburg, with no serious resistance, and in Moscow, with bloody street fighting.

The most visible leader of the St Petersburg Soviet was Trotsky, a man the same age as Koba who had been a protégé of Lenin but had broken with the Bolsheviks in 1903. For his part, Lenin was able to accomplish little in the revolution of 1905. But these two Marxists shared the belief that the end of the old regime was at hand, and both believed that the next stage need not be mere 'bourgeois democracy'. Lenin proposed that the new regime should be 'the revolutionary dictatorship of the proletariat and peasantry'.[19] Trotsky also concluded that some kind of workers' regime must follow directly from the overthrow of tsarism, with no intervening bourgeois stage – an 'uninterrupted [later called 'permanent'] revolution'. But he attached his hopes not to an alliance of the Russian workers and peasants but rather to the assistance of a proletarian revolution in the West.[20] Years later Stalin was to make effective use of this difference between the formulations of Lenin and Trotsky although it could be argued that their similarities were more significant at the time.

In this period Koba adhered to a staunchly Bolshevik, militant line, and in October 1905 won the warm praise of Lenin for an article that had come to the attention of the leader. For a short time in late October and early November he seems to have believed that the overthrow of the tsar was at hand. He urged the people to arm: 'The great Russian Revolution is beginning!'[21] In Georgia Koba was far from successful in promoting this violent line, for here the less belligerent Mensheviks had established themselves as the predominant party among all contenders. All the Georgian deputies to the four successive Dumas which sat between 1906 and 1916 were Mensheviks. The frustration of being a rejected leader among his own people surely helped to toughen Koba's already-combative nature, to harden his animosity toward any sort of democratic politics.

In Georgia Koba soon established a reputation as a nasty antagonist. Arsenidze recalls that the phrase 'a Menshevik Koba' was used to indicate any disagreeable comrade in that faction. There are various tales of his abrasive, disruptive conduct at Social-Democratic meetings of either faction. On one occasion the chairman called his behaviour 'indecent', to which Koba replied that he had not yet dropped his pants. Reproached, he soon stalked out of the meeting. In the same crude tone he referred to Martov and other Menshevik leaders as 'circumcised Yids'.[22] According to another account, he told a gathering that Marx was a 'son of an ass' (a choice epithet in Georgian) if the master had in fact written something or other that an opponent quoted against Koba. Meeting derisory laughter, he left.[23] Still another departure, following his defeat in debate, took a curious form: he arranged to have several of his confederates carry him out as in triumph, supposedly to impress the residents of the neighbourhood.[24] His open bitterness toward his enemies gave rise to stories that Koba had no scruples about using the police against them, and in later years, after Stalin had driven the Georgian Mensheviks into exile, these were embellished. In the mildest version an unknown person sounded a false alarm that the police were coming, just after Koba had left a meeting.[25] Much more sinister was the story that he betrayed a secret Menshevik printing press in Baku in 1909.[26] Still worse was the report that Arsenidze claims to have heard from Bolsheviks: that those among them who quarrelled with Koba often seemed to get arrested. When, supposedly, his comrades set up a 'court' to try him, the police arrested its members.[27] Beyond this there are many Koba-and-the-police stories in which he ceases to be merely a ruthless factional antagonist and becomes an outright agent of the tsar's men.[28] In dealing with a world of conspiracy incriminating suggestion is easy and definitive refutation next to impossible. But no reliable documentary evidence that Koba was a police agent has yet appeared, even though many researchers have sought it in the archives of the secret Paris office of the police, a rich body of material that has been available for many years at the Hoover Institution.[29] And the fact that the police arrested Stalin in 1913, sent him to a particularly remote place in Siberia and did not release him or allow his escape as long as the regime survived demonstrates that by this time, at least, the police did not treat Stalin as one of their agents.[30]

Koba was an important figure among the Bolsheviks of Georgia, few as they were, and was able to attend three major meetings of the party outside Georgia in 1905–7, his first view of the world beyond Transcaucasia, apart from his brief sojourn in Siberia as a prisoner. In December 1905 he went to Tammerfors in Finland, nominally part of the Russian Empire but not securely under police control at this point. Here he attended a 'conference', presumably less important than a 'congress', and for the first time met Lenin. After Lenin's death, Stalin, who was building the image of a loyal heir, described how impressed he was with Lenin's modesty, once he had overcome his disappointment in seeing that his leader was physically so ordinary. If they had any serious conversation at this stage of what was to be a long and complex relationship, no record of it has survived.[31] Koba then returned to Georgia for the first three months of 1906 before departing for Stockholm to participate in a so-called 'unity congress' of the party, which met in April 1906. His maiden address to a party congress, the first of many over almost half a century, was short but notable for its bold self-assurance. 'Ivanovich', Koba's pseudonym of the day, scornfully dismissed the arguments of the two most eminent Russian Marxists, Plekhanov, now a Menshevik, and Lenin, concerning the agrarian programme of the party. In his opinion they quibbled over the desirability of 'nationalizing' or 'municipalizing' the land (that is, placing it under the control of the central or the local government), but missed the basic point: the peasants wanted the land divided among their households. If they did not get this, he said, they would not support the workers' revolution. The leading theoreticians had missed the fundamental Marxist concept of stages of history. In the capitalist stage, he argued, it would be reactionary to partition the land among peasant households, but in the pre-capitalist stage, the position of Russia in 1906, this would be a revolutionary step. Otherwise Koba's participation in the proceedings of the congress was sharply factional, contrasting the 'path of false reform' and 'the path of revolution'. The Mensheviks had charged that the Bolshevik tactic of boycotting the elections to the Duma was merely words, while their tactic of taking part constituted deeds. 'Where is the difference?' asked Ivanovich. 'Is it really that you throw a shard in the urn and we do not?'[32]

At the next party congress, which met in London in April–May 1907, the Georgian Mensheviks succeeded in preventing the election of

Koba/Ivanovich as a delegate, but the mandate commission at the session seated him as a delegate with only a consultative vote. He sought revenge by accusing the Georgian Mensheviks of backing liberal slogans, of having merely petit bourgeois support. But these were written statements to the congress, signed by several comrades. Koba chose not to address this body, which had slighted his credentials.[33] This visit to London, then the centre of the capitalist world, seems to have left no particular impression on the poor lad from Gori. No references to Stalin's recollections of this trip crop up in the memoirs of his daughter or of Khrushchev. The one anecdote of the journey that he mentioned repeatedly in later years concerned his passage through Leipzig. Here he observed a group of German workers who failed to catch a train to a party rally because no railway employee was on hand to punch their tickets. Stalin formed a poor opinion of western radicals.[34]

While not travelling to one of these meetings, Koba tried settling down, albeit secretly, in Tbilisi. His home during much of 1906–7 was on the second floor of an obscure blind alley (3 Fresilsky St.), the only fixed address that he is known to have had between his departure from the observatory in 1901 and the Russian Revolution, apart from jail and Siberian exile.[35] At some time in 1905 he had married Ekaterina Svanidze, born in 1882 into a family that became active in the Georgian Marxist movement. To please her mother Koba even consented to a church wedding.[36] Taking up residence on Fresilsky St., he tried to establish himself as a Marxist theoretician, writing a treatise entitled 'Anarchism or Socialism?', which appeared in instalments in illegal Georgian Social-Democratic publications in 1906–7. It was at once a polemic against anarchists, who were appearing among Georgian radicals, and a general discourse on Marxist theory. While hardly a major work, it shows considerable application to the study of Marx and Engels, probably undertaken in this first relatively stable phase in Koba's adult life. The unabashed didacticism of the work, the enumeration of three anarchist 'accusations' and their five misunderstandings of dialectical materialism, the heavy literary allusions ('they are fighting not Marx and Engels but windmills, as Don Quixote of blessed memory did in his day'), all foreshadow the Stalin of later years, the author of a similar essay on 'Dialectical and Historical Materialism', which millions were obliged to study.[37]

Almost immediately after returning from the London Congress, Stalin left Tbilisi and moved to Baku, the centre of the oil industry. His motive may have been fear that the police would take special pains to find him because of a successful armed robbery on 12 June 1907 of a delivery of money destined for the state bank. This was an 'expropriation' by the Bolsheviks, a fund-raising device that the Mensheviks abhorred and Lenin found useful. It is unlikely that Koba had any role in this affair, which was under the command of a specialist in such matters, one Semion Ter-Petrossian, alias Kamo. But in the wake of this capital crime Koba could not afford to assume that the police would share this judgement.[38]

In moving to Baku he probably had to leave his wife and their son Yakov, who had been born in Tbilisi on 22 March 1907. According to one activist who as in Baku at the time, Koba lived in such secrecy that not even his close comrades knew his address, and he met them on a pier where there were crowds of passengers – no kind of life for a mother and infant. Ekaterina died in Tbilisi on 22 October 1907, and Yakov was brought up by one of her sisters there, rarely if ever seeing his father until he was about 20.[39]

In Baku, Stalin later recalled, 'I became a journeyman for the revolution', implying that the previous ten years had been merely an apprenticeship.[40] There is some justice in this, for Dzhugashvili enjoyed some success in Baku and developed a more mature capacity for political analysis. Leaving Georgia, where his Menshevik foes were well entrenched, he had a much better opportunity to influence workers of diverse ethnicity: Russians, Armenians and, especially, Azerbaijani Turks. This required that Koba conduct most of his work, including his political writing, in Russian, the lingua franca of the Empire and his normal working language for the rest of his life.

Aided by a friend and compatriot, Sergo Ordzhonikidze, Dzhugashvili succeeded in gaining control of the regional party committees of the city. This was possible because the Mensheviks had concentrated on skilled workers, leaving the unskilled open to Bolshevik attention. With the regional committees under control, the Bolsheviks called for a city-wide conference to elect a new committee to run the movement in Baku. There also was a question of worker participation in a legal conference of workers' representatives which the government wanted for the purpose of approving a general labour contract for the oil industry, thereby stabilizing labour relations. Koba, an ultra-militant, opposed participation in this conference. At first he succeeded, for the workers voted to boycott the election to the legal conference. But some of his comrades wavered, and in a clandestine meeting in the laundry of a hospital Koba was obliged to compromise. The workers would participate in the legal conference if certain conditions were met, such as the right of the workers to hold meetings. This would have improved the opportunities for radical agitation and placed on the regime the odium of breaking off negotiations. Koba was learning the value of manoeuvre.[41]

His effectiveness seems to have attracted the attention of the police, who arrested him on 25 March 1908. Koba had done well to evade them since fleeing Siberia in 1904, but in the wake of the revolution of 1905 the police intensified their activities against revolutionaries. Paradoxically it was legal after 1905 to form a Marxist political party and campaign in the

Duma elections, but it was unsafe to be a leader or a professional organizer in the same party. To improve their ability to apprehend such people the regime greatly increased its use of informers planted in the Social-Democratic organization. For years Lenin was hoodwinked by a member of his hand-picked Central Committee, who was also the leader of the small Bolshevik group in the Duma, one Roman Malinovsky.[42] It was extremely difficult for the revolutionaries to maintain any effective counter-intelligence operation against this well-financed programme, and underground operatives like Koba found it increasingly hard to maintain their cover, despite the use of a long list of aliases in his case.[43] If in later life Stalin seemed to suspect enemy agents within the party and even its upper echelons, this may owe something to the experience of working in an organization that really was seriously infiltrated with traitors.

After holding Koba in jail for over seven months following his arrest in March 1908, the authorities ordered him to reside under surveillance for two years in Solvychegodsk, almost 900 km north-east of Moscow. Following a stay in hospital with an attack of fever, he arrived there at the end of February 1909. Escape was quite simple, for the town was not in Siberia, and he turned up in Baku once again in July. In addition to agitating vainly for a industry-wide strike in the oil fields, Koba, signing himself 'K.S.', made his first contribution to a major Russian-language periodical, *Sotsial-Demokrat*. In these 'Letters from the Caucasus' he not only provided a fairly objective survey of the economic situation but also gave serious attention to the opportunities for legal action by the labour movement, which he considered greater in Baku than elsewhere in the Empire.[44]

The police caught up with him again in March 1910, returning him to Solvychegodsk to finish his sentence, which he did. Released in June 1911, he was forbidden to reside in St Petersburg, Moscow or the Caucasus region. The authorities need not have worried about his returning to the latter region, for Koba had decided to move closer to the centre of politics. He told the police that he would live in Vologda, a city located on a direct rail line to St Petersburg, about 500 km to the west.[45]

According to the report of a police spy named Ilchukov, a man he called 'the Caucasian' left Vologda on 6 September 1911 by third-class carriage on the 4.15 train for St Petersburg, carrying 'one small suitcase and a knotted bundle, evidently bedding'. This was not much to constitute the total worldly possessions of a man of thirty-one, but it was not wealth that aroused this Caucasian's ambition. By 1911 the activities of the Bolsheviks in the capital were acquiring new importance. True, Lenin and some other intellectual leaders of the movement lived abroad, but there now was increased opportunity for legal and covert activity. There were a few Bolshevik Duma deputies, Lenin having ended his boycott of the elections, legal publishing was possible and the mood of the workers was recovering from the depression if suffered following the revolution of 1905. Koba apparently decided on his own that he wanted to be part of this and set out to seek party assignments in the capital.[46]

But nothing came of this first attempt, for Ilchukov took the same train, and when it arrived in St Petersburg the next morning entrusted the surveillance of Dzhugashvili to a local spy who was waiting at the Nikolaevsky Station. This man lost his prey in the crowd but picked him up again in the evening when Dzhugashvili returned to claim his modest luggage. During the day Koba had been roaming the streets in a drizzling rain, hoping to find a comrade who could help him, fearing to go to the home of any activist who might be under surveillance. He did find a friend, Sila Todria, and together they returned to the station at 12.15 p.m. to get the luggage. The police then trailed him to the Hotel Rossiia, no. 3 Goncharnaia Street, a seedy place beside the railway yards, and resumed surveillance the next morning, 8 September. On the 9th they arrested 'the Caucasian'. He was found to be carrying the passport of a former political exile, presumably still a radical sympathizer, named Chizhikov. His possessions included five books: volume I of *Capital*, works on economics, sociology and history and a German phrase-book. If these were carried in the 'small suitcase', one may surmise that there was little enough room for a change of clothes. The police held Dzhugashvili in jail until 14 December, when they returned him to Vologda under orders for him to stay there for three years.[47]

He stayed two months, leaving his rented room at 2 a.m. on 29 February 1912, having told his landlord that he was taking only his 'valuables' and would be gone on personal business for about a week. How he actually left Vologda this time the police did not learn, but they speculated that he was headed for Moscow or St Petersburg. Actually he was headed for Tbilisi and Baku.[48] He had not given up his aspiration of a career in the capital but was spending a month in the Caucasus in a new capacity, member of the Central Committee of Lenin's version of the party. In January 1912 Lenin held a 'party conference' in Prague, at which he went as far as he could toward the exclusion of his opponents from the Social-Democratic Party. Even the selected delegates at this meeting balked at simply expelling all Mensheviks, and Lenin was obliged to claim that he aimed at the reunification of the party. But, he asserted, Mensheviks would have to recognize the Central Committee elected in Prague, and they would have to expel all 'liquidators', meaning certain Mensheviks who wanted the party to cease all illegal activity. Lenin loaded the new Central Committee with his own people, including six who were appointed, not elected, shortly after the Prague Conference. Dzhugashvili was one of these, and he was also named to the underground centre of the party, its 'Russian Bureau'.[49] This promotion was the first definite sign of personal favour by the founder of Bolshevism. Lenin may have been displeased by Koba's disagreements with him on agrarian policy in 1906, and Koba's later dismissal of Lenin's philosophical polemics against certain comrades as 'a tempest in a teapot'.[50] But the leader was bound to recognize that the Georgian consistently had fought the Mensheviks.

Koba's first assignment in his new capacity was to impress on the activists of Tbilisi and Baku the correctness of the Prague Conference. Judging by a report in the party organ *Sotsial-Demokrat*, he was successful in this. In Baku the leading Mensheviks stayed away from the city Social-Democratic conference because they were 'afraid' of the outcome and as a result were unable to prevent the Bolsheviks from passing resolutions in support of the Prague Conference. Only on one point did the Baku conference disappoint Lenin. It would not agree to exclude from any future party elections the 'liquidators'. This does not suggest that Koba himself deviated from Lenin's wishes, but that he was unable to persuade all of his comrades on this point.[51]

Returning to the capital in April 1912 Koba was arrested once again. After holding him in jail until July they decided to send him for three years residence in Narym, on the River Ob over 300 km north of Tomsk, the nearest railway station. *En route* he persuaded the Menshevik Nicolaevsky, whom he met in a transit jail, to give him a 'good blue enamel tea kettle'. Koba argued that he had none, while Nicolaevsky was with a group bound for another destination and well-equipped with kettles. He left Tomsk by steamer on 18 July and so must have reached his destination around the 21st. But he stayed in Narym little more than a month, disappearing from his lodgings on the night of 31 August and making it back to St Petersburg by 12 September.[52]

This time he enjoyed almost six months of liberty before the police caught up with him again. They almost took him on 29 October, when an agent spotted him in the Nikolaevsky Station and tailed him for a while, but lost him in a crowd.[53] In this period Dzhugashvili undertook new responsibilities. He made two difficult trips to visit Lenin in his latest place of exile in the Austrian Empire, and he served as the chief political adviser of the party's new legal, daily newspaper, *Pravda*. Lenin had been frustrated in his attempts to ensure that this organ pressed the point of the Prague Conference, that the party consisted only of members who recognized the supremacy of Lenin's Central Committee. Koba was supposed to impress this line on an editorial staff that was less sectarian than Lenin on this point and more inclined than he to the use of parliamentary means in the workers' cause. While Koba, as a member of the Central Committee, supposedly outranked the members of the editorial board, he was not an established party leader, especially in St Petersburg, and was not an experienced editor. While his own few contributions to *Pravda* in fall of 1912 castigated 'liquidators' and implied that all Mensheviks deserved this label, the editors and also the five Bolshevik Duma deputies moved away from Lenin's schismatic line and engaged in conciliatory talks with the Mensheviks. They even agreed to work toward the establishment of a single, united newspaper for both factions.[54]

Sorely disappointed, Lenin summoned Koba and a few others to a one-day meeting in Cracow in November 1912. This was a burdensome trip, for he had to risk arrest when he departed the Russian Empire at Abo in Finland.[55] Returning to St Petersburg in early December, he was there for only two or three weeks before Lenin called him back to participate in a slightly more ambitious meeting of the members of the Central Committee, Duma deputies and a few other activists. Now Koba had to cross the border again, this time at night in the hill country of Galicia. The second Cracow meeting passed several resolutions, one of which attacked 'liquidators' and another reprimanded the editorial board of *Pravda* for being 'insufficiently firm in party spirit. . . . Full compliance with the decisions of the Central Committee is obligatory.' This was not an implied reproach to Koba. Lenin's letters to him in St Petersburg were consistently friendly in spirit, urging him on against the 'liquidators' but not reproaching him for the insufficient militancy of the editorial board. The problem was Koba's lack of personal authority at this stage of his career, which Lenin attempted to remedy by appointing another person, Yakov Sverdlov, to the job of supervising *Pravda*.[56]

To avoid a personal slight to Koba, Lenin found a new assignment for him and a change of scene. The job was the composition of an essay on the problem of the minority nationalities in the Russian Empire, a matter that greatly interested Lenin at this time. During the first half of January 1913 Koba stayed in Cracow and discussed the topic with Lenin. Then he moved to Vienna where he spent about a month researching and writing the essay that in later years was known as 'Marxism and the National Question'.[57] This was a considerable task, for the essay was the longest that Stalin ever wrote in Russian and it required some research in German, which he read haltingly at best. Lenin wanted him to tackle the ideas of two major Austrian Marxists, Rudolf Springer and Otto Bauer, who proposed that nationalities that lived in scattered enclaves might satisfy their aspirations by forming not separate states but legally constituted cultural unions. Koba found fault with this scheme but seemed much less concerned with the fate of the national minorities of the Austro-Hungarian Empire than with the fact that some Marxists in the Russian Empire wanted to write the Austrian plan into the programme of the Russian party. The chief culprits were members of the Jewish Bund, the separate, Yiddish-speaking branch of the Russian Social-Democratic Party, which consistently had sided with the Mensheviks against Lenin. If one cannot say that Stalin's discussion of the Bund's espousal of the

Springer–Bauer idea was overtly anti-Semitic, it at least displayed a degree of antagonism toward advocates of Jewish interest. He had no patience with the unwillingness of the Bund to accept the proposition that 'the Jewish nation is coming to an end. . . . The Jews are being assimilated.' This, he found, led them to demand not the 'general right of all nations to use their own language, but the particular right of the Jewish language, Yiddish!'[58]

Apart from the Bund, some Social-Democrats in the Caucasus, in which ethnic groups indeed dwelled in scattered enclaves, favoured the Austrian scheme. Worse, a 'conference of liquidators' agreed that it was compatible with the party programme. Here Stalin was back to standard Leninist polemics, for the conference in question had been organized in August 1912 by Trotsky as a riposte to Lenin's Prague Conference. The nationality question thus served as a stick with which to beat Lenin's factional rivals. Concerning nationalism, Stalin supported the orthodox Marxist position of the day that nationalism and nations were a transient feature of capitalism, which would cease to be a serious problem by the time of the proletarian revolution. This was all very well if one accepted the assumption of the party programme of 1903 that Russia was still in the early part of a more or less protracted era of capitalism. In this framework Stalin spoke of the slogan of 'national self-determination' as good in theory but not in practice. The slogan could reassure nationalists of the good intentions of the socialists, but the actual dismemberment of the Russian Empire was undesirable. Better stick to some sort of ill-defined 'regional autonomy' within the Russian Empire until the end of capitalism, when no serious question of nationalism would remain.

When this essay was published in three instalments in March, April and May 1913, the author's name was given as 'K. Stalin', presumably 'K' for 'Koba', the author's best-known name within the underground. This was not the first time that he had signed 'K. Stalin', for that distinction belonged to a short article that appeared in *Pravda* in 1912. In any case the new pseudonym stuck. In selecting a name based on the Russian word for steel, he was, with what degree of deliberation one cannot tell, engaged in a major act of image-making that would serve him well in years to come. Most party pseudonyms were ordinary Russian names, such as Trotsky, Kamenev and Zinoviev. 'Lenin' was derived from the name of a Siberian river near which he was once exiled, and evoked nothing in particular as a political symbol. But 'Stalin', 'the man of steel', was superlative stagecraft for a would-be strong-man and, eventually, the builder of a great industrial economy.[59]

By the time the essay on nationality was in print its author was once again in jail. Back in St Petersburg he had been rash enough to attend a fund-raising concert for the party where the police picked him up on 23 February 1913. They were assisted in this by information provided by

Malinovsky, the informer who had been with Stalin at the meetings in Cracow.[60] This time the police decided to settle him in a region so remote that escape would be extremely hard, the Turukhansk region of northern central Siberia. Within this vast, almost unpopulated, frozen area he was assigned to live first in a hamlet called Kostino, then in early March 1914 in another called Kureika, which was north of the Arctic Circle. At the end of 1916 the authorities brought him south over 1000 km to Krasnoyarsk on the Trans-Siberian Railway to give him an army physical. By this time the First World War had killed over a million Russian males of Stalin's generation, so the Turukhansk region was perhaps not the worst place to reside. The potential conscript was, however, rejected because of the permanent damage to his left arm which he had sustained in childhood. After this the authorities permitted Stalin to finish his remaining half-year of exile in Achinsk, a town somewhat west of Krasnoyarsk on the rail line.[61]

At the beginning of his term in Siberia, the party made an effort to organize Stalin's escape, along with Sverdlov, who was in the same locality. This failed, for the police learned from Malinovsky of the efforts of the party to send money to the exiles.[62] Once the war started, communications with the leaders in exile were disrupted, and the police suppressed a great part of the underground organization in Russia. Stalin settled down to sit out his term, a fate made easier by his good relations with the natives, Ostiaks, a people resembling Eskimos or North American Indians. He joined them in fishing, kept a dog called Tishka, to whom he became much attached, and also a peasant mistress who bore him a son. At least his daughter states that her aunts, one of whom had been in fairly close touch with Stalin in this period, said that he fathered a son while in Siberia, and it seems unlikely that he did so during either of his previous, brief sojourns in Siberia. It is unlikely that he found a woman in this remote area who was not an Ostiak.[63]

Not that it was an easy existence. Apart from the climate and the dreary, flat, almost treeless scenery, of which Stalin complained in a letter to his friends the Alliluevs, there was the fact that his career in the party was stalled. In 1916 he had made an effort to advance his cause, writing to Lenin to propose the publication of an anthology consisting of his essay on nationality and a few of his shorter pieces that touched on this question. But nothing came of this.[64] Personal relations with other political exiles were poor, especially with Sverdlov, with whom Stalin shared the hamlet of Kureika for two years. In a guarded letter to his wife, Sverdlov complained that Stalin was 'too individualistic'.[65] The description was apt, not only because it implied an abrasive personality but also because it suggested that this obscure man was a ruggedly independent character.

3 Petrograd

As it turned out Stalin did not have to wait until July 1917, when his term of exile would have expired. On 2 March Nicholas II abdicated the throne of Russia, and a Provisional Government of liberals assumed precarious power. The capital to which Stalin returned on 12 March was a very different place from the city he had known, quite apart from the fact that the tsarist government had renamed it 'Petrograd' as part of the anti-German mood of wartime. Not only did the new government support a full range of civil liberties for all political factions, they had no choice but to permit the existence of a rival authority, the 'Petrograd Soviet of Workers' and Soldiers' Deputies', which had taken form as the old regime collapsed. Although composed of elected delegates from factories and military units of the capital city only, it possessed from the outset enormous prestige as a symbol of some kind of radical democratic order for all Russia.

This situation posed anew the problem that had from the founding of the party beset Russian Marxists. Presumably Russia had now thrown off the political vestiges of feudalism, but had by no means finished with capitalism and a bourgeois-democratic order. Should the leaders of the proletariat in Russia accept this Provisional Government as the logical product of economically determined evolution, or should they try to take advantage of the fluidity of the circumstances to take power themselves? Should they utterly reject the war as imperialist or should they support defensive operations as long as revolutionary Russia was threatened by reactionary Germany? In March 1917 most Russian Marxists took a qualified revolutionary stance on both issues. They accepted the liberal Provisional Government pending the fuller organization of socialist forces. But they opposed the participation of socialists in the liberal government, considering that the initial pact by which the Soviet accepted the Provisional Government constituted 'the conditions of a duel'. Concerning the war, they pledged to 'firmly defend our own liberty against all reactionary attempts both from without and within' and at the same time called on their 'brother proletarians' on the other side of the lines to 'throw off the yoke of your semi-autocratic rule'.[1]

Contrary to many later allegations by Leninists, this did not represent a sell-out of revolution, and it is not surprising that the main thrust of this policy at first won the support of a large part of the Russian socialist movement, including Bolsheviks. There were some Bolshevik activists in Petrograd who took a more impulsive radical stance, calling the Provisional Government reactionary and urging its replacement by a revolutionary republic. But even among Bolsheviks this line had limited support. Half

of the forty Bolsheviks who were members of the Petrograd Soviet at the
time of its founding voted for the resolution supporting the Provisional
Government.[2]

Arriving in Petrograd on 12 March, Stalin rejected the ultra-left
position in favour of the more moderate position of the Soviet majority.
This was to cause him considerable embarrassment in later years, because
it put him at odds with the line that Lenin enunciated a few weeks later
when he returned to Russia. When Stalin's writings from this period were
collected in 1924, he found it necessary to include an apologia for his
moderation in March 1917, and when his *Works* appeared after the
Second World War the offending words vanished.[3] In March 1917 his
stance aggravated his relations with the radical Bolshevik leaders in
Petrograd whose ascendency in the local party organization was interrupted
by the return from Siberia of Kamenev and Stalin, members of the
Central Committee and hence senior in party rank. Because of the
friction between the local leadership and the returnees, Kamenev was not
given a seat on the 'Russian Bureau of the Central Committee', which
was in effect the leading party body, and Stalin was given only a
consultative vote 'in view of certain personal characteristics'. This probably
referred to the abrasive style that he had displayed when he had been
Lenin's agent in St Petersburg in 1912. But the senior men soon overcame
their opponents and established their control over the revived party
organ, *Pravda*. In addition Stalin became a full member of the 'Russian
Bureau' and its representative on the Central Executive Committee of the
Petrograd Soviet. Just how this reassertion of seniority was accomplished
is unclear. The defeated Bolsheviks in Petrograd passed a resolution
condemning Kamenev's 'strong-arm' methods in taking over *Pravda*, but
this did not mean physical force. More likely the two had threatened to
appeal over the local leaders to the rank and file, who were inclined to
the policy of the Soviet.[4]

In the short time between his assertion of control over *Pravda* and
Lenin's return to Russia Stalin took a qualified stance concerning both the
Provisional Government and the war. He attacked the government as
non-revolutionary and urged that it be replaced soon by a democratically
elected Constituent Assembly. He also wanted an All-Russian (that is,
Empire-wide) Soviet, but called neither for the overthrow of the
Provisional Government nor the establishment of the Soviet as its
successor. The war he characterized as 'imperialist'. Backing the appeal
of the Soviet to the masses of the enemy countries to force their
governments to end the war, he opposed the slogan 'Down with the war!'
as impractical and instead called for pressure on the Provisional
Government to start peace negotiations at once.[5]

Another volatile issue was the question of reunifying the Russian
Social-Democratic Labour Party. After all, the various factions still shared

this name, and many rank and file members, including a flood of new recruits, considered bygone factional quarrels unimportant in the new situation. In many places in the Empire 'unification committees' of Bolsheviks and Mensheviks appeared. The Petrograd Bolshevik leadership was fairly reserved on this matter, but voted to accept in principle unification with one of the branches of Menshevism, the 'Inter-District Committee', and to open the door for negotiations with another branch, the Menshevik-Internationalists. Stalin did not initiate this trend or these particular overtures, nor did he oppose them. In a Bolshevik conference he supported further talks with the Mensheviks, but one should not necessarily conclude that he was going soft on these rivals. Stalin said that the line of demarcation between Bolsheviks and those Mensheviks with whom they would not join should be 'anti-defencism'. This meant that the Bolsheviks should continue to oppose the mainstream of the Menshevik Party, which espoused the policy of 'revolutionary defencism', while wooing the left-wing Mensheviks to defect and join the Bolsheviks. In the course of 1917 such defections did occur and with Lenin's blessing, the most notable case in point being Trotsky. At the Bolshevik conference in March Stalin moved a resolution that favoured a unification conference among socialists, which passed by a vote of 21–1. His calculation probably was that such a gathering would lead to a split among the Mensheviks to the advantage of the Bolsheviks.[6]

But there was no unification conference. Only a few days later, on 3 April, Lenin returned to Russia, thanks to the willingness of the German General Staff to allow this radical foe of the Russian war effort to pass across the territory of the Reich, *en route* to Sweden and thence Petrograd. Lenin brought with him a new set of answers to the question of Marxist theory and Russia's situation in 1917. These 'April Theses' took a line at once bold and ambiguous.[7] 'The specific feature of the present situation in Russia', said Lenin, 'is that it represents a *transition* from the first stage of the revolution, which, owing to the insufficient class consciousness and organization of the proletariat, placed power in the hands of the bourgeoisie, *to the second stage*, which must place power in the hands of the proletariat and the poorest strata of the peasantry.' Thus, as in 1905, Lenin was not content to accept an era of bourgeois rule, but he specifically denied that he was proposing to 'introduce socialism'. Land and banks should be nationalized, the police, army and bureaucracy should be abolished, officials should be paid no more than the 'average competent worker', but he said nothing about the nationalization of industry.

Concerning immediate tactics, the April Theses also combined bold radicalism and practical ambiguity. Lenin called for no support for the Provisional Government and the transfer of power from it to the Soviets. This sounded clear and strong, yet he did not call for insurrection at once or at any particular time in the future. Until he had succeeded in 'explaining' to the masses the need for the second stage of the revolution he evidently assumed the continued existence of the Provisional Government. In the same way he seemed ultra-radical concerning the war, opposing 'defencism' and insisting that only the spread of revolution to other countries could bring peace. To this end he proposed that Russian troops fraternize with their enemies, spreading subversive propaganda. But he could suggest no alternative to defensive war until the desired revolt in the West began, and he did not propose to accept the enemies' peace terms.

Some socialists considered Lenin mad, and even within Bolshevik ranks he had at first some difficulty in persuading comrades that he was right. Stalin's initial reaction was cool. The first indication of Lenin's new line was several 'Letters from Afar', which a comrade brought to Petrograd from Scandinavia before Lenin's return. *Pravda* published them, but Kamenev and Stalin deleted one passage that castigated the Mensheviks as traitors to the proletariat. When Lenin did reach the capital, Stalin was one of the few who met Lenin at Beloostrov to accompany him on the remainder of the trip. It could not have been an easy reunion, for the founder evidently used the occasion to scold his lieutenants for their errant politics.[8]

Apparently this was not enough fully to win Stalin to the line of the April Theses. In 1956 the Soviet historian E. N. Burdzhalov produced a short excerpt from the terse record of a meeting of the Russian Bureau of the Central Committee that occurred three days after Lenin's return. In Lenin's presence Stalin bluntly said that the Theses were 'a schema, there are no facts in them, and therefore they do not satisfy. No answers concerning small nations.' Burdzhalov intended to show that Stalin had persisted in opposing Lenin's views even after the leader had returned. During Stalin's era in power and after, this was regarded as a serious misdeed for a Bolshevik, which no doubt explains why the document was unknown before 1956. Ironically, Stalin's cultivation of the myth of his devotion to Lenin led him to conceal a quality that impartial people might consider more useful than mere obedience: intellectual independence.[9]

Such a critique might well be defended, but it missed the tacit key to the April Theses, a point too bold to be articulated in the spring of 1917 and still too strong for some of Lenin's comrades in the fall: the Bolsheviks should aim at taking power on their own. Twenty years of feuding with other Russian radicals, who seemed wrong-headed if not downright traitorous, had been enough for Lenin. He had wanted to seize control of the whole Marxist movement in 1912–14 and was still less willing to compromise with the Mensheviks now that there was a practical possibility of establishing a government of the Left. The immediate point of the April Theses was not to bring about some particular policy concerning the Provisional Government, the making of peace, the distribution of land or any other issue. It was to distinguish the Bolsheviks from other parties of the Left, enabling them to become the radical alternative. Convinced that all the other parties on the Russian scene would fail to deal effectively with the pressing issues of the day, Lenin wanted to be ready to offer the masses a clear-cut alternative, his leadership, his organization. But this programme was too bold to be revealed in the spring of 1917, and it is not surprising that Stalin took some time to grasp it.

He persisted in his cool attitude toward Lenin's Theses for three weeks after the leader's return, failing to mention the man or his proposals in four brief articles in *Pravda* during this time. True, Stalin did move toward Lenin's positions on several points, but on balance his acceptance of the April Theses was qualified. He mentioned in passing the desirability of a 'new, revolutionary International', a goal dear to Lenin's heart but not supported by most Bolsheviks for many months to come. Stalin's agreement with Lenin on this matter did not necessarily mean that he shared Lenin's passion for a revolution in the West at an early date. More likely it reflected a deep contempt for the Social-Democratic movement that had dominated the Second International. Stalin moved to a more radical stance on the agrarian question, urging peasants to cultivate landlords' land without awaiting a Constituent Assembly, but he completely ignored Lenin's proposal that all land be 'nationalized'. Similarly, he took a stronger line against the Provisional Government, stating that 'the workers and soldiers can support only the Soviet of Workers' and Soldiers' Deputies which they themselves elected'. But this fell short of clear acceptance of Lenin's line on the transfer of 'the entire power of the state to the Soviets'.[10]

In the course of April the most powerful force that drew Stalin and most Bolsheviks to Lenin's position was the politics of the Provisional Government, along with the Mensheviks and Socialist Revolutionaries in the leadership of the Soviet. The liberal ministers of foreign affairs and war, Miliukov and Guchkov, offended the Left by assuring the western allies that they would fight on to victory, with a thinly veiled hint that they expected in return the territorial rewards that had been promised to the tsar. When they were forced to resign in the ensuing furor, the Soviet leadership decided to form a coalition with less expansionist liberals, following the lead of Alexander Kerensky, who became war minister and the leading personality in the new cabinet. He was a member but not effectively a leader of the Socialist-Revolutionary Party and a Soviet leader who had defied the wishes of its Central Executive Committee by taking the portfolio of justice in the first version of the Provisional Government. The coalition represented the collapse of the policy of the early leadership of the Soviet, which Stalin had in the main supported:

temporary acceptance of the Provisional Government, pending the readiness of the Left to govern. The idea of establishing the Bolsheviks as the only radical alternative no longer seemed presumptuous when the other socialist parties were entering a coalition with the liberals. The crucial point was that the socialists in the coalition could not control the policies of Kerensky and the liberals. 'Control' was the key word in Stalin's short intervention in the discussion at the party conference that met in late April. He rejected any continuation of the idea that the Soviet could control the Provisional Government, preventing its slide toward reactionary policies. Recent government pronouncements on the war and land had convinced him that the policy of Soviet control could not work because the present leadership of the Soviet was supine. 'The government attacks the Soviet. The Soviet retreats.' With this new perspective Stalin joined the majority at the conference in supporting Lenin on most points of his April Theses.[11]

Despite these criticisms of the Soviet, Stalin was closely associated with this body for at least the first five months of its existence. As a Bolshevik representative on the Central Executive Committee of the Soviet, he regularly attended their meetings, although he rarely spoke. His role seems to have been to observe and keep his party current on the affairs of the Soviet. One report that he wrote on a crucial meeting between the Central Executive Committee and the Provisional Government showed that he was listening attentively to what his party's rivals had to say and could provide a clear, concise and, if one ignores the partisan adjectives, even an objective account of what was happening.[12]

Stalin's work in the Soviet increased in importance during 3–24 June when the First All-Russian Congress of Soviets met in Petrograd seeking to co-ordinate the far-flung movement and to endow a new Central Executive Committee with greater legitimacy than the previous, Petrograd-based one, could claim. The principle that all socialist parties should be represented in this assembly of the Left still held sway, so Stalin was elected to the new Central Executive Committee. During the congress Stalin once again demonstrated his independence within his own party. He now joined the militant wing with respect to tactics, advocating an anti-government demonstration including armed soldiers, contrary to the wishes of the still-moderate Kamenev. Lenin at first went along with the plan for the demonstration, and Stalin was authorized to write the principal party appeal to the masses. This turned out to be a violent attack on 'blood-sucking bankers', 'lockout capitalists' and 'marauding profiteers', ending with the slogan 'Down with counter-revolution!' While not explicitly a call to insurrection, the moderate socialist leaders of the Soviet thought that the demonstration might become a revolt and they pressured the Bolsheviks to cancel it. In Stalin's absence Lenin and the Central Committee agreed to do so, although not before some copies of the appeal had been printed and distributed. Angry at this retreat, Stalin and one other supporter of the demonstration submitted their resignations as members of the Central Committee. This was the first of several occasions in his career when Stalin made this gesture, reasonably sure that it would not be accepted.[13]

Had it been accepted, he would have missed his first opportunity to appear as a major leader in the party. This came about as a result of a confrontation between the Provisional Government and the more militant elements among the soldiers, sailors and workers, who in early July held the demonstration that they had been denied in June. Although numerous Bolsheviks of the 'Military Organization' of the party, the fairly autonomous branch that had grown up in the armed forces, favoured the confrontation, Lenin did not. Nevertheless, when it developed into violent conflict with the government, which it wished to overthrow, Lenin concluded that he must back the demonstration if he were to retain credibility as a radical leader. As he feared, the movement lacked enough popular support to succeed in toppling Kerensky, who was able to find loyal military units, especially after he charged that Lenin was a German agent. Facing arrest, Lenin had to decide whether to stand trial or go into hiding. He met with Stalin and a handful of associates in the apartment of Stalin's friend Sergei Alliluev. There Lenin decided in favour of hiding, and to camouflage his identity Stalin shaved off the famous beard. Then these two, along with Alliluev and one other, walked by a devious route through the night to the Primorsky Railway Station, whence Lenin departed for Finland.[14]

Throughout this crisis Stalin's main task was to minimize the damage to the party by attempting to persuade the leaders of the Soviet to restrain Kerensky, who was attempting to press a campaign against the Bolsheviks. On 3 July, at the beginning of the turmoil, Stalin broke his usual silence in the meetings of the Central Executive Committee by denying that the Bolsheviks were planning a coup. Although this was true concerning the plans of Lenin and the Central Committee of the party, it did not prevent Stalin from drafting a leaflet calling on the workers and soldiers to establish a Soviet government. He then met with Tsereteli to try to prevent the publication of the charges that Lenin was a German agent. Although he persuaded this Georgian Menshevik, the accusations were published anyway, arousing a substantial body of public opinion against the Bolsheviks. Stalin continued to try to persuade the Central Executive Committee to protect the Bolsheviks from their foes. 'Counter-revolution', he said, 'is strangling us, and you [the other parties of the Left] are next in line; give us a hand for the struggle with counter-revolution.' But the other socialists, as Stalin told a Bolshevik conference, 'ridiculed us'. Years later, when compiling his collected writings, this scene evidently struck him as beneath his dignity, and it was expunged from the record.

But in truth it was a loyal effort on behalf of his party, though largely unsuccessful. The remainder of his task was a rearguard action. He tried, again unsuccessfully, to prevent the eviction of the Bolsheviks from the mansion that they had expropriated in February as their headquarters, warning the Soviet leaders that it would be defended by force, a bluff. He did, however, succeed in obtaining the release from prison of some radical sailors.[15]

He may also have succeeded, inadvertently, in warding off his own arrest. While he was not popular with the Menshevik and Socialist Revolutionary leaders of the Soviet, Stalin was a familiar presence in its Central Executive Committee and in the July crisis had been the accepted link between this body and the Bolsheviks. Kerensky might have wished to crush the Bolsheviks as a party, but the Soviet would not permit this, nor the arrest of the most important Bolshevik who had remained in its midst following Lenin's departure.

By 6 July things had quietened down. Loyal troops had disarmed radical soldiers and sailors, Lenin was in hiding and several Bolshevik leaders were in jail. Also incarcerated was Trotsky, who had returned from western exile in May and had taken a radical line in the Soviet, but was still outside the ranks of the Bolshevik party at the time of the July upheaval. This left Stalin and his rival Sverdlov more or less at the helm of the party through most of July and August. Sverdlov was concerned mainly with internal organizational affairs, attempting with the assistance of perhaps a dozen amateur adminstrators to bring some semblance of order to a movement that had grown two and one-half fold between April and July 1917. Stalin and Sverdlov collaborated in managing a party congress, which met in Petrograd on 26 July–3 August, the first such meeting since 1907. Having visited Lenin in his hiding place in order to discuss the new party line, Stalin assumed the unenviable task of justifying Lenin's leadership in a time of defeat and uncertainty. This was all the harder because Lenin had advised his comrades to drop the slogan 'All power to the Soviets'. This was a sharp reversal of one of his most important theses of April and hence confusing to his followers. Lenin justified the switch on the grounds that the Soviet was now in the hands of opponents, but this had been the case since the beginning. And what was the party to propose as an alternative to the despised Provisional Government? Stalin tried to skirt this question at the party congress and also at a Petrograd conference that preceded it, but in both cases questions from the floor obliged him to admit that the party was abandoning its former slogan. Loyal to Lenin, he weakly tried to justify the switch by explaining that what was important was not the form of a revolutionary organization but its content. Confused as it was, the party congress was indecisive. Stalin was one of seven on the committee that drafted its inconclusive resolutions, statements representing compromises between more or less militant Bolsheviks.[16]

The congress had been difficult for Stalin, but he survived it as an accepted leader of the party and was elected to the new Central Committee. Another member was Trotsky who, though in jail, was now enrolled as a Bolshevik. Because of its size the new Committee, at its first meeting on 5 August, elected an 'Inner Committee' of eleven, also including Stalin. At this time he proposed and his comrades agreed that the new body 'work on the principle of strict division of functions'. If observed in practice this would have meant that the Committee would have left to Stalin, along with two unimpressive comrades, Miliutin and Sokolnikov, control of the function that had been assigned to him, the party organ. Since the organ enunciated party policy for the rank and file, this would have been tantamount to control of the party, had this principle been observed, which it was not. In any case, Stalin first had to find a functioning newspaper to serve as a party organ, *Pravda* having been closed down by the government as part of its anti-Bolshevik campaign. Armed with a resolution of the Central Committee, Stalin attempted to solve this problem by expropriating the organ of the Bolshevik Military Organization. According to a letter of protest from the proprietors of this newspaper, Stalin and another colleague violated 'the elementary principles of party democracy' by walking in, stating that they were taking over and that 'there was nothing to discuss'. Rather than alienate its soldier-Bolshevik comrades, the Central Committee then retreated and established a new organ for Stalin to edit.[17]

In the period August–October the political editorship of this organ, and the contribution of over forty articles, essentially editorials, occupied a great part of Stalin's time.[18] He also had to attend meetings of the Central Committee, which became more frequent and important than they had been.[19] Another responsibility that probably absorbed a good deal of his energy was a commission, established by the party congress, to manage Bolshevik participation in the elections for the long-awaited Constituent Assembly. Whatever they had said about giving power to the Soviets, the Bolsheviks, like all other parties, claimed to regard the Assembly as the legitimate expression of the popular will. They had protested that the elections were not held soon enough, but accepted the democratic procedures that the Provisional Government at length prepared and gave every sign of attempting to mount a vigorous campaign for delegates. It was a large and unprecedented job to draw up a list of Bolshevik candidates for all the electoral districts in the land. Stalin himself was named on a select list of twenty-five 'candidates of the Central Committee' and was placed on the ballot in four far-flung electoral districts in an attempt to ensure that he won a seat somewhere. One of his new-found constituencies, Stavropol, was obliged to write to the Central Committee to learn the real name, not the political pseudonym, of their candidate, and also his age, occupation and address, so that they could register him officially.[20]

But Lenin was not counting on these elections to put his party in power. Watching developments in Russia from his refuge in Helsinki and later Vyborg, Lenin in September and October 1917 became increasingly obsessed with the idea that his party could lead a successful insurrection. In late August the commander-in-chief, General L. G. Kornilov, made an attempt to establish a more authoritative government that would suppress the Left, especially the Bolsheviks. This proved abortive, owing to the unwillingness of his troops to carry out the seizure of Petrograd, but not before the Soviet had become alarmed and had called on the Bolsheviks to join a common effort to defend the revolution. The episode seriously undermined Kerensky's government, for Kornilov was his appointee, and it began a trend toward further radicalization of the soldiers, sailors and workers. In the Petrograd Soviet this led to the election of Trotsky, whom the government had released from jail, as chairman of the Central Executive Committee. With this position, and also membership on the Central Committee of the Bolshevik Party, this firey personality became the most eminent leader of that faction, apart from the absent Lenin. Although he did not complain at the time, Stalin had some cause to regard Trotsky's elevation as a grievance, especially considering that this man had for a decade been one of Lenin's most vociferous factional opponents.

In mid-September Lenin wrote two secret letters to the Central Committee, urging the party to seize power soon. Not one of the sixteen leading comrades, including Stalin and Trotsky, who discussed these documents were willing to accept Lenin's injunction without qualification. The idea that the Soviets, meaning some kind of Left coalition, would form a new provisional government, pending the Constituent Assembly, was widely accepted in the party. But many Bolsheviks were unready to contemplate rule by their party alone, confronting the opposition of all the other forces in Russian politics at a time when the Empire was facing grave economic and military crises. A majority of the Central Committee obviously was unwilling to accept Lenin's proposal, yet equally unready to affront him with a blunt rejection. Temporization took the form of a resolution, evidently passed unanimously, in favour of a meeting 'very soon' to consider tactics, a second resolution that the Committee postpone until the next session Stalin's motion that they discuss Lenin's letters, and a third that they merely file the letter. This meant that Lenin's ideas would not be disseminated throughout the party. This last resolution was passed by 6–4 with six abstentions, evidently Committee members who preferred to avoid the troublesome issue. Stalin's motion in favour of immediate discussion of Lenin's letters indicates that he was relatively favourable to the leader's intentions. But he did not pursue the matter, absenting himself from the next meeting of the Committee, which was to have dealt with his motion but in fact forgot to do so. Kamenev was willing to reject outright Lenin's proposed insurrection, but this was too much for the Committee majority. Kamenev had to settle for the part of his original proposal which called on the Military Organization and Petrograd Committee to 'take measures to prevent demonstrations of any kind in barracks and factories', which was tantamount to blocking an uprising.[21]

The most that Lenin could achieve at this time was the publication of an article that at least implied insurrection: 'Can the Bolsheviks Retain State Power?' Frustrated, he warned the Central Committee that he would bypass it and take his proposal to the party rank-and-file if he were not permitted to risk returning to the capital to participate in the work of the Committee. This they accepted, and on 10 October Lenin for the first time since June was able to address his leading comrades in person. By force of personality and argument he was able to persuade them to approve by a vote of 10–2 a resolution that put 'insurrection on the order of the day'. This could be interpreted as a victory for Lenin or merely as a sop offered by those who wanted to placate him without committing themselves to any specific action. Stalin seems to have been among the non-committal at this stage, attending the meeting that voted the resolution but not participating in the discussion. He was, however, included in a 'Political Bureau' of seven that the meeting elected, a body that does not appear to have become a reality in 1917.[22]

When the Central Committee next met on 16 October it was joined by representatives of several bodies that were on the whole more aggressive, notably the Military Organization, the Petrograd Committee of the party and various factory committees, at least twenty-five people in all. The mood was mixed, but many spoke of the probable success of an insurrection. This appears to have decided Stalin in favour of Lenin's tactics. He argued that the Bolsheviks should not wait for the government to attack them because the existing situation already constituted an attack. He took issue with the two chief opponents of insurrection, Kamenev and Zinoviev, arguing that their proposal that the party bide its time would allow 'counter-revolution . . . to organize itself'. This must have gratified Lenin, but the party leader still could obtain nothing more specific from the meeting than a confirmation of the previous resolution that a rising be placed 'on the order of the day'. The nearest thing to a concrete tactical measure that the meeting accepted was the establishment of a 'Military Revolutionary Centre', consisting of Sverdlov, Stalin, Bubnov, Uritsky and Dzerzhinsky. There is, however, no good evidence that this body actually met or acted in any way, although in later years it was associated with Stalin's alleged leadership of the Bolshevik Revolution.[23]

The indecision within the leading ranks of the party placed Stalin, as chief editor of its official organ, in a difficult situation. Following the resolution of 16 October Kamenev and Zinoviev sent a letter to party bodies in Petrograd in which they argued against any insurrection in the near future. A Menshevik newspaper learned of this and made mention of it, which prompted Kamenev to publish in that paper a denial that the Bolsheviks had decided on insurrection and his conviction that they should not do so. Lenin was outraged and demanded the expulsion from the party of the 'strikebreakers'. Kamenev and Zinoviev responded that they had been misunderstood, and Stalin, as editor of the party organ, published both sides of the exchange, adding an unsigned note in which he expressed hope that the incident was closed. It was not. Lenin was absent because he thought the police might find him when the Committee considered the case on 20 October. As Lenin expected, so he told Sverdlov, Stalin continued his mediatory approach and in an apparent effort to let both sides cool off proposed that the matter be deferred to a later meeting. He maintained that 'expulsion from the party [of Kamenev and Zinoviev] is no remedy, what is needed is to preserve party unity', and he assured the meeting that the pair would submit to Central Committee decisions. But the majority of those present, while not disposed to expel the dissidents, were less moderate. It rejected Stalin's motion to postpone and passed a decision that accepted Kamenev's proferred resignation from the Central Committee and commanded the pair to refrain from any statements against Committee plans. This rebuff to Stalin was amplified by statements by Trotsky and by Stalin's co-editor, Sokolnikov, attacking Stalin's handling of the matter in the party press. Stung, Stalin announced that he was leaving the editorial board, but the meeting resolved to pass on to other business without discussing his remarks or accepting the resignation. This was the second time in 1917 that Stalin's comrades had declined to accept his resignation, putting up with his abrasive conduct in order to retain his services.[24]

The lukewarm attitude of most members of the Central Committee toward Lenin's proposal of armed insurrection was not based on any sympathy toward Kerensky's government. A meeting of the All-Russian Congress of Soviets, consisting of delegates from many parts of Russia, was scheduled to begin about this time, and it seemed quite probable that this body would decide to replace the Kerensky cabinet with a new one, perhaps entirely socialist.[25] This presumably would not involve armed force because it was generally accepted that the Soviet had to approve the composition of any particular Provisional Government. Such a change might satisfy most Bolsheviks, but not Lenin, who wanted a Bolshevik government, rather than some sort of coalition of the Left. Trotsky did not completely share this outlook and favoured the postponement of any action against Kerensky until the Congress of Soviets met. Stalin, among others, seems to have found acceptable the prospect of a Left cabinet. On 24 October, the day before the actual seizure of power, he wrote and published an editorial maintaining that, if pressured by the masses, the Congress of Soviets could 'elect' a suitable new government. 'The stronger and more organized and more powerful your action,' he told the party faithful, 'the more peacefully the old government will make way for the new.'[26] By the time this appeared in print there was already armed conflict in Petrograd, for Kerensky, anticipating a Bolshevik coup, in the early hours of 24 October had sent troops to close down the Bolshevik press. In response Trotsky, as chairman of the Military Revolutionary Committee of the Petrograd Soviet, ordered army, navy and workers' militia units to take counter-measures, which soon amounted to the seizure of Petrograd. Lenin got his armed insurrection but as a defensive measure against Kerensky's feeble initiative rather than a deliberate offensive by the Bolsheviks.

On the afternoon of 24 October, the day the struggle for the city began, Stalin reported on the current situation to a caucus of Bolshevik delegates who had assembled in preparation for the opening on the next day of the Congress of Soviets. This report, along with the continuing responsibility for the editorial line of the party organ, disposes of the idea that Stalin was inactive during the seizure of power. In the speech he displayed a knowledge of the details concerning both the political and military aspects of the insurrection, which indicates that he was in close touch with the headquarters of the operation in Smolny Institute. In keeping with Trotsky's line that he was merely taking defensive measures against Kerensky, Stalin's report was deliberately vague on the question of whether the party was indeed carrying out a coup. The Socialist Revolutionary members of the Military Revolutionary Committee had decided against walking out in protest, said Stalin, because they had accepted Bolshevik assurances that the armed action was for 'order, defence'. He saw two tendencies in the Military Revolutionary Committee, 'immediate insurrection and concentration of forces', and the Bolshevik Central Committee favoured the latter. This seemed to mean that the party, and Stalin, stood for delay. But there was another aspect of his report, which leaned in the direction of insurrection at once. Front-line units were coming to help; one Latvian regiment was being delayed. Sailors had arrested fifty officer-trainees who were loyal to Kerensky. The cruiser *Aurora* was ready to fire if the government attempted to open the draw-bridges across the Neva, although the party advised her crew to hold their fire because the revolutionaries were taking the bridges anyway, and were relying on the Saints Peter and Paul Fortress to cover the Trinity Bridge. Some of the armoured car units were for the revolt, the uprising had 'special weapons' for use against armoured cars. The revolution was taking over railway stations, the telephone building and the post offices. Troops that had been called from the front to suppress the rising were actually sending delegates proclaiming their support for it. While saying nothing explicit to contradict the line that all the action was 'defensive', Stalin left it to any sensible delegate to conclude that the Bolsheviks had nearly completed the capture of Petrograd.[27] By the end of 25 October the more or less ceremonial capture of the Winter Palace did indeed complete the Bolshevik seizure of power in the Russian capital. At about the same time Lenin emerged from hiding and proceeded to the Smolny Institute to make sure that his comrades used this opportunity to proclaim a new government, 'Soviet' in name, Bolshevik in personnel.

Stalin did not play a glorious role in this action, a point that rankled in later years when it became important to his image to demonstrate that he was Lenin's close collaborator in the 'Great October Socialist Revolution'. The truth is that Trotsky commanded the military side of the operation, to which Lenin imparted its final political point. But this did not diminish Stalin's place near the top of the winning party. And there was not a lot for him to do in the actual take-over. The same could be said of Sverdlov and Dzerzhinsky, his comrades on the inactive Military Revolutionary Centre of the party (not to be confused with the really active Military Revolutionary Committee of the Soviet, chaired by Trotsky). After Stalin was dead and his myth dismantled, Soviet historians laboured to find at least a few respectable lieutenants, excluding both Stalin and Trotsky, to place beside Lenin at the time of the October Revolution. As a result Sverdlov and Dzerzhinsky emerged with enhanced reputations, but not even the most diligent researchers could say much about their hour-by-hour activities during the crucial days. As with Stalin, there was not a lot that required their attention in the overthrow of the unpopular Kerensky government.[28]

The main thing for Stalin's career was not his role in the operational side of the insurrection but his emergence on 26 October as a member of the cabinet of the new government of Russia. This body was called the 'Council [Soviet] of People's Commissars', soon given the acronym 'Sovnarkom'. Thus Stalin became a 'people's commissar' or 'narkom'. In its original form the Sovnarkom consisted of fifteen members, including Lenin as chairman and thirteen colleagues who directed departments that already existed in Russian government, such as foreign affairs, finance and the military. Only one narkom was responsible for a department that had not existed in the previous regime. This was Stalin and the field was nationality affairs. Because of the peculiarity of this area and its vital importance at a time when the Russian Empire seemed likely to shatter along national lines, Lenin at first labelled the new office not 'people's commissar for nationality affairs' but 'chairman for nationality affairs'. Implicitly this made Stalin a kind of co-chairman with Lenin, a mark of esteem for Stalin, but not one to be overrated. Most likely Lenin saw him as the natural man for the job, considering his Georgian ancestry and his theoretical writing before the war, and wished to strengthen Stalin's hand in dealing with the increasingly obstreperous national minorities.[29]

In practice Stalin's title of 'chairman for nationality affairs' was replaced with the ordinary title of 'people's commissar' or 'narkom'. Regardless of the exact title, there is some reason to think that Stalin was at first reluctant to take the job. The Georgian Sagirashvili, who was in Petrograd at this time, maintains that his compatriot Ordzhonikidze, a close friend of Stalin, said that the latter wanted to continue to concentrate on party affairs. Perhaps he noticed that Sverdlov, who was to some extent Stalin's rival in the party organization, did not take up a people's commissariat. Stalin's success thus far had been within the party, and he may have had a shrewd premonition of the role this body was to play in the long run.[30]

In the short term it was questionable whether the all-Bolshevik Sovnarkom would last long. A number of Bolsheviks, headed by Kamenev and Zinoviev, wanted to transform it by the inclusion of representatives of the Menshevik and Socialist Revolutionary parties. The Bolshevik Central Committee, meeting in the absence of Lenin, Stalin and Trotsky on 29 October, voted unanimously for this principle. Lenin, strongly supported by Trotsky, fought back. At a meeting on 1 November the Committee resisted the leader's efforts to terminate negotiations with the other two parties, but agreed to impose conditions that amounted to acceptance of Bolshevik leadership. On the next day, the Committee majority was persuaded to take a tougher attitude toward Kamenev and those who still supported the goal of a genuine coalition. Stalin showed no enthusiasm for leaping into this fray. If he was present at the Central Committee meeting of 1 November, which is not quite certain, he remained silent. The fragmentary record does not make it possible to say what stance, if any, he took at the session of 2 November. But on 3 November, after having been called personally to Lenin's office, and knowing that Kamenev and Zinoviev were now isolated, he signed Lenin's ultimatum to them. Only on 6 November did he make a public and explicit defence of Lenin's position in a speech in the Central Executive Committee of the Soviet. Here he rejected a Menshevik demand that, as a condition for coalition, the new government release arrested liberals and permit freedom of the press.[31]

By this time he had concluded that he must take his chances on the all-Bolshevik government and see what he would make of his difficult job within it. Lacking any extant administrative machinery, Stalin's commissariat, while it remained in Petrograd, consisted of little more than a room in the Smolny Institute and one assistant. The task of the narkom was to minimize the defections from the multinational Russian state, relying mainly on propaganda, for the armed forces of the new regime could not yet impose imperial continuity. A first step was the 'Declaration of the Rights of the Peoples of Russia', signed on 2 November 1917 by both Lenin and Stalin and probably drafted by the latter.[32] This proclamation sought to assuage the fears of the national minorities by promising them the right to national self-determination, including secession. But the Soviet government did not wish to encourage the exercise of this right. On 14 November Stalin went to Helsinki to address the congress of the Finnish Social-Democratic Party on this matter. Taking an optimistic view of the impact of Bolshevik–Soviet promises of national self-determination, he asserted that the new policy would create 'mutual confidence among the peoples of Russia. . . . That is why we smile when we are told that Russia will inevitably fall to pieces if self-determination is put into practice.' But he went on to hint that trust was not the only means by which the Soviet Russian government might influence the affairs of the national minorities. Finland, he said, seemed to be on the verge of its own October Revolution. The Finnish Social Democrats should practice audacity, and if they needed help would receive from Russia a 'fraternal hand'.[33]

On 18 December, however, the non-socialist forces of Finland declared the independence of the country, and Lenin and Stalin signed a document recognizing Finnish independence. This act, said Stalin in a newspaper article a few days later, should show that the Soviet government keeps its promises.[34] It did at this point, but in January 1918 attempted to keep the somewhat different promise that Stalin had made to the Finnish Social Democrats. When the Finnish Left attempted to take power, the Soviet government quickly gave diplomatic recognition to the 'Finnish Socialist Workers' Republic'. But at this early point in its own struggle to survive the Soviet state could not provide effective military aid to the insurgents, who were suppressed.

Meanwhile the nationalists of the Ukraine were at odds with the Soviet regime and on the verge of declaring their independence. This large, populous and rich territory was far more essential to the future of the Soviet state than was Finland, and Stalin was unwilling to recognize the right of the Ukrainian 'Rada' (national assembly) to exercise the right of self-determination in the form of secession. In a series of articles he reiterated the assertion that the Rada was 'counter-revolutionary', and that the socialists in its ranks were 'traitors'. The overthrow of the Rada by the Ukrainian 'workers and soldiers' would settle its fate, he argued.[35]

Stalin summarized his experience with the Finnish and Ukrainian nationalist movements in two basic points that constituted the core of his major speech to the Third All-Russian Congress of Soviets in mid-January 1918. First, only proletarian governments, as defined by the

Bolsheviks, could exercise the right of national self-determination. Second, the national components of the former Russian Empire should remain joined in a federal union, the details of which were not yet worked out. This represented an about-face for Stalin, who previously had regarded federalism as an unacceptable bourgeois concept. But in the face of incipient fragmentation of the territory that the Soviet state hoped to control, and which it badly needed for military and economic reasons, federalism no longer looked so bad.[36]

The same flexibility and practicality appeared in his support of Lenin's position concerning relations with Germany. On 27 October the Sovnarkom and Military Revolutionary Committee empowered Lenin, Stalin and Krylenko to deal with the Russian military commander in starting armistice negotiations. The next day Lenin and Stalin went to the radio station to issue the necessary orders. It was probably because of the urgency of this issue that Lenin gave Stalin, and only two other people, a pass that permitted him to enter Lenin's personal apartment, which recently had been established in the Smolny Institute.[37] Stalin's activity as an intermediary between the Soviet authorities in Petrograd and the peace negotiators seems to have lapsed between mid-November and the end of December, as Trotsky, the narkom for foreign affairs, took charge of the proceedings. But in January and February 1918, during the periods when Trotsky was away at the peace negotiations in the city of Brest-Litovsk, Stalin again became actively involved as Lenin's closest collaborator in the crucial affair. On 1–2 January Stalin twice served as Lenin's spokesman in sending messages to the negotiators. On the 2nd the negotiating team at Brest-Litovsk addressed an important message to 'Lenin and Stalin', and on 5 January Lenin implied to Trotsky that Stalin was his chief councillor on the peace negotiations. Trotsky wired for permission to adjourn the talks without a treaty. 'Stalin has just arrived', wired Lenin in reply. 'We will look into the matter with him and let you have a joint answer right away.' Later that day the two did authorize Trotsky and his colleagues to walk out of the negotiations with the Germans and their allies.[38] The same close association of Lenin and Stalin in handling Trotsky appeared once more on 28 January after Trotsky had returned to Brest-Litovsk for a last try. Failing to reach agreement, he wired, 'What further is to be done?' This implied to Lenin and Stalin that Trotsky intended to startle the enemy by announcing the principle of 'No war, no peace'. This formula, which Trotsky had proposed before leaving Petrograd, meant that the Soviets would declare that the war was over, even though no peace treaty had been signed. Lenin and Stalin replied, 'You know our standpoint; it has lately been formed'.[39]

The standpoint in question was scepticism concerning 'no war, no peace'. Lenin and Stalin doubted that the Germans would acquiesce to the formula, that Soviet Russia could withstand a renewed German attack and that they would be rescued by a revolution in Germany. In a Central Committee meeting on 11 January Stalin had expressed his doubts about Trotsky's proposal in terms that can hardly have improved their relations: 'Trotsky's position is no position.' Russia must make an odious peace because 'There is no revolutionary movement in the West, nothing exists, only a potential, and we cannot count on a potential.'[40] Such a flat dismissal of the orthodox Marxist hopes for proletarian revolution in the lands of advanced capitalism went too far for Lenin who disassociated himself from Stalin's statement. But he seems to have valued both Stalin's vote in the Central Committee during the controversy on peace, and his willingness to insist that they face a painful decision, to persist against the comrades who resisted Lenin's disagreeable logic. These tough qualities Stalin demonstrated in the crucial Committee meeting of 18 February, brushing aside with harsh realism the objections of idealistic comrades who wanted to continue a 'revolutionary war': 'We want to talk straight, go to the heart of the matter: the Germans are attacking, we have no forces, the time has come to say that negotiations must be resumed.'[41] This meant the signing of the punitive terms that the enemy presented at Brest-Litovsk, the acceptance of Lenin's bold gamble of trading a vast amount of space for a little time. The treaty brought the Kaiser's armies to within about 125 km of Petrograd, which persuaded Lenin to move his fledgling government to Moscow. Thus it was that Koba, who had come to St Petersburg by third-class carriage some six years before, departed from Petrograd on 10 March at 10 p.m. by special train no. 4001, which was reserved for the government of the new Russia.[42]

4 Narkom

Leaving Petrograd, Stalin retained no sentimental attachment to the city of the revolution. He returned to Russia's second city on only three occasions during the rest of his life.[1] Moscow, in contrast, became his home for life and the city on which he lavished much personal attention and the wealth of the state. He did, however, bring with him from Petrograd one souvenir of his sojourn there, a bride. This was Nadezhda Sergeevna Allilueva, who, in the spirit of the socialist emancipation of women, retained her birth-name after marriage. She was the youngest daughter of Sergei and Olga Alliluev, whom Stalin had known since 1900 and his Tbilisi days, a year before Nadezhda's birth. Having seen the family intermittently in the following years, Stalin had made their apartment in Petrograd his home around the beginning of August 1917. Sergei was a skilled electrician who worked in a power-plant and ran a small repair business on the side, his wife working as a nurse. So the family, though 'proletarian' in some sense, could afford a spacious apartment on Rozhdestvennsky Street. Stalin's room was small but large enough to contain all his belongings in one wicker basket that he had brought with him from Siberia. It probably was the most comfortable and sociable residence he had ever known, admired by the two girls of the family, pampered by their mother. It was she who tried mending his one suit and found it so threadbare that she insisted on buying him a replacement. This probably was the last 'bourgeois' or 'business' suit he ever owned. Stalin evidently had strict scruples about dressing in the style of the oppressing class, and, though he had until 1918 worn a dark two-piece suit, he would never put on a white shirt or necktie with it. Olga made him some kind of 'black velvet protectors with a high neck', partly to warm his throat, which was giving him trouble that winter. Even this eccentric adaptation of the bourgeois style seems to have displeased him, and after the move to Moscow and his involvement in military affairs Stalin assumed the garb that became habitual for him, a military tunic without insignia and military breeches stuffed into high-topped black Russian boots.[2]

With Nadia Allilueva, who was only fifteen when Stalin moved in with the family, a romantic attachment developed. She was a bright, idealistic student in secondary school, an ardent partisan of the revolution. Nadia could hardly have seen much of the 38-year-old widower, who was absorbed by politics in this crucial time and often did not return to the Alliluev apartment to spend the night. But she saw in him a hero of the liberating cause to which her father was devoted. If one may rely on the recollections of Nadia's sister Anna, their romance grew out of domestic

banter. On one occasion Nadia was noisily cleaning the apartment. Stalin
put his head out of his door and asked 'What's all the noise? . . . Oh, it's
you! A real housewife has settled down to work.' Nadia, like most women
of the radical intelligentsia, saw herself as a worker for the new society,
not a housewife, and she 'bristled' in reply, 'Is there anything wrong
with that?' Certainly not in Stalin's opinion, for he never envisaged
the revolution as a drastic transformation of the status of women. He
encouraged her to keep on with her house cleaning, and may have
misunderstood her reply. In the long run their relationship was to founder
on such a misunderstanding.[3]

But at the time he was drawn to this attractive, spirited and admiring
girl who was less than half his age. Against the wishes of her mother, he
married Nadezhda, now sixteen, at some time during the last month
before the government moved to Moscow.[4] In the new capital the couple
were privileged personages. Presumably they lodged initially in the Hotel
National, then (and, arguably, to the present day) the premier hostelry of
the city, facing the Kremlin and Red Square. In a few weeks Lenin's
inner circle was able to move into apartments that had been readied for
them in the Kremlin. Stalin's attraction to Russian nationalism, already a
feature of his personality, surely was enhanced by the powerful Muscovite
atmosphere of this fortress, which was obsolete for modern warfare but
eminently practical as protection against assassins or mobs. Appreciating
both its atmosphere and security, Stalin remained closely attached to the
Kremlin for the rest of his life.[5]

As for Stalin's youthful wife, she was at first able to fulfill her dreams of
service to the revolution. When her husband went off to war at Tsaritsyn
(later named Stalingrad) in the spring of 1918, she accompanied him,
probably as a secretary, and she joined Lenin's personal staff in that
capacity in 1919, having returned to Moscow. At some point in 1918 she
joined the Communist Party. Considering her devotion to the cause and
her high connections it is surprising to learn that she was expelled from
the party in 1921 and had to appeal to Lenin himself for a letter
requesting reinstatement. Who would dare to expel a member of Lenin's
staff, the wife of an important member of the government and daughter
of an influential old Bolshevik? It is hard to conceive that any member of
the commission that was then purging the party of undesirables (mainly
opportunists, alcoholics, embezzlers and the inactive) could have been so
stupid or audacious as to select Nadezhda for expulsion. Who indeed but
Stalin could have initiated this action? If he had not favoured it, Nadia
surely could have reversed it through his influence, which was immense
by 1921, and she would not have had to bother Lenin about the matter.
The most likely explanation of the incident is that Stalin wanted his wife
to settle down to a domestic existence at this time, the year of the birth of
their first child, Vasily. A similar crisis between them erupted after the

birth of their daughter Svetlana in 1926, with Nadezhda leaving for Leningrad (as Petrograd was called after 1924) to start an independent life. Stalin then telephoned her and persuaded her to return, probably by promising her the employment of a governess and a chance to pursue a higher education, both of which soon followed. In 1921 he may have been so angered by her refusal to drop her career in order to become a housewife-mother that he decided to clip her wings by the one administrative means at his disposal, expulsion from the party. It was, of course, beyond even his powers to have her fired from Lenin's office staff. And it appears that, despite Lenin's letter, Nadia regained full membership only in 1924. In August of that year she asked an old family friend and Bolshevik for a letter of recommendation for admission to the party as a full member, specifically noting that she was currently a candidate member.[6]

In the very period in which Lenin was requesting Nadia's reinstatement in the party, Stalin was in fact pressing Lenin for a favour concerning his family affairs, but this was quite a different matter: the acquisition of a better apartment in the Kremlin. With the arrival of a son Stalin must have found his old quarters cramped, and he complained to Lenin that the noise of the communal kitchen was hard to bear in the early mornings. But even Lenin had trouble getting the custodians of the Kremlin to move rapidly in preparing the new apartment. Three times between November 1921 and February 1922 Lenin wrote to his officials to complain of their slowness and red tape in this matter. The Stalin family apparently did move into their new quarters by March 1922, for the last note from Lenin is February. The apartment seems to have been the one that Svetlana describes in her memoirs as her mother's in the Poteshny Palace. This overlooks the bridge by which tourists now enter the Kremlin through the Troitsky Gate, somewhat to the right of the bridge as one enters.[7]

Living in an apartment in one of the Romanov's palaces in the Kremlin obviously was a mark of high rank and privilege. The very fact that the Stalin family had enough to eat during the terrible years that followed the revolution was also a mark of the highest status, although the leading Bolsheviks lived modestly in the first years of Soviet rule, compared to the leaders of most states. In any case, the goal for Stalin was at this time, as always in his life, not affluence but power. And in this he was brilliantly successful in the five years that lay between the October Revolution and the onset of Lenin's physical collapse. This period, and the five years following Lenin's death in January 1924, witnessed Stalin's rise to supremacy in the new Soviet–Bolshevik political system. His one serious rival since they both joined the Central Committee in 1912, another man who understood power, Sverdlov, died of an illness at the beginning of 1919, leaving the way open for Stalin to emerge at the top of the system when Lenin had reached his physical limit. Before

October 1917, Stalin, like other Bolsheviks, had never had to administer anything substantial, for the party was not a large operation. The October Revolution saddled this small organization with a stupendous task, and it is remarkable that Lenin could find even a bare minimum of comrades capable of doing the job at all. That the regime survived owes much to people like Stalin, in whom previously untapped qualities were discovered, most especially an aptitude for exercising power. Stalin's affinity for authority began with a zest for it. This sounds obvious enough, but there are serious grounds to doubt that many of the leading Bolsheviks, Trotsky, Zinoviev and Bukharin among them, fully shared this quality. Certainly none of them displayed in the five years of Lenin's rule the capacity for politics and administration that Stalin revealed in this time.

Lenin, a connoisseur of power, had the best opportunity to evaluate Stalin in this respect, and he rendered his judgment in a debate in 1922. Replying to a complaint about the concentration of power in general and in particular Stalin's responsibility for two peoples' commissariats, Lenin called Stalin 'a person of authority'. On what did this aura of authority rest? Not on a heroic image. Stalin was not a highly visible hero of the revolution and civil war in these years. The fame of Trotsky, the organizer of the Red Army and eloquent speaker and writer, was far greater, and a number of others – such as Zinoviev, Kamenev and Bukharin – probably received more attention in the Soviet media than did Stalin. This, incidentally, suggests that he was in these years, at least, much more concerned with getting on with his practical work than in preening himself in public. An unbalanced thirst for popular glory, a 'cult', could more easily be attributed to some of his comrades than to him. Nor did his authority within the party–state system rest on actual or threatened physical repression. The question of 'class enemies' is another matter, on which Stalin shared with his mentor and colleagues an ample degree of cold-bloodness. In dealing with Bolsheviks, however, his authority rested mainly on personality, on decisiveness and that capacity for non-physical intimidation that has served well so many successful bosses throughout history. Lenin was relying on this quality in January 1922 when he entrusted Stalin with an important commission concerning grain purchases abroad, a vital matter in a time of famine. 'Every day lean on Litvinov [concerning foreign exchange] and check *personally* two or three times a week.' Stalin was the man you counted on when the job was leaning on somebody. In the area of famine relief Lenin had already seen his cool toughness as a negotiator when Stalin had proposed that the Soviet state profit by the philanthropy of the American Relief Administration by charging them for the transport of emergency food supplies on Soviet territory.[8]

Among other signs of Lenin's regard for Stalin's ability to get results from people was a curious affair in 1920 concerning the possibility of a devastating secret weapon. This was the concept of a Soviet engineer, S. I. Botin, who believed that he could use electromagnetism to explode ammunition a considerable distance from the power source. In general a zealot for the use of electricity as a means of overtaking the advanced capitalist countries, Lenin must have had the greatest enthusiasm for the picture of imperialist armies collapsing as their own munitions exploded in their hands. Obviously he wanted practical results in the shortest possible time. Stalin had no scientific or technical background, and this kind of thing was not a part of any of his regular jobs. But it was Stalin whom Lenin assigned as the expediter of this key project, simply because he was the person most likely to get the impoverished and bureaucratized Soviet state machinery moving. Experiments were carried out, but failed. At the end Lenin wrote to G. M. Krzhizhanovsky, whom he considered a technical expert, that if he did not find the scheme promising, 'I will turn him [Botin, who had been bothering Lenin with complaints] back to Stalin and liquidate the "experiments." ' Obviously Stalin could be counted on to deal effectively with complainers.[9]

All of this meant that Stalin was well adapted to survival in the environment of bureaucracy that inevitably grew up as the Soviet–Bolshevik regime adapted to the task of ruling a large country. This was what Lenin had in mind in 1921 when he wrote of Stalin to another comrade, concerning work assignments, 'Really, of course, he in particular would stand up for himself.' There are fragments enough in Lenin's papers to show that he was right: Stalin trying to enhance the budget of one of his agencies, trying to have a free hand in picking capable personnel for another, asking to be relieved of some of his jobs because of overwork, asking to be reassigned from regional work to 'the centre', protesting that his requests for military supplies bring promises but not supplies.[10]

But a capacity for antagonistic working relations was not the only aspect of Stalin's personality as a boss. Those who were loyal and hardworking in Stalin's interest received his protection. Testimony that Stalin displayed this valuable and by no means contemptible characteristic comes from a witness who was not partial to Stalin, Trotsky. Despite the fact that he protested to Lenin in January 1919 that 'I consider the protection given by Stalin to the Tsaritsyn trend the most dangerous sort of ulcer, worse than any act of perfidy or treachery', nothing serious happened to the careers of these Stalin loyalists. During the five years of Lenin's reign Stalin's diverse activities put him in touch with a substantial number of Bolsheviks, including all of his future Politburo of the early 1930s, and those who were not previously acquainted with him appear to have been drawn into his orbit at this time.[11]

The early Soviet years also served as the best first-hand introduction that Stalin had ever had to the geography of European Russia. Previously he had lived in Transcaucasia, St Petersburg/Petrograd and a few scattered places of exile, with connecting journeys that gave him only limited glimpses of the land. From 1922 to the end of his life, he stuck close to Moscow, except for vacation trips to the south and wartime conferences. But in 1918–20 he was on the road more than he was in Moscow, his assignments requiring him to travel extensively in European Russia. Whatever he understood of this vast area was surely acquired mainly as an administrator who was required to arrive in some particular trouble-spot, form an impression of local problems, resources and people, and get something done. It was in this manner that Stalin encountered the Lower and Upper Volga regions, the Ukraine and the North Caucasus, along with areas that he already knew, Petrograd and Transcaucasia. (See map, p. xvi.)

Above all, Stalin's rise as an effective administrator depended on his capacity for work, unrelenting and immensely varied. Here was a man, perhaps the only one at Lenin's disposal, who could take on almost any kind of job, whether or not he had any background in the matter at hand, learn enough about it to make definite decisions under severe pressure of time and deal with the most pressing problems. The results were not necessarily ideal, but on balance they were successful, sometimes brilliantly so, and the principal thing was to maintain the offensive if possible, to substitute direction for drift. The years 1918–22 were a matchless education for Stalin in the direction of the new Russian Empire, exposing him, often for the first time in his life, to a wide variety of issues, and almost always under emergency conditions. If he, and perhaps the party as a whole, in later years displayed a strong inclination to 'campaignism', the all-out drive under quasi-military command and contempt for the opinion of 'specialists', this owes much to the atmosphere of these first years in power.

The weight and intensity of the burdens that Stalin carried in this period seem to have taken a physical toll. The evidence is fragmentary, but Lenin's papers include various references to some kind of medical problem that Stalin suffered in 1919–21. The founder expressed concern for the matter and at one point insisted that Stalin consult a specialist. The ailment was not one of the infectious diseases that were rampant in Russia in this period, such as influenza, cholera and typhus. Unlike these, Stalin's illness was chronic over several years but not disabling. Several times Lenin referred to the prospect of surgery, which suggests the possibility of ulcers. Such an ailment would be consistent with the alternative treatment that finally seems to have solved the problem, a cure at a mineral water spa, Nalchik, in the North Caucasus. This leave was ordered by no less an authority than the Politburo on 30 April 1921 and lasted from late May until early August.[12]

The only administrative realm that was assigned to Stalin when the Soviet government settled in Moscow in March 1918 was his established speciality, the affairs of the minority nationalities. His new start in this field was not entirely auspicious. He had an office in the Kremlin, but the various sections of his people's commissariat at first lacked any working quarters at all, then received several expropriated houses in widely scattered parts of the city. 'Make sure they don't swipe them from us', said Stalin to his assistant S. Pestkovsky, who proceeded to 'hire' some Latvian riflemen, the toughest of the soldiers at the disposal of the government, to guard his acquisitions, not from 'Whites' but from his fellow Soviet bureaucrats. But this dispersed domain did not please Stalin, and in the best tradition of bureaucratic empire-building he attempted to annex from the nascent 'All-Russian Council of the National Economy' the Hotel Siberia, a better located, more spacious headquarters. He took personal command of the attack, telling Pestkovsky, to have Allilueva type up some papers saying 'These premises are occupied by Narkomnats', and to bring along some tacks to post these notices. Thus armed, the pair proceeded to the unguarded hotel at night. Stalin tore down some signs claiming the place for the economists, posted his own signs and with his aide found an unlocked back entrance. But they could not turn on the lights and had to stumble through the corridors until their supply of matches ran out. Then they 'almost broke their necks falling into the cellar'. It was all for naught. Somehow the Council of the National Economy managed to retain title to the hotel. But this, said Pestkovsky, 'was one of the few instances in which Stalin suffered defeat'.[13]

But not quite the only instance. Shortly after his arrival in Moscow, Stalin somewhat cantankerously tried to press a libel suit against the Menshevik leader Martov. In March 1918 this defeated anti-Bolshevik tried to demonstrate the low character of Lenin's cabinet by making passing mention of the allegation that the narkom of nationality affairs, Stalin, had once been expelled from the party because of his connection to 'expropriations', that is, robbery. At this time Soviet 'revolutionary tribunals' were not yet reliable instruments of the regime, and Stalin had to make two court appearances to attest that Martov lied, only to have the court conclude that the case was not in its jurisdiction because it was a political matter, which enabled Martov to exult in print, 'I am satisfied.' After a stormy debate the Central Executive Committee voted to have Stalin's complaint reopened, but nothing came of this.[14]

In the spring of 1918 Stalin carried out two substantial tasks in the field of nationality affairs. In April he participated in three sessions of the commission that was drafting the first constitution of the Soviet state, the Russian Soviet Federative Socialist Republic, which was formally adopted in July. Here he stood for a centralist interpretation of the federal principle, rebuffing the members of the commission that wanted to grant considerable authority to the minority nationalities in the new state. He argued that in all events the history of federations, including the United States, shows that it is merely a transitional form on the path to unitary government, and that no bicameral legislative system was necessary to represent the interests of the minorities. Nor was he referring merely to the smaller ethnic groups, such as the Volga Tartars, that were already subject to the Moscow government. He foresaw the integration of Poland, the Ukraine, Finland and Transcaucasia into a unicameral Soviet state. In a few years this 'Great Russian chauvinist' approach was to involve him in a serious quarrel with Lenin, but in 1918 Ilyich made no objection. The second task of this period was the first of Stalin's numerous trips into the field during these years, a sojourn in Kursk around 1 May to negotiate with the Ukrainian government, which had come into being under German patronage.[15]

For about two and one-half years beginning in June 1918 Stalin had little time for the business of Narkomnats. Military assignments took priority in his work during most of that time. But in February–March 1920 the occupation of the Ukraine by Soviet forces once again involved Stalin in the affairs of this nationality with the object of reintegrating it into the Soviet Russian state. Although there was at this time a theoretically independent Ukrainian Soviet Republic, Stalin (no Ukrainian and a member of the Russian Sovnarkom) became a member of two vital Ukrainian bodies: the Council of the 'Ukrainian Labour Army' (an attempt to use military organization as an emergency measure to restore mines and industry) and the Central Committee of the Ukrainian Communist Party.[16]

By the fall of 1920 the successes of the Red Army brought him in contact once again with the affairs of his native region. At the opening of that year there were three small, independent, non-Communist republics in Transcaucasia: Azerbaijan, Armenia and Georgia. Stalin believed that small nations could not be truly independent but would fall under the sway of the imperialists if they did not become Soviet. This principle led to the Sovietization of Azerbaijan in April 1920 through a co-ordinated Communist rising in Baku and an invasion by the Red Army. In November Soviet troops entered Armenia and established a parallel 'independent' Soviet republic there. That left Georgia, governed by Mensheviks, many of them Stalin's personal enemies in his early career.[17]

In May 1920 the Moscow government had granted formal recognition of Georgian independence. But there were ominous signs. The Soviet–Georgian treaty included a secret protocol obliging the Georgians to permit the Communist Party freedom of action. Moreover, in a meeting with Georgian emissaries to Moscow Stalin referred to his concern about the possibility of 'anti-Soviet' forces operating in Georgia. This alleged threat to Soviet interests surfaced in Stalin's communications with Lenin in October–November 1920 when Stalin visited Baku and various nearby centres. He had gone to the region with the assignment of improving petroleum deliveries to Russia proper, but he succeeded in linking this matter to the Georgian question. There was a serious danger, he wired Lenin, that Georgia would invite the western capitalists to take over Batumi, the Black Sea port on the western end of the rail line leading to Baku and its oil fields. Did Stalin actually believe this? It is true that as recently as July 1920 the British had maintained a mere brigade in Batumi, a vestige of a force that had occupied the Transcaucasian railway shortly after the end of the war with Germany. But the Atlantic allies had been unable to agree on any commitment to defend the newly founded non-Soviet republics of Transcaucasia, and in withdrawing were obviously backing away from armed confrontation with the Red Army. That they would suddenly reverse direction and invade the area was far from likely. Still more implausible was Stalin's assertion in the third of these messages that 'Menshevik Georgia, the former actual tool of the Entente' was by itself a threat to Baku. To believe that little Georgia would try to wrest the main Soviet petroleum source from the Red Army requires a heroic leap of credulity, comparable to the wilder accusations that appeared years later in the great show trials of the 1930s.[18]

Pressed by Stalin, Lenin vacillated. His first response was: 'I consider it undoubtable that Georgia will give Batumi to the Entente, probably secretly, and that the Entente will move on Baku.' But Lenin was also concerned about the opinion of west European socialists, for he was at this time attempting to win over a large part of these movements to the newly founded Communist International, the apple of his eye. He temporized in his next two replies to Stalin, asking about the possibility of peaceful relations with Georgia, and he declined to support any decisive action without a full discussion in the Politburo. At the opening of December 1920 Lenin consented to Stalin's requests for the reinforcement of the Red Army in Transcaucasia. But in the middle of that month Lenin expressly forbade Stalin's friend, Ordzhonikidze, the party boss for Transcaucasia, to invade Georgia. It appears that Stalin was incapacitated by illness at this point, but on 24 January 1921, after he had returned to action, Stalin bypassed Lenin and wrote a letter to the Central Committee, proposing that the Military Revolutionary Council prepare measures to assist an insurrection in Georgia. Since the Communist Party of Georgia was a subordinate part of the Soviet party, reporting to Ordzhonikidze, such an insurrection could occur only on orders from Moscow. Soviet editors are withholding evidence on this matter, but it appears that Lenin accepted Stalin's plan to take over Georgia. On 27 January Stalin ordered Ordzhondikidze to prepare to defend 'the sovereignty and security of Soviet republics' against the 'anti-Soviet' policy of Georgia, and asked for a report on the status of Red Army forces. For some reason, probably poor communications facilities, no reply came from Ordzhonikidze, and on 5 February Lenin demonstrated that he had been won over to Stalin's position by pressing Ordzhonikidze for a reply, for 'we are very worried'. Less than a week later a feeble Communist uprising in Georgia evoked the 'defensive' measures that Stalin had been working for during the several preceding months. There was armed resistance, but the outcome in this grossly unequal contest was never in doubt.[19]

Lenin's scruples about the suppression of Georgian Menshevism required Stalin's ruthless hand in July 1921, about six months after the Communization of the country. At this time Stalin was taking a cure on the northern slopes of the Caucasus and received an invitation from Ordzhonikidze to visit Tbilisi and explain to their compatriots why it had been necessary to return them to the Russia orbit. Very likely Ordzhonikidze was concerned by the survival of Menshevism and nationalism and hoped that the personal authority of the world's most important Georgian would have a salutory effect. But the reception that Stalin received at a mass rally was anything but satisfactory. A witness recalls that a number of Menshevik activists, who were still at liberty in their homeland, openly attacked Stalin for betraying the treaty by which the Soviet state recognized Georgian independence, and easily aroused strong hostility toward the guest of honour. Stalin responded at a special meeting of the Georgian Communist organization, upbraiding the local leaders for their softness, ordering them to 'cauterize with red-hot irons' nationalist survivals, to 'crush the hydra of nationalism'. Such is the language of the official version of the speech. According to reports circulating in Tbilisi at the time, Stalin was in reality still more violent:

> You hens! You sons of asses! What is going on here? You have to draw a white-hot iron over this Georgian land! . . . It seems to me that you have already forgotten the principle of the dictatorship of the proletariat. You will have to break the wings of this Georgia! Let the blood of the petit-bourgeoisie flow until they give up all their resistance! Impale them! Tear them apart! Make them remember the days of Shah-Abbas!

Whether or not this version is strictly accurate, it was followed up by a severe sweep of the political opposition by the Cheka.[20]

Like his comrades among the Bolshevik leaders, Stalin lacked any sort of military experience before 1918, but the Russian civil war abruptly immersed him in this field, which he took to with zest and talent. His literal and intense understanding of class struggle imparted a taste for combat, the Leninist emphasis on central authority whetted his appetite for authority. The experience also encouraged his self-confident belief that the opinions of professional experts were not to be trusted when they differed from his own. Many of the officers with whom he worked in the civil war were former tsarist commanders who had been pressed into service in the Red Army with threats and promised rewards. Such men were suspect in Stalin's eyes because of their social origins, previous political connections and tendency to assume that they were in charge. He summarized his convictions on this matter most clearly in June 1919, following the capture of a coastal fortress by naval action: 'The naval experts assured that the capture of Krasnaia Gorka from the sea runs counter to naval science. I can only deplore such a so-called science.'[21]

In June 1918 there was no reason to consider Stalin a military leader, and he was dispatched by Lenin to Tsaritsyn on the Lower Volga to expedite the shipment of foodstuffs to the hungry cities of the north, not to command military operations. From the start, however, there was a military aspect of the trip, owing to activities in the region of the forces of the Don Cossacks, now an independent state of sorts, and the embryonic 'Volunteer Army' further south, both anti-Bolshevik. To protect Stalin and to impress the populace with his importance, Moscow gave its emissary an armoured train and a bodyguard of 400 men, of whom not less than 100 were to be Latvian riflemen, the Red Praetorian guard of the time. He needed such protection on one occasion, for White Cossacks attacked his train while he was on tour of inspection. This appears to be the only time in Stalin's experience in the Civil War that he was actually under fire. At first Stalin concentrated on unsnarling food transport, and seems to have made some progress in this. But in July the advance of the Cossack forces obliged him to give priority to defence, and on 19 July he took charge of a new 'North Caucasian Military District'. But how clear was his authority? This became an increasingly sore point in the summer and autumn of 1918. Trotsky, the narkom of war, dealt with the acute shortage of politically reliable officers by dividing unit command between a trained man, who often was a former tsarist officer, and a 'political commissar', who was supposed to be Red rather than expert. The former was to have the initiative in military command, but the latter was to co-sign all orders and if necessary countermand them or even execute a traitorous commander. This worked well enough to see the Soviet state through its civil war, but the system contained plenty of room for friction. One problem was determining the level at which the political authorities ran the military campaign, taking counsel with professionals but acting as the highest command.[22]

In September 1918 a Military Revolutionary Council assumed overall control as a supreme council of war. It included Lenin, Trotsky, Stalin and other Communists and no professional officers. Below this the major zones of operations, 'fronts', were directed by councils in which party officials held sway, Stalin prominent among them. But in the summer of 1918 the workings of such bodies had not yet been defined. Stalin and his two comrades on the 'Military Council of the North Caucasus Military District' asserted that 'All operational orders and all command of all troop units of the military district henceforth originate with the Military Council.' This body included one veteran soldier, at first an obscure ex-officer, Kovalevsky, followed by a former NCO in the tsarist army, Klimenty Voroshilov, Stalin's future crony and narkom of war. Orders were signed jointly by the military member and Stalin, with Stalin's name first. Incidentally, the content of these commands makes it clear that Stalin wanted to deal with conventional, full-scale military units, including artillery, not some sort of 'revolutionary' guerrilla force. There were 'vocates of partisan warfare among the Russian Communists, but Stalin the first seems to have wanted the weightiest, most conventional , that he could get, and bombarded Moscow with requests for all ..rts of heavy reinforcements, even including aircraft, destroyers and submarines.[23]

Trouble for Stalin's command began on 30 August 1918 when a former tsarist officer, P. P. Sytin, was appointed supreme commander for the southern front. According to his understanding of the new system, he was the operational commander of a large area including Tsaritsyn, which he proceeded to assert in a series of orders during his first visit to that centre on 29 September. Stalin and his two associates, a Communist named S. K. Minin and Voroshilov, were taken aback to find themselves mere subordinates. After considering the decisions of Sytin in the name of the Military Revolutionary Council of the Southern Front, they formally declared that they did not accept that he had 'full authority in the conduct of operations' and that the minutes of their meeting with him did not constitute a binding order. Lacking political authority over Stalin, Sytin appealed to the Military Revolutionary Council of the Soviet state. This outraged Trotsky, who on 4 October wired Lenin from Tambov, where Trotsky was inspecting operations on the eastern front: 'I insist categorically on Stalin's recall.' He then disparaged Voroshilov as a commander, insisting that he take orders from Sytin and ending by appealing to Lenin for his personal support: 'This can be put to rights within 24 hours given firm and resolute support at your end.' The next day he followed up with a wire demanding that one of Stalin's orders be countermanded: 'Stalin's actions are disrupting all my plans.' Stalin was far from inactive in his own cause. He had been in Moscow from about 14 until 22 September, during which time he had conferred with both Lenin and Sverdlov. This probably helped to blunt Trotsky's attack, for Lenin was far from quick in acceding to the War Commissar's demand for Stalin's dismissal. Returning to Tsaritsyn, Stalin and Voroshilov made their arguments against Sytin's authority in another wire to Lenin dated 3 October. Three days later Stalin again went to Moscow and conferred with Lenin with some success, it seems, for on the 8th he was appointed to the Military Revolutionary Council of the Republic, the highest organ of political control over military affairs. Returning to Tsaritsyn on 11

October, he had the good fortune to be present at the rout of the Cossacks, for which he claimed credit over Sytin. This probably helped to strengthen Stalin's hand when he returned to Moscow for his last shuttle-trip in this series, arriving 23 October. By now he had become deeply drawn to the military sphere and told Sverdlov that he wanted to continue to work on the southern front. He even sought, through Sverdlov, reconciliation with Trotsky, offering to come to the war narkom, to talk matters over, 'put aside former differences and arrange to work together as Stalin so much desires'. There is no record that Trotsky even acknowledged this overture, a rebuff that Stalin was not likely to forget.[24]

Lenin and Sverdlov attempted to resolve this quarrel by separating the disputants and withholding complete victory from either side. They appeased Trotsky by the denial of Stalin's request to return to the southern front and the transfer of Voroshilov to another assignment. But Sytin was also recalled and given a desk job in Moscow. The main result was that, far from concluding that Stalin was basically mistaken in his methods at Tsaritsyn, Lenin regarded 'the measures decided on by Stalin' as a model, urging these measures on the commanders in that area in May 1919 when a new and more powerful enemy force threatened the city.[25]

In January 1919 Stalin received an opportunity to obtain some measure of revenge against Trotsky's management of the war against the Whites, which, however, he exploited with restraint. The army of Admiral Kolchak, moving west from Siberia, had in December 1918 inflicted a major defeat on the Red Army, capturing the city of Perm and large quantities of supplies. Before sending anyone to investigate the causes of this calamity Lenin diplomatically wired Trotsky, asking his opinion about entrusting the job to Stalin, explaining that the local party boss would be too lenient with the professional commander who was said to be drunk and unable to restore order. Trotsky, perhaps innocently, accepted the nomination of Stalin, even implying that he shared Lenin's respect for his toughness. In fact, Stalin was teamed with Dzerzhinsky, who had to interrupt his work in building up the secret police in order to take on the assignment. The two spent the better part of a month in Glazov and Viatka studying the organization, or lack of it, of the party and army in the area. Perhaps Dzerzhinsky's influence moderated the partisan tone of their report, which did not mention Trotsky unfavourably, but it did refer contemptuously to his choice of commander-in-chief, the professional officer I. I. Vatsetis. His orders were 'ill-considered' and 'unpardonably thoughtless', but the report did not demand his removal. It may be, too, that Stalin was more interested in establishing himself as a competent analyst of military problems than in settling scores, for the general tone of the document was technical, professional.[26]

Evidently Lenin was favourably impressed, because he turned to Stalin in May 1919 when the White army of General Yudenich threatened

Petrograd with a drive based on nearby Estonia, which was under British protection. In fact the attack force was not large and it lacked any population base. The real danger was the panic and disarray which the party boss of Petrograd, Zinoviev, had permitted, according to Stalin. Zinoviev supposedly had permitted the military command to leak reports that they were preparing to evacuate Petrograd and had detached the commander from his staff, making him into some sort of personal adjutant. If Lenin and Stalin themselves did not panic, their darkly suspicious attitude toward the situation anticipated the atmosphere of Stalin's purges many years later, ready to see the encircling capitalists at the gate and their agents penetrating everything. According to Lenin's wires to Stalin, the imperialist foe was ready to spring. He believed that the attack of a British fleet of twenty-three ships would be co-ordinated with 'organized treason'. 'Mensheviks and Socialist-Revolutionaries' were 'blowing up bridges and conspiring'. Stalin agreed. 'We have unearthed a big conspiracy. . . . The battery commanders of all the forts in the entire Kronshtadt fortified area are implicated. The aim of the conspiracy was to seize possession of the fortress, take control of the fleet, open fire on the rear of our troops, and clear the road to Petrograd.' After the White capture of the city the British fleet would appear 'with the object of "helping the Russian people" to establish a new "democratic system"'. Not only the British but the bourgeoisie of numerous states (even Denmark, Greece and Switzerland!) had used their former embassy staffs in Petrograd, who 'scattered money left and right, buying everyone in the rear of our army who was open to be bought'.[27]

Such nightmares were not without some basis. The British fleet *was* nearby and, without committing major forces, did attack Soviet ships, inflicting serious damage. The British had sent money and supplies to Yudenich. There were cases of treason, the most important being the surrender of two coastal forts, and the populace as a whole could not be trusted fully. Stalin's state of mind probably was affected by the knowledge that in Baku the local commissars had been executed by their enemies, with British acquiescence, in September 1918. On the other hand, Lenin and Stalin were allowing old intra-party feuds to dominate their judgement when they included the Mensheviks among the alleged class enemies, for the Mensheviks steadfastly supported the Soviet state against its capitalist enemies despite their disagreements with Lenin.

In any case, Stalin overcame the crisis in Petrograd. He was for one thing a highly visible representative of the central authority, touring front-line areas all around the area during late May and June: south to military headquarters at Staraia Russa, back to Gatchina near Petrograd, the vicinity of the main White spearhead, out to Kronshtadt, the naval base in the Gulf of Finland, north to the Karelian border with Finland, west along the gulf to Narva and back nearer to Petrograd to participate in the command of the operations to recapture the forts that had been betrayed to the enemy. By 18 June he was able to wire Lenin that Petrograd did not need reinforcements, which should be sent east to deal with greater danger of Kolchak, a most welcome message for the hard-pressed Lenin and a sign of Stalin's self-confidence. In his public report on the situation, a *Pravda* interview, he made a point that contained two important implications for future reference. First, he seemed to invite congratulations for having revived the fleet, which he treated as a major arm, a point that not every analyst of Russian defence investments would agree on, given Russia's geographical situation. Nevertheless a yen for warships, which had possessed Peter the Great and Nicholas II, among others, was to reappear later in Stalin's career. Second, in connection with the navy, he observed that the officers of the Baltic fleet had not sold out to the foreigner. 'Here we have men who, to their honour be it said, prize the dignity and independence of Russia higher than British gold.' This unadulterated appeal to Russian nationalism was by no means unique among Stalin's pronouncements during the civil war and looked forward to future years and a future war.[28]

Stalin was back in Moscow for less than a week before returning to military–political duty, this time at Smolensk, the headquarters of the front facing Poland and Lithuania, where he appeared on 9 July 1919. Until 10 September he divided his time between that centre and Minsk, the capital of a supposedly independent Soviet Lithuanian–White Russian government. Matters had not gone well for this creature of Moscow, and Stalin presided over its dissolution. Nor were matters going well for the Red Army in the area. Despite the feebleness of the White forces of Yudenich in the north and of Poland and Lithuania, both of whom had been in existence for less than a year, Stalin considered the situation precarious. He concluded his report to Lenin, 'Now consider for yourself: can you let us have one division, if only in successive brigades, or are you going to allow the enemy to smash the already crumbling Sixteenth Army?' This grim appraisal was based on the belief that the 'enemy in the West, who is united under a single command, has not yet brought into action those *Russian* corps which he has ready, or nearly ready, in Riga, Warsaw and Kishinev'. This gross exaggeration of the evil competence of the imperialists was characteristic of Stalin's, and many others', outlook at this time. A united command that could make co-ordinated use of the various anti-Red forces was precisely what the enemy lacked, and existence of 'Russian' armies in Warsaw, Kishinev or Riga was fanciful.[29]

Returning to Moscow on 26 September for a Central Committee meeting, Stalin found himself assigned to an area of much greater immediate danger, the southern front, which faced the largest of all White armies, that of General Denikin. Having broken through Red Army positions in May 1919, this force was spreading to the Volga on its right flank and the Dnieper on its left, the centre heading ominously toward Moscow. And Denikin had received substantial supplies from Britain. After a four-day round trip once again to Smolensk, 28 September–1 October, evidently to wind up his business there, Stalin left Moscow for the most extended of all his military missions. On 3 October he reached the town of Sergeievskoe, the headquarters of the southern front. Ten days later the Whites captured Orel, about 200 km south of Moscow, which they hoped to reach by Christmas. Although the situation appeared grim, the basic fact was that the Whites had greatly over-extended their forces and supply-lines and were ripe for counter-attack. The plan for this operation and the accumulated military reserves were already in place when Stalin joined the Military Council of the Southern Front. The Red attack was a great success, piercing the thin White line and sending them into headlong retreat all the way beyond the Don River by the end of 1919. It is difficult to appraise Stalin's personal contribution to this campaign. As the principal political member of the council in charge, he co-signed many orders, but this was mainly in support of the military commander. Probably his main role was liaison with Moscow, especially the task of procuring from the impoverished regime the minimum material support necessary to keep the attack rolling. To this end he made six short trips to Moscow from the front headquarters which moved south, from Sergeievskoe to Serpukhov to Kursk to Kharkov. The second trip, 16–18 November, was mainly to gain permission for the establishment of the 'First Cavalry Army' as an independently operating force, commanded by a former cavalry sergeant of the tsar, Semen Budenny, a grandly moustachioed, swashbuckling figure who became one of Stalin's cronies. Often operating deep behind enemy lines, this army proved a highly effective force in a war that was the last great opportunity for the mounted soldier. In his pressure to obtain from Moscow what 'his' front needed, Stalin in mid-November even threatened to resign if he did not receive 83 000 reinforcements, a step that drew a rebuke from the Politburo. This did not prevent him from assuming a testy tone toward the Central Committee in early February 1920, asking that they not order him to take another tour of the front, something he already had done during 5–12 January 1919 and 11–14 January 1920. 'It is not journeys by individuals that are needed but the transfer of cavalry-reserves', complained Stalin. By February 1920, after the basic outcome of the campaign had been settled, his attitude toward the central authorities had turned downright sour, or so Lenin thought. On one occasion Lenin informed the Politburo that Stalin was 'carping' and that he should not be allowed to return to Moscow to discuss the matter at issue, the disposition of the 'Ukrainian Labour Army'. The second time the boss bluntly rebuked his field-representative: 'What is required is to help in every way one can and not pick a quarrel about departmental fields of competence' (meaning Stalin's assignment to the Council of the Caucasus Front). Probably it was a relief to both of them when Stalin resumed his work in Moscow in April 1920, after spending February and March in Kharkov dealing with political-economic affairs of the Ukraine.

But circumstances did not permit him to settle down in the capital. The fledgling Polish state rashly attacked the Soviets in late April, seeking to obtain for itself a swathe of White Russia and the Ukraine, while assisting the Ukrainian nationalists who had retreated to Poland to establish their government in Kiev. Facing only weak Red Army units at the opening of the campaign, the Poles were able to move rapidly as far as Kiev and beyond Minsk. The Polish threat to the Soviet Ukraine was compounded by the presence of Wrangel's White Army in the Crimea, a force composed of the remnants of Denikin's army that had been evacuated from eastern Black Sea ports to the peninsula. The south-western front, to which Stalin was assigned as the principal political supervisor, thus consisted of two quite separate enemies, either of which might strike a dangerous blow. Departing Moscow on 26 May 1920 by a special train provided by the Central Committee, Stalin proceeded to Kharkov, headquarters of the front, and thence to Kremenchug on 29 May. This place was better sited for dealing simultaneously with both the Poles and the Whites, lying about 250 km south-east of Kiev and only slightly further north of the Crimea. By the time Stalin arrived there a Red Army counter-offensive was already beginning against the Poles in Kiev, aiming at their envelopment and destruction. This plan succeeded in part, for the Poles suffered heavy losses and retreated from Kiev on 10 June, but they escaped with a large part of their army, partly because of the mismanagement of Budyenny's First Cavalry Army by Egorov and Stalin. Having broken through south of Kiev, this mobile force deviated from its original plan of circling west of Kiev and instead turned south to try to cut off the southern flank of the Polish army. Not only did this lead to inconclusive and costly fighting, it allowed the main Polish group to withdraw from Kiev. In a wire to Lenin, Stalin excused this by saying that the original plan was 'impractical' owing to the weakness of the Red forces, claiming that if in a week they took Fastov, the Kiev operation would be a success. Since Fastov lies south-west of Kiev, off the main line of retreat for the Poles, this was not a very convincing argument.[32]

Despite these mistakes, the Poles had been forced back from Kiev, and the prospects for the south-west front would have been good had it not been for the presence of Wrangel on the Crimea. He was building up his army just as Stalin's main forces were being drawn further away to the west, and even slightly north, for their orders were to occupy the Brest-Litovsk area on the road to Warsaw. In a message to Lenin on 3 June Stalin complained that he was scheduled to receive no more than five regiments when he needed at least eighteen, and he proposed two drastic alternatives to deal with the threat from the Crimea: either conclude an armistice with Wrangel or attack and destroy him. Concerning this proposed attack Lenin wrote to Trotsky, 'This is an obvious utopia. Will it not cost too many casualties?' But he did not wish to offend Stalin with such language and proposed that they tell him that such a serious question would require careful study. On the next day, 4 June, before anything could come of this, Stalin received new intelligence that Wrangel was about to attack, breaking out of the peninsula into the mainland. Lenin asked Trotsky what they should do, but the latter evidently was more absorbed with his feud with Stalin than with the threat from Wrangel, for he merely replied that Stalin was violating proper channels of communication in dealing directly with Lenin rather than with the military high command.[33]

The Wrangel offensive was contained, but it required most of Stalin's attention from late June to mid-August 1920. He was particularly concerned with the success of the Whites in capturing the territory just north of the Sea of Azov, rich country from which they might link up to the east with the Don Cossack land, still rife with anti-Bolshevism. Stalin travelled to Kharkov and from that base made three inspection tours of the Wrangel front. Considering his almost continual movement, it is not surprising that by early August he wired Lenin that he needed a rest and could continue to supervise the front for no more than two additional weeks. By this time his tone in dealing with Lenin was acrid. In response to notification that the south-western front had been partitioned into separate southern and south-western fronts, he brusquely said that the Politburo should not concern itself with 'trifles'. Concerning promised reinforcements: 'I do not believe the promises of the High Command for a minute; they only deceive with their promises.' On possible peace with Poland: 'our diplomats very often successfully spoil the results of our military victories'.[34]

The conclusion of his tour of duty was linked to an episode that Stalin's detractors have often held against him. In early July M. N. Tukhachevsky, commanding the 'western front' on the main Warsaw–Moscow axis, launched an offensive against weak Polish forces and ordered a march on the Polish capital. In Lenin's optimistic imagination, this might conquer Poland for the revolution and open the way to Germany. The offensive was an enormous success for about a month, by mid-August reaching almost to Warsaw. But the Reds now were exhausted, over–extended and poorly controlled by Tukhachevsky, who remained far in the rear. A Polish counter-blow completely reversed the momentum in the latter part of August, pushing the Soviet forces back to Minsk by mid-October. Out of this came a peace treaty and a boundary that survived until 1939. The involvement of Stalin in this disappointment of Lenin's hopes for the Russo–Polish War concerns the assignment of the First Cavalry Army to the capture of Lvov in southern Poland (or western Ukraine, as you prefer), rather than its northward swing to assist Tukhachevsky's forces in taking Warsaw. Trotsky, among others, blamed Stalin, claiming that he had sought the glory of taking Lvov, and failed in that, when he should have been helping with the main thrust further north. But less partisan study of the case places much of the responsibility for this muddle with the Soviet commander-in-chief, S. S. Kamenev (not to be confused with the party eminence L. B. Kamenev) and Tukhachevsky himself. The whole thing might be passed off as a trivial wartime quarrel, were it not for the fact that Tukhachevsky went on to become a marshal of the Soviet Union in 1935 and was executed as an alleged traitor two years later.[35]

On 17 August 1920, just after this latest eruption of friction between himself and supreme headquarters, Stalin returned to Moscow to attend the Ninth Party Conference. While he was there he arranged for the Central Committee to grant him two weeks leave from military work, but before this expired he asked the Politburo to relieve him altogether from military assignments. This appears to have been accepted.[36] Not until 1941 was Stalin to participate again in military command. His introduction to this art in 1918–20 had not been without its frustrations and defeats, but Stalin had emerged not only on the winning side but also as a political–military chief whose contribution to the Red victory was second only to Trotsky's. Stalin had played a smaller role than his rival in the overall organization of the Red Army, but he had been more important in providing direction on crucial fronts. If his reputation as a hero was far below Trotsky's, this had less to do with objective merit than with Stalin's lack of flair, at this stage of his career, for self-advertisement.

In the middle of the Civil War, 30 March 1919, while Stalin was working in Moscow between his assignments to the eastern and southern fronts, Lenin arranged for his appointment to a second cabinet post, narkom of state control. This appointment came about partly as a result of Stalin's investigation of the military failure at Perm. In their report of 31 January 1919 he and Dzerzhinsky had stressed the weakness of central authority over the regional branches of the party and state, the need to give the inexperienced local officials more guidance. To improve matters they proposed the establishment of a 'Control and Inspection Commission' under the Council of Defence. In essence Stalin's conception at this point anticipated the work that he later assumed as General Secretary of the Party: the construction of a reliable, authoritative, centralist network of administrators, a task that had barely been started in early 1919. But under the influence of Lenin the proposed reform took a different direction. He was drawn to the doubtfully practical idea that state administration could become 'merely a matter of accounting' under socialism, and that workers could take over this process, forestalling the rise of a new bureaucracy. He made this aspiration clear in his instructions to Stalin on the reform of state control: workers, especially women, must participate in this process, which would deal with citizens' complaints and improve productive efficiency. That Lenin would entrust this idealistic project to Stalin suggests that at this point he had no doubts about his lieutenant's moral suitability, and also that Lenin misjudged the far more authoritarian goal of Stalin's proposal.[37]

Stalin was appointed to head the People's Commissariat of State Control on 30 March 1919 and a few days later reported on this subject to the Sovnarkom and Central Executive Committee. But he soon had to return to military affairs, and nothing much seems to have happened in the new commissariat until February 1920 when, with Stalin still absent at the front, the body was reorganized as the 'Worker–Peasant Inspection' (*Raboche–Krest'ianskaia Inspektsiia* or RKI or Rabkrin). On this occasion Lenin again sent Stalin a summary of his idealistic goals for the new body. It is hard to say how Stalin regarded his new fief. At least he valued it enough to block a proposal to establish a separate People's Commissariat of State Accounting, telling Lenin that this represented merely 'the careerist striving of groups of bureaucrats who are striving to create sinecures'.[38]

Returning from military to civilian duties in September 1920, Stalin did not devote much effort to Rabkrin. He attempted to expand its staff, asking Lenin to assign 1000–1200 of the best 'Soviet worker-Communists', an impractically large demand on the limited pool of able and reliable people. He was authorized to add 250 party functionaries, but it is not clear that he could find that many. Trotsky formed the opinion that the staff of this agency was chiefly 'officials who have come to grief in various fields of activity'. Apart from the establishment of a complaints bureau, evidently no major operation, Rabkrin under Stalin's direction was largely a conventional bureaucratic inspectorate, which attempted to 'protect state property' and see that officials obeyed the rules. But as late as March 1922 Lenin still was expressing hope that a way could be found to recruit workers and peasants to Rabkrin. By about this time Stalin apparently concluded that the direction of this agency was not contributing to his career, nor was it capable of dealing with the task that had originally interested him: the construction of an effective administrative hierarchy. When on 3 April 1922 he became General Secretary of the Communist Party, Stalin accepted the post on the understanding that within a month he would be relieved of responsibility for Rabkrin, as he was on 25 April.[39]

His path to the post of General Secretary, a position which really could control the whole Soviet system, was the logical culmination of his experience as a generalist in the emerging Soviet–Communist Party system. As a narkom he was a member of the Sovnarkom, and when in Moscow he attended its meetings. Before his first trip to the front in 1918, and probably thereafter as much as his travel permitted, Stalin was one of the most regular attenders of this key policy-making body. He also was a member of the 'Little Council' of the Sovnarkom, an inner circle that spent much of its time trying to resolve expeditiously petty administrative problems – 'vermicelli' in Russian bureaucratic slang. Quite possibly his experience with this business was important in revealing to Stalin that the official who can control the 'vermicelli' has an important degree of authority over the whole machine, as he later demonstrated as General Secretary. In addition he was an active member of the two ancillary organs of the Sovnarkom, both headed by Lenin, which dealt with military matters, the 'Revolutionary Military Council of the Republic' (for political direction to military operations) and the 'Council of Labour and Defence' (for economic support for the armed forces). Stalin was deputy chairman of the latter body, which involved him in a number of special commissions, such as accountancy, clothing, munitions, railways and fodder. Such experience no doubt helped to qualify him for membership in the presidium of the commission that attempted to organize famine relief in the disastrous year 1921. One aspect of this work that Lenin specifically assigned to Stalin was the liquidation of the small relief committee that had been established by some precariously surviving Mensheviks. Lenin believed that these people were 'playing with fire', possibly using relief work for 'counter-revolutionary' aims at a time when 'foreigners were arriving', that is, representatives of Herbert Hoover's American Relief Administration, which saved vast numbers of Soviet citizens. At someone's instigation the Cheka would have executed these Mensheviks had it not been for the intervention of Hoover and the Norwegian humanitarian Fridjtof Nansen.[40]

While it was not one of his day-to-day responsibilities, Stalin acquired considerable acquaintance with the Cheka. Following the attempted assassination of Lenin in August 1918, he called for 'open, mass, systematic terror against the bourgeoisie and its agents', a perspective that qualified him to serve on three different short-term commissions of inspection of the activities of the secret police, as well as the task of refereeing a jurisdictional dispute between the People's Commissariat of Justice and the Cheka. At the end of 1921 Stalin, with Kamenev, was entrusted with a sensitive public-relations task in connection with the activities of the Cheka: the decision on when to publish the fact that the regime was holding a trial of Socialist-Revolutionary activists who were accused of treason. Stalin does not appear to have been the main instigator of the trial, but his conduct in later years suggests that he found merit in the propaganda value of such spectacles.[41]

Although highly varied, Stalin's activities between the October Revolution of 1917 and April 1922 did not focus on the party as a particular institution. Despite Lenin's theoretical commitment to the

construction of a party that would be the 'vanguard' of the proletariat, a
body of professionals, it was not clear in the year or two following the
revolution that this institution would be the key to power in the new
system. Lenin concentrated his own work in the Sovnarkom, which was
not an organ of the party, and there was as yet only a feeble system of
intra-party administration. But the need to place Communists in all the
organs of the regime to ensure some minimum of political reliability, the
need to co-ordinate the actions of these cadres and the need to have a
high-level, authoritative apparatus to make decisions in the light of
Communist ideology, inexorably led toward the establishment of a
strengthened party organization. By the early 1920s it must have been
clear to Stalin that the development of the party machinery was the
crucial aspect of the Soviet political system. For the good of the system
and his career it was important for him to become more deeply involved
in this sphere.[42]

He already had a foothold in the party, membership in the Central
Committee, but this was not enough. As the committee grew in size and
met less frequently, its role as the inner council of Bolshevism diminished.
In large measure power passed to three smaller bodies that were elected
by the Committee, the Secretariat, Organizational Bureau and Political
Bureau. The first of these had been in operation continuously since 1917,
the latter two coming into being informally around the end of 1918. In
December 1919 the Eighth Conference, which Stalin did not attend,
formally established the 'Orgburo' and 'Politburo' in the new party
statutes. From this time Stalin was a member of both bodies, the Orgburo
dealing with the assignment of party members to jobs inside and outside
the party apparatus itself, the Politburo fairly well replacing the Central
Committee as the effective inner council of Bolshevism. Both were highly
sensitive politically and correspondingly secretive. A rare glimpse of
Stalin's skill in manipulating these new instruments comes from a terse
note by Lenin, 'I agree with Stalin, Lenin.' The setting was a disagreement
in the Politburo over the composition of the 'Little Sovnarkom', a vital
body. Stalin proposed to break the deadlock that existed among the
leading politicians in the regime by referring the matter to the Orgburo.
Since the latter body supposedly dealt with personnel assignment, this
might seem reasonable, but the critical political consideration was that
Stalin was the most influential member of the Orgburo and could hope to
have his way there much more easily than in the Politburo.[43]

As for the Secretariat, Stalin had no formal role until April 1922,
although his work in the Orgburo and Politburo involved him in some of
its activities. For example, V. M. Molotov, who was a member of the
Secretariat, and Stalin jointly submitted for Lenin's approval the agenda
for the party conference of December 1921. It is hard to know when
Stalin decided that he wanted to concentrate his activity on party

administration. It may have been the subject of an interview that he sought with Lenin as early as November 1920 concerning 'his work in the centre'. It probably lay behind his request to the Politburo a year later to relieve him of the People's Commissariat of Nationality Affairs, a request that was not granted at the time. In any event the Secretariat became his domain on 3 April 1922, just following the Eleventh Party Congress, which elected a new Central Committee. This body in turn voted to establish the post of General Secretary to run the Secretariat and named Stalin to this office.[44]

It is highly probable that Lenin initiated this decision. Shortly before, in January 1922, he had shown his confidence in Stalin by naming him, together with Kamenev, to form a duumvirate (*dvoika*) while Lenin tried to regain his faltering health by taking a complete rest. The practice of this arrangement during February and March is well documented, Kamenev supervising the state apparatus, Stalin the party. Evidently Lenin was satisfied with Stalin's work and regarded his appointment as General Secretary as the beginning of a reform in the administration of the Secretariat. A decree that Lenin drafted and submitted to the Central Committee in April required that agency to publish and observe hours when it would be open to receive officials. The leading secretaries – Stalin, Molotov and V. V. Kuibyshev – should delegate to assistants all except major questions, and Stalin, whom Lenin mentioned by name, should quickly find and appoint his deputies and assistants, who should be transferred to the Secretariat from other bodies. This somewhat fussy directive does not appear to have been adopted by the Central Committee, but when Stalin announced his new position to the party in *Pravda* he did observe Lenin's point about having stated office hours: noon until three, six days a week. But Stalin deviated from Lenin's intent that the secretaries of the party should delegate routine matters, as most of the callers' business was bound to be. The General Secretary himself, said the notice, would be on duty on Tuesdays, Wednesdays and Saturdays. Whether he actually kept to this over a protracted period is impossible to determine, but it was a shrewd move on Stalin's party to build his image as a hard-working, accessible servant of the party. It was to prove a major weapon in his rivalry with other Bolsheviks during the next few years.[45]

5 Deathwatch

Lenin was only nine years older than Stalin. As founder and unchallenged leader of the Bolsheviks, maker of the world's first dictatorship of the proletariat, it was reasonable to assume in, say, 1920 that Lenin would have many years as effective head of the Soviet regime, that Stalin would spend most of his career in Lenin's shadow and that he might be too old to be a plausible successor to Lenin by the time the founder's career did reach its end. Not that Stalin in 1921 was by any means the heir apparent among Lenin's lieutenants. But Lenin was not genetically fortunate. The same premature arterial sclerosis that had felled his father at the age of 54 announced its claim on him during 1921 through headaches, insomnia and – so unlike Lenin – apathy toward his work. From early December to 1 March 1922 he spent much of his time on leave, living outside Moscow, trying to rest and regain his vigour. Then, on 25–7 May, he suffered a cerebral haemorrhage that temporarily paralysed his right arm and leg and impaired his speech.[1] For Stalin, and perhaps others, a whole range of new opportunities suddenly appeared.

With these opportunities came problems. The very novelty of the Bolshevik–Soviet system of government made it difficult to know just where the focus of authority was, and Lenin's unique career as founder did not provide a repeatable pattern of ascent to the top. The constitution of the Soviet state indicated the method for the selection of the chairman of the Sovnarkom, Lenin's paramount formal position, but the party statutes provided for no nominal chief. Most perplexing, the relation between the party and state had not been clarified in practice. For Stalin, another major uncertainty was the conduct of Lenin's other leading lieutenants, especially Trotsky and Zinoviev, who in 1922 were better known to a broad Soviet public. And all potential successors to Lenin had to consider the uncertainty concerning Lenin himself. Would he recover for a considerable period? Exert intermittent authority as an invalid? Resign? Name a successor? Die quickly? No such questions could be discussed openly, nor could any ambitious contender show any eagerness to make a move. Until the very end, which turned out to be a year and nine months following the first stroke, the regime felt obliged to maintain an optimistic pose, even ignoring as much as possible the fact that the leader was seriously ill. Lenin encouraged this sham, resigning no offices, making no farewell statements for delivery in his lifetime. Had he taken such a step before March 1923, it would have forced the question of succession on the regime while he was still able to speak. This would have given him some chance to influence events. But he chose to cling to his offices in the apparent hope that he might be able to return to active leadership, which obliged his lieutenants to sustain the pretence that he would recover.

Although he was not formally appointed to the task, Stalin, probably by virtue of his party functions, became the principal political guardian of the sick man. He was Lenin's first visitor, apart from doctors and family, calling on him on 30 May 1922.[2] This was barely three days after the potentially mortal strokes had abated, and the patient was not well enough to deal with politics. Probably Stalin wanted to see for himself just how much life seemed to be left, and his Politburo colleagues may have asked him to report to them on this interesting topic. Their uncertainty about the case is implied by the postponement of any public announcement of Lenin's illness until 18 June, when a cheerful, vague report was issued.[3] They let him convalesce in peace until 11 July when it was again Stalin who went to see Lenin. The leader was strong enough to be allowed two hours of political conversation, and in the next week also received Kamenev and Bukharin.[4] It was, however, Stalin to whom Lenin reported on 18 July, 'Congratulate me: I have been permitted *newspapers*! [that is, to read them] The old ones beginning today, and on Sunday the *new*!' This seems less a mark of special friendship than a report to the person Lenin understood to be politically responsible for his treatment.[5] In the same sense Lenin wrote to Stalin in August to arrange visits with several Soviet political figures. But it was only Stalin among them who visited Lenin fairly regularly at his country estate at Gorki. It appears that from early August until Lenin could return to work in Moscow on 2 October Stalin scheduled a weekly visit to the leader, seeing him on 9, 15, 23 and 30 August, 12, 19, 26 September.[6]

Following his visit on 12 September Stalin wrote an article for a special illustrated supplement to *Pravda*, which appeared on 24 September to reassure the populace that Lenin was not in danger. In this public display of solicitude Stalin's leading role as the link between the Politburo and Lenin was not revealed, and Stalin's article appeared with several others by party magnates, each with a photograph of the author and the recuperating patient. But it was in some other respects a revealing piece. Its opening paragraph used a theme that Stalin was often to repeat in the future to project the image of a humble servant of the party: after noting that it is difficult to convey such numerous and 'precious' impressions, he admitted 'I must write for the editorial board insists on it.' Later in the piece Stalin chose a significant aspect of Lenin's concerns to emphasize: the 'rabid agitation' of the 'Socialist-Revolutionaries and Mensheviks.' They are facilitating the imperialists' fight against Soviet Russia. They have been caught in the mire of capitalism, and are sliding into an abyss'. That Lenin could have said something of the sort is quite probable, for he had expressed keen interest in the trial of the Socialist-Revolutionaries during the summer. But the turn of phrase sounds more like Stalin. Finally,

Stalin informed his readers that his conversation with Lenin also had touched on 'The whiteguard press . . . the *émigrés* . . . the incredible fairy-tales about Lenin's death, with full details.' Comrade Lenin smiled and remarked, 'Let them lie if it is any consolation to them; one should not rob the dying of their last consolation.' This was a curious theme for Stalin to raise with Lenin. Had Stalin been trying to sound out the sick man on the question of succession?[7]

The official confidence that Lenin could resume his authority was justified between 2 October and 15 December when Lenin was able once again to live in the Kremlin and carry out something resembling his normal work routine.[8] One of the issues before him was the planning of the new Soviet federal constitution. At this point the legal position was that there were in addition to the Russian Soviet Federative Socialist Republic (that is, the Great Russian nationality and a number of relatively small ethnic minorities, such as the Bashkirs) three other Soviet Republics: the White Russian, Ukrainian and Transcaucasian (a federal amalgam of Armenia, Azerbaijan and Georgia). While supposedly independent states, these last three bodies were in reality occupied by the Red Army and ruled by subordinate branches of the Russian Communist Party. There was no doubt that their theoretically independent statehood was a transitional phase and that they would somehow be absorbed into the multinational, federal Russian state. The question was Stalin's special sphere, for he was still narkom of nationality affairs in 1922, as well as a participant in the nine different commissions that dealt with the making of the new constitution during 1922–3.[9] While neither Lenin nor Stalin had any use for the nationalist movements of the non-Russian peoples of the former Empire, they increasingly differed concerning the speed and manner with which Moscow's rule should be asserted over them. As early as 1920 it appeared in private correspondence between the two that Lenin envisaged a novel, multi-tiered federation, in which the Russian republic and the larger non-Russian republics would form a new federation. Stalin, however, believed that the Ukraine and other larger nationalities should simply be included in the existing Russian federation. He frankly said that the status of the Ukraine would in this arrangement differ not at all or hardly at all from that of Bashkiria, a much smaller nationality that was already in the Russian federation.[10] A similar divergence appeared in 1921 following the Sovietization of Georgia. Stalin wanted to order the creation of a Transcaucasian Soviet Federation, ending the separate 'independence' of Armenia, Azerbaijan and Georgia, but not yet annexing them to the Russian federation. This was a blunt exercise of power, and Lenin told him that the proposal was 'premature'. As a result Stalin's plan for the Transcaucasian Federation was postponed for about a year.[11]

But it was only at the end of Lenin's recuperation in September 1922 that the definition of the new federal system was faced squarely. At this time Stalin headed a commission representing the four Soviet republics that were to federate: the Russian, Ukrainian, White Russian and Transcaucasian. Perhaps apprehensive about Stalin's handling of this matter, Lenin wrote to him from Gorki on 22 September, asking how the matter had been settled.[12] Stalin's answer came by the 26th, and it showed that he had imposed his will on the three non-Russian republics. They would be incorporated into the existing Russian federation, on a par with the relatively minor nationalities that it already included. In the process they would abolish their extant parliamentary bodies ('central executive committees') and receive representation in the unicameral assembly of the Russian republic. This was not federalism as the term is usually used, but more like the diluted version of unitary, centralist rule that Stalin, before and after 1917, had called 'regional autonomy'. Lenin was displeased, and the log of his activities suggests that he argued the matter with Stalin for the better part of two hours and forty minutes on 26 September.[13]

In the main Lenin had his way, and later that day reported this to the Politburo, sending his memo via Kamenev, probably because he did not trust Stalin to disseminate material unfavourable to himself.[14] Stalin, said Lenin, 'has some tendency to hurry', but he 'has already agreed to make one concession', the establishment of a new federation that all four extant states would enter together. Moreover, this new entity would not be called a 'Russian' federation. Stalin had indeed conceded this, but did so neither gracefully nor completely. Having received Lenin's note, he dispatched to the Politburo a cantankerous rejoinder. In it he noted that one of Lenin's points was 'superfluous' and that in another 'Comrade Lenin himself "hurried" a little'. More importantly, he continued to oppose Lenin's wish to establish a bicameral legislature, one chamber to represent citizens on a uniform mathematical basis, the other to represent separately each federating state. In 1918 Stalin had asserted that bicameralism was in 'complete non-conformity with the elementary demands of socialism', and in September 1922 he argued that two chambers would divide into 'lower' and 'upper' houses, which 'will give us nothing but conflict and debate'. This seems to be one way of saying that interests of the minority nationalities could be effectively maintained against Great Russian dominance. Hoping to avoid a bicameral system, Stalin nevertheless proposed a contingency measure in case he lost on this issue, a measure that would vitiate Lenin's intent. If there were to be a chamber for national representation, then it should include as equals the larger and smaller national republics. The point of this was that the Russians presumably could line up the votes of the smaller nationalities, the leadership of which was likely to consist of ethnic Russians or co-operative local people. Furthermore, Stalin argued, the other chamber in such a system would have to be 'Russian'. There was no quick resolution

of the issue of bicameralism. As late as 18 November 1922 Stalin told
Pravda that 'a bicameral system is incompatible with the structure of the
Soviet system, at all events, in its present stage of development'.[15]

In laying out his plan for a Russian-dominated federation Stalin had
been applying strong pressure on the representatives of the non-Russian
republics. Wielding the authority of the party and dealing with
Communists, he seems to have had his way – except with his Georgian
compatriots. They were unhappy not only with the prospect of joining
some new form of Russian state but also with the idea of amalgamation
with their Armenian and Azerbaijanian neighbours into a Transcaucasian
Federation. On 27 September, the day after Lenin's argument with Stalin
about the new federal system, the convalescent received the leading
Georgian Bolshevik spokesman, Budu Mdivani. He evidently reinforced
Lenin's belief that Stalin was treating the minorities, and Georgia in
particular, high-handedly. Encouraged by Lenin's expressions of sympathy,
the Georgian Communist leaders organized to overturn the decision that
they were to join a Transcaucasian Federation. Following an angry
meeting with Ordzhonikidze, who was Stalin's main agent in the
reorganization of Transcaucasia, several Georgians wired a protest to the
Central Committee on 19 October. Here they overreached themselves,
using such intemperate language concerning Ordzhonikidze that Lenin
at once reproached them. Thus encouraged, Stalin sent a wire to
Ordzhonikidze that they should 'thoroughly punish the Georgian Central
Committee', transferring out of that republic the worst offenders. But
before this could happen the whole Georgian Central Committee resigned,
an unheard-of step that persuaded the Politburo to establish an
investigation commission. To head this commission, Stalin shrewdly
proposed Dzerzhinsky, a personal friend who was, like himself, a non-
Russian by origin but had no sympathy for the nationalists of his
ancestral land, Poland. This commission evidently did as Stalin expected,
for one of the Georgian spokesmen later complained that the commission
had heard only Ordzhonikidze's side of the story.[16]

But Stalin did not escape so easily. Lenin anticipated a whitewash and
sent Rykov to Tbilisi to investigate the matter on his behalf. While
present with Ordzhonikidze at a more or less social gathering, Rykov
witnessed a petty incident. One of Mdivani's faction insultingly referred
to the fact that Ordzhonikidze had received a white horse as a gift from
one of the mountain peoples, whereupon the angry Sergo slapped him.[17]
Like so much in the whole affair, this might have been passed off as one
more example of the Georgian national stereotype, hotheaded and
prideful. But it distressed Lenin. While having no scruples about the use
of force in class war, he was a proper bourgeois in personal style. Unlike
Stalin, who years later was quite capable of slapping his grown daughter
in anger, Lenin did not admit casual physical violence into relations

between members of *his* vanguard of the proletariat. He was outraged and – his overreaction perhaps exacerbated by his medical condition – sought to pursue the matter and punish Ordzhonikidze together with the man who was less directly involved but probably more responsible: Stalin. On 12 December Lenin talked with Dzerzhinsky and ordered him to return to Georgia and look into the affair of the slap, but on the night of 15–16 December, before anything could come of this inquiry, Lenin again fell ill, not with a paralytic stroke but with the less-debilitating symptoms of arterial sclerosis.[18]

Ill though he was, Lenin's mind and speech functioned, and even on the 16th he was able to dictate a letter and dispatch various messages, including one to Stalin telling him that his health would not permit him to attend the forthcoming Congress of Soviets.[19] But the recurrence of the arterial disease made it clear to the Politburo that his political future was in doubt. On the 18th a plenary session of the Central Committee made Stalin 'personally responsible' for the observance of the regime prescribed for Lenin by the doctors. This formalized the role that Stalin had played in practice during Lenin's previous incapacitation. The assignment was strictly secret, for no published admission that Lenin was ill again appeared until 13 March 1923.[20]

Though virtually Lenin's legal guardian, Stalin never saw his charge in person. A two-hour meeting between them on 13 December, before the renewed onset of the illness, turned out to be the last time Stalin saw Lenin alive. As official warder, Stalin now had substantial control over Lenin's household, which consisted of the invalid, his wife and his sister Maria, and over Lenin's personal staff of female secretaries. Until Stalin was given formal authority over Lenin's treatment, Nadezhda Allilueva remained on this secretarial staff, but her name disappears from Lenin's log after Stalin took control of the ménage. Perhaps he had been waiting for an opportunity to oblige Nadezhda to give up this career outside their domestic hearth. He probably did not need her as an informant in the Lenin household, if indeed she would have consented to play such a role. The doctors reported to Stalin, and at one point Lenin, with what justification one cannot say, told one of his secretaries, Lydia Fotieva, 'I know that you are betraying me.'[21]

Lenin, feeling that his hours might be few, wanted to give his party some last words of advice and fought against the restrictions that the doctors and Stalin placed on him. At one point he even threatened to refuse medical treatment if he were not given more time for dictation.[22]

'If only I were free', said Lenin during this time.[23] He knew that he was a virtual prisoner and that Stalin was his warder, but he did not learn at once of the first overt crisis in the relationship. On 21 December he dictated to his wife, Nadezhda Krupskaia, a short note to Trotsky, congratulating him on winning the approval of the Central Committee for the continuance of the state monopoly on foreign trade, a matter that had concerned Lenin deeply during the autumn and on which he had differed with Stalin. Through his anonymous informants, Stalin quickly learned of this, telephoned Krupskaia and threatened her with disciplinary action by the Central Control Commission. Concern for Lenin's health was not quite Stalin's only motive, for the doctors had approved this dictation. Stalin's threat was a move to isolate Lenin from Trotsky or other rivals. Deeply upset, Krupskaia wrote to Kamenev to ask for his protection, but this was futile, for at this time Kamenev was well disposed toward Stalin.[24]

On the night of 22–3 December Lenin suffered another stroke, which paralysed his right arm and leg. Aware that the end might be near, and that Stalin and the doctors might withdraw the privilege of dictating to his secretaries, Lenin made a desperate effort to influence posterity. On the 23rd, only hours after the stroke, he called in a secretary, whom he told, 'I want you to take down a letter to the [party] congress. Write!' The message turned out to be a rather confused version of his pet idea that the appointment of ordinary workers to important posts, the Central Committee in this variant, would correct the shortcomings of party rule. The letter was sent to Stalin, no doubt in his capacity as General Secretary, the same day. Lenin's idea was not new, no other members of the Politburo took it seriously, and the memo represented a danger to none of them.[25] But the next day, 24 December, Lenin resumed dictation, this time emphasizing to the secretary that it be '*absolutely* secret' and ordering its retention in five sealed copies, one kept by Lenin, one by his secretaries and three by Krupskaia. This 'Testament', as it is called, damaged the reputations of all the major political figures of the day. It noted Trotsky's bygone 'non-Bolshevism'. True, Lenin said that this should not be held against him, but mere mention of it implied otherwise. Trotsky was 'prone to excessive self-confidence' and was 'excessively involved in the purely administrative aspect of affairs'. The deviation of Kamenev and Zinoviev in the October Revolution also should not be held against them, but it was 'not, of course, accidental'. Bukharin was doubtfully Marxist in some of his ideas and had not understood the dialectic:

> Comrade Stalin, on becoming General Secretary, concentrated boundless power in his hands, and I am not sure whether he will always know how to use this power with sufficient caution.

On balance Stalin could take satisfaction in the appraisal. He and Trotsky appeared as 'the two outstanding leaders of the present Central Committee', and Lenin expressed grave concern that their rivalry would split the party. If Trotsky was called the 'ablest', Stalin emerged as a worthy rival, and the shortcomings that Lenin attributed to him were less likely to harm his image with party loyalists than those ascribed to Trotsky. The following day, 25 December, Lenin oddly saw fit to evaluate, rather negatively, G. L. Piatakov, who was not important enough to sit on the Politburo.[26]

The next day, 26 December, Lenin resumed his harmless hobby of advocating worker membership in the Central Committee and Rabkrin. Then he spent four days ineffectually worrying about the problem of finding adequate leadership for Gosplan, the economic planning agency – nothing to alarm anyone in the Politburo. On 29 December he once more turned his attention to the workers who should join the Central Committee and Rabkrin – they should be well paid. On the last three days of 1922 Lenin took up a new problem, Russian and minority nationalism, with much greater clarity and vigour. This posed a potential threat to Stalin because of Lenin's attack on the 'great power chauvinism' that Ordzhonikidze, backed by Stalin, had displayed in handling their native Georgia. Both, it seemed, should be held responsible, whatever that meant.[27]

With these nine days of dictation Lenin seemingly had satisfied himself and stopped. Then, on 4 January, he added a short postscript to the dictation of 24 December concerning personalities. Now he dealt only with Stalin, saying he was

> too rude and this failing, entirely tolerable in the party milieu and in relations between us Communists, becomes intolerable in the post of General Secretary. I therefore recommend that the comrades consider the step of transferring Stalin from this job and nominating to it another person who would in all other respects differ from Stalin only in having one advantage, namely that of being more tolerant, more loyal, more polite and more attentive to comrades, with less capriciousness, etc.

The proposed demotion left Stalin with his other important posts. Lenin did not call for the end of his political career and neither insisted absolutely that Stalin be ousted as General Secretary nor nominated any replacement. But in the hands of a shrewd and determined enemy this document was potentially dangerous for Stalin. What accounted for Lenin's abrupt turn against a man whose career he had hitherto fostered? Considering the emphasis on personal manners, it is hard to resist the supposition that Lenin had learned from his wife how Stalin had treated her in the telephone call, even though there is no explicit evidence that she told him about the incident until 5 March, when Lenin specifically referred to the affair. It may seem excessive to fire a politician from his most important post because of rude manners, especially in a political culture that prided itself on being 'proletarian', but Lenin certainly was shocked to think that his devoted, inoffensive spouse should have been verbally abused. The repeated reference to 'loyalty' is particularly persuasive evidence that Lenin was inspired by the affair of the telephone call. He could not, of course, be referring to political or ideological loyalty. That would have called for sterner punishment. But for a man who was to a considerable extent his protégé to treat Krupskaia so heartlessly . . . that was personal disloyalty in the extreme.[28]

One of the most important concerns of Lenin in his Testament was the possibility of a split in the party between its two ablest surviving leaders, Stalin and Trotsky. This was not based merely on prescience, but on a quarrel that Lenin had a chance to see develop in the fall of 1922, one that was renewed after his collapse in December disabled him. The origin of this quarrel was Lenin's attempt to improve the administration of the Soviet state, and to relieve some of the burdens that he was finding increasingly hard to carry, by establishing 'deputy chairmen' of the Sovnarkom. At first there were two, Rykov and A. D. Tsuriupa. The position was by no means a supreme honour, especially after Lenin in April 1922 offered a draft job description which Rykov, Trotsky and Tomsky found wanting. Rykov said that proper co-ordination between the deputies would be as 'rare as Siamese twins'. Trotsky noted that the conception was 'a Utopia', in which a special department 'peeps in [on other agencies] from time to time and takes note of everything that is needed'. While still convalescing at Gorki, Lenin on 11 September 1922 told Stalin to invite both Kamenev and Trotsky to become deputy chairmen, partly because Rykov was going on leave. This circumstance certainly did not make the post seem more honorific. Kamenev accepted and Trotsky did not, which gave Stalin an opportunity to focus on Trotsky the displeasure of the Politburo. Trotsky later maintained, perhaps rightly, that Stalin put the invitation to him on the telephone, and the rejection merely took the form of a postponement of the question. But Stalin proceeded to poll the Politburo, excepting Zinoviev, on the question of whether Trotsky should become a deputy chairman. Stalin and Rykov voted in favour and the rest raised no objection. Stalin could then inform the Politburo on 14 September that Trotsky was not taking the appointment, which led that body to resolve that 'it notes with regret Comrade Trotsky's categorical refusal'. This put Trotsky in the role of a petulant, uncooperative prima donna, an impression that was confirmed when Lenin on 15 October repeated the invitation with the same result.[29]

Stalin revived this sore point in January 1923 with a memo that proposed a merger of the 'collegium' of three deputy chairmen and a trimmed-down version of the Council of Labour and Defence, with Trotsky joining it as a deputy chairman, reminding the Politburo that Lenin had asked Trotsky to take this post. This particular deputy was to be the supreme economic co-ordinator, seemingly a handsome offer. This was doubly shrewd. Stalin knew that Trotsky was pretty certain to turn down the position again, further aggravating his relations with his colleagues, while Stalin could appear a model of impartial generosity. Trotsky took the bait and refused in a long-winded memo that claimed the original credit for advocating a strong economic authority. In a following memo to the Politburo Stalin not only reviewed Trotsky's rejection of Lenin's wishes the previous autumn, he introduced a theme that was to become central in his polemics against Trotsky after Lenin's death. Trotsky was portrayed as a defeatist concerning the prospects for the Soviet state. 'Comrade Trotsky, it seems, sought to assure us in the Politburo a year and a half ago that the days of the Soviet regime were numbered – the cock had already crowed.' Trotsky retorted that he had indeed told the Politburo that they endangered the revolution by casually settling ten or twelve major economic questions in a single session with no preparation and only ten minutes discussion for each.[30] This apparently led to Stalin's acrimonious remark in a Politburo meeting that 'Either the party must make Trotsky the *de facto* dictator in the areas of economic and military affairs, or he must really renounce work in the economic area, retaining for himself only the right of systematically disorganizing the Central Committee in its difficult everyday work.'[31]

Meanwhile Lenin's condition improved enough that he took to writing articles and planning a speech that he hoped to deliver at the party congress scheduled for April 1923. Publication of the articles was useful to the Politburo in that they suggested to the public that Lenin was well and in charge of things. No medical report had been published since September, and the Politburo in 1922–3, as during the last months of Brezhnev, Andropov and Chernenko, hoped to avoid any impression that there was no leader at the top. But the content of the articles was inconvenient to the Politburo, and especially Stalin. Lenin attacked bureaucratism and especially Stalin's erstwhile agency, Rabkrin. Along with some others, Stalin attempted to block publication of this article, but merely succeeded in delaying it. At least Lenin had not mentioned Stalin by name in the article.[32] Much more dangerous was the speech that Lenin hoped to give at the party congress, dealing with the problem of Russian chauvinism and the Georgian affair. After pestering his doctors, secretaries and Stalin for almost a month for permission to read the latest reports on this matter, Lenin finally obtained some of the pertinent documents on 26 February.[33]

On 5 March Lenin seems to have felt the now-familiar signs of an oncoming stroke and he lashed out at Stalin for the last time. Referring to Stalin's verbal abuse of Krupskaia the previous December, Lenin threatened to break off personal relations if Stalin did not 'retract his words' to Krupskaia and apologize. Lenin's opening line echoed his earlier reference to personality: 'you permitted yourself a rude summons to my wife'. The previous allusion to personal loyalty surfaced again in Lenin's statement that 'I have no intention to forget so easily that which is being done against me'. The next day Lenin, aware of the seriousness of the step he was taking, re-read the note and ordered it to be sent by hand to Stalin personally, the courier waiting to receive an answer.[34]

Because he was too ill, Lenin never saw Stalin's reply, which seems to have disappeared from Lenin's meticulously maintained files for the period. On 10 March his right side was paralysed and he lost the power of speech, which he never really recovered. The Politburo now was obliged to face the political–medical facts and decide how to deal with the public. On 11 March they met and established a medical board to make the best possible diagnosis of Lenin's state, and the next day determined to publish a medical bulletin, which appeared on the 13th. Although these actions were collective, one may assume that Stalin, as the established supervisor of Lenin's medical care, played the guiding role.[35]

The same day that Lenin sent Stalin the demand for an apology, 5 March 1923, he also sent Trotsky a note asking him to take over the 'Georgian affair', providing him with the dictations of 30–1 December on the problem of minority nationalism. Trotsky declined this commission, thus missing a fine opportunity to deal Stalin a serious blow. His excuse was illness, and it is true that he intermittently ran a debilitating fever during most of the 1920s. But he was not too ill to report to the congress of April 1923 on a different topic, and he at least could have read the dictations to the congress, thus presenting himself as a close ally of Lenin. One explanation of Trotsky's self-defeating decision might be the excessive self-confidence that Lenin had noted in his dictation. Trotsky perhaps could not conceive that he would have to exert himself to be recognized as the principal successor to Lenin. Another explanation might be that Trotsky was not interested in belabouring Russian chauvinism and defending minority nationalism. He had turned his back on the Jewish culture of his ancestors but to many Russians might seem an objectionable person to attack his adopted nationality.[36]

Trotsky's rejection of Lenin's request was at least as serious an example of disloyalty to the founder as Stalin's insults to Krupskaia, but the latest decline in Lenin's health closed that issue. Nothing happened until the eve of the party congress when Lenin's secretary Lidia Fotieva bravely took the initiative in trying another means of fulfilling Lenin's wishes. On 16 April she telephoned Kamenev, explaining the matter, and on the same day sent him Lenin's 'article' and a covering letter explaining the background of the business. She also sent Trotsky a copy of this letter, which mentioned that he had declined Lenin's earlier invitation to deal with the subject at the party congress. Kamenev at once sent the material to Stalin, and Trotsky, embarrassed by this revelation of his inaction on

Lenin's request, sent the Central Committee a letter. In it Trotsky proposed that if the rest of the Committee would keep quiet about Lenin's message to the congress concerning Russian chauvinism and the national minorities, so would he. This, he said, would absolve him from further responsibility in the matter. But Stalin did not miss this opportunity to attack Trotsky's concealment from the Central Committee of Lenin's message, even though it had been critical of Stalin himself. Upon receipt of the material from Kamenev he induced Fotieva to state that it was 'not ready for the printer'. Thus protected from a general airing of the affair, he sent a memo to the Central Committee in which he concentrated on Trotsky's alleged misconduct. In reply Trotsky issued a weak apologia to the Committee and attempted to obtain Stalin's commitment to withdraw his charges. He thought that Stalin agreed to this in a telephone conversation on 17 April, but the next day found Trotsky complaining to Stalin that he had not fulfilled his promise.[37]

The party congress itself was an understated success for Stalin. Lenin's material on the Georgian question and Russian chauvinism was disseminated at a meeting of leaders of provincial delegations, about forty people, who then reported this gist of the business to their delegations. Stalin did not press his advantage over Trotsky concerning the history of the documents, and he even showed his magnanimity on the eve of the convocation by proposing Trotsky to give the general report, which had been Lenin's function. But Trotsky declined and Zinoviev had the honour.[38] Stalin gave two major addresses to the congress. One was the 'organizational' report, which contained the classic description of the relation of the party to the state and all of society, using the image of a power source and 'transmission belts'. This was in part skilful self-promotion, Stalin presenting himself as a reliable, competent technical servant of the party which served the people. But it was also an important piece of political analysis, the first authoritative statement of the unwritten constitution that had developed in Russia since the revolution. If the presentation was, like most of Stalin's, pedestrian, he should get some credit for the appropriateness of his industrial metaphor, the right model for a party based, supposedly, on the industrial workers and destined to direct a massive programme of industrialization. Lenin's criticism of bureaucraticism in the party in recent articles did not bother him. Stalin presented himself as a model of forward-looking reasonableness on this issue. The leading organs should bring in new talent for the future, although there was no suggestion that these appointees should be Lenin's ideal workers and peasants. At Stalin's suggestion the Central Committee was expanded to forty members and sixteen candidate members. Since he controlled appointments through the Orgburo, this supposed realization of Lenin's programme could be turned to Stalin's advantage by shrewd selection of personnel. Not that the older leaders needed to be replaced.

In Stalin's presentation there was a 'core' of between ten and fifteen leaders who had become so experienced that they could make the right decision nine times out of ten.[39]

Nor did Lenin's criticism trouble his other report, which dealt with nationality affairs. Why, he himself was an opponent of 'Great Russian chauvinism'. Some Georgians did not want to be lumped into a Transcaucasian Federation, but it was necessary to prevent them from dominating lesser ethnic groups in their midst. The 'local chauvinism' of the larger minority nationalities was also an evil. The image of a strong, knowledgeable, moderate, modest leader came across convincingly.[40]

At one point during the discussion at the congress Stalin reassured the delegates that, contrary to an apprehension that Lenin had expressed in his article of January on Rabkrin, there was no split in the party leadership. On this the Central Committee was unanimous.[41] This, of course, was one of those denials that should be understood as confirmation of that which is denied. The New Economic Policy, which involved limited toleration of private enterprise, was cited as the reason that people might have suspected some sort of division. While not implausible, this was a necessary evasion of the more fundamental reason why factionalism could be anticipated: the anticipated death of the single strong-man who had imposed unity. What would be more natural than rivalry among the possible heirs of such a dominant figure? Stalin was in effective control of the party, but there was no constitutional succession mechanism, if only `because Lenin's dominance rested not on any one office, certainly not the chairmanship of the Sovnarkom, but on his historically acquired prestige. Knowing that he was dying, the second-rank leaders could not but engage in at least some discreet jockeying for position against one another.

It is customary to maintain that the first manoeuvre was the formation in early 1923 of a *troika* or triumvirate of Zinoviev, Kamenev and Stalin as an anti-Trotsky coalition. While not without foundation, this interpretation must be qualified. The *troika* was not an arrangement made by Lenin to fill in during his absence, comparable to the Kamenev–Stalin *dvoika* (duumvirate) of early 1922.[42] Nor was it possible for the three to connive frequently, for Zinoviev, the ostensible leader, was responsible for Petrograd and spent most of his time there. Nor was the group limited to three. When Trotsky later made common cause with Zinoviev, he learned that the *troika* actually consisted of seven, the whole Politburo except for Trotsky himself.[43] Nor was the *troika* a close-knit bloc. In the late summer of 1923 Zinoviev ineptly attempted a manoeuvre against Stalin that was at least as serious as any that the *troika* attempted against Trotsky. While on holiday in the North Caucasus spa of Kislovodsk, Zinoviev held an informal meeting with Bukharin and Voroshilov, along with some lesser figures. They discussed the reorganization of the party executive so as to 'balance' Stalin's power with some other leaders, such as Trotsky, Zinoviev, Kamenev and Bukharin. One idea was to make the Secretariat into a 'little Politburo', but Voroshilov cemented his ties to Stalin by objecting to this. The meeting did not present Stalin with a solid front and agreed to send their proposals to him via his friend Ordzhonikidze. The General Secretary replied, as Zinoviev put it, in a 'rudely-friendly' telegram: 'They say, boys, that you're mixing up things. I will come quickly and then we will talk.' He did, and persuaded his weak-willed foes to allow him to straighten out their confusion. To 'link organizational with political work' Trotsky, Bukharin and Zinoviev formally joined the Orgburo (not the Secretariat), but of these only the last bothered to attend as many as one or two meetings. Perhaps Stalin had loaded the agenda with trivia, or perhaps the others simply lacked persistence in this vital matter.[44]

Stalin at this time was consolidating, not yielding, his bastion, the Secretariat. In the summer of 1923 he moved it from cramped quarters at 5 Vozdvizhenskaia Street (now Kalinin Prospect) to an unpretentious but spacious office building at 4 Old Square, which to this day has remained the administrative headquarters of the party. Stalin's office as General Secretary was there on the fifth floor and remained his main place of work until the 1930s, when he shifted to the Kremlin, five blocks away.[45]

The new headquarters housed not only the top-level party administration but also Stalin's personal secretariat, a secretive but powerful agency that took definitive shape around 1923. The key personnel were Stalin's 'assistants' (their formal title), in the early stages a core of perhaps four tough, able and experienced Communists. I. P. Tovstukha, an intellectual who had been in the underground, Siberian exile and Parisian emigration before the revolution, was the most important organizer of Stalin's secretariat. He was to some extent a scholar and for a number of years was the director of the Institute of Marxism–Leninism, which collected and published the works of those giants, among other learned activities. L. Z. Mekhlis, a Jew by origin, an important political commissar during the civil war, served as personal secretary to Stalin, with the vital function of guarding jealously access to him. I. K. Ksenofontov was an experienced leader in the Cheka before joining Stalin's staff, so it seems reasonable to guess that one of his special responsibilities was liaison with the secret police, a business that surely was one of Stalin's major concerns from the beginning. There also was A. M. Nazaretian, an Armenian intellectual Communist, who had known Stalin in their years in the Transcaucasian underground. His main job was to prepare daily news communiqués for Stalin, which attempted to report the truth rather than the latest official line. To this number might be added G. Kanner, a particularly shadowy figure, who may have been second in line behind Mekhlis as a personal aide, possibly with special responsibility for clandestine and more or less illegal affairs.[46]

The whole operation was a closely guarded secret and Stalin's working area a special security zone within the Central Committee building, so it is impossible to describe with much confidence the personnel arrangements and table of organization of Stalin's secretariat. One can at least note, however, that he seems to have been neither anti-intellectual nor anti-Semitic in choosing his personal staff, at least in its early years. Tovstukha and Nazaretian were cosmopolitan intellectuals in style. According to one story, Stalin once said to Tovstukha, 'My mother had a billy-goat who looked exactly like you, only he didn't wear a pince-nez.' Not only Mekhlis, but also at least two second-level aides were Jewish by ancestry.[47] Unlike Lenin, who relied on a number of important female secretaries, apart from one male executive secretary, Stalin seems to have wanted only men as his responsible assistants, perhaps even as stenographers and clerks. His senior staff members were expected to hold important appointments outside that agency, either while they were his assistants or subsequently, and Stalin never appointed women to senior political positions. For example, Ksenofontov was the head of the important 'Administration of Affairs' section of the party (not Stalin's personal) Secretariat, and Mekhlis served after 1930 as editor of *Pravda*, head of the party Central Control Commission and chief political commissar of the Red Army. Among assistants who joined the staff after its formative phase the two most famous are N. I. Yezhov, who became head of the secret police during its most notorious years, and G. M. Malenkov, who was, very briefly, Stalin's principal heir, among other distinctions. At least four of the assistants became members of the Central Committee. No other official in the party–state system had such a substantial and well-organized personal organization, an inestimable advantage.[48]

Nevertheless he chose not to initiate quarrels with other politicians. Much better to leave that to others. Anyone who wished to attack the status quo would have serious difficulty demonstrating that either the leadership personnel or the policies were not those established by Lenin, the barely surviving founder whose image was increasingly revered. Had not Lenin, while still active, participated in the election of the present Central Committee, Politburo, Secretariat? Had he not inaugurated the New Economic Policy? Had he not established a correspondingly moderate foreign policy, which favoured co-operation with reformist socialists in the West and with nationalist revolutionaries in semi-colonial countries, such as China? And had he not shaped the domestic political order, whatever he might say about its 'bureaucratism'? Most particularly had he not banned 'factions' within the Communist Party? In 1920 there had been a real degree of pluralism among Bolsheviks, with two small groups openly criticizing the party leadership for what they regarded as excessive authoritarianism. Not that they wished to restore a multi-party system nor to oust Lenin, whom they accepted as the party leader. But they did argue that the party should allow the workers, especially trade unions, more initiative and autonomy and more freedom to dissenters within the party. It was exactly the latter point that vexed Lenin. In March 1921 there was a serious mutiny of sailors of the Kronshtadt naval base near Petrograd, previously noted for their ardent radicalism. This was not the doing of the Bolshevik dissenters, but at the party congress of March 1921 Lenin used it as an example of what dissent could lead to, thanks to the machinations of the Mensheviks, Socialist Revolutionaries and imperialists. The congress passed a resolution forbidding intra-party factions, with a secret article that permitted the Central Committee to discipline, even to expel from the party (that is, remove from political life), any factionalists, including Central Committee members.[49] Those who wish to portray Lenin as a pluralist at heart have observed that this was an exceptional measure during a crisis at the end of a devastating civil war and that it was not intended to be a permanent feature of Bolshevism. But Lenin never suggested in the two years following this resolution that he thought it might be rescinded, even though the crisis had passed. Which Communists, then, were a 'faction', and which 'the party'? Any comrade who opposed the status quo in the party was vulnerable to charges of forming an 'opposition,' or worse yet a 'faction'.

In the autumn of 1923 and January 1924 Trotsky ensnared himself in this problem. In two more or less open letters to the Central Committee and a collection of writings entitled 'The New Course' he attacked the bureaucratism within the party, especially the 'special party secretary psychology'. This was hardly likely to win to his side the very people he was lambasting, the party *apparatchiki* (full-time officials), who were heavily represented in the Central Committee and party congresses. Worse, he openly approved of 'just and healthy' aspects of the criticism of the particular opposition groups that Lenin had banned. That ban, he said, 'can have only an auxilliary character'.[50] The rest of the Politburo did not fail to strike at the vulnerabilities in Trotsky's position, so Stalin by no means appeared to be the most quarrelsome of the leadership. He was, however, the most astute in his polemic at the Thirteenth Party Conference, which met on 16–18 January 1924. Here Stalin could count on a particularly receptive audience, for he had a hand in selecting its members. The specifics of this arrangement cannot be documented, but a year before he had told his junior colleague Anastas Mikoyan that 'we are concerned about the kind of delegates who will come to the forthcoming [Eleventh Party] congress and whether there will be many Trotskyists among them'.[51] He expressed special concern for the delegates from Siberia and dispatched Mikoyan there to arrange the election of suitable people. At this time the delegation from the province of Samara was elected by the committee, meaning established leadership under the control of the secretarial hierarchy, rather than by a conference of electors who were elected from below, as provided in the party statutes. Such rigging was still simpler for the Thirteenth Conference because the delegates to this type of assembly were not required by statute to be elected by any particular procedure. Presumably the secretarial apparatus could simply select them.[52]

Stalin's speech was his first major public attack on Trotsky. In typical didactic fashion he enumerated the 'six errors' of his opponent. In truth this rhetorical device was merely a multiplication of the charge that Trotsky was violating the Leninist ban on factions: 'And, finally, Trotsky's sixth error lies in his proclaiming freedom of groups. Yes, freedom of groups!' In his closing remarks Stalin gave the oppositionists a whiff of what they could expect. He referred to the officially secret article of Lenin's resolution that authorized expulsion from the party. When one of Trotsky's supporters interjected, 'You are intimidating the party', Stalin's reply admirably stated the ground on which he intended to meet his opponents in the next few years: 'We are intimidating the factionalists, not the party.'[53]

6 Heirs

Shortly after Lenin's medical crisis in March 1923 the Politburo had started to issue regular medical bulletins, seemingly preparing the Soviet public for his death, but in mid-May these ceased and were not resumed even when his condition declined again in the first half of June.[1] Evidently Stalin thought it not in his own or the state's interest to ready the public for a succession of power. Much better for him if there were no pressure either from the masses of the governed or from senior party and state officials squarely to face the need to establish a new arrangement of power. Stalin held the high cards and wanted no new shuffle and deal.

Thus it was that Lenin's death as the result of another cerebral haemorrhage on 21 January 1924 came as a sudden blow to a public that had been permitted to think that their leader was in no immediate danger during a prolonged convalescence. This delusion has been utilized by various writers, Trotsky the most eminent, who have argued that Stalin murdered Lenin. Lenin was not in such bad shape, they maintain, so is it not strange that he died so suddenly?[2] In the nature of things Stalin's innocence cannot be proven, and in history, unlike some judicial systems, it cannot be presumed. But it strains the imagination to believe that the official account of Lenin's arterial sclerosis was fabricated. Furthermore the general impression of Stalin's tactics in this whole period, roughly 1922–8, is that he considered time to be on his side and was remarkably patient in waiting to see whether events would unfold to his advantage. It is unlikely that in early 1924 he feared that Lenin might revive and cause trouble.[3]

When death came to Lenin it was received not as pretext for political reorganization but as a time for consolidation, just what Stalin should have wanted. He was prominently involved in the official obsequies but not in the role of prime mourner nor heir apparent. The other leading figures probably were ready to block such a move, and for his part Stalin seems to have been willing to exercise patience and modesty. He was among the dignitaries who carried the coffin from the country estate where Lenin died to the nearest railway station, from the Pavletsk station in Moscow part way to the Trade Union House for the lying-in-state. Here Stalin did his turns in the honour guard and on 27 January, the day of the funeral, shared with Zinoviev and six ordinary workers the eminence of carrying the coffin out of the Hall on its way to Red Square. Following the ceremony, at which the main speaker was a second-ranker chosen for his powerful voice, Stalin was one of eight politicians who lowered the coffin into its vault.[4]

All this demonstrated status. But he was not on the funeral commission and did not have a memorial article in *Pravda* on 24 January along with those by Trotsky, Zinoviev, Kamenev, Bukharin and several lesser figures.[5] It is hard to believe that he simply did not bother or could not find time to write something: *Pravda* allowed two days for individuals and organizations to prepare copy by not mentioning Lenin's death in the issue published on 22 January and by skipping publication the next day. Moreover, Stalin produced a memoir of Lenin as leader at a speech to a memorial session of the Kremlin Military Academy on 28 January, one day after the funeral. Quite possibly it had been intended for *Pravda* on the 24th but had been omitted then. Apart from an unverifiable claim that he had received a letter from Lenin as early as 1903, the most interesting aspect of this memorial is the assertion that one of Lenin's attributes was 'hatred of the whining intellectual, faith in our own strength, confidence in victory'. Was this a shrewd stroke in Stalin's campaign to cultivate the increasing number of Communists who were not intellectuals? Was not 'faith in our own strength' a precursor of 'socialism in one country'? And was there not a deliberate echo of his earlier charges that Trotsky was a defeatist, charges then made in confidential circles, later to a large public? This piece finally appeared in *Pravda* on 12 February, but one wonders if the editor, Bukharin, was part of an effort to minimize Stalin's eminence as a mourner of Lenin.[6]

There is no persuasive evidence that Stalin was busy plotting to keep Trotsky away from the funeral. In his autobiography Trotsky says that he wired 'the Kremlin' and that 'the conspirators' falsely told him that the funeral would be on the 26th, which would not premit Trotsky to return in time from his sick-leave in Georgia. No substantiating documents have turned up in Trotsky's archive, although one might expect that he would have taken some pains to preserve such a communication. Even if true, his report does not mention Stalin by name and tends to inculpate other comrades. Stalin's office was not in the Kremlin at this time, and if Trotsky had contacted Lenin's office, the office of the Sovnarkom, which was in the Kremlin, he would not have been dealing with Stalin.[7] In any case it was a remarkable political error on Trotsky's part not to make every effort to get the date of the funeral changed or to attempt to get back to Moscow. After all, the narkom of the armed forces could commandeer special trains or even aircraft.

Stalin's main move to make political capital out of the ceremonies came on the evening of 26 January, the eve of the funeral itself. The occasion was the special session of the Second All-Union Congress of Soviets, which among other gestures renamed Petrograd 'Leningrad'. The meeting was indoors, not in the arctic temperatures of Red Square, which made oration more convenient. Kalinin, chairman of the Congress, opened, followed by Lenin's widow and then Zinoviev. Although often regarded as a disagreeable personality, Zinoviev was a noted orator and rose to the occasion with a lengthy eulogy which evoked the image of a father and a quasi-folkloric vision of the feats of the hero, an important part of the Soviet civic cults of the future.[8] No spellbinder, Stalin was at a disadvantage in following Zinoviev, but he attempted to compensate for this with a shrewdly chosen theme, Lenin's behests, presented with effective brevity. While it was eulogistic enough to suit the occasion, Stalin's address was basically a reaffirmation of the mission and glory of the Communist Party. It began: 'Comrades, we Communists are people of a special mould. We are made of a special stuff.' The format of the talk consisted of six brief points, each ending with Lenin's supposed departing behest and a pledge to fulfil it: 'Departing from us, Comrade Lenin enjoined us to hold high and guard the purity of the great title of member of the party. We vow to you, Comrade Lenin, that we shall fulfil your behest with honour!' Such was the conclusion of the section on the party membership, followed by similar affirmations concerning party unity, the dictatorship of the proletariat, the alliance of workers and peasants, the union of the national republics and the Communist International. In its setting this was astute, well-crafted rhetoric.[9] The use of repetition might resemble in a general way Orthodox Christian liturgy, and, naturally, the whole atmosphere of the funeral was reverent, but Stalin did not draw specifically from Christian funereal tradition, which stresses neither behests of the deceased nor the church as an organization. What Christian rites for the dead do stress is immortality, and this theme soon became a commonplace in the Soviet cult of Lenin. The most famous evocation of this idea, by the poet Mayakovsky, ran, in part:

> Lenin –
>   lived.
> Lenin –
>   lives.
> Lenin –
>   will live.[10]

Stalin, on the other hand, reiterated the all-too-mortal fact that Lenin had 'departed from us'. There appears to have been some equally earth-bound political manoeuvring connected with Stalin's address. For one thing, he had to compete with Lenin's widow for the privilege of interpreting the 'testament' of the deceased. She, too, drafted an address based on this format. Its political content did not differ substantially from Stalin's version, and did not touch on Lenin's secret dictations, but it was not in Stalin's interest to permit anyone else to define Lenin's ideas – 'Leninism' in the word that was gaining currency even before his death.[11] Stalin's eulogy was delivered 'by commission' of the Central Committee of the party, which was not said of any other eulogist. The implication of this curious note seems to have been that Stalin did not have a personal right to interpret Lenin's parting commands to the party. The impression that somebody was attempting to counter Stalin's use of 'Lenin's behests' is bolstered by the fact that *Pravda* did not print the full text of his address, although it published in their entirety the others that were delivered at the Congress. And the condensed version substantially diminished the force of Stalin's rhetoric. Moreover, his eulogy was not republished along with other addresses in the immediate aftermath of the funeral.[12] It seems especially significant that Stalin's speech did not appear in the anthology that the party press of Leningrad, Zinoviev's fief, produced. This book found room for three pieces by Zinoviev, one by Zinoviev's wife and one each by Trotsky, Kamenev and Bukharin, but none by Stalin. Such tricks, incidentally, help to show that the *troika* was far from being a close-knit, anti-Trotsky cabal.[13]

Lenin's funeral was neither the beginning nor the end of the development of the practices that came to constitute a major civic cult in the Soviet Union and world Communist movement. His achievements were immense by any mortal standard, and it was inevitable that many people who believed in the revolution but had little feeling for dry theory would look to Lenin with awe. The first major manifestations of a Lenin cult came in the summer of 1918 when he was seriously wounded by an assassin. Gifts and letters poured in from humble folk. Local party activists may have played a role, but at this early point in the growth of the Communist apparatus it is not credible that the following message was centrally stage-managed:

> Dear teacher, permit the predominant majority of the citizens of the first Lopukhovskaia county to express to thee a deep feeling of sorrow and a deep feeling of hatred and indignation toward the social enemy. . . . We have the pleasure to send to thee to mend thy health, which is so dear to us, 360 pounds of millet flour.[14]

The strongest proof of the rustic innocence of this tribute is its implied admission that the district included some people who had nothing kindly to say to Lenin even after an assassin had wounded him. This could never happen in the professional propaganda that resonated with the naive on this topic, for example the pamphlet of Yemilian Yaroslavsky, entitled 'The Great Leader of the Worker Revolution':

> He is alive, he is with us. . . . The wounded leader of the working class, standing at his post without relief. . . . The wounded, lucid head, the mind of genius, in which is accumulated, ordered and in these hours burns feverishly the thoughts of all fighters for the liberation of mankind.[15]

Judging by a large Soviet anthology of letters of the people to Lenin, published after Stalin's death, the stream of such expressions of respect that started with the assassination attempt continued afterwards in steadily growing numbers. An increasingly formalistic quality became apparent in them, even though this craft was not yet centrally managed, and the letters were not published as propaganda at the time. It became more or less customary for various minor conferences to send Ilyich a greeting. Often there was a pledge to fulfil some sort of economic task. Letters such as these set a precedent for millions of similar litanies addressed to Stalin in later years.[16]

Stalin did not play a major role in the rise of the Lenin cult during the leader's lifetime. Nor did he play a leading role in the establishment of the enhanced cult when Lenin died. As we have seen, Stalin's eulogy was more concerned with the ongoing authority of the party than with any superhuman qualities of the departed. Nor did Stalin have a central role in the early stages of the construction of the Lenin mausoleum, a task entrusted to the Funeral Commission, soon renamed the Immortalization Commission, the leaders of which were Bonch-Bruevich, Krasin and Lunacharsky – not Stalin.[17]

He may or may not have played a crucial role in the decision to embalm Lenin. Nikolai Valentinov, a generally respectable memoirist, claims that Bukharin told him that in the autumn of 1923 Stalin had offended Trotsky, Kamenev and Bukharin by opposing the cremation of Lenin and stating that people in the provinces wanted him 'buried' in the Russian custom. Trotsky supposedly accused Stalin of wanting to preserve the relics of Lenin in the manner of Orthodox saints. But this report loses credibility when one learns that there was at this time no crematorium in Russia. Furthermore, the official expectation for some time after the funeral was that the body would either be buried or placed in a coffin in a crypt, rather than embalmed for indefinite display. But so many people had been unable to get into the lying-in-state that the commission decided to extend the viewing for forty days, re-embalming the body with this limited period in mind. The decision to attempt long-term preservation came only in March, and Stalin evidently wanted to take credit for this when his collected works appeared in the 1940s. According to this source, he ordered the Immortality Commission to consult scientists on the possibility of such embalming. If true, this suggests that he was responding to a demonstrated popular demand rather than taking an initiative to gratify his own wishes. And he certainly was not the only advocate of corporeal preservation. The main responsibility for the decision to embalm seems to belong to Leonid Krasin, an intellectual Old Bolshevik and personal friend of Lenin.[18]

Although it was the model and buttress of the later Stalin cult, the cult of Lenin was not established primarily by or for Stalin. It grew out of popular yearning for an individual hero–leader, which dialectical materialism did not provide. Before Stalin had exercised personally any substantial influence on this development many of its forms were well established: the omnipresent statuary and paintings, the icon-like portraits carried in processions, the devotional poetry and songs, prose fiction, with special folkloric and children's subcultures, historical plays and films and such knick-knacks as lapel buttons and decorated ceramics. Stalin's agency, the Secretariat, exercising the authority of the Central Committee, in June 1925 attempted to assert its control over 'the distribution of lapel buttons, small flags, etc. bearing the picture of V. I. Lenin'.[19]

This subject probably did not occupy much of the General Secretary's attention, but there was one vital aspect of the Lenin cult that did: ideology. In a political culture based on purportedly scientific theory it was natural that the writings of the pre-eminent thinker of the era would be revered, and managed by those who wished to make use of this reverence. The republication of various works by Lenin already was a large enterprise in his last years, and after his physical collapse the party leadership took a keen interest in this activity. The collection and publication of Lenin's 'complete' works was the basis of this activity, and Stalin made at least a formal appearance in this as signatory of appeals from the Central Committee to people who possessed any Lenin papers to turn them in. More important, he obtained a significant degree of control over the then-infant 'Lenin Institute', the scholarly body charged with the production of the 'complete works'. Although Kamenev founded this body and was the nominal editor of the first version of the Lenin works, in October 1923 the Institute was placed under the Central Committee, meaning its standing executive. Stalin joined the board of the Institute but probably exerted more direct influence through his assistant Tovstukha, who spent a good deal of time in this work.

But the collected writings of Lenin could not define 'Leninism'. That required an authority who could interpret this great mass of material. Stalin wasted little time in staking his claim to be such an authority. The medium that he used was, in its initial form, a speech delivered in early April 1924 to the party 'university', really a school for functionaries, named for the deceased Sverdlov. Entitled 'The Foundations of Leninism', it ran serially in *Pravda* in that month and May, and in May also appeared as a brochure, which included his eulogy of 28 January on Lenin's supposed behests. In 1926 it became the basic statement in an anthology entitled *Questions of Leninism*. For the rest of Stalin's life this book, updated, expanded and issued in over 17 million copies, served as the basic one-volume collection of his thought and for many years was one of the two most widely studied books in the Soviet Union. The speech at Sverdlov University was dedicated to the Lenin Enrolment, that is, the recruitment of about 200 000 new members to the party as a tribute to Lenin. Few of these newly fledged Communists had much education concerning the doctrines of the movement, and so presented a population that probably was receptive to whatever authority would define for them the ideas of the venerated founder.[21]

'The Foundations of Leninism' was Stalin's main attempt to reconcile traditional Marxism and Bolshevism. Before 1917 Marxists generally believed that the proletarian revolution would start with an economically advanced country, which Russia was not. Lenin had challenged this belief by seizing power, but he had never offered a clear or extended Marxist explanation of his revolution. While not admitting any shortcoming of the master in this respect, Stalin set out to fill in this gap. In a few pages, quoting Lenin only once, Stalin legitimized the October Revolution by arguing that Russia, although not economically advanced, had become 'the focus of all these contradictions of imperialism'. Russia was 'the home of every kind of oppression – capitalist, colonial and militarist – in its most inhuman and barbarous forms'. Tsarism was 'the concentration of the worst features of imperialism'. This Russo-centric interpretation of Marxist orthodoxy even maintained that the very predominance of the peasant was not a drawback to the revolution, because the Russian peasant, 'schooled in three revolutions', was a 'reserve of the proletariat'. On such a basis the working class not only could make a revolution but also could move ahead toward a socialist society. Mindful of the strong assumption among Bolsheviks that there would have to be a revolution in the West to assist them in this process, Stalin was guarded on this point. The Russian revolution, he said, showed that the proletariat of a single country could overthrow the bourgeoisie. But 'the organization of socialist production', was impossible for a single, peasant country like Russia. To attain this goal – which he equated with the 'final victory of socialism' – 'the efforts of the proletariats of several countries are necessary'.[22]

This vestigial element of traditional Marxism did not last long in Stalin's exposition of Leninism. In subsequent editions of 'The Foundations of Leninism' he revised the passage in question, admitting that the 'complete and final victory of socialism' in one country required revolutions in several countries, but not in relation to the construction of a socialist economy, only in relation to external security – a 'guarantee against intervention' and the consequent restoration of capitalism. Stalin laid particular stress on another element in the Russian context that would enable the proletariat 'to achieve the complete victory of socialism': the party. This was, of course, Stalin's speciality and a legitimization of his authority. It was also a reasonable extension of Lenin's life-work and ideas, even though the founder had never provided an extended explanation of the post-revolutionary role of the party. When Stalin said that the party was the 'advanced detachment of the working class', the 'organized detachment of the working class', the 'highest form of class organization', he was summarizing Lenin's own well-established doctrines. But when he went on to identify the party as 'an instrument of the dictatorship of the proletariat', which that class needs to 'maintain the dictatorship and expand it in order to achieve the complete victory of socialism', Stalin was extrapolating from Lenin, who had ignored the party in his main discussion of the dictatorship of the proletariat, *State and Revolution*. Nor had Lenin flatly stated that the party was needed to build socialism. In 1924 Stalin made only a passing reference to this mission of the party, but it was to become a central feature of his career and Bolshevik orthodoxy down to the present day.[23]

According to Stalin's definition of Leninism, 'the party represents unity of will, which precludes all factionalism and division of authority in the party'. By itself this seems close enough to Lenin's position in the decree of 1921 abolishing factions, but Stalin elaborated on this theme in a way that may or may not be part of Lenin's conception. This was the argument that

> Petit-bourgeois groups penetrate the party and introduce into it the spirit of hesitancy and opportunism. . . . To fight imperialism with such 'allies' in one's rear means to put oneself in the position of being caught between two fires, from the front and from the rear. Therefore ruthless struggle against such elements, their expulsion from the Party, is a prerequisite for the successful struggle against imperialism.

The notion that such enemies could be defeated simply by ideological struggle within the party, he said, 'is a rotten and dangerous theory'. Here Stalin anticipated the ideological and moral basis of the great purges of the 1930s. 'Rotten theory' is precisely the reiterated catchphrase of his main justification of the bloodletting as he explained it in 1937. It may be regarded as the logical extension of Lenin's strictures against deviation, or it may seem a dangerous distortion of Leninism in its assumption that the class struggle must continue within the vanguard of the proletariat for an indefinite period after the revolution.[24]

Having asserted his authority to define Leninism, Stalin did not seek any confrontation with other leading Bolsheviks who might challenge this right. Probably he believed that he already held the high ground and that his image would gain if he appeared to be a defender of ideological orthodoxy against heretical initiatives. In the fall of 1924 Trotsky took such an initiative, providing Stalin with a splendid opportunity for counter-blows. In this period the hero of the October Revolution seemed adrift, unable to mount any serious campaign to gain supremacy and uncertain whom to attack. One step that he had taken, perhaps thinking to enhance his position as a great Marxist thinker, was to arrange publication in 1924 of his own collected works. Zinoviev and Kamenev did likewise, but Stalin modestly did not.[25] Trotsky's publication was one of his many tactical errors, for he not only revived memories of his differences with Lenin but also made it easier for his critics to find quotations useful to their polemics against Trotsky. One such reader was Stalin, but when Trotsky launched his own polemic it was not against him. Trotsky may have continued to disdain Stalin as a mediocrity, or he may have judged him less vulnerable than Zinoviev and Kamenev. They, after all, had sinned demonstrably against Leninsm in 1917 by opposing armed insurrection. This was the main point of Trotsky's essay 'The Lessons of October', which implied that the two sinners of 1917 were unimproved in 1924. In this connection Trotsky made a few references to the abortive German revolution of October 1923, a fiasco first supported by Zinoviev, then called off.[26]

In the ensuing uproar Stalin could attack Trotsky's deficient Leninism as part of a defensive response by the party leadership to 'The Lesson's of October'. Stalin's first blast came right to the point in its title, 'Trotskyism or Leninism?', published in *Pravda* and also in an anthology. It was followed by 'The October Revolution and the Tactics of the Russian Communists'. Both catalogued Trotsky's disagreements with Lenin, taking special satisfaction in the polemics against Lenin just before the First World War. Stalin's sharpest dagger consisted of a sentence from a previously unpublished letter of 1913 from Trotsky to a leading Menshevik: 'The entire edifice of Leninism at the present time is built on lies and falsification and bears within itself the poisonous elements of its own decay.'[27]

Then there was 'Trotskyism' as 'a peculiar ideology that is not compatible with Leninism'. The notion that no Russian Marxist except Lenin deserved the suffix '-ism', was a basic assumption of the time. This had been turned against Trotsky in the polemics at the end of 1923 and now was revived with increased zest by a variety of Trotsky's enemies, of which Stalin was only one. They had Trotsky in a corner, for he wanted people to understand that he had made important contributions to the development of Marxist theory. But what if these were to some extent incompatible with Lenin's contributions? Here lay a mortal vulnerability, which Stalin shrewdly seized on in his polemics of late 1924. In particular he focused on Trotsky's theory of 'permanent revolution', which had appeared in 1906 as a response to the Russian revolution of 1905. Like Lenin, at that time and in 1917, Trotsky had not permitted traditional Marxist ideas about economic development to prevent his finding reason to hope for a successful workers' revolution in Russia. But Trotsky's explanation of this development was not the same as Lenin's, the former stressing more the possibility of a western revolution coming to the aid of backward Russia; the latter the revolutionary potential of the poor Russian peasantry as an ally of the proletariat. One might argue that Lenin's actual tactics in 1917 resembled Trotsky's concept. Had not Lenin advocated a 'proletarian' revolution, while acknowledging that Russia was economically backward and hoping for an early western revolution? But

Lenin had never said that he found merit in the theory of 'permanent revolution', nor had Trotsky revived it during 1917–18, although in 1924 it reappeared in Trotsky's collected works.[28]

Having merely touched on this supposed non-Leninism in the first of the two polemics of late 1924, Stalin emphasized it in the second. Trotsky's theory, he maintained, always had belittled Russia's revolutionary potential, especially the peasantry. Small wonder that in the post-revolutionary period, in the absence of a western revolution, Trotsky had talked about the ' "degeneration" of our party', had 'prophesied the "doom" of our country'. 'Trotsky's theory of "permanent revolution" is a variety of Menshevism', alleged Stalin. In this single stroke he implicitly combined reference to Trotsky's former factional position and the belief of the Mensheviks that Russia of 1917 was not economically ready for proletarian revolution. To this defeatist ideology Stalin juxtaposed 'Lenin's thesis on the possibility of the victory of socialism "in one capitalist country taken separately" ', elsewhere contracted by Stalin to 'socialism in one country'. Although this famous phrase is usually considered quintessential Stalin, he presented it as 'Leninism'. Stalin's reading of the master's famous writings on imperialism was that proletarian revolution might come first not in the most highly developed capitalist countries, but in the weakest link in the world-wide imperialist system. This had happened in Russia, the weak link and a setting in which the revolution had the advantage of working-class and soldier support, a 'tried and tested Bolshevik party', weak internal enemies, vast space for manoeuvre and vast resources in food, fuel and raw materials. Not that this interpretation of Leninism turned its back on 'world revolution'. On the contrary, the October Revolution was a 'precondition' for world revolution. Socialist Russia 'is the first centre of socialism in the ocean of imperialist countries . . . it constitutes the first stage of the world revolution and a mighty base for its further development'. Only after the world revolution had secured the Soviet Union against imperialist intervention could that 'final victory' of socialism be attained.[29]

In one sense this distorted both Trotsky's and Lenin's ideas. There was, it seems, only one sentence in all the master's works that perhaps said that one could build socialism in a single country.[30] On the other hand, Lenin had shown unqualified zest for the seizure of power in the name of the proletariat. In 1917 this had been linked to the expected appearance of the western revolution, but in 1923, after the prospect of an early revolution in the West had vanished, Lenin still heaped contempt on Mensheviks who doubted that he had been correct in his decision to exploit the chance that 1917 presented to his party.[31]

Whatever relation 'socialism in one country' had to Lenin's beliefs, it harmonized well with Stalin's. True, he never offended orthodox sensibility by renouncing the eventual victory of the revolution on a world scale, and probably believed in it himself in a vague, long-term sense. As late as October 1923, when the western revolution showed scant signs of life, he even wrote to the leader of the German Communist Party in support of the intended insurrection that Zinoviev was supporting in that country. This was an inexpensive gesture that may have been simply a means of maintaining tolerable relations with the then-leader of the Communist International, Zinoviev.[32] But Stalin probably had been expressing his real beliefs in 1920 when he told a conference of party workers in the North Caucasus that events had refuted the assumption of many Bolsheviks that 'The socialist revolution in Russia could be crowned with success, and this success could be lasting, only if the revolution in Russia were directly followed by the outbreak of a more profound and serious revolutionary explosion in the West.'[33] It may be significant that he made this observation deep in the provinces, for in Moscow the likes of Lenin and Trotsky might have considered that they were among the comrades whom Stalin considered mistaken. Apart from this exceptionally clear declaration of Russian revolutionary independence, there was a long string of expressions of a Russo-centric world-view, including his appraisal of the nationality question in 1913, his statement to the party congress in 1917 that Russia might be the country 'to lay the road to socialism' and a variety of more-or-less patriotic expressions during the civil war.[34]

Stalin's outlook was far better adapted than Trotsky's to Soviet Russia's circumstances in the mid-1920s, surviving but politically isolated. It not only appealed to the self-confidence and national pride of Russian Communists, but also encouraged Stalin to assert that Trotsky's theory of permanent revolution meant that 'the only "choice" that remains for the revolution in Russia is: either to rot away or to degenerate into a bourgeois state'; that there is a 'yawning chasm which lies between the theory of "permanent revolution" and Leninism'; that 'It is the duty of the party *to bury Trotskyism as an ideological trend.*'[35]

Trotsky, in truth, did not despair of the ability of the Soviet Union to progress toward socialism, and at this stage he advocated a faster pace of economic advance than did Stalin. But Stalin's polemic exposed Trotsky to charges of 'defeatism' any time he criticized the existing leadership and their policies. And it baited this highly egotistical Marxist with a dilemma that he could never evade: either recant his earlier doctrines as non-Leninist or defend 'Trotskyism' as a separate and superior ideology. When Trotsky in a letter of 15 January 1925 tried to solve this problem by insisting that 'permanent revolution' was merely a matter of historical interest, which he did not mean to apply to the situation after October 1917, Stalin replied that

Trotsky does not understand, and I doubt whether he will ever understand, that the party demands of its former and present leaders not diplomatic evasions but an honest admission of mistakes. Trotsky, evidently, lacks the courage frankly to admit his mistakes. He does not understand that the Party's sense of power and dignity has grown, that the Party feels that it is the master and demands that we should bow our heads to it when circumstances demand.

Sensing his advantage, Stalin pursued the issue of the 'Trotskyist' permanent revolution and 'Leninist' 'socialism in one country' in the first half of 1925, while Trotsky, probably sensing his disadvantage, retired to the south with his fever and kept his silence on the debate at this time.[36]

On 27 January 1925 Trotsky admitted defeat in an important practical political matter: he allowed himself to be forced out of the post of narkom of defence. It is doubtful that there ever was any likelihood that he could have used this authority to organize a military coup. The primacy of the party and the very mixed popularity of Trotsky among the Red Army commanders argued strongly against such a move. Nevertheless it was an important strategic bastion, representing Trotsky's past glory as the defender of the Revolution and his right to present himself as the man primarily responsible for the military security of the Soviet Union. In his autobiography Trotsky claimed that he 'yielded up the military post without a fight', even relieved that this deprived his opponents of the opportunity to charge him with Bonapartism. In reality there seems to have been a campaign, instigated by Stalin, to remove Trotsky from this post for about a year before the 'resignation'. There were allegations that the state of the country's defences was poor, and a commission that included Voroshilov, Ordzhonikidze, Shvernik and Andreev (established and rising Stalinists) investigated the matter. Within the commissariat Trotsky's authority was undermined in March 1924 by the appointment as deputy narkom of M. V. Frunze, a Bolshevik who had become a military officer in the civil war and who was to be Trotsky's replacement.[37]

Stalin could scarcely have foreseen that his stance on 'socialism in one country' would lure Zinoviev, and also Kamenev, into the trap that had caught Trotsky. But in the autumn of 1925 this is what happened, probably because these two erstwhile members of the anti-Trotsky bloc had reached the conclusion that Stalin was becoming too powerful. That Zinoviev took the bait of 'socialism in one country' may be a mark of recognition that if Stalin were permitted to define Leninism he would be in a commanding position. In a sense it mattered less *what* 'Leninism' was said to be than *who* was able to say it. That seems to have been implicit in Zinoviev's publication of an article 'The Philosophy of an Epoch' and a book, *Leninism*, in the autumn of 1925. Neither of these specifically attacked Stalin, but they did stake their author's claim to define Leninism. Zinoviev's attack on 'socialism in one country' came in his speech at the Fourteenth Party Congress in December 1925. Here he denied only the proposition that the socialist economy could be *finally* built in one country, 'and that not such a country as America, but in our peasant one'. This position, like Trotsky's, stressed the domestic economic obstacles to the building of socialism in Russia, and, also like Trotsky, Zinoviev stressed the 'delay in the world revolution' as a serious problem. Since Bukharin had written at much greater length than Stalin on the economics of transforming the New Economic Policy into socialism, Zinoviev devoted the preponderance of his long-winded polemic to him rather than the General Secretary.[38]

Stalin responded with heavy artillery. In February 1926 a long essay entitled 'Concerning Questions of Leninism' appeared as a booklet, a magazine article and in the anthology that was to be the standard record of Stalin's teachings, *Questions of Leninism*, with one chapter getting still broader circulation in *Pravda*. For the convenience of party agitators a set of fifty magic-lantern slides illustrating Stalin's report to the congress also went on sale. Sensing that he was in a strong position, he did not alter the main line of his argument, apart from changing the name of the enemy from Trotsky to Zinoviev, with a few mentions of Kamenev as well. Like Trotsky before him, 'Zinoviev is deserting Leninism and slipping to the standpoint of the Menshevik Sukhanov' (who did not think the October Revolution properly Marxist). This meant that Zinoviev must think that the Bolsheviks never should have seized power (an implied dig at Zinoviev's tactical position in October 1917), that they must now 'capitulate to capitalism'. As usual the debate was couched not in terms of Stalin versus his opponent but of that oppositionist against 'Leninism' and 'the party', which Stalin claimed (with some exaggeration) had endorsed 'socialism in one country' at the Fourteenth Congress of December 1925. All of this was backed by an increased volume of direct quotations from Lenin, counterbalancing Zinoviev's efforts to establish mastery in that scholastic occupation. This technique Stalin extended to one issue that he had not raised with Trotsky, the idea that the 'dictatorship of the proletariat' in Russia meant 'the dictatorship of the party'. In truth Zinoviev had not flatly made such an assertion, although a lesser figure, V. G. Sorin, had done so. Stalin evidently found this issue attractive because it gave him the opportunity to demonstrate, with many dogmatic definitions and fine distinctions, that he, and not his critics, was opposed to arbitrary authority within the party and in relations between the party and mass organizations such as Soviets and trade unions.[39]

The next stage in the debate on Leninism came in the autumn of 1926, following the formation of a 'united opposition', led by Zinoviev, Kamenev and Trotsky. Whatever they gained through coalition they lost by their obvious reversal of positions toward one another. It was only recently that Zinoviev, in the heat of anti-Trotsky polemics, had even called for his expulsion from the party. Stalin was not one to miss an opportunity to exploit such a weakness, referring sardonically to their 'mutual amnesty', to Kamenev as 'Trotsky's janitor', to Trotsky as 'Zinoviev's teacher'.[40] This time Stalin's chosen medium of attack was not merely articles or books but a formal resolution of a party conference (the fifteenth, 26 October–3 November 1926), transforming the debate on theory into concrete political action. He provided this assembly with a draft resolution, supported it in a lengthy speech and saw it voted through unanimously. Now he was able to claim truly that the party had embraced the idea that Leninism meant the building of socialism in the USSR and that those who said otherwise were undermining 'the will of the proletariat to build socialism', that they had created 'a Social-Democratic deviation in our party'.[41]

The extent of Stalin's victory on the issue of 'socialism in one country' is better illustrated by Trotsky's rambling, inconsistent and apologetic speech than by Stalin's address. On the one hand Trotsky tried to demonstrate that he actually favoured building socialism in Russia no less than his opponent, then quoted Lenin against the prospects for success in this without the aid of western revolutions; then he tried to resolve this contradiction by forecasting that it would take at least between thirty and fifty years to build socialism in Russia, within which time the West would surely have its proletarian revolution. At this point Trotsky gratuitously insisted on precisely the point that Stalin wanted to attribute to him: if western capitalism could show that it was 'still on the upgrade, creating economic and cultural progress . . . this would mean that we have appeared too early on the scene'. This implied that the Mensheviks were right in calling the October Revolution historically premature. A corollary of this was another of Stalin's propositions about Trotsky – that he did not want to rely strictly on Russia's own resources in building socialism.[42]

Stalin evidently was enjoying himself. In the course of a lengthy reprise of his version of Leninism he mocked his enemies. Trotsky's ideas about the necessity of the western revolution meant, he said, that if the western revolution did not follow immediately upon the Russian, 'What then? Then, chuck up the job. (A voice from the audience [perhaps planted for this moment?], "and run to cover".) Yes, and run to cover. That is perfectly correct (*Laughter*).' Trotsky might claim that he believed in building socialism in Russia, but 'Sinner that I am, I suffer from a certain scepticism on this point', for Trotsky had failed to assert that Russia could actually '*arrive* at socialism'. Stalin's conclusion was the demand that Trotsky, Zinoviev, Kamenev and their followers admit their error and accept party 'unity', meaning not only Stalin's doctrines but, implicitly, his authority to define Leninism. If you do not accept these conditions for the complete unity of our Party, said Stalin, 'then the Party, which gave you a beating yesterday, will proceed to finish you off tomorrow'.[43]

The meeting of the Executive Committee of the Communist International in December 1926 witnessed a repetition of these polemics. Stalin's summation of Leninism as socialism in one country now assumed its most finished form, which linked the current alleged anti-Leninism of the opposition to the long-term behaviour of Trotsky and others and to its supposed social roots in bourgeois influence.[44] Beyond this point Stalin did not find it necessary to repeat or elaborate this doctrine, although it was kept before the public in reprinted works and commentaries. In its final year, 1927, the Trotsky–Zinoviev opposition, tacitly conceding that 'socialism in one contry' was a bad point on which to attack Stalin, attempted to shift the debate to other issues. But it was hard to get at him in any fundamental Marxist sense without suggesting some kind of degeneration of the revolution, exactly the crime with which Trotsky and Zinoviev had been charged during the debate on socialism in one country. This emerged in 1927 when various oppositionists alluded to the French Revolution, which had degenerated from radicalism to conservatism. The key word was 'Thermidor', meaning the shift from the revolutionary Robespierre to the moderates in 1794. In fact, the opposition was undecided about the existence of a Thermidorean situation in Russia, but Stalin was assiduous in associating them with that notion;[45] he told the Fifteenth Party Congress in December 1927,

> The opposition says that we are in a state of Thermidorean degeneration. What does this mean? It means that we have not got the dictatorship of the proletariat, that both our economics and our politics are a failure, that we are not moving towards socialism but towards capitalism. That, of course, is strange and foolish. But the opposition insists on it.[46]

He connected such talk of degeneration to Trotsky's ill-considered statement in July 1927 that if the imperialists invaded the USSR the opposition would have to save the country, emulating Clemenceau in France during the First World War. A few years previous it would have been difficult to heap scorn on Trotsky as a possible leader of national defence, but by 1927 Stalin rightly believed that he had sufficiently discredited his opponent that he could ridicule him as

> a comic-opera Clemenceau. . . . Trotsky wants, with the aid of a small group which signed the opposition's platform, to turn back the wheel of our party's history at a time when the enemy will be 80 kilometres from the Kremlin; and it is said that some of the comrades who signed the opposition's platform did so because they thought that if they signed they would not be called up for military service (*Laughter*).[47]

Only one of the new issues that the opposition sought to use against Stalin in 1927 bothered him enough to require any substantial new argumentation. This was the embarrassing state of affairs in China, following the occupation of Shanghai by the Kuomintang army under Chiang Kai-shek in April 1927. The Soviet Communists had been supporting Chiang as an anti-imperialist force, instructing the small Chinese Communist Party to join the Kuomintang and co-operate with it. But in Shanghai the Chinese nationalist leader began a slaughter of Communists, facing the Politburo with the unpalatable options of turning against Chiang and alienating this ally or of clinging to the alliance even at the expense of the Chinese Communists. Stalin chose the latter tack, for which he was vociferously condemned by Trotsky. It would have been unseemly for Stalin to say frankly what he probably thought: that the Chinese Communists would not amount to much in the short run, while the Kuomintang was a significant check against foreign imperialist depredations on Russia's long Asian flank. For this reason it was necessary to bury opposition criticism in a verbal avalanche on such matters as the proper comparison of China's historical situation in 1927 and Russia's in 1905, the underestimation by Trotsky of the peasantry, and the circumstances in which Soviets may be formed. This was not Stalin at his most astute in the manipulation of ideology, but it probably sufficed to convince almost all Russian Communists that the General Secretary was giving the Chinese question his close attention. And how many Russian Communists cared enough about China to make trouble for the General Secretary?[48]

Still, the very fact that Stalin felt obliged to prepare a substantial polemical barrage on the Chinese question, or any of the matters just discussed, demonstrates that he was functioning in a system that was in some sense parliamentary, if not democratic. The system in question was not the Soviet state, with its one-list elections in which almost the entire population voted. It was the much less publicized intra-party elections, in which all party members (about 800 000 in 1925) could cast ballots in the indirect elections that culminated in the selection of the highest level of leadership. In this system Stalin was elected General Secretary by the entire membership of the party, not directly but through four levels of electors: the cell, provincial conference, the Congress and the Central Committee. Since the party statutes called for annual elections of the congress, which was to elect a new Central Committee, which in turn elected new executive bodies (such as the Secretariat), one might say that Stalin had to stand annually for re-election.[49] But, as in many political systems, the written and real constitutions differed substantially, and in ways that benefited the General Secretary. There was a strong tradition that only one candidate would be nominated for any position, that the secretarial apparatus was nominated from the top down and that the secretary on any level controlled nominations to committees and conferences that functioned on that level. Upon becoming General Secretary, Stalin moved quickly to staff the level just below the centre, the provincial level, with new secretaries, appointees who presumably owed him something and also understood his power to demote. In 1924, two years after Stalin had assumed his post, 90.6 per cent of the secretaries in 55 provinces had been in the job less than two years and 69.2 per cent less than one year. In addition it appears that the Secretariat controlled the budgets of the regional party commands, disbursing to them the largesse that the party received secretly from the state.[50] Finally, the Secretariat exercised substantial control over the party's organs, especially *Pravda* and the network of agitprop workers. The power to suppress opposition propaganda was equally important. In September 1927 the party forbade publication of a long 'platform' that the opposition had prepared, and this goaded the dissidents into establishing an underground printing press, a step that enabled Stalin to accuse them of treason.[51]

The efficacy of all these advantages for the General Secretary became apparent in the one case in which Stalin confronted a significant bloc of oppositional votes in a party congress. The General Secretary had not, until the end of 1925, succeeded in imposing his authority on the Leningrad city and province organization because that area had been assigned to Zinoviev in Lenin's time, and this leader exercised much the same authority within his sphere as Stalin did elsewhere. As a major industrial area with considerable party membership, Leningrad was represented at the Fourteenth Party Congress largely by delegates who had the audacity, at least in the early stages of that meeting, to vote against the 'party line'. This was reflected in the record as 65 votes against the resolution to approve the Central Committee (that is, Stalin's) report – against a majority of 559. But during and after this congress 'the party', meaning the large majority that supported Stalin, brought considerable pressure to bear on the Leningraders, replaced Zinoviev with one of Stalin's protégés, S. M. Kirov, and subordinated that province to the secretarial apparatus in the normal way.[52] To consolidate his victory Stalin dispatched an élite team of speakers, headed by Molotov, Voroshilov and Kalinin, to Leningrad in January 1926. In April 1926, after the situation was well in hand, Stalin took the unusual step of travelling to Leningrad to lecture the provincial Committee and a meeting of the more important party members of the city. The Zinoviev opposition, he told them, had 'worked its own undoing' by acting 'pardon my bluntness – like policemen toward their party units'. Happily this was now replaced by 'intra-party democracy', which meant not 'factionalism' but 'raising the unity of the party, strengthening conscious proletarian discipline in the party'.[53]

Idealization of unity and disparagement of factionalism was a major myth in Bolshevism, a legacy of Lenin's struggle with his Marxist opponents and the concept of 'scientific socialism'. Perhaps it also owed

something to the Russian peasant tradition that the commune rules by
unanimity rather than mere majorities. As long as Stalin was perceived as
a servant of the party, it was impossible to attack him without appearing
to divide the party. The logical conclusion of this reasoning was that the
opposition was attempting to establish a new rival party, a point that
Stalin pressed on several occasions.[54] The practice of nominating only one
person for a given post (or as many candidates as were wanted to fill some
body) rested on this attitude towards unity, and it is reasonable to
suppose that factions would have appeared if the electorate at any level
found themselves choosing between alternative candidates. The power of
these assumptions explains the failure of the opposition ever to nominate,
or even attempt to nominate, a candidate to compete with Stalin for the
post of General Secretary. Such a step either did not occur to them, as
creatures of this culture, or (more plausibly) was not attempted because
they believed that most Bolsheviks would be offended by the very idea.

The unwritten constitution of the Russian Communist Party did, then,
afford Stalin a number of great advantages, but this is not the whole
picture. The reliability of the rank-and-file of the party was not absolutely
secure for him. The opposition leaders were able to speak out as late as
the autumn of 1927 through 'discussion sheets' which *Pravda* carried in
preparation for the Fifteenth Party Congress in December, and Trotsky
was able to publish a statement in *Pravda* as late as August 1927.[55] The
boldest attempt of the opposition to use the open press was the publication
in the literary journal *The New World* of 'The Tale of the Unextinguished
Moon' by Boris Pilniak (Vogau) in May 1926.[56] This was a barely
disguised version of the death on 31 October 1926 of Trotsky's successor
in the post of narkom of defence, Frunze. He had been operated on for a
gastric ailment, began to recover, then died. Frunze and Stalin were
supposed to have been on good terms and the General Secretary made
much of his attempt to visit the patient in hospital shortly after the
operation. The deceased, an old Bolshevik turned military man, received
the fullest possible honours, including an eulogy from Stalin and burial
near the Lenin mausoleum. But there was a rumour that it was a case of
medical murder. Frunze supposedly had been Zinoviev's candidate for
narkom, while Stalin backed Voroshilov, who in fact succeeded Frunze in
the post. Allegedly the General Secretary had arranged a Politburo order
to the unwilling Frunze to have the operation, during which he received
an overdose of an anaesthetic known to be bad for his heart, although he
apparently survived the actual operation for several days.

It is impossible in the nature of the case to exculpate Stalin. One might
even speculate that he did not feel able to oust Zinoviev from Leningrad
while Frunze headed the armed forces. On the other hand, the evidence
against Stalin is not strong, and it seems unlikely that he would have
risked murder of such an important personage at this stage in his career.

But the rumours that Stalin had murdered Frunze obviously served the opposition. One plausible theory is that Karl Radek, a friend of Trotsky who had lost his membership in the Central Committee in 1924, inspired the novelist.[57] It was in any case a demonstration of the absence of a reign of terror in the Soviet Union of 1926 that a writer, even a brash eccentric like Pilniak, would dream of publishing a novel that virtually accused of murder the man whom the writer called 'Number One' and 'the unbending man'. Or that a literary journal would accept it. In fact, one journal rejected it, and Pilniak cheekily dedicated the story to the rejecting editor when it was published, adding a preposterous denial than the plot was based on Frunze's death. This was going too far. The offending issue of the journal was withdrawn and apologies for such 'error' and 'slander', which could 'play into the hands of the small-minded counter-revolutionary', were forthcoming from both editors who were involved and the author. But the whole scandal served as much to advertise Pilniak's tale as to suppress it, and the matter was common knowledge. Pilniak, by the way, was arrested and shot in 1937.

The opposition could reach the rank-and-file Communists by means of the spoken as well as the written word. Important figures could on occasion visit and address party cells, but, lacking an agitprop machine (excepting Zinoviev's in Leningrad, while it lasted), this was limited in impact. More widespread was the presence of a minority of ordinary party members who adhered to the opposition in the cells, the lowest level of party organization. This is best documented for the period of the united Trotsky–Zinoviev opposition in 1926–7. Preceding the Fifteenth Party Congress of December 1927, the official press carried a great many reports of cell meetings to discuss the 'party line' in the form of theses on various policy issues. The point of these reports seems to have been partly to demonstrate that democratic discussion occurred, for Stalin could offend his own supporters if he appeared to be excessively undemocratic. Even the official statistics acknowledged that over 9 per cent of the speakers in the cells of Moscow on 13 November 1927 supported the opposition. The capital city district was in fact the area of most votes against the party line at this time, 1.8 per cent, while the national figures purportedly were 738 205 for the party (and hence Stalin), 4165 against and 2707 abstaining.[58]

In the party congresses and conferences, for which there are official stenographic records, it is clear that Stalin made use of a claque and hecklers. The General Secretary and other supporters of the party line benefited by applause and favourable interjections, some of which seem to have been planted to give him an opportunity to respond approvingly to a voice of 'the people'. Oppositionist speakers faced a barrage of interruptions. But this practice is not unknown in authentic parliamentary bodies, and there is evidence that not all those who voted for the party

line were so partisan that they did not want to give the opposition a
hearing. When the chair, usually a party-liner, would inform an opposition
speaker that his allotted time was up, there usually was an appeal for an
extension, which almost always carried. Trotsky received an initial
extension of thirty and then an additional five minutes at the Fifteenth
Party Conference in October–November 1926.[59]

Stalin faced his most serious problems in ensuring control of the body
that actually reconfirmed him in his offices after each party congress, the
Central Committee. Unlike other links in the indirect system of election,
it consisted of a relatively small number of influential Communists. Until
the end of the Fourteenth Party Congress in December 1925, ten of the
fifty-one committee members were opponents of Stalin – Trotsky and
Zinoviev among them. When the new Committee, expanded to sixty-
three, was elected, it did not include three former oppositional members,
and a fourth was dropped in July 1926, but six remained until October
1927.[60] The oratorical powers of these dissenters was perhaps a less
important obstacle to Stalin than the reservations that the party loyalist
majority entertained concerning their own tenure. The Central Committee
was a highly exalted body in party tradition, and its members had enjoyed
a degree of security. The impression that many were reluctant to expel
members of this club is confirmed by the disparity between Stalin's
condemnations of the opposition and the action of the Committee against
Trotsky and Zinoviev, who remained in the body until October 1927. A
year earlier Stalin was referring to the opposition as 'a Social-Democratic
deviation'. Given Lenin's condemnation of Social-Democrats as traitors
to Marxism, this implied grounds for expulsion. Stalin came close to
demanding expulsion when he listed eight things that the party 'will not
tolerate' from the opposition. The use of such expressions as 'smash',
'liquidate' and 'root out' added to the impression. The Central Committee
took this seriously enough to remove Zinoviev from the Politburo in July
1926, and Trotsky in October, but left them in the Central Committee,
which was hardly consistent with the notion that they were 'Social-
Democrats'.[61] Only in July 1927 did Stalin place the question of their
expulsion on the agenda of a Central Committee plenum, only to find that
he lacked the votes and would have to settle for a warning.[62]

To overcome this moderation he deployed a new weapon in October
1927: police 'evidence' that the opposition, in collusion with foreign
imperialists, was plotting an armed revolt and his own assassination. This
was a crucial moment in the history of Russian Communism and the
emergence of Stalinism. Previously the police had been ruthless in dealing
with real or imagined enemies outside the party, but there was a tacit
understanding that the party did not settle its internal disputes by police
measures. When he suppressed the 'democratic' opposition in 1921, Lenin
scrupled to cross this line. The Kronshtadt mutineers, he claimed, were

used by the imperialists, and the intra-party opposition was in danger of helping these enemies. But he did not charge the opposition with intentional treason or subversion, nor threaten them with arrest. Stalin went further. He accused the opposition of contact with the class enemy, or intent to commit treason and murder, and asked not only for their expulsion from the party but also their arrest on criminal charges.

In this Stalin collaborated with V. R. Menzhinsky, who had succeeded Dzerzhinsky as head of the police. It is hard to illuminate the relation between Stalin and Menzhinsky, but they must have become acquainted while the latter was working as the deputy of Stalin's friend Dzerzhinsky. That Stalin wished to reward the new police head for work well done is suggested by the celebration of the tenth anniversary of the founding of the police, with special attention to Menzhinsky, and his election to the Central Committee, both in December 1927.[63] His main service to Stalin in this period was the provision of several memoranda alleging that the opposition was plotting subversion and murder.[64] The case apparently rested almost wholly on 'depositions' from several low-level oppositionists. During the civil war the Cheka had acquired rich experience in interrogation, and it may be that their star witness had first fallen into their hands when the Crimea was captured by the Red Army in 1920. This was an anonymous 'Wrangel officer', actually a police agent, whom the opposition had employed in an illegal print-shop. Considering that captured officers were routinely shot by both sides during the civil war, with or without torture, it is not highly speculative to suggest that this prisoner of war was given a choice between becoming a corpse or an informer.

The text of the police report that Stalin submitted to the Central Committee meeting of October 1927 (jointly with the Central Control Commission) is unavailable. Evidently it referred to opposition plots for armed insurrection, although when pressed in the debate Stalin denied that he had levelled this charge.[65] But he did charge the opposition with illegal factional activity and leaking party secrets to foreign class enemies. This resulted (at last) in the expulsion of Trotsky and Zinoviev from the Central Committee.[66] But not from the party. This not only implied doubt concerning the charge of treason, it effectively protected the pair from criminal prosecution, for the common law of the party held that this could occur only *after* a party member had been expelled by his comrades. To overcome reluctance Stalin and Menzhinsky circulated to the Central Committee and Central Control Commission a pair of stronger reports, dated 10 and 11 November.[67] Stalin claimed that reliable evidence showed that the opposition had planned a coup to coincide with the tenth anniversary of the October Revolution on 7 November, but that Trotsky had called it off because the 'party' was ready for it. But a secret 'combat organization' (in the Russian radical tradition this implied terrorism) existed, and there was danger of subversion in the armed forces. In a few months, Menzhinsky asserted, there would be a real danger. It would be 'frivolous' to wait, especially because the foreign enemies of Soviet power would take this as a sign of weakness. But if the party 'liquidated' the opposition leadership, the danger would be slight. Along with this there was pressure from below, perhaps officially inspired, to expel Trotsky and Zinoviev. The Moscow province committee demanded this on 9 November, and various lower organizations supposedly asked, 'Why stand on ceremony this way with Trotsky and Zinoviev?'[68] A decree in the name of the Central Committee and Central Control Commission, dated 14 November 1927, expelled Trotsky and Zinoviev from the party. But even this did not demonstrate that Stalin had completely convinced the Central Committee that this step was justified. By persuading this body to expel the culprits from its midst, although not from the party, he had deprived his enemies of the special protection that party law gave to members of the Committee, the requirement that two-thirds of that body must vote for exclusion. Quite likely most members of the Committee had not realized that once Stalin had placed Trotsky and Zinoviev outside this protection he would expel them from the party by a decree in the name of the Central Committee and Central Control Commission without putting the matter to a vote, which is what he did.[69] He next recommended to the Central Committee in late November or early December that Trotsky and Zinoviev be arrested, noting the danger of spies and foreign agents, the role of the opposition in passing Soviet secrets to them and the need for a party purge. But the Politburo would not consent to the arrest of the oppositionists at this stage, and Stalin's premonitory vision of events a decade later remained only that.[70]

Did Stalin believe what he said or was it all a cynical tactical device? As with the accusation in 1920 that the Georgian Mensheviks were about to hand Baku to the British, or in 1938 that Bukharin was in league with the imperialists, it is impossible to be sure. Perhaps it was both cynical and sincere. On one level Stalin knew that evidence had been fabricated, charges exaggerated, while at the same time he probably believed them to be virtually true. Given the pervasive nature of class struggle and the identification of his own leadership with the interests of the party, it mattered less what Trotsky was actually doing than what his opposition meant *objectively*, what he *might* do in the future, if he followed to its conclusion the logic of his contumacy.

As the opposition's reputation waned, Stalin's waxed. This period of competition was the time when he first contrived a public image, a normal task for candidates who must sell themselves to an electorate. This was not yet a cult, for it lacked the reverence and pervasiveness to merit that label. The time of Stalin statues, paintings, films and all the other cultish trappings still lay in the future. Even the party organ *Pravda*, edited by his then-associate Bukharin, gave the name and visage of Stalin scant exposure. For example, in the year of his final triumph over the Trotsky–Zinoviev opposition, 1927, there was no picture of Stalin (or anyone) reviewing marchers on the anniversary of the October Revolution, and in December at the Fifteenth Party Congress, the culmination of his victory, he merited only two small photographs in *Pravda*. Several other politicians received as much publicity. Was this low profile entirely a result of his inability to impose a more visible campaign of self-promotion on the Soviet media? Considering the power of the Secretariat over the party's propaganda apparatus, this seems unlikely, and the modesty of Stalin's publicity harmonizes well with the image that he personally proposed: 'And what is Stalin? Stalin is only a minor figure.'[72] His use of the third person in reference to himself during the mid-1920s was an interesting touch. It did not by any means totally replace the normal use of the first person in his speeches, but it added an ambiguous flavour to occasions when he wished to discuss himself. Did the objectivity of the third person convey a healthy capacity for self-criticism, reinforcing the claim 'I have never regarded myself as infallible'? Or was the impression that the humble mortal who said 'I' was somehow separate from an unseen, greater power whom he called 'Stalin'?[73]

His projection of modesty served several specific political needs. He wanted to appear as the teacher of 'Leninism', not some theory of his own. He explicitly denied even a friendly suggestion that there was such a thing as 'Comrade Stalin's formula'. He also wanted to be perceived as the servant of the party, heatedly denying unfriendly suggestions that he stood for 'Stalin's faction'. Above all, he wanted to appear non-threatening to those comrades, lofty or lowly, who were potential supporters, a point that he made in the early part of the period by rejecting 'amputations' as a means of dealing with internal disagreements.[74] The Stalin of this period was above all presented as a man of moderation, diligent, reliable, expert – the embodiment of Bolshevik virtue. The very dullness of his reports at official meetings helped to reassure. Here was no flamboyant intellectual, obsessed with theoretical and literary brilliance. But not without ideas. Comrade Stalin could impress many comrades with his capacity to talk at length not only about Leninism, but also Chinese and European politics, Russian agriculture and Soviet–party administration, among many other topics. In truth, Stalin's reports of this period, the most voluminous of his life, represented a lot of homework and staffwork. His real capacity to assimilate a vast amount of information, much of it on subjects that he had barely encountered in his previous life, showed up clearly and no doubt impressed many. That his style was for the most part unadorned probably did him no harm, bespeaking the solid man of the people, not the kind of fancy intellectual who for generations had been trying to put himself at the head of the dark masses. Trotsky had the style of such an intellectual, and Stalin enjoyed mocking his adversary's use of expressions such as 'the splendid historical music of growing socialism' and the 'muscular sensation in physical labour'.[75] When Stalin employed an embellishment it was an artless peasant saying, such as 'Tell a fool to kneel and pray, and he will split his forehead bowing', or a literary allusion that would not baffle his less-educated comrades, such as a reference to the Krylov fable of 'The Hermit and the Bear'.[76] But these flourishes were few in Stalin's reports, and the main thrust was weightily didactic and businesslike, rich in explicit, enumerated outline forms, direct quotations and repetitious summations.

Despite the restraint in the official image of Stalin in the mid-1920s, the main themes just mentioned could be, and eventually were, adapted to the purposes of a cult. Even at this early time there were portents. Yuzovka, a coal-mining city named after a Welsh capitalist (Hughes), became 'Stalinsk' in 1924, and the next year Tsaritsyn – the scene of his first military success – exchanged its apparently monarchist name for 'Stalingrad'. In the second half of the 1920s other, humbler things were named for Stalin, such as the 'Stalin Railway Shop' in Moscow and a steamship *Stalin*.[77] But this was not exceptional, for there was also a Zinovievgrad, a steamer *Zinoviev*, a Piatakov sugar factory and a Mikoyan shoe factory.[78] When Stalin visited Tbilisi in 1926, it appears that the local dignitaries who introduced him to a meeting (possibly trying to make up for the fiasco of his visit in 1921) heaped on encomiums of the sort that became common a decade later: 'hero of the October Revolution, leader of the Communist International, a legendary warrior-knight'. But Stalin dismissed this as 'absurd', and it was exceptional at the time.[79] More important was the sustained, quiet campaign of fostering good public relations with diverse interests through brief greetings, formal, published congratulations and exhortations. There was a considered effort to reach a wide variety of constituencies in such notes: workers, peasants, women, youth, military, various nationalities, among others.[80]

Only in one practice did the Stalin image of the 1920s approach the style of the later cult, and this only by the close of his struggle with the opposition in 1927. This was the ritual celebrating the end of Stalin's addresses to major party assemblies. In 1924 at the Thirteenth Party Congress he received only the distinction of 'prolonged applause', and in May 1925 at the Fourteenth Party Conference no audience response at all was recorded. But by December that year the Fourteenth Party Congress gave him 'Loud and prolonged applause. An ovation from the entire congress.' By the next party congress, December 1927, the accolade had reached approximately the level of the great years that were to come: 'Stormy and prolonged applause. All rise and give Comrade Stalin an ovation. The "Internationale" is sung.'[81]

The particular occasion for this outburst was the final ratification of Stalin's defeat of the Trotsky–Zinoviev faction. Quite probably many Bolsheviks regarded him as a hero precisely because he had defeated the 'anti-party' enemy. Such was the main justification for the acceptance of Stalin's leadership that the Khrushchevists proposed to explain how they came to support a man who later killed so many good Bolsheviks.[82] In a sense, then, Stalin needed these enemies, should have invented them if they had not existed and certainly used them to his own advantage. His triumph in the mid-1920s lay not only in the defeat of Trotsky and Zinoviev but especially in persuading the majority of the party that he was the saviour of Leninism from its treacherous foes. The political value of enemies – the more abominable the better – must have been clear to Stalin by this time in his career, if not earlier. They were the nonpareil pretext for his own authority as leader. That he understood this is indicated by his persistence in finding such foes during the rest of his life, some enemies that were unquestionably real and others implausible, but perhaps useful in demonstrating the necessity of Stalin.

Was there not one counter-weapon that the Trotsky–Zinoviev opposition could have used against the image of Stalin as the disciple of Lenin? Was not the immortal Lenin's advice to the party, dictated as a last testament, that they replace Stalin as General Secretary, a trump card against Stalin? The party leadership first learned of this on 18 May 1924 when Krupskaia, following Lenin's advice, tried to transmit to the Thirteenth Party Congress his comments on leading potential heirs. She sent the documents to Kamenev, who transferred them to Stalin because he, as General Secretary, was responsible for the organization of the Congress, which was to begin on the 23rd.[83] It is probable that Kamenev was present when Stalin read the testament for the first time, bursting out, 'He shit on himself and he shit on us!'[84] Apart from the characteristic crudity, there is some merit in Stalin's point: the dying Lenin, in a surge of idealism, repudiated much of his life's work, blaming others for the Bolshevik authoritarianism that he had done so much to establish.

The handling of this document, which was potentially damaging to Trotsky, Zinoviev, Kamenev and Bukharin, as well as Stalin, was on 19 May entrusted to a six-person body that appears to have had no legitimate standing (and probably was organized by Stalin as General Secretary), the 'Commission of the Central Committee Plenum'. This self-interested group excluded Trotsky but otherwise consisted of the men on whom Lenin had commented, plus one less-important figure. On 19 May they determined to submit the notes 'to the nearest party congress for its information', but in practice they only sent them to a kind of informal steering committee. About forty senior party officials met in this body and heard Kamenev read the dying founder's judgements. Bajanov, one of Stalin's staff who was present as a stenographer, recalls that Stalin sat on the edge of the speaker's platform and maintained 'a forced calm'. Only fragmentary recollections of what was said have survived. Zinoviev, who had reason enough to deny publicity to Lenin's comments on his conduct in the October Revolution, assured the assembly that the experience of collective leadership had demonstrated that Lenin's apprehensions concerning Stalin were mistaken. Stalin implicitly disparaged Krupskaia, noting that the Lenin who dictated the testament had been 'a sick man surrounded by womenfolk'. The thrust of these arguments was that the document should be suppressed. By a vote of about 30–10 the group decided against open publication, but salved conscience by agreeing that closed meetings of the delegations from each province would hear the gist of the testament, with explanations that Lenin had been ill and that Stalin would mend his ways.[85]

So the one serious danger to the General Secretary passed off quietly. At the end of the Congress Stalin submitted his resignation as General Secretary to the Central Committee, which in fact re-elected him by unanimous vote.[86] Whatever version of Lenin's testament the 1000 or so delegates heard, it was still as good as secret when in 1925 the American journalist Max Eastman published a second-hand account of it that he had received from Trotsky. Somehow Stalin prevailed on Trotsky and Krupskaia to sign a statement calling this revelation a fabrication.[87] But in the July 1926 session of the Central Committee, the opposition accused Stalin of suppressing Lenin's Testament, and he replied by challenging them to ask the next party congress to publish it. The result was agreement that the Testament should be included in a future issue of the scholarly serial *The Lenin Collection*. This had not yet been done when the Committee met in October 1927, and the opposition again complained that the Testament had been suppressed. Now Stalin was sufficiently confident of his crushing superiority over the opposition that he read aloud and in full the passage in which Lenin recommended his replacement as General Secretary, publishing this in *Pravda* in the context of his speech. In a bold stroke Lenin's criticism now was transformed into evidence of the very qualities that marked the official image of Stalin. 'Yes, comrades, I am rude to those who grossly and perfidiously wreck and split the Party. I have never concealed this and do not conceal it now. Perhaps some mildness is needed in the treatment of splitters, but I am a bad hand at that.' He advertised his steadfastness as a public servant by recalling that he had offered his resignation as General Secretary, only to be unanimously re-elected:

> all the delegations unanimously, including Trotsky, Kamenev and Zinoviev, *obliged* Stalin to remain at his post. What could I do? Desert my post? I have never deserted any post, and I have no right to do so, for that would be desertion. As I have already said before, I am not a

free agent, and when the Party imposes an obligation on me, I must obey.[90]

And this was for all practical purposes the last time Lenin's Testament was heard of in Russia while Stalin lived. The party congress of December 1927, pursuant to the Central Committee's recommendation of July 1926, voted to publish the document in the *Lenin Collection*, but this did not happen. And when Stalin's own *Works* appeared after the Second World War, the unseemly portion of Lenin's Testament had vanished from Stalin's speech.

7 Kulaks

The years of struggle with the Trotsky–Zinoviev opposition, despite the stresses of the conflict, were a period of relative tranquility in Stalin's personal life. He had been impoverished for his first forty-odd years. At the end of the civil war his run-down physical condition required an extended rest-cure, which, along with a more settled life, seems to have done him a lot of good. Up until this time photographs show him as wiry, even undernourished, but by 1922 he had put on a becoming amount of weight and looked healthier, better suited for the handsome public relations photographs of his political campaign.

During the civil war he had acquired, for his use, not as a legal property, a villa near Usovo, about 25 km from the Kremlin. Was it coincidental that the handsome property had belonged to the Zubalov family, which had made its fortune in the oil refineries of Batumi and Baku, where Stalin had toiled in the revolutionary underground? Stalin's daughter recalled the house as gabled, of German design, surrounded by a massive brick wall with tiles on top. Stalin probably appreciated the value of the wall for security and ordered the woods around the house cleared, possibly to make the scene 'lighter, warmer', as Svetlana thought, but perhaps as an additional security measure. In later years he took the same precaution around other residences. Only after his life had settled down around 1921 could Stalin begin to enjoy 'Zubalovo', which became the centre of an active social life by the mid-1920s. His friends Voroshilov and Mikoyan lived in other buildings of the estate, and he had a string of visitors, including Ordzhonikidze, Budenny and Bukharin.[1]

Now he also could enjoy extended summer holidays on the Black Sea. In 1924 Stalin seems to have been too preoccupied with the politics of the early post-Lenin era to take a real vacation, but the following year he spent about two months, mid-July to mid-September, in the south, wholly or partly at the lovely resort of Mukhalatka, just east of Yalta along the Crimean coastline. In 1926 he vacationed for about the same period in a villa on the beach near Sochi, on the eastern, Georgian end of the Black Sea. It was convenient for the hot springs at Matsesta where he treated his achy left arm. The Sochi area became his vacation favourite, and he probably was there in 1927 for about two months and in 1928 for the month of August.[2]

Although he was engaged in a crucial political conflict in this period, Stalin seems to have been able to relax during his vacations. He produced no published articles and wrote few letters, as far as one can tell from the published record. He enjoyed some hunting, light games such as *gorodki* – a game of knocking down pins as in bowling – and a good deal of sitting around over meals. All of this had its political side, for Stalin entertained close associates, such as Molotov and Voroshilov, and also people whom he wanted to know better, such as the Finnish official of the Comintern, Otto Kuusinen, whose widow recalls that the Boss twice invited them to join him at his villa or on a small motor yacht. During their day-long cruise, she says, Stalin drank wine to excess and danced to a Georgian folk-tune played on a phonograph. His wife, he told his guests, was away visiting relatives – which probably refers to her attempt to leave him for good in 1926.[3]

There was, however, a reconciliation between Stalin and Nadezhda. When he told her that he wanted to come to Leningrad, where she was staying with her parents, she replied, 'I'll come back myself. It'll cost the state too much for you to come here.' And his domestic life was not all stormy, for Nadezhda joined actively in their social activities and persuaded Stalin to have his son by his first marriage, Yakov, come up from Georgia to live with them in the Kremlin.[4] If the family scene had been idealized in its description by Stalin's daughter, reflecting what she heard from her governess years later, it at least seems likely that the period from Lenin's death until perhaps the end of 1928 was the most normal and stable of his whole life. Moreover, his political situation seemed reasonably secure around the opening of 1928. He had eliminated his rivals and had won widespread acceptance in the party, which seemed in control of Russia as never before. The economy had recovered from the terrible devastation of world war, revolution and civil war. Why, then, did Stalin embroil himself in a new maelstrom of class war, exchanging the stability that had been achieved by 1928 for a new time of crisis? The motivation for this risky new departure involved his personal ambition, a drive for greater power, but it is hard to justify Bukharin's charge that Stalin was merely 'an unprincipled intriguer who subordinates everything to the preservation of his own power'.[5] Stalin could manipulate theory and policy for self-interested ends, but he was in his way a deeply committed Marxist–Leninist and a champion of class struggle. His profound absorption with enemies did not stop with personal political opponents but associated these with the orthodox Marxist–Leninist concept of the class enemy. Apart from the outside world of capitalist encirclement, which guaranteed Stalin a life-time supply of hostile imperialists, the Soviet Union of 1928 still contained a vast reserve of capitalism, the agrarian sector with its property-loving peasantry. In its first few years in power (the era later known as 'War Communism') the party of the proletariat had begun the assault on this enemy, just as it had against the urban capitalists. This attack set poor peasants against their more prosperous neighbours ('kulaks' – literally 'fists') and set urban workers against peasants in general by means of food-requisitioning detachments. The devastating economic collapse that ensued, though not

entirely the result of these policies, persuaded the practical Lenin to
introduce in 1921 the 'New Economic Policy'. By retreating from active
class struggle in the countryside he rescued his regime from economic
self-destruction.

The party had accepted its founder's decision on this critical issue, but
not with an unmixed sense of satisfaction. Many Bolsheviks, including
some of the intellectuals, some of the working-class recruits of the civil
war period, and certainly many of the younger members of the party and
its youth affiliate, the Komsomol, still retained an ardent Communist
idealism. Given the Bolshevik penchant for mass mobilization from
above, one must be guarded in speaking of spontaneous trends within the
party or working class, but it does appear that there was in the late 1920s
an authentic revival of enthusiasm for the domestic class struggle. In this
period there was still room for some degree of pluralism, if not organized
factions, within the party, and on the lower level activists pursued their
own initiatives on many matters. It would be going too far to maintain
that such zealots could impose their will on the Politburo, but they
created a mood that influenced the whole party and its leaders. Groups of
young radicals, often members of the Komsomol, calling themselves
'light cavalry', took it on themselves to intervene in the work of many
institutions, criticizing 'bourgeois' tendencies and particularly 'specialists',
such as professors, engineers and doctors, who were survivors of the old
regime. The anti-religious auxiliary body of the party, the 'Society of the
Militant Godless', increased its membership and activism. Factory
workers, especially in the metal and textile industries, without prompting
from above, began to form 'collectives' and 'communes' within their
factories, aiming at egalitarianism as well as improved production.
Workers also went to the countryside as agitators and managers,
sometimes with directives from above, sometimes on their own initiative.
There was among them a sense that the New Economic Policy had
permitted too great a revival of bourgeois elements, and in some cases
veterans of the civil war rekindled their zeal to finish with the class
enemy.[6]

All of this was to some extent inspired by the adoption of the First
Five-Year Plan, with its implied goal of providing the economic base for
the ideal society. Fulfilling a consensual assumption of Bolsheviks that the
transition to socialism required a statized, centrally planned economy, the
Plan was not particularly Stalin's doing. Gosplan, the State Planning
Commission, was an agency staffed largely with 'experts', including ex-
Mensheviks, which drew up the first real plan in the winter of 1925–6.
The party entered the process in a major ceremonial sense in December
1927 when the Fifteenth Party Congress adopted a resolution 'On the
Directives for the Establishment of a Five-Year Plan for the Economy'.[7]
This was a fairly general exhortation, neither an intervention in detail nor

an order to attain some sort of superhuman target, but it did give the weight of the party's will to the planning operation. Stalin, for his part, barely mentioned this new departure in his report of the Central Committee to the Congress.[8] Only in April 1929 at the Sixteenth Party Conference would the completed planning document, which sought to cover a five-year period beginning in October 1928, receive formal acceptance by the party.[9] By that time the propaganda apparatus of the regime had been emphasizing the concept of the plan for many months, and this appears to have evoked a wave of enthusiasm among workers, possibly the last time in Soviet history that the idealism of the proletarian revolution was successfully invoked on a large scale.

In its fullness this renewal of radicalism was not merely Stalin's creation, nor could he fully control it. In the longer run he even turned against some features of it. But the idea of sharpening the sense of class struggle appealed to him, and in the first half of 1928 he made a major contribution to the symbolic renewal of class militancy by sponsoring a major show trial. The accused were fifty Soviet engineers, primarily men who had held responsible positions under the old regime, and three Germans working in the Soviet Union under contract. The charge was that they had conspired, on the instigation of foreign capitalists, to sabotage the important coal-mines of the town of Shakhty in the Donets Basin.[10] One ingredient in the inception of the case was worker hostility to the management and engineers of the mines, where working conditions probably were no better and perhaps worse than they had been before 1917. Some miners suggested to the local office of the secret police that they investigate the possibility that the surviving bourgeois elements were deliberately disrupting mining operations. The regional police chief, E. G. Yevdokimov, took up the sensitive case with such determination that it seems likely that he had received some favourable signal from Stalin. Certainly Yevdokimov would have been taking a huge gamble to assume full responsibility for the possible disruption of a major industry and relations with Germany if he acted without any assurance of support from above. This he probably obtained as early as March 1928 when the police arrested some of the German engineers as crucial links to the alleged foreign masters of the saboteurs, hoping to supplement with confessions the feeble documentary evidence that the prosecution had obtained. Rykov, the chairman of the Sovnarkom, expressed indignation, treating the matter as a local error. Chicherin, the narkom for foreign affairs, also registered a strong complaint on the grounds that the case would jeopardize Soviet utilization of foreign economic assistance. If, as is often said, the police chief Menzhinsky initially had doubts about the case, these senior officials showed no sign that they had heard this. Documents obtained by German intelligence at this time show Menzhinsky to have been a consistent enthusiast in the hunt for agents of the class enemy, so it is likely that Stalin enjoyed his co-operation throughout the affair.[11]

In supporting the prosecution of the Shakhty trial Stalin enjoyed the psychological advantage over colleagues who did not care for it. Lenin had founded the party on the principle of class struggle. Its history since 1917 was replete with real or imagined efforts of the enemy to attack the proletarian state from within, and it was not easy for a leading politician to appear soft on the accused agents, especially those of undoubted bourgeois origin. Stalin made the most of this advantage in his address to a party gathering in April 1928, opening with the question, 'What was the class background of the Shakhty affair? Where do the roots of the Shakhty affair lie hidden, and from what class basis could this economic counter-revolution have sprung?'[12] At this point the trial had not yet started, but Stalin had no scruples about assuming the guilt of the accused, and could count on the unwillingness of any of his leading comrades to challenge this procedure. The trial itself, which opened in May, was imperfect in technique, especially with respect to the reliable extraction of confessions. While no doubt preferring to avoid such difficulties, Stalin could fairly conclude that the desired propaganda message reached the Soviet populace and that neither the humble nor eminent folk suffered from incredulity concerning sabotage by means of 'irrational construction projects, unnecessary waste of capital, lowering the quality of production, raising the cost of production'. Even Rykov, who had objected to the trial, voted for the death penalty, along with Bukharin, outdoing Stalin in this respect.[13]

Few Bolsheviks wanted to be backward in the class war when the particular foe was a small number of alleged agents with close ties to big business. But when it came to applying the same zeal to the Soviet peasantry, three members of the nine-man Politburo, Bukharin, Rykov and Tomsky, disagreed. The opening of this rift dated from the unsatisfactory marketing of grain by peasants following the harvest of 1927, down from 1926 by about 20 per cent.[14] The Politburo responded to this shortfall at the opening of 1928 by dispatching various members to grain-surplus regions to see what could be done to oblige the more prosperous peasants to sell grain to the state. In mid-January 1928 Stalin began a three-week tour of the Ural-Siberian district, a fertile and not overpopulated appendage of the Russian steppe that penetrates the western edge of the Siberian vastness. In the course of this trip Stalin addressed party organizations in Novosibirsk, Barnaul, Rubtsovsk and Omsk. His message was that the richer peasants had plenty of grain but were 'engaging in unbridled speculation on grain prices' rather than marketing it. The solution was to prosecute them under article 107 of the criminal code, which forbade hoarding. Party officials had better drop their usual work and start working on this, getting rid of any comrades who did not comply.[15] If one is to believe the editors of Stalin's collected works, who acknowledge that they compiled a composite document from 'statements made in various parts of Siberia in January 1928', he went on to say that such emergency measures were only a short-term solution, that large-scale state and collective farms with tractors must cover the country. Perhaps he did say this, for the ideal of replacing the family farm with large-scale collectives was familiar enough in Soviet Russia. But it was only significantly later that Stalin committed himself to ambitious goals in this matter, and one wonders if his editors, perhaps Stalin himself, were improving on the record of the Siberian trip in order to sustain the image that later became part of his myth.[16] When he returned to Moscow he issued a report to all party organizations on the grain procurement campaign, saying nothing at all about long-term collectivization and much about keeping pressure on kulak speculators. Indeed, he specifically denied that this policy meant the abolition of the New Economic Policy, which was based on the family farm.[17]

Nevertheless the agrarian crisis drew him into a major political quarrel with the 'Right' and above all with Bukharin. Nine years younger than Stalin, Bukharin had made his reputation mainly as a theoretician and publicist.[18] Although he had had serious differences with Lenin, especially in opposing the peace treaty with Germany in 1918, his talents were appreciated by the founder. They also were appreciated by Stalin, who must have supported Bukharin's promotion to full member of the Politburo shortly after Lenin's death and rewarded him for loyalty in the factional struggle of the mid-1920s by making him Zinoviev's successor as head of the Executive Committee of the Comintern in 1926. Bukharin was one of the men Stalin cultivated, and for a time they were on very friendly terms. According to Stalin's daughter, Bukharin often visited Zubalova, charming the little girl's nursemaid by teaching her to ride a bicycle and shoot an air-rifle. Perhaps it is also true, as Svetlana writes, that Bukharin on occasion brought pet hedgehogs, snakes, a fox and a hawk, but it is probably exaggerated to say that he 'often came for the summer'. In April 1929, after the break in this cordial relationship, Stalin acknowledged that he and Bukharin had been 'personal friends' 'quite recently', and he did not challenge the evidence of this that Bukharin provided at this time by reading to the Central Committee parts of their personal correspondence.[19]

While no mere client of Stalin, Bukharin was not, prior to 1928, the leader of an autonomous faction, nor was he a rival for primacy. It seems highly improbable that Stalin made his 'left turn' in 1928 with the intention of breaking off with this useful comrade as a preliminary to his destruction. True, when Bukharin, in a panicky frame of mind, went to Kamenev on 11 July 1928, he said that Stalin 'changes his theories depending on whom he wants to get rid of at the moment'. And at that time Bukharin was convinced that Stalin wanted to get rid of him. Four times in this conversation he spoke of Stalin 'cutting the throats' of the Right opposition. But this came after an angry confrontation, which probably changed Stalin's perception of Bukharin and his friends. Moreover, Bukharin himself acknowledged that Stalin had presented a coherent line of his own at the joint meeting of the Central Committee and Central Control Commission in July 1928. This consisted of three points: (1) the building of the socialist economy required the exaction of 'tribute from the peasantry'; (2) 'the farther socialism advances, the greater will be the resistance [of class enemies]'; (3) because of this situation 'a strong leadership is necessary'. As Bukharin observed, the first point was similar to one advanced previously by an economist who was close to Trotsky, E. A. Preobrazhensky, and in adopting this line Stalin was indeed changing his stance. But this shift was no mere manoeuvre against Bukharin, as was demonstrated in due course by Stalin's adherence to this line for many years after the removal of Bukharin from the Politburo. As for the second point, Bukharin considered it 'idiotic illiteracy', which was perhaps an unintended tribute to its originality. It proved to be a fundamental tenet of Stalinism, the basis for the execution of Bukharin a decade later and still close to Stalin's heart at the end of his life. So was the third point, strong leadership.[20]

In mid-1928 Stalin did not wish to precipitate a split with Bukharin by proposing anything as drastic as the liquidation of the New Economic Policy. For the moment he merely proposed the continuation of the 'extraordinary measures' to extract grain from the peasants in case of another shortfall in deliveries following the harvest of 1928, along with a moderate upward shift of collectivization and industrial investment.[21] But even these policies were enough to distress Bukharin, who was committed to the concept of developing the whole economy on the basis of an increasingly prosperous private peasant sector. According to his theory the transition to socialism required no renewal of class war, but could be accomplished through state manipulation of prices and taxes to extract the capital needed to finance industrial growth. To introduce forced requisition of agrarian production would be to restore 'War Communism and sure death', Bukharin told Kamenev, referring to the alienation of the peasantry that had endangered the regime at the end of the civil war.[22]

But there seem to have been personal factors as well as policy disagreement in the opening of the rift between Stalin and Bukharin. The latter preened himself on his theoretical gifts, especially in economics, and it must have come as a shock to him that Stalin would contradict him on such matters. Worse, Stalin's close associate Molotov, whom, said Bukharin, we call 'Stone Bottom', had 'presumed to instruct me in

Marxism'.[23] In June Bukharin sent Stalin a letter that protested not so much the specifics of the latter's policies as the alleged want of leadership in the party. We have 'neither a line nor a common opinion'; the party was becoming 'ideologically disorganized', claimed Bukharin. Such charges of aimless leadership may have annoyed Stalin, but initially he seems to have tried to smooth things out, telling Bukharin that 'You and I are the Himalayas [of the Politburo]. The rest are nobodies.' But Bukharin was not placated and repeated Stalin's invidious flattery to the 'nobodies' themselves during a session of the Politburo. Stalin angrily accused Bukharin of inventing the story to turn the Politburo against him. On this occasion Bukharin read a policy declaration on the economic issues, but refused to give Stalin a copy because 'You can't trust him with even the smallest document.' At this point the two leaders ceased to be on speaking terms.[24]

Evidently Stalin felt unready for an open struggle with the Right group that emerged at this meeting: Bukharin, Rykov and Tomsky among the full members of the Politburo, Uglanov, the party chief of Moscow, among the candidate members. Stalin told the Politburo that he accepted 'nine-tenths' of Bukharin's declaration, and for the next ten months he did not reveal publicly that he faced an opposition faction on the highest level. But within a few days of the opening of a week-long Central Committee on 4 July 1928 Bukharin became convinced that Stalin was manoeuvring to deprive the Right of control of the editorial boards of *Pravda* and *Leningradskaia Pravda* and to oust Uglanov from the direction of the Moscow party organization. Respecting Stalin's skill in such matters, Bukharin seems to have panicked, demonstrating his own vastly inferior political gifts by paying a clandestine visit to Kamenev to tell him of the impending struggle and to beg him not 'to help Stalin cut our throats by giving him your approval'. This was not only a vast overestimate of the influence of the defeated Trotsky–Kamenev opposition, but also a serious underestimate of the damage to Bukharin's position that would follow if the Politburo learned of his meeting with Kamenev. And it was almost certain to become known, for Bukharin indicated that his own telephone might be tapped and he knew that the police kept Kamenev under surveillance. For that matter, Kamenev was not impressed by Bukharin's performance, which he called 'fawning'. The Politburo learned of the conversation only in January 1929, but it is hard to believe that Stalin had not heard about it sooner and that he chose the moment to reveal it to his leading comrades.[25]

In the latter half of 1928 Stalin proceeded, as Bukharin had foreseen, to replace the 'rightist' personnel, apart from Bukharin himself, on the editorial boards of crucial party publications and on the Moscow committee. Thanks to the authority of the General Secretary, this was relatively simple, requiring little visible action by Stalin himself, apart from an extraordinary appearance at the meeting of the Moscow party committee in October, prior to the removal of Uglanov as its secretary. It appeared similarly easy to remove Tomsky from the leadership of the trade union movement.[26] Stalin's main problem was not the strength of his opponents, who were in truth feeble, but the unreadiness of many Communists to crush some new internal opposition, headed by a popular comrade. Bukharin probably was right in telling Kamenev that 'the average Central Committee member still doesn't understand the depth of the differences [between Stalin and the Right], and such members are afraid of a split'. Stalin was sensitive enough to this mood that he preferred to avoid a head-on attack on Bukharin until he had gradually prepared party opinion and had found a plausible way of demonstrating that the Right had violated Bolshevik ethics. This patient strategy explains Stalin's unwillingness to see the Politburo accept the proferred resignations of Bukharin and Tomsky when they offered them in November. If, as one often-quoted but unsubstantiated report claims, Stalin received the resignation 'paling and with trembling hands', it must have been not from fear but anger. Resigning in protest was not a done thing among Bolsheviks, even if Stalin himself had tried it on occasion – and had been turned down. One stayed on the assignment unless removed, and Stalin was looking forward to the humiliating removal of his foes when he was ready. His anger must have been aroused in any case by the epithet that Bukharin had hurled at him just before the meeting: 'petty Oriental despot'.[27]

At this point, early November 1928, Stalin was only beginning to prepare party opinion for the concept of a new deviation that must be extirpated. In his address to the Moscow party organization on 19 October he had dismissed as 'tittle-tattle' rumours of a split in the Politburo. Nevertheless this was the forum in which he first revealed to the party that there was a new 'right deviation', presumably on the lower levels. A shrewd pedagogue, Stalin introduced this new concept by relating it to a familiar one, the Left Opposition. While the Left erred in overestimating the strength of 'our enemies' and thus denied the possibility of building socialism in Russia, the Right reached the same result from a different direction, excessive concern with the problems of economic development. While out-and-out Right deviationist elements had been removed following the grain-procurement campaign against kulaks, there were still numerous Communists who were 'conciliatory' toward the Right. At this point Stalin asserted that 'one [deviation] is as bad as the other', but the next month in a lengthy address to the Central Committee he was ready to reveal that the Right deviation was 'the chief danger' of the moment.[28]

This priority did not, however, prevent Stalin from lashing out at the remains of the Trotskyist opposition in January 1929. Some of the more distinguished adherents of this deviation, including Radek and

Preobrazhensky, recanted and were readmitted to the party at about this time. To this limited extent Stalin fulfilled Bukharin's expectation, expressed to Kamenev, that Stalin would make a deal with the defeated Left. But for those Trotskyists who did not wish to repent or whose repentance was not wanted, there was a new wave of persecution. At about the end of 1928 several hundred were rounded up and deported to remote parts of the Soviet Union, not yet in labour camps, although that was to follow. In February Trotsky himself was removed from his place of exile in Central Asia and – deprived of his Soviet citizenship – deported to Turkey. Stalin personally drafted an editorial, which was published anonymously in *Pravda* on 24 January 1929, justifying these decisions in ominous language. The 'logic' of the Trotskyist struggle 'has brought them into the anti-Soviet camp', and has led them to form an underground. 'The revolutionary phrases in the writings of the Trotskyists can no longer conceal the counter-revolutionary essence of the Trotskyist appeals.' Here was the gist of Stalin's accusation against the large numbers of Bolsheviks who were to perish in the coming decade: their opposition to Stalin was tantamount to betrayal of the proletariat. Was this preposterous, warped? Stalin took pains to remind the reader that Mensheviks, former comrades in the single Social-Democratic Party, were not merely mistaken but actually collaborated with 'whiteguards' against the Soviet regime. And it was well known that Lenin had established this point.[29]

Having reaffirmed the alleged nature of Trotskyism, Stalin felt prepared to launch his attack on Bukharin and the Right by explicitly linking them to this treason of the Left. In January 1929 unnamed 'Trotskyists' supposedly distributed 'leaflets' containing Kamenev's account of his conversation with Bukharin the previous July. It is hard to believe that the timing of these leaflets was merely Stalin's good luck. By this time there surely were some ex-Trotskyists who were sufficiently frightened by the exile of their friends to be willing to co-operate with the authorities. And if 'leaflets' were produced, there is the question of who provided the printing press, considering that the Left no longer possessed one. The principal Soviet historian of this topic suggests that the 'Central Committee' was sceptical of the whole story and wanted more evidence. For this purpose the Central Control Commission, headed by Stalin's friend Ordzhonikidze, on 27 January asked Kamenev about his meeting with Bukharin, and was told that the leaflets were substantially accurate. Stalin then moved quickly to convene on 30 January a joint session of the Politburo and the presidium of the Central Control Commission. This was a peculiar combination, which he probably concocted to compensate for the narrowness of his majority in the Politburo alone. The meeting witnessed a sharp confrontation that lasted until 9 February. Stalin's side accused Bukharin of seeking 'a bloc with the Trotskyists against the Central Committee', Rykov and Tomsky sharing his guilt because they knew of the contact and did not report it. Bukharin used the occasion to present a general attack on Stalin, entitled 'On the Political Line of the Party'. In agrarian affairs Stalin was guilty of 'military–feudal exploitation'; in industry Stalin sponsored excessive goals that would disrupt state finance; in intra-party life he was suffocating democracy.[30]

If Stalin hoped that the majority of those assembled would at once rally to his side against the Bukharinists, he was disappointed. At some point in the proceedings the joint meeting referred the question to a subcommission. With the exception of Bukharin himself and a minor figure named Korotkov, this was ostensibly a highly Stalinist group: Voroshilov, Kirov, Molotov, Ordzhonikidze, Yaroslavsky and Stalin. Yet it would not ratify a resolution of censure that Stalin or one of his supporters proposed. Instead, after discussing the matter with Bukharin, the subcommission concluded that he sufficiently repented his error in meeting with Kamenev and in offering his polemic 'On the Political Line of the Party'. On this basis the majority proposed not to give the Politburo any resolution reproaching Bukharin and to recommend that all records of the affair be suppressed so that he could continue his career without embarrassment. This was a defeat for Stalin, but his campaign was rescued by Bukharin, who now overplayed his hand and said that he would agree to tell the full Politburo only that he regretted the excessive frankness of his talk with Kamenev.[31]

This enabled Stalin to win a majority in the subcommission in favour of submitting to the full Politburo a resolution censuring Bukharin, and this appears to have occurred on 9 February. The resolution was in some ways stern. In meeting Kamenev, it stated, Bukharin had displayed a 'total lack of principle', and it was 'absolutely impermissible' for Rykov and Tomsky to conceal their knowledge of the meeting. Bukharin's critique of the party line was 'absolutely groundless' with respect to both economic policy and intra-party democracy. But the resolution did not call the guilty 'deviationists', and the punishment was minimal. Bukharin and Tomsky were advised merely 'to carry out loyally' all party and Comintern decisions, and their resignations were rejected.[32] This time it is unlikely that Stalin wanted to avert their departure, and in his speech to the joint meeting, probably on 9 February, he complained about the 'mildness' and 'liberalism' of the treatment of the malefactors. Somebody, he noted, had asserted that 'Lenin would have acted more mildly'. But this was not true, said Stalin, for the resolution of censure did not exclude the guilty from the Central Committee, nor did it pack them off to Turkestan, a reference to a case in Lenin's time in which Tomsky had in fact been assigned to this backwater. 'Would it not be truer to say that we, the Central Committee majority, are treating the Bukharinites too liberally and tolerantly, and that we are thereby, perhaps, involuntarily encouraging their factional anti-Party "work"? Has not the time come to stop this liberalism?' Nevertheless he had to settle for the 'mild' resolution, which he recommended to the Politburo and presidium of the Central Control Commission.[33]

Stalin then proceeded to see what he could do with this resolution in order to win over a majority of the full Central Committee to a definite anti-Bukharin position. Contrary to all the traditions of intra-party procedure, the joint resolution of the Politburo and presidium of the Central Control Commission was submitted to the full Central Committee, meeting with the Central Control Commission on 16 April. This combined session of about 300 heard an open debate between Stalin's majority and eight vocal Bukharinists, including the man himself. This minority maintained the arguments that Bukharin had advanced previously.[34] Stalin delivered a lengthy polemic, over one hundred pages as published in his *Works*. While professing to be above discussion of 'the personal factor', he raked up Bukharin's disagreements with Lenin as a premonitory sign of the 'treachery' that Bukharin had committed in approaching Kamenev and in his illicit factionalism. But the Right deviation was not based on personality, said Stalin. It was a matter of 'Bukharin's incorrect, non-Marxist approach to the question of class struggle in our country'. With characteristic redundancy he hammered away at the charge that Bukharin was soft on kulaks, blind to the fact that they will not willingly yield their grain, foolishly optimistic in his belief that kulaks are 'growing into socialism', ignorant of the fact that dying social classes resist all the more furiously when 'they feel their last days are approaching'.[35]

The conclusion of Stalin's speech implicitly acknowledged that he could not persuade his comrades completely to quash the dissenters. Since he had accused them of factionalism, he could have asked for their expulsion from the party under the terms of Lenin's famous resolution of 1921 'On Party Unity', which was still in force. But this would have required a two-thirds majority, which was out of reach, so Stalin did not raise the question of expulsion. He did allude to the lesser step of removal from the Politburo, which would have been justified if one accepted the validity of all the charges levelled against Bukharin and the others. But Stalin evidently knew that this would not be easy to achieve and so merely issued a warning on this form of demotion, noting that 'some comrades' had called for this but he found it unnecessary 'for the time being'. He asked only that Bukharin and Tomsky, but not Rykov, be removed from their main non-party posts: the editorship of *Pravda* and chairmanship of the presidium of the Executive Committee of the Comintern in the case of Bukharin, and the chairmanship of the Trade Union Council in the case of Tomsky.[36]

The resolution of the Central Committee reflected the popularity in that body of the general idea of revived social radicalism. It fulsomely condemned the errors of right-wing moderation in the domestic or foreign class war, but it also reflected some mistrust of Stalin's draconian style in dealing with wayward comrades. The resolution did authorize the removal of Bukharin and Tomsky from their non-party posts, but it explicitly demanded that they not resign from the Politburo. This was an incongruous situation for men just condemned for factionalism and ideological deviation. The Committee did not wish the whole business advertised by the publication of resolutions, and Stalin concurred in this, probably not wishing to expose the gap between his accusations and Central Committee actions.[37]

Having been thwarted in his efforts to finish with these opponents at this time, Stalin appears to have withdrawn temporarily from the political scene. At the Sixteenth Party Conference, which opened the day the Central Committee session ended, 23 April 1929, he left it to Molotov to report on the political situation in the party and settled for yet another ratification of the inadequate resolution censuring the Right. Only once did he intervene in the discussion, observing that those who wavered in their policy toward the kulaks were vacillating like rabid dogs. It is hard to say just what he was doing from May to October 1929, an exceedingly important period in the development of the great transformation that is commonly associated with Stalin. Apart from a short foreword to an unimportant book and a greeting to the Ukrainian Komsomol, he wrote nothing for publication and delivered no speeches. It appears that he took a prolonged summer vacation on the Black Sea, in July watching naval manoeuvres from the deck of a cruiser, and did not return to Moscow until November.[38]

If in this interval he was directing from behind the scenes the early phase of the vast agrarian upheaval that soon was to engulf Russia, no evidence to this effect has turned up in the extensive and relatively forthright post-Stalin scholarship in the Soviet Union on the subject of collectivization. This research generally has not attempted to protect Stalin's reputation, and for a time even sought to emphasize his responsibility for the 'excesses' of the campaign. What has come out of Soviet research is a substantial body of evidence that the enthusiasm for collectivization and the destruction of the kulaks had generated considerable momentum on the lower levels before Stalin visibly attempted to intervene in the administration of the campaign. Part of this revitalized radical trend seems to have derived from the lower levels of party membership, among people whose zest for class war probably had been encouraged by Stalin's pronouncements but was not simply his creation. Then there was the class hatred of the poor peasants for the relatively well-off ones, a potent force that cannot be discounted merely because Soviet historians have emphasized it excessively. An added factor in the intensification of the conflict was the active and not infrequently violent resistance by kulaks to collectivizers, who were often erstwhile factory workers.[39]

There is no reason to believe that Stalin in June 1929 compelled the state agency 'Kolkhoztsentr' (Collective Farm Centre) to decide that it was necessary drastically to increase the goal of the Five-Year Plan for collectivization, embracing seven or eight million families in 1930 alone. Nor that Stalin was involved in the decision of the Khoper district, a large area in the former Don Cossack land, to declare that they would achieve complete collectivization by the end of the plan period. Nor is it plausible to attribute directly to Stalin the eviction of a substantial number of kulak families from their farms during 1929, which is to say before he had announced the drive to 'liquidate the kulaks as a class'. Yet the best Soviet study on the subject estimates that about 30 000 families or over 200 000 people were evicted in 1929.[40]

Thus in November 1929, when Stalin decided to break his silence concerning the agrarian upheaval, a strong radical movement already was in motion, involving elements of the peasantry, middle-level party officialdom and the central administration of the state. On the anniversary of the October Revolution, an occasion associated with class warfare, Stalin applauded this upsurge. The year 1929, he said, taking stock of the changes of the few months preceding, was 'a year of great change'.[41] He called for an end to the retreat that was embodied in the New Economic Policy and for a resumption of the attack on capitalist elements in both industry and agriculture. But he was non-committal on the extent and nature of collectivization in the immediate future and on the fate of the kulaks. His main point in this area was the alleged success of vast 'grain factories', contrary to the objections of 'science'. But such enterprises, requiring a high level of investment in mechanical equipment, were thus far a minor part of collectivization and would remain so for many years. Nor did Stalin call for a massive adoption of this form of organization in the short run. It may be, however, that the lower-level zealots were eager to find encouragement in his speech and, as Soviet writers assert, increased their efforts after reading it.[42]

At the Central Committee meeting of 10–17 November 1929 Stalin did not follow up his speech on the year of great change with any personal commitment on agrarian policy. In fact, he did not address this important session, even on the subject of the 'Right deviation'. Bukharin and his associates had been overwhelmed by the growing strength of party opinion in favour of some sort of radical policy on the agrarian question, and they submitted various recantations of their supposed errors. But Bukharin in particular did not go far enough to satisfy his comrades and was voted out of the Politburo by the November meeting of the Committee.[43] Stalin did not overtly urge this, nor did he have to exhort his comrades to achieve substantial support for an ambitious upward revision of the planned goals for collectivization. Even the relatively technocratic planner Gleb Krzhizhanovsky agreed in principle to this in his co-report, with Kuibyshev, on the economic plan.[44]

But there were different opinions on the tempo of the agrarian transformation. Molotov stood out as the most extreme zealot, calling for the collectivization of whole union republics 'in the near future' or even in the coming year, and not only in the regions of relatively modern grain cultivation, such as the North Caucasus, but in other regions too. In the early 1960s, when criticism of Stalin was encouraged by the Khrushchev regime, Soviet writers mantained that Stalin had backed this aggressive policy, but this seems to be mere assumption. Even if it is correct, it appears that Stalin was using Molotov as a spokesman whom he could disavow if the ultra-ambitious policy turned out to arouse too much opposition. Nor can one exclude the possibility that Molotov was following his own inclination in this matter and was at liberty to do so because of Stalin's non-committal posture. Speaking of Molotov at about this period, Khrushchev, who was not likely to overpraise a man who tried to overthrow him in 1957, recollected that around 1929 he regarded Molotov as a 'strong-willed, independent man who thought for himself'. In any case Molotov was not alone in his radical zeal. Among other advocates of an ambitious policy was G. N. Kaminsky, the head of Kolkhoztsentr, who maintained that in areas where collectivization had attained 50 per cent the job could be completed in a few months. But others argued that the technical and organizational base was not yet ready, and these included Mikoyan and Andreev, men who presumably were close enough to Stalin to know if he had made up his mind on the issue. Since he did not choose to intervene in this debate, the resolutions that emerged from it were generally enthusiastic about the socialization of agriculture but did not settle the question of tempo. Some passages spoke of various organizational measures, such as the establishment of a central school for collective farm organizers or the building of tractor factories, which seemed to imply a relatively long-term approach to the transition. However, the decision of the Committee at this time to send 25 000 industrial workers into the countryside within a few months to push collectivization seemed to imply a frantic campaign. So did some of the rhetoric of the resolution, particularly a favourable reference to 'complete collectivization of entire districts', marking 'a new stage, a new phase in the period of transition from capitalism to socialism'.[45]

Such ambiguous marching orders invited confusion among the middle- and lower-level party officials and the disruption of agriculture. Even by the time of the Central Committee session, and especially in its wake, there was increasing evidence that chaos was brewing. On one hand, radical zealots on the lower levels were in many areas deciding on their own to push for a high level of collectivization within a year or less. For example, at the opening of December 1929 the party leadership of the vast Lower Volga region decided to aim at 80 per cent collectivization by the spring of 1930 and 100 per cent by the autumn. Fearing the expropriation of the recent harvest by grain procurement teams and incipient collectivization, many of the more prosperous peasants resisted the authorities by non-co-operation and sometimes violence.[47]

On 5 December 1929 the Politburo concluded that the situation could not be allowed to drift any longer, that some order had to be imposed on an agrarian transformation that had departed entirely from the moderate goals of the plan and threatened not only agricultural production but the very existence of the regime. Some Soviet writings attribute this vital decision to 'the Central Committee', which is literally untrue, for that body did not meet between 17 November 1929 and July 1930. Others, more plausibly, attribute the decision to the Politburo. None comment specifically on Stalin's role in this, and it is not clear whether he took the initiative or merely agreed with the majority of his colleagues. In any case, there is no evidence that Stalin acted unilaterally or imposed his will on a reluctant Politburo. Had he been high-handed in this matter, Soviet historians of the early 1960s would have been quick to use this to bolster their argument that he and not the party was responsible for the 'excesses' of the early 1930s.[48]

The first step of the Politburo was the appointment of a commission of twenty-one officials, chaired by Ya. A. Yakovlev, the narkom of agriculture, and including the chief party secretaries of almost all the important agrarian regions. Two of these, Andreev and Kosior, were members of the Politburo. Stalin seems to have been content to delegate to this team the main responsibility for bringing order to collectivization. He did not meet with the commission, nor is it credible that he cowed them into taking the main decisions that emerged. Up to this point in his career, one should recall, Stalin had never jailed, let along executed, a senior party official, and on the issue at hand it is not at all clear that he knew what he wanted from the commission. This body assembled on 8 December, presumably allowing time for its out-of-town members to come to Moscow. They went about their business with a will, breaking into eight subcommissions to deal with such topics as the tempo of collectivization, the character of the collective farm and the fate of the kulaks. Only a week later, on 14–15 December, the commission reconvened to hear the results of these emergency deliberations, then appointed an editorial subcommission to write up a digested conclusion by the 18th. By 22 December a draft was ready 'for the Politburo', which in practice meant submission to Stalin. He read it and returned it to the commission, recommending that the document be significantly shortened by the removal of material concerning the nature of the collective farm, considering that another commission was drafting model statutes for this institution. This done, Yakovlev brought the revised version to Stalin on 3 January 1930, and together they gave it a final editing on the 4th, so that it could be issued bearing the next day's date and the title 'On the Rate of Collectivization and State Assistance to Collective Farm Construction'.[49]

Soviet historians who were allowed to sift the archives to construct this narrative deserve credit for beginning the illumination of the vast suffering and economic dislocation engendered by the crash campaign of collectivization in 1929–30. But they were supposed to demonstrate that the wisdom and rectitude of the party was never tarnished, that the 'excesses' were Stalin's responsibility. The distinction between the good ongoing institution and the fallible transitory leader is a familiar apologia in the history of many institutions in the world. But with respect to Stalin and the 'excesses' of rapid collectivization it does not bear examination. Although the Soviet historians tried to saddle him with responsibility for making rash changes in the resolution of 5 January 1930, transforming a prudent and humane plan into a drastic and excessive one, the evidence that they present scarcely sustains this contention. True, Stalin revised the schedule for the collectivization of 'the overwhelming majority of collective farms', as provided by the commission's draft, but his changes were slight and not always in favour of higher goals. For example, the Lower Volga region was to be collectivized by the autumn of 1930 according to the draft. Stalin changed this to read 'the autumn of 1930, or at any rate the spring of 1931', a reduction of tempo if anything. For the Middle Volga and North Caucasus he changed the target from 'spring 1931' to 'autumn 1930 or spring 1931', which merely raised the possibility of an increase in tempo.[50]

Stalin was criticized in the 1960s for removing from the draft of the resolution an article that exhorted the lower officials not to treat the drive 'with the excitement of a sporting event', replacing collectivist spirit from below with bureaucratism. But the same sentiment ended up in condensed form in the published version as the parting shot of the whole decree. As his latter-day Soviet critics asserted, Stalin did delete an article that permitted the collectivized household to retain some animals and implements. But this was merely an attempt to delay a decision on a disputed point until the commission on the draft statutes of the collective farm could reach a conclusion. In its draft statutes published in March 1930, no doubt with Stalin's approval, the right to possess such modest capital was restored.[51]

The fate of five or six million kulaks, as their number was estimated by the commission, raised such complexities that the commission could not agree on any formulation. There were, however, no tender hearts among these committed Bolsheviks, and Stalin was well within the limits of commission opinion when on 27 December he delivered his famous address 'On Questions of Agrarian Policy in the USSR' to a conference of some 300 Marxist students of the agrarian problem. The party, he announced, had 'passed from the policy of *restricting* the exploiting tendencies of the kulaks to the policy of *eliminating* the kulaks as a class'. The same violent phrase appeared in the party decree of 5 January 1930, and this double authority of the General Secretary and Central Committee may well have accounted for much of the chaotic, destructive, sometimes deadly attack on peasant families deemed by somebody to be kulaks. Stalin did not add any detailed instructions on the handling of the elimination of kulaks, nor their disposition after thay had been stripped of their possessions. In late December 1929 and early January 1930 he was aware that the commission had been unable to reach agreement on this topic, and evidently he did not want to settle it on his own responsibility. But the matter could not wait, for there were widespread attacks on alleged kulaks. Thus on 15 January the Politburo appointed Molotov to head a new commission that included many of the members of the previous one. By the 26th they had prepared a decree entitled 'On the Means for the Liquidation of Kulak Farms in Areas of Complete Collectivization', which the Politburo passed on the 30th. This efficiency owed something to the drafts inherited from the previous commission, particularly the idea of assigning all alleged kulaks to one of three categories of banefulness. Those who 'actively opposed the socialist order' were subject to arrest and/or exile, meaning labour camp. Those who submitted to complete collectivization were merely to be deported to remote areas, while those who were somehow still less pernicious could join the new collective farms without rights for a trial period, after which they could be fully accepted. This last point seemed too liberal to the Molotov commission, which changed the fate of the least pernicious kulaks to resettlement on new plots outside the collective farms but in the same vicinity.[52]

In so far as any order from Stalin was responsible for the vast and cruel assault on alleged kulaks during the next four years, this decree was it. A deliberate act of class war, it clearly had Stalin's approval, for he wrote a murky, hair-splitting article in the Red Army newspaper while the Molotov commission was at work. In it Stalin asserted that this class 'must be *smashed* in open battle and it must be deprived of the *productive* resources of its existence and development'. Why did Stalin choose to publish in this particular organ rather than in *Pravda*? Probably he wanted to respond to military officers who feared that the destruction of kulaks was dangerous because there were too many soldiers and officers whose families were among the victims. This was a serious issue, one that distressed Voroshilov, and in mid-March the party leadership finally decided that families of Red Army soldiers and officers should be exempted from the usual prohibition of the admission of kulaks to collective farms.[53]

By the time the decree on the deportation of kulaks appeared at the end of January the Soviet countryside was in a state of calamitous and violent chaos as peasants, willing and unwilling, were enrolled in collective farms, real and fictitious. The most prosperous 15–20 per cent were swept from their homes, their possessions transferred with great wastage to the new collectives. As early as 30 January Stalin showed some apprehension concerning excessive rates of collectivization, wiring orders to Central Asia to reject the request of local authorities for permission to complete the collectivization of thirty-two districts. This was 'mistaken', he said. His telegraphic order was to 'advance cause of collectivization to extent that masses really involved'. In early February his office ordered the Moscow region to cease the deportation of kulaks. This measure had been ordered only for regions of complete collectivization, which did not include Moscow. By the opening of March he had concluded that some degree of order and relaxation was essential before the spring planting if crop failure were to be avoided in 1930. His relative moderation owed something to the fact that he was the person best placed to learn of the destruction and disorder that collectivization was inflicting on the Soviet countryside. Stalin received weekly reports from the information section of the Central Committee, based on regional offices, and about 50 000 letters from the populace in general, which his staff presumably summarized for him. On this basis he concluded that a pause was necessary, and on 2 March he published in *Pravda*, over his own name, the famous short article 'Dizzy with Success'. While praising the great 'achievements' of the campaign, he called for consolidation rather than expansion of collectivization and sharply criticized violations of the voluntary character of the process and such excesses as the socialization of poultry and the removal of church bells.[54]

On 3 April, after the Politburo had followed Stalin in urging a moderation of the collectivization campaign, Stalin published a 'Reply to Collective Farm Comrades', in which he mentioned that 'some comrades' believed that he was personally responsible for the article on 'dizziness'. Nonsense, said Stalin. The 'Central Committee' had taken an analagous decision on 15 March. In fact this body did not meet between November 1929 and July 1930, and as for a relevant decree in the name of the Central Committee, that appeared thirteen days *after* Stalin's piece, which suggests that he had some difficulty in persuading the more zealous collectivizers on the Politburo that a retreat was necessary.[55]

It is customary to say that Stalin's article 'Dizzy with Success' was hypocritical in blaming lower officials for his own excessive enthusiasm for collectivization. The point has some merit. Stalin's general encouragement of renewed class war in 1928–9 had contributed to the stimulation of zest for the agrarian débâcle of 1929–30. By approving the party decree of 5 January 1930 on the tempo of collectivization he contributed to the chaotic and destructive events of the next two months. But the evidence does not sustain the notion that a single dictator was forcing his programme on a hierarchy of reluctant or intimidated officials. Stalin was slow to commit himself to any specific programme of agrarian transformation, even though an increasingly ardent radical movement was in progress. Even after he threw his support behind rapid collectivization and dekulakization his main role was to approve the plans that his colleagues on the commissions quickly put together. And in March, when the resulting possibility of economic disaster faced the regime, Stalin was ahead of the Politburo in calling for temporary retreat.

This is not to conclude that Stalin was an innocent bystander to the waste and carnage of the time, nor that he was moderate in his conception of class war. But opposing political camps have unwittingly conspired to sustain the conclusion that Stalin was the main force behind collectivization. First the Stalinists, pretending that collectivization was a great triumph for socialism, credited it to their all-wise leader.[56] The anti-Communists, more realistically treating collectivization as a human and economic disaster, agreed that it was his personal work, a great crime. After his death they were gratified to find Soviet historians agreeing that the 'excesses' of collectivization were Stalin's fault. But the substantial evidence provided by Soviet research actually presents a more complex case. What emerges is a Stalin who was at this stage of his career a 'chairman of the board', delegating most of the crucial work to commissions, listening to opposing viewpoints and acting to cut his losses when it appeared that the programme was headed for disaster.

In the party the decision to pause and allow unwilling peasants to withdraw from the collective farms produced a serious wave of indignation among lower officials.[57] Some of this anger was directed at Stalin for passing the blame for 'excesses' on to the lower echelons. But the main grievance, which was widespread, was simply that the leadership had interrupted and retarded the process of collectivization. In one district, for example, Stalin's article was treated as 'a retreat to capitalism'; in another as 'a backward step in the rates and methodology of collective farm construction, . . . crawling to the policy of the Right wing'. This was the most persuasive of all evidence that Stalin had not invented and foisted on a passive or unwilling bureaucracy the policies of class war and collectivization. His article of 3 April, 'Reply to the Collective Farm Comrades', tried to placate some of the irate zealots. Stalin addressed ten questions that, he said, had been raised in a number of enquiries addressed to him by 'practical workers', meaning organizers, in the collective farm movement. First he asserted that the main error had been that the movement at some point 'began imperceptibly to slip from the path of struggle against the kulaks on to the path of struggle against the middle peasant'. Then he went on to deny that the turn to moderation was 'a step backwards, a retreat', as some of his incoming mail no doubt said it was. This explanation, and other official publications, was not enough to eliminate the possibility that the Sixteenth Party Congress, scheduled for 15 June 1930, might be marred by protests from the zealots, so it was postponed for ten days.[58]

Stalin's critics were mistaken if they thought that he differed from them concerning long-term goals for the social transformation of the countryside. The campaign for the destruction of kulaks was considered complete by 1933 and by 1934 70 per cent of the peasantry was collectivized. There is no reason to doubt Stalin's determination in backing this unrelenting pressure, with its harsh impact on the peasants. Two major laws passed in 1932, no doubt with his consent, underscored the oppressed condition of the collectivized peasantry. One was the passport law, which treated the collective farm peasants as a separate and legally disadvantaged social estate. The other law dealt with 'theft of collective farm property', meaning, among other things, small-scale pilferage of crops by peasants who were unable to live on the meagre distribution of collective farm production. Although the maximum penalty for this offence was death, a stretch of forced labour was much more likely, thus providing the camps with one of their major sources of inmates for years to come.[59]

But the event that tested the full potential of Stalin's regard for the peasantry as a *petit bourgeois* class was the famine that followed the drought and crop failure of 1932, a famine that lasted into 1933. One of the principles of Soviet collectivized agriculture was that the farms should feed themselves, and that their inhabitants should not receive the food rationing documents that the non-peasant populace had received since the beginning of the grain-marketing problem in 1928. When crop failure hit large areas of south-central European Russia, especially the Ukraine, the rigid refusal of the regime to undertake substantial relief activities was calamitous, costing the lives of millions – six million by the higher estimates.[60] Stalin and his press pretended that there was no such problem, but in a confidential letter to the writer Mikhail Sholokhov Stalin justified state policy in harshly simple terms. Supposedly Sholokhov had been bold enough to write to Stalin, telling him of the misery of his home area near the River Don and of the callous refusal of local authorities to aid the victims. Stalin allegedly did authorize the dispatch of some relief in this case, and admitted that the local officials had to some extent engaged in 'deplorable' conduct, which 'accidentally hit our friends and stooped to sadism'. But this, he claimed, was part of a fight to 'bridle the enemy', for the farmers were actually 'waging an "Italian strike" (sabotage!) and were not averse to leaving the workers and Red Army without bread'. The whole confrontation was 'a war of attrition, dear Comrade Sholokhov'.[61]

8 Builder

Nothing was more generally or readily agreed among Bolsheviks than the proposition that Russia needed massive industrial growth in order to achieve a socialist society. While sharing this concensus, Stalin did not distinguish himself as an early or emphatic advocate of rapid industrial growth, once pre-war levels of production had been achieved in 1926. In that year he even opposed a proposal to undertake construction of a huge dam on the Dnieper River, comparing this to the folly of a peasant who invested precious savings in a gramophone when he should have used it to repair his plough. Perhaps Stalin, influenced by Bukharin, did indeed believe that the best investment strategy at that point was the renovation of existing plants rather than the expansion of electric power production before there was a market for it. Or he may merely have opposed the dam because Trotsky had proposed it.

In any case the following year he changed his mind and called Trotsky a liar when the latter asserted that Stalin had opposed Dneprostroi, as the project was called.[1] Also in 1928 Stalin moved to associate his image more closely with the concept of a powerful industrial drive, which was an integral part of the new radicalism of this time. The Shakhty trial in April placed industrialization squarely, and oversimply, in the context of class war, opening the way to a series of military metaphors that Stalin was to encourage in the coming years of economic development. In his interpretation of the trial at the April 1928 meeting of the Central Committee Stalin used the case to identify himself with the workers, who were being abused by 'bourgeois specialists', imported and domestic, but who did not complain. 'That's the stuff our miners are made of. They are not just workers, they are heroes.' This foreshadowing of the theme of 'shock-workers' and 'Stakhanovite' heroism also set the tone for future accusations against 'traitors' when industrial projects went badly. Equally important, the speech pointed toward the rejection of (possibly evil-intentioned) expert advice against setting excessive targets. 'There are no fortresses that the working people, the Bolsheviks, cannot capture', said Stalin, drawing applause for this slogan, which was to be repeated in the propaganda of the regime countless times in the coming years.[2]

At the following meeting of the Central Committee, in November 1928, he rounded out the basic ideology of rapid industrial modernization. The main point was the assertion that the final victory of socialism in Russia requires that she 'overtake and outstrip the advanced technology of the developed capitalist countries'. This was rooted in class ideology, but, characteristically, Stalin complemented this with a Russian nationalist argument. The precarious backwardness of Russia 'was bequeathed to us by the whole history of our country'. In what may have been the first favourable remark by a Bolshevik leader about a tsar he went on to point out that Peter the Great had understood this point and had 'feverishly built mills and factories to supply the army and strengthen the country's defences'. At the end of the 1920s, then, Stalin was well on his way to building an image of himself along the lines that Khrushchev perceived after hearing Stalin speak in 1930: 'Here is a man who knows how to direct our minds and our energies toward the priority goals of industrializing our country and assuring the impregnability of our Homeland's border against the capitalist world; the well-being of the people is obviously in firm hands!'[3]

Whether the outcome was so beneficient is debatable, but Khrushchev was right in emphasizing Stalin's concern for priorities. The highest was an obvious corollary of his sense of class war, the question of the military survival of the USSR in a world of capitalist encirclement. The imminence of this hostility Stalin projected not only in the Shakhty trial of 1928 but also in sequels in 1930, 1931, and 1933, the 'Industrial Party', 'Counter-Revolutionary Organization' and 'Metro-Vickers', respectively. The accused in these educational dramas were mainly Russian technical experts who were supposed to be agents of foreign capitalism, and in the case of the Metro-Vickers Trial, there were also some British engineers who were working under contract.[4] In this phase Stalin seems to have decided to treat France as the chief anti-Communist force, explaining to the Sixteenth Party Congress in 1930 that the depression in the West produced 'the tendency toward adventurist attacks on the USSR and towards intervention'; 'the most striking expression of this tendency at the present time is present-day bourgeois France'. Indeed, the second of the trials just noted linked the Russian traitors to ex-president Poincaré of France. For Stalin this continuing class war merged with an equally long-term *national* struggle between backward Russia and her enemies. In addressing a conference of economic administrators in 1931 he warmed to this nationalist theme:

> One feature of the history of old Russia was the continual beatings she suffered because of her backwardness. She was beaten by the Mongol khans. She was beaten by the Turkish beys. She was beaten by the Swedish feudal lords. She was beaten by the Polish and Lithuanian gentry. She was beaten by the British and French capitalists. She was beaten by the Japanese barons. All beat her – because of her backwardness, because of her military backwardness, cultural backwardness, political backwardness, industrial backwardness, agricultural backwardness. . . . In the past we had no fatherland, nor could we have one. But now that we have overthrown capitalism and power is in our hands, the hands of the people, we have a fatherland,

and we will uphold its independence. Do you want our socialist fatherland to be beaten and lose its independence? If you do not want this, you must put an end to its backwardness in the shortest possible time and develop a genuine Bolshevik tempo in building up its socialist economy. . . .

We are fifty or one hundred years behind the advanced countries. We must make good this distance in ten years. Either we do it, or we shall go under.[5]

More specific than this general goal of military security, Stalin's concern for priorities emerged in broad economic strategy, basic points such as 'the transfer of funds from the sphere of producing means of consumption to the sphere of means of production' or the recognition that 'the chief problem is to force the development of the iron and steel industry'. Still more specifically his priorities involved him in the direction of particular industrial projects. At the Sixteenth Congress he stressed one cluster of major new industrial undertakings that had a markedly easterly shift, an implicit recognition of the strategic character of industry: the Urals–Kuznetsk coal and iron combine, the automobile plant in Nizhnii-Novgorod, the tractor factory in Chelyabinsk, machine-building industry of Sverdlovsk and agricultural equipment projects in Savatov and Novosibirsk.[6] Others of particular note were Dneprostroi, already mentioned, the Stalingrad tractor factory, the Rostov agricultural machinery plant and the White Sea–Baltic Canal.

Apart from a spate of brief and ceremonial written greetings to various industrial plants in 1930–2, it is hard to know in any detail how Stalin went about the supervision of Soviet industry.[7] In any case it was neither by terrorizing the managers nor by personal inspections. Considering his unquestionable devotion to industrialization, it is curious that he showed no greater zest for seeing with his own eyes the fruits of his, and others, labours, the more so in cases of architecturally monumental works such as the Dnieper dam, the opening of which was treated as a first-rank pageant in 1932. Surely the Boss would have cut a fine figure here. But no, he apologized to the builders that 'my work makes it impossible for me to leave Moscow'.[8] True, he did find it convenient to visit one Georgian hydroelectric project while on vacation in the area, did travel a few hundred metres from his office to see the new Moscow Metro and was induced by the police to see one of their pet projects, the White Sea Canal. But basically it was not Stalin's style to chase around the USSR in a tiring effort to supervise things, or to appear to do so. Let Kalinin dedicate the dam, let Ordzhonikidze visit Magnitostroi, and the Stalingrad tractor works. Stalin evidently believed that authority should stay put in the centre and he with it.

The crux of his concern was party control over the planned economy. A consequence of the Five-Year Plan was the enhancement of the state agencies that drafted and implemented the plan: Gosplan, the Supreme Council of the National Economy and a number of people's commissariats. It was understood that the party should provide only the broadest statement of goals, and there was no expectation that the staff of the Central Committee would intervene in the specifics of planning, nor in its day-to-day administration. Marxists usually assumed that the economic superiority of socialism lay in its rationality, based on the ability of intelligent and benevolent planners to run the economy for the good of the people, not profit. And it had transpired that these experts were not working in the central party headquarters and in some important cases were not even party members. Very likely Stalin rejected both the economic and political consequences of this version of a socialist economy. These experts wanted to achieve 'equilibrium' among the many variables in the plan, such as investment, wages and output. They opposed the adoption of the industrial growth rates that Stalin considered necessary to make up between fifty and a hundred years in a decade. In the long run they undermined the authority of the party, perhaps even raised doubts about the need for such a party.[9]

In approximately the period of the First Five-Year Plan, 1929–33, Stalin overturned this traditional Marxist conception of economic planning and replaced it with something quite different, which in its main lines is still in place today in the USSR and other systems modelled on it. Without taking credit for the historic shift that he was promulgating, Stalin explained the essence of the matter in his major address to the Sixteenth Party Congress in July 1930:

> But the Party cannot confine itself to drawing up a general line. It must also, from day to day, keep check on how the general line is being carried out in practice. It must guide the carrying out of the general line, improving and perfecting the adopted plans of economic development in the course of the work, and correcting and preventing mistakes.
> *How has the Central Committee of our Party performed this work?*
> The Central Committee's work in this sphere has proceeded mainly along the line of amending and giving precision to the Five-Year Plan by accelerating tempos and shortening time schedules, along the line of checking the economic organizations' fulfilment of the assignments laid down.[10]

Here, as so often, in his usage 'Central Committee' referred not to that body as a whole but to his own apparatus, the Committee's Secretariat, with the possible involvement of Politburo in some instances. Examples of changed production goals that Stalin cited included a 59 per cent rise in the goals previously set for iron and steel, 324 per cent for tractors and about 100 per cent for motor vehicles, non-ferrous metals and farm machinery.[11] How this was to be achieved without a corresponding rise in fuel and transport or a decrease in, say, housing construction and shoes, Stalin did not say. The main thing was that the party decided these things, not the economists or the industrial administrators of the people's commissariats.

As for the establishment of 'Bolshevik tempos', the most famous was 'the Five-Year Plan in four years', which Stalin stressed at the same party congress. This transformation of the economists' plan into a slogan to promote labour heroism was supposedly the invention of factory workers in Moscow in early 1930. In any case this drastic shift in the timing of the plan would not have reached the pages of *Pravda* without Stalin's approval. Certainly it fit in with the concepts of 'socialist emulation', 'labour enthusiasm' and 'shock-brigade work', which he stressed at the 1930 congress. Such devices for labour mobilization were specifically regarded as ways in which the party and its youth wing, the Komsomol, functioned directly in the economy. 'Socialist emulation', the competition of industrial enterprises with one another, can be traced specifically to Stalin's door, for the first 'suggestion' of this practice appeared in February 1929 in a Central Committee publication.[12]

Stalin's enthusiasm for ever-higher tempos, or at least targets, emerged not only in his talk about fulfilling various aspects of the plan in even less than four years but also in his hostility to anyone who questioned the changes. This ranged from scorn for 'sages' who doubted the efficacy of labour 'shock-brigades' to something much more ominous concerning those 'who talk about the necessity of *reducing* the rate of development of our industry', who are 'agents of our class enemies'.[13] This was not idle talk. While the head of Gosplan, Lenin's old friend the engineer 'sage' Krzhizhanovsky, was removed from that job in 1930 without reprimand, others were tried and convicted in the new trials, in which the accused were mainly 'bourgeois specialists' or former Mensheviks who worked in the planning apparatus and suffered the misfortune of not anticipating Stalin's decision to replace the old conception of planned growth with the party-directed all-out drive.[14]

Apart from such dramatic interventions, the party's routine control of high-level state appointments enabled Stalin to dabble as much as he wished in this area. Although evidence is fragmentary to say the least, it appears that he personally handled a large number of promotions, demotions and transfers, often quite arbitrarily. For example, he first designated an almost uneducated Communist, D. E. Sulimov, for promotion to narkom of transport, and to prepare him for this post ordered him to take a crash course from a specialist in that department. But soon the Boss phoned Sulimov to tell him that he would not have to study transportation after all, he was to be chairman of the Sovnarkom of the Russian Union Republic. And shortly thereafter, Sulimov's erstwhile tutor, whose background was transportation engineering and mathematics, received personal orders from the Boss to become the deputy narkom of finance, despite his protests that he knew nothing about the field.[15] In this particular case, and no doubt in many others, Stalin was acting on a principle that he had enunciated in a note to Lenin in 1921, long before he had taken part in economic affairs. Speaking of the staff of Lenin's beloved GOELRO (State Electrification Commission), Stalin noted that some lacked 'healthy pragmatism', that people 'alive to politics, ready to act on the principle of "order carried out", "fulfillment on schedule", etc.' should be appointed.[16]

In addition to use of the party's control over personnel, Stalin intervened in industrial administration by means of specific decrees on the authority of the Central Committee. It is reasonably clear that the published documents are nothing like the full list of even formal 'party decisions', much less informal orders by letter, telegram and telephone.[17] But the number of published directives in the name of the Central Committee in 1929–33, even if only the tip of the iceberg, is adequate to demonstrate Stalin's abrupt turn toward direct intervention in industry. These decrees carried the full weight of party authority, but they were not submitted to meetings of the Central Committee for approval and were basically the work of Stalin's staff at Old Square. Perhaps the Politburo passed some or all of them, but the detailed evidence cited in the previous chapter concerning the vital decree on the tempo of collectivization shows that Stalin did not necessarily submit such documents to the Politburo. He did not, of course, do everything singlehandedly, and in this connection it is significant that at the beginning of 1930 he reorganized the apparatus of the Central Committee Secretariat in an attempt to adapt it better to industrial administration. The section of the Secretariat that dealt with the assignment of personnel now established specific economic subdivisions to enable it to focus more clearly on this kind of activity.[18]

Prior to 1929 there had been many published party directives, but none on the management of particular industries. Beginning with one on the Donets Basin coal industry, dated 17 January 1929, and ending in 1933, some thirty-five Central Committee directives were published, giving orders to the chemical, petroleum, railway, river transport, textile, rubber, coal, electrical, iron mining, metal smelting, automobile, paper and food canning industries, along with the Moscow Metro and Volga hydroelectric projects.[19] These were high priorities in Stalin's opinion, and he sought to give them a push on the authority of the party, regardless of the consequences for the equilibrium of the plan. The most striking in the list, and one that is most accessible in Soviet scholarship, a set-piece of labour heroism, is the decree of 25 January 1931 'On the

Construction of the Magnitogorsk Metallurgical Plant'.[20] This project was vital in several respects. It aimed at greatly increasing steel production. It was part of the strategic shift to the East, for the site was located in the southern Urals, far from the hostile West, and linked with the Kuznetsk coalfield project, still further east. And it was totally new, involving the construction of a city in the wilderness and the pioneering effort of large numbers of presumably enthusiastic labour heroes, including foreign volunteers and Soviet Komsomols. At the opening of the 1930s it was not going ahead fast enough to please Stalin. One of the problems was a series of unresolved planning questions, for example the relative desirability of separate Ural and Siberian projects, rather than a 'combine' in which coal and iron ore would be swapped between two centres. On 15 May 1930 the Party (evidently Ordzhonikidze was the crucial figure, reporting no doubt to Stalin to obtain Central Committee support) resolved this problem in favour of the combined approach.[21]

But the state agencies that were supposed to be building the plant did not satisfy Stalin with their progress, and in particular the engineering design that had been contracted out to two American firms. An internal report of the Central Committee apparatus in November 1930 excoriated the performance of the capitalist experts, noting that some of the American engineers whom they sent were not part of their regular staff but merely men hired through newspaper adverts.[22] This appears to have led Stalin's office to take over the direction of the operation, bypassing the foreign experts, and ordering a variety of Soviet state agencies to take specific steps. The decree of 25 March 1931 'On the Construction of the Magnitogorsk Metallurgical Plant' may have been planning in a sense, but it was quite different from the traditional socialist conception, having no direct connection with the attempt of the First Five-Year Plan to provide a series of nationally integrated and balanced developmental steps. Instead it was a command to drop whatever had to be dropped in other sectors in order to give priority to Magnitogorsk. The Main Administration of Geological Survey was ordered to submit by 1 March the necessary information on usable sources of limestone, dolomite, fire clay 'etc'. The implication seemed to be that these materials were under orders to be present in nature near Magnitogorsk. The Supreme Council of the National Economy had a month to assign the necessary technical staff, without concern, it seems, for the impact that this would have on other projects.

A corollary of the assumption of economic command by the Secretariat in a particular enterprise was the requirement of direct reports to that authority from the field. Detailed knowledge of the labour situation at Magnitogorsk was implied in another of its decrees, dated 5 April 1931. It castigated the local management for the presence of shortcomings that were rife in Soviet industry during the First Five-Year Plan: absenteeism,

high turnover and inefficient utilization. To remedy these disorders
Stalin's office issued fairly detailed commands that probably were
impossible to obey, including the transfer of 22 000 new workers in the
last two quarters of 1931, the training for industrial labour of 4000
workers, of whom at least 1500 should become skilled mechanics, and the
assignment by 15 May of 70 additional engineers and 190 new technicians
to Magnitogorsk.[23]

The 'Central Committee' completely discarded the original plan for the
Magnitogorsk plant, which aimed at a productive capacity of 665 000 tons
per year by 1932. In 1929 the state agencies that had drawn up this target,
swept along in the drive for 'Bolshevik tempos', raised the goal to 750 000
and then one million tons. But this did not suit the 'Central Committee',
which on 15 February decreed that by 1 October 1932 a capacity of 2.5
million tons should be on line, with a later increase to four million.[24]
Perhaps Stalin actually regarded such goals as primarily inspirational,
reflecting the arguable idea that people would work harder for heroic
dreams, expressed in vast, round numbers, than for carefully calculated
targets which perhaps could be attained. That he had encountered
objections was acknowledged in a speech of June 1931. 'There are certain
near-party philistines who assert that our production programme is
unrealistic, that it cannot be fulfilled. They are somewhat like Shchedrin's
"sapient gudgeons" who are always ready to spread "a vacuum of
ineptitude" around themselves. Is our programme realistic or not? Most
certainly it is.'[25]

But this was for public consumption. When in April 1932, only about
six months before the Magnitogorsk plant had been ordered to start
producing at the high levels, he did not reproach the director of the
project, Ya. Gugel, when the latter came to call, for the first time, and
presumably knew very well that he could not meet the inspirational target
figures. If Gugel's recollection of the conversation may be believed, they
talked amicably about various technical aspects of the project, on which
Stalin was well informed, such as the piping of gas and the building of
reservoirs. When Stalin asked him how long it would be before the
project was finished, Gugel answered 'half a year', but Stalin was less
optimistic: 'More, I think. It seems to me that the actual, complete
putting into production in the conditions of Magnitostroi must take more
time. It will be good if things go as you think, but it seems to me that you
have been carried away.' 'It turned out that Stalin was right', recalled
Gugel. And indeed the 1933 production figures for Magnitogorsk were
quite close to the original plan target, though even achieving this much in
so short a time may have owed much to the zeal that Stalin's propaganda
generated.[26]

Magnitogorsk illustrates the impact of Stalin's transformation of the
concept of a planned socialist economy. Whether the resulting economic

system really can be considered to be planned is debatable. A British economist who worked for Gosplan in 1936–7, Jack Miller, concluded that 'a coherent planning system did not exist. What existed was a priorities system of a fairly simple kind. The effective priorities were limited to products and services important enough to merit decisions by the Politburo and its permanent staff (the relevant Departments of the Central Committee and Stalin's personal secretariat).'[27]

The impact of Stalin's transformation of socalist planning was as great for the party as for the economy. The Sixteenth Party Congress in 1930 produced the slogan 'Face to Production!', which meant that henceforth the Communists legitimized their power through an economic argument: only the party possessed the inspiration to set heroic goals and the authority to lead the masses to fulfill and overfulfill them. With this alleged responsibility went a vested interest. The party bureaucracy came to owe much of its power and privilege to its economic role, and in the 1930s a certain degree of gratitude to Stalin for arranging this. However dysfunctional the Stalinist economic system may be (and sooner or later many economists, including Soviet ones, concluded that it was extremely inefficient), it has served party officialdom well.[28]

On 7 January 1933 Stalin celebrated the completion of the First Five-Year Plan in agriculture and industry in a widely publicized address to the Central Committee. Before the plan, he claimed, the Soviet Union lacked iron and steel, tractor, automobile, machine-tool, chemical, agricultural machinery and aircraft industries; in electric power, coal and oil production the country had been 'last on the list'; it had only one coal and metallurgical base, one textile centre. All these deficiencies, asserted Stalin, had been rectified in the Five-Year Plan that had been completed in four years. The effect of all this was to create factories that could be quickly switched to defence production, thus transforming the Soviet Union from 'a weak country, unprepared for defence, to a country mighty in defence, a country prepared for every contingency'. Without this, he added, 'our position would have been more or less analogous to the present position of China, which has no heavy industry and no war industry of its own and which is being molested by anyone who cares to do so'. Stalin concluded with a flourish on behalf of his own bastion: 'Finally, the results of the Five-Year Plan have shown that the Communist Party is invincible, *if* it knows its goal, and *if* it is not afraid of difficulties.'[29]

But Stalin's evaluation of the party-dominated command economy that he had created was mixed. While one part of his heart gloried in the all-out Bolshevik campaign, another part loved good order, recoiling from the confusion, waste and shortfalls that resulted from his disruption of the economists' attempt at a rational plan. On 5 December 1929, just as his intervention in the economy was in full swing, his office issued a major decree, entitled 'On the Reorganization of the Administration of Industry', which attempted to offset the disruption of good order.[30] More personally he stressed the same point in his major speech to industrial administrators on 23 June 1931. Far from exhorting these officials to set production records, Stalin provided six points that constituted a litany of managerial sobriety. Significantly these points were by far the most highly publicized teaching that he had to offer concerning industrial management, an important early harbinger of the cult of his personality. Stalin told the administrators to 'recruit manpower in an organized way; mechanize labour'; stop excessive labour turnover and 'organize wages properly'; 'end the lack of personal responsibility'; create a 'working-class intelligentsia'; show 'greater attention and solicitude' to engineers and workers of the old school; 'introduce and reinforce business accounting'.[31]

The dichotomy between all-out drive and good management was not new in Stalin's thinking at the time of the First Five-Year Plan. When he wrote his major treatise on Leninism in 1924, he had expressed clearly his attachment to both 'Russian revolutionary sweep' and 'American efficiency'. The former stood for boundless heroism, the latter business-like organization. Without American efficiency, said Stalin, the Russian revolutionary sweep might degenerate into 'fantastic scheme-concocting', and without Russian revolutionary sweep American efficiency might sink into 'narrow and unprincipled practicalism'. Properly synthesized, the two constituted the proper 'style in work' for Bolsheviks.[32] Like most schemas of this sort, Stalin's conception oversimplified the cultures that he used as models, but it was respectable as an intellectual ideal. In practice its realization was unattainable. The engineers, economists and managers who had received professional training in the old regime were cowed by treason trials and 'specialist-baiting' (*spetsedstvo* – literally 'specialist-eating'). As for the new working-class successors to these suspect ex-bourgeois, they tended to be recruited from among the most zealous Communists, people distinguished by their ample 'revolutionary sweep' and rarely by their technical qualifications. Stalin seems to have been permanently frustrated by the failure of his minions to achieve the synthesis of 'Russian revolutionary sweep' and 'American efficiency'. Indeed, this failure and his frustration probably had something to do with his application of police terror methods in dealing with industrialists in the latter half for the 1930s.

Perhaps there was one branch of the industrial economy that could approach the synthesis that Stalin sought: Gulag (an acronym for State Administration of Camps). The forced labour camp, primarily for political convicts, emerged in Lenin's time, but it was only in the midst of the First Five-Year Plan that it flowered as an economically important institution. In this period the regime faced the question of what to do with a substantial increase in the Gulag population, largely as a result of dekulakization, and to a lesser extent the arrest of clergy, lay believers, minority nationalists and 'bourgeois specialists'. The party decree ordering the deportation of kulaks, it will be recalled, specified that the most pernicious should be sent to labour camp. Officially there was a quota of 63 000 but it surely was exceeded. The leading Soviet scholar on this matter, acknowledges that about 300 000 families, which works out to over two million people, were deported to remote areas, but he does not state what proportion were actually in Gulag.[33] According to an official Soviet source, 'It was Comrade Stalin's idea and order that we build the [White Sea–Baltic] canal with the labour of prisoners, thus reforging them into honest workers.' Gulag folklore maintained that the police official (an erstwhile capitalist and camp inmate) N. A. Frenkel conceived the idea, no doubt submitting it to Stalin, which comes to much the same thing.[34]

It was not only the manual labourers on the canal project who were prisoners. Excepting a small number of police officers and guards, the inmates constituted almost the entire enterprise, including planners and engineers. This innovation in the use of forced labour was a logical consequence of the Bolshevik revolution. As Marxists have always noted, the bourgeoisie has been underrepresented in the convict population of most countries. This was not so in the Soviet Union, and a more or less unplanned by-product of the revolution, in particular the arrests and trials of 'wreckers', was that a wide array of technical specialists was at the disposal of the police. Hence the decision in 1931 to give Gulag exclusive responsibility for building one of the most spectacular projects of the First Five-Year Plan, the canals that would link the various lakes and rivers between the White Sea and the Baltic Sea, traversing sparsely inhabited Soviet Karelia, a land of severe winters and rocky geology. And all this between early 1931 and mid-1933, a canal in 500 days, as the slogan put it.[35]

Was Stalin unusually cruel or ideologically warped to conceive of socialism based on forced labour? Some Marxists no doubt would say that he was, but not Trotsky, who had ample opportunity to identify Gulag among Stalin's betrayals of the revolution and did not. Among the Stalinists, three men who sometimes received credit for moderating his ruthlessness paid fulsome tribute to Gulag. Two of them, Kirov and Voroshilov, accompanied the Boss in July 1933 on a steamer trip through the newly opened canal linking the Baltic and White Seas, the first major construction of Gulag. It was an exceptional junket for Stalin, who almost never paid personal visits to industrial construction sites but now spent an entire week admiring the fruits of convict labour and on one 'white night' at about 3 a.m. he was to be found sitting on the deck of the *Anokhin* and sketching plans for an industrial 'combinat' based on the canal, and presumably involving Gulag. (Apart from his satisfaction with this institution, Stalin was indulging his penchant for naval affairs, inspecting small warships that had passed from the Baltic Sea to the White through the canal and getting a look at Murmansk. The summer of 1933 was indeed the high point of his enthusiasm for cruising. In August he made his way south for his annual holiday by steamer on the Volga from Gorky to Stalingrad, visiting a stud farm in the former Don Cossack region on his way overland to the Black Sea.)[36] The third among the eminent, supposedly moderate, men who seemed enthusiastic about the work of Gulag was Gorky, who visited the canal on his own, and, with the literary critic I. L. Averbakh and the Gulag official S. G. Firin, edited the book *Belomor*, supposedly the collective work of thirty-four more and less well-known writers. This work sums up Stalin's conception of the construction of socialism. The camp is a society that combines 'Russian revolutionary sweep' in the workers, who are being 'reforged' through joy in socially useful labour, and 'American efficiency', which the police officials impose. There is strict accountability, for the authorities permit no *tufta* ('the falsification of production figures') and otherwise live up to Stalin's famous six points for management. There is 'socialist competition' between the 'women's and national minority brigades', urged on by cultural workers, who produce entertainments, posters and at the dam of the 'sixth fighting section' a 48-metre-high portrait of Stalin. As in Soviet society as a whole, socialist construction involves not only the creation of new physical plant but also new men and women.[37]

In publishing this book in English as well as Russian Stalin presumably assumed a favourable reception abroad. Who but hardened class enemies could reject this edifying story? Perhaps the response did not fulfil his hopes, for, apart from a sequel on the Moscow–Volga Canal, the genre dried up and the existence of Gulag became an official secret.[38] But the idea of building the good society with massive forced labour remained central to Stalin's conception of his mission. Gorky's speech to the police at the Moscow–Volga canal construction site captured the spirit of the future: ' "Ah, you devils – you don't know yourselves what great things you've done." The Chekists smiled. They were concerned over their new tasks.'[39]

Stalin enjoyed a close association with the police in the early 1930s, but this did not give him the unrestrained authority to apply police measures against intra-party opposition. As we have seen, his comrades in the Politburo and Central Committee were far more inclined to think that the deviationists should be obliged to follow the line of the majority than they were to approve the extirpation of these comrades. Evidently there was considerable opinion that the more or less repentant sinner should be restored to the party and some degree of responsibility, rather than dispatched to jail or labour camp. Even Zinoviev and Kamenev were permitted to re-enter the party in 1928, and the repentant leftist Piatakov became a deputy narkom of heavy industry. The main 'right deviationists' were not even expelled from the party, nor required to make full confessions of error. True, they were sharply criticized at the party congress of 1930, but Rykov made some defence of his record and Bukharin merely signed a vague statement some months after the congress, calling for support of the Central Committee. These two and Tomsky actually remained members of the Central Committee from 1930 to the next party congress at the beginning of 1934, when they were demoted to candidate membership. Stalin put up with this, though it represented the excessive 'liberalism' that he had criticized in 1929.[40]

In dealing with various adherents of a more or less 'rightist' programme who would not keep quiet, Stalin sought approval for severe punishment. The first such case involved two members of the Central Committee, S. I. Syrtsov and V. V. Lominadze. The former had been an orthodox supporter of the 'general line' and in 1929 had become chairman of the Sovnarkom of the Russian republic within the Soviet Federation and a candidate member of the Politburo. Evidently he reconsidered his politics during the following, turbulent year, made a speech calling for reduced rates of industrial investment and, if he did not form a faction, at least held conversations with Lominadze and some other dissidents. Stalin moved against these opponents in October–December 1930. Within the party statutes it was possible to expel some minor supporters of Syrtsov without the consent of the Central Committee, but the rules required Committee action to deal with members of the Committee. Stalin seems to have succeeded in bending the rules, probably by referring the matter to a joint meeting of the Politburo and the presidium of the Central Control Commission, the device formerly applied with limited success to Bukharin. Somehow the two dissidents were removed from their important positions by 2 December 1930, the Central Committee possibly ratifying this decision in its session of 17–21 December.[41]

The second case of repression of an unrepentant 'rightist' centred on one of Bukharin's erstwhile supporters in the Moscow party organization, M. N. Riutin. Apparently he had some links to the Syrtsov group, because in October 1930 he was expelled from the party along with two minor figures associated with Syrtsov.[42] Once out of the party Riutin enjoyed no immunity to police action and was exiled to some remote place. Here he had the contumacity to write and smuggle out a 'platform', which circulated secretly in the party in Moscow and other cities. Supposedly this was a long document, sharply critical of Stalin as an individual. The Boss must have found it highly objectionable, for it was suppressed so thoroughly that no copy reached the West at the time, nor has it turned up in any post-Stalin scholarship, dissident or official. When the identity of the author was discovered, Riutin was sent to jail – one of the 'isolators' in which troublesome Trotskyists resided. According to a leading *émigré* Menshevik Kremlinologist of the 1930s, Boris Nicolaevsky, Stalin asked the Politburo to authorize Riutin's execution, arguing that the illegal platform was tantamount to a call for the assassination of Stalin. Perhaps. Nicolaevsky later said that his information came largely from Bukharin, who saw Nicolaevsky in the course of a visit to western Europe in 1936. But Nicolaevsky admitted that he mixed in material from other sources, and one wonders how well-informed Bukharin was on such sensitive details as conversations in the Politburo, from which he had been expelled in 1929.[43]

Quashed though Riutin and his platform was, it may have helped to stimulate the third episode of rightist opposition that Stalin experienced in this period, the 'Anti-party Grouping of Eismont, Tolmachev, A. P. Smirnov and others'. A Trotskyist who was in jail then maintains that Riutin and some associates were tried and imprisoned at this time, but official publications show that they were merely reprimanded by the Central Committee, not expelled from the party. Smirnov, the only one who had been on the Central Committee, was removed from it and threatened with expulsion from the party if he did not mend his ways. The same resolution was also relatively mild in merely reprimanding Rykov and Tomsky, who supposedly had been in touch with this group. Once again, the majority in the Politburo and Central Committee seems to have opposed harsh sanctions.[44]

If Stalin was experiencing difficulty imposing his will on the party in the matter of repressing dissent in the early 1930s, it seems that there was a parallel difficulty with the enlargement of his own stature. The two problems were inevitably linked, for a leader-cult would make opposition all the more baneful and resistance to the leader's wish to crush opposition all the more unlikely. Research on policy concerning the evolution of the cult is hampered by Soviet sensitivities. In Stalin's day the subject did not exist, because no cult was acknowledged. Later Khrushchev attacked it, but with scant discussion of its management, partly because this would have raised awkward questions about the image of Lenin and of Khrushchev himself. It is nevertheless clear enough that Stalin sought the establishment of heroic status for himself by the opening of the 1930s. This would be an understandable corollary of the officially sustained cult of Lenin. If the regime implicitly reinterpreted the Marxist idea of the class struggle to mean that the proletariat would overcome the bourgeoisie with heroic leaders in the vanguard, then the Soviet Union clearly needed more heroic leaders. With the coming of the era of Five-Year Plans and new historic struggles, the time had come for Stalin to set aside the guise of humble disciple that he had cultivated for about five years after Lenin's death.

This change in image burst upon the Soviet public abruptly on 18 December, the beginning of a ten-day extravaganza of praise in honour of

Stalin's fiftieth birthday, which fell on the 21st. This was almost wholly a matter of printed words, not meetings, parades, museums, artistic works or any of the other media that later characterized the Stalin cult. The shape that the celebration took leaves no doubt that it was the work of the central authority of the party, which in turn implies Stalin's personal approval, which he provided explicitly in a short letter of thanks to well-wishers. In it Stalin retained his claim to modesty by crediting his achievements to 'our glorious Leninist party' and by pledging to its cause 'all my strength, all my ability and, if need be, all my blood, drop by drop'.[45]

One of the principal expressions of the celebration was the dispatch of over 350 greetings from diverse groups, foreign and domestic, some of them real, such as the 'Bauman district committee' of the party, others patent inventions for the occasion, such as the 'women collective-farm workers of Armenia', which never existed as a corporate body. The weight of these messages, apart from general admiration, was the portrayal of Stalin as 'Lenin's faithful pupil' and 'faithful companion-in-arms'. The other main effusion consisted of articles by various political magnates and a few professional writers, but not serious artists. The only poet in the number was the political versifier Demian Bedny, who contributed prose. These articles, published in newspapers and then in most cases collected in an anthology, provided the main ideas of the image of Stalin that was to dominate Soviet and Communist consciousness in the future. True, there were imperfections, such as Yenukidze's over-familiar 'I knew him when' tone in recalling how in 1900 a senior activist had told him to 'Find Soso Dzhugashvili, he's a good lad', and to give him instructions. The main themes were Stalin's commitment to Lenin and their close association as leaders of the revolution, his heroic stature as military leader against the class enemy (Voroshilov's speciality), his genius as a theoretician and his status as party leader – not merely in the formal office of General Secretary but as the *rukovoditel'* and *vozhd'*, the Russian terms that in Bolshevik usage had special association with Lenin.[46]

The birthday celebration was impressive as a harbinger of things to come, but it was not followed immediately by a sustained civic ritual honouring Stalin. Evidently his influential comrades, while willing to countenance special recognition for this occasion, were not yet disposed to permit this to become the daily norm. Only on a few set occasions, such as the anniversary of the October Revolution and Red Army Day, or some especially contrived ones, such as the twentieth anniversary of *Pravda* or the fifteenth of the Sixth Party Congress, did Stalin's name and visage appear prominently in the press and in huge, temporary public portraits.[47] Otherwise Stalin's image received scant attention. Readers of any American daily newspaper in the first three years of the decade surely would have seen greater attention (albeit not entirely favourable) to their president than *Pravda* gave to Stalin in this period. A study of the Soviet press reveals that Stalin's photograph appeared on the front page of the party organ only eight times in 1930, six in 1931 and eighteen in 1932, including its publication in connection with special meetings or anniversaries. There were only four occasions when Stalin's picture appeared solo (not as part of a group) in *Pravda*. Similarly a search for references to Stalin in the lead articles of that organ in the sample month of May found none until 1932, when the name appeared twenty-three times during the month, still a feeble premonition of the 127 appearances that it achieved in May 1938.[48] During January 1930–June 1933 Stalin wrote no articles and delivered only five speeches that appeared in *Pravda*. He did not yet receive letters in the press but had to write them if he wanted this kind of publicity. His wisdom did not appear in school textbooks, and there was hardly any art – graphic, performing or literary — devoted to Stalin.[49] True, the Georgian painter I. Toidze as early as 1931 immortalized an alleged visit by the leader to a hydroelectric project in the Caucasus, presumably on one of his vacations, an expression of national pride that was to flower somewhat later. In 1932 the Russian painters I. Brodsky and S. Gerasimov finished portraits of Stalin, important harbingers of the future but at this time isolated events.[50]

One might even argue that Stalin himself did not favour an enlargement of his public stature in this period, were it not for a short but persuasive document that has slipped into Soviet scholarship on Maxim Gorky. Disenchanted with the Bolshevik regime, this erstwhile supporter of the Russian Social-Democrats had been living in Italy for about ten years when Stalin began to pay court to him in 1928. In the spring and summer of that year the expatriate writer was lionized during a tour of his homeland and for the first time met Stalin. The process was repeated the next year. Gorky really had not become very well acquainted with Stalin, having been travelling most of the time he was in the USSR, but the leader assumed the tone of an old friend when he wrote to him in January 1930, responding favourably to some proposals that Gorky had submitted concerning publishing. He also offered to send the best Russian doctors to Italy if Gorky, who had arrested tuberculosis, wanted them. Stalin was even able to work in a display of modesty on matters literary, perhaps an implication that he would leave these matters to Gorky if the latter would come back to his homeland. Stalin declined the suggestion that he write an essay on the party view of literature with a self-deprecating 'What sort of critic am I, devil take it!'[51]

What did Stalin want from Gorky? In general there was the immense prestige of a literary giant in a culture that honoured such figures. And Gorky was a friend of Lenin. Granted, he had become a sharp critic of Bolshevism in the early Soviet years, but these differences could be buried to enable Stalin to enjoy the friendship of Lenin's friend. More specifically Stalin wanted Gorky to write a biography of him, and set about persuading the writer to do this only a few months after Gorky had made Moscow his home, or at least summer home, in May 1931. The approach was tactfully indirect. Stalin himself said nothing, but at some date near the end of that year his specialist on historical research and personal secretary, Tovstukha, sent Gorky a batch of research material on the life of Stalin, presumably with some sort of indication of the book that it might make. Since Gorky did nothing, a literary functionary who often represented Stalin in dealing with Gorky, A. V. Khalatov, sent the writer a letter on 15 January 1932 in which he referred to the previous dispatch, asking if the writer wanted more material. Khalatov was at pains to imply that Gorky's silence did not mean rejection. Of course it was a result of Gorky's heavy work-load, which had merely led him to 'wait a bit'. There was also an allusion to Gorky's debt to Stalin, not for a stylish town house and country villa, which were not mentioned, but for the publication of Gorky's collected works and the celebration of the fortieth anniversary of the start of his literary career. All of this was a bold manoeuvre by Stalin to enhance his image. Gorky had dabbled in short political pieces, but he had never written a biography, nor had any Bolshevik personality been the subject of a book by a prominent author. But in exile Trotsky had written his autobiography in 1929, and it may be that Stalin wanted to eclipse this work. And if the Politburo had reservations about the glorification of Stalin, how could they object to the publication of a book that the great Gorky chose to write? Of course there were risks. If the book turned out somewhat less glorious than desired, what was to be done? As it turned out, this was not a problem. Roy Medvedev quotes a friend of Gorky to the effect that the writer, after much urging, did make the effort, but dropped it because the result was too saccharine. If true, this came later, after Stalin had established more control over Gorky. In 1932 there was no biography but merely a covert demonstration of Stalin's efforts to establish himself as the heroic leader.[52]

During that year and the first months of 1933 there was little change in the situation. Stalin remained the acknowledged party leader, but his public image could scarcely be called a cult. The change, when it came, was not as abrupt as the sudden effusion of birthday sentiments in 1929, but this time it proved durable. The nearest thing to a precise turning point was Voroshilov's ceremonial address in Red Square on May Day. He had given this speech on the two preceding years without mentioning Stalin, but in 1933 Voroshilov included in his finale: 'Long live its [the party's] leader, the leader of the workers of our countryside and the whole world, our glorious, valorous Red Army man, fighter for the world proletarian revolution COMRADE STALIN!'[53] This was important but only one short tribute by one man. The humbler expression of mass admiration that took the form of the ritual greeting-pledge was more significant. There were many precedents for this in Lenin's day, and Stalin's fiftieth birthday had briefly revived the institution. Perhaps local bodies had been sending in such greetings regularly, but it was only in 1933 that they began to appear in *Pravda* with some degree of regularity. The first was from the meeting of the Kharkov province and city party committee, appearing on 6 February on an inside page of the newspaper. It was followed by two such communications in March and one in April. Not all of these closed with what was to be the obligatory series of ejaculations: 'Long live . . .' this or that, including something like 'Long live the beloved leader of the toilers of the whole world – Comrade Stalin!' Only in May, following Voroshilov's tribute, did it appear that some authority had decided to encourage more of this, as *Pravda* published greetings from a conference of rectors of agricultural schools, the New Lessner factory, the shock-workers of the Kuznetsk basin, the Middle Volga and Tartar kolkhoz shock-workers, a machine-tractor station, a group of Leningrad factory directors and the professors and students connected with the first all-union music competition.[54] The way was now open for the establishment of a ritual as widely practiced in the USSR as the pledge to the flag in the USA, no doubt repeated billions of times by meetings of one sort or another in the next nineteen years, but not all published and never answered by Stalin. Although the wording varied slightly depending on the nature of the group dispatching the greeting-pledge – potato-farmers referring to their zeal to grow tubers, soldiers to slay the enemy – the shape of this artefact became highly formalized. It usually stayed in the range of 250–350 words and invariably ended with the enthusiastic 'Long lives', one of which was devoted to the leader.

The new civic cult devoted to Stalin was not full-blown by the end of 1933, partly because various art-forms, such as sculpture and the film require some time to produce, but it was well on its way. The journalist Eugene Lyons counted the number of busts or portraits of various leaders that appeared in five or six blocks of Moscow's main thoroughfare on the eve of the anniversary of the October Revolution in 1933. Stalin bested Lenin by 103 to 58, followed by 56 for Kaganovich (the Moscow city boss), 33 for Voroshilov and, among lesser lights, 5 for Marx.[55] It was in this period that Stalin's name began to join Lenin's in elementary textbooks, such as a Russian grammar of 1933 which included a poem with the lines:

> He is to me a father and a brother,
> And he is a comrade –
> Stalin.

Among similar poetic tributes, *Pravda* carried one in January 1934 which came close to stating explicitly the nature of the recent shift in civic cults:

> Now when we speak of Lenin
> It means we are speaking of Stalin.[56]

At about the same time painters joined in the celebration. Gerasimov's portrait of Stalin addressing the party congress of 1930 dated from 1933 and was publicized in *Pravda* on 1 July of that year. The following year he had added its sequel: Stalin addressing the congress of 1934. Brodsky seems to have been under pressure to produce a new portrait in a hurry in 1933. The frontispiece for the book on the Belomor Canal, signed that year, presents a technically detailed head attached to a quick sketch of the tunic. The first chapter of that book, by the way, signed by Gorky on 20 January 1934, set the tone for countless other books in the next nineteen years, opening with a paean to Stalin as Lenin's true heir.[57] In June 1933 a major art exhibition, a retrospective on painting in the Russian republic since 1918, was able to include separate halls devoted to Lenin and Stalin. It was, however, necessary to fill in the Stalin section with painting of factories, because not enough of the leader yet existed. But some did, including portraits by Brodsky and Gerasimov and the heroic action scene of Avilov, showing Stalin greeting 'The Arrival of the First Cavalry Army in 1919'. Also in 1933 A. Mizin and G. Klutsis placed Stalin in the foreground, with Lenin, Marx and Engels behind him, in widely distributed posters. By 1934 it was possible to publish a book of reproductions, entitled *Stalin. Paintings, Posters, Graphics, Sculpture.* The dates that this book assigned to the creation of the artistic works testified to the existence of a frantic effort in 1933 to make up for lost time in the creation of a cult of Stalin in the visual arts. Only one statue, representing Stalin and Voroshilov together, had been completed in time for depiction in this book. Apparently commissions in this art-form took longer to complete, and it was only in 1934 that the sculptors S. Merkurov and G. V. Nerod produced their first full-length statues of Stalin, precursors of many more to come.[58]

The impact of all this lay not only in its growing diversity but also in the exalted tone of references to Stalin. Kirov conveyed well the spirit of the cult in his speech to the Leningrad party conference that preceded the Seventeenth Congress in January 1934:

> It is hard to conceive such a gigantic figure as Stalin. For years past, starting with the time when we worked without Lenin, we have not known one turning in our work, not one great initiative, slogan, direction in our policy, the author of which was not Stalin, but someone else. . . . I must say that this relates not only to the building of socialism as a whole but to the separate questions of our work. For

example, if one takes the question of the defence of our country, then one must underscore with all one's might that all our successes, of which I have spoken, we owe as a whole and completely to Stalin.[59]

Why did this change in Stalin's public image occur in roughly the last half of 1933? One possible ingredient may have been Hitler's unexpected success in establishing his power in Germany in the first half of 1933. The apparent popularity of the *führer-prinzip* may have so impressed the Soviet Politburo that they decided that the proletariat could ill afford not to use this instrument of mass mobilization. In this connection advocates of cult might have noticed signs that this conception already had mass-level support in Russia, and not entirely with respect to Lenin. An American volunteer worker at Magnitogorsk noted that workers there liked to post pictures of Kalinin and Kirov. Ella Winter found that Soviet women workers decorated their communal residences with portraits of 'Stalin, Molotov, Kalinin or Marx'. Samuel Harper and Lyons found that peasants often kept icon-like pictures of Lenin and Stalin in their homes. Corliss and Margaret Lamont noticed floral portraits of Marx, Lenin and Stalin in parks in Kiev and Samara and that young people named their organizations after Lenin, Stalin and Voroshilov. In the first half of 1933 the workers of the Cheliabinsk Tractor Works, which was named for Stalin, struck a bronze medallion of Stalin, a rough representation that was not much like the standardized, more professional versions that came later.[60]

If the matter was ever discussed in the Politburo, an advocate of establishing an official pantheon of the living might well have argued that there was authentic popular demand for such an institution. Better to encourage and regulate it than to allow spontaneous expression to take its course. Such a mistrust of local initiative concerning the image of Lenin had produced a Central Committee resolution of 1925 to claim control over this enterprise, however praiseworthy its intentions.[61] Perhaps some members of the Politburo formerly had doubts about such a course. It may be significant that neither Molotov nor Kirov contributed laudatory essays to the volume in honour of Stalin's fiftieth birthday. But they could be certain that the new plan was not merely to pay tribute to Stalin. All members of the Politburo could be honoured by the new civic cult at a slightly lower level, appearing in photographs and paintings along with Stalin and having places and factories named in their honour. This principle was even extended downward to such obscure officials as the chairman of the Belorussian Republic, Cherviakov. He had several collective farms named for him in Belorussia at some point before 1937, when he was 'unmasked' as an 'enemy of the people', which required the renaming of these institutions.[62]

This civic cult could be expanded still more broadly to the 'labour heroes' of the workforce, who participated as 'shock workers' and, from

1935, as 'Stakhanovites' – the name given to labour heroes in honour of the coal-miner who set a stunning production record. All of this suggests that the coming of a cult of leadership was far from being simply a reflection of some pathological condition of Stalin. His appetite for glorification probably was an ingredient, but even this was not out of control. He could cajole Gorky to write his biography, fail in this without visibly losing his temper, then persevere with the project. Evidently there were volunteers who helped him sell the whole idea of heroism. Voroshilov, who delivered the first May Day tribute to Stalin, seems to have greatly enjoyed appearing on horseback on such occasions and sitting for his portrait. According to Khrushchev, Kaganovich urged Stalin to replace 'Leninism' with 'Stalinism', only to be rebuffed by the Boss, who in fact never sanctioned the use of this term, so honorific in a highly ideological culture.[63]

Barely below Stalin and closely associated with him in the pantheon was Maxim Gorky, for whom the city of Nizhnii Novgorod, one of the most important centres of industrialization (and Gorky's home town), was renamed in 1932. His presence in the Soviet Union was useful to Stalin as a means of enhancing his own image, and the leader arranged to appear beside Gorky at such major public festivities as May Day and a massive parade of physical culture enthusiasts. In 1932 Stalin, rather incongruously, had his own picture paired with Gorky's on the front page of *Pravda* in connection with the celebration of the fortieth anniversary of the beginning of Gorky's literary career.[64] Stalin wanted to use Gorky to facilitate the establishment of party control over Soviet culture. Since the revolution and especially during the period of the new Economic Policy, the arts and intellectual life had enjoyed a considerable degree of autonomy. True, open political opposition was forbidden, and the regime could use the power of the purse to support this or that tendency. But direct political supervision was sporadic, and diverse schools of thought and art could and did contend, even forming separate organizations in literature, for example. Stalin did not like this situation, nor did he care for some of the 'modern' artistic trends of the time. Literature, which had occupied such a central place in Russian life for a century, was the flagship of the whole cultural sphere, and if it could be subject to party supervision the rest would follow. To ease this process Stalin needed the prestige of Gorky, not only a literary giant but also a non-party humanist – the only non-Communist admitted to the new Soviet pantheon. This worked on several levels: the writer's supposedly close personal association with Stalin implied that the General Secretary possessed some credentials to be a cultural leader in his own right. The association of Gorky with the reorganization of Soviet artistic life added respectability to this political take-over. And to literature itself Gorky's own style, which was direct and accessible rather than 'modern' and obscure, could help provide a model.

The organizational form that Stalin established for supervised Soviet literature was the 'Union of Writers', the stylistic canon 'socialist realism'. Although Gorky became president of the Union when it held its inaugural congress in 1934, thus giving his blessing to the canon, Stalin was not interested in bringing Gorky into the decision-making process itself. The writer, after all, had shown himself to be soft on bourgeois ideas of artistic freedom. The initiative for the establishment of institutionalized party control over culture came in a decree of the Central Committee on 23 April 1932, 'On the Reconstruction of Literary–Artistic Organizations'. The Orgburo of the party was instructed to take practical measures to carry out the change, and it established an 'organizing committee' to construct a new union and with it a new artistic canon. The initial work of this body was conducted in May 1932 at a joint meeting of this 'organizing committee' and a commission of the Central Committee. Stalin participated actively, but Gorky was not invited, despite his presence in Moscow at the time. During the discussion Stalin asked the editor I. Gronsky, who was the principal spokesman for the literateurs, to provide a label for the new artistic creed. When Gronsky proposed 'communist realism', Stalin 'tactfully' explained that this did not rest on 'real foundations and did not answer the historical conditions for the development of Soviet art'. Gronsky then suggested 'socialist realism', and the Boss must have been satisfied, for it stuck, although it was adopted officially only in 1934 when the new union held its first congress. Stalin evidently conceived of socialist realism simply as art serving politics, but he chose to explain this to a gathering of intellectuals at Gorky's home on 26 October 1932, thus associating the new doctrine with their host's 'humanism'. 'The artist', said Stalin, 'must give first priority to the truthful presentation of life, and if he truly portrays our life, then he cannot but note, cannot but show, that it leads to socialism. This will be socialist art. This will be socialist realism.' It was on this occasion that Stalin offered the opinion, often cited subsequently, that writers are 'engineers of the human soul', an accurate synopsis of his utilitarian concept of art.[65]

Stalin had motive enough to foster the idea that he was a close friend of Gorky, while the writer's prestige among Soviet writers gained much from the impression that he was on close terms with 'the Boss' or 'Iosif ' as Gorky referred to Stalin in correspondence with those who sought favours from the writer.[66] His influence was able to secure support for various publishing enterprises, and even Central Committee decrees to speed up work on two of them. But Soviet scholarship, which at one time would have been delighted to show that the two men met frequently, demonstrates that the relations between Gorky and Stalin were in reality scant and formal. There had been a celebrated visit by Stalin to Gorky's town house on 11 October 1931 when the writer read his poem 'Death and the Maiden' and the politician wrote his critical evaluation on the text: 'This piece is stronger than Goethe's *Faust*.' Possibly there was another visit about this time. In a note to a friend on the 17th Gorky noted that Stalin did not come for a visit the previous night because of an illness, but he expected to go to Stalin's residence the next night. There was a reason for the flurry of socializing at this time: Gorky was about to return to Italy for the winter, and Stalin wanted to ensure his return to Russia the next spring. Beyond this, it is established that the two were together only in various groups, on public occasions such as May Day 1934 and at closed affairs such as the editorial committee of the *History of the Civil War* and a meeting with Romain Rolland.[67]

Among other reasons why the two probably did not see each other often in the early 1930s was Gorky's absence from Moscow for considerable periods. He spent the six months of winter in 1931–2 and 1932–3 in Italy and much of the summer-time in his country estate, in addition to several extended trips within the Soviet Union. After 1933 Gorky was not allowed to leave the Soviet Union, which may have ended whatever personal cordiality there had been between him and Stalin. In May 1935 a tough party functionary, A. S. Shcherbakov, curtly informed Gorky that he, Shcherbakov, was taking over cultural and educational affairs within the Secretariat of the Central Committee and found this field in an 'unsatisfactory condition'. Literature, he said, was part of his job, and by implication he made it unmistakably clear that Gorky should deal with him, not Stalin. Evidently Gorky accepted this, for in July he contacted Shcherbakov to see if Stalin would come to the writer's reception for Rolland. Stalin did, probably the last time he saw Gorky alive.[68]

Nicolaevsky and others have asserted that Gorky moderated Stalin's conduct, but this does not seem to have been the case. Stalin established his authority in his letter to Gorky in 1930, bluntly telling him that Radek could not be trusted with sensitive assignments because of the factional struggle and chiding the old humanist for his propensity to 'bourgeois pacifism'. Shortly thereafter Stalin further sought to educate Gorky by telling an aide to send him a packet of materials compiled by the police on the 'wreckers'. Gorky must have been impressed by this sort of thing because in 1932 he wrote to Rolland (from the safety of Italy) that the White generals were plotting to assassinate Stalin. The apogee of Gorky's espousal of Stalin's politics was his participation in the glorification of Gulag. Not only did he contribute to the collective book on the Baltic–White Sea Canal a foreword and an afterword, but he also travelled to the site of the Moscow–Volga Canal, which was the follow-up project. Here he addressed a meeting of police and forced labourers, plainly stating that he understood that there were many kulaks among them and that they had been 'the hardest to educate'.[69]

Literature was not the only branch of culture on which Stalin began to exert his influence in the early 1930s. In 1930 and 1931 he dealt with philosophy and history, respectively, excoriating what he took to be departures from orthodox Leninism. In neither case was there any explicit reference to Stalin's genius in these fields, but it was significant that he extended his authority as the definer of Leninism from politics to academic subjects. And in both cases there were immediate and serious consequences in the professions, the heterodox falling from influence amid confessions of error, the orthodox assuming new power.[70]

Concerning education he had nothing substantial to say in person, but his interventions through the medium of decrees in the name of the Central Committee had a major impact on policy. During the 1920s, as in literature and various arts, diverse modernist and experimental schools of thought competed in Soviet education, including advocates of Tolstoy's 'free school' and even of the abolition of schools as part of the 'capitalist superstructure'. Some of these ideas even penetrated Stalin's home, for his wife was attracted to them and was on good terms with a more or less Tolstoyan educator, Regina Glass. 'Father', recalls Svetlana, 'could not stand her and her "pedagogical tricks" and soon insisted that she no longer frequent our home.' He also sought to banish such policies from Soviet schools and move back to basics as he had known them, not necessarily a bad idea for a country that needed to bring elementary education to large numbers of people, and fast. One of the more radical conceptions, 'paedology', a Central Committee decree crushed as a 'perversion', mandating the restoration of compulsory subjects of instruction such as mathematics, geography and history. Somewhat ahead lay the reintroduction of school uniforms of the sort that Stalin had known as a lad, and the segregation of boys and girls.[71]

Another sphere of culture that Stalin helped to return from modernism to tradition was architecture. It appears that this, along with urban planning, appealed strongly to his zest for building on a monumental scale. It was a shrewd insight by the repentant Trotskyist Radek that he entitled a major cult article 'The Architect of Socialist Society', for Stalin must have fancied the metaphor. (He may not have liked Radek's literary device, an imaginary historical lecture given in 1967 to the 'School of Interplanetary Communication', marking the fiftieth anniversary of the October Revolution. While Radek paid fulsome tribute to Stalin's continuation of Lenin's work, he neglected to assure his audience that Stalin was still, at a robust eighty-eight, leading the country.[72]) In the 1920s Soviet architecture, like other branches of culture, had been dominated by bold modernism, heavily influenced by cubist concepts which the Russians shared with their western contemporaries. During the 1930s the USSR turned away from this trend in favour of its own, eclectic version of neo-classicism. This did not happen quickly and was not the topic of a clear-cut order from the Central Committee. Very likely it reflected (like much of this whole shift away from modernism to more traditional forms in various areas of culture) the taste of the great majority of the rising élite in Stalin's Russia. Unlike the radical intelligentsia of Lenin's generation, the new élite was not much influenced by the culture of western Europe, and they were quite sure that they preferred a pseudo-classical temple with muscular figures perched on its roof to an unadorned concrete box.[73]

Stalin shared this opinion and made his influence felt by offering advice on the design of the greatest architectural project of the time, the Palace of Soviets. This was to be the largest building in the world, one of the great construction projects in the land during several Five-Year Plans, with its own ancillary factories to manufacture various parts. Since the Palace was to be the centrepiece of Stalin's Moscow, presumably his office, it is plausible that he gave it painstaking attention. The chief architect of the Palace, Boris Yofan, recalled that Stalin attended all the meetings of the construction council, which Molotov chaired, and personally settled a large number of technical questions. He cut through a debate among the architects on the placement of the Palace by deciding that they would demolish the largest cathedral of Moscow, named for Christ the Saviour, noting that only this would give the new monument the necessary grandiose dimensions. Then he walked over the area and decided that the main entrance to the Palace should face the Kremlin. There followed a debate between architects who advocated a rectangular structure and those who wanted to build the largest round building ever seen. Stalin chose the latter, asserting that a rectangular building would seem 'American', 'commercial'. Thus emerged a plan for a main structure consisting of cylinders stacked on one another, but there was no agreement on the number of these until Stalin chose a sketch showing three main ones, which he considered more 'simple and clear'. Atop the highest cylinder was to be, he decided, a steel statue of Lenin 100 metres high, weighing 6500 tons. On the ground level would be statues of such heroes as Marx, Engels, Fourier and Chernyshevsky, and in the main hall, which he ordered to be capable of seating 21 000, there would be an ensemble of sculpture showing 'Lenin Leading the Peoples to Communism'. Nowhere was Stalin's visage to appear, according to these plans, drafted in the early 1930s, but the main approach to the Palace was to be flanked by six great pylons, each inscribed with one of the 'behests of Lenin' that Stalin had enunciated in 1924. Was this building technically possible, Stalin asked the architects? They replied that it was, but it now seems likely that they were too eager to please the Boss and underestimated the problems of foundation engineering. Although the cathedral was demolished and excavation begun in 1939, the project stalled. Today what was to have been Stalin's greatest monument is a large swimming pool.[74]

Had it ever been built, the Palace would have been the focal point of Moscow, so it was natural that Stalin was keenly interested in the reconstruction of the city. Considering that Moscow had not served as Russia's capital between 1703 and 1918 and that much of the bureaucracy worked in an assortment of antique structures, former commercial buildings and expropriated mansions, it was clear that a major investment in urban renewal was inevitable. In early discussions of the new Moscow a number of the city planners advocated radically 'modern' or 'futuristic' concepts, including the abolition of cities. One such school of thought proposed the replacement of the city with collectivized population centres of about 50 000 persons, another with 'linear' settlements criss-crossing the landscape. These radical visions impressed Stalin no more favourably than analogous ones in painting, education and architecture, and in May 1930 his office issued a decree attacking them.[75]

Perhaps it was to ensure that such dreamers did not take charge of urban planning in Moscow that in 1931 the party Central Committee and its Moscow committee assumed responsibility for this work. Stalin's apparatus, the Central Committee staff and Moscow party committee, rather than the city administration, set up the offices that were to draught the master plan for Moscow. One of the largest projects in Moscow was the construction of the Metro, which had already started in 1931 but two years later was making such slow progress that the party annexed it to its sphere. Soon the work was assigned to Khrushchev, the rising second secretary of the Moscow province. Around 1 April 1935, shortly before the public opening, Stalin came to try out the new monument to modernity. Alas, the train went only some 200 metres before coming to a halt. 'What's going on with you?', asked the Boss. 'Something jammed', was the vague reply. It turned out to be a minor defect in the safety signals, and Stalin was soon able to reach the next station, depart the train and ascend the escalator. 'And here nothing jams on you?', he asked – 'with gentle humour', says the memoirist, whose state of mind at this point could hardly have been jolly. Stalin clearly regarded the opening of the Metro as a major civic ceremonial, and he was not going to put up with any embarrassment. After his visit he ordered the builders to take another six weeks to check over the system to make sure that 'there will be no hitches'.[76]

When the first section was officially opened Stalin not only walked from the Kremlin to the nearby station where the ceremony occurred, but also saw to it that his image was closely linked with this project, though it was named for Kaganovich. The importance that Stalin attached to the Metro is also implied in the remarkable speed with which he promoted Khrushchev for getting results in a short time. He advanced to first secretaryship of the Moscow party organization and candidate membership in the Politburo before the end of 1935.[77]

As for the master plan for Moscow, the radical visionaries had not totally surrendered. From abroad Le Corbusier proposed to preserve old Moscow as a museum-city and build a new metropolis nearby. Another scheme was to raise the population to ten million in order to overtake in size any then-extant capitalist city, with the corollary, it appears, of demolishing much of the old city. Still another aimed to rebuild the city as a community of one- and two-storey structures spread over a circle of 200 km in diameter. A memoirist notes that Stalin personally scuttled this last idea at a meeting with the planners on July 1934, showing in his comments the kind of respect for historically evolved institutions that he also accorded the family, the school and the army. The city, said Stalin, was not defined accidentally but as the most economic form of settlement, the most rational with respect to transport and water. He also told the more than fifty urban planners who had been brought to the Kremlin in buses for the occasion that he did not want tall buildings or exceptionally wide boulevards and did insist on greenbelts in the residential areas. With this the draft was returned to the planners for revision.[78]

In the spring of 1935 Stalin met again with the planners and architects. Evidently he now was satisfied with the main lines of their proposed 'Plan for the Reconstruction of Moscow', for it was adopted by the Central Committee and the Sovnarkom in July. At the meeting he was able to concern himself more with particular details, such as the need to widen Gorky Street (at great cost) near its junction with Okhotny Riad. The plan itself provided a revealing glimpse of Stalin's values. The model city was to be modern, equipped with such amenities as the Metro, sanitary water and sewage systems, spacious apartments and office buildings, cinemas and stores, parks and promenades, with the Moscow River channelled between stone embankments and crossed by numerous bridges. Judging by the architects' sketches that accompanied it, and some of the buildings that were later completed, a neo-classical trend was to overtake the modernism of the 1920s. It seems that Stalin wanted an impressive but fundamentally conventional city, and that a general tone of modernity and power was more important to him than social egalitarianism, a consideration that the officially approved planning documents did not address.[79]

The Moscow plan, perhaps the largest of Stalin's construction projects, was to be completed in ten years, that is in 1945. Stalin told the builders, 'One must build strictly according to the plan. Anyone who tries to violate this plan must be called to order.' But the Palace of Soviets proved impractical and World War Two intervened, following which Stalin decided he wanted the six skyscrapers that now mark the Moscow horizon. Eventually, long after Stalin's death, the Museum of the City of

Moscow dismantled its substantial exhibit on the future Moscow, based on the plan of 1935. But so much of the plan was carried out, especially the demolition of old areas, the construction of boulevards, the Metro, the parks, and the reshaping of the Moscow River, that the present-day Moscow remains in many ways a monument to Stalin that his successors could not dismantle.[80]

9 Murder

In a letter to Gorky in 1930 Stalin made it clear that he scorned 'bourgeois pacifism'. Like most non-pacifists he obviously thought that killing people might be justified in war, and as a militant Marxist he saw class struggle as the highest form of war.[1] As a combatant Stalin was by the opening of 1934 more or less responsible for the killing of a large number of the enemy, mainly members of the White forces of the civil war and peasants who had the misfortune of being classified as kulaks. Still, it is difficult to demonstrate that he had, by the start of his fifty-fifth year, committed what non-pacifists would normally call murder. Not only were his killings wartime acts in a Marxist–Leninist perspective, the lacked the individualized character that common usage attributes to murder.[2]

There is some reason to suspect that the first person whom Stalin murdered, and the only one he killed with his own hands, was his wife, Nadezhda Allilueva, who died on the night of 8–9 November 1932. The published announcement of the death of this woman (aged only thirty-one) mentioned no cause at all, and officially inspired rumours that she died of appendicitis merely stimulated dark suspicions. Given Stalin's reputation within a few years, it was inevitable that he should be accused of killing her, and that stories to this effect should flourish in the camps, where his real victims were plentiful and ready to give credence to stories about a prisoner who met another prisoner who had this or that inside information. One weakness of these reports is that they tend to contradict one another, variously attributing the death to shooting, bludgeoning and strangling.[3]

The much greater likelihood that Nadezhda died by her own hand rests partly on the background of her life and personality, both troubled. As we have seen, her marriage to the domineering and male-supremacist Stalin had been a trial. In 1926 she tried to leave him and in returning seems to have attempted a new arrangement. This involved employing a governess for infant Svetlana, Alexandra Andreevna Bychkova. This warm-hearted peasant woman joined the substantial domestic staff that was already in place: a cook, a housekeeper, a serving woman, and Vasily's tutor. These were soon joined by Svetlana's tutor and part-time instructors in music and French for Nadezhda, not to mention the separate domestic staff at her country house. As an adult Svetlana wrote that her mother 'genuinely believed in the rules of party morality which required members to live modestly', but some party members seem to have lived more modestly than others.

This domestic help permitted Nadezhda to devote herself little to child-rearing and much to her higher education. After a stint on the editorial staff of a periodical she enrolled in the Industrial Academy, specializing in synthetic fibres and chemical engineering. Trying to practice the party's rules for modest living, she commuted to her studies by streetcar and mixed with other students as an equal, using the name Allilueva. As an active Communist, she headed a party group at the Academy, reporting to a young organizer named Nikita Khrushchev, who gained the impression that she spoke well of him to her husband.[5]

But by the end of the 1920s life seems to have lost its savour for Nadezhda. Although Svetlana tried to idealize her mother, the image that emerges frankly in her memoirs is that of a remote and judgemental parent, whose main message was 'let me know whether you've decided to be good or not'. Her father, in contrast, 'was always carrying me in his arms, giving me loud, moist kisses and calling me pet names like "little sparrow" and "little fly" '. Nadezhda's marriage was miserable for her and may have ceased as a sexual relationship. Svetlana recalls that her mother had her own bedroom, while her father slept more or less as an outcast 'either in his office or in a little room with a telephone next to the dining room'. According to rumour he had a mistress, in one version Kaganovich's sister Rosa, who seems never to have existed, or in another version a ballerina. Although this story is mere gossip, it might have reached Nadezhda, adding to her distress.[6]

And there was the problem of alcohol. Nadezhda could not drink without becoming ill, and rarely did. 'Don't touch alcohol' was the main message that she wanted to give her daughter in a talk that she seems to have intended as a farewell. Such is certainly the tone that Svetlana gives to her account of it, adding that 'I saw my mother so rarely that I remember our meeting very well.' Drink had been and was to be a powerful destructive force in Stalin's family. His father was a violent alcoholic, his youngest son died of alcoholism and his daughter was to seek relief from alcohol dependence through Christian Science in Princeton, New Jersey. It is reasonably clear that Stalin himself was a functioning alcoholic, able to stay sober when necessary, not infrequently inebriated. The development of this condition in him is hard to trace. According to Khrushchev, Stalin said that his father 'was teaching me to drink when I was still in the cradle', and that as a young revolutionary he had joined with non-political convicts on their way to exile in drinking up whatever money they could obtain. In the early Soviet regime he is reputed to have been allowed a stock of wine despite the existence of prohibition. The Finnish Communist Aino Kuusinen says that Stalin was obnoxiously drunk when he entertained her and her husband Otto in 1926. In 1928 Bukharin, talking with Kamenev, made allusion to a 'drinking bout', in which Stalin and other leaders participated. Otto Kuusinen's aide Tuominen, who saw Stalin in the 1930s, maintained that Stalin did not hold many drinking parties but recalled an incident in which

Kuusinen and Stalin became drunk together, the Boss drinking 'much more' than Kuusinen, who 'was not one to shy away from a drink, and for a small man held up splendidly'. On this occasion the drunken Stalin insisted that he and Kuusinen do some shooting on his rifle range, waving off his deeply worried bodyguards. In 1940 Stalin's teenage daughter on one occasion left him a note saying that she could not wait up for him, but that 'you may eat and drink – though not a lot – and talk'. This sounds like the classic plea of the child of a heavy drinker. Near the end of his life his doctors persuaded Stalin to cut down, but the last time that Khrushchev spoke with him Stalin was 'pretty drunk'. Like many drinkers he wanted those around him to drink too, sometimes to see what his men would say in their cups but also because he was comfortable in an alcohol-soaked atmosphere. Svetlana recalls that he was continually offering wine to her and Vasily, to the horror of their mother, and this was surely not politically motivated. Non-drinkers seem to have annoyed him, and both his one-time secretary Bajanov and Milovan Djilas claimed that they resisted with difficulty his attempts to oblige them to drink. All this lends credibility to Svetlana's version of the final break between her parents, as it reached her through Molotov's wife. Stalin curtly, and very likely drunkenly, told Nadezhda, 'Hey you, have a drink!'[7]

By this time she was probably suffering from depression. If genetic factors are involved in mental illness, it is pertinent to add that her sister Anna and brother Fyodor both were incapacitated by psychiatric conditions, probably schizophrenia. While resisting the opinion of her in-laws of later years, the Zhdanovs, that her mother was 'neurotic', Svetlana herself refers to her mother's 'depressed' state of mind. Nadezhda's sister-in-law told Lidia Shatunovskaia that Nadezhda had gone to Berlin in the late 1920s to consult a neurologist, staying with her brother Pavel (Evegeniia's husband) who was stationed there. Svetlana confirms that her mother went to Berlin, but seems unaware that it was for medical reasons, even though the trip, Svetlana recalls, included a stay at Karlsbad. If so, this might have been the occasion on which Pavel gave Nadezhda the little Walther pistol with which she probably shot herself, although Svetlana believes that Pavel brought it to Moscow on a visit there. This was a strange gift for a person suffering from depression. Is it possible that Nadezhda purchased it herself, or asked Pavel to obtain it for her? In any case, Svetlana is credible in writing that her mother had said 'again and again that "everything bored her", that she was "sick of everything" and "nothing made her happy" ' – ' "Even the children" '. This fits with Svetlana's recollection of the valedictory tone of her mother's warnings on alcohol, and it fits all too well with the book that Nadezhda chose to read just before her end, *The Green Hat* by Michael Arlen. Svetlana attaches no special importance to this book, but notes that in his last years her father was obsessed with the idea that it turned

Nadezhda to suicide. This is a persuasive indication that Stalin considered the death to have been suicide. It is far-fetched to think that he would have introduced the novel into his talks with his daughter just for the purpose of persuading her that her mother's death had been suicide and not murder. Svetlana needed no such persuasion, and Stalin was right in thinking that *The Green Hat* glorifies suicide. Very little happens in this novel about the pointless lives of wealthy English people except for three suicides. Of these the climactic one seems to Arlen to be unspeakably noble, perhaps the one meaningful act open to a person who finds life empty. ' "But that death!" Hilary stammered. "That death!" ', after the heroine has proven her purity of soul by crashing a sports car into a large tree. No doubt Stalin, in his groping for an answer to the question of Nadezhda's self-destruction, attached too much importance to the novel, but his reading of it was by no means foolish.[8]

Nadezhda took her children to the 7 November parade on Red Square and the next day saw them for the last time, looking into the nursery while wearing a bathrobe, evidently preparing to go out to a social function. This probably was a small reception, which would have occurred on the evening of the 8th. The custom then and now in the Soviet Union is to give everybody a two-day holiday, the first involving formal public events, the latter private relaxation. For the General Secretary, whose social friends were his political lieutenants, this probably took the form of an intimate banquet at the Voroshilov apartment in the Kremlin, along with the Molotovs.[9]

At this party Stalin offended his wife with the command to drink and she, according to Molotov's wife Polina (speaking to Svetlana after Stalin was safely dead), left in a rage. Polina, a close friend, followed Nadezhda and walked with her around the Kremlin Palace until she seemed calmer. Nadezhda spoke with some satisfaction of her studies and the prospect of a career, perhaps trying to convince herself that life was worth living – and failing, although she reassured her friend. The next morning, according to the post-Stalin statements of Polina and Svetlana's governess, Nadezhda was found dead on the floor of her room, the Walther pistol beside her. The housekeeper found the corpse and, horrified, called the governess. They called for the head of the guard, and also Avel Yenukidze and Polina Molotov. Soon Molotov and Voroshilov were there.[10]

When Stalin awoke and learned the news he was both outraged and crushed. Svetlana believes, with many others, that there was a suicide note attacking Stalin personally and politically, but the contents of this document, if it ever existed, remain poorly substantiated. Svetlana heard of it from her aunts, who were not residents of the Kremlin at the time and not among those first on the scene after the suicide. Stalin later jailed them, explaining this to his daughter by saying, 'They babbled a lot', an appraisal that seems well justified by Shatunovskaia's account of all the gossip (including the story of the ballerina-mistress) that she heard from Evegeniia Allilueva. Having been jailed, Stalin's sisters-in-law gained both fresh motivation to blacken his name and access to the rich store of rumours that circulated among prisoners. The story goes that the suicide note was seen by only a few unidentified people (and who would have had the opportunity to read it and the nerve to gossip about it?) and then quickly destroyed. According to Svetlana, the letter was 'liberal' in tone, but there is no good evidence about its content, if it existed at all. The question of political differences between Stalin and his wife remains conjectural, on a par with the rumours that Stalin offered his resignation as party leader following Nadezhda's death.[11]

The death of Nadezhda ended a period in which Stalin had lived a fairly conventional and settled family life, albeit with its stresses, and ushered in a new way of life that was eccentric, isolated and probably steeped in alcohol. Celibate it was not. Someone on Stalin's staff, probably his bodyguard and major domo, Nikolai Vlasik, seems to have presented the Boss with a new crop of waitresses at his country house, Zubalovo, and he made his pick, 'a young one with a snub nose and a gay ringing laugh called Valechka' (Valentina Istomina). She became his housekeeper and, by the time of his death, Stalin's accepted widow, though without the benefit of marriage. This was no 'woman with ideas . . . herrings with ideas – skin and bones', as Stalin contemptuously called Vasily's first wife. Valechka, says Svetlana, was 'corpulent, neat, served deftly at the table and never joined in any conversation'. And she remained fiercely loyal to her master to his death and after.[12]

Valechka was settled in the new home that Stalin built for himself in 1934 in the village of Kuntsevo, incorporated into the city limits of Moscow as these were redefined in 1935. The location was undramatic but, before the expansion of the city in recent years, rustic and convenient. The grounds form the south-west corner of the Mozhaisk highway and the Minskaia, 8 km from the Kremlin by a straight run down the Kalinin Prospect—Kutuzov Prospect–Mozhaisk highway. The motorcades bearing Stalin, his cronies and security men raced down roads that the police had cleared of all other traffic. Svetlana and her friends called it a 'dogs' wedding', referring to the howl of sirens. It should not have taken Stalin more than ten minutes to get from his Kremlin office to 'Nearby' (*Blizhny*), as his regular guests called it to distinguish it from other villas at considerably greater distances. In 1983 a visitor could not see the 'modern' wooden house, originally single-storey, then expanded to two-storey, but it was quite possible to see the green-painted wooden wall surrounding it, rotting away after many years of neglect. About three metres high, except in the north-west corner, evidently near the house, where it rose to about four metres, this gave Nearby discreet privacy within a rectangular area, largely wooded, about 240 metres on a side.

Along with a service entrance, flanked by a small barracks for security personnel, there was the main gate – simple wooden doors in the wall, flanked by a guardhouse window and decorated with only a pair of three-hole fixtures for flags, probably for festive occasions. Only Stalin's car was permitted through the gate, no doubt for security reasons. Having walked to the house, the visitor entered an oak-panelled foyer flanked by separate cloak-rooms for Stalin and his guests and also by his office. Then one entered a large multi-purpose room – austerely furnished with a long table, some divans and straight-backed chairs – in which he did his entertaining. Colour reproductions of photographs from a popular journal adorned the walls, strips of rose-coloured carpet on the floor. By the standards of many stockbrokers, Stalin's suburban home was modest.[13]

Stalin retained both office and flat in the Kremlin, which by the early 1930s had replaced his offices at the Secretariat as his usual workplace.[14] Officials who came there regularly called his office the 'nook', for it was tucked in a corner formed by the Kremlin wall, the Arsenal and the Sovnarkom building, in which the office was located. Callers entered the Kremlin at its opposite end through the Borovitsky Gate, drove across the interior expanse of the fortress and stopped just under the Nikolsky Tower, which abuts Red Square near the Lenin Mausoleum. They then entered a ground-floor reception room where police officers checked their papers, then ascended two floors in a lift and passed through a corridor to a reception room presided over by no less a personage than General Vlasik. This room contained a good collection of Soviet and foreign magazines, including some forbidden to the population, such as *Life*. Attached to this room was the office of Stalin's principal secretary, Poskrebyshev, the wall of which was decorated with a water-colour of Stalin during the defence of Tsaritsyn. Also attached was what its familiars called 'the changing room', meaning that they virtually disrobed in the course of a body-search by police with the rank of colonel. 'One was not supposed to go in to see Stalin carrying a gun', recalled one visitor.[15]

The Boss's office was a large room with a high, vaulted ceiling. Large windows overlooked the Arsenal, and the walls were panelled in dark oak. The decorations emphasized Lenin, whose death-mask was exhibited in a glass case, along with a large portrait on the wall and a smaller one on Stalin's desk. Marx and Engels appeared in other portraits, but there was nothing of Stalin or his family. The furniture was 'old-fashioned and bulky', consisting of Stalin's desk, usually bearing a large pile of work, a conference table with chairs, a divan, an overstuffed chair and a tall clock. During meetings Stalin 'did not like to sit', roaming the room while his colleagues debated, alighting briefly on the divan or easy chair. He rarely if ever chaired meetings, often delegating that function to Molotov. In talking with visitors individually or in small groups he was inclined to sit and doodle, but not always the sketches of wolves' heads that some observed in his later years. Adjacent to the office was a dining room, one wall of which was occupied by a buffet containing an array of wine bottles in the tradition of Georgian hospitality. There was a table that seated ten and a divan. When Stalin invited some of his comrades for a meal late at night, the table would be laden with wine, vodka, cognac, champagne, cold dishes and soup. The meal was self-served, except for the occasional appearance of 'a woman in a white smock carrying some hot dish'.[16]

The office suite also contained a room where Stalin might sleep if he did not drive out to Kuntsevo, but he did not spend his nights in the flat that he maintained one floor below the office. This had been Bukharin's until 1933, at which time Stalin occupied it in exchange for the one in which Nadezhda had died. He did, however, join Vasily and Svetlana for dinner quite often, signing their homework assignments like millions of other Soviet parents. But he no longer shared an apartment with his children, nor his holidays, which he passed at Sochi, usually sending Vasily and Svetlana to the Crimea.[17]

By the mid-1930s Stalin seems to have found a settled daily and annual cycle. Arising near noon, he would be driven from Kuntsevo to the Kremlin, where he would work until six or seven in the evening. Political lieutenants were often present for dinner and stayed on into the evening to talk shop or see a film – Soviet or American – in the Kremlin's private cinema. In this case Stalin would, until the war, tell Svetlana, 'You show us how to get there, Housekeeper. Without you to guide us we'd never find it.' And so a procession of Politburo members would follow the girl to the former Winter Garden in the Kremlin. Around midnight Stalin would leave for Nearby in an armoured Packard automobile, one of the best American cars of the day. This eccentric schedule kept the upper echelons of the party and state, at least in Moscow, at their desks until midnight or perhaps later, awaiting a possible phone call from the Boss. This may have been deliberately planned, for another ritual of Stalin's life showed his acute awareness of the role of symbolic subordination in politics. In this instance Stalin played an ostensibly jovial paternal game with his daughter, who signed herself 'Secretary no. 1', and issued 'orders' to her father, who replied as 'wretched secretary', 'I submit'. Furthermore he drew his political cronies into the game, calling them 'secretaries' or 'wretched secretaries' of 'Setenka-Housekeeper'. It is easy to imagine a response to Svetlana's remark, 'I have no idea whether it amused them or not', but this insistence on mock-submission to the Boss's young daughter was a shrewd means of reminding people of their place.[18]

Although his wife's suicide altered Stalin's way of life, and his daughter thought it had a 'traumatic' effect on him, it is not evident that his political conduct changed drastically in the two years after the tragedy.[19] His relations with his immediate subordinates seemingly remained stable. The new Politburo that was elected in February 1934, following the

Seventeenth Party congress, retained all of the men who had risen with him: Kalinin, Voroshilov, Molotov, Rudzutak, Kuibyshev, Andreev, Kirov and Ordzhonikidze. There was scant turnover in the Central Committee, considering the severe demands that many of its members bore in their daily assignments: fifty-six out of seventy-one full members who had been elected in 1930 were re-elected in 1934.[20] The same spirit of stability was apparent in the policies that Stalin supported in the mid-1930s. He now showed less inclination to issue arbitrary commands to raise the targets of the plan, and in 1933 he even consented to a reduction of some of the goals that had been set in the earlier versions of the plan. Stalin no doubt wanted to complete the process of collectivization but sought to moderate its harshness, signing a secret decree that limited the number of arrests of alleged kulaks, and in a secret speech to party functionaries urged them to avoid 'administrative measures', that is, coercion.[21] A party purge was announced on 28 April 1933, but this was not then an ominous sign. The Russian word *chistka* that usually is translated as 'purge' does not in general imply violence. In the party it had come to mean a weeding out of unsuitable members, mainly for non-political reasons such as apathy or ignorance, and rarely with arrest on criminal charges following the expulsion. These reviews had followed previous periods of rapid recruitment, such as the civil war and the 'Lenin Enrolment', and it was predictable that one would follow the hasty growth of the party during the enthusiasm of the First Five-Year Plan. Far from appearing to presage renewed turbulence, it seemed to fit in with the sense of consolidation that prevailed in 1933. The decree of 28 April seemed to sustain this point by urging party officials to stick to fair and reasonable procedures, creating 'a comradely atmosphere for the purge', avoiding 'captious', 'tricky' questions. True, it also referred to 'class alien and hostile elements', 'double-dealers' and 'moral degenerates', but this was well-established rhetoric, which omitted references to foreign capitalists and their agents or to Trotsky, Zinoviev or Bukharin. The decree provided for the readmission of expelled members and candidate members after a year, providing that they 'improved their knowledge of political fundamentals', which clearly implied that it was not expected that they would be dead or in Gulag.[22]

The death of Nadezhda Allilueva was not, in all probability, murder, and it did not lead quickly to a morbid deterioration of Stalin's dealings with his political associates. That change seems to date from 1 December 1934 and the murder of Kirov, party boss of Leningrad, member of both Politburo and Secretariat, long-term, protégé of Stalin, and one of his cronies. Or was Stalin really behind this killing?[23] By all accounts the act itself was carried out by an obscure young man named Leonid Nikolaev, who shot Kirov in the back of the head at close range in the party headquarters building of Leningrad, the former Smolny Institute. Beyond this there is little enough firm information on the case. Kirov was at the peak of his career at the time of his death, after which he was elevated to a position right behind Lenin and Stalin, and ahead of all others, in the Bolshevik pantheon of the living and dead. It might be argued that in respect to the naming of things in his honour Kirov equalled or surpassed Stalin. Between 1934 and 1953 there were named for Kirov eight cities and at least fifteen towns, two large administrative regions, a gulf in the Caspian Sea, a peak in the Pamir Mountains, a group of islands in the Arctic Ocean, a mineral, the former Mariinsky Ballet Company, the vast former Putilov Factory in Leningrad, among countless other factories, educational institutions, collective farms, streets and squares. One cannot tell if this flowering of the Kirov cult was entirely obedience to orders from the centre or whether, as is possible, it also reflected some degree of genuine popular feeling for the man, the very thing that would have troubled Stalin – until Kirov was dead. His ashes were immured in the Kremlin wall in Moscow, but it was his last fief, Leningrad, that paid him the most redundant tribute in place-names and statues. To this day one senses in that city some authentic popular pride in Kirov.[24]

Of course Stalin gave no hint that he was anything other than a loyal comrade of the deceased, and it is remarkable that during his lifetime there was almost no inclination in the non-Soviet world to believe that he was responsible. This reflects a degree of innocence concerning Stalin, rooted in the reality that thus far in his life he had no record as a murderer of his comrades. Moreover Trotsky, respected in the West as a presumed expert on Soviet politics and surely a man with a motive to blacken Stalin, did not accuse Stalin of arranging this murder. This appears to stem from Trotsky's profound hope that there was a rising tide of worker radicalism against the Stalinists, which, he persuaded himself, was demonstrated by the assassination. Only with the death of Stalin and especially Khrushchev's attack on 'the cult of personality' were there serious allegations that Stalin arranged Kirov's death.[25] For his part, Khrushchev did not take a definite position, merely stating in 1956 that aspects of the case were 'inexplicable and mysterious' and five years later that there 'were still many, a great many, unclarified circumstances', which were then the subject of investigation. This inconclusiveness might reflect Stalin's success in covering his tracks, or Khrushchev's difficulty in persuading his Politburo colleagues to authorize him to reveal so shocking a crime. It was one thing to announce that such rehabilitated 'enemies of the people' as Rudzutak or Tukhachevsky had been murdered, and something else to reveal Stalin as the killer of Kirov, who had been venerated ever since 1934.[26]

The best evidence that Stalin was behind the assassination of Kirov is circumstantial. On the most general level the probability of Stalin's responsibility lies in the character of the Soviet system in 1934. One need not subscribe to a simple or unadulterated 'totalitarian' model of this system to believe that the security apparatus was extremely powerful, highly centralized and controlled by Stalin. For a leading member of the Politburo, one of the four or five most important men in the system, to be killed by a lone assassin with a handgun was possible only if the killer enjoyed incredibly good luck. And there is good evidence that Nikolaev did not depend wholly on luck and that there was some kind of conspiratorial activity within the security forces. According to Khrushchev, the post-Stalin investigation showed that the head of Kirov's bodyguard had not been, for some reason, close to his charge at the time of the shooting and that when he was being driven to the interrogation the next day he was murdered in a crudely staged, but at the time secret, car accident. Khrushchev also believed that the police who had been escorts during this 'accident' were later eliminated. Furthermore Nikolaev had on two occasions been found by the police in the building carrying a revolver and yet was released, said Khrushchev, 'upon someone's instructions', an unthinkable breach of security in a state which tightly restricted even gun ownership.[27] In addition to these official revelations the dissident historian Anton Antonov-Ovseenko maintains that there were attempts on Kirov's life earlier in 1934, and Roi Medvedev believes that Kirov's bodyguard warned him that a plot seemed to be afoot.[28] This part of their versions of the affair gains credibility from a curious bit of archaeological evidence. In the Kirov museum in Leningrad, which occupies his former apartment, one exhibit in 1976 consisted of the tunic that he was wearing on his last day, along with a blood-encrusted visored cap. The neatly tailored garment, which was not damaged in the shooting, bears a highly visible line of professional stitching from the left armpit in a curve to a point about 20 centimetres below, where it joins the front opening of the tunic. It is hard to imagine what purpose this custom-tailored reinforcement serves if it is not to provide an interior pocket for a good-sized handgun. The victim, it appears, did indeed think that he should be ready to defend himself.[29]

Beyond this there is a frustrating, tantalizing and contradictory body of evidence that Kirov was becoming a sufficiently serious rival to Stalin to create a reasonable motive for murder. There *may* have been serious friction between Stalin and Kirov before the party congress of January–February 1934. Nicolaevsky may have been right in stating that Kirov led the opposition to Stalin's proposal to execute Riutin in 1932, but there are the usual problems of knowing if this came from Bukharin and if Bukharin was in a position to know the facts. Khrushchev seems more reliable in recollecting a less serious incident that year in which Stalin spoke insultingly to Kirov about the report that one of the latter's aides had made to the Politburo concerning food rationing in Leningrad, a report that Kirov evidently regarded favourably. Kirov often has been depicted as a 'liberal' in contrast to Stalin's despotism, but this is hard to demonstrate. Stalin as much as Kirov appears to have supported the various forms of relaxation that appeared in 1933. In his own right Kirov seems to have been a tough Bolshevik and a staunch supporter of Stalin's policies and emergent cult. The notion that Kirov represented some sort of 'liberal' alternative to Stalin rests in considerable measure on the desire of latter-day anti-Stalinists such as Khrushchev and Roi Medvedev to find such an alternative within the movement.[30]

Wishful thinking of this sort may have informed the report of Medvedev and Antonov–Ovseenko that on the eve of the Seventeenth Party Congress, about January 1934, a small group of leading Bolsheviks proposed to Kirov that he assume the post of General Secretary, which he declined to consider. Neither writer reveals the source of this story, and it is curious that neither Khrushchev nor the official historians of his era made reference to such a meeting, even though one would think that they would have welcomed any evidence of resistance to Stalin by 'good Bolsheviks' during this period. The official history of the party published in 1962 refers vaguely to the wish of 'many delegates' to the Congress 'to transfer Stalin from the office of General Secretary to some other post'.[31] Unofficial reports maintain that a significant minority of the almost 2000 delegates attempted to vote against Stalin as a member of the new Central Committee. Exclusion from this body would have ruled out his re-election as General Secretary. Each delegate received a list of candidates for election to the Central Committee, which contained as many names as there were seats on the Committee, and negative votes were cast by crossing out names. Medvedev and Antonov-Ovseenko maintain, respectively, that 270 or 292 ballots came in with Stalin's name thus deleted – far from a majority but a lot of dissent by party standards. To avoid embarrassment, this version goes, Kaganovich told the head of the electoral commission to destroy the ballots and tell the Congress that only three votes were cast against Stalin. This is close to Khrushchev's recollection that the congress was told that Stalin received six negative votes. He also states that Stalin personally collected all the ballots, 'looking each delegate squarely in the eye so as not to see his ballot'. To Khrushchev this implied probity, but it could also be taken as an indication that Stalin knew that he faced some dissent and wanted to intimidate the voters. Certainly the process of taking ballots from each of almost 2000 voters would have been a memorable and even eerie procedure.[32]

The announcement of the composition of the newly elected executive organs of the party also suggests that Stalin had some difficulties with Kirov in relation to the Secretariat. This body now consisted of Stalin, Kaganovich, Kirov and Zhdanov. According to the official announcement, Zhdanov was relieved of his previous assignment as secretary of Gorky province, a normal step in view of his new job in Moscow. But Kirov was made a member of the Secretariat 'while remaining secretary of the Leningrad provincial committee', an unprecedented arrangement. This could reflect an attempt by Stalin to bring Kirov more directly under his supervision, contrary to Kirov's wishes, or a manoeuvre of those who wanted Kirov to take over as General Secretary. There have been unsubstantiated rumours in both directions. At the very least there was some unsolved problem concerning Stalin, Kirov and the Secretariat.[33]

Even if this entire jumble of debatable evidence is worthless, which seems improbable, it remains that Kirov was Stalin's principal potential rival. Aged forty-eight at the time of his death, Kirov was seven years younger than Stalin. In almost ten years as party chief of Leningrad province he had become a well-established national figure. If he wanted a turn at the top, he could not afford to wait for Stalin to die, but perhaps his relative youth might recommend itself to a number of party activists. He was good-looking and a powerful speaker. Most important, he was a Great Russian. Despite public professions of internationalism by Bolsheviks, the Soviet state remained Russian at its core. The appearance of Russified Jews like Trotsky and Zinoviev or a Georgian like Stalin at the top of the movement was an anomaly of the revolution, which temporarily overthrew all sorts of established norms. After Stalin died the unwritten rule that only a Great Russian could lead the Communist Party of the Soviet Union became firmy established. Stalin himself seems to have been acutely aware of this weakness and tried to compensate by cultivating the idea that he was a Russian nationalist Bolshevik.

It may or may not have been coincidental that in mid-July 1934 he had occasion to demonstrate his concern for this image when the editor of the party's theoretical journal, *Bolshevik*, proposed to observe the twentieth anniversary of the outbreak of the First World War by printing in Russian translation an article that Engels had written in 1890, 'The Foreign Policy of Russian Tsarism'. Marx and Engels had been ardent enemies of Imperial Russia, and in this piece Engels treated the Russian state as the worst of all imperialists. Stalin in a letter to the Politburo recommended that the article not be published because Engels supposedly exaggerated the evil of tsarist foreign policy. It would be fine, said Stalin, to publish it in a collection of Engels's works or a historical journal, but it would not do to make it appear as a directive of the party. Stalin could not have been deeply concerned that the party members who read *Bolshevik* would form an excessively low opinion of the old regime. More to the point was the prospect that they would think that the regime of a Georgian in the Kremlin scorned the historical defenders of Russian national interest. This was only one of the ways in which Stalin manifested his support for Russian nationalism, but the fact remained that he could never be a real

Russian, that many Russians privately laughed at his accent, that they might find a real Russian leader more to their liking. Even if only a small part of the anti-Stalin, pro-Kirov feeling that has been alleged was real, or considered real by Stalin, he had reason to regard Kirov as a serious potential threat.[34]

Kirov was killed at 4.30 p.m. on 1 December 1934, and Stalin acted with haste to travel to Leningrad to start the investigation, covering the 600-plus km by special train in time to arrive 'when it was nearly dawn' (perhaps 8 a.m. at that time of year) on the 2nd.[35] No doubt this could be interpreted as Bolshevik zeal, but it is doubtful that Stalin, if surprised by the news of the killing and informed that there had been a breakdown of security, would have been so quick to put himself in the midst of a potential nest of armed traitors. True, he took with him the head of the police, G. G. Yagoda, and also Voroshilov and Zhdanov. But if Stalin really was in the dark concerning the murder, and especially concerning the reliability of the police, Yagoda's presence would have been an additional risk. Stalin stayed in Leningrad for only two days. In this time he probably participated in the opening of the interrogation of Nikolaev, which probably presented an unexpected difficulty. According to a plausible report, the killer said that a police officer, Ivan Zaporozhets, put him up to the killing. This would have upset any previous deal, if one existed, to have Nikolaev incriminate Zinoviev and Kamenev.[36] Soon these former opponents of Stalin appeared as the main culprits in the case, but the first published statements displayed some confusion concerning the question of political responsibility, assigning it to 'enemies of the working class', then to 'White Guards'.[37]

During his short stay in Leningrad Stalin found time to be photographed as a member of the guard of honour at Kirov's bier. '. . . together with Stalin the great and formidable Soviet country pressed its lips on his cold lips', said *Pravda*, although it is impossible to say if this traditional Orthodox leave-taking actually occurred. It was not this gesture that the artist N. Kh. Rutovsky depicted in his painting *Stalin at the Bier of S. M. Kirov*, a now-vanished work that, a commentator claimed, conveyed 'great human grief'. On 4 December Stalin arrived back in Moscow, never again to see Leningrad. He travelled on a special train which bore the body of Kirov and was pulled by a locomotive named *Iosif Stalin*. Neither in Leningrad nor in Moscow did he deliver any eulogy on Kirov. The last such address by Stalin had been at Dzerzhinsky's funeral in 1926, so the omission was normal by 1934. He did, however, appear prominently at Kirov's obsequies, taking the lead position among those who carried the cremated remains from the Hall of Columns to the grave near the Lenin Mausoleum. Apart from this kind of prominence at the funeral, *Pravda* from 3 to 10 December carried a special feature, 'Telegrams to Stalin', in which appeared a total of one hundred short messages from a great variety of party and other public bodies concerning the assassination. These were not condolences but statements on the need for struggle against 'the class enemy' and for 'vigilance'. The absence of any specific culprit in these notes created the impression that Stalin was getting a mandate from the Soviet populace to take severe action against whomsoever he identified as guilty.[38]

Quite a different political message appeared on 8 December when the death of Kirov abruptly disappeared from the front page of *Pravda*, which it had almost monopolized since the 2nd. This was a long state decree ending bread rationing in cities, which had been in effect since 1929, and also promising an increase in wages. This significant amelioration of living conditions had been decided in principle in November, but the timing of the detailed decree seems too precise to have been accidental. It read as an implied message that Kirov was not, contrary to any rumour, the main advocate of relaxation of the austerity of the previous few years. Surely Stalin wanted it known that even without Kirov his regime would try to ensure that 'life becomes better, life becomes more joyous', to paraphrase slightly a much-publicized remark of Stalin in 1935.[39]

The tone of the press had established an official mood of severe vigilance toward hidden class enemies, but when Stalin sought action in this spirit in the conduct of criminal justice, he seems to have encountered difficulties. On 5 December *Pravda* carried a state decree dated 1 December, which sought to hasten the arrest, trial and execution of 'terrorists'. Stalin seems to have experienced some friction concerning this decree, if not in the Politburo then with Yenukidze, the secretary of the Central Executive Committee of the Congress of Soviets and therefore the administrative officer of the legislature. Khrushchev said in 1956 that Yenukidze signed the decree on 'the evening of 1 December', which is physically possible only if Stalin or his staff composed it immediately after receiving the grim news from Leningrad and just before departing Moscow. Khrushchev maintains that the Politburo approved it 'casually' on the 3rd. Moreover the version of this decree that appeared in the press four days after Stalin drafted it was not identical with the original draft. It appears that somebody, probably Yenukidze or his legal staff, revised the original draft considerably and perhaps moderated its impact. The three points that Stalin originally wanted were elaborated into five, with an added preamble. One point that in the original had vaguely ordered the police to 'speed up' investigations of terrorists instead specified that the police had ten days in which to handle such investigations. This maximum term was little enough, but did offer the police an excuse to take ten days, which in important cases might allow time for influential friends of the accused to organize opposition to a drumhead trial and execution. It is not certain that Stalin was displeased with the changes in his draft, but it is well documented that Yenukidze was removed from his job and the party within the first half of 1935.[40]

The spirit of this decree, ruthless speed in the liquidation of 'terrorists', was applied to substantial numbers of 'White Guards', leftovers from the civil war, who were initially blamed for the assassination of Kirov.[41] It is doubtful that Stalin was particularly interested in these obscure victims. Possibly these executions were the work of police officers who were trying to give satisfaction but did not yet understand that the investigation was supposed to inculpate Kamenev and Zinoviev. In any case, the investigators soon purported to discover links between the assassin and former Zinoviev oppositionists in the Leningrad Komsomol organization, and thence to Zinoviev and Kamenev themselves. It was easy enough to apply the decree on rapid prosecution of terrorists to the assassin and his alleged Komsomol accomplices, who were executed on 29 December. But Stalin encountered difficulty in achieving comparable haste in the cases of the two former members of the Politburo, and several fairly eminent associates, who stood accused in the Kirov case. The zig-zag careers of Zinoviev and Kamenev since their defeat in 1927 suggests that there had been elements in the Central Committee that had opposed consistently the severe measures that Stalin wished to visit upon errant comrades. The pair had been expelled from the party in 1927 and readmitted in 1928, only to be re-expelled, and exiled within the Soviet Union, in 1932 on charges that they failed to report what they knew about the Riutin platform. But in harmony with the relaxation of 1933 they again were pardoned and appeared at the party congress of early 1934 as repentants. But on 16 December, following the death of Kirov, they were arrested once again along with several associates on suspicion of involvement in the Kirov case.[42]

They were held secretly until the 23rd, by which time *Pravda* tried to demonstrate that the workers wanted stern and swift justice for the killers of Kirov. More specifically the party organ maintained that Zinoviev and his friends were responsible for the formation of an opposition group that had turned to 'double-dealing, treason and spying', and that Nikolaev had emerged from this group. But police investigation did not sustain this charge. A terse announcement on 23 December stated that there was insufficient evidence to continue the investigation of the cases of Zinoviev and Kamenev, which were being turned over to a 'conference' of the police. This was not exoneration, but it showed that somebody was buying time for the more prominent accused. Only on 16 January 1935 did Zinoviev, Kamenev and seventeen others come to trial for complicity in the Kirov murder. By this time a large number of lesser fry who were in the hands of the police appear to have testified against the main figures, who were now found guilty of indirect responsibility for the assassination. But the court explicitly exonerated them of actually planning the murder. Supposedly their worst crime was to have known of the terrorist inclination of some of the oppositional youth groups called 'the Leningrad Centre'. It allegedly operated under the direction of a 'Moscow Centre' of Zinovievites, which did not know about the actual assassination plot but only of the 'terrorist state of mind' of the youths, which the leaders 'inflamed'. For this Zinoviev was sentenced to ten years imprisonment, Kamenev five, evidently less than Stalin wanted, for on 27 July 1935 Kamenev was re-sentenced to ten years. The entire development of this affair, from the drafting of the decree on speeding up the prosecution of terrorists, strongly suggests that Stalin was pressing for severe action against his former political enemies, while other influential figures were succeeding in moderating the action of the judicial process.[43]

On 23 January 1935 a separate trial dealt with police officials in Leningrad whose alleged negligence made possible the shooting. Among those convicted was Stalin's putative chief agent in the assassination, Zaporozhets, who received a sentence of only two years, a mild punishment in view of the grave consequences of his supposed negligence. But in 1937, according to Khrushchev, these men were shot 'to cover the traces of the organizers of Kirov's killing'. This trial ended for the moment the arrests of important people in connection with the Kirov assassination, although many humbler folk continued to be swept in for some months to come as the police continued to try to demonstrate zeal. During the rest of 1935 and the first half of 1936 the propaganda campaign stressing vigilance continued, but neither prominent figures nor ordinary citizens were subject to any fresh upsurge of police action.[44]

There was, however, in June 1935 one political case, not involving criminal prosecution at the time, which is of singular importance for Stalin's biography. It began with the dismissal on 3 March of Yenukidze from the important position that he had held since 1918: secretary of the presidium of the Central Executive Committee of the Congress of Soviets. This removal was followed on 7 June 1935 with his expulsion from the party and its Central Committee. The importance of this case lies in Yenukidze's long and intimate personal relationship with Stalin, dating back thirty-five years to the time when both were young activists in the Georgian Social-Democratic movement. In later years he was a friend and important associate of Stalin, but not in work that involved him heavily in factional politics, certainly not as any kind of oppositionist or rival. The resolution passed by the Central Committee session of June, 'On the Office Staff of the Secretariat of the Central Executive Committee of the USSR and Comrade Yenukidze', tersely approved unspecified improvements in that body and the expulsion from the party of the erstwhile secretary. There was also a brief allegation that he had fallen into 'a degenerate life-style', and this probably was amplified in a whisper-campaign. It may be that the bachelor Yenukidze, with his eminent

Stalin's birthplace in Gori, Georgia, as it appeared at an indeterminate date, probably in the early 1930s, before its enshrinement.

The improved birthplace and its pavilion as they appeared in December 1983.

3   Pupils and teachers of the 'Gori Ecclesiastical Seminary'. Stalin is fourth from the left in the back row.

4   'Koba', the young revolutionary activist (1903).

5   Stalin in exile (1915), in the Siberian hamlet of Monastyrskoe, with fellow Marxist Suren Spandarian.

6   A meeting of the Sovnarkom in Smolny Institute, Petrograd (early 1918). Stalin is standing behind and to the right of Lenin.

7   Portrait in pencil and pastel by N. Andreev, autographed by Stalin and dated 1 May 1922, which is about three weeks after he became general secretary of the party.

8 Stalin with workers of the 'Stalin Railway Shops' (1 March 1927). He spoke there in connection with the election of the Moscow Soviet. His willingness to engage in this kind of politicking may have owed something to his desire to overcome the Trotsky–Zinoviev opposition.

9 A cartoon of December 1927 ridiculing Trotsky (the organist), Zinoviev (the singer) and Kamenev (the parrot). The caption reads: 'We play and play, but nobody comes to us.'

10 Nadezhda Allilueva, Stalin's second wife (c. 1930).

11 Avel Yenukidze, Stalin and Maxim Gorky near the Lenin Mausoleum, Red Square (May Day 1932).

12   Soviet drawing of Kirov showing Stalin and Klimenty Voroshilov the White Sea–Baltic Canal, built by Gulag, during Stalin's tour of this project (July 1933).

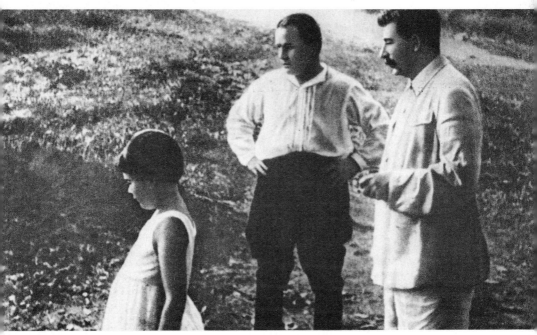

13   Svetlana, Stalin's daughter, with Kirov and her father on holiday at Sochi on the Black Sea coast (c. September 1934), about three months before the assassination of Kirov.

14 Painting by G N Gorelov of Stalin and his entourage, including Gorky, admiring a model of the planned 'Palace of Soviets'.

15 The heroic aviator Valerii Chkalov, receiving congratulations on 10 August 1936 upon his return to Moscow from his flight to the arctic island of Udd and Kamchatka peninsula.

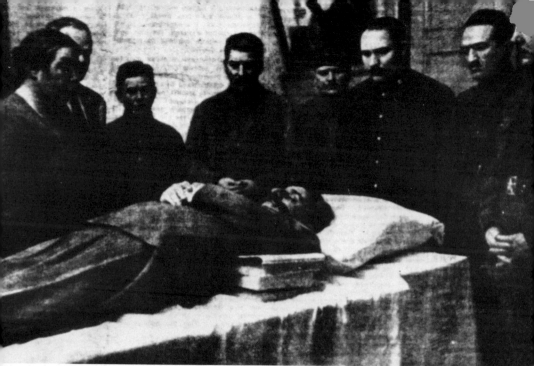

16 The corpse of Sergo Ordzhonikidze lying in his apartment, viewed by his widow, Molotov, Yezhov, Stalin, Zhdanov, Kaganovich, Mikoyan and Voroshilov. One might wonder why the picture on the wall in the background has been knocked askew.

7 An example of mass-produced cult statuary of the late 1930s.

18   Stalin and Hitler's foreign minister, Joachim von Ribbentrop, at the signing of the Soviet–German treaty (23 August 1939).

19   Churchill, Roosevelt and Stalin at the Yalta Conference (February 1945).

20 Oil painting by F. P. Reshetnikov, dated 1948, showing Stalin, in the Kremlin in 1942, planning the counter-attack at Stalingrad, which appears on the map before him.

21 Stalin passing a British guard of honour at the Potsdam Conference (July 1945). His principal military staff officer, General Alexis Antonov, is on his left, followed by the portly Aleksandr Poskrebyshev, Stalin's long-time secretary.

22 A poster of 1950, in which Stalin contemplates a map showing his scheme to transform nature by planting huge shelter-belts.

23 A Chinese painting which presents a fanciful version of the Mao–Stalin talks of December 1949–February 1950. It appears that Mao, holding a volume by Lenin, is instructing Stalin.

24 Stalin's picture, hanging from an invisible tethered balloon, shimmers in spotlights on his 70th birthday in December 1949. Although the photograph may be a montage, this airborne icon was in fact used.

25 G M Malenkov delivers the principal report to the Nineteenth Party Congress, 5 October 1952, watched by Stalin and, in the front row, Kaganovich and Molotov.

26 Beria, Malenkov and Bulganin at Stalin's bier.

position and access to material privilege, cut a wide swathe among actresses and ballerinas – but then so did other dignitaries who were not punished. Stalin, it seems, had some scores to settle with his old friend.[45]

Soon after the June meeting of the Committee, Khrushchev and Zhdanov, two of Stalin's rising clients, proved their loyalty to their patron by amplifying the official line on Yenukidze, delivering parallel speeches in Moscow and Leningrad. Yenukidze, said Zhdanov, had in the course of his 'infamous subversive work against the party and state gathered together the contemptible remnants of Fascist–Zinovievite–Kamenevite–Trotskyite groups and the chaff of bourgeois-landlord counter-revolutionaries'. Khrushchev alleged that Yenukidze, 'losing all the qualities of a Bolshevik, wished to be "the good uncle" for the enemies of the party'. Unlike Zhdanov, Khrushchev did not in his own speech state explicitly that Yenukidze was on the side of the class enemy. But a 'worker' who spoke along with Khrushchev alleged that the culprit had formed a 'counter-revolutionary nest' of 'former princesses, ministers and noblemen, Trotskyites and all sorts of scum'. Stalin's tendency to lump all his enemies together into one enormous plot, now coming into full flower, makes it difficult to know what actual differences he had with Yenukidze. Apart from the allegations cited, Yenukidze probably was in a better position than anyone else in the Central Committee to have foreseen the menace in the evolution of Stalin's personality. And if the Zinoviev–Kamenev case and the decree on speeding up the prosecution of terrorists had led him to talk with others about this evolution, this would inevitably have turned Stalin against him.[46]

This speculative train of thought connects with another intriguing aspect of the affair: Yenukidze's relationship with Nadezhda Allilueva and involvement at her death. He was an old friend of the Alliluev family, for Nadezhda's father, though not a Georgian, had lived in Transcaucasia for a number of years early in the century. Nadezhda's mother, Olga Allilueva, was a Christian, despite her marriage to a Marxist, and she persuaded Yenukidze to be Nadezhda's godfather. Though not a believer, he took seriously the human side of this responsibility and was something of a second father to his godchild throughout her life, and was regarded by Stalin's daughter as an 'uncle'. He was, in Svetlana's recollection, a regular participant in their family life, and one wonders what Nadezhda, as a troubled young woman, may have told her godfather about the drift of her husband's personality in the early 1930s. When she committed suicide, Yenukidze was one of the first people called in by the household staff, and with Stalin in a state of shock it fell to 'Uncle Avel' to make the funeral arrangements. Formally he was chairman of a 'funeral commission', informally he assumed the paternal role of comforting Stalin's children. Probably it was he who commissioned the memorial statue that marks Nadezhda's grave in the cemetery of the

New Virgin's Convent, a simple and graceful marble evocation of a vulnerable young woman. It is a work that has little in common with Stalin's artistic taste, and it may be that he found in the statue an implied reproach. Svetlana maintains that her father was looking for somebody other than himself to blame for the tragedy. Who was a more likely candidate than Yenukidze?[47]

A man whom Nadezhda had disliked intensely, another Georgian Bolshevik, probably played some role in Stalin's turn against Yenukidze. This was Lavrenty Beria, twenty years younger than Stalin, who in 1935 was close behind Zhdanov and Khrushchev among the new lieutenants whom Stalin was adding to his original team. A man with many enemies throughout his life, Beria was executed in 1953, accused by his former comrades of striving over many years to restore 'bourgeois rule' in Russia. From that time until 1956 Beria was held responsible for most of the wrongful killings of the Stalin era. While Beria was no doubt a cruel killer, a sycophant and careerist, it does not follow that he was in fact guilty of all the crimes attributed to him. It seems unlikely, for example, that he was during the civil war period an agent of both the Armenian and Turkic nationalists. More plausible is the widespread assertion that he used his power to obtain the favours of women, and particularly girls. Svetlana, who knew Beria's wife fairly well, probably is right in believing that this woman married him because he held her brother hostage. Stalin, who did not have to rely on mere gossip to learn about these things, seems to have taken very seriously the stories about Beria's taste for young girls. This is unwittingly confirmed by Svetlana, who recalls that when she was fifteen she paid a social visit to Mrs Beria, sat up late and was persuaded to stay the night. 'Next morning my father called up in a fury. Using unprintable words, he shouted, "Come back at once! I don't trust Beria!" ' It seems to have been this aspect of his character that had so upset Nadezhda, who would not have Beria in the house.[48]

Beria's rise began with police work in Communist Georgia, and Stalin later credited him with an important role in the repression of an anti-Bolshevik revolt in 1924. As police chief in Georgia, Beria had responsibility for Stalin's safety during his vacations there, which gave him the opportunity to cultivate his personal relations with the Boss. He so ingratiated himself with Stalin that in 1931 he became the party secretary for all of Transcaucasia. With this fief Beria enjoyed special opportunities to direct the development of the cult of Stalin with reference to the first three decades of the Leader's life. Even after Beria had moved his own work to Moscow in 1938, he retained supervision of this enterprise, ordering the construction of a very large Georgian branch of the Institute of Marxism–Leninism in Tbilisi, which specialized in Staliniana, and at the end of Stalin's life the elegant Stalin museum in Gori. In the mid-1930s he saw to it that Georgian painters were in the forefront in the production of oils depicting Stalin in Transcaucasia. There was, for example, Eristavi's *Stalin Leading the Workers of Batumi*, Nadoreishvili's *Stalin Addressing the Workers at Chiatura*, Eristaveli's *Stalin Addressing the Workers at Baku* and Kutateladze's *Stalin Addressing the Workers of Adzhariia*, not to mention major portraits of Beria by Magilachvili and Gzelichvili.[49]

In 1935, the year of Yenukidze's fall, Beria scored a major success in cult-building by opening the restored and enshrined birthplace of Stalin in Gori. In 1938 he added the announcement of a plan to rebuild the whole town, which was to become a showplace of the socialist future, centred on a statue of Stalin some 20 metres tall. This monument, like much of the plan, was never to be completed, though a much smaller statue of Stalin still stands in Gori. Incidentally, the restoration of Lenin's birthplace and its development as a tourist attraction came only after Stalin's death. Beria took custody not only of Stalin's birthplace but also of his aged mother. She had never learned Russian and declined her daughter-in-law's invitation to move to Moscow. Attached as she was to her ways it seems unlikely that she would have wanted to move to Tbilisi and the former viceregal palace, which, however, she did at some point before 1934. Probably this was Beria's idea, just as Svetlana suspects that it was his doing that she and her brother visited the old lady in 1934, accompanied by Mrs Beria and lodging in Beria's 'magnificent apartment' and 'sumptuous villa'. If Stalin had seen his mother since the revolution, it was never noted in the press until 1935 when *Pravda* printed an interview with Stalin's mother which discussed his recent visit to her. The object seems to have been the humanization of Stalin's image, and one wonders if Beria had not suggested to Stalin how heart-warming this filial gesture would be for the Soviet public. When Yekaterina Dzhugashvili died in 1936, Stalin did not attend her funeral and probably left it to Beria to arrange for her burial in particularly hallowed ground near St David's Church. In all of this it seems likely that Beria was able to ingratiate himself with the Boss by appearing to join the family circle and to remind Stalin of his special loyalty as a Georgian.[50]

These various manoeuvres not only enhanced Beria's status, they played an important role in the fall of Yenukidze, who appears to have been an obstacle to his younger compatriot. In January 1935 Yenukidze, still in full possession of his offices, signed an article in *Pravda* which amounted to a confession of grave errors in his own treatment of the history of the revolutionary movement in Transcaucasia. In particular he supposedly had exaggerated his own role and had glossed over his deviations from true Bolshevism. He had written a short work in 1930 on illegal Bolshevik printing presses in Transcaucasia and had provided himself with highly favourable entries in some reference books. Most important, he had not taken sufficient pains to emphasize Stalin's stature.

It must have been about the time of Yenukidze's apology that Beria had his staff preparing his lectures 'On the History of the Bolshevik Organizations in Transcaucasia', delivered in Tbilisi in July 1935 and quickly published as a book that remained a staple of the Stalin cult until 1953. One by-product of Beria's questionable research presumably was the accumulation of a file of Yenukidze's 'errors', which he presented to Stalin to discredit his foe and exact the humiliating self-criticism. The linkage of Yenukidze's decline and Beria's rise was next implied in the official announcement of 3 March 1935 that Yenukidze was relieved of his post as secretary of the Central Executive Committee, for it attributed this change to the request of the Transcaucasian Federal Republic to make him its president. This was not ostensibly a clear-cut demotion, but the hegemony of the party over state institutions implied that in this case Yenukidze would become the subordinate of the party chief of Transcaucasia, Beria. It is clear that Yenukidze was not in fact elected to this presidency, and possible that Beria humiliated him, in the short period before his expulsion from the party in June, by assigning him to manage sanatoria. Yenukidze was, then, in disgrace by mid-1935, but he was not arrested until about February 1937. An announcement dated 16 December of that year stated that Yenukidze and several others (including a Georgian opponent of Beria, M. D. Orakhelashvili) had been shot as spies and traitors.[51]

We cannot know what relative weight Stalin attached to various possible black marks against Yenukidze: his treatment of personalities in the history of Transcaucasian Bolshevism, his close connection with Nadezhda, his softness on oppositionists, perhaps some expressed concern about the menacing evolution of Stalin's personality. But the dismissal and disgrace of Yenukidze, leading to his arrest and execution in 1937, is a persuasive indication that Stalin's attitude toward his close associates had taken an ominous turn by 1935. The Stalin who could round on Yenukidze in this year was quite capable of plotting to murder Kirov a few months earlier.

10 Yezhovshchina

Did Stalin turn insane around the mid-1930s? The scope of his killings among his own comrades in the last half of the decade inevitably raises this question. One might argue that his conduct for many years previous would justify the diagnosis of insanity, but it is hard to sustain this opinion unless one considers the mainstream of Soviet Communism up to that point to have been mad. Stalin succeeded in making himself the leader of this movement by articulating the widespread opinion of psychologically normal people and by providing stable administration, not by imposing on the party and the bulk of the populace notions that most people perceive as deranged. True, he repeatedly had pushed for harsher punishments of defeated Bolshevik opponents than the party élite was willing to approve. The élite realized this, and they probably reasoned that Stalin's conduct on this matter was extreme but not threatening. He had, after all, no record of imprisoning or killing those who followed the 'general line' and he had accepted the restraint of his comrades concerning defeated oppositionists for about ten years prior to the mid-1930s. Some may have been sufficiently disenchanted with Stalin for one reason or another to contemplate parliamentary means of reducing his power or replacing him as leader, but none of the bits of arguable evidence that have reached us concerning such ideas have suggested that there was any serious notion that the issue was Stalin's sanity. The very absence of any substantial concern on this issue very likely helped to disarm Stalin's high-level comrades when his conduct toward them did indeed turn vicious rather abruptly after the middle of the decade.

Even after this point it is hard to find a person who saw him at close quarters who was willing, after Stalin was safely dead, to say that he was mad in the later 1930s. The person who had the best opportunity to observe him at close range in this period and who had the best motivation to decide that his homicidal actions were the result of mental illness is his daughter. While party spokesmen might be reluctant to admit that the Bolsheviks could not defend themselves against the ministrations of a single lunatic, Svetlana's chief wish is to be considered a human like other humans. It would be natural for her to want to attribute the tragedies of her family to mental illness, which is all too commonplace among ordinary people. But Svetlana Alliluyeva has not made this argument. On the contrary she maintains that Stalin was sane, that 'under no circumstances could one call him neurotic' – until his last few years. She granted that he was given to occasional outbursts of rage, but well within the range of normal human behaviour. For example, he threw an uncooperative telephone at the wall, an unwanted boiled chicken out the window.

Nevertheless Svetlana believed he possessed powerful reserves of self-control.[1]

The one witness to Stalin in the later 1930s who has alluded to possible mental illness was Khrushchev. In his secret speech of 1956, without referring to any particular stage of Stalin's life, Khrushchev described Stalin's suspiciousness as 'morbid' and 'sickly'. 'Why are you turning so much today and why do you avoid looking directly into my eyes?' were characteristic questions posed by Stalin, according to Khrushchev. A decade later, dictating his confidential memoirs, Khrushchev seems to have said flatly that Stalin was mentally ill, but he did not elaborate the vital point and placed the crisis *after* the later 1930s: 'it was during the war that Stalin started to be not quite right in the head'.[2]

Given the paucity of intimate personal evidence, it is difficult to reach a definite conclusion on the question of Stalin's mental condition. It is reasonably clear that he did not suffer from such obvious pathological symptoms as hallucinations or depression, that he remained highly functional as a personality right through the worst slaughter of his own people in 1937–8. There is an obvious argument that his cruel and abnormal behaviour was politically rational, at least up to a point: it reinforced Stalin's personal authority. And this self-serving calculation could merge with a higher ideal. The Bolshevik idea not only assumed a titanic struggle of bourgeois and proletarian throughout the world but also held that self-styled Marxists who differed from the truth as scientifically determined by 'the party' were either traitors or deviators who 'objectively' served the bourgeoisie. So if it was in some sense madness to believe that a large portion of the Soviet establishment had become 'enemies of the people' by the mid-1930s, this was compatible with the traditions of the movement. In Lenin's opinion the Menshevik portion of the Social-Democratic Party had turned out to be bourgeois in essence, fit only for suppression. The opposition that emerged after Lenin's death was similar and also had to be excised. The logic of the terror of the 1930s had been well established before the large-scale killing started.

If Stalin was mad, he possessed the genius of projecting his own reality onto large numbers of normal people. They were ready, for the most part, to believe that large numbers of their erstwhile comrades were traitors. They were ready to denounce, to turn away from the incriminated and even from their spouses and children. Here Stalin's success in implanting in the minds of many party members his own heroic image played a helpful role. One could not be 'right against the party', as Trotsky had once put it, and the righteousness of the party could not be separated from its leaders, Lenin and Stalin. The atmosphere of devotion to the leader and alienation from suspect 'comrades' led to the atomization of members of the Soviet élite. Normal human relationships, within a certain level of society, dissolved. As the wife of an old Bolshevik and important military officer put it after her husband's arrest,

> Under the tsar it didn't matter what they did to us, it did not affect our personal relations. The tsar could throw us into prison, lock us up in fortresses, send us to Siberia, but he could never sever the ties that bound us together. On the contrary, whenever we suffered a blow we moved closer together, helped each other. But now? What is happening to us all?[3]

Was Stalin unaware that his regime of terror worked such results? One cannot say, for he never acknowledged that the good Bolsheviks who escaped prosecution had any reason to feel insecure. But his ruthless commitment to the construction of a classless society inevitably guided him toward a hostile attitude toward the class of privileged people that the economic build-up of the country inevitably produced. Stalin did not discuss his response to this inner contradiction of his Communism, but a passionate rejection of the new élite seemingly burst out when, during the war, his daughter told him of the highly privileged arrangements that had been made for the children of the Moscow upper crust. 'Ah, you damned caste!' he exploded. Trotsky, though anything but an admirer of Stalin, accepted the premise that the police terror was a perfectly sound means of dealing with the problem of social differentiation. 'The purge', he wrote, 'by one stroke of the pen throws thousands and thousands of the bureaucrats into the greatest poverty, demonstrates how entirely fragile are the links between the bureaucrats themselves and all the more so between their families and state property.' The same point was clearly perceived by a high official's wife, according to Lidiia Shatunovskaia, a member of the new élite. Bluntly asked by Shatunovskaia why she engaged in brazen 'speculation', the woman replied, 'We are caliphs for an hour. Today my husband is a minister and we have everything, but tomorrow he might arrive at the ministry and find that they are disillusioned with him.' For all his discretion on this matter, it is unlikely that Stalin understood less well than Trotsky and the bureaucrat's wife what he was doing.[4]

And so terror, rationality and insanity appear as inextricably intertwined in Soviet society under Stalin as in his persona. It is difficult to demonstrate his insanity in the late 1930s on the existing evidence, and yet difficult to believe that his psychological condition was normal around 1937. The suspicion that he was failing by that time is enhanced by the comparative normality, even of increasing relaxation, of the regime in 1935 and the first half of 1936. Along with the amelioration of food supply with the ending of rationing, the political climate seemed more tranquil than it had been since the late 1920s. True, the party purge that had started in 1933 dragged on, owing to the dissatisfaction of Stalin and other administrators with the administrative ineptitude of the lower party bodies. At his decree in May 1935 the previously ordered winnowing of the membership by purge commissions was to be repeated by a 'verification' carried out by the hierarchy of party secretaries. This was supervised by the head of the Central Committee Department of Leading Party Organs, N. I. Yezhov, an obscure functionary who was soon to become infamous. A further extension of this check began in February 1936 with the issuance of new party membership cards to those deemed worthy, an 'exchange of documents'. As a result of these steps about 20 per cent of party membership was expelled, but this was not to any significant degree mixed up with arrests or charges of treason. Nor was there any wave of demotions in the senior levels of the party and state apparatus through 1935.[5]

But Stalin had not been entirely idle in his quest for severe punishment of former opposition leaders. Just following the Zinoviev–Kamenev trial of January 1935, his office sent to lower party bodies a secret letter that did not contradict the finding of the court that the pair were only indirectly responsible for the Kirov shooting, but evidently sought to dispel any impression that their guilt was relatively minor. In the ensuing months the secret police engaged in some efforts to find proof of a 'Trotskyite' plot to assassinate Stalin, but could not come up with enough to merit a public trial. In November 1935 an obscure Trotskyite from the city of Gorky, A. A. Lavrentev, supposedly confessed that he and others had tried to finance terrorism by plotting the robbery of funds from a village soviet treasury. The absurdity of the idea that one could obtain thus a large sum of money may account for the fact that this finding never surfaced in a public trial.[6]

It seems to have been just a little later that Stalin obtained some evidence that was considerably more authentic and potent. The timing suggests that it came from an agent named Mark Zborowski, who around 1935 succeeded better than any predecessor in becoming the confidant of Trotsky's son, Lev Sedov, who operated the small secretariat of the Trotskyist movement, first in Berlin, then in Paris.[7] What Zborowski, if it was he, learned was that in 1932 Trotsky, communicating through Sedov, had formed what they called a 'bloc' with dissident elements in the Soviet Union. There a Trotskyist named I. N. Smirnov had proposed to form a coalition of underground opposition to Stalin. Only after a previously closed section of the Trotsky archive at Harvard University was opened in 1980 was it demonstrated that this bloc, although feeble, actually had existed. The evidence is incomplete because somebody, quite possibly Trotsky himself, had removed from the file the letters that he had attempted to send to Sokolnikov, Preobrazhensky, Radek, Kollontai and Litvinov. Nor is there direct evidence in the archive that Stalin came into possession of this material, but the resemblance between the account of the formation of this bloc, as it appears in the Trotsky papers and as it emerged in the show trial of August 1936, makes it reasonably clear that the trial was based on this evidence.[8] This implies significant revision of the previous interpretation of the trial of 1936 by non-Stalinists, for it shows that the confessions were not totally fabricated by the police. It also demonstrates, by the way, that Trotsky did not tell the precise truth to the 'Dewey Commission', a counter-trial that he arranged in 1937 to exculpate him of Stalin's charges, before which he testified that he had not been organizing an underground.[9]

On the other hand, traditional belief that Stalin and his police fabricated confessions is by no means wholly overturned. The Trotsky papers do not at all substantiate charges of terrorist conspiracy, collaboration with Fascists and other imperialists, 'wrecking', the dismemberment of the Soviet federation of nationalities and the restoration of capitalism. At most the 'bloc' of 1932 was an attempt to establish communication between Trotsky, living in exile, his few followers in the USSR who were not in 'isolator' prisons and other oppositional elements that formerly had existed within the Communist Party, going back to the Workers' Opposition of 1920. It is not clear that all of these elements agreed to participate, and it appears that Trotsky specifically excluded those who had 'capitulated' to Stalin, presumably including Zinoviev, Kamenev, Bukharin and Rykov. The result of these covert negotiations was at best a miniscule force, which never achieved any serious level of organization. I. N. Smirnov himself was jailed in 1933, not because his communication with Sedov had been discovered but, according to the latter, for some other reason. Trotsky vastly overvalued the political importance of this coalition, for in the early 1930s he entertained the fantasy that he might be able to return to Moscow and participate in party leadership, not necessarily to the exclusion of Stalin, to whom Trotsky was willing to offer an amnesty. Thus in 1932 he advised Sedov against the slogan 'Down with Stalin' on the grounds that they might soon wish to support Stalin against a serious threat from political forces well to the right of the party. So Trotsky's bloc with Zinovievites and others was not particularly concerned with overthrowing Stalin, much less assassinating him. Its purpose was to 'exchange information', presumably in preparation for the legal re-entry into party leadership.[10]

It may be that Trotsky's optimistic exaggeration of the importance of the bloc that he had joined was matched by Stalin's exaggeration of the threat that it posed to him, at least as a potentiality. If his mind was slipping toward pathological anxiety, he may have taken the bloc seriously, considering that all this had occurred in 1932 and had not, most probably, come to his attention until about the opening of 1936. One cannot be sure of the timing, but the bloc did not appear in Soviet accusations against

Zinoviev and Kamenev in their trial of January 1935, nor the extension of Kamenev's sentence in July of that year.[11]

It is reasonably clear that by February 1936 the police had started a new investigation, beginning with the attempt to link Zinoviev and Kamenev to Trotsky through contacts with Sedov in Berlin – that is, to utilize as a starting point the actual formation of the bloc in 1932. The first known subject of interrogation on this line was one V. P. Olberg, who had been sent by the Soviet police to try to penetrate Sedov's operation, had failed and moved to the Soviet Union. That the police were using one of their own unsuccessful agents rather than a real oppositionist suggests that they were unable to get much out of Smirnov, a tough nut throughout the affair, and lends credence to the report of the defector Alexander Orlov that Olberg was promised a soft berth as a reward for co-operating in making a fraudulent confession. The strategy of the police appears to have been to use this 'confession' and whatever real evidence they had, along with promises, threats and such pressures as protracted interrogation, to break down some minor oppositionists. With these confessions in hand they could oblige even Zinoviev and Kamenev to admit that they had been involved in a terrorist, treacherous plot. This took time, and it was only by July 1936 that the police received a spate of confessions, culminating in those of Zinoviev and Kamenev on 23–5 July. The case against these two, the absent Trotsky, and their alleged accomplices went far beyond the fact of a secret oppositional bloc. The prosecution alleged that it constituted a 'Trotskyite–Zinovievite Terrorist Centre', which successfully plotted the assassination of Kirov and planned to kill Stalin, Voroshilov, Zhdanov, Kaganovich, Kirov, Kosior, Ordzhonikidze and Postyshev. In the subsequent 'confusion' the bloc hoped to seize power, not as some alternative Communist élite, but rather as depraved seekers of power who no longer had an ideology and who had entered into collaboration with the Nazis.[12]

Having obtained Zinoviev's and Kamenev's consent to confess to this concoction, Stalin, in the name of the Central Committee, sought to prepare the party rank and file for the trial by dispatching on 29 July a secret circular letter describing in some detail the 'guilt' of the accused and above all Trotsky.[13] The trial itself did not begin until 19 August and lasted until the 24th. Stalin probably wanted the three weeks that elapsed between the sending of the circular letter and the start of the trial to allow his message to be absorbed and to finish dealing with some of the less co-operative witnesses.[14] But in addition he wanted time to permit the aviator Valerii Chkalov and his two crew-members to provide an edifying example of the heroic in Soviet life just before the trial, so that good and evil would stand in vivid contrast. According to Chkalov the order to depart on the first 'Stalin *marshrut*' (literally 'march route') came from Stalin in conversation during an intermission in the Central Committee session of 1–4 June 1936. This implies that Stalin had been circulating among members of that body some preliminary findings of the Zinoviev–Kamenev investigation and felt that he had enough support to plan on a trial by mid-summer. The aviators suggested that they fly to the North Pole, the kind of obvious exploit dictated by geography, but Stalin instead ordered them to go to the symbolically meaningless island of Udd in the Arctic and thence to Kamchatka. The length of such a trip and the return to Moscow along the line of the Trans-Siberian Railway could stretch the whole thing out to whatever duration the timing of the trial required, and it probably was a more reliably achievable feat than going to the Pole. Stalin wanted neither a failure nor a successful completion at the wrong time – that is, too far in advance of the trial nor simultaneous with it, when the media of propaganda were reserved for the trial. The aviators set off on 20 July and returned to Stalin's embrace, literally, on 10 August. There was a flood of publicity about the 'Stalin *marshrut*' and the ultimate hero who had inspired them. This was but one of the characteristic festivals of the Stalin cult as it emerged by the mid-1930s, the Leader as commander of his 'falcons'. In 1933 he challenged Soviet aviators to fly 'farther than anyone, faster than anyone and higher than anyone' and instigated the establishment of an annual 'aviation day'. By the eve of the Second World War the Soviet Union claimed sixty-two specific records. Each victory was the occasion for a celebration in which Stalin was closely associated with the heroes of the sky. Even when things went badly he could gain something. In 1934 after the death of the three crew-members of a record-setting high-altitude balloon, the poet M. Zenkevich asserted that the dying gasps of the heroes included 'Stalin . . . Stalin . . . Stalin . . .', and when their ashes were placed in the Kremlin wall 'Stalin himself! Stalin himself carries them!'[15]

The timing of the positive and negative sides of Stalin's summer programme was adroit. On 15 August, while the celebratory atmosphere surrounding Chkalov and his Leader was still intense, including a triumphal parade in Moscow, *Pravda* published a short notice on behalf of the Central Executive Committee of the Soviet concerning the forthcoming trial of Zinoviev, Kamenev and others. Had any party members been distressed by this news, they must have found it particularly hard to challenge Stalin amid such national rejoicing.[16]

With all in readiness for the trial, Stalin departed Moscow for an extended vacation near Sochi. One who testified to his presence there was Chkalov, who recalled being invited with his two fellow-fliers and their wives to Stalin's villa. It was, he said, surrounded by an orchard, for Stalin was an 'expert' on trees and intended to wipe out malaria by planting groves of eucalyptus. After dinner there was dancing, Stalin choosing the records and singing along with them. This memoir does not specify the date of Stalin's departure from Moscow, but it must have been

before the opening of the trial on 19 August. This is established by
Khrushchev's memoirs, in which he recalls joining in a conversation that
his immediate boss, Kaganovich, and Ordzhonikidze were having with the
party poet Demian Bedny. The latter had been told to write something
appropriate for the trial, but the result had not proven satisfactory. Bedny
said he felt 'impotent toward' the accused, his erstwhile friends. Actually,
said Khrushchev, Bedny had used a 'cruder, more manly expression'. The
political magnates, and especially Ordzhonikidze, gave the poet his
orders, which Bedny had followed by 21 August, when *Pravda* published
a suitable verse entitled 'No Mercy!' By this time Stalin must have been
out of Moscow for several days, for Khrushchev specifies that Kaganovich
at the time of the conversation with Bedny (that is, about 18 August) was
Stalin's deputy in charge of affairs in Moscow, as was normal when Stalin
and Molotov were both away.[17]

The poem itself, so important to Stalin that Kaganovich and
Ordzhonikidze felt it necessary to make sure it was done properly, may
(in excerpted, prose form) serve as a synopsis of what Stalin wanted to
convey through the trial:

There they all are, like flies in honey,
Like flies stuck in glue.
They carried on their villainous policies
And finally found
The place their villainy deserved . . .
Fascists . . . Himmler . . . How do you like that?!
The incredible suddenly became clear fact,
Recorded in the transcript of the trial:
Betrayers of the Soviet motherland,
Pseudoparty traitors, liars,
Devoted clients of all hostile offices,
Underground enemies, Fascist agents,
Murderers of Kirov . . .
    Here are the ones who murdered Kirov! . . .
They were going for Stalin!
But they failed to get their bandit mugs to him!
        WE HAVE GUARDED STALIN
        WE ARE UNABLE NOT TO GUARD HIM!
        WE GUARD HIM AS OUR HEAD,
            WE GUARD HIM AS OUR OWN HEART! . . .
Where is Trotsky? Without him your poisoned – filthy,
        Your foredoomed group
        Is lacking, empty, –
        But Proletarian wrath will pursue
            The hated Judas everywhere . . .[18]

In the Hall of Columns the prosecutor Andrei Vyshinsky, using scarcely less lurid language, made the same points. The sixteen accused (with some backsliding by Smirnov) confessed. And the judge imposed 'the supreme penalty – to be shot', while ordering the arrest of Trotsky and his son if they should appear on Soviet territory. This they were unlikely to do, but it should not have been hard for Stalin's 'proletarian wrath' to pursue Trotsky to Norway, where he was living at the time of the trial and until the beginning of 1937, when he found a new refuge in Mexico. His followers feared for him particularly while he was in Norway, for he had almost no protection against possible assassins and might face a threat of extradition should Stalin's government wish to argue that Trotsky was an accomplice to simple murder. But neither legal nor covert efforts to kill him occurred until 1940. Evidently Stalin preferred to have Trotsky alive in exile as long as there were public trials of his alleged allies in the Soviet Union. The existence of a living villain, plotting as well as he could against Stalin, even founding a miniscule Fourth International in 1938, would do more to add verisimilitude to Soviet accusations (especially in the eyes of the Left in the West) than would a corpse. Moreover Trotsky persisted during his exile in trying to contact various former oppositionists, and such correspondence, even if it was rejected by the addressee, could be useful in deciding who was incriminated.[19]

This is conjectural, but it is definite that Stalin was not satisfied that the Zinoviev–Kamenev trial of August 1936 had settled his score with the former opposition. On 25 September, while still at Sochi, he, along with Zhdanov, wired the Politburo that Yagoda had 'definitely proved himself to be incapable of unmasking the Trotskyite–Zinovievite bloc', that the police were 'four years behind in this matter' and that Yezhov should replace Yagoda. 'Four years' was an allusion to the bloc between Trotsky and the Zinoviev group in 1932, which had been strongly emphasized in the trial.[20] Had Yagoda been doing his job properly, Stalin implied, he would have uncovered this plot when it first was hatched. Moreover, Yagoda seemed reluctant to follow the Zinoviev–Kamenev trial with a sequel, even though the leaders of the former 'Right opposition' had been implicated in the pre-trial investigations and the trial itself. One leader of the former Right opposition, Tomsky, committed suicide shortly after testimony in the trial implicated him on 19 August. On the 23rd *Pravda* briefly reported his death, asserting as an established fact that he had been linked with 'counter-revolutionary Trotskyite–Zinovievite terrorists', a clear indication of what Stalin wanted to do with Tomsky's former colleagues Bukharin and Rykov. At the same time, workers' meetings called for an investigation of these two and also of Radek and Piatakov, even though the latter tried to demonstrate his orthodoxy by contributing to *Pravda* a piece headed 'Mercilessly Destroy the Despicable Murderers and Traitors'. Since the 'workers' did not mention the investigation of

Tomsky, it must be assumed that he died before 21 August, probably the 19th or 20th.[21]

Despite this obvious pressure for another trial, *Pravda* on 10 September revealed that the investigation of Bukharin and Rykov had been dropped for lack of evidence. Which among the influential men in Soviet politics had managed this reversal of Stalin's wishes is not clear, but any member of the Central Committee might have felt uneasy about the prosecution of men who were still sitting in their midst. Piatakov, who was perhaps the most important administrator of heavy industry in the whole system, was a full member of the Committee, Bukharin and Rykov candidate members. It is plausible that many Committee members had hoped to appease Stalin by giving him what he had sought for so long, the heads of the unpopular and discredited Zinoviev and Kamenev. But Piatakov and the former Rightist leaders were another matter. Possibly Stalin struck a bargain with the moderates: he would relent on Bukharin and Rykov if they would agree to replace Yagoda with Yezhov. This was done on 26 September, the very day after he had wired his demand from Sochi.[22]

Stalin's elevation of Yezhov was wondrously rapid. Just over forty in 1936, this protégé was a former factory worker who joined the party in 1917 and worked for some years as a regional official in its apparatus before joining the staff of the Secretariat. About 1930 he took on the important job of running the personnel section, a post in which Khrushchev, as Yezhov's subordinate, found him 'diligent and reliable'. This administrative specialty involved Yezhov in the purging of the party in 1933–6 and in 1935 led to his assumption of the additional job of heading the Commission of Party Control, which dealt with disciplinary infractions in the party. But none of this involved him directly in police work, nor did he have a reputation for bloodthirstiness in dealing with Bolsheviks. In 1936 Stalin evidently decided that Yezhov was the man to clean up the opposition once and for all, entrusted him with the supervision of the August trial and then promoted him to narkom of Internal Affairs – the police and Gulag. Georgy Malenkov, who was also on his way up in the staff of the Secretariat, succeeded Yezhov as head of the personnel section, but, Khrushchev recalls, Yezhov 'kept his seniority over Malenkov, which explains why the supervision of personnel fell under the control of the NKVD [police]'.[23]

Only thirteen months after becoming head of the police Yezhov became a candidate member of the Politburo and a full member of the Secretariat, the first police boss to enjoy these distinctions.[24] But the most glorious aspect of his success was his association with Stalin in the official imagery of 1937, standing as close to the Leader as Voroshilov and Molotov, or perhaps ahead of them in that he alone rejoiced in the informal title of 'Iron Commissar' and Stalin's references to him as 'our mailed fist'. Yezhov appeared beside Stalin on a variety of important occasions, such as the reception of newly heroic aviators, and he particularly benefited from the opening of the Moscow–Volga Canal, the second major waterway built by Gulag. Still delighted with the achievements of this institution, Stalin, who so rarely visited economic achievements, personally inspected the new canal on 22 April 1937 in the company of Voroshilov, Molotov, Zhdanov and Yezhov. The latter, incidentally, was a small man in physique, barely reaching to Stalin's chin in some photographs, and the military-style hat and overcoat that he wore in April 1937 seemed several sizes too big for him. This gave Yezhov a deceptively comic, harmless appearance. The canal also brought him an Order of Lenin and a gala celebration at the Bolshoi Theatre in July, honoured by Stalin's attendance. Before the year was out he stood at the centre of another major festivity at the Bolshoi, the twentieth anniversary of the founding of the police. But by this time something seems to have soured in his remarkable career. Stalin was absent.[25]

Any implication that Yezhov and not Stalin was supreme is unjustified, but the most widespread arrests, deportations to Gulag and executions among the Soviet élite did occur during Yezhov's tenure as head of the police, September 1936–December 1938, and it is highly probable that the violence and scope of these repressions owed something to his personal management or mismanagement of Stalin's terror. Although the number of arrests of 'enemies of the people' cannot be documented on a monthly basis, it seems that Yezhov's first few months in police work were relatively restrained. True, there was in November a publicized trial of alleged wreckers in a coal-mine at Kemerovo in the Urals, and a continuation of a campaign of arrests, already in progress under Yagoda, against 'Trotskyites' in various provincial cities.[26] But 1936, unlike 1937, is not a year remembered with mythic dread by the Soviet élite of that generation. According to Khruschev's speech to the party congress of 1956, the number of arrests for counter-revolutionary crimes increased tenfold from 1936 to 1937. But, given the extremely high (though unknown) figure that the latter year represents, it is hard to account for even one-tenth of its casualties in 1936.[27] The closing months of that year were indeed the time when the party purge that had started in 1933 finally drew to a close, as the admission of new members was resumed in November. About the end of the year the 'exchange of documents' was completed, ending the 'purge' in its traditional, non-violent form.[28]

Former 'Right deviationists' seem to have been left alone in late 1936, and Stalin went out of his way to demonstrate that he had accepted Bukharin's innocence, inviting him to stand on the Lenin Mausoleum during the observances in November of the anniversary of the revolution. But if the investigation of Bukharin and Rykov had been ended in September for 'lack of evidence', no such grace had been extended to Radek, Piatakov, Serebriakov and Sokolnikov, whose investigation the chief prosecutor had ordered during the August trial.[29] These four were the principal victims of the trial of the 'Trotskyite Centre' in January 1937, which implied that they were arrested in the first month or two of Yezhov's career in the police, since some time was required to arrange their confessions. According to the trial record, Sokolnikov was under interrogation as early as 30 November. The official name of the trial reflects Stalin's calculation that he would have a much easier time persuading influential party members of the need to quash 'Trotskyites' than to execute former Rightists.[30] This probably helped him to get away with a striking violation of intra-party legality when Piatakov was arrested without having been expelled from the party by a two-thirds vote of the Central Committee. At this stage it seems that Stalin did not want to have any of his policies discussed by the Committee, for he did not convene it between June 1936 and February 1937, breaking the pattern of the two previous years in which there had been three regular sessions per year. Excepting Piatakov, no other member of the Central Committee seems to have been arrested in 1936, but that precedent and the omission of regular sessions of the body was an ominous sign of Stalin's developing attitude toward the party élite.[31]

The 'Trial of the Anti-Soviet Trotskyite Centre' went off in reasonably good form on 23–30 January 1937, despite some lapses in the planning of the confessions. For example, the script had Piatakov flying to visit Trotsky in Oslo in 1935 and landing at an airport that in fact recorded no activity at all during anything resembling the period in question. The prisoners confessed. Vyshinsky and Demian Bedny, among others, excoriated the Trotskyites' treasonous deeds, the latter publishing a poem entitled 'A Steel Fortress', making the obvious pun on the name Stalin. Piatakov and twelve others were sentenced to be shot, while Radek and Sokolnikov, probably as a reward for co-operation, were merely given ten years, of which they actually survived very few. The main idea was that a Trotskyite conspiracy had tried to carry on separately after the murder of Kirov and the break-up of the former bloc of Zinovievites and Trotskyites. But not quite alone, for the confessions reintroduced the Rightists, and especially Bukharin, with whom the Trotskyites supposedly maintained contact. The familiar accusation of murder was still present, and the list of intended targets now was expanded to include Molotov (whose absence from the list of 1936 may have been a sign that Stalin was displeased with his chief lieutenant at that time) and Yezhov, a sign of his new eminence. But wrecking, the sabotage of industrial operations, displaced assassination as the chief activity of the enemies of the people. This had several advantages from Stalin's perspective. It was familiar, thanks to various previous trials. There were real mine disasters and railway accidents to 'prove' that the criminals had actually carried out some of their plans. And various calamities and chronic shortcomings of the economic system could be blamed on the class enemy; for example, 'At the Kemerovo mine the Trotskyites gassed pits and created intolerable conditions for the workers.' As in the 1936 trial the Trotskyites supposedly had collaborated with Nazis, and now the Japanese and Poles. Not only did they gather intelligence from the Trotskyite agents, they plotted war, which would, so the Trotskyites hoped, bring down the socialist government and enable the Trotskyites to take over, returning the country to capitalism.[32]

It is easy enough for the outsider to deride all this as farcical, but it may be argued that Stalin had greatly improved his use of show trial confessions as propaganda. No longer was the supposed struggle primarily a shoot-out between a few top-level leaders. It involved the suffering of large numbers of ordinary citizens, killed or maimed in 'accidents', and a threatened invasion by foreign armies. The theme of patriotism against treason was greatly enhanced in the supporting propaganda, which repeated charges that the Trotskyites were selling out the Motherland. Winter was an inclement season for patriotic exploits by aviators, but the centennial of Pushkin's death, starting a week after the trial was over (and off the pages of *Pravda*), and lasting two weeks, replete with public gatherings, served to celebrate Russian nationalism. The commemoration of deaths is customary in Russian culture, but the stress on this one, and its unnecessary use of patriotic references ('Glory to Russian People!' read one headline), suggests some deliberate manipulation of the occasion.[33]

Piatakov was shot on 1 February, his appeal for clemency having been rejected along with others. On 18 February Sergo Ordzhonikidze, his immediate superior in industrial administration, who had relied heavily on him and regarded him as a friend, shot himself.[34] Stalin inspired suicide, or attempts thereat, in a number of people who were closely associated with him: his son Yakov, Nadezhda Allilueva, Tomsky, Orzhonikidze and Bukharin. Not as close to Stalin among the suicides were the oppositionist Lominadze, the military commissar Yan Gamarnik and Mikhail Kaganovich, brother of Lazar and a member of the Central Committee, not to mention the obscure people who took their lives in despair in Gulag or in dread of being sent there.[35] It is unlikely that Stalin desired the self-destruction of all of these people, but in the case of Ordzhonikidze it is plausible that he pressed his old friend in that direction.

Sergo had been too long a hero and comrade-in-arms of the Leader to be killed as an enemy of the people without creating problems of explanation that should have troubled even Stalin. Yet Ordzhonikidze must have been causing serious difficulties around the opening of 1937, objecting strenuously to the intended execution of his friend and valued assistant Piatakov and of other industrial administrators who now were being arrested in serious numbers. As usual, information on who was arrested and when is insufficiently precise, but it seems fairly clear that before February 1937 there was no great wave of arrests among high party officials, military leaders, national minority élites and the police themselves. But the *Yezhovshchina* (an unofficial term which perhaps is translatable as 'the dreaded reign of Yezhov') already was under way among economic administrators. This was a campaign against 'wrecking' in industry, closely linked to the public trial of the industrial administrator Piatakov in January 1937.[36]

Khrushchev called Sergo 'chivalrous' and maintains that he had appealed to Khrushchev to try to mitigate the fate of Lominadze, a participant in the opposition of 1930. This in itself is revealing concerning the decline of Ordzhonikidze's relations with Stalin. Why should he, who was senior to Khrushchev in political rank and, especially, in friendship with Sergo's compatriot Stalin, have to try to seek the aid of Khrushchev, who had not yet reached the Politburo? In another anecdote about Sergo's efforts to save those threatened by Stalin, one of Svetlana's older friends told her of seeing the writer Maria Shaginian kneeling before Sergo in his office, begging for the life of an engineer who was accused of sabotage. A passionate and sometimes violent man, influential among important party members, Ordzhonikidze could cause Stalin trouble in ways that went beyond the saving of a few 'wreckers'. As an old friend of both Stalin and Yenukidze, Ordzhonikidze might have spread the word that Koba's personality was deteriorating, that he was capable of turning on anyone. A meeting of the Central Committee, scheduled for 19 February 1937 might have given Sergo the opening to do Stalin some serious harm.[37]

By January 1937 Stalin was subjecting his friend to vicious psychological pressure. One of Sergo's brothers, who also was an industrial administrator, was arrested. Medvedev, citing no sources, says that Stalin sent Ordzhonikidze transcripts of police interrogations of his friends that even implicated Sergo, and at the same time ordered him to give the forthcoming Central Committee meeting a report on wrecking in industry. On 16 January the police even searched Ordzhonikidze's apartment. Outraged, he tried to reach Stalin by phone, was stalled for hours and then told 'The NKVD can even search my apartment.' There was a violent face-to-face confrontation later that day, following which Sergo told Mikoyan that he 'couldn't go on living, . . . that it was impossible to tolerate what Stalin was doing to the party, and he didn't have the strength to fight it any more'. Possibly Stalin hoped to induce a heart attack in Ordzhonikidze, who was indeed suffering from a cardiac condition for which he had recently been on a rest cure in the Caucasus. But the evidence that Sergo shot himself is persuasive. Whatever Stalin's objective in his dealings with Ordzhonikidze, he seemed unruffled by the news of the suicide, coming quickly to the dead man's apartment along with Molotov and Zhdanov, ordering that the press announce a heart attack and publish a suitable physicians' report. To the objection of the widow that nobody would believe this, Stalin rightly replied, 'Why won't they believe it? Everyone knew he had a bad heart and everyone will believe it.' And so Ordzhonikidze joined the party pantheon beside the Lenin Mausoleum, Stalin participating prominently in the full-scale obsequies. The day after the press ended the tributes to Ordzhonikidze, candidate member of the Politburo Eikhe contributed a signed article to *Pravda* about the danger of Trotskyite saboteurs in industry.[38]

Delayed by the funeral, the Central Committee convened on 23 February. Despite the secrecy that still surrounds this crucial meeting, there are definite signs that Stalin encountered serious difficulties with the Committee concerning his determination to smash various alleged enemies. The formal resolutions of the meeting are one indication of the conflict. Normally such decisions of the Central Committee are published, but in this case only one of three was. It was based on the relatively harmless report presented by Zhdanov concerning elections within the party. Of the two others, one was based on what must have been a sensational and menacing report by Yezhov, 'Lessons Flowing from the Harmful Activity, Diversion and Espionage of the Japanese–German–Trotskyite Agents'. It became known only through Khrushchev's secret speech in 1956 and remains unpublished apart from a short excerpt that he provided, referring to the backwardness of the police in unmasking 'these most inexorable enemies of the people'. The third was based on Stalin's report, to be considered momentarily, 'On Deficiencies in Party Work and Measures for Liquidating Trotskyites and Other Double-dealers'.[39]

Another sign of difficulty in the session was its length, eleven days (23 February–5 March), which is much more than the longest session since 1934, which was only five days. This extended span probably included a two-day intermission while a subcommission, itself an exceptional measure, considered the 'guilt' of Bukharin and Rykov. They were allowed to speak in their defence but in the end were voted out of the party and thus placed on the path to trial and execution. There must have been some discussion of other cases too, for at some point P. P. Postyshev, a candidate member of the Politburo, defended an accused comrade named Karpov in a way that challenged the very foundations of Yezhovshchina:

> I personally do not believe that an honest party member who had trod the long road of unrelenting struggle against enemies for the party and for socialism, would now be in the camp of the enemies. I do not believe it. . . . I cannot imagine how it would be possible to travel with the party during the difficult years and then, in 1934, join the Trotskyites. It is an odd thing. . . .

This official confirmation that Postyshev spoke out against Stalin's ideas on class enemies adds credibility to reports circulating in the Vorkuta labour camp that there had been a broad agreement in the committee to remind Stalin that this body, and not any individual dictator, held power in the party. Normally Gulag rumours must be treated with great reserve, but in this case the story was correct concerning Postyshev's role, long before the Khrushchev speech of 1956.[40]

Stalin's two speeches to the Committee also imply that he encountered there serious resistance to the Yezhovshchina. These addresses, the only substantial published statements Stalin ever made on the subject of his reign of terror, appeared belatedly in *Pravda* on 29 March and 1 April, respectively. Evidently it was necessary to sanitize the speeches to some extent before they could be published, removing some of the more threatening passages. In 1956 Khrushchev unintentionally showed that this was the case: 'in one of his speeches [to the Central Committee in 1937] Stalin expressed his dissatisfaction with Postyshev and asked him, "What are you actually?" ' (The doomed man replied, 'I am a Bolshevik, Comrade Stalin, a Bolshevik.') No such passage appeared in the version of the speeches that was published in 1937, and one cannot say how much additional material, menacing to Stalin's opponents or his reluctant supporters, may have been excised.[41]

What was published is a lengthy discourse by Stalin on the need to crush 'spies, wreckers, diversionists, double-dealers, Trotskyites' who have penetrated 'all or almost all our organizations, both economic and administrative and party . . . not only the lower organizations but also some responsible posts'. Stalin attempted first to dispel scepticism concerning the alleged presence of so many and such influential enemy agents. We are encircled by capitalist states, he argued, and it is natural for them to try to infiltrate and destroy us with their agents. Thus it was in the time of the French Revolution, thus it is in relations among the capitalist states today. And these enemies of socialism have a new ally, Trotskyism, which has degenerated from being a tendency in the workers' movement, as it was seven or eight years previously, to being 'an unprincipled and ideology-less band of wreckers, diversionists, intelligence agents, spies, murderers'. The danger, said Stalin, had been underrated by Soviet officials because they were too absorbed in domestic concerns, especially economic achievements, falling prey to 'political blindness', despite the series of warnings that they should have heeded: the Shakhty trial, the Kirov assassination, the Central Committee letters of 1935 and 1936, the Zinoviev–Kamenev trial.[42]

Stalin was at particular pains to convince his audience of the transformation of Trotskyism. 'The mistake of our party comrades is that they are oblivious to this deep distinction between Trotskyism in the past and at present.' That such blindness was commonplace Stalin implied in his weighty, redundant conclusion to his speech of 3 March, consisting of six 'rotten theories' that must be 'smashed and thrown out'. These theories seem to have been arguments that he had heard in the Committee, perhaps in reply to Yezhov's report. Stalin's conception of these errors was menacing indeed, providing a theoretical basis for the expectation that the enemy was everywhere. First, it was a 'rotten theory' to think that growing Soviet success led to the class enemy becoming less dangerous. 'On the contrary,' said Stalin, 'the more we advance, the more we are successful, the more wrathful will become the remnants of the detested exploiting classes, . . . the more they seize on the most desperate means of struggle as the last resort of the doomed.' Second, third and fourth, Stalin proposed a conception of economic wrecking that left no executives invulnerable. Were they successful sometimes? That might be just a ruse. Did they fulfill plans? Perhaps they had deliberately arranged lowered targets or perhaps they only fulfilled some of the targets. Did they support the Stakhanov movement, the form of socialist competition named for a record-setting coal-miner and the focus of much attention from 1935? 'Noise and chatter' about Stakhanovism merely served to conceal wreckers. The fifth 'rotten theory' wrongly held that the Trotskyites have no 'reserves' left, the sixth that the enemy agents could do little harm because they were few and we many.[43]

Two days later, on 5 March, Stalin, having heard members of the Committee debate his report and a related draft resolution, appeared to soften his stance, perhaps in response to the discussion. It was agreed, he claimed, that we must 'mercilessly destroy and comb out, as enemies of the working class, as betrayers of our motherland', Trotskyites and Bukharinites. But did the draft resolution mean that this should be done not only to actual Trotskyites but also to those who might have sometimes 'wavered to the side of Trotskyism'? Of course not, claimed Stalin. There were some fine comrades who had once been Trotskyites or who had maintained personal ties with Trotskyites. While some participants in the debate (perhaps Yezhov and Molotov?) had been calling for the blood of these people, that would be an incorrect interpretation of the draft resolution. Those on the other side of the debate, he implied, had not dared openly to defend class enemies but had argued that the draft resolution stressed politics (a code-word for the Yezhovshchina) at the expense of effectiveness. On this Stalin claimed to be a moderate. The resolution did not mean that political considerations should be ignored in appraising the trustworthiness of officials, but the 'businesslike qualities' also should not be ignored. As if to solidify the impression that he was not threatening loyal Bolsheviks, Stalin concluded his remarks with an extended disquisition on the need for leaders to show consideration for the lower ranks, to learn from the people, like Anteus, drawing strength from the soil, to avoid 'formal and soulless bureaucratic attitudes' especially in the manner of expelling members from the party. But even in this display of compassion and moderation, there was a veiled threat to party officials. The lofty ones, such as provincial secretaries, acted as arbitrary authorities, building up 'families' of client-officials. Stalin implied that they should be taken down a notch, their shortcomings exposed by 'verification from below', which was a code-word for denunciation as class enemies. And as for those who committed excesses in the expulsion of party members, they assisted the Trotskyites by fomenting discontent.[44]

Perhaps Stalin's display of reasonableness won a unanimous vote for the resolution he wanted, but the fact that it has not been published, apart from snippets that run in opposite directions, suggests that it was in his eyes an unsatisfactory document. This, and some of the other signs that Stalin had trouble with the Central Committee, may be debatable evidence. But his subsequent actions toward the Committee demonstrated all too plainly that he was sorely displeased: he killed almost all of them. Khrushchev's statement to the party congress of 1956 that 98 out of 139 Committee members and candidates, 70 per cent, were arrested and shot, 'mostly in 1937–1938', does not do justice to this carnage.[45] Consider those whom he spared. Four were harmless old Bolsheviks. Three were people with special symbolic importance for various interests. Another was Stalin's, and Voroshilov's, military crony Budenny, and two were minor, unaccountably lucky men. The remaining fourteen were his close henchmen, all of them Politburo members (if not in 1937, then in a few years), excepting one of Beria's closest associates and two members of Stalin's personal secretariat. All the rest were killed. The survival of those closest to Stalin seems politically rational. If he meant to weed out a large number of officials who stood below the apex of the pyramid, he needed a reliable cluster of deputies, men whom he had known well since the 1920s or before (Andreev, Voroshilov, Kaganovich, Kalinin, Mikoyan, Molotov) or those whom he had selected in the early 1930s (Beria, Zhdanov, Khrushchev, Shvernik – and one should add Malenkov, although he was in Stalin's personal secretariat and not yet in the Central Committee in 1937). With respect to psychopathology the most obvious point here is that Stalin's suspicions were under control, that he could bring himself to repose great trust in his cronies, that he was not turning viciously on them, as he had on Kirov, Yenukidze and Ordzhonikidze. Later in life he would again begin to kill or threaten those closest to him, but during the height of the Yezhovshchina Stalin showed substantial restraint in this respect. This is not to say that the Politburo offered reliable protection to its own. Two members, V. Ya. Chubar and S. V. Kosior, and four candidate members, R. I. Eikhe, Postyshev, Ya. E. Rudzutak and eventually Yezhov himself, fell victim.[46]

Nor did Stalin spare other full members of the Central Committee who never held Politburo rank but must have worked personally with Stalin over a number of years. Among these were three heads of subdivisions of the party Secretariat, nine narkoms or deputy chairmen of the Sovnarkom, eight secretaries of provincial or federal republican party organizations, and the heads of the Commission of Soviet Control and of the Komsomol, the secretary of the Comintern, the chairman of the Council of People's Commissars of the Russian Federal Republic and his deputy.[47]

These and other Committee members were 'shot' according to Khrushchev, which is to say that none of them were sent to Gulag to expiate their sins, the fate of a vastly larger number of victims of the Yezhovshchina. That Stalin meted out certain death (not merely the likelihood of it in the camps) to 'enemies of the people' who stood so high in the pyramid of power seems to reflect a conviction that such influential figures were too dangerous to be spared on any terms. And, as Khrushchev also said, and studies of individual cases confirmed, most of the victims were arrested in 1937–8, which is to say in the year and a half or so after the February–March session of 1937. There is no reason to think that any Committee member was arrested before the end of the session, except for Piatakov, who was tried in January, and Bukharin and Rykov, who were arrested during the session. But during the next meeting of the Committee, 23–9 June 1937, the depredations of Yezhov must have been well started, and one can only speculate on the mood of the dwindling band of survivors as they debated the improvement of seed for grain agriculture and a few other innocuous matters.[48]

If it was not entirely as a result of the February–March session (and its long string of antecedents in which Stalin found his punitive wrath partially frustrated), it was surely in the wake of this event that the Yehovshchina swelled mightily, spreading out beyond the search for 'wreckers' in economic administration and into every other sector of the upper orders of Soviet society. Stalin's speech at the session had singled out senior regional party officials as a suspect category. According to *Pravda*, these potentates had been slow in rooting out wreckers. This implies that the same shortcoming had been manifested in the Central Committee by those among the regional secretaries who were members of that body. They were also guilty, so Stalin had told the Committee, of becoming satraps who obeyed orders from the centre more or less as they pleased. Thus his wrath on the issue of oppositionists merged with his frustration toward the general problem of insubordination. Stalin alluded acerbicly to this matter in his report to the February–March session, linking the questions of political vigilance and administrative insubordination. The attitude of the regional potentates to his central authority was, in his caricature of it, insufferable. 'Capitalist encirclement? That's rubbish [say the regional bosses]. . . . New forms of wrecking, struggle with Trotskyism? All that's trivia! . . . Strange people sit in Moscow, in the Central Committee: they concoct some kinds of questions, nag about some sort of wrecking, they don't sleep themselves and they don't let others sleep.' This last reference was no metaphor but an unmistakable allusion to Stalin's own, eccentric work pattern and his practice of telephoning officials after midnight.[49]

Given these frustrations and the flowering of Stalin's homicidal tendency, it is not surprising that the regional party leaders suffered severely in 1937–8. Medvedev has identified 206 secretaries of regional party organizations (down to the rural and city district level) who perished. To remove the top level of regional satraps, potentially a difficult operation because these men had political machines of their own, Stalin dispatched members of his own inner circle as special legates. The discovery that a regional party boss was an 'enemy of the people' inevitably led to the liquidation of most of his staff, the 'family' that Stalin had castigated at the February–March session of the Central Committee. At that time he still referred to L. I. Mirzoyan as 'comrade', but there could be little doubt that this experienced party administrator was in deep trouble when Stalin observed that Mirzoyan, when appointed party boss of Kazakhstan, had taken with him '30–40 of "his own" people' from his former baliwicks and had 'placed them in responsible posts in Kazakhstan'. It was not necessary for Mirzoyan, psychologically and physically pressured by interrogators, to incriminate these staff members, although he may have done this. Their association with an 'enemy of the people' could condemn them.[50]

Thus did the Yezhovshchina expand by geometric progression. It would be far too simple to say that the arrests started at the top and expanded downwards as administrative subordinates were inculpated by their supervisors. But it is probably safe to say that Stalin's decision to have done with oppositionists within the Central Committee guaranteed a massive wave of arrests, executions and sentences to Gulag in all branches of the Soviet system. It was, in T. H. Rigby's terminology, 'mono-organizational'.[51] All institutions, except, perhaps, the churches, were integrated into a single complex, with the party and its Central Committee at the centre. A round-up of economic 'wreckers' who were not in most cases at the top level was bound to lead through painfully extracted confessions up the chain of command to the people at the centre. Incrimination of these would lead down the hierarchies beneath them as their staff and the staff of their staff were involved. Given that party officials were responsible not only for the party itself, but also for agriculture, industry, education, science, public health, the arts, and almost every other sphere of life, it was inevitable that their contagion would infect the professions that had not been involved with the original drive against economic 'wreckers' or the party bosses who 'sheltered' them.

The emergence of a highly uniform pattern in the handling of information about the Yezhovshchina is persuasive evidence that Stalin himself was responsible for its design.[52] A few selected events, especially the three show trials of 1936–8, received massive publicity, while the disappearance of unknown thousands of other people officially never happened. Arrests usually took place in the middle of the night, or in any case in circumstances that caused the ingestion of the victims into the police system with few witnesses to their actual departure. Communication between the victims and their friends and relatives almost totally ceased after the arrest, although the fortunate might be permitted some correspondence if they became settled in Gulag. In many cases, especially on the higher levels, the spouses and children of the victims also vanished from society, transported to Gulag or, in the cases of many children, into state homes for orphans. The main advantage of this cruel arrangement was that it reinforced the superficial impression that Soviet society was its normal, joyous self, for the visible residue of bereft widows, widowers and orphans was minimized. The survivors readily understood without being told that the terror was not something that they should discuss, even to comment upon favourably, except behind the closed doors of a party meeting at which it appeared timely to denounce this or that comrade. Other denunciations, to be sure, went on in the privacy of police offices.

Meanwhile, the press rarely mentioned the terror. Apart from the fairly brief, intense propaganda campaigns at the time of the four main trials, there were only occasional articles on vigilance against the class enemy, containing few references to particular cases, and by no means providing a record of the enormous personnel turnover in high places. True, in September 1937 a spate of articles in *Pravda* revealed the unmasking of Fascist–Trotskyite–Burkharinite agents among minority nationalities, from Karelia to Uzbekistan, although this did not reveal the scope of the massacre of the minority élites.[53] Much more prominent in the press than negative communications about the class enemy were exceptionally long lists of recipients, mainly ordinary citizens, of labour awards, or (in season) reportage of fresh exploits of heroic aviators, or historical pieces on notable men of letters and science, such as Pushkin, Gogol and Mendeleev. One ingredient in the positive propaganda that seems to have been somewhat diminished in 1937, but certainly not absent, was the personal image of Stalin. Quantified studies of *Pravda* show a sharp drop in verbal and pictorial references to the Leader, and a sharp increase in the emphasis placed on ordinary proletarians, in 1937–8.[54] He published next to nothing over his own name between March 1937 and September 1938. This represented no curtailment of Stalin's status, merely a fine-tuning of the official myth to suit grim events. Best to provide reinforcement of the notion that this was the workers' state and their own struggle, while avoiding any impression that it was basically Stalin's affair.

And what was Stalin doing personally during the Yezhovshchina? On the whole he appears to have maintained his normal work routine in

Moscow, departing for his accustomed holiday in the south between late
August and October in 1937, but not in 1938.[55] The direction of the terror
must have required a substantial effort, so it was necessary to delegate a
good deal of the work. Kaganovich, Malenkov, Mikoyan and Beria were
dispatched to direct major purges of regional party organizations. Yezhov,
of course, was responsible for the mainstream of arrests, interrogations
and sentences, submitting for Stalin's approval in 1937–8 383 lists
containing 'many thousands' of individual names and proposed sentences.
Considering that Yezhov probably was not in charge of such operations
beyond the middle of 1938, this appears to mean that the perusal of such
a list was almost a daily feature of Stalin's routine. It should have been
simple enough for the Khrushchevian investigators to add up the total
number of names that crossed Stalin's desk in this way, but no sum was
released, probably because it was so embarrassingly immense. In February
1956 the number of 'rehabilitated' persons stood at 7679, according to
Khrushchev, but he noted that the review of the convictions was still in
progress and that 'a great portion of them' were being overturned. It
therefore seems safe to conclude that the total number of convictions
approved by Stalin was at least in the tens of thousands, which is not to
say that the procedure gave all of the less-important victims the
questionable benefit of his personal approval of their fates.[56]

Capacious though his memory was, it is impossible that he could have
known much, if anything, about most of these victims, and the only
available example of the kind of list Yezhov sent him shows that the
format did not provide any individual detail (certainly not evidence of
guilt) but merely lists of names according to category ('general', 'former
military personnel', 'former police personnel', 'wives of enemies of the
people'), followed by the request for conviction 'in the first degree' (to be
shot). Stalin strongly discouraged any complication of this procedure
through appeals by victims or their friends. When a regional party official,
I. M. Vareikis, tried to intercede by telephone on behalf of some accused
officers, 'Stalin shouted, "It's none of your business! Don't interfere
where you don't belong!"' And Vareikis was soon arrested. At least three
members of the Politburo – Eikhe, Rudzutak and Chubar – managed to
reach Stalin with appeals by letter to the Politburo. Eikhe and Rudzutak,
and the military leader Yakir, managed to reach Stalin with unsuccessful
appeals on their own behalf, but this seems to have been an exceptional
privilege of rank.[57]

Stalin seems to have kept his distance from the physical reality of the
terror. There is no reliable evidence that he ever attended an interrogation,
an execution or a trial. He did, however, find merriment in a black joke
about a professor, the neighbour of a police officer, who once told the
latter that he was so ignorant that he did not know who wrote *Eugene
Onegin*. Thereupon he was arrested and the officer soon boasted that the

professor had confessed that *he* wrote it. But usually no one laughed, Stalin's daughter recalled. This is not surprising, because Stalin generally did not permit in his presence any cynical discussion of the innocence or guilt of the victims of the terror, maintaining the pretence that he took seriously the entire lurid ritual, with its Nazi–Jewish blocs, herds of poisoned pigs, butter laced with glass and nails, and vast numbers of would-be assassins, plotting against him and his friends, even against Kosior and Postyshev who themselves turned out to be enemies of the people. Molotov, Voroshilov and other members of the Politburo had to co-sign at least some of the lists of victims, and on at least one occasion Stalin even asked Molotov 'What to do?' But actual discussion of the merits of any case seems to have been rare.[58]

But if Stalin delegated much of the work of the great terror of 1937–8, he no doubt paid close attention to both of the last two major trials of the period. The first of these destroyed most of the high command of the Red Army. Despite the presence of a special apparatus for political control within the army, the Main Political Administration and its network of political officers, the army possessed a greater sense of *esprit de corps* than other state agencies, not to mention weapons. The case of Marshal Tukhachevsky, a candidate member of the Central Committee, required special attention. Stalin had long been on poor terms with this talented, somewhat erratic leader. Ever since the Soviet–Polish war of 1920 there had been recriminations concerning Tukhachevsky's failure to take Warsaw, or Stalin's failure to give him adequate assistance, depending on one's perspective.[59] The friction was renewed in the early 1930s. Tukhachevsky was responsible for the modernization of the Red Army and pressed Stalin for massive expenditure, which the latter rejected as incompatible with the needs of civilian industrial investment, branding Tukhachevsky's plan as 'Red Militarism'. With some petulance and insubordination Tukhachevsky in 1930 protested to Stalin that the decision prevented him from dealing with vital questions, that he was excluded from the Military Academy, and that his proposal had suffered 'unprincipled distortion'. At the time Stalin snubbed this complaint, but in 1932 he reversed himself and wrote to Tukhachevsky that he had been wrong about the latter's plan and offered his apologies for taking so long to correct his mistake. Stalin had become an ardent advocate of a major military build-up and for the time being found Tukhachevsky useful, but it is highly unlikely that he forgave the officer's insubordination. It is significant, too, that they communicated by letter, implying that Tukhachevsky was not among the senior personnel whom he chose to meet personally.

Stalin linked the high command in the alleged network of treason by implicating in the trial of August 1936 the military attaché to Great Britain, V. K. Putna. This was a bad sign for Tukhachevsky, who had visited this officer in London the previous February while serving as Soviet representative at the funeral of King George V. At the second purge trial of February 1937 there was a new menace when the defendant Radek mentioned that Putna had come to him once with 'some request from Tukhachevsky'. While Radek added that Tukhachevsky was not an enemy agent, in the circumstances this was far from reassuring to the marshal. In the following months Tukhachevsky was the victim of a rumour campaign and on 11 May was transferred to an unimportant regional command. Deeply depressed, he wrote a letter to Stalin, but received no known reply, unless his arrest on the 26th was the reply.[60]

Meanwhile Stalin had been preparing on a broader front for the purge of the officers. Soon after the Central Committee meeting of February–March 1937 the police 'discovered' a 'Counter-revolutionary Military Fascist Organization', a normal prerequisite for a major trial, paralleling the 'Trotskyite–Zinovievite Terrorist Centre', for example. Evidence on this was extracted from prisoners and, perhaps, provided by the fabrication of documents prepared in Germany by Nazi intelligence in collaboration with White Russian emigrant officers who had links with both the Germans and the NKVD. These forgeries were then leaked to the Czechoslovak government which helpfully submitted them to its Soviet ally. This elaborate ruse may not have worked well enough to satisfy Stalin, and he may or may not have used the documents in putting the case before the military authorities (that is, those not about to be liquidated) or the party.[61] In any case it indicated his apprehension concerning the potential power of the military and the possibility that the officers would be less malleable confessors than the civilians. The same concern was manifest at the beginning of June when Stalin made a personal appearance at the session of the Military Council, an advisory body of the People's Commissariat of Defence, to deliver a report on the alleged military conspiracy, something that he never did with any civilian body after the Central Committee session of early 1937. He even replied to 'numerous' questions about his charges, using 'the fabricated testimony of repressed military figures', material that he also circulated among members of the Politburo.[62] On 11 June 1937 Tukhachevsky and seven other senior officers (not to mention Gamarnik, head of the Main Political Administration, who had committed suicide in anticipation of his fate) were secretly tried by a court consisting of Voroshilov and about nine other officers. Justice was swift; the accused were convicted and found guilty within an hour or so, sentenced to death and shot. The public learned of the trial and its outcome on 11–12 June only through short notices which provided no details.[63] This procedure stood in contrast to the civilian trials, but the subsequent spasm of mass meetings, resolutions and letters to newspapers concerning the 'traitors' followed the established pattern, as did Demian Bedny's poem. There was also a magnificent aviation exploit – surely arranged to turn mass opinion back to the positive side of Soviet life – a flight by Chkalov and two comrades across the North Pole to the United States, probably the most impressive feat of 'Stalin's falcons'.[64]

The purge that had started at the top of the officer corps spread downward in the year following June 1937, gradually diminishing in force in 1938–9. In an unusual personal intervention Stalin pushed it along in early August 1937 by delivering a secret speech to a conference of political officers. When one of them asked, 'Can one speak without reservation of "enemies of the people?"', Stalin replied, 'To the whole world . . . it is an obligatory duty.' In December 1937 he placed the political administration of the army under his former personal secretary, Mekhlis, who intensified the campaign by discovering a new enemy, the 'Anti-party Army Belorussian–Tolmachev Group'. The following April Stalin was still pressing for 'the Bolshevization of the Red Army' in a letter entitled 'On Inadequacies in Party-political Work in the Red Army', addressed to a special conference of political workers in the military. The last top-level military arrest, that of Marshal V. K. Bliukher, commander of the Far East, did not come until October 1939.[65]

Bukharin and Rykov had been arrested during the February–March session of the Central Committee in 1937, but it was only a year later, 2–13 March 1938, that they were tried along with nineteen others. This turned out to be the last of Stalin's show trials on Soviet territory, and it seems clear that he intended it as the climax of this form of mass education. Along with Bukharin and Rykov, Yagoda, the former chief of police, was among the accused. This was a bravura feat of confession-management, considering that Yagoda knew enough about previous trials to do serious damage if he departed from the script. In addition to these three, there were among the defendants three more full members of the Central Committee as elected in 1934: V. I. Ivanov, Ya. A. Zelensky and A. Ikramov. Like Yagoda, they had not been expelled from the party by a two-thirds (or any other) vote of the Central Committee, as required by the party statutes. Apart from those indicated, all the important men convicted in the two preceding trials were once again condemned in the testimony, as were some prominent victims – especially Tukhachevsky and Yenukidze – who had fallen after secret trials in 1937. For them and also for Rudzutak, the first Stalinist member of the Politburo to become an enemy of the people, the Bukharin trial served as a surrogate trial.[66]

The prosecution case was more than an elaboration of the alleged link between the 'Rights' and the supposed Trotskyite–Zinovievite–Fascist coalition. It strained to establish that diverse culprits had been covert enemies at varying times in the relatively remote past. Yagoda, for example, admitted that he never had been a Bolshevik, having been a bourgeois from birth, which helped explain why he had become infatuated with Hitler. Bukharin and Rykov had been deviators from Leninism as far back as 1909 and, most importantly, Bukharin and Trotsky supposedly had plotted in 1918 to kill Lenin. While confessing to general responsibility for the crimes of the Right, Bukharin steadily denied all charges of terrorism. But the prosecution produced from the jails former Left Socialist Revolutionaries and Left Communists to bear witness to Bukharin's conspiracy. The state also found, outside the court-room, the means of persuading another uncooperative defendant, Krestinsky, to withdraw an embarrassing recantation of his entire pre-trial confession.[67]

A particular novelty of the 1938 trial was its emphasis on the alleged use of poisons and medical maltreatment by the assassins of Soviet leaders. This heightened the sense of horror that the public was meant to feel toward the enemy, assuming that people would believe that Menzhinsky was murdered by exposure to the fumes of ordinary house paint. It also had the advantage of compensating for the previous absence of any actual victims of assassination, apart from Kirov. Thanks to the appearance of three Kremlin physicians among the accused, as tools of the political masterminds, it was possible to show that Gorky and his son, Menzhinsky and Kuibyshev, had all been poisoned by various means. This has led to speculation that the charge might be true and that Stalin was responsible for these killings. There is no way to prove his innocence, but it is hard to see why he would have ordered these murders, even taking into account his penchant for killing during the latter half of the 1930s. Gorky had disappointed Stalin, but the elderly writer seemed under control and still a propaganda asset in 1935–6. In June 1935, for example, the relatively non-partisan image of Gorky played a major and successful role at the anti-Fascist 'First International Congress for Writers for the Defence of Culture'. Maxim did not attend, but his name and a message that he sent to the Congress were prominent features of the affair. The whole tale of medical murders probably was introduced at the 1938 trial to lend credibility to the charge that assassins really had killed some notables. It also is possible that Yezhov invented at least part of this business to enhance his own importance. The prisoners confessed that Yagoda, upon learning that he was losing his job, plotted to kill his successor, Yezhov, by spraying his office with 'mercury solution'.[68]

Eighteen of the defendants, including Bukharin, Rykov and Yagoda, were sentenced to death, the other three to prison, and the established rituals of public indignation ran their course. This time, however, there was no poem by Demian Bedny. He had been on troubled terms with Stalin for years, and despite his efforts to please, was now an outcast, but not an enemy of the people. As for feats of heroism that could serve to balance the revelations of treason, the season was inclement for polar aviation. But Stalin had arranged a convenient alternative. He had been keeping the Arctic explorer I. D. Papinin literally on ice, awaiting the time when the public needed something to cheer about. Papinin and three comrades had been camped for nine months on an Arctic ice-flow which had drifted nearly to southern Greenland. In early February 1939, by which time the schedule of the Bukharin trial had been determined, Papinin was notified that he would be brought home by ice-breaker. This was done, and he arrived in Moscow for a mass welcome and reception by Stalin in the Kremlin just on the heels of the executions.[69]

11 Peace

On 11 December 1937 Stalin gave a speech that should have caused the perceptive listener to fear that the Leader's mental state was slipping wholly out of control. The setting was the ornate Bolshoi Theatre, and the occasion was meant to be joyous, optimistic. It was a special meeting of the voters of the 'Stalin' electoral district, assembled to hear speeches on the eve of the election of deputies to the Supreme Soviet, the parliament established by the 'Stalin Constitution' which had been adopted the previous year. Stalin had been nominated by 3346 districts as their deputy, but could stand as a candidate only in one, which turned out to be central Moscow. The build-up for the election had included speeches by all the political magnates except Stalin, and on this occasion those among his lieutenants who were in Moscow were not required to speak again. They merely sat in the audience to hear appropriately grateful, celebratory speeches by two factory workers, a physician, a teacher and a housewife.[1]

Then Khrushchev, who as party boss of Moscow was serving as master of ceremonies, called on Stalin to speak. Stalin's style on this occasion was not that of a major set-piece address, such as a report to a party congress, but seemed to be an ad lib talk, like one he had given at the ceremony marking the opening of the Moscow Metro in 1935. It was rambling enough, personal enough, and sufficiently at odds with the optimistic character of the occasion that one wonders if he was quite sober.[2]

Stalin began in a familiar, joking tone, saying that 'the esteemed Nikita Sergeevich [Khrushchev] had used force, you might say, to drag him into coming here, to the meeting. Give, he [Khrushchev] said, a good speech.' Here Stalin attributed to Khrushchev use of the familiar second-person singular, as if he often gave orders to the General Secretary. Stalin continued this humble tone, denying that he was able to give some kind of ceremonial repetition of all that others had said about the constitution. From such modesty he then shifted to a solemn reaffirmation of his greatness, humbly thanking the electors for their confidence. 'I know what confidence means. Naturally it places on me new, additional responsibilities . . . among us Bolsheviks, it is inadmissable to decline responsibilities. I accept it willingly.' Then the ordinary first-person usage vanished: 'you may confidently rely on Comrade Stalin. You may count on it that Comrade Stalin is able to fulfil his duty to the people.' Here his rhetoric evoked a being far above the ordinary mortal that stood before the audience, a power to be addressed in the third person in a spirit of awed detachment.

Following a few words about the merits of the constitution, Stalin then shifted to a wholly unexpected theme, incongruous in the festive, self-congratulatory and optimistic mood of the occasion: the weakness of the human material at his disposal and the division of the universe into the forces of God and the devil. Had he planned this strange, self-revelatory excursion? Setting an unattainably lofty standard, Stalin asserted that deputies to the new soviets should be like Lenin, 'clear and well-defined persons', 'fearless in battle and merciless to the enemies of the people, like Lenin', 'free from any panic', like Lenin. Given the impossibility for most mortals of living up to heroic myths, it is not surprising that Stalin had to advise his listeners that there were candidates for election who did not meet this standard: 'There are people of which one cannot say what they really are, if they are good, if they are bad, if they are brave, if they are cowards, if they are for the people to the end, if they are enemies of the people. We have them even among us, among Bolsheviks.' Folk-wisdom expressed this, said Stalin, in the saying 'such a person is neither fish nor meat, neither a candle for God nor a poker for the devil'. The last phrase so attracted him that he repeated it a moment later: 'among our candidates and our prominent personages' there were those who 'by their character, by their physiognomy, remind one of people of that type of which the people say, "neither a candle for God nor a poker for the devil"'.

How were Stalin's listeners to respond to this cloud of pessimism and hint of rejection by the remote being whom Stalin called Stalin? The audience in the Bolshoi Theatre could only follow the accepted norms and greet the speech with 'stormy, long, unsubsiding applause, turning into an ovation'. Among other ejaculations one supposedly heard, 'Long live the first Leninist candidate for deputy to the Soviet of the Union, Comrade Stalin, Hurrah!' The editorial in *Pravda* the next day skirted the ominous implications of his remarks, blandly noting that Stalin advised electors to keep their deputies under control.[3]

For Stalin's lieutenants, and indeed all officials of the regime, the tone of the speech had been a portent of continued or even more devastating slaughter. Stalin, it seemed, no longer felt sure of anybody. There were enemies of the people among the nominees to the Supreme Soviet, and all surviving Central Committee members were nominees. The devil was abroad within the party, contending with . . . God? Stalin? Was it Stalin who encouraged chief prosecutor Vyshinsky to mention in the trial of 1936 'Trotsky's cloven hoof'?[4] But not all unsatisfactory comrades served Satan; some were merely uncommitted, worthless. This seems to be an allusion to officials who had not defended the class enemy but had been reluctant to give the Yezhovshchina unlimited support, the kind of foot-dragging that Stalin had excoriated at the February–March session of the

Central Committee. But what was one to do with these people? Folk-wisdom seemed to imply that it was better to be one thing or another than a worthless opportunist. Despite Stalin's suggestion that you can identify opportunists by their physiognomies, the speech seemed to imply that he no longer was sure that he could tell who these people were, and might kill any number to be on the safe side.

The surviving members of the Central Committee, and we cannot say how many there were at the time, must have had such concerns very much in mind when that body met in January 1938, a month after this speech. Direct evidence on this assembly is scanty. Until 1971 no particular dates for the meeting were published, a unique usage concerning the Central Committee. Then it was revealed that the body met on 11, 14, 18 and 20 January, that is on four days separated by three intervals of two or three days, a unique pattern. Most likely this reflected the creation of a subcommission on some issue and difficulties of such a body in producing a consensual policy statement. If so, the problem probably centred on the one resolution that emerged from the session, 'On Errors of Party Organizations in Expelling Communists from the Party, on Formal Bureaucratic Attitudes toward the Appeals of Those Expelled from the VKP(b) [the party], and on Measures to Eliminate these Shortcomings'.[5]

In the setting of January 1938 'expulsion from the party' was tantamount to arrest, but the document took care not to challenge Yezhov or the police, who in fact were sweeping up party members and ordering party officials to expel them retroactively. Such a confrontation with Stalin would have been too hazardous. Instead, the drafters of the resolution apparently tried to moderate the Yezhovshchina by appealing to points that Stalin himself had made at the session of February–March 1937. Some party officials were guilty of a 'formalistic and soullessly bureaucratic' attitude toward members who were expelled. Worse, there were 'cleverly disguised enemies who try to disguise their hostility with shouts about vigilance. . . . This disguised enemy – the most vicious traitor – usually shouts louder than anyone else about vigilance, hastens to "unmask" the greatest number possible, and does all this to cover up his own crimes before the party.' For the advocates of moderation this had the advantage of discouraging the wave of panicky and self-serving denunciations that was claiming so many victims, and it specifically attempted to repair some of the damage by readmitting wrongly expelled members. But it also called for additional arrests, including those who had been disguising their 'hostility' by denouncing others, and that could run to a substantial number. According to a relatively frank Soviet history of political work in the armed forces, the resolution brought some moderation of the Yezhovshchina among military officers, but 'the repressions did not stop'. This appears to have been generally the case in the Soviet establishment.

The advocates of moderation were, however, unable to stop the Bukharin–Rykov–Yagoda trial in March and the arrest of five members of the Politburo in the spring of 1938.[6] Such arrests demonstrated the serious danger that Stalin was losing any kind of discrimination between 'loyal' and 'disloyal' comrades and might destroy the whole system if not checked. But at this late hour Stalin drew back; why, one cannot be sure. Perhaps he recognized the risk to his whole structure, especially against the background of the growing danger from Nazi Germany, which in March 1938 had annexed Austria, her first territorial move to the east. Along with this it appears that his morbidly suspicious tendency itself manufactured its own anti-body, distrust of Yezhov, a sentiment that Stalin's lieutenants would have been well advised to encourage. Khrushchev recalls two incidents that reflect the development of Stalin's doubts about his police chief. In one case, soon after Khrushchev had arrived in Kiev to take charge, he encountered the case of an innocent official who had been arrested, resisted torture and (why it is not clear) had been released. When Khrushchev mentioned this to Stalin, the latter replied, 'there are these perversions. They're gathering evidence against me, too.' In the same period Stalin phoned Khrushchev about the planned arrest of the police chief of the Ukraine, who, however, got wind of his fate and tried to flee. After the victim had been caught, Stalin told Khrushchev that he suspected that the man had fled because Yezhov had been listening in on their earlier telephone conversation and had tipped off his subordinate.[7]

By the time these incidents had occurred, Yezhov had a new deputy narkom, who may well have encouraged Stalin's suspicion of Yezhov. This deputy was Beria, who was appointed on 20 July 1938 and over the next fifteen years, as head of the police apparatus, was to build a reputation at least as odious as Yezhov's. But he may have been sincere (and fishing for support) when he told Khrushchev shortly after his appointment 'This whole business has gone much too far. We've got to stop it before it's too late.' This was a reasonable, self-serving proposition. Beria's own chances of survival stood to gain from stabilization of the police regime, and also from the removal of Yezhov, who was not accustomed to having such a politically important deputy. Stalin was already on good personal terms with Beria, who soon became one of his closest cronies. A special mark of his trust of this compatriot was Beria's ability to infiltrate Stalin's household with his own staff, who were Georgians. The first was Alexandra Nakhashidze, a relative of Beria's wife and an NKVD officer, who took over as housekeeper. Evidently Beria intended to remove Svetlana's beloved nanny by discovering that the old woman's one-time husband had worked as a clerk for the tsar's police, but Svetlana thwarted this – 'my father could not stand tears'.

Sooner or later almost all the household around Stalin consisted of Georgians appointed by Beria.[8]

Perhaps to provide a pretext for the transfer to Beria of day-to-day administration of the police, Stalin appointed Yezhov in March 1938 to an additional people's commissariat, water transport.[9] By the autumn Beria was investigating the activities of the police in the recent past and, apparently, encouraging the supreme court to do likewise. Both appear to have found many 'errors'. The court reported this in a letter to Molotov and Stalin, asking permission to reopen cases in which there had been violations of legality. There was no reply, but at some point in late 1938 the Central Committee or its apparatus adopted one or two resolutions condemning errors of the police, implicitly under Yezhov's leadership.[10]

Isolated, and with many of his former subordinates arrested in a purge of the NKVD, Yezhov crumbled without a struggle. A few years later Stalin told the aircraft designer Yakovlev that Yezhov stopped showing up for work and was at home, drunk, all day. 'The wretch, he killed many innocent people in 1938,' said Stalin, 'for that we shot him', implying that the slaughter of 1937 was a different matter.[11] On 8 December 1938 Beria was named head of the police, and some time early in 1939 Yezhov was arrested. There are various tales about the particular circumstances, none of them verifiable, but it is clear that he had vanished by the beginning of March when regional party meetings elected the delegates to the forthcoming Eighteenth Congress and Yezhov was not chosen.[12]

Emboldened by the fall of Yezhov, various party leaders sought to persuade Stalin to moderate the depredations of the police against Communists. Khrushchev relates how he demonstrated to Stalin's satisfaction that a horse plague was not the work of Jewish veterinarians in the pay of Germany, but of a fungus in improperly dried hay. Andreev, a secretary of the party, promoted a young officer in the military engineers to the important post of party secretary of Yaroslav province as a result of his defence of the innocence of a comrade officer. Stalin received enough messages from regional party officials protesting the use of torture by the police that on 20 January 1939 he felt obliged to dispatch a circular telegram defending 'methods of physical pressure' on the grounds that 'bourgeois intelligence services' used them, and claiming that in 1937 the Central Committee had authorized torture.[13]

In 1939–41 Stalin even showed a degree of forgiveness toward some 'enemies of the people'. In some cases he seems to have regarded the unwillingness of the accused to sign confessions as some kind of evidence on their behalf, evidently regarding the torture to which they had been submitted as a kind of lie detection test. One such case was an important aircraft motor engineer V. P. Balandin. When Yakovlev asked Stalin to return Balandin to duty, the Boss, showing that he was keeping an eye on such an important case, said, 'Yes, he's sat [the jargon for being under arrest] for about 40 days and hasn't given any evidence. Perhaps there's no case against him. . . . It's very possible.' And the engineer was released. Another prisoner who may have benefited by heroic unwillingness to confess was General A. V. Gorbatov. He was not spared Gulag, but, like some other officers who may or may not have confessed, was returned to duty as the war approached. In still another case of clemency, Stalin's daughter in 1940 brought home a written plea from the mother of a schoolfriend concerning her diplomat-husband. This happened at dinner when Molotov, who had been watching the case and apparently was favourably disposed to the accused, was present. Stalin accepted his judgement, and the man was released, but Svetlana was sternly ordered not to deliver such letters in the future.[14]

If Stalin had pulled himself from the brink of self-destruction, or if he had allowed his minions to nudge him back toward normality, he nevertheless proceeded to finish off a number of the more important men who had been arrested during the Yezhovshchina and were still being held at the beginning of 1939. Among those executed in that year or 1940 were former members of the Politburo, Chubar, Kosior, Eikhe and Postyshev. Another was Alexander Svanidze, Stalin's brother-in-law through his first marriage and head of the bank for foreign trade. Arrested in 1937, he was not shot until February 1942, refusing a proferred pardon (perhaps spurious) if he would ask forgiveness.[15] In addition it appears that Stalin was willing to authorize Beria to purge his new fief of those whom he considered too close to Yezhov, along with some diplomats who were no longer wanted following the deposition (but not arrest) of Litvinov, the narkom of foreign affairs. Gulag probably expanded under Beria because of the addition to its population of many victims from the western territories that the Soviet Union annexed in 1939–40. Under Beria a peculiar institution within Gulag flourished as never before, the *sharashka* or privileged prison for technical specialists, who continued their professional work under the aegis of the police. Stalin took a special interest in the work of military aircraft designers, many of whom toiled in *sharashkas*, including the famous A. N. Tupolev. Their fighters had disappointed Stalin in the Spanish civil war, where they encountered German adversaries, and many designers had been arrested; quite a few were shot in 1937 and early 1938. But Beria saw the irrationality of this waste and established various *sharashkas* in later 1938 and the following year.[16]

This appears to have harmonized with Stalin's emerging perspective on rule by terror: resignation to the impossibility of wiping out all potential traitors and the use of means short of execution or life-destroying labour to deal with people of doubtful reliability. By 1939 the adult population had learned the lesson of the Yezhovshchina and needed only occasional reminders. Stalin provided these throughout the rest of his career. When in January 1940 he wanted to persuade Yakovlev to accept the hazardous position of deputy narkom of aviation, it was only necessary for Stalin to note that 'we do not fear force, we do not stop short of using force when it is necessary'. Sometimes he would merely make playful allusion to his reputation, apparently enjoying the effect. In April 1941 in a small group discussing serious problems in the rubber tyre industry in Yaroslavl he was sharply critical of the work of the provincial party secretary, N. S. Patolichev, who recalled the incident: 'Finally he said, "Patolichev ought to be punished." All were waiting for what he would say next. He paced the room for a few minutes, deep in thought. These minutes seemed incredibly long to me. Stalin suddenly smiled and said: "Patolichev should be placed on the commission for drafting a resolution." '[17]

In this spirit Stalin did not find it necessary to call for new campaigns against the domestic class enemy in his major report to the Eighteenth Party Congress on 10 March 1939. A pair of references to 'fiends', a justification of 'the purging of Soviet organizations of spies, assassins and wreckers like Trotsky, Zinoviev, Kamenev, Yakir, Tukhachevsky, Rosengolts, Bukharin and others' was sufficient to remind his audience of his capacity for terror. The 2035 delegates had reason to get the point. Only fifty-nine of them had been delegates at the previous congress in 1934, almost all of the balance having been arrested in the interim. The main thing for the delegates was that Stalin treated the acute danger from within as history and took a positive view of the security outlook, owing to the success of the purge in strengthening the system. The 'drivel' of 'foreign pressmen' that the experience had shaken the Soviet Union deserved only 'laughter and scorn', as demonstrated by the overwhelming support of the electorate for the system in the 1937 elections, in which 98.6 per cent voted for the official slate. He admitted that in the party purge of 1933–6 there had been 'more mistakes than might have been expected,' but was so confident that the task of 'culling the staunchest and most loyal' had been done so successfully that 'undoubtedly we shall have no need to resort to the method of mass purge any more'. Here his specific reference was to the more or less traditional party custom of expelling substandard members without arrests or charges of treason, but he noted that it had dealt with 'directly hostile elements' as well, so his listeners had reason to take the remark as an assurance that their heads were relatively safe. Stalin made no explicit reference to Yezhov, his erstwhile close comrade, whose disappearance had never been noted or explained in the press. As for Trotsky, the diabolical figure in the mythology of the past few years, Stalin referred to him only allusively in lists of villains already dead, an ominous portent for Trotsky.[18]

Having decided to stabilize the system and have done with great public trials of traitors, Stalin had no more need of a living arch-enemy. The first attempt on Trotsky's life came on 23 May 1939, two and one-half months after Stalin's report. The machine gunners who got into Trotsky's guarded compound near Mexico City missed on this occasion, and it was not until 20 August 1940 that an alternative plan succeeded in finally settling scores with Stalin's best-known opponent. Although neither the unsuccessful nor the successful attempts to kill Trotsky received much publicity in the Soviet Union, the decision to liquidate him was the best possible assurance that Stalin was sincere in his decision to wind down the active killing of his own people.[19]

This meant that those who were now elected by the congress to the new Central Committee had a reasonable hope of actually benefiting by this promotion, and promotion it was for almost all of them. Only 23 out of 139 on the new Committee had served previously on it as member or candidate. The comparative security of the place-holders who had advanced to fill the vacancies caused by the Yezhovshchina was illustrated in 1940 in the re-election of party secretaries from the primary and district levels. Over 60 per cent were re-elected. Owing to Stalin's preservation of an inner core of the Politburo, even in 1937–8, that body did not change so drastically when it was reconstituted in 1939. There were, however, some vacancies in this body, which were filled by Zhdanov and Khrushchev as full members, Beria and Shvernik as candidate members. In 1941 Malenkov and another former member of Stalin's personal staff, A. S. Shcherbakov, also became candidate members.[20]

The Eighteenth Party Congress stood for the restoration of the position of the party, which had been reeling under the impact of the Yezhovshchina. Yet Stalin chose to conclude his report with a somewhat unexpected discourse on the importance of the Soviet state. It is sometimes asked, said Stalin, 'why we do not help our socialist state to wither away?' Perhaps – although it was preposterous to think that during the recent terror anyone had been so brash as to challenge the regime on its failure to wither. With a display of Marxist–Leninist erudition Stalin explained that in conditions of capitalist encirclement it was impossible for the Soviet state to die away, that it had evolved into a new socialist form as the need for internal repression of hostile class elements diminished. This, by the way, was an implicit moderation of his thesis of 1937 that these elements became increasingly dangerous as society approaches Communism. Even under Communism, said Stalin, the state would remain until 'capitalist encirclement is liquidated and replaced by socialist encirclement'. Perhaps Stalin threw in this digression, and a comment on the need to drop the former hostility to the intelligentsia, in order to add assurance that the time of terror was over. Reference to the importance of the state also may have reflected a realization that the threat of war might enhance the importance of the state apparatus. This, in any case, seems to have been Stalin's conclusion on 6 May 1941 when he took over from Molotov the post of chairman of the Sovnarkom, the premiership.[21]

The hazardous international situation was on Stalin's mind on 8 August 1939 when he wrote to his thirteen-year-old daughter: 'I don't plan to come south this year. I'm busy. I can't get away.' For Stalin to give up his annual holiday was unusual, but so were the circumstances, for he was arranging one of the greatest diplomatic revolutions of modern times. Stalin came fairly late to the personal conduct of diplomacy, which became one of his major occupations during 1939–45. In this field he displayed a formidable array of talents. Anthony Eden was impressed by Stalin's personality, which 'made itself felt without effort or exaggeration' and by his 'natural good manners'. Even the Finnish envoy J. K. Paasiviki, who met Stalin in circumstances that were grim for Finland, noted Stalin's recourse to humour. In this his style was heavy-handed but well calculated to distract or impress his opposite numbers. On at least two occasions he made Maisky, the inoffensive Soviet ambassador to Britain, the butt of approximately the same sardonic, implicitly murderous, pseudo-joke. In 1935 he illustrated the idea of collective security by telling Eden that there were six in the room, 'if Maisky chooses to go for any one of us, then we must all fall on Maisky'. (At which Maisky 'grinned somewhat nervously'.) Eight years later at the Tehran Conference he rhetorically asked Roosevelt and Churchill who among them might threaten the peace? Could it be Maisky? And he sought to amuse the humourless de Gaulle in 1944 by suggesting that they should shoot all their diplomats.[22]

He could be soft spoken, so much so in meeting Eden that even Stalin's foreign minister, who was serving as interpreter, had trouble hearing him. Or he could be angry, as in the instance when Roosevelt affronted him by revealing that he and Churchill called Stalin 'Uncle Joe' in their correspondence. He also had devices to put certain visitors in their place, for example stalking around the room behind the backs of a Finnish delegation, which felt obliged to remain seated at the bargaining table. This, by the way, was also his practice in meetings with his Soviet subordinates who, like the Finns, were expected to keep their seats while Stalin strolled. All his foreign visitors were impressed by his mastery of the factual material related to the case at hand. Above all, he knew what goals he considered essential in any negotiation and struggled with unyielding determination to obtain them.[23]

Until 1935 Stalin seems not to have regarded relations with capitalist states as a high-priority concern, leaving the conduct of diplomacy to the experienced narkom of foreign affairs, G. V. Chicherin, or his successor, in 1930, Maxim Litvinov. In the main they were permitted to follow the policy established in Lenin's time: correct formal relations with most capitalist states and something closer with Germany, and support for anti-imperialist governments of Asia. Stalin's comparative passivity concerning foreign relations before the mid-1930s reflected not only his preoccupation with other matters, but also the relatively secure situation of the Soviet Union in world politics once the period of the civil war and foreign intervention had ended around 1920. Much as Bolshevik propaganda might rail against it, the Versailles system unintentionally provided Russia with a secure situation in Europe, better than the one she had lived with during the second German Reich and the one she was to experience following the Second World War. A large, chronically anti-Russian Austro-Hungarian state had been reduced to a number of harmless, mutually contending successors, and the trimmed-down German state was restricted to an army of 100 000, lacking tanks and aircraft, among other weapons. As long as this lasted, Russia's western frontier was secure against any great-power attack, the more so considering that only France among the Versailles powers maintained a relatively large peacetime army. Continuing the tradition of Lenin, Stalin never spoke favourably of this situation, occasionally inserting a jibe against Versailles into his speeches. He even professed concern for the threat of war in the late 1920s. It is hard to believe that he took this seriously. More likely it was merely a way of demonstrating his Marxist–Leninist orthodoxy to the party rank and file.[24]

Although it would not have been politic for Stalin to break with Leninist tradition and say so openly, the real danger to Soviet security lay not in the Versailles system but rather in the possibility that it might be overturned, that a coalition of Germany with Britain and France would unite the three main west European powers against Russia. This was the worst case, which Stalin sensibly and consistently strove to avoid throughout his career at the head of the Soviet Union, adding the United States to the possible hostile coalition after that country ended its isolation in the 1940s. The problem presented itself in various guises over the course of Stalin's career and invited varying responses in different periods. One basic response was to make common cause with humiliated Germany against the victors of Versailles, as Lenin did in the Treaty of Rapallo in 1922 and Stalin was to do in the Molotov–Ribbentrop Treaty of 1939. But in 1925 the German Republic had signed the Locarno agreement with Britain and France, opening the possibility of reconciliation of victor and vanquished and the replacement of the Versailles order with an anti-Communist alliance.

Stalin's concern about this possibility appears to have informed his policy in the early 1930s. At this time depression-ridden Germany was in disarray, and one of the possible results was the formation of a Nazi government. Stalin has been criticized for not ordering the German Communist Party to make common cause with the Social-Democrats in an all-out attempt to block the Nazis. On the contrary he ordered the German Communists to treat the Social-Democrats as enemies, accepting the risk that Hitler would come to power. The key to his hard-headed analysis of this issue, which he could not discuss in public, he revealed to a German Communist leader who visited Moscow in late 1931: 'Don't you believe, Neumann, that if the Nationalists [meaning Nazis] come to power in Germany they will be so completely preoccupied with the West that we will be able to build up socialism in peace?' The Nazis, in other words, were so bent on forcibly demolishing the Versailles order that they would ensure the continuation of German–Anglo-French hostility. If the Versailles order was doomed, it would be better for the Soviet Union if this came about in a way that divided the main capitalist powers of western Europe against one another. True, Hitler had written about the need for German annexations to the east, but this was not the main line of his appeal to the German public, which was doubtfully interested in the conquest of the Ukraine but unquestionably indignant over the humiliation of 1919. By any reasonable calculation Hitler in power would give priority to his quarrel with Britain and France, thus inadvertently restoring the Versailles system in so far as it kept Germany and Britain/France divided against one another.[25]

Compared with the problem of preventing a broad coalition of anti-Soviet powers, including Germany, the fate of the German, or other foreign Communist parties was minor in Stalin's eyes. His public stance around 1930 was that the economic crisis in the capitalist world portended a new revolutionary upsurge, for which Communists must be prepared. The depression was real, and Stalin may have believed that political upheavals would follow, but it is highly unlikely that he took seriously the idea that Communists might come to power in western countries in the near future, nor that the Comintern would direct such revolutions. Stalin did not share Lenin's commitment to the idea of the Communist International and was not active at its seven 'World Congresses'. His aversion to the Comintern derived partly from his unfavourable impression of the revolutionary toughness of the European leftists who made up its main force and partly from his mistrust of organizations that he could not control by direct means. In the 1930s the potentiality for discord in the World Communist movement was outweighed by the prestige of the October Revolution, but there was the possibility that at some time non-Soviet Communists might appear at a World Congress of the Comintern as troublesome dissenters from Moscow's line. Stalin had a glimpse of this potentiality in the 1920s when various foreign Communists backed his opponents in the Soviet party. This had required his personal intervention in Comintern assemblies, such as the Executive Committee meeting of December 1928, in which he attacked the 'Right Danger' in the German Communist Party. But for Stalin the Comintern generally remained a second-rate concern, as witnessed by his non-appearance at the Seventh World Congress in Moscow in 1935, the only such meeting he permitted after 1930. The one respect in which he did not overlook the Comintern in the 1930s was the terror. A large part of the expatriate Communist population in the Soviet Union perished in 1937–8.[26]

Whether or not Stalin or the German Communists could have done anything about it, Hitler did come to power in Germany in January 1933, and set about fulfilling his pledge to dismantle the Versailles system. A year later Stalin sought to reassure the Seventeenth Party Congress on the consequences of this change. Fascism, a particular form of bourgeois politics, rather than any basically new force in the world, was 'far from being long-lived', and there was nothing inevitable about a Nazi–Soviet war. After all, said Stalin, Italy had been Fascist for years, and we have 'the best relations' with her. We have no orientation toward one European power or another, he insisted.[27]

This was an overture to Hitler, not the proposal of any special deal, but merely an expression of readiness for *détente* between the powers. Hitler, however, ignored this, continued to rebuild German military power and to fulminate against Bolshevism. Stalin responded by embracing the policy of a united front against German revanchism, the policy that Litvinov articulated most effectively in public and urged on Stalin privately. This involved joining the League of Nations (dropping Stalin's former characterization of it as 'rotting alive'), ordering Communists in Spain and France to make common cause with socialists and signing mutual defence treaties in 1935 with France and Czechoslovakia. In this connection Stalin made his debut as a diplomatic representative of the Soviet Union, in 1935 meeting with French foreign minister Pierre Laval, British foreign minister Anthony Eden and Czechoslovak foreign minister Edvard Beneš. The real work of negotiation had been done before the French and Czech representatives visited Moscow for the signing, and Stalin, who did not yet hold any major state office, did not sign the treaties. But he demonstrated the importance of the new security system by his public participation and broke out of his long isolation from 'bourgeois' political leaders. In his meeting with Laval Stalin adopted the misleading image that he was to maintain thereafter in foreign dealings: 'I cannot talk in diplomatic language, I am not a diplomat.' The issue at hand was Laval's goal of obtaining a communiqué in which Stalin would give his blessing to French military preparations, thus implying an order to French Communists to cease their opposition to legislation for an increased term of conscription. When Laval explained that he could not accept that Stalin had nothing to do with French Communists and that French public opinion required that Stalin give appropriate orders to his French comrades, Stalin replied 'I agree'. Judging by the conduct of the French Communists, they received such orders.[28]

But the Franco-Soviet alliance did not prevent the further increase of German military power, its annexation of Austria and the dismemberment of Czechoslovakia. The Munich agreement of September 1938, from which the USSR was excluded, seemed to show that the Soviet Union could not rely on the Atlantic democracies. Regardless of Munich, it is highly probable that Stalin consistently regarded Germany as a more suitable diplomatic partner for the Soviet Union.[29] In August 1939 when Stalin was entertaining Joachim von Ribbentrop, Molotov toasted Stalin for having initiated the improvement in Soviet–German relations in his report to the Eighteenth Party Congress in March 1939. In this speech Stalin had reproached Britain and France for abandoning 'collective security' and 'encouraging Germany to attack the Soviet Union'. At Munich they had given Germany portions of Czechoslovakia 'as the price of undertaking to launch war on the Soviet Union' but the Germans were not delivering their end of this bargain. Stalin's asserted policy, therefore, was 'to be cautious and not allow our country to be drawn into conflicts by warmongers who are accustomed to have others pull the chestnuts out of the fire for them'.[30]

Among various diplomatic overtures that followed, the replacement on 3 May 1939 of Litvinov, known for his anti-Fascist stance, by Molotov as narkom of foreign affairs was only the most visible. Seeing the prospect of a thorough partition of east-central Europe with Soviet co-operation and the exclusion of Britain and France, Hitler moved swiftly in August. On the 15th the Germans secretly informed the Soviets that they should 'clarify their relations' because war was possible, and that foreign minister Ribbentrop would like to visit Moscow for this purpose. A condition for the visit was a personal meeting with Stalin. Now Stalin skilfully avoided any appearance of eagerness. 'Careful preparation' was necessary. But he was generally agreeable and on the 17th made a formal reply that included a reference to a 'special protocol' that might be appended to a mutual non-aggression treaty, 'defining the interests of the contracting parties in this or that question of foreign policy' – a polite way of suggesting that Stalin wanted a secret partition of east-central Europe. Molotov also was able to assure the Germans that 'Stalin was following the conversations with great interest, he was informed of all the details.' Having allowed Stalin to establish himself as the one who was being wooed, Hitler on 20 August ignored protocol and dispatched a personal telegram to Stalin, appealing to him to receive Ribbentrop no later than the 23rd. Stalin replied in his only personal message to Hitler, dated 21 August. It was brief, courteous and optimistic, thanking Hitler for his note, emphasizing the need for 'peace and collaboration between our countries' and inviting Ribbentrop for the 23rd.[31]

Considering the magnitude of the issues at stake, the negotiations themselves were smooth and quick. Ribbentrop arrived at the Kremlin at

3.30 p.m. on 23 August, and before midnight he and Molotov put their signatures to a non-aggression treaty, which was published, and a protocol, which was not. In this negotiation Stalin played an active role, for the deal was too vital to delegate entirely to his foreign minister. After the signing Stalin displayed his accustomed late-night conviviality at a social gathering that lasted until almost 4 a.m. It was here that he raised the toast, 'I know how much the German nation loves its Führer. I should therefore like to drink his health.' Was this sheer diplomacy, or did Stalin express a sincere respect for the strong leader, ideology aside, as did Hitler in 1942: 'Stalin, too, must command our unconditional respect! In his own way he is a hell of a fellow! He knows his models, Genghis Khan and the others, very well, and the scope of his industrial planning is exceeded only by our own Four-Year Plan.' Stalin sought to seal the agreement with a personal pledge to the departing Ribbentrop: 'He could guarantee on his word of honour that the Soviet Union would not betray its partner.'[32]

The published mutual non-aggression treaty had the implied result of freeing Hitler to invade Poland without fear of Soviet opposition, and the secret protocol in effect drew a line from the Arctic to the Black Sea, leaving Finland, Estonia, Latvia, central Poland (including Warsaw) and the Romanian province of Bessarabia in the Soviet sphere, and points west to Germany. So eager were the negotiators to reach agreement that they worked without adequate maps, as Molotov observed in a letter of 25 August to the German ambassador, requesting that the name of the River Pissa be inserted retroactively in the treaty to fulfil the intentions of the negotiators. The Germans agreed. The question of what sort of Polish rump state, if any, would be permitted, was left to future negotiations. But for all his eagerness to reach an accord, Stalin delayed the agreement by holding out for two Latvian ports that had not been mentioned in the original draft of the treaty. This required an intermission from about 8 to 11 p.m. while Ribbentrop obtained Hitler's consent.[33]

Stalin seems to have made this fateful treaty in consultation with Molotov and no other member of the Politburo. Khrushchev recalls that the Boss explained it to him, Voroshilov, Beria and several others by observing that the real goal of the British and French was to incite Hitler against the Soviets, hence the talks that were in progress concerning a possible Anglo-French–Soviet defence treaty were fruitless. The treaty with Germany, said Stalin, would keep Russia out of the anticipated war for a while, enabling her to save her strength and see how things developed.[34] It seemed likely that the Germans would do most of the fighting that would bring the Soviet Union its share of eastern Europe, especially against the largest power in the zone of change, Poland. This advantage, however, implied a dilemma: if Russia attacked Poland more or less simultaneously with Germany, this might lead to unwanted conflict with Britain and France. On the other hand, a delay in moving into Poland might allow Germany to take more than her agreed share, which she might then be reluctant to hand over.

This was on Stalin's mind when he ordered the Red Army into Poland on 17 September, sixteen days after the German invasion of that country. Hoping to minimize the offence to Britain and France, he tried to see if he could slip past the Germans a draft of a Soviet public explanation of their action which implied that the Russians came as rescuers. But in response to German objections, he retreated from this gambit in conversation with the German ambassador whom he had invited for a talk at the congenial hour of 2 a.m. In any case, by this time the extent of the German victory diminished the inclination of the British and French to declare war on Poland's second invader. For Stalin the more pressing problem was now the presence of German troops in the Polish territory that had been assigned to Russia. On the 17th he told the German ambassador that he had no doubt that the German government would honour its word, but it was 'a well-known fact that military men are loath to give up occupied territories'. Three days later he was less amicable in having Molotov inform the ambassador that Stalin 'personally was astonished at this obvious violation of the Moscow agreement'. Despite German assurances that they would keep their promises, Stalin on 25 September called in the ambassador, this time at the relatively humane hour of 8 p.m., and proposed a fundamental revision of the partition of Poland. He would swap Warsaw and other portions of the Soviet sphere that the Germans now occupied for the greater part of Lithuania, which the treaty had placed in the German sphere. He did not say so, but this would provide Russia with a straighter, more defensible frontier with Germany in case of war. He also mentioned two other points, avoiding any sense that he was a supplicant in dealing with his triumphant partner. First, there should be no 'independent residual Poland'. Since the Germans would have the Polish heartland under the new agreement, this meant that they would forego the possibility of emulating Napoleon in harassing Russia by sponsoring some sort of 'Grand Duchy of Warsaw'. Second, Stalin planned to 'take up the solution of the problem of the Baltic countries immediately' and he expected 'the unstinting support of the German Government'.[35]

In response Ribbentrop went to Moscow for the second time and spent three hours in tough bargaining with Stalin and Molotov on 27–8 September. 'Stubborn efforts on my part', reported Ribbentrop, to gain ground for Germany 'failed because of even more stubborn resistance on the part of Stalin.' The Reich foreign minister doubted whether he could obtain even a small strip of Lithuania 'in view of Stalin's great obstinacy', although this was in fact accepted by the time the new agreement was signed at 5 a.m., followed by a reception that lasted until about 6.30 a.m.

This resembled a normal night's work for Stalin, who probably relished the opportunity to grind down the will of an adversary at an hour when Stalin was accustomed to work, while the other side was drooping with fatigue.[36]

After the fall of Poland the Germans opened a peace offensive diplomatically, to which Stalin gave verbal support. He even approved a draft of a German speech in this sense that Ribbentrop tactfully sent to him in advance of delivery, making a minor change in a statement Ribbentrop attributed to Stalin concerning the need for a strong Germany. But it is unlikely that Stalin really wanted to see Germany disentangle herself from the war in the west at this time. He needed a secure opportunity to reap the rewards that his agreement promised in the Baltic area, and he set about this in a series of personal negotiations with Estonian, Latvian, Lithuanian and Finnish delegations, mainly in October and November 1939. From the three smaller states he demanded and obtained mutual assistance pacts and bases, maintaining that Soviet strategic security demanded it. He was brutally frank concerning the price of non-co-operation, telling the Latvian foreign minister, for example, 'As far as Germany is concerned, we could occupy you.' He was less honest in assuring his visitors that the Soviet Union would not annex their states, which it did in 1940.[37]

The Finns were stubborn and required more attention. Stalin had held seven inconclusive talks with their representatives in the spring of 1939 and on 12 October resumed the dialogue. Attempting a conciliatory approach, he told the Finns that they were 'a remarkable people' who had come to hate the Russians in tsarist times and 'now carried over your hatred to the Soviet Union'. Seeking a mutual defence treaty, a base at Hango and part of Karelia near Leningrad, Stalin assured the Finns that he meant them no harm and was merely concerned about the possibility of a British or German naval attack through the Gulf of Finland, citing Soviet experience in this area during the Russian civil war. It was impossible to take seriously the idea that the British could come so far without Hitler's permission, but the remark illuminates Stalin's mistrust of his German treaty partner. Would the tsarist government have dealt so reasonably with Finland, asked Stalin? 'There is no doubt on this', he replied. Would any other great power offer 5500 sq. km in exchange for 2700 (for the Soviets were willing to compensate the Finns in the north for the territory that the Finns were asked to cede in the south)? 'No. We are the only one that is so stupid.' But as the talks dragged on his tone hardened: 'Finland is small and weak', he said. Then, pointing on a map to Hango, 'A great power lands here and marches further without troubling itself over your protest', a remark that could apply equally to Germany or the Soviet Union.[38]

Not even Stalin's persuasive gifts could move the Finns to settle peacefully, so he ordered an invasion in November. He had hoped to obtain his goals without this, and his comparative patience in negotiation suggests that he had not completely underestimated the Finns. But the course of the winter war of November 1939–March 1940 showed that he nevertheless had rated the Finns too low and the Red Army too high, although the Soviet Union ended by getting what it required.

In early 1940 Stalin found time to continue personal diplomatic negotiations with Germany on the question of their delivery of various items of naval equipment. This was only a part of a programme of economic collaboration between Germany and Russia, but the one closest to Stalin's heart, for in the late 1930s he had decided to make the Soviet Union a major naval power. Specifically he wanted a first-rate fleet of large surface vessels, heavy cruisers and battleships, not aircraft carriers, for Stalin was among the numerous naval strategists who did not anticipate the revolution that this weapon was soon to bring about. He seems to have reached this decision, with its major implications for the Soviet defence budget, on his own, unable to obtain from his admirals a firm recommendation. 'You yourselves don't know what you need', he grumbled to a meeting of officers in 1936 or 1937. No doubt he thought he had sound strategic reasons for building capital ships, but the decision fits well with his general taste for the monumental, as in the great dams and other construction projects, the plan for the Palace of Soviets and the 'All-Union Agricultural Exposition' that was opened in Moscow in 1939. As Admiral N. G. Kuznetsov recollected, 'Stalin devoted no small attention to the ship construction programme and was very interested in the fleet.' When, at a naval gathering at Stalin's villa in the autumn of 1939, the admiral expressed doubts about the usefulness of large ships on the small Baltic Sea, 'Stalin got up from his chair, paced the room, crushed two cigarettes, poured out their tobacco, stuffed it in his pipe and smoked. "We will gather the money penny by penny and build them", said he, measuring out each word and staring sternly at me.'[39]

The possibility of accelerating this naval programme by purchasing assistance from Germany was not the least of the attractions for Stalin of the pact of 1939. He wanted to buy the plans for the *Bismarck*, the greatest battleship of the day, succeeded in obtaining the unfinished hull of the heavy cruiser *Lützow* and various items of equipment, such as turrets. But the Germans did not satisfy Stalin's zeal for haste, and on 29 January 1940, though barely recovering from a week-long attack of flu, he joined a conference with the Germans on this matter, followed by another on 8 February. The Germans were impressed by Stalin's mastery of technical detail, much of which concerned turrets for 28- and 38.1-cm guns, and by his becoming 'quite agitated' concerning what he regarded as German delays, for which he 'excused himself later'. He was at pains to offer the Germans compensation in grain, oil and strategically vital ores such as wolfram, even the right to station near Murmansk a submarine tender, euphemistically called a mother-ship for German fishing boats. But Stalin was avid for the prompt delivery of naval equipment. 'One should not take advantage of the Soviet Union's good nature', he brusquely told the representative of the world's greatest, and most aggressive, military power.[40]

These talks turned out to be the last of his formal meetings with representatives of the Reich. This was not the Germans' wish. In March 1940 Ribbentrop was even planning to invite Stalin to Berlin, advising his ambassador in Moscow that, 'The Führer would not only be particularly happy to welcome Stalin, but he would also see to it that he would get a reception commensurate with his position and importance, and he would extend to him all the honours that the occasion demanded.' Considering the Nazis' gift for pageantry, Stalin missed an opportunity for a glorious, if politically incongruous, occasion. Indeed, Ribbentrop, who made it clear that he did not want to deliver an invitation that would be declined, evidently thought better of the idea. In casual conversation with the German Ambassador Stalin agreed in principle to accept the invitation, but it is unlikely that he meant it and the Germans dropped the idea. By the spring of 1940 Stalin seems to have decided to keep the Germans at arm's length from his person, despite all the continued professions of Russo-German amity. Only after fifteen months and repeated requests did he deign to accede to Ribbentrop's request for an autographed portrait, which was finally delivered by a new Soviet ambassador in December 1940.[41]

Stalin's increased personal coolness to his diplomatic partner was a reaction to a growing series of irritations in the relationship, concerning trade and territory among other matters. For Stalin the unexpectedly rapid German victory over France in the spring of 1940 upset the military balance in Europe on which he had been relying. He probably had been sincere in telling Ribbentrop in August 1939 that 'France still had an army worthy of consideration' and 'England despite her weakness would wage war craftily and stubbornly.' Like many other people, he had not expected these opponents of Hitler to collapse so quickly in France. 'Couldn't they put up any resistance at all?', he complained.[42]

Stalin never found time after February 1940 to receive the German ambassador, but he did confer with a new British ambassador, Sir Stafford Cripps, and the Japanese foreign minister, Yosuke Matsuoka, in July 1940 and March–April 1941, respectively. The Soviets treated Cripps coolly, and Stalin sent Molotov a copy of his version of the talk for transmission to the Germans to reassure them of this reserve, and perhaps to remind them that he was independent. Since the Japanese were allied with Germany, it was permissible to join them in a mutual non-aggression pact, which in effect neutralized the boundaries of their respective spheres in case of a Japanese–American or Soviet–German war.[43]

By this time, the spring of 1941, Stalin indeed had ample reason to worry about the success of his deal with Hitler. But he left it to Molotov to handle the direct contacts at the highest level. In the autumn of 1940 the Germans, apparently the rulers of Europe from the Soviet frontier to the English Channel, wanted to talk privately with their Soviet partner about plans for the partition of Eurasia between their two countries, and also Italy and Japan. Ribbentrop sent Stalin a lengthy letter surveying the world situation and was annoyed to find that his ambassador did not even try to obtain a personal audience to deliver it. 'Stalin has recently been showing a strong reserve in public, and I was therefore justified in assuming that he would avoid a personal meeting with me on some pretext or other', reported the embarrassed ambassador. This was disingenuous, for the meeting would scarcely have been public. The real point was that Stalin did not want to link his personal prestige to the German connection any more than was necessary. He did, however, reply briefly by letter to Ribbentrop, and authorized Molotov to go to Berlin, a trip which the latter made in November 1940. Molotov obviously was not empowered to agree to anything and was under orders to see if Hitler would gratify Stalin's interest in the Turkish straits. Unlike the brief and productive meetings of 1939, this discussion, in which Hitler did much of the talking, dragged on and decided nothing. There were ample signs of German–Soviet tension by early 1941, but Stalin now had no reasonable alternative to a policy of maintaining peace with Germany. Britain was the only readily available ally against Germany, and she was weak. Soviet military preparations were going forward but needed several years at least.[44]

Nevertheless Stalin's foreign policy was an apparent success, substantially expanding Soviet territory while keeping the country out of the war among the great powers. This achievement reinforced the glorification of his person that had attained new heights by the end of the 1930s. The rituals that had been established by the mid-1930s remained in place and grew in amplitude. But along with quantitative expansion there were qualitative changes. For one thing, the relationship between Stalin and the other personal cults – of Lenin and the members of the Politburo – underwent a subtle change. Lenin still occupied the mausoleum. His visage and his collected works were still a major part of Soviet culture. And it remained good form to refer to Stalin as Lenin's successor, to depict the two together in statue, film and other media. But the image of the living Stalin, who was guiding the nation and the international Communist movement day by day, overmatched the shade of Lenin. Not only was his cult a matter of the past, it also was mummified, like his mortal remains. Stalin's cult, on the other hand, was alive and growing.

To a certain extent this was inevitable, but Stalin took some deliberate measures to ensure that the volume of publications concerning Lenin was restricted and that some were suppressed. This began as early as 1938 when a Politburo resolution forbade publication of a novel about Lenin's family and continued in the post-war years with the suppression of a memoir by Lenin's chauffeur. As for the lesser cults, they continued, and some new dignitaries, such as Yezhov and then Beria, were able to join this circle. But the volume of attention given to these secondary heroes was rationed and the sense of collectivity dwindled.[45]

As for the enhanced glorification of Stalin's image, one feature was the differentiation of subcultures, adapting the same basic message to different audiences. There was, for example, an immense special effort to teach children the benign glories of their ultimate father. Stalin personally determined that this myth should not emphasize one of the obvious devices at the disposal of the propagandists: didactic legends about the young Soso. In 1938 the editors of the state publishing house sent Stalin a book manuscript entitled *Stories of Stalin's Childhood*, which he rejected, observing that it was harmful 'to inculcate in the consciousness of Soviet children (and people in general) a cult of personality, of leaders, of flawless heroes'. This, he said, was not Bolshevik but Socialist-Revolutionary, meaning non-Marxist, in its concept of historical determination.[46]

Despite this display of ideological orthodoxy and personal humility, Stalin permitted the profusion of a pervasive, cloyingly sweet image of himself as the loving protector of all children, so vague on human particulars that it evoked the divine. 'Thank you, Stalin, for a happy childhood', was a vastly repeated slogan that summarizes the sense of this subcult. The image of Stalin and joyful children was propagated in the later 1930s through the graphic arts and poetry. There was a spate of staged photographs of Stalin and children, some of which inspired paintings, such as a shot of him smilingly holding little Galia Markizova in his arms. No nursery could be without a copy of this, reported Margaret Bourke-White. The poetry consisted of vague raptures about the great man, such as 'Lullaby' by V. Lebedev-Kumach, ten stanzas in length, one of which ran:

> Within the walls of the Kremlin there's a fellow
> He knows and loves all the land;
> Happy and fortunate are you because of him;
> He is Stalin and great is his name![47]

Children themselves composed poetic tributes, such as the following excerpt from the work, rhymed in the original Russian, of twelve-year-old Lina Tartakovskaia:

> Stalin! Thou art dearer to us than anything in the world.

> Stalin! Thou art sweeter to us than anything in the world.
> We know that thou lovest us, too,
> Lovest thou the children of the proletariat.

Ten-year-old Kostia Orlov called his verse 'A Dream':

> You know, Vania, today
> I had a dream.
> It was as if the great Stalin himself
> Came to visit me.[48]

Another newly emergent folkoristic subculture resembled the children's in its contrived simplicity, treating the ordinary folk, especially peasants and members of non-European ethnic groups, as mental children. One was to believe that the upwelling of love for the leader among these folk generated anonymous epics, such as a Russian *bylina* entitled 'The Glory of Stalin Will Be Eternal' or a work in the Oi rot language, 'There Is a Man in Moscow', ending

> Who is that man who appears to the toilers,
> Spreading happiness and joy all around?
> It is Stalin, I shout, so the whole world will hear,
> It is Stalin, our Leader and Friend![49]

Sometimes these bards received personal recognition, as in the case of 'decorated story-teller F. A. Konashkov', author in 1937 of 'The Most Precious Thing'. This was a story about some collective farmers who could not decide what is the most precious thing: cows, fish or grain. One recalled that her dying grandmother had told her that if she could not find her way, to take the old woman's magic ball, roll it and follow it. They do this, come to Moscow and take the Metro to the Kremlin, where Stalin genially receives them. After hearing his wisdom – exactly what is not stated – the farmers conclude that what he told them was the most precious thing. This title suited the tone of this kind of literature so well that it was used as the title for a substantial anthology of such works, verse and prose.[50] Still less spontaneous were the non-literary expressions of folk-art devoted to Stalin. The depiction of Stalin in an oriental rug from Central Asia or in a tapestry from the Ukraine tried to evoke the style of various traditional forms, but they were obviously professional productions.[51]

There were certain difficulties, never openly acknowledged, in the subculture that was created for educated people. Stalin seems to have taken some time to make up his mind about the desirability of having a substantial official biography, and this presented his propagandists with an uncomfortable ambiguity. Following his failure to induce Gorky to write a biography, Stalin appears to have turned away from the idea of a full-length work. Two very brief, elementary Stalin biographies appeared in 1939, one by the propagandist Emilian Yaroslavsky, the other anonymous. Henri Barbusse, the prominent French Communist and novelist, was commissioned to write a book on Stalin, but the result, published in Paris in 1935, implies that the author was given neither material nor encouragement to make it a biography. *Stalin, A New World Seen through a Man*, while laudatory in its references to Stalin, is basically a propaganda tract for Soviet Communism. It appeared in Russian translation in 1936 but never became a staple of indoctrination in the USSR, serving mainly to reach foreign audiences.[52]

Lacking a reliable guide to the presentation of Stalin's life or personality as a whole, the authors of historical fiction for the printed page, stage and screen were constrained to portray the ultimate hero in cameo roles. These were common enough, and a whole school of actors specialized in playing Stalin, M. G. Gelovani perhaps leading the way with credits in this role in twenty plays and films. The one important work that is known to have deviated from this norm was a play entitled *Batum*, by one of the major literary figures of the generation, Mikhail Bulgakov. Stalin greatly admired his play, *Days of the Turbins*, first produced in 1926, later banned, then in 1932 permitted again with Stalin's blessing. Moreover Stalin had in 1930 telephoned the then-desperate playwright to tell him that work had been arranged for him at the Moscow Art Theatre. In 1938 the managers of that institution, who evidently had not understood the canons that were emerging, urged Bulgakov to write a play about the young Stalin. He did, but its hero vetoed its production, commenting that, 'All children and young people are alike. There is no need to put on a play about the young Stalin.'[53]

What was wanted was not an extended narrative, however hagiographic, of Stalin's life or personality, but incantations on a few basic virtues of the Leader: wisdom, kindness, courage. Stalin apparently reached the conclusion that in advertising a strong, simple message is the best. And poetry was one medium that was well suited to this end. There were, of course, phalanxes of hack versifiers who sometimes performed literally in formation, for example, the nine Uzbeks who filled a whole page of *Pravda* with a poem entitled 'Letter from the Fortunate Uzbek People to the Leader of Nations, to the Great Iosif Vissarionovich Stalin on the opening of the Eighteenth Congress of the All-Union Communist Party (Bolsheviks)'.[54] But he also wanted the most gifted poets of the time to contribute to the cult. He took a serious interest in this art and intervened in 1936 to establish the suicide Vladimir Mayakovsky as the premier poet of the Soviet era.[55] Although Stalin had not written poetry since his youth, he found diversion from the anxieties of the hour in May 1941 by making critical comments on the translation into Russian of the Georgian classic *Tamariani* at the request of Sh. Nutsubidze, a scholar who had prepared the work.[56] So great was his respect for poetic talent that he dealt personally with the case of Osip Mandelshtam, the most gifted Russian poet of his generation, who in 1934 had rashly recited to presumed friends a short poem that referred to Stalin as 'the Kremlin mountaineer', with fingers 'fat as worms', a killer surrounded by 'half-men'.[57] On learning of this from some informer, Stalin phoned Boris Pasternak, another great poetic talent, to ask if the culprit was really a genius. There are various versions of the conversation, but it is agreed that Stalin at one point said that Mandelshtam would be 'all right' and at another told Pasternak that if he (Stalin) were somebody's friend in such a 'dangerous situation' he would know better how to defend him. For the present Stalin spared Mandelshtam, who was released from arrest and encouraged to make good his repentance by writing an ode to Stalin, which, with much anguish, he did. The result lived up to the standards of Stalin cult poetry. For example:

> By Stalin's eyes in the mountain put assunder,
> And the plain peered into the distance.
> Like the sea without wrinkles, like tomorrow out of yesterday.

But Mandelshtam had too much artistic integrity to release this work and, like many other writers, died in Gulag.[58]

Pasternak, too, was obliged to contribute, greeting 1936 with two untitled poems in *Izvestia*, one of which merely made passing reference to Lenin and Stalin, the other carrying on for a number of stanzas, including:

> Within that antique stronghold
> Dwells Action Man in person –
> The essence of a doer
> Swollen to global bulk. . . .
>
> And he remains so human.
> If he should shoot a hare
> In the winter the woods would echo
> His shot like any other.[59]

To demonstrate that some of the diverse artistic creations devoted to Stalin were high culture, the discipline of criticism was also mobilized. This, however, presented a serious problem. How could the critic say anything negative about an artist's depiction of the Leader without any hint that he was demeaning the artist's subject? Thus the literary critic S. Balukhaty, in discussing Gorky's poem 'Song of the Falcon' (not about Stalin), was inspired to remember that the poet Umurzak had written, 'Stalin, my falcon, my eagle!', while a Kazakh poem said 'Stalin is such an eagle with a thousand thousand eaglets', and so on through other writers who had used this metaphor. But he dared not offer any opinion about which usage was more beautiful. Similarly one of the premier historians of art in Russia, K. S. Kravchenko, devoted a whole book to painting (and a little sculpture) on Stalin, with 106 illustrations but had trouble offering any critical judgement beyond the safe statement that the 'Stalinist epoch' posed artists with 'a historical task of the highest significance – to embody in art the image of Stalin, the beloved friend of the people, leader of [and so forth]'. After a hundred pages of merely naming works, she ventured to complain of the artistic technique with which one painter treated some parachutists who appeared in the background of a painting that focused on Stalin. At last she was emboldened to assert that *Comrade Stalin Smokes a Pipe* is distinguished by its 'freshness' and might be ranked 'among the best portraits of Comrade Stalin'.[60]

Another difficulty arose when the leading sculptor, Merkurov, attempted an ideologically correct interpretation of his numerous statues of Stalin. Neglecting to mention that he had put aside work on the immense statue of Lenin that was to have crowned the Palace of Soviets, he noted that he had been absorbed with 'the solution of the problems of the monumental likeness of the Leader'. 'The likenesses of the Leader of a free, progressive country,' wrote Merkurov, 'striding forward in the century, inspired the artist to depict this in sculpture. This is the characteristic feature that distinguishes Soviet sculpture from the sculpture of earlier epochs.' The trouble with this vaguely Marxist interpretation was that the canon of Stalin statuary in reality was rigidly static. Far from striding forward, the Leader's feet were firmly rooted beneath a bolt-upright body, arms by its side, which frequently was draped in a full-length overcoat that reached to the pedestal, suggesting an immobile power attached to the ground. Such, for example, was Merkurov's enormous statue of Stalin in the All-Union Agricultural Exhibition.[61]

The flourishing of the cult in the latter half of the 1930s not only involved established forms but also some special occasions. The first of these was the adoption of a new constitution of the USSR. This may have served several purposes, but one of these certainly became the glorification of Stalin. He chaired the drafting commission that was established on 6 February 1935, perhaps a symbolic function but an important one in that it represented the General Secretary's supremacy in the state. At the beginning of June 1935 the draft was ready, and Stalin submitted it to the Central Committee, which approved it and called for a final session of the Congress of Soviets to ratify the new constitution. It was at this point that the name 'Stalin Constitution' appeared as the standard reference to the document, a reverent appellation that remained in use throughout the leader's life.[62]

On 12 June the most innovative aspect of the process began: the submission of the published draft to meetings all over the country. It must have been the rare citizen who was not rounded up to participate in at least one discussion on the Stalin Constitution in factory, collective farm, school, military unit or other body. The press devoted itself unstintingly to this process during most of June and July, concluding on 7 August – evidently to avoid competing with a trial of alleged traitors – and in particular saturated the public with letters simply in praise of the Stalin Constitution, which now appeared as a kind of donation from on high. Along with this, 154 000 amendments were proposed by the populace, none known to be unfriendly but surely a significant part of the attempt to persuade the masses that they were collaborating with Stalin in the political process.[63]

Following an interval in which enthusiasm for the Constitution was allowed to lie fallow, the ratification ceremonies began on 25 November 1936 at an 'Extraordinary' session of the Congress of Soviets. Among the many speeches praising the Leader, one by A. O. Avdienko hit some kind of high point when he stated that he was in love and that when he married and his wife gave birth to a child 'the first word that it utters will be "Stalin"'.[64] The main event of the Congress was, predictably, Stalin's speech, in which he presented the constitution as his gift to the people, dealing authoritatively with thirteen proposed amendments, determining which were acceptable and which were not. His main point came as a revelation, not something that had been made clear in all the previous publicity on the constitution. The USSR, said Stalin, had achieved 'socialism' as a stage of development, marking the beginning of the transition to the higher and final stage, 'communism'. This was an important ideological dogma. Previous Marxists had recognized that there would be some sort of transition from the proletarian revolution to the completion of the ideal society. Marx had once referred to a transitional stage under the slogan 'From each according to his abilities, to each according to his work', and an ultimate one under the slogan 'From each according to his abilities, to each according to his needs.' In a speech of 17 November 1935, Stalin had alluded to this schema, defining the first period as 'socialism', the latter as 'communism'. But it was only in presenting the constitution that he emphasized that the USSR had entered socialism. This implied a claim by the Leader that he had led the country across a divide that was as important as the one that the Russian people had crossed under Lenin's leadership when it left behind the capitalist epoch. It was generally understood that Lenin's revolution had ushered in a transitional stage that aimed at the construction of socialism under 'the dictatorship of the proletariat'. Such an authoritarian form was needed because of the supposed threat of hostile elements in society, and this was reflected in the Soviet constitutions of 1919 and 1924 by the disenfranchisement of some categories of people, such as former capitalists, and by the unequal weighting of proletarian and peasant votes. But, said Stalin, the achievement of socialism in the USSR meant the elimination of all exploiting classes and any further need for such inequalities. In his constitution all citizens voted and their votes weighed equally in the election of officials. Classes did remain: the working class, peasantry and the intelligentsia. But there were no economic contradictions between these groups, which were all serving the goal of building a classless society.[65]

Stalin's speech was treated with maximum fanfare. It reappeared not only in print but in film and on phonograph record. Everyone stopped to hear him deliver it over the radio, his first important use of this medium. *Pravda* recounted how 250 collective farmers in the hamlet of Strizhova listened to it on the radio of their club, the crew of the ship *Kharkov* heard it in the English Channel and (as the poet Aleksei Surkov put it in a 'lyric reportage') 'The Congress met in Prigorovka', which is to say that the wonders of radio brought Stalin personally among the awe-stricken teachers and students of 'The Pedagogical Institute named for Bubnov' on 'Little Prigorovka Street, Moscow'. An editorial commission of 220, chaired by Stalin, put the final text in order, and it was ratified by the congress on 5 December. This signalled the opening of a new phase in the process, mass meetings throughout the country to celebrate the Stalin Constitution and its maker. A final flurry of glorification of the Constitution and its namesake came in October–December 1937 with the nomination and election of delegates to a new Supreme Soviet.[66]

The following year brought another special event in the evolution of the cult, the appearance of a textbook entitled *History of the All-Union Communist Party (Bolsheviks)*. When this work of some 350 pages first appeared in September 1938 it was attributed to a commission of the Central Committee, but a section of twenty-six pages 'On Dialectical and Historical Materialism' was specifically credited to Stalin, with much ado. This was a summation of Marxist theory, embellished with quotations from Marx, Engels and Lenin, which makes dry reading but nevertheless covers its subject respectably. The ideological specialist Yaroslavsky, who may well have drafted much of the book, claimed that Stalin spent four months going over the book as a whole, rewriting most of the draft that was submitted to him. In 1946 he claimed credit for the whole, which it certainly was in a spiritual sense, permeated with deadly hatred for the foes of 'the party', starting with the narodniks and ending with the Bukharinists, and treating Lenin and Stalin as invincible heroes.[67] This was only the most widely disseminated, authoritative part of a much broader campaign to reinterpret history in Stalin's favour. All manner of works showed him as Lenin's partner in revolution and a more-than-worthy heir in the march to socialism. Apart from those Bolsheviks, Trotsky chief among them, who had turned out to be 'enemies of the people', all other historical figures were relegated to a lowly or invisible role.

The *Short Course*, as it usually was called, was more than a book. It became the main educational device of the Soviet Union and Communist movement elsewhere for the rest of Stalin's life. Despite its narrow concern with the history of factional disputes, the Soviet cultural establishment was obliged to act as if they believed what one character in a Stalinist novel said of the *Short Course*: 'it contains everything that a man needs'. By 1948 its 234 printings in 66 languages had sold 34 million copies in the Soviet Union and over two million elsewhere. Stalin seems to have felt a sincere authorial attachment to the book, whatever portions he actually wrote, for he gave his twelve-year-old daughter an inscribed copy of the first printing, instructing her to read it. Svetlana was perhaps the one person in the country who could defy such an order, suffering only her father's anger. Even at twelve she was becoming an apolitical, and also headstrong, person.[68]

The culmination of the pre-war Stalin cult was the celebration of his sixtieth birthday in December 1939. That he had waited a whole decade since there had been any public observance of his birthday testifies to Stalin's patience and his shrewd understanding that, along with daily rituals, the cult needed high points that would lose their potency if overworked. The senders of birthday tributes ranged from the Politburo, each member of which contributed a suitable essay, to the 192 859 Turkmen people who signed a greeting. Amid the flood of verbiage in Stalin's honour one major theme was reverent accounts of meetings with him, some of which turned out to be nothing more than presence at some large assembly where he appeared. An important writer, A. Fadeev, edited an anthology of such material and it dominated the most impressive example of bookmaking of the occasion, a weighty, illustrated volume of 481 pages entitled *Stalin. On His Sixtieth Birthday*. Other memoirs, for example the recollections of film directors and architects of the Boss's benign interest in their work, appeared in the appropriate specialist journals. Another theme was the cataloguing of works, literary and graphic, devoted to the cult. The leading examples of this reverent research were a substantial volume called *Stalin and About Stalin* and another entitled *Stalin and Pictorial Art*.[69]

Less ephemeral than these tributes was the new official biography of the Leader, short enough to be published in a single issue of *Pravda* and simple enough to be understood by a graduate of a four-year elementary school. According to Khrushchev, Stalin personally embellished the lavish praise that this slim work heaped on him. Finally, another birthday memorial that lasted while Stalin lived was the creation of 'Stalin Prizes' in twenty-one categories of the arts and sciences, as well as several thousand stipends in his name for deserving students.[70]

And what did Stalin think about this massive celebration of his greatness? His only published response was a single sentence of thanks, but his museum in Gori now contains a document that suggests a gloomy reaction to the cult that he had fostered. This is the typed text of a speech that he gave on 22 April 1941 to participants in a conference on a decade of Tadzhik art. After thanking them for their confidence, sympathy and good wishes, Stalin, without mentioning himself, said that

> People have a bad custom – to commend the living, if they of course are deserving, but to consign the dead to oblivion, as idols as was said in olden times, or as Leaders as they say now; to commend, to express sympathy for them as long as they have not died, but when they die to forget them.

Like the speech that began this chapter, with its references to God and Satan, this unexpected self-revelation of Stalin suggests a troubled, pessimistic man behind the façade of joyful self-confidence . . . and a premonition of the eventual fate of his cult.[71]

12 War

Although Stalin's last formal meeting with a representative of Hitler's Reich occurred in February 1940, there was one more, ostensibly impromptu, occasion when he addressed the German ambassador. When the Japanese foreign minister departed from Moscow after signing a treaty with the USSR in April 1941, Stalin emphasized the importance of the agreement by seeing him off at the railway station. Also present was the German ambassador. Stalin sought him out and embraced him, saying, 'We must remain friends and you must do everything to that end!' He then repeated the performance with the German military attaché, a lowly personage to receive such recognition, but the only direct link that Stalin had to the German officer corps.[1] He had good reason to be concerned with the preservation of peace between Russia and Germany. The Soviet Union now faced victorious German forces along a frontier that stretched from the Arctic to the Black Sea at a time when the modernization of the Red Army was still incomplete.

Stalin saw to it that his military build-up went forward at an imposing pace, personally approving every new weapon that was adopted. The total manpower of the army and navy increased to about 4.2 million by the onset of the German invasion. By that time the Red Army had more tanks than the rest of the world combined. Granted, many of these were obsolete, but about 1500 of the excellent T-34 and KV had been delivered. Later critics of Stalin complained, with reason, that this was not enough, but it does not seem bad compared with a German tank force of about 3350, including many older models. Soviet aircraft lagged further behind, although models fit to fight the *Luftwaffe* were coming into production in 1941. Just how much Stalin's penchant for sending aircraft designers into penal institutions impeded progress is hard to appraise. Equally hard to evaluate is his tendency to get involved personally in technical decisions. After Stalin's death a number of specialists recalled cases in which he had imposed bad decisions on his designers, if only experimentally; for example, double-hulled armour for tanks, a fighter model that some ambitious designer sent to him outside regular channels. No doubt there were mistakes, which are inevitable in any large military programme, and no doubt Stalin contributed to them, but the results were not bad on balance. Given another year or two for modernization, and especially the training of officers to replace the victims of the Yezhovshchina, the Soviet armed forces should have become an effective deterrent against any invader. This calculation was basic to Hitler's decision to attack Russia in 1941, and in this sense the source of the Soviet calamity lay not in the inadequacy of Stalin's military preparedness, but in its achievements.[2]

Stalin may have underrated this point. His error may have derived partly from overrating the capability attained by the Red Army in 1941, despite its poor showing in the war with Finland. Soviet forces were immense, they had large stockpiles of equipment, and the deal with Germany had given them a large territorial buffer. In a secret address to Red Army commanders on 13 January 1941 Stalin estimated that in the existing conditions the invader would have to muster a two-to-one numerical superiority along the entire front. Stalin was right in doubting that the Germans could achieve such an advantage even with the aid of European allies. He alluded to the possibility of a two-front war involving Japan, but this was before the signing of the Soviet–Japanese non-aggression treaty. Following that agreement, when he gave another confidential speech to officers on 5 May, he could take a more confident tone, stressing the improvement of the Red Army, the vincibility of the Germans, and the need to improve political awareness in order to avoid the collapse of the will to fight. This, he thought, had played a major role in the German victories in the west.[3]

Stalin's optimistic appraisal of the military balance between Germany and Russia in the first half of 1941 was matched by his political outlook. According to his daughter, he repeatedly said after the war, 'Ech, together with the Germans we would have been invincible.' Indeed, continued co-operation of these two powers would have provided ample security against any coalition. Hitler for his part might have looked forward to a long reign over a huge empire. Stalin did not think that the Führer would be so rash as to lightly discard this situation, a point that he made in conversation with Roosevelt in 1943. His words were not transcribed, but Charles Bohlen, Roosevelt's interpreter at the time, believed that Stalin meant to convey that he 'considered that Hitler through his stupidity in attacking the Soviet Union had thrown away all the fruits of his previous victories'. In the spring of 1941 this calculation was sustained, independently, by both British and Japanese intelligence.[4]

These fundamentals in Stalin's appreciation of the broad background of international affairs in the spring of 1941 conditioned his reaction to the signals of military intelligence. Warnings from Britain and America that the Germans would attack were worse than useless, given their desperate desire for war between Germany and Russia. Stalin assumed that their efforts to make trouble between him and Hitler took the form not only of information supplied through official channels but also through covert disinformation. On one report from a Czech agent of Soviet intelligence, forecasting a German attack on Russia, Stalin noted, 'This informant is an English provocateur. Find out who is making this provocation and punish him.' It was reasonable to suspect that the British had planted disinformation on such agents, or even on Richard Sorge, a German who was a Soviet spy in Japan and who warned of a German attack. And, despite various forecasts of invasion on particular dates in the spring of 1941, weeks passed without action and the time remaining for a summer campaign diminished. As events were to demonstrate, Hitler needed as much time as possible if he were to take Moscow before winter set in. Stalin was justified in thinking that the delay through May and much of June meant that he was in the clear for another year. Even if Hitler had been contemplating a drive to the east, his decision to invade the Balkans and even Crete, with the resulting loss of time and also of German paratroops, should have persuaded him to call off the Russian campaign. There was also German disinformation – such as the printing of large quantities of maps of Britain – which was planted on Soviet intelligence and read by Stalin, who wanted to believe it. He could not deny that German forces were massed in eastern Europe, but this might be explained merely as a threat that could be useful in diplomatic negotiations. Hitler might, for example, want to renegotiate the 1939 deal, obliging the Soviets to yield their interest in Finland, where there was now a German military presence. This was also the general conclusion of British military intelligence,[5] despite the contrary warnings sent to Stalin.

In these circumstances it is not surprising that Stalin avoided as much as possible any appearance that he was preparing for immediate war. Had not Nicholas II brought about the German attack in 1914 by mobilizing his army? Considering that it was well known that Soviet military doctrine stressed the offensive, would not an increase in Soviet battle-readiness have invited a German pre-emptive blow? This was the sense of Stalin's response to the proposal of the narkom of defence, Marshal S. K. Timoshenko, and General Zhukov on 14 June that the Red Army should undertake full mobilization. 'That's war,' replied Stalin, 'Do you understand that or not?' Even on the evening of 21 June, by which time reports of imminent attack had intensified, Stalin rejected the recommendation of these military men. Full wartime mobilization would be 'premature'. The question still can be settled by peaceful means', said Stalin, and he approved a compromise order that ambiguously acknowledged the possibility of German attack in 22–3 June and urged troops not to yield to 'provocation'.[6]

Stalin's judgement concerning Hitler's intentions in the spring of 1941 turned out to be calamitously wrong, but in the long run it turned out to be Hitler who had made the more serious miscalculation. This, however, was not the appearance of things on 22 June 1941. In a few hours the German onslaught destroyed a large part of the Soviet air force, had penetrated the positions of forward Soviet formations and, perhaps, most important, had smashed Soviet communications, which depended heavily on vulnerable wire lines to Moscow. The first reports to reach the capital were treated as provocation, but within only about an hour Stalin had accepted Zhukov's affirmation of their validity and at 4.30 a.m. convened the Politburo. Stalin was 'pale', Zhukov recalls, and his first thought was that they must contact the German ambassador. Evidently he still hoped to find a diplomatic alternative. Within an hour or two Molotov had received what amounted to a declaration of war in the name of the Führer. Stalin reacted to this news with a prolonged silence, which Zhukov broke to propose that they order the troops to fight. Stalin then approved orders for the Red Army to destroy the invader on Soviet territory but not to pursue him to the west. As matters turned out, this was an irrelevant constraint, but it reflected Stalin's intent, even in the circumstances, of leaving open the door for a negotiated settlement.[7]

The following week or so was a time of utter confusion in the Soviet high command, which scarcely knew what was going on at the fronts. Stalin appears to have been stunned and, soon, exhausted, but it is unlikely that he suffered a complete nervous collapse or abdicated all leadership. Zhukov recalled that Stalin seemed 'depressed' on 22 June. But he also portrays Stalin as active in a series of meetings that day. The next day he participated in the framing of the order that established the General Headquarters of the High Command, called Stavka. Zhukov next saw Stalin on the 26th and found him 'not in the best shape', which in context seems to mean exhausted. But he was able to hear Zhukov's report on the southern front, whence he had just returned. Three days later Stalin impressed three of his generals as vigorous and ill-tempered, in the words of Voronov, 'depressed, nervous and of uneven disposition. When he assigned missions he demanded that they be carried out in unbelievably short periods without taking into account the actual possibilities of doing so.' General Chakovsky recalls that, upon hearing of the threatened encirclement of Soviet forces near Minsk, he 'burst out with angry, insulting scolding. Then, without looking at anyone, head down and stooped over, he left the building, got into his car and went home.' It may have been in such a confrontation that he burst out, 'All that which Lenin created we have lost forever', intended as a rebuke to the generals, but this alleged expostulation is provided by Khrushchev, who was in the Ukraine and could not have heard it personally. In this angry humour, Stalin ordered the execution of General D. G. Pavlov, who commanded the Soviet forces on the main route from Warsaw to Moscow, and several of his subordinates. This was not, however, the beginning of a new purge of the military. During the rest of the war Stalin often proved himself a tough taskmaster, but he did not act as if he imagined his officer corps to be riddled with traitors.[8]

Although it is probable that Stalin experienced some intervals of complete exhaustion during the first ten days of the war, this does not account for the near-disappearance of his image from the official media during this period. Even if he had been totally prostrate, it would have been easy for the press to rally the populace around Stalin's name and visage. And only Stalin himself had the authority to cut off the predictable flow of leader-cult material in the dire circumstances. But the Soviet press, which normally spent so much effort assuring the public that Stalin was in complete charge, quickly dropped any such notion once the news of defeats began to pour in. Stalin assigned to Molotov the task of announcing on the radio at noon on 22 June that there was a war. When this short statement appeared in *Pravda* the next day, it was accompanied by Stalin's photograph, implying that he was in command. On the 24th a banner headline referred to the war effort 'headed by the great Stalin', among other ritual references to him, including some in hastily composed poems. But for the next nine days *Pravda* scarcely indicated that he was alive. Apart from an occasional allusion to 'the party of Lenin–Stalin', his name was almost wholly absent, even in the spate of topical poems.[9]

His image as leader was also absent from the formal arrangements for military command that were adopted at the start of the war. The Soviet armed forces lacked any office of commander-in-chief when the Germans attacked, and Timoshenko and Zhukov proposed to remedy this by naming Stalin to the post with a 'Stavka of the High Command'. But when a draft of this plan was presented to Stalin at 9 a.m. on 22 June, he said that the Politburo would consider it. The next day, whether or not he had discussed it with anyone, Stalin approved the plan in amended form, naming no commander-in-chief, and made Timoshenko chairman of a Stavka that included Stalin, Molotov, Voroshilov, Budyenny, Kuznetsov and Zhukov. At first glance Stalin's supremacy was established on 30 June when the party and state jointly appointed a 'State Committee of Defence' with Stalin as chairman. But the official presentation of this war council was guarded on the question of ultimate authority. Stalin's name as chairman was presented once in *Pravda*'s official announcement and once in the lead editorial hailing this new body. Far from stressing Stalin, the editorial went on to emphasize collective leadership, taking heart in the presence on the committee of men 'who are devoted to the cause of the people, Molotov, Voroshilov, Malenkov, Beria'. All of this suggests not that Stalin was in a state of paralysis, but that he had calculated that the news was going to be bleak for some time to come and was loath to identify his carefully nurtured image with terrible defeats. Shortly after the ultimate victory over Germany he came close to acknowledging that he had been concerned about the popular response to his leadership in a time of military disaster. In a toast to the Russian people Stalin paid tribute to their steadfastness, noting that the government had made many mistakes and there had been desperate situations. 'Another people might have said to the government, you have not justified our confidence, get out.'[10]

Perhaps he overreacted to his fear that the Soviet people would tell him to get out. The masses had been conditioned to rely on their 'Leader,

Teacher and Friend' in all matters, and such an abrupt withdrawal of Stalin's image could only bewilder them in time of crisis. This may have been the message that some members of the Politburo delivered to Stalin at about this time. Khrushchev's secret speech of 1956 claims that such a delegation went to him early in the war, urging 'certain steps . . . to improve the situation at the front'. In the context of a speech attacking 'the cult of personality', Khrushchev could hardly say that the Politburo told Stalin that the people were addicted to the cult and could not fight without it.[11]

Such a message would explain Stalin's re-emergence as Leader on 3 July when he delivered his first wartime radio address. The delivery was far from rousing, but if, as has been alleged, there were sounds of nervousness, such as the clinking of a water glass and gulps of air, these have been removed from the recorded version.[12] Style aside, it is clear that Stalin had given serious thought to the image that he wished to assume in his début as wartime leader. Opening with an appeal to 'Comrades! Citizens! Brothers and sisters!', the speech barely implied that the Soviet Union purported to be a Communist state. Stalin evidently believed what he told Averell Harriman two months later: 'the Russian people were fighting as they always had "for their homeland, not for us", meaning the Communist Party'. The speech referred not to class war but to the struggle of the Russian and other nations against German Fascism. But the Germans were not invincible, said Stalin. They had gained an advantage by attacking, but this did not discredit the Soviet–German treaty of 1939, a peace-loving measure that had won time for the improvement of defences. Stalin was sure that the Germans would be defeated, but by the most sacrificial means: the Red Army would retreat and destroy everything as it went, and 'our forces are numberless'. In short, a war of attrition. Britain and America, Stalin noted in passing, had said that they would send aid, but his message to the Soviet people was that their sacrifices alone would overwhelm the Germans.[13]

Soon after the radio address *Pravda* announced that Stalin had assumed the post of narkom of defence. In fact he also became 'Supreme Commander' and 'chairman' of Stavka on 10 July and 8 August, respectively, but these responsibilities were not made known to the public at the time. As Khrushchev recalled, Stalin's name never appeared on specific orders in the first year or more of the war, in Khrushchev's opinion a carefully considered decision concerning the Stalin image.[14]

Stalin's routine of work was adjusted to wartime conditions. Although he had offices in a bombproof command centre in a Metro station and another shelter in the Kremlin grounds, the enemy did not bomb Moscow heavily or often, and most of Stalin's work continued in his accustomed office. The stream of visitors was modified, military men supplanting many of the civilians. Zhukov, for example, recalls going there at least once, sometimes twice a day, for reports. His description of the office indicates that it was little altered from its pre-war state, apart from the appearance of a teletype device and the addition of portraits of the victorious tsarist commanders Suvorov and Kutuzov, somewhat incongruous companions for Marx, Engels and Lenin. Here Stalin worked from between twelve and fiften hours a day, following his eccentric habit of starting late in the morning and finishing in the small hours of the next day. Apart from spending most of his nights at Nearby, Stalin scarcely stirred from his office, 'the nook'.[15]

His style of command in war was much as it had been in peace, reserving for himself not only the ultimate authority but also the prerogative of intervening at any level if it pleased him. According to Zhukov, Stalin 'mastered questions of the organization of front operations [there being about a dozen large sectors, or "fronts", at any given moment] and groups of fronts', a point sustained by chief-of-staff Vasilevsky. Lest this be dismissed as mere post-Khrushchev propaganda aimed at rehabilitating Stalin's image as a war leader, consider that General Alan Brooke, who encountered Stalin in 1943, judged him 'a military brain of the very highest order'. And Brooke was arguably the keenest British military mind of the war, a professional who held in contempt politicians who dabbled in strategy, and also the one western general whom Stalin accused to his face of being unfriendly to Russia.[16]

But both Zhukov and Vasilevsky consider that Stalin's martial competence did not mature until about the time of the Battle of Stalingrad in late 1942, and this implies that the first year and more of the war was a time of education for him, at terrible cost to the Red Army and the Soviet people. The improvement in Stalin's performance owed something to the arrival in December 1942 of A. I. Antonov as chief of operations of the General Staff. This well-organized military administrator saw to it that Stalin received his reports in files coded red for urgent action, blue for matters of lower priority and green for promotions and assignments, which required careful attention and proper timing. Antonov alternated with General S. M. Shtemenko as Stalin's principal duty officer, the former covering from noon until 5 or 6 a.m. and the latter from 7 p.m. until 2 p.m. Thus both officers were available when Stalin was at his best, from 6 or 7 p.m. until 5 a.m. They reported on the military situation three times daily, with a joint summary somewhere around midnight, using maps on a scale of 1:200 000 for each army group, showing the position of each division and sometimes of regiments. Shtemenko notes that there was indeed a globe in Stalin's Kremlin office, but he never saw it used in discussions of operations. This is one of several sources that discredits Khrushchev's polemical assertion in 1956 that Stalin planned Red Army operations on a globe.[17]

Stalin's remarkable memory, which Vasilevsky considers the best he ever encountered, enabled him to deal personally with the assignment of his high command.

> Stalin knew not only all the commanders of the fronts and armies, and there were over a hundred of them, but also several commanders of corps and divisions, as well as the top officials of the People's Commissariat of Defence, not to speak of the top personnel of the central and regional party and state apparatus. Throughout the war Stalin constantly remembered the composition of the strategic reserve and could at any time name any particular formation,

recalled Vasilevsky. With this knowledge of individual personalities Stalin engaged in frequent reshuffling of commands, probably more than was useful. He usually preceded a new senior posting with an interview and often discharged unsuccessful officers the same way, or by personal telephone call.[18]

His vast knowledge of the war concerned the enemy, too. During daily reports if the briefing officer omitted reference to any particular German army, Stalin would prompt him to deal with it. Evidence of his intervention in details, especially in the first year or so of the war, abound and suggest excessive meddling. In the beginning of the war he tried to watch over the work of the General Staff in detail by assigning six officers as his personal deputies in the staff, but this proved so disruptive that the practice was disbanded. But he never yielded a close and detailed control over war matériel, personally authorizing the defenders of Leningrad to take for themselves four days' production of KV tanks, or allocating 160 cannon to specific units in the Battle of Moscow. He took a particular interest in aircraft supply, keeping a personal notebook on daily production of fighters. At one point he authorized the air force to train fighter pilots in intra-mural dogfights with live ammunition.[19]

Stalin controlled the armed forces not only through the military hierarchy but also through techniques that were not a standard feature of modern armies. One was his use of Politburo members or other senior party officials as representatives with military fronts. Not only did he keep men like Zhdanov and Khrushchev in the councils of the front, holding military rank, he also sent Politburo members who normally worked in Moscow on special missions to key areas. For example, Malenkov was dispatched to the Stalingrad sector during the height of the battle, and Beria to the Caucasus when it was threatened. As General Secretary of the party he still controlled the actions of regional party secretaries concerning military affairs. Thus, when Zhdanov took the initiative to establish a special council for the defence of Leningrad, Stalin wired a rebuke for not first obtaining his consent. A more prudent provincial secretary, Patolichev in Yaroslavl, remembered to ask permission to integrate militia units into the Red Army as the enemy approached. Then there was Stalin's practice of sending his senior military assistants, especially Zhukov and Vasilevsky, to front-line areas to supervise the command during major battles. Since he insisted on receiving daily reports by wire, this provided Stalin with a direct presence in regional commands. Stalin's physical performance over four years of war was formidable. Perhaps it owed something to a reduction of alcohol consumption. At least General Shtemenko discovered that Stalin's special decanter, which was present at his night-time meals with his officers, contained iced water. In a sense he personally wore down Hitler, a man ten years his junior, who also insisted on a high degree of personal authority and drove himself into serious physical decline long before his suicide.[20]

During the first months of the German onslaught the Red Army was in such a state of disarray, its communications so badly disrupted, that it was difficult to determine the impact of Stalin's leadership on the course of the disaster. But by the end of July the invader had to pause to regroup, which permitted the Red Army to assume some semblance of order and Stalin to exercise more deliberate control over it. Far from showing that German success had intimidated him, he was intent on halting their advance at once and in some areas counter-attacking. He had been 'beside himself' at the failure of Timoshenko, commanding the central front, the main road to Moscow, to stop the Germans and was barely dissuaded by Zhukov, supported by Kalinin at a Politburo meeting, from dismissing Timoshenko and assigning Zhukov to the post. When evidence mounted that the next phase of the German offensive would turn their main forces from the Moscow road to the south, forming one claw of a pincer movement around Kiev, Stalin became obdurately aggressive. He ordered an attack on this northern force, and was irate when this failed. 'Stavka is much displeased with your work', he wired Yeremenko. 'Guderian [the German commander] and the whole of his group must be smashed to smithereens.' As the Germans were closing their pincers around Kiev the Soviet generals proposed withdrawal to a new defensive line, while Stalin wanted an attack. 'What sort of counter-blow is this?', he fumed to the frontal command. 'How could you dream up the idea of surrendering Kiev to the enemy?' Angry in turn, Zhukov offered to resign as chief-of-staff and to take command of a front, which is just what Stalin arranged in less than an hour. On 8 August 1941 he accused the command in Kiev of 'light-heartedly' planning to surrender the city and promised them fresh forces for the defence in two weeks. It must have been about this time that Khrushchev, as senior political member of the military front committee in Kiev, received from Stalin a wire accusing him of cowardice and the intention of surrendering Kiev. It threatened to 'take action' against Khrushchev. By 11 September the German encirclement of Kiev was so far advanced that Stalin ceased his fulminations against the advocates of retreat, but he showed fatal indecision. His new orders called for the preparation of defensive lines to the east, but also stated that Kiev should not be surrendered nor the bridge across the Dnieper destroyed without direct orders from Moscow. Five days later the Germans closed their trap and by the end of the month had crushed their prey, taking about half a million prisoners. This was Stalin's worst defeat of the war.[21]

In conversation with his ambassador to Great Britain, Ivan Maisky, Stalin acknowledged that his strategy in 1941 resembled that of Kutuzov, who drew Napoleon to Moscow and eventual destruction. In both cases, said Stalin, the retreat was not the result of prior planning, but he saw a major difference: while Kutuzov's defence had been passive, Stalin's involved a battle for each position. To this one might add that when Kutuzov stood against Napoleon at Borodino, on the western approaches to Moscow, both armies were relatively intact. In contrast, the Red Army had suffered vast losses by October 1941 when the Germans, whose casualties were large, too, broke through and threatened the Soviet capital. At this juncture Stalin recalled Zhukov from Leningrad, where he had been commanding the city that was starting its long ordeal by siege. Though ill with influenza, Stalin's charge to his best trouble-shooter was to organize the defence of the capital. But the Red Army was in disarray, the weather still favourable for tank operations, and the Germans drove toward Moscow from three sides. At some point around 10 October Stalin evidently was driven to consider that he might have to evacuate his capital and high command to Kuibyshev, about 800 km to the east on the Volga, truly a strategic retreat in the manner of Kutuzov. Foreign diplomats, many women and children, key factories, some government offices, and even the general staff, Stalin's daughter and his large personal library were moved to Kuibyshev. On 15 October Molotov told the British and American representatives that Stalin also would leave in a day or two. Office and residential accommodations were indeed made ready. What started as an orderly withdrawal became a panicky flight for many civilians on 16 October, but Stalin was not among them. Although German planes bombed Moscow frequently at this time, forcing Stalin into his shelter, he had not given up on the defence of his capital.[22]

The psychological importance of holding Moscow no doubt weighed heavily in his calculation, as became evident on 30 October when Stalin informed General P. A. Artemev that the traditional parade in honour of the October Revolution would be held as usual on 7 November. Stalin determined to make this an occasion for a display of personal determination. Previously he had appeared on the Lenin Mausoleum at the observances of the October Revolution and May Day and left the speech-making to others. But in wartime he regularly presented major addresses on each of these holidays. The first of these, on 6 and 7 November 1941, occurred in dire and dramatic settings. With the Germans at the outskirts of Moscow, Stalin made one speech on the eve of the anniversary, holding the meeting in the vestibule of a Metro station in case German planes appeared, and another in Red Square in broad daylight. Both speeches breathed defiance, hatred and Russian patriotism. Reversing the true figures, Stalin claimed that German casualties far outweighed Soviet, and, more accurately, that the enemy had left his original bases far behind. In this, said Stalin, Hitler was following Napoleon, but 'Hitler no more resembles Napoleon than a kitten resembles a lion, for Napoleon fought against the forces of reaction and was supported by progressive forces, and Hitler, on the contrary, is supported by reactionary forces, is waging a struggle against progressive forces.' This was as close as the Communist leader came to inspiring his people with the Marxist–Leninist creed. The main thrust of his rhetoric was that 'the great Russian nation, the nation of Plekhanov and Lenin, Belinsky and Chernyshevsky, Pushkin and Tolstoy, Glinka and Tchaikowsky, Gorky and Chekhov, Sechenov and Pavlov, Repin and Surikov, Suvorov and Kutuzov' would give the Germans 'a war of extermination'.[23]

This he wished to provide not only through stubborn defence but by counter-attacks, even contrary to the advice of his military experts. The first of these commands during the Battle of Moscow came on 13 November, despite Zhukov's insistence that it was folly to commit the last reserves at this stage. 'Consider the question of the counter-blow settled. Communicate the plan to me tonight', said Stalin, ending the conversation. In truth the attack did not succeed, except perhaps in demonstrating the reckless determination of the Red Army, and about a week later Stalin telephoned Zhukov to ask him to say, 'Honestly, as a Communist', if he was convinced that they would hold Moscow. Perhaps Stalin was just checking Zhukov's nerves, for when the latter asserted his assurance that they would hold but needed two reserve armies and 200 tanks, Stalin promised him the soldiers by the end of November, adding that they did not have the tanks. Zhukov was right. Bitter weather, for which the Germans were ill prepared, the attrition of men and weapons, and Soviet determination stalled the German attack by the opening of December.

Stalin gave Zhukov additional forces to enable him to counter-attack once again on 5 December. As 1941 ended Stalin ordered attacks on a number of other fronts, extending from the Crimean Peninsula to besieged Leningrad. There were some limited successes, but the action failed to break the blockade of Leningrad and the Red Army incurred further heavy losses. This did not deter Stalin, who on 5 January 1942 told a meeting of senior officers that because of German exhaustion and unpreparedness for winter, 'This is the most suitable time to go over to a general offensive.' No doubt he had a point concerning the Germans, but, as both Zhukov and the chief of war industry, N. A. Voznesensky, observed, the Soviets needed time to re-equip before they could attack effectively. No, said Stalin, 'It is necessary to quickly grind down the Germans, so that they will be unable to attack in the spring.' The issue, explained Marshal Shaposhnikov to an exasperated Zhukov, had already been decided by 'the Supreme', so objections were in vain. And Zhukov had occasion to confirm this a little later when he tried to explain on the telephone that his forces were stretched too thinly to support a successful attack: Stalin did not argue but simply hung up. And so in 1942 the winter months, not traditionally a season for heavy campaigning in Russia's wars, were a time of continued slaughter. Stalin's hope that the enemy would be too weakened to attack in the spring proved excessive, and it probably would have been more effective for the Red Army to rest and rebuild during the winter. On the other hand, some ground was gained, which was at least beneficial for morale.[24]

Since neither Hitler's plan to crush the Red Army in 1941 nor Stalin's attempt in early 1942 to smash the Germans had succeeded, the resumption of heavy fighting was guaranteed with the coming of spring and dry weather. As before, Stalin was convinced that the best defence was to attack first, while his generals believed that their forces needed more time to repair the grievous damage they had suffered. Stalin had his way and ordered offensives at various points, some of which enjoyed some success, inspiring him to mutter about the 'uselessness' of the General Staff. But the Red Army was in truth not yet ready to drive back the re-equipped Germans, and Soviet penetrations were either stopped or threatened with enveloping counter-attacks. The most serious case in point was a drive in May 1942 aimed at the industrial city of Kharkov. Contrary to Shaposhnikov's warnings, the Red Army tried to extend a salient that it had won during the winter. It soon became evident that the Germans could close pincers on the advancing Soviet forces, a point that the political representative on the council of the front, Khrushchev, tried to get through to Stalin by telephone. But the Supreme Commander would not accept the call and had Malenkov inform Khrushchev that 'the offensive must continue'.[25]

The resulting defeat gravely weakened Soviet forces in the eastern Ukraine, through which Hitler planned his major drive. By good luck, Red Army intelligence had obtained a complete copy of this plan, but Stalin discounted it, believing that the main attack would come further north. At the opening of July the Germans knocked a vast hole in Soviet lines in the south, enabling one large force to head for the Volga and Stalingrad, the other for the Caucasus and its oil fields. As in the early months of the war, Stalin witnessed the disintegration of his plans and army as the enemy plunged ever deeper into Russia. Having no fresh forces with which to check the German advance, he tried to substitute exhortation, especially in his order of 28 July 1942, best known for its slogan, 'Not a step backward!' This was signed 'Supreme Command', not with his own name. But it was only about a month later that natural obstacles – the Volga and the Caucasus range – enabled the Red Army to block the invader's progress.[26]

In this desperate period Stalin's anger often burst out at his subordinates, though not to the extent of ordering executions. One of his victims was his former secretary Mekhlis, who had been posted to supervise what turned out to be a disaster on the Kerch Peninsula. When Mekhlis asked Stalin to send a brilliant general to save the situation, the Supreme sardonically replied, 'We have no Hindenburgs in reserve', and soon proceeded to demote Mekhlis and remove him as head of the political directorate of the army. Another recipient of Stalin's wrath was Vasilevsky, the chief-of-staff, who had the unpleasant task of reporting the entry of German troops into Stalingrad. This was bad enough, but a break in the telephone lines prevented Vasilevsky from making his report from the front on time, always a grave sin in Stalin's opinion. When communications were restored they burned with 'painful, insulting and mostly undeserved abuse, directed not only at the Chief of the General Staff but at all Red Army commanders'. But Zhukov had won Stalin's confidence and in the crisis of August 1942 Stalin made him 'deputy supreme commander', a singular mark of esteem.[27]

As in 1941, German victories had forced the strategy of retreat upon Stalin, and once again the elongation of German supply lines and the attrition of battle wore down the invader, who had compounded his difficulties by sending his two main armies in widely divergent directions. as soon as the German advance had reached its limit Stalin was once again plotting a counter-offensive, meeting in his quarters with Zhukov and Vasilevsky on 12 September to lay plans for their attack. This time Stalin was willing to listen to the professionals and accept their proposal to take forty-five days to prepare their forces for the counter-blow. He also dropped his own idea of attacking near the city of Stalingrad and accepted the professionals' plan to strike much further west along the flank of the German salient. This patient mood persisted while a Soviet assault force of over a million men was assembled. About a week before the operation, Zhukov, who was at the front, and Stalin adopted special pseudonyms in their mutual communications, the latter signing 'Vasilev', a cover he had used for a time in the pre-revolutionary underground, and the former 'Konstantinov'. In May 1943 they changed this code, Stalin becoming 'Ivanov', which was another one of his pre-revolutionary covers, while Zhukov became 'Yurev'. There was little likelihood that any of this would have fooled the Germans, should the messages have been intercepted. It seems to have been more a gesture of comradeship on Stalin's part, combined with a sentimental regard for his earlier life.[28]

The Red Army opened its attack on 19 November and by the 23rd had closed pincers around the large German force in the vicinity of Stalingrad. Moreover the possibility of a westward push to the Sea of Azov threatened to trap the other prong of the German offensive in the region north of the Caucasus. In the frenzied fighting of the next two months the Germans succeeded in extricating this army but not the one trapped in Stalingrad, which was crushed by the end of January 1943. The enormous victory of Stalingrad must have been all the sweeter for Stalin because it focused on the city bearing his name. This was a remarkable bit of luck, considering how unlikely such an event was when the city assumed his name in 1925 and how far it had been from Stalin's mind, even in early 1942, to permit the Germans to advance so far. The mythic qualities of this victory also resonated with those of his success at the same place in the civil war, long a part of his cult. With his second, greater triumph accomplished at this place on the Volga, he was willing to appear publicly in the guise of 'Supreme Commander'. But neither this title nor his later assumption of the rank of 'Marshal of the Soviet Union' was formally announced; references to his name along with these dignities simply appeared in the press without comment. Evidently Stalin did not want to call attention to his reticence in assuming publicly the full responsibility for the conduct of the war.[29]

Although the war now seemed nearly hopeless for Germany, her troops still were deep in Soviet territory and by the summer of 1943 had sufficiently recouped their strength to attempt a final major offensive, this time aimed at the bulge that the Red Army held around Kursk. Although Stalin was tempted to try once again to strike first, he was at length induced by the professionals to fight a deliberate defensive battle. The result in July 1943 was a vast encounter of tanks, grim for both sides, but ending without a German breakthrough. This encouraged Stalin to open a new propaganda campaign. In early August, when the Red Army took Orel and Belograd, he surprised his headquarters staff by asking them, 'Do you read military history? If you had, you would know that in ancient times, when troops won victories, all the bells would be rung in honour of the commanders and their troops. It wouldn't be a bad idea for us, too, to signify victories more impressively.' And he proceeded to elaborate a plan by which important victories would be celebrated in Moscow by artillery salvoes, broadcast over the radio to the whole country, accompanied by fireworks. The hierarchy of honours ranged up to twenty-four salvoes from 324 guns, preceded by an official message in Stalin's name. Only he could authorize such a salute, and he signed the published orders as 'Marshal of the Soviet Union'. Henceforth military uniform with the rank of marshal was his accustomed dress. His enhanced status as war leader was also manifest in the publication at the end of July of his book *On the Great Patriotic War of the Soviet Union*, which consisted of his speeches since the start of the war. The title of this book bestowed on the war its new official Soviet name, which captured well the nationalist spirit that Stalin wished to invoke and which has endured to the present in Soviet usage. The book was treated as the principal writing on the war, was the subject of mass meetings, and later was brought up to date in new editions.[30]

It was just after the victory at Kursk that Stalin on 3 August 1943 undertook his only look at the front. His exact itinerary is unclear, but he definitely went to the small city of Yunkov on the Roslavl highway, about 200 km west and somewhat south of Moscow. Here he summoned two senior commanders and told them twice over that they must plan to recapture Smolensk, a point that he could easily have made by wire. Stalin's motivation for the trip seems to have been personal curiousity, not propaganda, for it was not publicized at the time.[31]

The Soviet populace needed all the encouragement it could get in order to struggle through almost two more years of war with Germany. Although it was capable of wearing down its adversary in massive frontal attacks, the Red Army was unable to sustain a deep drive behind a point of breakthrough. This being the case, Stalin probably was well advised to attack at various times along the full extent of the enormously long front, keeping the Germans strung out as much as possible. Thus it was that his military historians glorified 1944 as the year of 'the ten Stalinist blows'. Of these the most crushing was 'Operation Bagration', as Stalin named it in honour of the Georgian general who had fought against Napoleon in the same region, Belorussia. Beginning on the third anniversary of the German invasion, this enormous offensive inflicted about as many casualties on the Germans as had the Battle of Stalingrad. In this and other major operations in the closing phase of the war Stalin maintained the centralized pattern of control that he had established, but managed to collaborate with his senior officers without any serious quarrels on strategy. True, there were occasional outbursts, such as the time he called his aircraft experts 'Hitlerites' because of a flaw in a fabric paint that was causing fighters to break up in the air; or the formal reprimand to Voronov, his marshal of the artillery, and Zhukov because they had issued new field regulations without his approval; or the cold sarcasm of his message to General Tolbukhin, which began, 'If you are thinking of extending the war by five or six months then please do withdraw your troops behind the Danube.'[32]

As the war drew to a close in the spring of 1945 Stalin's military concerns shifted from the defeated enemy to his western allies. On 29 March he told Zhukov, 'I think that Roosevelt will not break the Yalta agreements, but Churchill, that one might do anything.' In particular he wanted the honour and political leverage that went with the conquest of Berlin. On 1 March 1945 he had asked General Konev who was going to take the city, 'we or the allies?' When Konev said it would be the Red Army, Stalin said with sarcastic satisfaction, 'So that's what you're like.' But he was afraid that the Germans would bend every effort to defend Berlin from the Red Army, while opening the gates to the west. This inspired Stalin to deceive General Eisenhower, when the latter took the initiative on 28 March in communicating about plans for the joining of Soviet and western forces in central Germany, not at Berlin. Stalin replied that this fitted in with Soviet plans, because 'Berlin has lost its former strategic importance. The Soviet High Command therefore plan to allot secondary forces in the direction of Berlin. . . . The beginning of the main blow by Soviet forces is approximately the second half of May.' Shortly after the war he assured Eisenhower that the Berlin operation had been the result of 'last-minute changes' in the military situation, a transparent deception. In fact he was directing the preparation of an enormous Soviet offensive aimed at taking Berlin in early May. With the death of Roosevelt on 12 April, Stalin was apprehensive about the situation and told Zhukov that he thought 'a serious scuffle is in prospect'. But the western forces did not try to beat the Red Army into Berlin, and Stalin had his triumph.[33]

On May Day 1945 Zhukov dared rouse Stalin from his sleep to inform him by telephone that Hitler was dead and the German commandant of Berlin asking for an armistice. 'He's caught it at last, the scoundrel', said Stalin and expressed regret that they had not taken Hitler alive. Stalin's satisfaction that it was the Red Army that took Berlin was vitiated by the fact that the initial surrender of the Third Reich was to Eisenhower. What made this particularly aggravating to him was the fact that a Soviet liaison officer, General I. A. Susloparov, signed the instrument of surrender. Stalin angrily phoned his marshal of the artillery, Voronov, to inquire who was 'this celebrated general of the artillery Susloparov who, without even telling the Soviet government and certainly without its authority, had dared to sign a document of such tremendous international importance'. The culprit was ordered to return directly to Moscow for punishment, and Stalin insisted on a second surrender ceremony with the high commands of all the Allied armies present, Zhukov signing for the Soviets.[34]

Stalin's suspicions in the spring of 1945 concerning Britain and the United States were not new. From the German invasion of Russia his relations with those two Atlantic powers were among his overriding concerns, a question that he handled personally, despite the pressures of military affairs. Even with so trustworthy a deputy as Molotov serving as narkom of foreign affairs, Stalin did not wish to delegate the conduct of diplomacy at a time when the world was in flux. His work therefore involved many more meetings with representatives of capitalist states than it had in his previous career, including the period of the German–Soviet treaty. The most frequent top-level caller was Winston Churchill, who came to Moscow on his own in August 1942 and October 1944, and was one of 'The Big Three' at Tehran in November 1943, Yalta in February 1945 and Potsdam in July of that year. When a visitor remarked to Stalin that Churchill, Roosevelt and Stalin had been referred to as the Trinity, Stalin noted that Churchill must be the Holy Ghost, because he flitted around so much. Roosevelt came to Tehran and Yalta, Truman to Potsdam, where Clement Atlee became Churchill's successor during the conference. Apart from summit meetings, Stalin maintained a voluminous personal correspondence with the British and American leaders, although he wrote fewer and briefer letters than his allies most of the time, which helped to create a sense that he was the benefactor and they the supplicants.[35]

The British foreign secretary, Anthony Eden, visited Stalin on his own in December 1941 and along with his American counterpart, Cordell Hull, in October 1943. At least as important were the visits of presidential emissary Harry Hopkins in July 1941 and May–June 1945. W. Averell Harriman first called on Stalin along with Lord Beaverbrook in October 1941 when the two were dispatched to discuss war supplies. Harriman went again with Churchill in 1942 and returned as ambassador in October 1943, staying in this capacity until January 1945. Including several personal meetings with Stalin and attendance at larger meetings, he probably spent more time in Stalin's presence than any other representative of a foreign state. The Soviet leader seems to have liked this authentic capitalist banker and multimillionaire, who was far from pliant as a diplomat. Stalin's parting words, after receiving Harriman at his vacation villa in October 1945, were, 'I have received you not only as the ambassador of the United States but as a friend. It will always be so.' For his part, Harriman rated Stalin 'better informed than Roosevelt, more realistic than Churchill, in some ways the most effective of the war leaders'. Harriman's predecessor, Admiral W. H. Standley, and the British ambassador, Sir Archibald Clark Kerr, also called on Stalin during the war.[36]

Then there was a stream of visitors who came with more or less official credentials and more or less serious business: Wendell Wilkie, Patrick Hurley, Joseph Davies, Donald Nelson, Eric Johnston, Air Marshal Tedder, Mrs Winston Churchill, General Eisenhower and, just after the war, Senator Claude Pepper and a committee of the House of Representatives. This group went to see Stalin immediately following a bibulous reception in the Moscow Metro, inspiring one of their number to say something, just before the audience, about punching Stalin in the nose. The most exotic of Stalin's American visitors during the war was a priest from Springfield, Massachusetts, Father Orlemanski, who had no official credentials but provided Stalin with an opportunity to assure Polish-Americans of his benevolence. But there was one aspiring visitor whom he evaded. In June 1945 Churchill wrote to Stalin that King George VI 'would be glad if you invited him to luncheon' during the forthcoming conference in Germany. Stalin ignored this overture, but after the prime minister repeated the proposal, now offering the monarch's hospitality to the Bolshevik, the latter replied that he 'had no objection . . . if you think it necessary'. The king decided that he had other pressing engagements. In addition to the many hours spent with these Britons and Americans Stalin also received the presidents of four European states that Germany had occupied: from Poland Władysław Sikorsi and his successor Stanislas Mikołajczyk, from Czechoslovakia Eduard Beneš, from Yugoslavia Ivan Subasič, and from France Charles de Gaulle. There also were separate audiences for two successive Polish ambassadors and the Chinese nationalist foreign minister, T. V. Soong.[37]

Taken as a whole, this personal diplomacy involved a formidable effort in briefing. Stalin was, for example, able to speak with authority on such arcane matters as the status of Ratisbor and the kind of coal produced by certain German coal-mines. On the other hand, he did not expend much time or energy in travelling to meet these foreigners. With the exception of the three meetings of the Big Three, all had to come to him. In the first of these summit meetings Stalin achieved some psychological advantage by obliging Roosevelt to back down from his sustained efforts to arrange a meeting at any place that would not imply that Roosevelt was travelling at Stalin's convenience: the Siberian–Alaskan border, the Arabian Near East, North Africa, Iceland, Scotland, Italy or the French Riviera. No doubt there was some validity in Stalin's argument that his command responsibilities would not permit him to travel very far, but his assertion that he was 'obliged to be with the troops and visit this or that sector of the front more often than usual' was sheer invention. Equally contrived was Roosevelt's claim that he could not go as far as Tehran because the American Constitution required that he 'act on legislation within ten days'. In fact article 1, section 7 states that if a bill is passed by Congress and not returned by the President, signed or vetoed, within ten days, it becomes law automatically. What the President might have said truthfully was that he would be unable to veto legislation that had been passed by Congress if he did not return within ten days. But Stalin did not argue the American Constitution with Roosevelt. He merely continued to insist on Tehran, until Roosevelt decided that he could, after all, fulfill his duties from that remote place.[38]

Stalin not only had to take the longest journey of his years in power, but also had to fly from Baku to Tehran and back. This was his first and last venture aloft, an exercise which he regarded with caution. On being offered two planes, one piloted by a lieutenant-general, the other by a colonel, he chose the latter, noting that generals have less chance to practice their flying skills. Even in Tehran, Stalin was able to operate on his own ground, for he persuaded Roosevelt that there might be German assassins in the city, making it dangerous to alternate meeting places and thus face a long drive from one embassy to another. Therefore the meetings were held in the Soviet compound, where the President was lodged in guest quarters. This surely improved the opportunities for eavesdropping, a practice that Stalin jovially confirmed when Churchill and Eden were visiting Moscow in 1944. When they joined Stalin in his Kremlin apartment he told them, 'That's where you can wash your hands if you want to, the place as I understand it where you Englishmen like to conduct your political discussions.' His understanding rested on an attempt by the British visitors to find some political privacy in the lavatory of the Bolshoi Theatre three nights earlier. Having done so well in establishing himself as host to the president in Tehran, Stalin could afford to try one of Roosevelt's infamous, personally mixed martinis which involved two kinds of vermouth. He said that he found it 'all right, but it is cold on the stomach'.[39]

Many topics were discussed in Stalin's wartime meetings with his allies, but there was one nearly taboo subject: the conflict between capitalism and Communism. True, Churchill in November 1941 asserted in a letter that 'the fact that Russia is a Communist State and that Britain and the United States are not and do not intend to be is not any obstacle to our making a good plan for our mutual safety and rightful interests'. Stalin made no reply to this, but he did needle Churchill on the subject of his past anti-Communism when the two had settled down to drinks and relative conviviality. Stalin recalled that when Lady Astor had visited him years before the war she had suggested that he invite Lloyd George to Moscow. Stalin had objected that Lloyd George had been the head of the intervention in the Russian civil war, to which Lady Astor had replied, 'That is not true. It was Churchill that misled him.' Stalin added, in Churchill's recollection of their conversation, 'We like a downright enemy better than a pretending friend', which apparently placed the prime minister squarely in the former category. Churchill acknowledged that he had been active in the intervention and asked, 'Have you forgiven me?' Stalin evaded the question: 'All that is in the past, and the past belongs to God.'[40]

On their side, Churchill, Roosevelt and the others did not wish to introduce an issue that might disrupt the coalition. The president in particular hoped to overcome ideological enmity by establishing warm, personal ties, confident, as he told Churchill, that 'I can personally handle Stalin better than either your Foreign Office or my State Department. Stalin hates the guts of all your top people. He thinks he likes me better, and I hope he will continue to do so.' It appears, however, that Roosevelt reinforced Stalin's preconception that the founder of the New Deal fell into the category of 'pretending friends'. Probing Roosevelt, Stalin asked him if there was a substantial 'labour party' in America. This was disingenuous, for Stalin knew about the two-party system and in 1927 had explained to an American labour delegation why there was no labour party in their country. The president's evasive reply probably conveyed to Stalin that this capitalist leader was too devious to confront the issue of class struggle. It was therefore unlikely that Stalin was impressed, at dinner at Yalta, when Roosevelt attempted to use a parable to show that personal trust can overcome ideological differences. He once had attended a dinner, Roosevelt said, in the American South, where it was fair to assume that most of the prominent citizens were members of the Klu Klux Klan. Yet the head table included an Italian-American, presumably Roman Catholic, and a Jew. Roosevelt quietly asked one of the local leaders how this could be, given the beliefs of the Klan, and was told that the men in question were 'all right since everyone in the community knew them'. This showed, said Roosevelt to Stalin, that prejudices, 'racial, religious or otherwise', did not last 'if you really knew people'. The president was mistaken if he assumed that Stalin would be willing to regard his ideological convictions as a mere 'prejudice'.[41]

Even though the weight of Stalin's wartime exhortations to his own people was on patriotism rather than Marxism, he made it clear in his major speech of 6 November 1941, with the Germans at the gates of Moscow, that he still took seriously the danger of an imperialist crusade against Communism. He maintained that the Germans had calculated that they could win the war in two months because they expected 'to create a universal coalition against the USSR, to draw Great Britain and the United States into this coalition, and, preliminary to that, to frighten the ruling circles of these countries by the spectre of revolution'. This policy, he said, had already worked in France and it was to this end that 'the not unknown Hess was actually sent to England by the German Fascists to convince the British politicians to join the universal campaign against the USSR'. Here they had 'gravely miscalculated', but on what grounds Stalin did not say. He gave the British and Americans credit for having 'elementary liberties', trade unions and parliaments, but this fell far short of an assertion that there was no major difference between their prevailing social system and Russia's. At best Stalin implied a distinction between more and less pernicious forms of capitalism. The Germans were 'the most rapacious and plunderous imperialists among all the imperialists of the world', but this formulation by no means placed the British and American states in the camp of the proletariat. Nor did it mean that Stalin had much confidence in the intentions of the less pernicious imperialists in the world war. 'The paucity of your offers', he told

Beaverbrook and Harriman in 1941, 'clearly shows that you want to see the Soviet Union defeated.'[42]

Throughout the war, then, ideology was the great unmentionable. But it was never remote from Stalin's mind and shaped his approach to the most important military issue between the Allies during most of the war, the question of the 'second front'. The very acceptance of this expression, which Stalin introduced to the public in his speech of 6 November 1941, was a propaganda success. It implied that nobody had been fighting Hitler before June 1941 and dismissed the existence of a British front in Africa since 1940, later an Allied front in Italy. The result of this verbal device was to turn the terms of negotiation against the British and Americans, who were uncomfortably aware that the Soviets were in truth engaging the greatest part of the German army. Stalin probably considered the early establishment of a second front in France as a crucial test of the intentions of his co-belligerents. Did they really wish to defeat Hitler as quickly as possible, or were they using Germany as the first wave of an attack on Communism, which they might join if the Red Army did too well or if Germany was so worn down that she no longer threatened other capitalist states?[43]

In his first message to Churchill, dated 18 July 1941, Stalin proposed that the British establish a front (he had not yet invoked the advantages of calling it 'second') in northern France or the Arctic. Despite Churchill's explanations of Britain's difficulties, Stalin returned to the matter on 3 September, now speaking of a 'second front' in France or the Balkans. Ten days later he even proposed that in place of a second front the British send a force to the Soviet Union as an alternative means of 'rendering active military aid against the common enemy', as if the British were inactive. When the United States entered the war Stalin did not at once press Roosevelt for a second front, perhaps recognizing that America was ill prepared for war. The president, however, in May 1942 gave Molotov something resembling a promise of a second front by the end of that year. The British, too, gave some encouragement to his idea, but avoided commitment.[44]

Stalin may or may not have taken this seriously, but in August 1942, when Churchill paid his first visit and explained that the western attack would be in North Africa, the Soviet leader reacted angrily. Why, he repeatedly taunted, were the British so afraid of fighting the Germans? This came close to implying what he had said openly to Harriman and Beaverbook about their wishing the defeat of the Soviet Union. By about the beginning of 1943 Stalin was showing signs of doubt that a landing in France was being planned for that year, and in letters to both Churchill and Roosevelt he raised the matter of 'promises' that they had made. The Casablanca conference of Roosevelt and Churchill in February 1943, with its non-committal references to the invasion of France in August or

September, inspired Stalin to reproach Roosevelt directly for the first time. His letter argued that the delay of a second front had enabled the Germans to transfer thirty-six divisions from the west to the Russian front, and he concluded with 'a most emphatic warning' that 'further delay' was fraught with 'grave danger'. But Stalin really boiled over in June 1943 when the two western leaders informed him of their plans for the rest of the year, which envisaged an invasion of Sicily and ignored the question of a landing in France. In a bitter letter to Roosevelt Stalin imputed not merely inadequate vigour but deliberate ill will, 'the withholding from our Army, which has sacrificed so much, of the anticipated substantial support of the Anglo-American armies'. His impression of the president probably was not improved by the latter's decision to ignore the whole issue in his subsequent letters. Churchill, in contrast, tried to argue that the time was not yet ripe for the invasion of France. He received in reply a lengthy recrimination, which referred to 'disregard of Soviet interests' and 'the preservation of confidence in its Allies' on the Soviet side. This was late June 1943, and it does not seem coincidental that the following month Stalin christened the war 'The Great Patriotic War of the Soviet Union', implying much about the importance of the British and American contributions.[45]

Nor was it coincidental that in his May Day speech of 1943 Stalin had mentioned the question of an Anglo-American separate peace with Germany and the possibility of a Soviet–German deal. The treacherous German imperialists, he said, expected 'some one of the Allies to swallow the bait'. While referring to this as 'babble', Stalin did not claim categorically that such things were impossible. The next month there were highly tentative Soviet–German contacts in neutral Sweden. Considering that Hitler still held a vast expanse of Soviet territory, it is unlikely that Stalin was seriously interested in negotiations at this time, but the leaks about the contacts served to notify London and Washington that Russia could not be taken for granted. When Secretary of State Hull came to Moscow in October 1943, Stalin obliquely gave him the same message, pouring sarcasm on reports of a separate peace between Russia and Germany. Hull accepted this at face value, but the fact that Stalin would gratuitously raise such a nasty topic and his somewhat excessive denials suggest that he wanted to keep the question alive. Soviet publications continued to needle the British about the possibility of a separate deal between them and the Germans. Churchill complained about this in January 1944, noting that even when Britain stood alone and 'could easily have made one [a peace settlement] without serious loss to the British Empire and largely at your expense' it had not done so. Stalin's reply, far from repudiating the Soviet press, asserted that the reports came from 'tried and tested correspondents'. And he bluntly pushed home the theme that Russia could not be taken for granted: 'But if, nevertheless, we grant that Britain could have managed without the USSR, exactly the same could be said about the Soviet Union.'[46]

In November 1943 at the Tehran conference, Stalin did not repeat this point, although at one time he seemingly alluded to the possibility that his allies would make their own peace with Germany: 'just because the Russians are simple people, it was a mistake to believe that they are blind and could not see what is before their eyes'. On the whole, however, he was reserved, waiting to see what his allies wished to propose. The main issue turned out to be more a disagreement between Britain and America than between themselves and Russia. Churchill was still advocating a Mediterranean strategy and wanted to postpone a cross-channel invasion, while Roosevelt wanted to ensure that D-Day would come in France in the spring of 1944. Stalin firmly supported the president and they carried the day, but the debate gave Stalin opportunity to prod Churchill concerning his real intentions. Did the British 'really believe in OVERLORD [code name for the cross-channel operation] or are they merely saying so to reassure the Russians', asked Stalin? And at dinner he repeatedly alleged that Churchill 'nursed a secret affection for Germany and desired to see a soft peace'. An appropriate peace in Stalin's opinion would include the 'physical liquidation' of 50 000 to 100 000 German officers. This so offended Churchill that he nearly left the room and was persuaded to stay with the explanation by Roosevelt that the proposal was a joke. But, considering Stalin's treatment of his own élite a few years previous, there is no reason to doubt that he was in earnest.[47]

The fate of the German officer corps was only one dimension of Stalin's concern that Germany should not revive as an anti–Soviet power. Another means of achieving this was the dismemberment of the German state, a proposal that the Big Three agreed on in general terms at the Tehran and Yalta conferences. Still another was the imposition of enormous war reparations on Germany. But the British and Americans had other ideas on this issue, remembering the failure of the reparations agreement that followed the First World War. Their reluctance sorely vexed Stalin, who at one point said that 'if the British felt that the Russians should receive no reparations at all, it would be better to say so frankly', and, after finally gaining assent to the principle of reparations, ironically asked his allies, 'You will not go back on this tomorrow?' One particular form of reparation must have impressed Stalin as evidence of his allies' basic ill will. This was the question of sharing out the Italian and German fleets, on the face of it a simple matter of sailing particular vessels to Soviet ports, without raising any fiscal complications. When the British and Americans found it politically inconvenient to deliver to Russia the Italian ships that had been promised, Stalin protested vehemently and haggled at length concerning the substitute vessels that his allies offered him from their own fleets. At the Potsdam conference he asked 'Why does Churchill refuse to give Russia her share of the German fleet?' When the prime minister raised the possibility that it should be destroyed, Stalin replied, 'Let's divide it. If Mr Churchill wishes, he can sink his share.'[48]

The collapse of German military power in the spring of 1945 gave rise to one final and particularly acrid display of Stalin's suspicion that the western powers were plotting to use Germany against Russia. The occasion for this outburst was the opening of secret talks in Switzerland, in which the German command in Italy discussed their possible surrender to the British and Americans. Informed of this through diplomatic channels, Molotov demanded the suspension of the talks because they included no Soviet representatives. In a letter to Stalin Roosevelt protested that this surrender was in the common military interest, but he can scarcely have assuaged Stalin's suspicions by arguing that there had not yet been any 'negotiations'. In fact there had been a secret meeting between German and American representatives, but it is possible that Stalin, through his intelligence agencies, was better informed on this than was Roosevelt, whose men in the field were not reporting everything to Washington. In reply Stalin maintained that the Germans were using the negotiations as a cover for the transfer of troops to the Russian front as part of 'some other, more far-reaching aims affecting the destiny of Germany'. This allusion to a separate deal with Germany angered Roosevelt, but he could not move Stalin with an assertion of his innocence. On the contrary, the Soviet leader added that the Germans had 'in fact ceased the war against Britain and America', while 'they fought desperately against the Russians for Zemlenice, an obscure station in Czechoslovakia, which they need just as much as a dead man needs a poultice. . . . You will admit that this behaviour on the part of the Germans is strange and unaccountable.'[49]

The unmentionable question of Communist–capitalist enmity also lurked not far below the surface of another question that occupied much of Stalin's attention during the war: Poland. The Soviet Union had annexed a large swathe of eastern Poland as a result of the Molotov–Ribbentrop treaty of 1939, land which Stalin was determined to regain after the defeat of Germany. Even with the Germans close to Moscow, he pressed this point with Anthony Eden. It was bound to be a sore issue between Moscow and the Polish government-in-exile in London, but in the dark month of November 1941 both saw some advantage in restoring relations. Stalin personally received the new Polish ambassador, Kot, and attempted to establish a cordial mood by observing that their countries were not only neighbours but also were 'of the same blood'. On 3 December the dialogue was resumed with a Polish delegation headed by President Sikorski. Here the main issue was the formation of a Polish army in exile, consisting mainly of Poles who were on Soviet territory. This was a painful matter for the Poles, because so many of their people,

especially officers, had been held in jail or labour camp. Stalin blandly
asked one of these, General Anders, who came with Sikorski, how long
he had been in prison and how conditions had been. Twenty months, and
the jail was 'exceptionally bad' in Lvov, somewhat better in Moscow, was
the reply. 'Well, it couldn't be helped; such were the conditions', said
Stalin without apology. His attitude was equally unhelpful when the
matter of 4000 missing officers was raised. 'They've fled', he claimed.
Where? 'Well, to Manchuria, for instance.' His concern was not with
those who had disappeared but with the soldiery that he hoped to raise
among the Poles. In particular Stalin did not agree with Sikorski's wish to
evacuate the men to the Near East for training by the British, and he
skilfully needled the Polish president with the idea that the British might
send the Poles to fight Japan.[50]

These strained relations ruptured entirely when the corpses of most of
the missing Polish officers were exhumed in the Katyn forest by the
Germans in April 1943. If Stalin had entertained the possibility of doing
business in the long run with the non-Communist Polish leadership, this
foreclosed that option. When the Polish government in London showed
interest in an impartial investigation of the massacre, Stalin called them
'Fascists' and accused them of preparing an anti-Soviet campaign of
slander, abetted by the British.[51]

Thus when the Big Three convened at Tehran in November 1943 the
Polish questions was doubly vexed: the Soviets wanted a promise that
they should be awarded the eastern portion of the Polish state, and there
was no Polish government that both the Soviets and the western allies
recognized. Roosevelt futilely attempted to enlist Stalin's sympathy for
his plight as a politician in a country in which there were six or seven
million Polish-American voters, along with others from the three small
Baltic states that the Soviets had annexed. On the latter point Stalin
noted that during the First World War nobody had pressed the tsarist
government to part with territory, so he did not see why the matter was
being raised now. If the American public did not understand the situation,
Roosevelt should undertake 'propaganda work'. Only Eden among those
present was willing to be so disagreeable as to observe that the boundary
Stalin wanted should be called 'the Molotov–Ribbentrop line', to which
Stalin returned, 'Call it what you will, we still consider it just and right.'[52]

The conference ended by accepting in principle that Stalin would
receive approximately the territory he wanted, and Poland would be
compensated with land to be taken from Germany. But what Polish
state? Churchill and Roosevelt continued to press Stalin to accept the
London-based government, and in March 1944 Churchill, through
diplomatic channels, attempted to apply pressure by suggesting that, if
Stalin was uncooperative, the military operations that Britain and America
had agreed to at Tehran might not be carried out. Stalin angrily replied

that the British message 'bristled with threats against the Soviet Union', but 'threats as a method are not only out of place in relations between allies, but also harmful, for they may lead to opposite results'. In this spirit Stalin now began to construct a predominantly Communist Government in exile for Poland, considering it the only alternative to a hostile Anglo-American satellite astride the traditional path of invasion of Russia. In the spring and summer of 1944 he invested substantial personal effort in discussions with Communist or other co-operative Poles who were on Soviet territory and in July established a 'Polish Committee of National Liberation'.[53]

At the same time as he was establishing his Polish government Stalin had to contend with the western allies and the Polish government of their preference. This was particularly awkward in the summer of 1944 when the Red Army reached the Vistula River across from Warsaw and the underground armed forces loyal to the London government-in-exile rose against the Germans. Stalin understood clearly the political implications of the rising and showed no remorse when the Germans proceeded to destroy the flower of the anti-Soviet political forces in Poland. To him the Poles who were fighting to liberate Warsaw were 'power-seeking criminals'. Only with reluctance did he agree to pleas from Churchill and Roosevelt to give western aircraft permission to land on Soviet airfields after they had tried to drop supplies to the resistance forces in Poland. He also consented to receive a delegation from the Polish government in London. His object, he explained to President Mikołajczyk, was to replace the two rival governments of Poland with a fusion of the two, and he denied that his objective was to give power to the Communists alone. When Mikołajczyk observed that the Soviet-backed Committee had scant public backing and contained 'no serious socialists', Stalin sharply interrupted, informing his visitor that his criterion of seriousness was 'not up to the mark. . . . Political trends in Poland under the occupation have undoubtedly shifted to the Left.'[54]

On the last day of 1944 the Soviet-backed Polish Committee declared itself a provisional government, Stalin brushing off British and American objections with the observation that it had 'won great prestige' in Poland and was keeping the rear of the Red Army secure against the 'terrorists' supported by the London Poles. He hoped to gain some leverage in the West by persuading General de Gaulle to recognize the Soviet-backed Polish regime. The French leader came to call in December 1944, hoping to restore French prestige as a great power by signing a mutual defence treaty with the Soviet Union, and Stalin tried diligently to trade recognition of his Poles for this treaty. But de Gaulle was unwilling to become reliant on the Soviet Union as a superpower patron and resisted Stalin's overtures. When Stalin skilfully tried to play on de Gaulle's bitter relations with the British and Americans, the French leader simply denied that such antagonism existed. Indeed, he insisted so strongly that he had no differences with these allies that he found it necessary to delete such statements from the record of the conversation when it was published in France years later. At length de Gaulle threatened to go home empty-handed if the treaty he sought depended on his commitment to the Moscow-backed Polish government, and it was Stalin who gave way.[55]

At Yalta in early 1945 Stalin tenaciously defended what he had achieved in Poland. When Roosevelt and Churchill tried to persuade him to concede to Poland the district of Lvov, he gave Roosevelt a taste of his own argument that the question involved his own domestic political prestige. The boundary that Stalin wanted, he said, had been fixed 'not by the Russians but Curzon and Clemenceau', that is by British and French statesmen at the end of the First World War. 'Should we be less Russian than Curzon and Clemenceau? We could not then return to Moscow and face the people who would say Stalin and Molotov have been less sure defenders of Russian interest than Curzon and Clemenceau.' On the issue of the composition of the Polish government Stalin conceded that some of the London Poles should be included in a new cabinet but gained the much more valuable point that the resulting provisional regime should receive the recognition of the British and Americans. They swallowed this on the understanding that this regime would hold free elections to establish a more permanent government. Roosevelt pleaded that the elections should be 'like Caesar's wife. I did not know her but they said she was pure.' 'They said that about her', retorted Stalin, 'but in fact she had her sins.' Later in 1945 when the western powers pressed for the establishment of an international commission to observe these Polish elections, Stalin claimed that this would be 'an affront and gross interference in their internal affairs'.[56] The unmentionable subject of ideology also permeated Big Three discussions of the concept of global security. At the Tehran conference Roosevelt proposed to Stalin a scheme in which the peace would be kept by 'Four Policemen', the United States, the Soviet Union, Britain and China, which would be the leading members of a global 'executive committee' of ten. While Stalin may have seen advantages in the concept of 'policing' a sphere of influence, he was wary of the preponderance of capitalist, or American, power with which the proposal seemed loaded. Would the international organization have the right to make decisions binding on the nations of the world, asked Stalin? Roosevelt thought not, but at the same time believed that the new body, unlike the League of Nations, should be able to take decisive armed action, including 'bombardment and possible invasion' in the case of serious threats to peace.[57]

At the Yalta conference Stalin warily sought to discover if this proposal meant that the international organization might be mobilized as a crusade against Communist Russia. This was the thrust of his warning that it was necessary to preclude a repetition of the situation during the Russo-Finnish War, in which 'British and French had roused the League of Nations against the Russians, isolated the Soviet Union and expelled it from the League of Nations'. He also tried to draw out his allies on their attitude toward the idea that the Soviet Union was striving for world domination. Churchill provided the opening by expressing concern that the plan for the new international organization might create the impression that the Big Three 'wanted to dominate the world without letting the other countries express their opinion'. Stalin twisted this into a suggestion that it was really the Soviet Union that Churchill had in mind, asking rhetorically if it was the United States that had such intentions, and answering in the negative. Britain? Also not so. 'That left the third – the USSR', said Stalin, now putting a more serious edge on his enquiry. 'So it was the USSR that was striving for world domination?' But his allies would not confront this challenge to discuss their apprehensions concerning the Soviet Union and world Communism, replying only with 'general laughter'. Stalin, having confirmed that Churchill and Roosevelt were less than forthright on this issue, was content to resume his jocular tone and let the matter pass. And he was willing to join the United Nations Organization despite the inherent risks involved, presumably reasoning that it was still more hazardous to leave it entirely to American management.[58]

In 1939 the Soviet Union had been one of perhaps seven states that were considered great powers. By 1945 the United States and Russia were alone in the newly emerged category of 'superpowers'. This transformation was not the work of one man alone, but it represented a real achievement for Stalin as architect and chief executive of Soviet foreign policy. Yet the cult of Stalin, while paying tribute to all manner of questionable contributions by the leader, had little to say about his role in this great advance. The reluctance of the cult to speak of this can only have been Stalin's choice, and it reflected his painful experience in dealing with the imperialists, above all with Hitler. He had seen that even the most promising arrangements could turn sour at any moment, thanks to the treachery of the imperialists, and he was not one to permit his personal prestige to become hostage to the goodwill of the class enemy.

13 Generalissimus

Victory over Germany and Japan brought Stalin various personal rewards, apart from the vast increase in the power of the Soviet Union. There was a triumphal parade on Red Square, the planning of which he personally initiated, instructing Zhukov to appear on horseback in the interests of tradition. There were more medals to add to his substantial collection: the Order of Victory, another Hero of the Soviet Union with the Order of Lenin and a Gold Star. Although he was to be embalmed wearing numerous medals, Stalin while alive customarily displayed only a single Hero of the Soviet Union award. The most elevated of all his new honours was a specially created military rank, 'generalissimus' – 'the superlative general'. This dignity was proposed by his commanders at a banquet following the victory parade, with what inspiration one cannot say. At least he exercised some restraint in the design of the uniform of the new rank. Marshal Shtemenko relates that he once called on Stalin's office and found in the waiting-room the commander of the intendancy of the Red Army, wearing an archaic costume in the style of Kutuzov, with a high collar and gold stripes on the trousers. This was somebody's proposed design for Generalissimus Stalin, who, on seeing it, asked, 'Who got you dressed up like that?' On learning what was going on, he sensibly decided to stick to the existing uniform of a marshal, simply adding a new shoulder insignia.[1]

Along with this formal military honour, the cult of Stalin emphasized his role as victor. This was, of course, reflected in any number of routine works, such as updated editions of the official biography that was first published in 1939 and in Voroshilov's tract on Stalin and the armed forces. More interesting were the grandiose new monuments to his martial glory. The largest of these was the principal war memorial of the Soviet Armenian republic, a statue of Stalin, by the tireless Merkurov, 16.5 metres tall, standing on a 33-metre-high pedestal. Under the feet of the victor, in the stone pedestal, was a hall in which the names of the fallen were inscribed. This took until 1950 to complete, as did the epic cinematic monument to Stalin the victor, M. Chiaureli's *The Fall of Berlin*, in which Stalin not only defeats Hitler but also reunites two lovers who were separated by the war, a steel-worker/tank-driver and a woman collective farmer who was carried away as a forced labourer.[2]

As leader in the 'Great Patriotic War', Stalin's image was more closely associated with nationalism, specifically Great Russian nationalism, during and after the war. In 1944 he personally directed the adoption of a new national anthem to replace the 'Internationale', at one point ordering Shostakovich and Katchaturian to collaborate in composing an entry in the competition. His ultimate choice, unsurprisingly, was an anthem by the director of the Red Army Chorus, G. Aleksandrov, the words to which included the line 'Stalin raised us'.[3] More importantly, the Russian Orthodox Church, that bastion of the national tradition, was associated with the cult of Stalin. On 4 September 1943 Stalin met with Metropolitan Sergei and two other hierarchs and granted them permission to convene a *sobor* (assembly) of the church to elect a patriarch, which had not been allowed since the death of Patriarch Tikhon in 1925. Following this reconciliation the church was granted a synod for administration, a regular publication, theological academies and religious instruction for children. The clerics gratefully hailed Stalin as 'the Supreme Leader of the Russian People', among other accolades. Thus it was appropriate that Stalin invited Metropolitan Nikolai to join him in celebrating the victory over the Germans at a reception in the Kremlin. The clergyman described this occasion in the conventional language of the Stalin cult. The leader 'simply and sincerely' greeted Nikolai 'with a smile', and soon invited him for 'an unrestrained conversation between father and son'. In this case it was not the priest but the ex-seminarian who was the figurative father. The Metropolitan honoured the occasion by presenting Stalin with a decorated cup.

In 1947 the 800th anniversary of the founding of Moscow provided Stalin with a further opportunity to associate his name with Russian nationalism. Although he was out of town on vacation during the festivities in Moscow, his image was as much a part of the occasion as that of Ivan Dolgoruky, the founder of the city, and Stalin's widely disseminated message paid tribute to Moscow as the 'base and initiator of the creation of a centralized state in Rus [medieval Russia]'. The celebration included an innovation in iconography, a huge portrait hung from a tethered balloon, the picture illuminated by searchlights to create the illusion of a benign presence hovering over the people.[4]

Having clinked glasses with his commanders in celebration of the great victory, Stalin soon set some distance between himself and them. Zhukov, the best known and probably the most popular, was in 1946 dispatched to the Odessa military district, later to the Ural district on the edge of Siberia. Other military figures soon ceased to be regular callers at Stalin's office or guests at nocturnal parties. These were attended mainly by Stalin's established political pals, although sometimes there were a few foreign or domestic guests as well. The tone of these gatherings seems to have become increasingly coarse and drunken, as Stalin obliged his guests to imbibe heavily and engage in juvenile song and horseplay. The Yugoslav emissary Milovan Djilas recalls, for example, that Stalin commanded all present to guess the temperature outdoors under penalty of drinking a shot of vodka for every degree of error. According to Khrushchev, Beria, Malenkov and Mikoyan sought to spare themselves such abuse by persuading waitresses to fill their glasses with water, but were caught and reprimanded. He considers that two members of the inner circle, Zhdanov and Shcherbakov, drank themselves to death because of Stalin's soirées. Svetlana recalls that toward the end of the proceedings it was customary for each dignitary's bodyguard to carry home their ill or semi-conscious charge. As for Stalin's own drinking, several witnesses agree that most of the time he drank only wine and remained sober, but there seem to have been exceptions. Once, for example, he and the minister of health joined in inebriated folk-songs, and the admiring Albanian visitor Hoxha noted that a general was assigned to watch what Stalin imbibed and became agitated when the Boss began to stray from what was approved. These parties no doubt included political and general conversation, but the impression is that there was less serious content than in earlier years and more buffoonery, such as practical jokes involving tomatoes on chairs or salt in wine. There was music, much of it recorded and played by Stalin, either on a gramophone that the Americans had given him or on an older model which he personally cranked. He received a copy of most new Soviet records and rated them 'good', 'tolerable', 'poor' or 'trash'. One that he found highly amusing involved dogs howling along with an operatic diva. There was also dancing, which sometimes meant that Stalin commanded a guest to do a difficult feat, sometimes that the individual did what he wanted and sometimes that Stalin paired off his all-male gathering for ballroom dancing.[5]

If Stalin became ever more dependent on these inebriated gatherings for sociability, it may have been because his relations with his family had become increasingly remote and embittered. Yakov, with whom he had never been close, came to a tragic end. Following his attempted suicide in about 1928, he moved to Leningrad where his step-mother's parents, the Alliluevs, still had an apartment, even though they had for years lived in the Kremlin. This, incidentally, was a remarkable privilege, considering the housing conditions that most citizens faced. Yakov, following in the footsteps of Sergei Alliluev, became an electrical engineer and was employed in a city power plant. Returning to Moscow in 1935, he rejoined the family circle to the extent of spending summers at Stalin's country villa, Zubalovo, and becoming friendly with his half-sister Svetlana, eighteen years his junior. He offended his father by marrying a previously wedded, and abandoned, Jewish woman named Yulia, who bore a daughter, Stalin's first grandchild, in 1938. About this time Yakov changed careers, attended the Dzerzhinsky Artillery Academy and was commissioned in the army on 6 May 1941. Two or three months later he was captured in combat. The Germans seem to have considered using him in some kind of prisoner exchange or as a propaganda mouthpiece, but neither Stalin nor his son would deal with them, and Yakov died in a prisoner-of-war camp. Zhukov says that Stalin was proud of Yakov's refusal to betray his country and that he suffered for his son's fate. Svetlana, on the other hand, maintains that he regarded Yakov as a disgrace and told a foreign correspondent that there were no 'Russian prisoners of war, only traitors', and that 'I have no son called Jacob.' Such was his attitude towards prisoners of war in general, but the story is not sustained by any known interview. In any case, Yakov's wife was incarcerated for two years beginning in October 1941, evidently because Stalin suspected that she had somehow betrayed Yakov to the enemy. Stalin provided a nurse for her child, who was evacuated to Kuibyshev at this time, along with Vasily's wife and child, their nurses, Svetlana and her nurse. After the war Stalin occasionally gave his daughter some money with instructions to give it 'to Yasha's daughter'.[6]

Vasily Stalin, who was always a lazy student, became an artillery cadet, like his elder half-brother, but failed – which must have given his instructors nightmares. He then succeeded in becoming a fighter-pilot and heavy-drinking womanizer before the war. By the Battle of Moscow in 1941 he was a major and 'inspector-in-chief' of the air force, and reported directly to his father. Although Vasily was evacuated to the safety of Kuibyshev at that time, Stalin seems to have decided not to spare his younger son the hazards of war during the Battle of Stalingrad. General S. D. Lugansky recalls that when Malenkov paid a visit to the embattled city he carried a message of reproach for Major Stalin because his unit had not destroyed any German planes. When not occupied with the war, Vasily was busy carousing in the apartments of his aunts in Moscow while these ladies were evacuated. His partners in drink and philandering, then and later, were fliers, athletes and police officers. Along with these entertainments Vasily managed to marry, and in October 1941 this union produced a daughter. Torn between pride in the 'achievements' of his son, as proclaimed by sycophants, and despair at his weakness, Stalin alternately promoted and punished Vasily. During the war he sentenced Vasily to ten days imprisonment for 'depravity', afterwards posted him to conquered Germany, then brought him back, too alcoholic to fly a plane, as a lieutenant-general and air-commander of the Moscow Military District, only to dismiss him in 1952 after Vasily nearly caused a major disaster by ordering a low-level fly-past on 7 November in bad weather. Toward the end of his life Stalin was especially frustrated by Vasily's unwillingness to attend the General Staff Academy, in which he was reluctantly enrolled.[7]

Svetlana presented different problems. Unlike Vasily she was a successful student and graduated from Moscow State University, specializing in history to please her father. She preferred literature and did well in foreign languages, learning English well enough to do professional translating. She also acceded to her father's wishes, contrary to her own, in joining the party in 1949. But Svetlana had to take the entrance exam on party history three times in order to pass, even though it must have been set at an intellectual level far below hers. That was part of the trouble. Her intellectuality was non-political and aesthetic, becoming religious in time, quite different from the official culture of the party. This was but one ingredient in her adolescent rebellion. Another was the stifling domestic life that her father imposed on her, assigning bodyguards who infuriated her even as a schoolgirl by insisting that she have a segregated cloak-room and that she eat behind a screen. Before the war one of her means of evading this oppression was abetted by her brothers who secretly taught her to drive. Only after the war did Stalin, who never learned this skill, discover that his daughter had a licence. By that time Svetlana's coming of age as a woman had estranged them. Stalin was the kind of man who used a choice collection of obscenities when it pleased him, who could defend the tendency of Red Army soldiers to 'have some fun' with unwilling women, and at the same time wanted his daughter raised on Victorian standards. On one occasion he accused the ten-year-old Svetlana of going 'naked' when they were at Sochi and ordered her nurse to make some bloomers to cover her knees, even though such garments were long gone in Russia. As she matured, the order was to wear loose-fitting clothes, which Svetlana evaded as she could.[8]

All these differences between father and daughter exploded in 1942–3 when she fell in love for the first time. Her choice could not have been better calculated to enrage Stalin. He was Alexei Kapler, a man of forty, an intellectual, specifically a writer, and a Jew. What sort of blind love or utter miscalculation led this man to risk his life for the sake of such a romance is impossible to fathom. Vasily introduced them, having met Kapler when he was working on a film script about pilots in 1942. They were quickly attracted as Kapler, 'who had an easy, natural way with men and women of the greatest diversity', introduced the girl to the cultural world that she had never known in her father's house. They would meet when she left school, despite the presence of her bodyguard. Recklessly, he even published in *Pravda* on 14 December 1942 a scarcely veiled reference to their love, a letter from a fictitious lieutenant at Stalingrad, closing with a reference to his beloved's room overlooking the Kremlin walls. Only one young woman in all the world had such a room.[9]

Upon his return from Stalingrad, where he had been a journalist, not a combatant, Kapler resumed his trysts with Svetlana, now meeting in an apartment that Vasily and some of his comrades had used for their revels. With a bodyguard in the next room, the lovers may merely have kissed, as Svetlana says, but that was not what Stalin concluded when he learned about it. Evidently his personal security chief, General Vlasik, had hoped to avoid a confrontation on the Kapler affair, with its unpredictable consequences for his own career. One of his aides had phoned Kapler around late January, urging him to leave town, but, amazingly, was rebuffed. By 3 March 1943 Vlasik had decided to inform his Boss, who angrily descended on his daughter that same day with the news that he knew everything, had transcripts of her phone conversations with Kapler, and had jailed the lover because he was 'a British spy'. When the girl of sixteen protested her love, her father struck her twice across the face. 'Just look at her, nurse, how low she's sunk. Such a war going on, and she's busy the whole time ——.' The word omitted from Svetlana's memoirs can only have been, in English, 'fucking'. That summer Stalin ordered the closure of the villa Zubalovo on the grounds that his children had made it 'a den of iniquity' and 'moral depravity'.[10]

But Svetlana had her revenge. Having started university studies later in 1943, attending without a bodyguard, she defied her father by marrying one Gregory Morozov, a student whom she had known for years and a Jew. Stalin may or may not have mentioned this last point, but he did observe that the young man was 'too calculating', sitting out the war as a student (with what kind of exemption is not clear) while others died. It also seems that Stalin wanted his daughter to marry Andrei Zhdanov's son. Despite his power, including the options of dispatching Morozov to jail or to the front, Stalin seems to have sensed defeat at the hands of his adolescent daughter. 'To hell with you. Do as you like', was his conclusion. He made it clear that he would never meet his son-in-law, but did provide the couple with an apartment outside the Kremlin and, after the birth of their son, Iosef, in the spring of 1945, two nurses to care for him while Svetlana continued her studies. The marriage, which seems to have been more a manoeuvre in the war between Stalin and his daughter than a romance, ended in divorce in 1947, and the following year Svetlana's ex-father-in-law was arrested. With this, father and daughter enjoyed a measure of reconciliation, sharing his annual autumn holidays in 1947 and 1948. Svetlana tried to please him by marrying Yuri Zhdanov in the spring of 1949, a union that produced another child and, in 1952, another divorce. But Stalin had lost interest in this match, perhaps because Andrei Zhdanov had died in 1948, and he warned Svetlana that the Zhdanov women would 'eat her alive'. The relation of father and daughter remained strained, though he made one further effort to reach out to his aggravating children in the autumn of 1951 when both Vasily and Svetlana joined him on holiday at Borzhomi. Stalin showed little interest in the eight grandchildren who were born in his lifetime. Evidently he never saw Vasily's five children. Svetlana took her two along with Yakov's only child to see their famous ancestor perhaps twice. She thought that he was genuinely pleased, but that was that.[11]

As for Stalin's other surviving relatives, all contact seems to have lapsed by the time the war began. His parents-in-law, Sergei and Olga

Alliluev, survived until 1945 and 1951, respectively, living in an apartment in the Kremlin, but rarely if ever seeing Stalin. Their son-in-law, Stanislav Redens, was executed in 1938, and their son Pavel died of a heart attack the same year. Their daughter and daughter-in-law, widows of Stanislav and Pavel, were arrested in 1947–8 and given ten-year jail sentences. Just what the charges were is unclear. The daughter-in-law, Evgeniia appears to have been intimidated into making some sort of confession, while their daughter Anna lost her mind in prison. The most that Stalin would tell his daughter about her aunts was that they had 'babbled a lot' and 'helped our enemies'. In Anna's case this evidently referred to her memoirs, published in 1947, which treated in a favourable, but rather informal spirit, Stalin's early connections with the Alliluev family. Evgeniia wrote no memoirs, but seems to have been quite a gossip. It may also be relevant that she remarried in Stalin's lifetime, and her second husband was Jewish.[12]

Stalin was sixty-five years old when the war ended. When Zhukov visited him at Nearby in early March 1945, after having been away at the front for some time, he noticed signs of exhaustion in Stalin's 'aspect, movements and speech', an opinion sustained by Patolichev when he saw the Boss a year later. On 10 October 1945 *Pravda* carried the unprecedented announcement that Stalin was going on vacation and that Molotov was temporarily assuming responsibility. This naturally inspired rumours that Stalin was critically ill or was retiring. He had indeed made some remarks about retirement to his commanders at the end of the war. His daughter, although she did not see him for a considerable time after August 1945, believes that he 'fell ill and was quite sick for months' in the latter part of the year. No doubt he was physically debilitated in this period and may have suffered from some specific condition or disease, but the seriousness of Stalin's decline should not be overrated. The American ambassador Harriman found him looking well in October 1945 when they met during Stalin's vacation. Three years later the incoming American ambassador, Alan Kirk, reported, 'I thought he looked in good shape. He carried his years well, his black hair is silvered somewhat on the tips but his face is not particularly lined, and, while his eyes are tired, he seemed fully alert.'[13]

During the post-war years Stalin extended somewhat his annual vacations on the Black Sea coast of Georgia. In 1945 he left on 10 October and returned on 17 December, which was perhaps not much more time off than was customary before the war, but in 1947–51 he left around the end of August and did not return until late November or early December. This meant that he was absent from the Lenin Mausoleum for the 7 November parade in these years, but in 1952 he entirely missed the vacation and did watch the parade. Stalin made the first of his post-war vacation trips by car, staying with party officials along the way and having a rare opportunity to see something of the condition of the war-ravaged land. Subsequently he travelled by special train.[14]

These three-month sojourns in the south did not spare Stalin the severity of the Moscow winter, nor were they respites from work. Rarely he received foreign visitors in the south: Harriman in 1945, a British Labour Party delegation in 1948, the Albanian leader Hoxha in 1949 and Zhou En-lai in 1950. More frequently he had the company of his Soviet political cronies. One of these, Khrushchev, thought that Stalin could not stand being alone, which may be so, but he probably wanted to keep an eye on these men and give them orders, too. He kept up at least a part of his normal paper-work while on holiday and in 1950 attempted to speed this activity by introducing an air-courier service to his door. According to the aviation designer Yakovlev, Stalin heard that Hitler had been able to send and receive papers from his besieged chancellery by means of a short-take-off plane and so ordered production of one that required only 50 metres of runway. Unfortunately when the 'Yak-12' was put into this service in 1951, Stalin was staying in the Georgian mountains near Borzhomi where his residence was set in such a valley that the plane could not function. The designer was reprimanded at a meeting chaired by Beria. This change from Stalin's accustomed holiday area near Sochi was perhaps one sign of a restlessness that grew on him in the post-war years, impelling him to order the construction of new villas that he rarely or never visited – at Novy Afon, on Lake Ritsa and in the Valdai Hills.[15]

For at least four or five years following the war Stalin was fit enough to continue to carry a substantial burden of administration, but the arrangement of his authority was somewhat altered. He divested himself of the wartime titles of chairman of the State Committee of Defence and supreme commander at the end of the war, and ceased to be minister of the armed forces in March 1947. He remained chairman of the Sovnarkom (renaming this body, without explanation, 'Council of Ministers' in 1946), General Secretary of the Central Committee, and member of the Politburo and Orgburo. But the meaning of this array of offices was not what it had been before the war. Most importantly, the leading organs of the party did not resume their pre-war, statutory functioning. The last pre-war party congress had met in 1939, the last meeting of the Central Committee in 1941. It was understandable that these assemblies were suspended during the war, when so many responsible party officials were engaged in war-related assignments that prevented their coming to Moscow. But this does not explain the atrophy that Stalin imposed on them after the war. The Central Committee did convene twice, and undertook little important business, in March 1946 and February 1947, but it did not meet again until late 1952, when there was at last a party congress. Something similar also seems to have hapened to the Politburo, although here the matter is blurred by the traditional absence of formal announcements of meetings and the uncertain status of the many gatherings that Stalin had with his political cronies, often in the middle of the night. Did anyone know which of these might be called sessions of the Politburo? In 1956 Khrushchev maintained that it had met 'only occasionally, from time to time', and was indignant that much of the work of this supreme party council was delegated to subcommissions known by the number of members appointed to them, 'the five', 'the six' and so on. These seem to have been standing bodies, each of which dealt with a large area such as foreign affairs or economic planning. Stalin's point in handling matters in this way seems to have been to avoid dealing with a legally authoritative gathering that might cause him trouble, to 'make it difficult', as Khrushchev said, for 'any member of the Politburo to take a stand against one or another unjust or improper procedure, against serious errors and shortcomings in the practice of leadership'.[16]

Through this manipulation of the leading organs of the party Stalin was able to avoid confrontation with any opposition. This enabled him to forego any substantial purge or blood-bath within the party–state élite in the first post-war years. This is not to say that this was a relaxed time for the citizenry at large. On the contrary, the population of Gulag probably was at its all-time peak, owing to the presence of vast numbers of Soviet citizens who had been prisoners of war, forced labourers, real or imagined collaborators in German-occupied territories or 'bourgeois' inhabitants of the annexed territories in the west, along with German, Japanese and other prisoners of war. At the same time Siberia and Central Asia also contained hundreds of thousands of ethnic German Soviet citizens, various peoples of the North Caucasus, the Crimean Tartars and even ethnic Greeks who were collectively deported on Stalin's orders during or shortly after the war. Moreover the Soviet populace as a whole was sealed off from the outside world as never before in peacetime, and any past or present links with or inclinations toward the West could be a mortal threat to a denizen of Stalin's Russia. Above all it was a harsh time because of the massive human and material costs of the war, which made the first post-war years a period of dire penury for most Soviet citizens and 1947 a time of incipient mass famine.[17]

But, having taken into account all these grim facts, it remains that Stalin's dealings with his élite were not bloodthirsty in roughly the first five post-war years. Responsible officials might well recall with trepidation what Stalin had done to their kind in 1937, but their own job tenure, and security of party membership, was not under serious threat. No member of the Central Committee was removed from the end of the war to 1949, when several members fell foul of Beria and Malenkov more than Stalin. Studies of the lower ranks of party and state administration indicate a high level of job security for incumbents, greater than the Khrushchev years soon to follow. There was no general purge of the party, despite the expansion of the party membership as a wartime measure from 3.8 million members and candidates in 1941 to 5.7 million in 1945.[18]

While retaining effective ultimate authority, Stalin played a smaller role in the administration of domestic affairs than he had before the war. During the war he had concentrated on military and diplomatic matters and to a substantial extent left domestic issues to the leading members of the State Committee of Defence. Though this body was disbanded, its members continued to function with much of the delegated authority that they acquired in wartime. Khrushchev recounts that many decrees that Stalin never saw appeared over his name, and he believed it possible for Malenkov and Beria to take such a major step as authorizing rationing in the famine-stricken Ukraine without ever mentioning it to the Boss. This reliance on a circle of deputies had particularly important implications for Stalin's leadership of the party. In 1944 he brought Zhdanov back from Leningrad and in effect placed him in charge of party affairs, the senior member of the Secretariat despite Stalin's nominal status in that body. Stalin wanted to 'restore the power of the Central Committee [meaning Secretariat] to control the work of local party organizations', he explained to Patolichev in March 1946. Indeed, he spent some time discussing the problem with this newly fledged member of the Secretariat, who was assigned the task of running a network of 'inspectors' who would represent the centre to the regional party organizations.[19]

But Stalin appears not to have wanted day-to-day responsibility for the management of the party nor to have the party play an autonomous role in economic affairs, as it had before the war. The Fourth Five-Year Plan, begun in 1946, was never submitted to a party congress or other party meeting for ratification, and the resolutions issued in the name of the Central Committee in the post-war years included only a few commands concerning economic matters, specifically agriculture, and many on ideology, propaganda, culture – the area that Stalin allocated to the party and Zhdanov. Popular belief attached to Zhdanov responsibility for the ideologically severe, but not bloody, campaign against creative intellectuals whose work was insufficiently Marxist–Leninist – the 'Zhdanovshchina'. It is safe to assume that Stalin approved of the general drift of this campaign, but the fact that it dwindled after Zhdanov's death in 1948 suggests that it was in large measure something that he undertook under the terms of the broad authority that the Boss delegated to him.[20]

Nominally the administrative head of both the state network of ministries and of the party, Stalin had ceased to be either. He was simply Stalin, a true autocrat in the sense that his power derived from his person and not from any legal or institutional base. He sat at the centre of a vast array of agencies, of which the party was but one, allowing his senior deputies great latitude on many matters. But when he bestirred himself to intervene, he could command attention. In 1947, for example, he phoned the party boss of Dnepropetrovsk, L. I. Brezhnev, to berate him for the supposedly insufficient speed with which the steel plant there was regaining its pre-war productivity. He took the occasion to impress on this rising young official that the danger of the Cold War required increased pressure. One example of Stalin's personal direction of a major domestic operation began in January 1943, with the Battle of Stalingrad nearing its close and prospects for ultimate Soviet victory greatly improved. At 5 a.m. Stalin phoned his narkom of finance, A. G. Zverev, and spent about forty minutes in a deeply secret conversation about a matter dear to Stalin's heart: currency reform. This was no mere replacement of one issue of paper money with another bearing fewer zeros. It was a deliberate act of class war. Throughout the 1930s there had been a steady increase in the total wage bill of the Soviet Union as industry and the state grew. This created a supply of money in private hands which greatly exceeded available goods and services. During the war this imbalance had increased, and various state loan campaigns, including compulsory ones, were inadequate to deal with the problem. Stalin believed that this threatened the whole economy and in particular benefited speculators, especially peasants who sold scarce products that they had raised on their small private plots. While he might have wished to apply severe legal sanctions against those who had accumulated the surplus money in the economy, the speculators, especially the peasants, were too valuable to be liquidated in this way.[21]

And so Stalin ordered Zverev to begin planning a currency reform that would wipe out excess purchasing power. He closed the conversation with the shrewd advice that the scheme should appear to demand the people's sacrifice for the last time as part of the rebuilding of Russia, and he thrice repeated the command that the whole business should be kept a deep secret until the plan was ready. A year later Stalin introduced Zverev's draft to the Politburo, and in the autumn of 1945 invited him to come to Sochi to discuss their plans. He continued thereafter to keep a close watch over details of the plan. On one occasion he phoned Zverev in a rage because the latest draft of the public announcement made reference to certain price reductions, which Stalin had not authorized. In the final stage of this operation, ever conscious of images, he considered the design of the new currency and the propaganda campaign that would accompany its launch. On 16 December 1947 the populace learned abruptly that all the existing currency was defunct, and that it could be exchanged for the new issue on a one-to-ten ratio for currency in hand, the medium preferred by 'speculators', who did not trust the state bank. On the other hand, the first thousand roubles that a person held in a bank account could be exchanged at par, the next 7000 at three-to-two and above that at two-to-one.

One wonders, incidentally, how this affected Stalin's own financial standing. Although this was irrelevant in the sense that all his needs were provided by the state, it appears that someone was using insider knowledge to protect Stalin's assets from the full force of the currency reform. His daughter recalls that he received packets of currency from time to time, in keeping with a practice permitted the managerial class as a whole. This money he dumped in a drawer, and at intervals somebody deposited it in a bank account. This did not, however, include the enormous royalties that accrued from the *Short Course* on party history, which he donated to the state. Svetlana writes that she learned of a bank account that had been established in her father's name in 1947, the year of the currency reform. Although the unworldly Svetlana did not understand this, the effect of this move would have been to minimize the impact of the reform on Stalin's savings. But such a move seems likely to have been the work of some retainer rather than Stalin himself. Although he lived comfortably and even indulged in a spree of superfluous dacha-building, he seems to have remained, on balance, a non-acquisitive person, sincere in his indifference to roubles and in his reminders to his daughter that none of their real estate was personal property.[22]

The laggard agricultural sector of the Soviet economy attracted Stalin's personal intervention in the late 1940s. A disastrous crop failure of 1946 was followed by very slow recovery, especially in animal husbandry. Stalin tried changing his chief deputy for agriculture, appointing in turn Malenkov, Andreev and Khrushchev, with no favourabie results. He tried verbal abuse, for example sending Khrushchev 'the rudest, most insulting telegram' concerning crop failure in the Ukraine. He pressed them to impose harsh exactions on the peasantry and to punish the impoverished victims of his policy who resorted to 'pilferage of collective farm property'. Both Khrushchev and Zverev claim to have protested to Stalin about the severity of the taxes on private household plots of peasants. He was unmoved. 'It is enough for the peasant to sell a chicken to satisfy the Ministry of Finance', he replied to Zverev.[23]

Dissatisfied with the results of such policies, Stalin began to look for a fundamental scientific breakthrough that would rescue collectivized agriculture. Like many self-educated people he had developed both a contempt for academic specialists and a vaulting self-confidence. This was present in his support for the 'cultural revolution' of the late 1920s, which had pitted proletarian radicalism against 'bourgeois' scientists and technologists. In the post-war years he chose to assert himself in three disparate fields as the teacher of the professional experts. In each case his pronouncement took the form of a reply to one or more specialists who were wrestling with theoretical problems and had asked for his advice. The first was a military historian named Razin, who in 1946 needed some clarification of the theory of warfare and especially the validity of the ideas of von Clausewitz.[24] In Stalin's opinion the ideas of the German theoretician were obsolete. This at least had some bearing on important issues of Soviet defence policy. But the sequel, comprising four letters to a total of five scholars in linguistics was far removed from any pressing practical matter. It was evidently a reflection of Stalin's amateur interest in the field, which appeared in his editing of Georgian-to-Russian poetic translation, his enquiries of Enver Hoxha concerning the Albanian language, and his questions to the Indian ambassador Menon about the languages of India. The main point of Stalin's disquisition on linguistics was to overturn the prevailing theory in Soviet scholarship since the early 1930s, the eccentric notions of the Georgian N. Ya. Marr, who had died in 1934.[25] Finally, in 1952 Stalin dealt with the difficulties that Soviet economists were having in agreeing on a general textbook in their field, magisterially correcting their numerous 'mistakes'.[26]

He did not publish any analogous pronouncements in his own name on agriculture and related sciences, but by 1948 endorsed the theories of three Soviet pseudo-scientists who had challenged the orthodox academic establishment. Two of these were deceased by this time, I. V. Michurin and V. R. Viliams. The former was a self-taught breeder of fruit trees who began this work before the revolution and established a state-financed nursery after it. Even though scientists belittled his findings he gained the patronage of the narkom of agriculture, Yakovlev, who probably was attempting to follow Stalin's inclination for the 'practical'. Although Michurin never actually produced any new varieties of fruit trees, the official view was that 'Michurinism' was an important Soviet, proletarian contribution to science, demonstrating the ability of man to control his environment. In the early post-war years this was reinforced by the Russian nationalist trend in science and technology, which proclaimed Russian innovative genius in all the sciences. Viliams was an agronomist who in the 1930s had pushed the idea that the planting of grasses on fallow land would improve fertility more than the use of chemical fertilizers, manure or conventional cover-crops. The scheme proved ineffective, but it offered an alternative to major investment in the chemical industry, and it was a 'discovery' by a 'practical' worker who defied orthodox agronomical science.[27]

The third, and crucial, figure in Stalin's espousal of an unorthodox scientific approach to the agrarian problem was very much alive in the 1940s, Trofim D. Lysenko. A peasant by birth, he had attended the Kiev Agricultural Institute, received only a modest scientific education and became convinced that the mainstream of genetics, with its determinist implications, was wrong and perhaps malevolent. Genes and chromosomes, he maintained, were the figments of reactionary imaginations which sought to limit the prospects for the socialist transformation of nature. During the First Five-Year Plan he had proposed to revolutionize grain agriculture by 'vernalizing' wheat, that is, moistening and chilling winter wheat seed and planting it in the spring. This simple treatment supposedly changed the nature of the plant and protected it from winter-kill. When this did poorly in practice, Lysenko claimed that he had 'vernalized' spring wheat and would produce a hardy strain of cotton that could grow in the Ukraine. His promises and more or less fraudulent reports of experiments sufficiently impressed non-scientist officials to keep his work going through the 1930s. But he had not triumphed over the scientific establishment. His main opponent was N. I. Vavilov, who defended orthodox genetics. The conflict between these two became embroiled in the Yezhovshchina, which claimed some geneticists and agronomists on both sides. But Lysenko's charges that Vavilov was supporting 'bourgeois idealism' could not have helped the scientist's standing with the police. In 1940 he was arrested and soon died in camp, having received a death sentence which was commuted to imprisonment.[28]

Lysenko's status with the political leadership seems to have declined just before the war, but in the calamitous post-war agricultural situation he found a chance to recoup his fortunes. In addition to his attacks on 'bourgeois' genetics he now proposed that a sufficiently vast planting of trees, especially oak, in the Russian steppe would moderate the cold of winter and heat of summer. The seedlings, he maintained, should be planted in clusters and allowed to thin themselves, which they could do better than man. Existing evidence does not make it clear just how Lysenko managed to get Stalin's ear, but by 1948 he had a convert. The general drift of Lysenko's thinking harmonized with Stalin's preference for the 'practical' worker over the academic and for the innovative genius of Soviet experts over westerners. Most particularly this peculiar idea came just when Stalin desperately needed a quick solution to the agrarian problem. Perhaps Stalin even fancied himself a practitioner of botanical transformation, for his secretary Poskrebyshev claimed that the Boss was 'a scientific innovator in specialized branches of science' who had long engaged in 'the cultivation and study of citrus crops in the region of the Black Sea coast' and 'proved in practice that it is possible to produce types of citrus crops capable of withstanding frost'. He also had played 'a decisive role in the matter of planting eucalyptus trees on the coast of the Black Sea, cultivating melons in the Moscow region and extending the cultivation of branched wheat'. Gardening was just about his only hobby, though his daughter maintained that his activity did not go beyond occasionally pruning 'a twig or two'.[29]

By July 1948 Stalin definitely had given Lysenko his support, overriding scientists and party officials who had doubts. One who capitulated was Andrei Zhdanov's son Yuri, Svetlana's husband a year later. A rising young man trained in chemistry, Yuri recently had become the chief of scientific affairs in the party Secretariat and had attempted to resist

Lysenko and the 'Michurinism' that he expounded. Young Zhdanov, very likely with his father's consent, criticized Lysenko's ideas in a lecture to party propagandists. Stalin let it be known that this would not do, and on 10 July Yuri addressed to Stalin a craven letter of repentance for having 'underestimated my responsibility', for having made 'a sharp and public criticism of Academician Lysenko' and for having 'insufficient preparation for the struggle for Michurin's teachings'. Evidently Stalin accepted his closing statement that 'all this was because of inexperience and immaturity', for the only punishment given Yuri was the publication of the letter in *Pravda* on 7 August 1948.[30]

The day this appeared was the last in a week-long conference of the Lenin Academy of Agricultural Sciences, at which Lysenko delivered a report on the Situation in Biological Science', At the time of Stalin's death Lysenko maintained that Stalin had personally edited this polemical document, which castigated the supposedly reactionary, idealistic (non-materialist), metaphysical, Weismannist–Mendelist genetics. For the rest of Stalin's life Soviet biological science was harried into accepting Lysenkoism. Non-conformity was particularly dangerous because the issue was linked to the Cold War. Michurinism was Soviet while Mendelian genetics was sponsored by 'Carnegie and Rockefeller' – defenders of the bourgeois idea of immutable heredity.[31]

The larger economic implications of Stalin's espousal of Lysenko's ideas appeared on 24 October 1948 in a decree announcing a plan to transform nature, partly by the application of Viliams's theories on grasslands and partly by a massive campaign to plant shelter-belts. Maps now appeared showing how this 'Stalinist Plan' would consist of three great belts running roughly north–south in the south-eastern portion of European Russia, each consisting of three strips 60 metres wide, totalling 5320 km. This enormous project, which was to require massive peasant labour, was to occupy fifteen years starting in 1950. At the same time collective farms were to plant their own, local shelter-belts, largely at their own expense. 'Stalin transforms nature' was one of the slogans in support of this plan, which was supposed to improve the climate and crop yields in a vast area. By the anniversary of the October Revolution in 1949 Malenkov claimed that half a million hectares of trees had been planted and by the end of 1951 three times as many. But problems emerged: many seedlings died of the dry climate that they were supposed to transform. Perhaps it was in response to this that in 1950 four state decrees announced a new wave of hydraulic projects, the 'Great Stalinist Constructions'. These included five canals and four dams: the south–Ukrainian Canal, the north–Crimean Canal, the Volga–Don Canal, the Stalingrad Canal and the main Turkmen Canal, the Kakhovsky Dam on the Dnieper River, the Tsimliansky Dam on the Don and the Stalingrad Dam on the Volga. These projects were already partly in progress in

1950, but they now assumed mythic status as part of the Stalinist transformation of nature. He probably conceived these as his last great monument of economic development, and indeed ordered that the point where the Volga–Don Canal joined the greatest Russian river be marked by a towering statue of himself, high on a bluff.[32]

Foreign affairs continued to absorb much of Stalin's attention after the war. True, in dealing with capitalist powers his reliance on personal diplomacy was much less than during the war. His correspondence with the American and British leaders ceased in 1945, and there were no more summit meetings, even though Stalin told President Roosevelt's son Elliott in December 1946 that there should be 'not one but several conferences of the Big Three'. But when President Truman in April 1946 sent Stalin an invitation to visit the United States, the Generalissimus told the bearer, Ambassador Walter B. Smith, that his doctors would not allow him to travel and had him on a diet. The last part of this excuse was plainly diplomatic rather than medical. Stalin did, however, have substantial meetings with two American secretaries of state, James F. Byrnes and George C. Marshall, and with British foreign minister Ernest Bevin when they were in Moscow in December 1945 and February– March 1947. He also kept in touch with the American and British ambassadors until early 1949. Harriman called at Stalin's vacation villa in October 1945 and paid a final visit to the Leader in Moscow in January 1946, as did Clark Kerr the same month. Although Stalin was not 'head of state' according to protocol, he received the incoming American and British ambassadors Walter B. Smith and Sir Maurice Peterson in April and May 1946 and their successors, Alan Kirk and Sir David Kelly, in the summer of 1949. He also dealt with Smith, joined by the British representative, F. K. Roberts, and the French ambassador, Y. Chataigneau, on the Berlin crisis in August 1948. Throughout 1946 Stalin evidently wished to be fairly accessible to diverse visitors from the capitalist world. These included Chiang Kai-shek's son, Chiang Ching- kuo, the secretary-general of the UN, Trygve Lie, the prime minister of Iran, Ghavam, and also an Iranian princess, representatives of Finland, Denmark and Sweden, Elliott Roosevelt and an obscure American labour leader named Leo Krzycki.[33]

This open-door policy all but disappeared in 1947, although he did receive Field Marshal Montgomery in January, the French foreign minister G. Bidault in March, presidential aspirant Harold Stassen in April and a group of seven British Labour Members of Parliament, who had the honour of an invitation to Stalin's vacation villa at Sochi. Apart from the ambassadorial contacts already mentioned, Stalin received nobody from the non-Communist world in 1948–51 except for the ambassador of India, once in 1950, and the president of Finland in the same year. In 1952–3, however, he again seemed interested in meeting foreigners, receiving the outgoing and incoming ambassadors of India, the French ambassador, the Italian socialist Pietro Nenni and, curiously, the Argentine envoy.[34]

During the post-war years Stalin did not meet with the press, Soviet or foreign, unless Elliott Roosevelt is considered a journalist. But he did reply in writing to written questions, all on international relations. In this, too, 1946 was the peak year, in which four foreign journalists and also *Pravda* had such scoops. Only *Pravda* was thus favoured in the next four years, and only twice, but in 1952 Stalin reopened this kind of dialogue with one American group of journalists and with James Reston individually.[35]

In all this activity, and also in open letters to presidential candidate Henry Wallace and to Prime Minister Nehru, Stalin presented himself as a man of peace. This theme paralleled various major peace campaigns that he sponsored in the same period. In these he generally kept his own name in low profile, presumably to avoid offence to various non-Communists whom he hoped to win to the campaigns against capitalist armament. A sketch of a dove by Picasso, not the image of the Leader, was the main symbol of this enterprise, although there was a Stalin Peace Prize, established in 1949. Unlike earlier Stalin prizes for Soviet citizens, this recognized deserving people from all over the world and thus acted as an antidote to the capitalists' Nobel Peace Prize.[36]

The irenic style also predominated in his personal diplomacy. This stands in contrast to the acrimonious tone that he often adopted during the war, the last outburst of which occurred on 22 August 1945, when Stalin rebuffed a request from Truman for bases in the Soviet Union's newly won Kurile Island: 'demands of this kind', replied Stalin, 'are usually laid before a vanquished country or before an allied country that is unable to defend a particular part of its territory. . . . I do not think that the Soviet Union can be classed in either category.' Despite the chilling of US–Soviet relations in the ensuing years, Stalin showed that he could match his language to his purposes and avoided such expressions. In this spirit he took George Kennan aside in September 1945 to say, 'Tell your fellows not to worry about those eastern European countries. Our troops are going to get out of there and things will be all right.' He seemingly tolerated lengthy expositions of American grievances by Smith and Marshall, rebutting the former 'quietly and pleasantly'. Stalin even accepted Marshall's unconvincing statement that the delay in the American reply to the Soviet request for economic credits had been unintentional: 'such [devious] tactics were not characteristic of United States policy', said Stalin, apparently concealing the sarcasm that he surely felt.[37]

He was at pains to assert that there was no need of conflict between the Soviet Union and the capitalist powers on ideological grounds. True, his first post-war speech, in February 1946, reaffirmed his commitment to Marxism–Leninism, attributing the world war to 'contemporary monopolistic capitalism', which in general leads to a 'general crisis' and 'military conflicts'. But in this speech he still spoke of the British and Americans as allies, as 'freedom-loving states'. In his approach to various Americans he treated the economic crisis of capitalism as useful for world peace because it would induce the capitalists to give Russia large credits to absorb overproduction in their own countries. Stalin told Alexander Werth in 1946 that he doubted that America wanted to establish 'capitalist encirclement' (Stalin supplying the inverted commas), that 'Communism in one country' was 'entirely possible' and that possibilities for 'peaceful collaboration' between the two economic systems were increasing. Stassen in 1947 elicited from Stalin a fuller statement on the subject. Yes, the United States could collaborate with the Soviet Union despite their differing economic systems. Lenin had said so, neither Stalin nor the Central Committee had ever said otherwise. It was for the American people to decide if their system was good or bad for them. Marx and Engels could not have foreseen circumstances '40 years' after their deaths. Stalin, he said in the third person, was not a propagandist but a businesslike person. When he and Roosevelt had talked, they had not abused one another as 'monopolist' or 'totalitarian'. Several years later, in a short written response to questions from American journalists, he characterized the proper relationship between Communism and capitalism with the term that Khrushchev was to popularize, 'peaceful co-existence'.[38]

According to Stalin, those who thought otherwise were warmongers, but until the autumn of 1948 he refrained from attributing this sin to the American or British governments. Churchill, now out of power, was the chief culprit. His 'Iron Curtain' speech in February 1946 brought a sharp rejoinder from Stalin, who found it a 'dangerous act', 'sowing discord among the allies'. 'Churchill now assumes the position of an instigator of war.' He had led the anti-Soviet intervention in the early days of Soviet power and, as Stalin told Ambassador Smith, 'lately he has been at it again'.[39]

One obvious motivation for Stalin's conciliatory stance from the end of the war until well into 1948 was the relative military weakness of the Soviet Union, above all its lack of atomic weapons until the first successful test in September 1949. During the Potsdam conference Truman had, in vague terms, informed Stalin of the first Anglo-American atomic explosion. The Soviet leader, who probably knew about the weapon from his intelligence service, showed no special interest in this news, and in 1946 told Werth that he 'did not consider the atomic bomb such a serious force. . . . Atomic bombs are intended to terrify the weak-nerved, but they cannot determine the outcome of wars.' That, he said in his pronouncement on military theory, is more likely to be determined by the 'counter-offensive', such as the Parthians had used against the Romans, Kutuzov against Napoleon, and – he might have added but did not – such as Stalin had used against Hitler and might yet use against the Americans. But this belittling of atomic weapons seems to have been a tactical cover for the interval in which the Soviet Union lacked them. Stalin told a Yugoslav delegation that the bomb was 'a very powerful thing, pow–er–ful!', and as early as the summer of 1942 the Soviet Union had its own Manhattan Project underway. According to Zhukov, Stalin turned to Molotov in the privacy of their quarters at Potsdam, following Truman's revelation, and said, 'tell Kurchatov [the scientist in charge of the atomic project] to hurry up the work'. With obvious satisfaction Stalin told *Pravda* in October 1951 that the danger of an American atomic attack obliged the Soviet Union to develop its own bombs and that the American leaders were 'displeased that the secret of atomic weapons was possessed not only by the USA but also by other countries, and, first of all, the Soviet Union'. By this time he had ceased to find it necessary to parlay with American diplomats, or to assure them that he respected their good intentions.[40]

Another matter may have been more important than atomic weapons in determining Stalin's withdrawal from personal diplomacy and the hardening of his line toward the capitalist states. This was the German question, the principal unresolved issue created by the war. Stalin evidently had trouble making up his mind about the future of Germany. In his meeting with Eden in 1941 and at the Tehran and Yalta conferences he had advocated the dismemberment of Germany, but in his victory address in May 1945 he gratuitously noted that the Soviet Union intended neither 'to dismember nor to destroy Germany'.[41] Nor did he urge dismemberment at the Potsdam conference. Probably the main reason Stalin changed his mind on this matter in the spring of 1945 was his recognition that the capitalists were going to have effective control of the most industrialized part of Germany when the fighting ceased, an outcome that would have seemed improbable a year earlier and far from certain even at the opening of 1945. This posed the possibility of the formation of a single capitalist west German state, including the industrialized Ruhr, as the Anglo-American interpretation of dismemberment. To prevent such a development, the Soviet Union had to become the defender of German unification, albeit without Austria. This stance could gain the support of almost all Germans, winning them away from the idea of a new west German rump state. Perhaps Stalin was sincere in 1947 when he told Marshall that he opposed dismemberment because 'he was afraid of losing control of the instrument of German unity and handing it over to the militarists and chauvinists'. At least he sincerely did not want the capitalist West to have a monopoly on this instrument. Perhaps he was sincerely willing to gamble on the harmlessness of a 'democratic and demilitarized' Germany in which there would be no 'strong centralized German government'. If this arrangement left Soviet occupation forces in the eastern zone of the country, it would always be possible to prevent a German government from rearming.[42]

Was it even possible that Stalin contemplated the creation of a unified, demilitarized Germany from which almost all occupation forces had been removed? Molotov made such a proposal at the Council of Foreign Ministers in March 1947. Such a German state would have had the attraction of transferring American and other capitalist forces fairly far from eastern Europe and the Soviet Union, but on balance it is hard to conclude that Stalin would have accepted a plan that left the continuation of German demilitarization to the goodwill of a conjectural German government. During the meeting of the foreign ministers at which this proposal appeared, Stalin told Bevin that the failure of the other powers to occupy Germany after the First World War was responsible for the revival of the German military. This implies that Stalin did not propose to repeat that mistake and had authorized Molotov to make his suggestion as one more means of distracting west Germans from the allurements of a state of their own.[43]

When such a state seemed about to take shape, Stalin demonstrated his repugnance for it by imposing a blockade of the western enclaves in Berlin. The goal of this uncharacteristically risky move was not to eject the paltry capitalist forces from these enclaves, but, as Stalin said repeatedly, to oblige the suspension of steps toward the formation of West Germany. In the course of the futile negotiations in which Stalin participated in August 1948 he showed that he was still capable of mastering complex information, such as the currency question that served as a pretext for the blockade. He also showed that he was capable of nimble manoeuvre, at one point asking 'suddenly whether we wanted to settle the matter tonight', thereupon proposing a formulation that seemed to leave open the establishment of a west German state. But at the next session, which started at 9 p.m., an agreeable time of day for Stalin, he began, 'quite jovially', 'well, I have a new draft'. This included wording that might have permitted the western countries to retreat on the west German issue with diminished embarrassment, but, as Stalin no doubt hoped, with some chance of losing the confidence of west German opinion. The West would not accept this proposal, and Stalin soon departed for his vacation, evidently convinced that he could not prevent the formation of a potentially dangerous West Germany. His next public comment, an interview in *Pravda*, for the first time in his personal usage referred to 'the aggressive policies of Anglo-American and French ruling circles', 'instigators of a new war'. Excepting short meetings with new British and American ambassadors in July and August 1949, Stalin had no more direct contact with his adversaries. In March 1949 he appointed as foreign minister, replacing Molotov, a man more suited to propaganda than purposeful bargaining, the prosecutor in the show trials of 1936–8,

Andrei Vyshinsky. Only in the last months of his life did Stalin suggest that he would be willing to meet with President-elect Eisenhower, but death intervened before this overture could be tested.[44]

It was not only the capitalist states that involved Stalin's personal diplomacy in the post-war years. By 1949 there were Communist governments in Poland, Romania, Bulgaria, Hungary, Yugoslavia, Albania, Czechoslovakia, East Germany, North Korea, North Vietnam and China. Previously there had been many Communist parties outside the Soviet Union, connected to Moscow through the Comintern. Now eleven of these parties ruled states that ranged in size from tiny Albania to immense China. Previously Stalin had given fairly low priority in his own work to Comintern affairs. Now he was obliged to take seriously the relations of the Soviet Union to this Communist sphere. The emergence of a 'Soviet bloc', as it was once miscalled by its opponents, has often been regarded as one of Stalin's greatest triumphs, but his own propaganda did not take this line, nor did his own comments reveal much of his thinking about the new situation. The inventor of 'socialism in one country' was, it seems, willing enough to encourage the spread of Soviet-model regimes but reluctant to provide any ideological framework for the Communist sphere as a whole. Stalin evidently approved of the concept of 'People's Democracy' as a form of socialism that was somehow less mature than the Soviet form, but he left it to an old Comintern functionary, the Bulgarian Georgi Dimitrov, to enunciate this somewhat fuzzy formulation.[45]

Stalin's reluctance to provide a clear and comprehensive ideological explanation of the nature of the Communist sphere presumably owed something to his desire to avoid stirring up excessive American antagonism. Thus, in discussing the situation in eastern Europe with Byrnes at the end of 1945, Stalin played the innocent. He denied that Soviet troops exercised pressure on elections and claimed that the Soviet Union considered some non-Communist parties to be 'friendly'. The Soviet Union, having suffered much from invasion from the west, merely wanted 'loyal' governments there. He did, however, drop a hint of his potential power, noting that in Hungary there were Soviet troops and 'in actual fact the Soviet Union could do pretty much as it wanted there' – but had shown restraint. In Bulgaria, he claimed, certain 'disloyal' parties were not following the model of Thomas E. Dewey, who had pledged the loyalty of his party to Roosevelt after losing the election. This was tendentious, but in truth the Soviet Union backed a policy of 'front' governments in which Communists at first shared power with other elements, then moved to establish Communist hegemony. Stalin frankly proposed this tactical plan to the Yugoslav Communist Kardelj: 'Take the king back as a matter of form, give some minor state positions to a few of the old politicians, and when the time comes you can easily eliminate both the king and his ministers.'[46]

But it was not only caution concerning the American response that induced Stalin to avoid an unrestrained and open commitment to the proliferation of Communist states. There was also his mistrust of Communists who were not under his direct control. His most vivid, if implicit, demonstration of this was the formal dissolution of the Comintern on 15 May 1943.[47] It is often suggested that Stalin did this to please his capitalist allies against Hitler, and he may have considered this a useful by-product of the dissolution. But Stalin would never have conceded something that he valued without receiving compensation, especially when there had not been any request from his allies that he make such a concession. A more plausible explanation for his decision was his concern for the post-war situation among Communists. A number of parties, including the Yugoslav, French and Chinese, had developed some sort of military capability, and also considerable experience in running their own affairs, partly owing to the poor communications of wartime. Who could say in May 1943, shortly after the victory at Stalingrad, where there might be independent Communist regimes following the war? And if the Comintern continued, who could say what the independently minded parties might do within this body, which was parliamentary in form? True, the Soviets had dominated the Comintern in the past by playing host to its executive and congresses, but could it count on doing so indefinitely in a world of numerous Communist states? From Stalin's perspective it was better to liquidate an organization that he had never esteemed before it became an embarrassment in the post-war world.

Thus Stalin faced a dilemma, one horn of which was his sincere antagonism to capitalism and preference for a Communist regime over any potentially anti-Soviet American satellite, the other his apprehension concerning the reliability of independent Communist states, the larger the less trustworthy. A partial solution lay in controlling nominally sovereign Communist states, operating mainly through three administrative hierarchies that reported to Stalin: the Soviet embassies, which kept an eye on political trends in general; the Red Army, which was the ultimate force where it was present and the patron of the reformed armed forces of the Communist states; and the political police, which directed Soviet-model security establishments in a number of countries. But what of the Communist party itself, the key institution in Stalin's experience in the formation of the Soviet Union? In the early 1920s the separate parties of the Ukraine, Georgia and so forth were treated as strictly subordinate units of the Russian party, subject to direct control from the Secretariat in Moscow. In contrast, the Communist parties in power outside the Soviet Union after the Second World War did not report directly to the Soviet party headquarters at 4 Old Square, Moscow, which contained no apparatus adequate to administer such an empire. True, the party leadership in a number of east European countries at the end of the war was heavily loaded with 'Muscovites', long-term *émigrés* to the Soviet Union who were dispatched to their homelands when this became possible. But once exported, the pool of 'Muscovites' was used up, and there was no regular chain of command linking these people and the Soviet party.

The shortcomings of this situation led Stalin to establish a 'Communist Information Bureau', or Cominform, in September 1947. Attempting to allay the reluctance of other parties to join what might be a new instrument of Soviet domination, Stalin tactfully placed the founding conference, which he did not attend, in Poland. The conference then agreed to place the standing Bureau of the organization in Belgrade. Nevertheless Zhdanov, Stalin's leading emissary to the conference, had to work hard to overcome objections to the formation of any Bureau at all. The result was an office that could at least serve as a disseminator of Moscow's line, openly through a newspaper (*For a Lasting Peace, For a People's Democracy*, a cumbersome name devised by Stalin) and secretly through circular communications. This at least might prevent a repetition of the embarrassing situation that existed shortly before the Cominform was established, when several east European Communist parties had expressed interest in participating in the Marshall Plan for European economic recovery, evidently lacking any clear directive from Moscow on this matter until the Soviet press had taken a stand.[48]

Stalin's personal prestige was one of his major instruments for controlling the new Communist states, which emulated the Soviet Union in the propagation of the Stalin cult, replete with portraits, statues (the one in Prague reputedly the largest in the entire world), street names, Stalin prizes and translations of the Teacher's classics in the local languages. Admiration for Stalin seems to have been not merely a cynical display for the rank and file but a genuine sentiment among foreign Communist leaders, who had ample reason to admire his success. In personal diplomacy, especially in the first few post-war years, Stalin attempted to make use of the respect that he enjoyed among the leaders of the new Communist states. The Soviet press recorded his participation in fifteen bilateral meetings in 1946–8 with representatives of Bulgaria, Hungary, Poland, Czechoslovakia and Albania.[49] Thereafter *Pravda* reported only one more meeting between Stalin and an east European Communist, Hoxha, which was in 1949. This does not, however, mean that Stalin ceased to receive European Communist leaders, for various memoirs report such meetings, which were secret at the time.[50]

One purpose that these audiences served was to permit Stalin to gather intelligence. How many Macedonians were there in Yugoslavia? How many Jews in the Yugoslav Central Committee? What did the Yugoslavs think of Hoxha? What was the potentiality for ship-building in Albania? How had the Albanians dealt with 'internal reaction'? Another purpose was to give advice or orders, often dealing in exceedingly casual style with major issues. Thus he proposed without ado that Yugoslavia 'swallow' Albania; told Dimitrov that he should arrange the election of a few opposition parliamentarians; advised Hoxha to go slow in collectivizing agriculture in the mountains, to call his movement not the 'Communist Party' but the 'Party of Labour in Albania'. Much less genial was his handling of the idea of a federation of two or more east European Communist states. In December 1944–January 1945 he approved a Yugoslav–Bulgarian federation, then summoned delegations from the two countries and cancelled the idea. In January 1948 Dimitrov spoke vaguely in public of a federation of eastern Europe from Poland to Greece. Stalin abruptly demanded a trilateral discussion with the Bulgars and Yugoslavs and there proceeded to browbeat Dimitrov, first for acting too independently, then for apologetically assuring Stalin that 'we all learn from you'. 'What are you talking about?' snapped the Boss, 'What can you, an old man, learn from me? You're behaving like an old woman on her way to market, saying the first thing that comes into her head to everyone she meets.' He then proceeded to propose the immediate absorption of Bulgaria into Yugoslavia as one of the components of the existing Yugoslav federation. This was not the only case in which Stalin played arbiter between two east European parties. In 1951 he sat as judge in a dispute between Hoxha and the leaders of the Greek Communist army, who had been defeated by the American-backed Greek army. According to Hoxha, Stalin found the Greeks at fault for having signed a capitulation to the enemy when they should have waged guerrilla war. This, incidentally, reversed Stalin's earlier position, as stated to the Yugoslavs, that the Greek civil war should be terminated because the Anglo-Americans would never permit a Communist victory there. But Stalin's justice was even-handed, for he ruled against Hoxha's accusation, which was highly Stalinist in spirit, that the Greek leader Nicos Zachariades was a British agent.[51]

Stalin's prestige among the foreign Communists was great, but there were limits to his personal authority, as the Yugoslav case demonstrated. There had been friction between Tito's regime and the Soviets almost as soon as the Yugoslav partisans established themselves as an independent force in the war. Tito had annoyed Stalin by not accompanying the obedient Dimitrov to the conference with the Bulgarians in February 1948. In March Stalin sought to apply pressure by sending the Yugoslav party a letter in the name of the Central Committee of the Soviet Communist Party, upbraiding the Yugoslavs for 'creating an anti-Soviet atmosphere which is endangering relations' between the two parties. In conclusion the letter ominously compared Tito's alleged criticisms of the Soviet party with those of Trotsky, 'when he decided to declare war on the Communist Party of the Soviet Union. . . . We think that the political career of Trotsky is quite instructive.'[52]

But there were no Red Army units in Yugoslavia, and the police reported to Tito. The Cominform could not command the Yugoslav party, which absented itself from a meeting of the Bureau in Bucharest in June 1948. This gathering urged the Communists of Yugoslavia to 'replace the present leadership' if it did not correct its 'nationalist line', which 'can only lead to Yugoslavia's degeneration into an ordinary bourgeois republic and to its transformation into a colony of the imperialist countries'. Such ideological pressure fits in with Stalin's boast to Khrushchev: 'I will shake my little finger and there will be no more Tito. He will fall.' It was not rash of Stalin to think that his personal prestige was so great among Communists that a suitable proportion of the Yugoslav party would take action against its leaders. Tito seems to have feared as much, for in December 1948, despite the poor state of relations with Moscow, the Yugoslav party organ fulsomely hailed Stalin's sixty-ninth birthday – an event that was not celebrated in the Soviet Union that year. But in the end they had to choose between defiance of Stalin and probable execution, the fate implied by a Cominform resolution of November 1949, 'The Communist Party of Yugoslavia in the Power of Murderers and Spies'. They chose defiance, and Stalin evidently decided not to respond with invasion, explaining to Hoxha that such a thing never crossed his mind.[53]

Tito's heresy opened a new period in Stalin's dealings with the east European Communist states. Having experienced the consequences of not having physical control in Yugoslavia, he sought to demonstrate for the benefit of satellite leaders the consequences for them of the presence of physical control, especially the presence of Soviet police 'advisers'. In Bulgaria, Hungary and Czechoslovakia a series of public trials of major Communists exposed a network of alleged 'Trotskyite–Titoist–imperialist' agents, who confessed and were executed.

The Tito affair was a timely lesson for Stalin, for the victory of the Communists in China faced him with the potentiality of a similar problem on a disastrously larger scale. Mao Zedong and his lieutenants were accustomed to independence, and they had various grievances with the Soviet Union, going back to Stalin's costly advice in 1927. At the end of the Second World War Stalin had signed a treaty with the government of Chiang Kai-shek and had received Chiang's son. Stalin told Harriman that he had told Chiang Ching-Kuo that he would willingly advise the Chinese Communists to end the civil war, but they had not asked for his advice. The Soviets, said Stalin, 'had poor contacts with the [Chinese] Communists'. Stalin was doing little to provide military aid to them, and probably doubted that they could win the civil war. When Byrnes told him that Mao claimed to have an army of 600 000, Stalin 'laughed heartily and repeated his assertion that all Chinese were boasters'.[54]

But Mao did win, and in July 1949 deferentially sent Liu Shaoqi to ask Stalin's advice on the establishment of a 'People's Republic'. In this meeting the Generalissimus admitted his past errors and apologized for the resulting interference and damage, an exceptional thing for Stalin, who may have been contemplating the possibility that Mao would be another Tito. That is exactly what Mao later said he believed Stalin was thinking, and he tactfully tried to overcome this apprehension.[55]

Thus Mao was received with special consideration when he arrived in Moscow on 16 December 1949. The Soviets timed the arrival of his train to coincide with the chiming of noon by the Kremlin bells. Stalin never met visiting comrades at railway stations, but Molotov was on hand and arranged that the planned formalities were curtailed to accommodate Mao, who was suffering from an indisposition. At 6 p.m. the same day Stalin and the Politburo gave a reception for Mao, evidently at Nearby. 'I never expected you to be so young and strong', said Stalin. 'You have won a great victory, and victors are above censure.' Behind this cordiality there was, however, a serious disagreement about the purpose of Mao's visit. He seems to have been invited, like all leaders of major Communist parties (except Tito), to pay homage to Stalin on the Leader's seventieth birthday. Mao did this, praising Stalin as 'the teacher and friend of the whole world, the teacher and friend of the Chinese people'. But Mao wanted something more practical than mere good wishes, specifically an alliance and economic assistance. Years later he claimed that Stalin had not wanted to grant these, and it seems that Mao had to apply pressure by virtually camping on Stalin's doorstep after the birthday festivities had ceased. On 2 January 1950 *Pravda* ran an interview with this inconvenient guest, trying to learn more of his intentions. How long would he stay? That 'depends on the time it takes to decide successfully the questions that interest the People's Republic of China', replied Mao. Stalin yielded to this bland threat to stay indefinitely, and by 10 January Premier Zhou Enlai was preparing a delegation to travel to Moscow to negotiate some treaties. The actual talks began on 20 January and culminated in the signing of a 'Treaty of Friendship, Alliance and Mutual Assistance', as well as economic agreements. The negotiations were delegated to Zhou and Vyshinsky but this may not have involved much bargaining because the Soviets drafted the main treaty and the Chinese adopted it with only minor changes in wording. They seemed pleased to have extracted a commitment from Stalin to come to China's aid in case of attack 'by Japan or states allied with it'. But Stalin could take satisfaction that this formulation left him considerable latitude to decide whether or not this covered the United States.[56]

To show his satisfaction Mao gave a reception on 14 February, the day of the signing of the treaty in the presence of the Soviet and Chinese leaders. Stalin came in a genial mood, but took the precaution of bringing his own bottle and drinking only its contents. In the course of the occasion he bantered with another Communist leader who was in Moscow but evidently had been unable to obtain an appointment with Stalin. This was the head of the new state of North Vietnam, Ho Chi Minh, who took the opportunity to request instructions. 'How could I instruct you, Mr President?' said Stalin, 'You are higher ranking than I am.' Ho was not the only Asian Communist asking Stalin for advice. In a filial gesture Mao told Stalin that he would like to have him send a 'political adviser' to China, but this wish was not fulfilled.[57]

Still another Asian Communist leader who came to Moscow for the birthday observances and stayed to ask advice was Kim Il-sung of North Korea. He wanted to use military means to reunify that country under his rule, assuring Stalin that this would go quickly and easily. Without consulting Mao, Stalin approved the plan, and the Korean war began in June 1950. Even if all had gone well for Kim, this affair wouild have aggravated Sino-Soviet relations, for the Chinese could not have been pleased with the presence of an enlarged Soviet client-state on their north-east, augmenting the Soviet presence in naval bases and along rail-lines in Manchuria. But Kim did not quite win in his initial offensive, and by autumn the American counter-attack threatened the Chinese border. Zhou secretly visited Moscow and flew thence to Stalin's vacation villa in the south to consult on the question of Chinese military intervention, with the accompanying risk of broadening war, perhaps involving the Soviets. Stalin and Zhou may have vacillated, but they ended by deciding in favour of Chinese intervention, which did indeed drive back the enemy to the middle of the Korean peninsula and led to a cease-fire in July 1951. Although this was a kind of triumph, Mao, whose son died in the fighting, cannot have been grateful to Stalin for getting his country into a costly war when China so badly needed peace. Nor did Stalin show any inclination to facilitate the signing of a more stable settlement in Korea, which is understandable considering that the precarious cease-fire occupied a large part of both the Chinese and American armed forces. Perhaps it was to stir him from this inaction that Zhou came to see Stalin in August 1952, a few months before Stalin wrote to James Reston that he was willing to discuss Korea with President-elect Eisenhower. In his lifetime, then, Stalin's prestige and diplomacy had avoided an open Sino-Soviet rift, but he had done much to prepare the way for such a calamity following his departure.[58]

14 Mortality

Stalin's seventieth birthday, which fell on 21 December 1949, was the high point of his claim to earthly immortality. Because praise for Stalin had been so profuse for so long, it was not easy to make the birthday a strikingly distinctive occasion, but the propaganda machine, co-ordinated by a committee of seventy-five dignitaries, including the Politburo, Lysenko and Shostakovich, rose to the challenge. The 'stream' (*Pravda*'s word) of greetings flowed on until 14 August 1951, published at the rate of a couple of hundred per day almost every day during those years. Poesy flourished in countless tongues, the Union of Soviet Writers offering a purportedly collective inspiration, concluding with an implied allusion to the role of the bow in Orthodox ritual:

> For all, for all, receive our bow;
> As the hearts' duty, as a mark of the people's love;
> From all the republics of the free Motherland,
> From all free nations and tribes –
> From all, from all, a filial bow to You![1]

The Tretiakov Gallery in Moscow devoted an exhibition to Stalin as a subject of the visual arts. The Academy of Sciences held a ceremonial meeting in honour of 'the greatest genius of mankind' and published a large volume that elaborated Stalin's contributions to each branch of learning. This was not easy, but the appearance of Stalin's *Works*, starting in 1946, at least simplified the task of finding statements that might be used to demonstrate the Leader's wisdom on this or that subject. Among composers who celebrated the occasion was Khatchaturian with 'Songs about Stalin'. The Orthodox Church, which had not joined the chorus in 1939, now added its voice. In the words of a cleric named Luke: 'And we raise to God our prayer of thanks that He has given us this pillar of peace, Stalin, this pillar of social justice. Amen.'[2]

The members of the Politburo each contributed an essay, the lot reprinted in many periodicals. Malenkov had pride of place. His 'Comrade Stalin – the Leader of Progressive Mankind' began: 'Comrade Stalin constantly warns us that not conceit but modesty adorns a Bolshevik.' But Beria, in the number three position, following Molotov, was the only one to achieve three paragraphs entirely in italics. These leaders were highly visible but not audible at the gala in the Bolshoi Theatre that culminated the festivities. The proceedings emphasized Stalin's global role, and by implication the subordinate status of other Communist leaders, interspersing speeches of such dignitaries as Mao Zedong, Togliatti and Ulbricht with those of obscure Soviet personages, none of Politburo rank, like P. A. Kruchenyuk of the Moldavian Republic. Stalin attended but merely smiled his thanks for the accolades.[3]

The central feature of the whole complex of celebrations, distinguishing it from the festivities of 1929 and 1939, was the presentation of gifts. This was a shrewd decision because it was possible to involve masses of people as donors. Thus in 'Gifts' by the Belorussian poet Anton Belevich the residents of a collective farm each consider what to give their 'teacher, friend, father'. After the woodcutter, milkmaid and beekeeper each have selected something appropriate to their occupations, a small boy vows that for his gift he 'will grow up faster so that he can become a Hero of the Soviet Union'. This was fiction, but real gifts were contrived and flowed to Moscow, where a selection was displayed in the Museum of the Revolution. A permanent museum was envisaged, but never materialized, although one room of the Stalin museum in Gori is devoted to birthday gifts. One of the largest gifts in the Moscow exhibition was a carpet 20 metres square from the Kirghiz Republic. 'In the centre of the rug is embroidered a portrait of Comrade Stalin. On the blue background under the portrait is written in the Kirghiz language: "To the Great Stalin from the Kirghiz people." ' An optical factory sent a microscope with a viewing slide that contained images of the busts of Lenin and Stalin, presumably the smallest among many thousand representations of these heroes, for they were only 0.03 millimetres high. Less manufacturered were the 'stacks of bound folios' of signed greetings, the illiterate making fingerprints. North Korea, a country of about ten million, managed to send sixteen million signatures. Despite the hostile regimes of certain countries, their toilers sent gifts to Moscow, 1500 from Hamburg alone, a feather war-bonnet from America, dedicated to 'the supreme warrior of the Indian tribes'. Ilya Ehrenburg wrote that 'an old Norwegian' had told him, 'I would like to carve a wonderful pipe for Stalin.' Burgundy vintners said, 'We put aside our best bottles for Stalin.' 'A Frenchwoman whose daughter had been shot by Fascists sent Stalin the only thing that was left of her child, her little hat.' Perhaps she sent it to the special exhibition of gifts to Stalin that the Communist Party of France organized in Paris, seven convoys of trucks bearing the diverse contributions to the display. The workers of the house of Schiaparelli, for example, made a small fashion manikin dressed in a gold lamé evening gown. This was far more stylish than the gift of the timber workers of Albania, a pledge to fulfil their plan by 210 per cent.[4]

This celebration of Stalin's birthday was the most eleaborate, far-flung observance of such an occasion in history. But it had this in common with the celebration of anyone's birthday: along with joy an implied reminder that life is fleeting. The chorus of tributes carefully avoided any reference to the idea that Stalin had attained a great age. Few came as close to touching on mortality as did Sholokov, who concluded his essay 'Father of the Toiling World!' with 'Father! Our glory, our pride, love and joy, live for many years.'[5]

The question of Stalin's age and life-expectancy, while unmentionable, could not but fascinate his small circle of lieutenants. Ambitious men, formed in an environment in which political murder had been common, they inevitably began to manoeuvre for position as the Boss grew older and less vigorous. The fact that he had not killed anyone of Politburo rank for about ten years may also have emboldened some of them in the early post-war years, not to move against Stalin but against one another. Not all the full members of the Politburo participated in the competition. None of the men who had become leading Stalinists in the 1920s were active in the game, perhaps partly because they were relatively near Stalin's age but more from a variety of individual reasons. Molotov, who should have been the front-runner on the basis of his status as virtual second-in-command for so many years and his age, eleven years Stalin's junior, was not among the contestants. Perhaps he had grown too accustomed to the role of deputy to retain a high level of personal ambition. In any case Molotov seems to have been in slow political decline since he yielded the office of chairman of the Sovnarkom to Stalin in 1941, and he lost the ministry of foreign affairs to Vyshinsky in 1949. While he remained a member of the Politburo and a deputy chairman of the Council of Ministers, his role and sphere of influence were uncertain. In the last few years of Stalin's life Molotov's life was at risk, for Stalin arrested his wife and excluded him from the late-night movies and revels. Another who sunk to this level around 1951 was Voroshilov. Even when he had been narkom of defence and one of Stalin's most visible comrades-in-arms in the 1930s, Klim lacked the personal attributes of a potential political force in his own right, and after his inept performance in the war was fortunate to retain his place on the Politburo. In contrast, the status of Kaganovich seems to have remained stable, and in 1947 Stalin demonstrated his trust in this old associate by sending him to the Ukraine to take over from Khrushchev, then under a cloud. But Kaganovich was Jewish by ancestry and probably sensed that the atmosphere of the post-war Soviet Union required a Great Russian as successor to the russified Georgian. Ethnicity presumably helped to keep Mikoyan, an Armenian, on the sidelines. Moreover he, like Molotov, lost his ministerial base, foreign trade, in 1949 while gaining no compensating position and in the last year or two of Stalin's life fell from social favour in the Kremlin.[6]

The participants in the pre-succession struggles were men who had reached the Politburo a decade or more after these elder cronies of Stalin: (in order of seniority) Zhdanov, Khrushchev, Beria, Malenkov and Voznesenky. They were not in all cases much younger than the men who had made it to the Politburo in the 1920s, but they seem to have preserved more sense of ambition and independence. The first three in the list all had spent a substantial period as regional bosses, operating with a considerable degree of independence in Leningrad, the Ukraine and Transcaucasia, respectively. Malenkov, in contrast, had come up through Stalin's personal secretariat, but his career had flowered as one of the main operatives in the State Committee of Defence, and it seemed by 1950 that he was Stalin's chosen heir. Voznesensky, too, had advanced rapidly during the war as the main economic boss. This was a somewhat specialized base, lacking influence in the party, but he compensated for this with a close working relationship with Zhdanov. Suffering from a heart ailment, it may be that this senior potentate set aside his personal ambition in succeeding Stalin, whose daughter states that Zhdanov often privately expressed the wish to die before his Boss. But he may have transferred such aspirations to the younger Voznesensky, or perhaps simply took up this ally as a necessary measure of self-defence in an increasingly feud-ridden atmosphere. The power of this combination, which claimed the loyalty of Zhdanov's successor as chief of the Leningrad area, A. A. Kuznetsov, may have induced Malenkov and Beria to make common cause against it. As members of the State Committee of Defence during the war these two, with their respective specialties in the party and police, had been delegated great authority in domestic administration, and must have been loath to see this reduced by the ascent of a man who had not even been a member of that committee. According to Khrushchev, Malenkov had even suffered rustication to Central Asia because of charges that he was responsible for defects in aircraft engines during the war. Such accusations might, of course, have been planted by Zhdanov or Voznesensky. For his part Beria had particular need for an ally because Kuznetsov had been promoted to the Secretariat with the particular function of supervising the security organs. Beria persuaded Stalin to bring Malenkov back to Moscow, and this coalition set itself against the Zhdanov–Voznesensky team.

The myth of party unity required that the conflict was covert, although Kremlinologists have detected various refractions of the struggle in ideology and changes of personnel. There is, however, no good evidence that Stalin chose sides, and it is reasonable to suppose that a balance between contending lieutenants suited him better than the emergence of one preponderant individual or coalition. But the death of Andrei Zhdanov on 31 August 1948 upset the balance in favour of Beria and Malenkov. Roi Medvedev believes that Zhdanov died alone at his villa near Moscow in mysterious circumstances, and it is possible that Beria used the nefarious agencies at his disposal to arrange this. But Zhdanov really did have a serious heart condition, and probably drank much too heavily. It seems that Stalin became aware of this problem, which he had encouraged over the years, and near the end of Zhdanov's life attempted to oblige him to give up alcohol, shouting at him to stop drinking. It is difficult to see why Stalin would have wanted Zhdanov dead.[7]

Zhdanov's demise not only removed the senior figure in one of the contending factions, it also deprived this group of its best access to Stalin. Voznesensky was a relative newcomer at the top, and was not a personal crony of the boss. Khrushchev's plausible testimony of what followed attributes to Beria and Malenkov the initiative in arranging the slaughter of Voznesensky, Kuznetsov, and a number of their subordinates. These executions required Stalin's assent, to obtain which the conspirators revived the traditions of the Yezhovshchina, complete with a 'Leningrad case', a 'Moscow case' and phony denunciations. One of these was directed against G. M. Popov, the Moscow party chief appointed by Zhdanov. The precise charges against the victims have never been specified, for there was no show trial. Stalin at first seemed reluctant to accept the allegations and thus upset the balance among his lieutenants. Khrushchev believed that Stalin recalled him from the Ukraine and placed him in the Secretariat as a counterweight to the victorious Malenkov and Beria. Having shown Khrushchev the deposition against Popov at the time he summoned him back to the capital, Stalin was still weighing its credibility somewhat later when Khrushchev settled into his new assignment at the end of 1949. Having heard Khrushchev's opinion that the charges were false, Stalin in fact spared Popov, as he did Kosygin, one of Zhdanov's clients from Leningrad. Khrushchev believed that Kosygin's life hung by a thread and does not purport to know what saved him. It may have helped that Kosygin had a chance to establish personal relations with Stalin while on vacation on the Black Sea in 1946. At the same time Stalin spoke of releasing from prison some officials of the aviation industry whom Beria and Malenkov had framed. Most important, Stalin was reluctant to make a decision against the talented Voznesensky. In March 1949 Voznesensky was relieved of his duties, but for a time was not arrested, while Stalin continued to ponder the case, suggesting several times that his ability should not be wasted, that perhaps he should be put in charge of the State Bank.[8]

At some point in 1950 Stalin made up his mind to accept the charges against Voznesensky, which evidently involved treason in some form, and he was sentenced to death. This penalty, by the way, had been suspended in Soviet Law in 1947, but in January 1950 was restored for 'traitors to the motherland, spies and subversive diversionists', an ominous sign of the shift in Stalin's mood. The principal police official working on the case was Beria's protégé and compatriot V. S. Abakumov, and the Politburo acted as the court, its members signing the order for execution. Khrushchev, who was far from attempting to exculpate Stalin for this judicial murder, believed that Beria had used his fine understanding of Stalin to find just the right moment to bring him to the desired conclusion.[9]

It is tempting to conclude that the 'Leningrad Case' played a role in unbalancing Stalin as well as the arrangement of power in the Politburo. For about a decade since the waning of the Yezhovshchina Stalin had been able to restrain his propensity to see traitors all around him. With the 'revelation' that there was an enemy agent in the Politburo, among other high places, his concern for his personal safety appears to have taken a new and phobic turn. Granted, his concern for security had been earnest for many years, and it may be that the particular eccentricities that Khrushchev and Svetlana associate with his last few years began earlier. But his Yugoslav guests, who were present as late as the opening of 1948, and who were amply willing in later years to recount any bizarre behaviour that they observed at Stalin's dinners, make no reference to the 'routine' that Khrushchev mentions. 'Let's say Stalin wanted something to eat; everyone was assigned a dish which he was supposed to try before Stalin would taste it.' If Khrushchev, for example, failed to sample the giblets assigned to him, he would notice that Stalin 'would like to take some himself but was afraid'. This, despite the presence of certificates, bearing official seals, stating 'no poisonous elements found,' on every item of food destined for his table. The air in Stalin's Kremlin quarters was also subject to tests for toxic substances. In the trial of Bukharin the prosecution had alleged that Yagoda plotted to murder Yezhov by spraying his quarters with poisons. It seems that Stalin in his later years began to place some credence in a tale that he, or Yezhov, had fabricated. If so, this was a bad sign for Beria, since he occupied the position as security chief that the deceased Yagoda formerly filled. Perhaps Stalin also became dissatisfied with the protection offered by his armoured car and its escort of bodyguards, for in 1949 he may have ordered the building of a special Metro line from the Kremlin to his residence at Kuntsevo, Nearby. This story, widely believed in Moscow, is apparently sustained by the existence of two parallel lines, one of them quite superfluous. As any visitor to Moscow can confirm, one end of the unnecessary line heads from the Lenin Library Metro station toward the Kremlin, a few hundred metres away, and the other end is at the Kiev railway station, evidently aimed at Kuntsevo, which it never reached.[10]

There is, however, another sign of Stalin's increasingly morbid apprehensions that seems to have pre-dated the 'Leningrad Case' by a short time, suggesting that the changes for the worse in Stalin's personality had already started when Beria and Malenkov began to fabricate denunciations against Voznesensky and Kuznetsov. This was Stalin's deadly attack on the leading figures in Soviet Jewish culture. In a country rife with anti-Semitism the Russian revolutionary movement had made opposition to this ethnic hatred a major issue. By the standards of the movement, Stalin in his earlier years had been at least impolite in making reference to the number of Jews among the Mensheviks, even speaking sarcastically of the need for a pogrom. And much later he had not been above a few remarks about the poor qualities of Jews as soldiers in an apparent attempt to add a note of cordiality in his dealing with the Polish ambassador. According to Khrushchev, Stalin sometimes indulged in mimicry of a Jewish accent, and he was pretty good at it. But his record was not actively anti-Jewish before 1948. He had not permitted open and official acts against Jews, and had chosen Jews among his close subordinates, including Kaganovich. While indulging himself in anti-Jewish remarks, Khrushchev recalls, Stalin would never countenance this sort of thing in the presence of Kaganovich.[11]

It was probably brooding on his family that set Stalin on his anti-Jewish course around 1947. His eldest son, Yakov, had married a Jewish woman whose loyalty was, in Stalin's eyes, questionable. His daughter had taken up with a middle-aged Jewish man while still a schoolgirl and then had married another Jew. 'That first husband of yours was thrown your way by the Zionists', Stalin told his daughter, evidently after she had married again in 1949. But whatever his dissatisfaction with Svetlana, he would never turn her over to the police for investigation. The same restraint did not, however, apply to his sister-in-law Evgeniia, who had married a Jewish man some time after her first husband, Pavel Alliluev, had died. Her interrogation may have helped to spread the wave of arrests of Jews, since she had many intellectual Jewish friends. One of these, Lidiia Shatunovskaia, believes that Vasily Stalin had a hand in Evgeniia's arrest, revenging himself for her complaints about his use of her apartment for his revels while she was living in Kuibyshev during the war. In this version Beria also had a score to settle because of insults from the sharp-tongued Evgeniia. She was, in any case, arrested, perhaps the only non-Jew to be included in this case of the 'Zionist centre'. As in the past, one arrest led to another through interrogation or simply association. None of the victims were high-level political figures, for it had been a number of years since Jews had been promoted to that sphere. One who perished, A. Lozovsky, had been a substantial figure in the Comintern apparatus, but had become a professor. Most of the others were intellectuals of one sort or another, although there was one air-force general in the lot. Stalin singled out Solomon Mikoels, the leading actor and director of the Soviet Yiddish-language theatre, for murder, announced as an auto accident, in January 1948. This is the one case out of many murders in Stalin's era concerning which there is a good witness to his complicity: his daughter, who walked into his office while he was issuing appropriate orders on the telephone.[12]

The arrest of those suspected of connection with the 'Zionist centre' was already under way when an incident occurred that evidently increased Stalin's apprehensions concerning Zionism. The Soviet Union had supported the establishment of the state of Israel, evidently reasoning that this would undermine British influence in the Near East. When Golda Meier arrived in Moscow in October 1949 as the first ambassador from the new country, a large and enthusiastic crowd of Soviet Jews greeted her appearance at a synagogue. One of her well-wishers at a diplomatic reception was Polina Molotov, whose ancestry was Jewish. Stalin now dispatched her to prison in Kazakhstan. But in the wake of the spontaneous demonstration of support for Israel, the Jewish Anti-Fascist Committee, a body established during the war by the Soviet regime, was dissolved and a number of its leading members, especially writers, were arrested, and some of them executed in a year or two.[13]

The 'Leningrad Case' and case of the 'Zionist Centre' appear to have had quite different origins: the former a manifestation of the pre-succession conflict among Stalin's lieutenants, which he approved with some reluctance; the latter a personal obsession that did not touch the higher levels in Soviet politics. But the two affairs converged in Stalin's mind, combining to concentrate his attention on real or imaginary domestic threats to his security. In this it seems that Beria and Malenkov achieved more than they had bargained for. Their victory not only upset the existing balance in the Politburo, it also contributed to the destabilization of Stalin's personality. The spectacle of his prospective heirs quarrelling over the disposition of his power may have alarmed him and impelled him to the conclusion that they had to be dealt with before they became too independent. As early as 1947 he had a curious conversation with the film director Sergei Eisenstein, who was working on a life of Ivan the Terrible, and the actor Nikolai Cherkasov, who was playing the tsar. Stalin saw clearly a parallel between Ivan and himself when he praised the tsar as 'a great and wise ruler who protected the country from the infiltration of foreign influence and tried to bring about the unification of Russia'. And did he not see some parallel, too, when he said that Ivan was mistaken in his 'failure to liquidate the five remaining feudal families. . . . There God stood in Ivan's way, for he would liquidate one boyar clan and then repent for a whole year and pray for forgiveness of his sins when instead he should have been acting with increasing determination'? Stalin knew well that 'family' was one of the terms used to described patronage groups in the Soviet hierarchy, and he had long since attacked this tendency. The notion that it was necessary to smash such independent centres of power to protect Russia from civil strife after the passing of the strong ruler was an attractive justification for harsh action against the boyars of the sixteenth or mid-twentieth centuries.[14]

Whether or not Stalin was contemplating such analogies in 1947, he began to take some steps against his ambitious deputies. Beria was the most threatening, having gradually taken control of Stalin's household by planting Georgian cooks and servants of his own choice throughout the establishment. At some point after the war, Stalin turned on Beria, asked 'Why am I surrounded by Georgians?' and proceeded to have them removed. But Beria's control, through fear of the police, of the political apparatus was not so easily reduced. In late 1951 Stalin moved deviously against Beria in two ways. First, he moved Beria's compatriot and protégé Abakumov, on whom he had placed considerable reliance in recent years, out of his post of minister of state security, which controlled the secret police. His replacement was S. D. Ignatiev, an official whose background was in party administration, and thus not under Beria's patronage. This seems to have been related to the concoction of yet another 'case', the 'Mingrelian'. It was alleged that one of the provinces of Georgia, Mingrelia, had been allowed to fall into the hands of anti-Soviet Georgian nationalists. Since Georgia was still regarded as Beria's sphere of influence, and he was responsible for security in general, this dereliction was discreditable to him. But at this point in his career Stalin had no need to discredit a subordinate in order to convince the Central Committee or public opinion to accept anyone's removal, so it is likely that the aim of the manoeuvre was to test Beria's commitment to Soviet Russia, to smoke out any partiality for Georgia that he might be harbouring. Or simply a test of his willingness to sacrifice his clients, especially Mingrelians, for that was Beria's own provincial origin. If such was the case, the ruthless Beria passed the test by personally travelling to Georgia to supervise the purge of the Mingrelian élite. That he did so unwillingly emerged shortly after Stalin's death, when Beria had a brief chance to rehabilitate some of those arrested earlier.[15]

Beria may have survived the 'Mingrelian Case' as much through Stalin's indecisiveness as through his own efforts. Khrushchev attributes Beria's survival to Stalin's weakening health and consequent inconsistency in action. The same weakness would explain the survival of Molotov, Voroshilov and Mikoyan in 1952, despite Stalin's belief, which he expressed before considerable numbers of people, that these old Bolsheviks were agents of imperialist states. Unwilling to decide which cronies to arrest, Stalin evidently determined to deal the lot of them a political blow. The instrument for this was the Nineteenth Party Congress. The Politburo had wanted such a gathering, now let them have it – but there would be some surprises for them before and after the meeting. Stalin did not feel strong enough to give the traditional, long report in the name of the Central Committee. This he awarded to Malenkov, while Khrushchev was assigned the second most important topic, the new party statutes. Beria was thus relegated to a less promising position. Stalin himself sat at a separate tribune during the proceedings and said nothing, apart from the brief concluding speech that ignored the others and stressed the continuation of the class struggle in the world. Evidently his concern for his health was such that he was pleased to be able to make even this oratorical exertion.[16]

But Stalin's words nevertheless dominated the scene during the congress. On 3–4 October, the eve of its convocation, his latest classic appeared in *Pravda*: 'Economic Problems of Socialism in the USSR'. Consisting of four replies to various economists, this work had been composed at intervals between February and September 1952, but had been held from the press until just the moment when it was most useful. All the principal speakers at the congress were obliged to improvise appropriate admiration for this work, which was the subject of an immediate campaign of study and praise throughout the country. Since the document did not deal with any of the specific issues of the day, it was not easy for Stalin's lieutenants to know what to say about it. But it was always possible to emulate Khrushchev's report to the congress, averring that Stalin's work was 'a new, invaluable contribution to the theory of Marxism–Leninism', which creatively develops 'Marxist–Leninist science, arming the party and the Soviet people with teaching on the laws of contemporary capitalism and socialism'.[17]

The other surprise that Stalin had for the party leaders came on 16 October at the first meeting of the newly elected Central Committee. This was the proposal that the old Politburo, which had eleven members and candidate members on the eve of the congress, be replaced by a 'Presidium' of twenty-five members and eleven candidates. Here was a promising step toward the reduction of the power of the leading lieutenants of the day, the creation of a larger pool of potential rivals or replacements for the *boyars* who might be liquidated. Stalin indeed implied that this might be the fate of some of the established figures, for he told the Committee that Molotov, Mikoyan and Voroshilov were agents of western governments. In keeping with his confused and indecisive handling of such matters at this stage, these three were still retained in this Presidium, although they were not on Stalin's list for a new inner group – the 'Bureau of the Presidium' – that he proposed at this time. A remarkable indication of Stalin's mental decline by this stage is Khrushchev's belief that Stalin could not have known all thirty-five of the men who were named to the new body. After all, ten had been on his old Politburo, and the others were not wholly obscure. There was, for example, a provincial party secretary, Brezhnev, who had talked at length with Stalin by telephone. Even if he did need help, and received it from Kaganovich, as Khrushchev suspected, it demonstrated that the aging dictator was not too enfeebled to spring a political coup on Beria, Malenkov and Khrushchev, who all agreed in private that they did not like the business.[18]

At about this time, the autumn of 1952, Stalin's physical health evidently took a turn for the worse, and with it his wavering mental stability. His daughter, seeing him for the first time in two years, was struck by his sickly appearance and impressed that he had given up smoking, a habit of half a century. The pipe was one of Stalin's well-known props, presumably a symbol of his wisdom, but he also smoked cigarettes and indeed used tobacco crumbled out of cigarettes to stoke his pipe. This probably played some part in the problem with high blood pressure that evidently was becoming severe by 1952. As befits a recently reformed heavy smoker he was in a foul humour on the occasion of Svetlana's attendance at one of his parties near the end of that year. She had been dancing to the customary music of her father's record player, tried to rest and was ordered to continue. When she protested Stalin dragged his daughter, now a woman of twenty-six, by her hair back to the dance-floor. He was 'lurching about', and it may be that in these final months alcohol had taken control of the dictator, who rarely left Kuntsevo.[19]

Also at about this time, Stalin turned viciously on his two most important personal retainers, Vlasik and Poskrebyshev. The former had started in Stalin's service as a bodyguard in 1919 and had become a kind of 'minister of royal domains', which included Stalin's residences, food supply system and transportation. The latter had joined Stalin's staff not long after Stalin became General Secretary, and for many years was his personal executive secretary. The two effectively guarded the approaches to Stalin's office, one as controller of security, the other of appointments. Yet both of these men were thrown out in 1952, Vlasik under arrest and Poskrebyshev suspected of leaking state secrets. Whatever may be said of Stalin's suspicious character over most of his career, it should be conceded that the retention of the same two men as chief of personal security and as political secretary shows not a pathological instability but a fairly steady hand throughout many crises. So much more threatening, then, was Stalin's belated, abrupt and menacing turn against such trusted aides.[20]

Stalin turned on still another man on whom he had relied for many years: his personal physician, Dr V. N. Vinogradov. He had little to do with doctors, it seems, and this older practitioner was, as Svetlana recalls, 'the only one he trusted'. But Vinogradov was swept up in a drastic purge of the 'Kremlin doctors', that is the staff of the special hospital-clinic next to the Kremlin, across the street from the Lenin Library, whose patients are the very top of the Soviet élite. The arrest of seven of these doctors was announced in the press on 13 January 1952, but they were not the only victims and the 'case' had been on Stalin's mind for over three months. Khrushchev had seen reports on some of the accused before the party congress, which opened on 5 October 1952, and had first been appraised of the case when Stalin read to some of his lieutenants a letter from one Dr Lidiia Timashuk. She accused her colleagues of bringing about the death of Zhdanov by administering the wrong medical treatment. In his secret speech of 1956 Khrushchev said that she 'was probably influenced or ordered by someone to write Stalin a letter' and that she was a police informer. According to his long-time housekeeper, Stalin himself harboured doubts concerning Timashuk's veracity. If true, this eliminates the likelihood that he had inspired her denunciations. Beria might have done this to discredit Ignatiev, showing Stalin that plots were going undetected, but he could scarcely have wanted to include evidence that such negligence dated back to Zhdanov's death in 1948, when security was Beria's own responsibility. Conceivably some daring would-be heir to the police job among the second-rank men in that field was behind the scheme. As for Ignatiev, Khrushchev maintained that he was 'mild' and 'considerate', not really well suited to his assignment with the police and unable to satisfy Stalin in producing confessions from the doctors.[21]

In any case, Stalin raged at Ignatiev and threatened to 'shorten him by a head' if the requisite confessions did not emerge. According to the resulting concoction, the assassins were connected with the 'American Joint Distribution Committee', a philanthropic body founded before the revolution to assist Jews in the Russian Empire. Because Beria had been responsible for security when this plot was hatched, the affair cast doubt on his loyalty. The confessions also 'revealed' that the doctors had been working on the assassination of a number of leading military figures, one of whom, Marshal Konev, wrote a letter to Stalin in which he maintained that the doctors were trying to poison him as they had Zhdanov. It could not have been reassuring to the leading members of the party Presidium that the masters of the fiendish doctors did not want to eliminate these leaders. Stalin's case was different. Presumably he was not included among the listed targets because this would have implied that his health required medical care, a highly sensitive point. 'The investigation will soon be concluded', stated the announcement of 13 January, leaving Beria and the others to guess what the conclusion might be.[22]

In openly associating Jews with disloyalty to the motherland or to Communism Stalin evoked a strain of popular anti-Semitism that was far from outlived in Russia, and aroused in the Jewish population a state of apprehension that gave birth to the report that all Jews were to be deported to Central Asia or Siberia. The main line of this report is that Stalin ordered a number of prominent Soviet Jews to sign a letter requesting that their people be moved east as protection against pogroms, which might have been permitted as a prelude. Perhaps, but testimony on this matter has become a classic example of the flowering of rumour in a system that restricts open research. Stalin might have been attracted to the removal of much of the Jewish population in European Russia, but it is hard to believe that he wanted to permit the non-Jewish Soviet population to engage in riots that might have been hard to control.[23]

The arrest of Ivan Maisky, Jewish by ancestry, around the beginning of 1953 fitted in with the trend of the time, but was more threatening to the political élite than the fate of doctors, writers or actors. Although not in the highest ranks of the ruling apparatus, he had served as ambassador to Great Britain and in 1944–5, as deputy narkom of foreign affairs, had assisted Molotov.[24] If he turned out to be a 'traitor', Molotov's already precarious position would become much worse. And what about the other members of the Presidium who had worked with Jewish subordinates at one time or another? More than at any time since 1938 Stalin's conduct was a threat to his colleagues. He was in a state of physical and psychological deterioration, probably aggravated by increasingly heavy drinking, but there was no way to retire him. Supposedly he had offered his retirement to the Central Committee at its meeting following the party congress of October 1952, but was begged to stay on.[25] If indeed he did make the offer, the response was predictable, given the awe and fear that he inspired. No legal means of deposing Stalin was available, and assassination or a *coup d'état* would be exceedingly risky. The preponderance of the population was too much in the thrall of the cult of Stalin, propagated for twenty years, to accept any explanations of why it was now necessary to remove him. Were such a thing undertaken, it would be impossible to answer for the stability of the regime or the safety of Stalin's successors. What was needed was a natural death, and soon.

On 4 March 1953 the Soviet newspapers for that day reached their destinations a few hours late. They carried a medical bulletin that began:

> On the night of 1–2 March, while he was in Moscow in his apartment, Comrade Stalin suffered a brain haemorrhage which affected vital areas of the brain. Comrade Stalin lost consciousness. Paralysis of the right arm and leg developed. Loss of speech followed. Serious disturbances of the function of the heart and breathing appeared.[26]

It is now reasonably well established by the accounts of Stalin's daughter and Khrushchev that this version includes three deceptions. First, Stalin was not in his Moscow apartment in the Kremlin, as implied, but at his usual residence, Nearby, at Kunstsevo. But the existence of this home was officially a secret, and for years the cult had stressed the image of the wise Leader in the Kremlin. So it was reasonable not to confuse people with new information at a critical time.

The second deception concerns the timing of the haemorrhage. The Russian expression used in the bulletin was *v noch' na 2-oe marta*, which may be translated as 'on the night of 1–2 March', for want of any more exact rendering. But to a Russian the phrase normally means the period beginning shortly before midnight and ending around the time of rising the next day. Anything before this period would be called 'evening' rather than 'night'. The bulletin conveyed to Russians the idea that the seizure occurred between about 11 p.m. on 1 March and 6 a.m. on 2 March. But Khrushchev says that the first sign of illness that Stalin's household staff noticed was that he did not call for tea and food at about 11 p.m. on 1 March. If true this suggests that the attack had occurred before that time, probably before early afternoon, when Svetlana had telephoned and had been told 'there is no movement right now', meaning that the staff guessed that Stalin was still in bed. In any case the author(s) of the medical bulletin could not have known when the seizure really occurred – unless somebody was secretly observing Stalin throughout 1 March, a possibility, but not something to be admitted in public.

The third deception in the official bulletin is the implication that Stalin was receiving medical care at an early point. The statements about the sequence of symptoms suggest that a competent physician observed the course of the attack. But the memoirs of the daughter and the political heir make it clear that in fact no physician could have arrived until the night of 1–2 March was over or almost over. Khrushchev does not mention specific times, but his narrative makes it incredible that the doctors arrived much before 5 a.m. on 2 March. This is many hours, perhaps over twelve, after the seizure. Both the second and the third deceptions noted seem to be motivated by the natural desire to show the Soviet public that the men who might stand to gain by his death had from the start done everything possible to provide medical attention to the sick Leader. Even if Stalin did indeed die of wholly natural causes, even if no amount of medical care could have affected the mortal consequences of his stroke, it is not true that he was under medical care soon after the seizure.

The narratives that emerge from the memoirs of Khrushchev and Allilueva do not both deal with all the same points, but these two mutually independent accounts are complementary in what they do cover. Neither wishes to argue that Stalin was murdered, yet the impact of their memoirs, along with the falsity of the official bulletin, suggests that suspicion is reasonable. On the evening of 28 February Beria, Malenkov, Khrushchev and Bulganin saw movies at the Kremlin (perhaps an unusual outing for Stalin in his last year or so) and then repaired to Nearby for dinner and drinks. Khrushchev maintains that Stalin was in a jovial mood that evening, if only because he was 'pretty drunk', an expression that carries weight in the usage of a Russian of Khrushchev's experience. The four guests departed around 5 or 6 a.m. on 1 March, the last time any known person saw Stalin in reasonably good health.

The next time any known person saw him was about 3 a.m. on 2 March, almost twenty-four hours later. According to Khrushchev, Stalin's guards said that they became concerned when he did not call for tea and food around 11 p.m. as he usually did. This is odd, not that Stalin would want to eat at that late hour, but that his guards did not expect him to eat something shortly after rising around midday, a well-attested habit. After this seeming delay the guards evidently waited almost four hours before deciding to look in on their charge, sending a not very competent emissary, an old and rather stupid serving woman. After this the guards, in their version to Khrushchev, entered the room, found Stalin asleep on the floor and lifted him onto a couch. Svetlana was told that this was at 3 a.m., which is compatible with Khrushchev's recollection that he awaited an expected phone call from Stalin on the previous evening, went to bed 'very late' and still later received a phone call from Malenkov reporting that 'the Cheka boys' at Stalin's villa 'think something has happened to him'. This, by the way, suggests that the communication was not from the guards to each of Stalin's drinking companions but through Beria, the obvious one for them to notify first. But the cronies, on arriving at Nearby – presumably around 3.30 a.m. – and hearing the guards' report, decided not to venture into the dining-room, in which Stalin now reposed on a sofa, while he 'was in such an unpresentable state'. This presumably refers to the assumption that he was still, almost twenty-four hours after they had been drinking with him, in the process of sleeping it off – unless they thought it plausible that he had resumed drinking at some later time. Either assumption would be eloquent testimony to the severity of Stalin's alcoholism at this point.

And so the cronies returned to their own villas, having done nothing about the sleeping Stalin. But 'later that night', which must mean not much after 5 a.m. at the latest, the guards phoned again. They had sent the old woman in to have another look, and she reported that he was sleeping soundly, 'but it's an unusual sort of sleep'. This time the party of Beria, Malenkov, Khrushchev and Bulganin decided to expand their council to include Voroshilov and Kaganovich and also some doctors, which must have added to the time it took to reassemble at Nearby. Taking into account all the foregoing events it could not have been significantly earlier than 5 a.m. on 2 March before this political–medical delegation ventured into the room where Stalin lay. In other words, Stalin had been wholly in the hands of his bodyguard, seen only by them and an old woman, during the twenty-four hours since Khrushchev had last seen him. Now the doctors diagnosed paralysis and moved him into the adjacent main room to the sofa where he usually slept. Why the guards, who surely more familiar with his ways, did not take him there in the first place is unclear and a little suspicious. It is still more peculiar that the doctors did not see fit to move the sick man to a hospital, if every possible means of saving him was to be available.[27]

He survived for just a few hours over three full days from the time the doctors first entered his quarters, dying in Kuntsevo at 9.50 p.m. on 5

March. In this interval his potential heirs set up a rotating death-bed watch of pairs: Beria–Malenkov, Voroshilov–Kaganovich, Bulganin–Khrushchev. It was highly unlikely that the partially paralysed man, who had lost the power of speech, would have anything to say, but presumably they wanted to watch one another. Only after medical facilities, including X-ray, cardiogram and artificial respiration equipment, were in place on 2 March did the politicians notify Stalin's son and daughter. It was not desirable to allow these two to form the opinion that the efforts to save their father were less than whole-hearted. It helped that Bulganin and Khrushchev were in tears when they greeted Stalin's children, which is not to say that their emotions, even if mixed, may not have been sincere. Nevertheless Vasily, drunk as usual, 'gave the doctors hell and shouted that they had killed or were killing our father'. After Stalin's death he persisted in saying that his father had been 'poisoned' or 'killed'. The new authorities would not permit this, warned Vasily to stop and, when that failed, ordered him to a post outside Moscow. He refused and continued to air his opinions to strangers in restaurants. On 28 April, less than two months after his father's death, Vasily was jailed, tried for 'corruption' and sentenced to eight years in jail, though soon transferred to a hospital. The opinion of this seriously alcoholic wastrel scarcely constitutes firm ground for thinking that Stalin was murdered – but Vasily was exceptionally well acquainted with Beria.[28]

And Beria was the member of the inner circle who was most threatened by the 'doctors' plot' and who had the greatest access to professional killers. He was also the one whose conduct at the death-bed suggested open hostility to Stalin. Svetlana presumably was not present at the time recounted by Khrushchev when Beria 'spewed hatred' against Stalin, then fell on his knees when the sick man seemed to regain consciousness, only to rise and spit when the appearance of lucidity passed. But her version is consistent in tone, referring to Beria's apparent lust for power, his staring into Stalin's eyes, when they opened from time to time, as if to convey loyalty, and his 'unconcealed' shout of triumph to his bodyguard in the silence just after Stalin died, 'Khrustalev, my car!'

But for all this and her general detestation of Beria, Stalin's daughter does not believe that he murdered her father. This makes all the more piquant her comments on the fate of her father's personal staff after his death. Long-time servants were discharged and 'sent away'. 'A good many of the officers of the bodyguard were transferred to other cities. Two of them shot themselves.'[29] It is not clear just how Svetlana Alliluyeva learned about these alleged suicides, which she did not regard as evidence of foul play. But if the men did indeed die at this time and if it was alleged that they committed suicide from grief, that would be the most persuasive of all indications that Stalin was murdered. Svetlana may be right in claiming that her father's personal staff was devoted to him, but it is grossly incredible that the feelings of these professional bodyguards were so sensitive that they could not bear life without their Boss. Such men had charge of Stalin for about twenty-four hours at a stretch, starting at about 5 a.m. when his companions departed from the inebriated dictator. This time should have been adequate for the guards, or some specialist whom they admitted to Stalin's quarters, to deal with the fairly sophisticated problem of stimulating or simulating a stroke. To be sure, such a task would be easier in dealing with a prime candidate for a stroke, but more difficult if the physicians who conducted the autopsy did an honest job in the few hours that they seem to have had to perform that function. Finally, the scenario of Stalin's hypothetical murder should refer to his last gesture, a possible attempt to indict Beria or a doctor (for it could be that the fabricator of the case against doctor-murderers was after all murdered by a rogue doctor), 'He suddenly lifted his left hand as though he were pointing to something above and bringing down a curse on us all', recalled his daughter.

Such speculation cannot settle the matter, which probably never can be settled. If murder it was, the prime suspect as master plotter is Beria, who had good motive not to reveal his secret to anyone but a few executioners, who probably became 'suicides' soon after the event. Beria himself may have perished at the time of his alleged arrest in late June 1953, or at least by December, the time of his announced execution.[30] But perhaps there was, concerning Stalin's death, no guilty secret to die with Beria or be passed on to interrogators. Stalin's general condition by March 1953 was such that a cerebral haemorrhage would be unsurprising. His daughter believes that he took a Russian steam-bath only twenty-four hours before his stroke, foolish for a man with high blood pressure, as was getting drunk.[31] Vasily was usually drunk, so his opinions can be discounted. Svetlana believes her father died of natural causes, and she has not revealed how she came to think that two bodyguards committed suicide in their grief. The slow action of the guards on the day he failed to get up might reflect their fear of his caprice, especially with a hangover. Khrushchev, who hated Beria, has not suggested that he murdered Stalin and says that at one point Stalin revived enough to shake hands with each of his cronies, presumably including Beria. This seemingly suggests that this highly suspicious man did not in his last hours suspect anyone of hastening his end. On balance the case for murder remains 'not proven', but even those who would rule out foul play must admit that the timing of Stalin's death was providential for some people.

Along with benefits, Stalin's death presented problems for his successors. Despite the medical opinion that Stalin was about to die, the inner circle did not inform the world of Stalin's illness until 4 March, two days after the first diagnosis. Even with this delay they were unable to say more about the new arrangement of authority than that Stalin would be unable to participate in the affairs of state for 'a more or less prolonged' period. On 5 March *Pravda* tried to deal with this problem in an editorial entitled 'The Great Unity of the Party and the People'. This was an attempt to revive the legitimacy of the party as an institution, a necessary step after so many years in which the idea of personal autocracy had been so strongly implied by the propaganda of the cult. Also on 5 March two more medical bulletins appeared, offering only bad news. These reports helped to prepare the public for the end and to protect the successors from public suspicion, for they detailed the measures that the doctors were taking.[32]

When death came, it posed the leaders with the task of writing a new chapter in the history of the image of Stalin. How to deal with the passing of a Leader who for twenty years had been represented as more than human? To stress too much the indispensable greatness of the departed might be dangerously demoralizing to the public, but to do too little might turn the people against Stalin's heirs. These men successfully steered a middle way, giving Stalin a fine funeral but in truth much less adulation than he had received on his birthday in 1949. The success of the new leaders in dealing with this touchy business seems to owe much to Khrushchev, who was chairman of the funeral commission of seven, of which only one other, Kaganovich, was a first-rate potentate. The main announcement of Stalin's passing, issued in the name of the party and state, informed the masses that 'The heart of the comrade-in-arms and genius-continuator of Lenin, the wise leader and teacher of the Communist Party and the Soviet people – Iosif Vissarionovich Stalin – has stopped beating.' Although the idea of a partnership of Lenin and Stalin was a staple of the cult, it was out of keeping with the usual style of Stalin's later years to open so important a tribute in this way. To begin the obsequies for Stalin with reference to Lenin was a good indication of the line that was emerging. The statement spoke of Stalin's role in founding the party, making the revolution, building socialism and winning the war, but then it moved on to a significantly longer discussion of the primacy of the party and its unity with the people.[33] The next day, 7 March, a party–state decree went about the practical business of handing supreme power to ten men, a new Presidium that replaced the swollen one that Stalin had introduced at the party congress of 1952. Of this group Malenkov, already a member of the party Secretariat, became chairman of the Council of Ministers and thus something like Stalin's successor. Beria regained control of the police as minister of internal affairs, which now embraced the Ministry of State Security. Khrushchev gained something, too, for he was freed of the task of running the Moscow party organization and allowed to 'concentrate' his work on the Secretariat. It may or may not be coincidental, by the way, that these three winners in the new arrangement, along with Bulganin, had comprised Stalin's drinking partners on that last night. The justification for the revised distribution of authority was that 'the difficult time demands the greatest unity of leadership and prevention of any kind of disorder or panic'. This was not entirely easy at the lying-in-state and funeral, owing to the massive outpouring of emotion: proof that the cult had struck root with the multitude. Harrison Salisbury, who had been a correspondent in Russia for almost nine years, wrote that the crush of people, young and old, men and women and some children, was something that he had never seen there before, 'a *spontaneous* crowd'. To attempt to curb the influx from the rest of the country, the authorities had to suspend incoming rail services, and the last trains that did arrive had people clinging in ice and snow to the roofs of the carriages. Despite the best efforts of police and troops, and the use of parked trucks to contain the crowd, the press of mourners crushed to death some of their number.[34]

At a funeral itself, on 9 March, the three representatives of the new leadership who delivered eulogies seemed less in awe of the departed than was the mass of the populace. While the formalities of funereal pomp were observed, including the bearing of the coffin to Red Square, artillery salutes and the tolling of the Kremlin bells, the total affair was somewhat short and understated. Malenkov and Beria, the first and second eulogists, gave political speeches that seemed more concerned with party unity and national security than with the superhuman greatness of Stalin. The last speaker, Molotov, whose wife Stalin had sent to Central Asia, at least gave the impression of emotion and said something about Stalin's career. At the end of the ceremony the embalmed body, in the uniform of generalissimus was placed beside Lenin in the mausoleum. But even before this enshrinement there had been a hint that it might not be permanent. On 7 March the decree ordering that Stalin's body be placed in the mausoleum was accompanied by another decree ordering the construction in Moscow, not mentioning Red Square, of a 'Pantheon – a monument to the eternal glory of the great people of the Soviet land'. It ordered that the sarcophagi of Lenin and Stalin be moved there along with the remains of all the other heroes memorialized at the Kremlin Wall – a chance to rearrange the ranking of the immortal. In practice, this plan has not been heard of since, but it illuminates the uncertainty of Stalin's successors concerning the fate of his cult.[35]

In the very short run the cult atrophied almost at once, at least in official media. No statues, pictures, place-names or prizes were removed or renamed, but the dynamic of the cult evaporated. On 11 March, only two days after the funeral, references to Stalin moved off the front page of *Pravda*, and a week later eulogies ceased to appear in the party organ. No new literary or dramatic works glorifying him appeared, nor did the fourteenth volume of his collected *Works*, which would have covered the years 1934–9. On 26 July *Pravda* ran a very long article on the entire history of the party, which barely mentioned Stalin but had much to say about Lenin and collective leadership. Meanwhile the collectivity of the leadership had suffered when Beria was arrested in June 1953. In the short term this retarded movement toward a revision of Stalin's image, for it became possible to blame a great number of evils on the discredited police boss. But in the longer run the end of Beria meant the end of police terrorization of the party. At some date prior to 1956 the party commissioned one of its historian-ideologists, P. N. Pospelov, to direct an investigation of the political crimes with which many former Communists, dead or surviving in Gulag, were charged. The result was a report that, while treating Beria as an ogre, placed the major responsibility for the slaughter of good Communists on none other than the centre of the cult of personality. On the night of 24–5 February 1956 at the Twentieth Party Congress, the first since Stalin's death, Khrushchev presented much of the Pospelov report in the form of a secret speech. Until the last minute the Politburo had been divided on the advisability of such a step: Molotov, Voroshilov and Kaganovich opposing Khrushchev, Malenkov, Mikoyan and others who wanted the report presented to the delegates. Logically this was the end of the Stalin cult. The man was depicted as a poor Leninist, an egomaniac and a sadistic murderer of good Communists, but, incongruously, the visible monuments of the cult did not disappear, and the body remained beside Lenin's. The anti-Stalin speech was circulated secretly to party and other groups and released to foreign Communist parties, whence it was leaked to the western press, to be published in June 1956. But no substantial, direct attacks on Stalin appeared in the Soviet Union, and the published resolution on 'On Overcoming the Cult of Personality and Its Consequences' was a compromise document. In it the emotional indignation of the Khrushchev speech was missing, there was much justification of party policy past and present, and a strong aversion to 'excessive' anti-Stalinism.[36]

Only five years later did the party, at its Twenty-Second Congress, confront the relics of the Stalin cult. Again Khrushchev was the key figure, and again he seems to have met strong resistance in the Presidium to the idea of assaulting Stalin. Only at the end of the agenda did he deliver an address on this problem, this time published and this time supported by several other speakers. But not all, for there were some, including Brezhnev, who held their peace on this subject. In the course of these deliberations the congress finally dared attack the magic of the cult as embodied in its visible symbols. Thus it determined that the body of Stalin should be removed from the Lenin Mausoleum, a symbolic step that opened the way to the removal of all the statues of Stalin except one in Gori, the dismantling of his pictures, even the chipping of his image from a mosaic in the Moscow Metro, and the renaming of thousands of places. A new wave of officially sponsored attacks on Stalin followed, including historical research and fiction. The most devastating of all blows was the officially permitted publication in 1962 of that brilliantly understated polemic *One Day in the Life of Ivan Denisovich* by Aleksandr

Solzhenitsyn. Ironically, this concentration on the demythologizing of Stalin enhanced his posthumous importance. Only a monumental historic figure, albeit evil in many respects (but not all, according to the official line) would require such a massive effort by the propaganda apparatus. With some justice, the whole anti-Stalin campaign implied that he was the central figure of the previous generation, and that Russia and Communism needed to come to terms with the Stalin legacy if they were to go forward.[37]

This was awkward, perhaps dangerous, for the regime. As Molotov and others apparently warned before Khrushchev's secret speech of 1956, it was hard to discredit Stalin without undermining the authority of the party at home and abroad. The party establishment attempted to fend off this threat by re-emphasizing the goodness of the party as an institution and by reinflating the cult of Lenin. But this failed to convince such dissident intellectuals as Solzhenitsyn, and by 1964 the attack on Stalin was turning into a critique of the whole system. This development was only one of numerous complaints that the Soviet establishment nursed concerning Khrushchev's leadership. Khrushchev was retired in October 1964, and a new phase in the evolution of the Stalin image began. Despite the wishes of some party hierarchs, Stalin's reputation was not substantially revived in the Brezhnev era. A marble bust, similar to others in the row adjacent to the Lenin Mausoleum, appeared in 1970, and, in keeping with an enhanced effort to glorify the patriotic war against Germany, Stalin was recognized favourably as the national leader in that struggle. But in the main the solution to the Stalin problem in Soviet mythology was denial that the problem existed. This required such feats of amnesia as the publication of a standard book of 550 pages on the history of the USSR during 1931–1941, in which 'the cult of personality of Stalin' is criticized in one and one-half pages and his name is otherwise mentioned perhaps a dozen times.[38] The Gorbachev leadership, while attacking some of the foundations of the Stalinist economic system and releasing some artistic works that deal with the terror, has not been eager to reopen the Stalin issue as a whole. Only after two and a half years as General Secretary did Gorbachev use the seventieth anniversary of the October Revolution as an occasion to speak in general terms of the need to reinterpret Soviet history, making brief reference to Stalin's personal responsibility for crimes, referring favourably to Bukharin and Khrushchev and promising some sort of continuing reappraisal of the past.[39] Whether this will lead to the release of substantial new information about the life of Stalin remains to be seen, but it is at least safe to say that the persistence of the Stalin issue as one of the central problems of Soviet politics, over thirty years after his death, is a more impressive, undoubtedly sincere, tribute to his historical impact than were any of the emanations of the Stalin cult.

15 Judgements

There is no point in trying to rehabilitate Stalin. The established impression that he slaughtered, tortured, imprisoned and oppressed on a grand scale is not in error. On the other hand, it is impossible to understand this immensely gifted politician by attributing solely to him all the crimes and suffering of his era, or to conceive him simply as a monster and a mental case. From youth until death he was a fighter in what he, and many others, regarded as a just war. As one of his comrades, and most important critics, Khrushchev, put it, 'The class war isn't a festive parade, but a long, tortuous struggle.' For all his denigration of Stalin, Khrushchev found in him a man who was 'incorruptible and irreconcilable in class questions. It was one of his strongest qualities and he was greatly respected for it.'[1] Stalin rose to eminence among people who subscribed to this outlook, not only party activists but many members of Russia's vast underclass, urban or rural. They were ready for bloodshed, little concerned with the suffering of the *burzhui*, to use the russification of the Marxist term that was popularized in the revolution. The greatest exponent of the class war in the first quarter of the twentieth century was, to be sure, Lenin, but neither he nor Marx was the inventor of class hatred. This was a powerful force in the world, no mere figment of the imaginations of radical intellectuals, and there is a growing body of scholarly opinion that in the early twentieth century class hatred was stronger in Russia than in any other country in Europe or possibly the world. In a broad sense there is much to be said for Stalin's thesis that Russia represented the 'weak link' in the world system of imperialism. He flourished in this environment and his success cannot be understood apart from the context of class hatred, to which he (and this book) frequently referred.

The class war in Russia was, then, authentic and essential to Stalin's ascent. But he was no mere passive beneficiary of the struggle and eventually was able to shape it according to his own definition. In Stalin's vision the conception of the class enemy expanded, while that of the proletarians and their party shrank. The bourgeoisie was perceived as not only the capitalists and those dependent on them, but also a large part of the peasantry and other elements, such as the intelligentsia, that did not fit into a bipolar model of society. There was also the category of 'bourgeois nationalists' that might include people of any social stratum. Stalin's enlargement of the conception of class enemy caused him no serious difficulty within the Russian proletariat itself, and at some points there may have been numbers of proletarians or their advocates who ran ahead of Stalin in their zeal to finish with the old 'bourgeoisie'. The industrial working class in Stalin's Russia rarely suffered at the hands of his police, and appears to have been receptive to his presentation of the idea of class struggle. Substantial numbers of poor peasants probably shared this outlook, though as a whole it was the peasantry that suffered the largest number of exclusions from the camp of the toilers, as officially defined. The dispossession and dispersal of the 'kulaks' was, on the whole, a popular policy among proletarians and party activists, by no means something that Stalin imposed on reluctant comrades. If he faced isolated opposition from the Bukharinists on this issue, he also moderated to a limited extent the zeal of some other Bolsheviks.

Although Stalin had opponents within the party before the assault on the peasantry, they had not argued that his fault was excessive brutality toward remnants of the bourgeoisie or *petit bourgeoisie*. Even Bukharin's case rested on utilitarian economic grounds rather than moral scruples. The tension between Stalin and the party élite stemmed instead from his tendency to transfer Bolsheviks from the sphere of the elect to that of the class enemy. Those who disagreed with him on this point had shown no reluctance to regard the Mensheviks as objective members of the enemy camp, even though these 'deviationists' had started as comrades in a single Social-Democratic Party. But they balked at applying this logic to defeated deviations within Bolshevism. From an early point after Lenin's death Stalin consistently had trouble persuading the higher party assemblies to accept the fullness of the argument that those who opposed 'the party' were as good as class enemies and should be treated as such. Repeatedly he had to settle for sanctions against various oppositions that were less than what he wanted. The Central Committee session of February–March 1937 was the last such frustration, for at this point he appears to have decided to treat as class enemies all those in the élite whom he suspected of thwarting him.

The subsequent Yezhovshchina was crucial in establishing Stalin's full-blown dictatorship, but the nature of his rule by terror can be misunderstood. After Stalin's death, the Khrushchevians and various surviving victims, in venting their indignation, created the impression that Stalin's police measures against the élite were at a high level over a protracted period. This exaggerates his actual record as an executioner of Bolsheviks. The bitter reference of victims to 'the call-up of 1937' testifies to the suddenness with which the blow fell on the élite, and the principal depredations lasted about two years. After decimating and intimidating the upper levels of Soviet society, Stalin resumed a more restrained attitude toward them for about ten years. If a new wave of 'cases' appeared in the late 1940s, the initiative seems to have owed much to Stalin's lieutenants, engaged in pre-succession manoeuvres.

But did Stalin really conceive of the Yezhovshchina, with its preposterous accusations, as class struggle? Could he really justify to

himself the killing of his old friend Yenunkidze, of Kirov, the murderous
psychological pressure on Ordzhonikidze, as necessary deeds in the class
war? Some argue that his conduct reflects nothing but self-serving
cynicism. There was indeed a cynical streak in his make-up, which in its
lighter expressions would relieve the deadly humourlessness of a Lenin or
Trotsky. 'The USSR always keeps its word . . . except in cases of extreme
necessity', Stalin told Charles Bohlen.[2] But such a frank attitude toward
politics does not preclude a profound devotion to radical principles. 'In a
party one must support everything that helps without having any boring
scruples there', Marx, who was not a mere cynic, once wrote to some of
his followers.[3] Like most strong political figures, Stalin identified the
cause and his own interest. The party and the Soviet system were in his
eyes all too vulnerable in a hostile capitalist world and could not afford
the luxury of bumbling leadership. 'You'll see, when I'm gone the
imperialistic powers will wring your necks like chickens', he told his
lieutenants, evidently more than once.[4] It was not necessary for a victim
to be literally in the pay of the class enemy. If he was thwarting or
threatening Stalin, he was objectively serving the imperialists. Moreover
the publicly prosecuted cases had great heuristic value, showing the
populace how any deviation from true Marxism–Leninism must lead to
service of the imperialists.

In general the concept of 'capitalist encirclement' was well established
in the Bolshevik world-view before Stalin provided this evocative
expression. The supposed imperialist threat justified not only his harsh
measures against internal dissent but also his demanding goals for
economic construction. Although Trotsky and some other Communist
opponents of Stalin attempted to argue that his foreign policies served
poorly the interest of the proletariat, they had difficulty in arguing against
his long-term success in maintaining the interests of the 'socialist
fatherland', the Soviet Union. True, Stalin's foreign policies involved
numerous deals with imperialist powers, conducted with a thoroughgoing
practical, or cynical, sense of the nature of the international game. But
throughout this record of changing alignments and hostilities Stalin's basic
commitment to the idea of two camps was unchanged. Circumstance
might require him to deal courteously with Eden and Laval, then
Ribbentrop, then Churchill and Roosevelt, but for him it was
fundamentally a continuum – the pursuit of the interest of the Soviet
state, the global base of the proletariat.

This identification of the USSR and the proletarian cause raised some
complications. His manipulation of Russian nationalism at times seemed
cynical, incompatible with any version of Marxism–Leninism, especially
in cordiality toward the Russian Orthodox Church during the Second
World War. But it is hard to believe that his espousal of Great Russian
nationality was wholly unprincipled. His personal identity as a Russian

was sufficiently firm that his young son had to inform his sister, 'you know, Papa used to be a Georgian once.'[5] And in his relations with capitalist powers in war and peace there was a sense of authentic national pride. In this matter Stalin must have found foolish or incomprehensible the debates of foreigners on the tension between Russian nationalism and Communism. But the newly emergent Communist states following the war posed his Russo-centric Communism with a serious challenge, which he seems never to have resolved in his own mind.

The logic of implacable class warfare was simple, the psychological element in Stalin's behaviour complex, perhaps beyond the reach of the historian with his limited research materials on Stalin's personal life. It is at least clear that he was not bothered by 'affect' in its current psychological usage. To order murder or torture brought no distress to Stalin, though he had no taste for administering or witnessing the actual deed. Up to a point this may be regarded as immoral but not particularly abnormal human behaviour. The society in which he was a youngster, with its public hangings, was not tender hearted, nor was the Russia of the civil war, with its mutual atrocities. But in 1937–8 the interaction of militant Marxism and personal cruelty led Stalin almost to the stage of dysfunction as a personality and a politician. The contracting circle of the elect was drawing so tightly around Stalin in the vision that he projected in his electoral speech of December 1937 that he was in danger of becoming totally isolated, unable to run a political machine because he could trust no one. This was the condition that he diagnosed in himself, according to Khrushchev, in 1951, saying, 'to no one in particular', 'I'm finished. I trust no one, not even myself.'[6] He had succeeded in restraining this psychotic vision of class struggle by 1939, but its return by the 1950s may have spelled his doom, driving Stalin to threaten mortally too many underlings, especially Beria, while retaining no core that he could rely on.

Stalin's identification of the cause of the proletariat and his own person was publicly symbolized in the cult. To the extent that he believed his leadership necessary to the movement he probably did subscribe to this official mythology. But it seems unlikely that he suffered from delusions in this matter. His daughter's opinion that he did not see himself as a demigod is confirmed by his sardonic references to the cult of Stalin in the presence of such diverse witnesses as the American Harriman, the Finnish Communist Tuominen and the Soviet minister Yakovlev.[7] The delusion that he was an infallible super-hero was not for Stalin himself but for the fallible human material that he had to work with as the builder of Communist society. Having spent his first four decades very much among the ordinary folk, not in an encapsulated society of emigrant radical intellectuals, Stalin did not idealize human nature among the proletarians. The cult was necessary as a beacon for the masses – who were too easily influenced by false movements and leaders – and was the guarantee that a reliable Marxist–Leninist would maintain supremacy. It was the necessary inspiration for those who could not derive it from Stalin's essay 'On Dialectical and Historical Materialism', despite his strenuous efforts to see that millions tried to master this dry tract, which made no reference to wise leaders. The cult as well as the killings, therefore, was part of Stalin's response to the gulf between human nature as he saw it, with cynical realism, and as it was supposed to become, according to Marxist eschatology. It was his personal dilemma and tragedy that he could never find a way to bridge this gulf, despite his enormous personal power and gift for politics and administration. And for the millions whom he ruled, Stalin's ruthless struggle to impose a solution to this problem was an incomparably greater tragedy.

Chronology of Stalin's Life

('Old Style' to February 1918)

1879
9 Dec   Born in Gori.

1888
Sept   Enters clerical elementary school in Gori.

1894
Sept   Enters theological seminary in Tbilisi.

1899
May   Expelled from seminary.

1900
Apr   Addresses worker demonstration near Tbilisi.

1902
Apr   Arrested in Batumi following worker demonstration of which he was an organizer.

1903
July–Aug   Appearance of Lenin's Bolshevik faction at the Second Congress of the Russian Social-Democratic Workers' Party (Stalin not present).

1904
Jan   Escapes from place of exile in Siberia and returns to underground revolutionary work in Transcaucasia.

1905
      Revolution, reaching peak in Oct–Dec, threatens the survival of the tsarist government.
      Stalin marries Ekaterina Svanidze.
Dec   Attends Bolshevik conference, also attended by Lenin, in Tammerfors, Finland.

1906
Apr   Attends 'Unity' congress of party in Stockholm.

1907
Mar   Birth of first child, Yakov.
Apr   Publishes first substantial piece of writing, 'Anarchism or Socialism?'
Apr–May   Attends party congress in London.
Jun   Moves operations to Baku.
Oct   Death of his wife, Ekaterina.

1908
Mar   Arrested in Baku.

1909
June   Escapes from place of exile, Solvychegodsk, returns to underground
            in Baku.

1910
Mar   Arrested and jailed.
Oct   Returned to exile in Solvychegodsk.

1911
June   Police permit his legal residence in Vologda.
Sept   Illegally goes to St Petersburg but is arrested and returned to Vologda.

1912
Jan   Bolshevik conference in Prague at which Lenin attempts to establish
            his control of party; Stalin not present but soon after is co-opted to
            new Central Committee.
Apr   Illegally moves to St Petersburg, but is arrested there.
Sept   Escapes from place of exile in Siberia, Narym, and returns to St
            Petersburg.
Sept–Dec   Edits *Pravda*, in this connection visiting Lenin in Cracow, Austrian
            Poland, in Nov and Dec.

1913
Jan   Stays in Vienna in order to write 'Marxism and the National
            Question', which Lenin commissioned.
Feb   Arrested in St Petersburg soon after return there.
July   Transported to exile in Siberia where he lives in Kostino, Kureika and
            Achinsk.

1917
Mar   Following the fall of the old regime in the 'February Revolution',
            returns from the last of his several places of residence in Siberia,
            Krasnoiarsk, to Petrograd, where he is elected to the editorial board
            of the party organ, *Pravda*.
Apr   Meets Lenin upon latter's return from exile in Switzerland.
July   Following abortive left-wing attempt to overthrow the Provisional
            Government, helps Lenin flee Petrograd; remains in capital
            representing Bolsheviks in the Soviet of Workers' and Soldiers'
            Deputies.
July–Aug   In the absence of Lenin plays leading role in the Sixth Party Congress,
            which elects him to new Central Committee.
Sept–Oct   Participates in party Central Committee meetings, which deal
            inconclusively with Lenin's demands that the Bolsheviks seize power.
Oct   Bolsheviks overthrow the Provisional Government and proclaim a
            Soviet government, headed by a 'Council of People's Commissars', in
            which Stalin heads the People's Commissariat of Nationality Affairs.
Nov   Visits Finland to address congress of Social-Democrats.

1918
Jan–Feb   Supports Lenin in his attempts to persuade party Central Committee
            to accept German peace terms.

('New Style' calendar in effect February 1918)

Feb(?)	Marries Nadezhda Allilueva.
Mar	Moves with government from Petrograd to Moscow.
	Peace of Brest-Litovsk signed with Central Powers.
June–Oct	In Tsaritsyn supervising defence against anti-Bolshevik forces.

1919

Jan	With F. Dzerzhinsky visits eastern front to report on reasons for failure of Red Army.
Mar	Elected to Politburo and Orgburo.
May–June	In Petrograd area supervising defence.
July–Sept	In Smolensk area supervising military activities on western front.
Oct–Jan	Travels in area south of Moscow supervising military efforts against anti-Bolshevik forces.

1920

Feb–Mar	In Kharkov dealing with political and economic affairs of Ukraine.
May–Aug	In Kharkov area supervising military efforts against anti-Bolshevik forces in south and Polish army in west.
Oct–Nov	In North Caucasus and Baku dealing with party affairs.

1921

Birth of second child, Vasili.

Sustained activity connected with the reintegration of minority nationalities with Soviet Russia.

Feb	From Moscow supervises occupation of Georgia by Soviet forces.
June–July	In North Caucasus for reasons of health, visiting Tbilisi in July to insist on tougher measures against Georgian nationalism.

1922

Apr	Elected General Secretary of party.
June–Sept	Serves as principal link between Lenin, who was incapacitated by a stroke in May, and the Politburo.
Sept–Dec	Quarrels with Lenin, partially recovered, about the status of national minorities in the new Soviet federation.

1923

Jan	In a postscript to secret testamentary dictations, started the previous month, Lenin proposes removal of Stalin as General Secretary.
Mar–Jan	Serves as supervisor of medical treatment of Lenin, who suffered another stroke in March and was unable to speak.
Apr	Reports to Twelfth Party Congress on party organization and on minority nationalities, manages to suppress Lenin's intended attack on his policies on national minorities.

1924

Jan	At Thirteenth Party Conference begins open attack on Trotsky.
21 Jan	Lenin dies; at funeral Stalin speaks on Lenin's 'behests'.
Apr	Publication of his 'Foundations of Leninism'.
May	Reports to Thirteenth Party Congress on party organization, having suppressed attempts on the eve of the gathering to publicize Lenin's testamentary recommendation that Stalin be removed as General Secretary.
Nov	Publication of his 'Trotskyism or Leninism?'
Dec	Publication of his 'The October Revolution and the Tactics of the Russian Communists', a polemic against Trotsky.

1925
Dec   At Fourteenth Party Congress directs attack on Zinoviev, who is deprived on his political base in Leningrad.

1926
Jan   Publishes anthology *Questions of Leninism*.
28 Feb   Birth of third child, Svetlana.
Apr   Visits Leningrad, now under command of Kirov.
Oct–Nov   At Fifteenth Party Conference attacks 'United Opposition' of Trotsky, Zinoviev and Kamenev.

1927
Oct   In attack on 'Trotskyist Opposition Before and Now' fends off attempt to use Lenin's testamentary recommendation that Stalin be removed as General Secretary.
Nov   Arranges expulsion from the party of Trotsky and Zinoviev on the authority of the Central Committee and Central Control Commission.
Dec   At Fifteenth Party Congress delivers main report on the work of the Central Committee.

1928
Jan–Feb   Visits western Siberia to press for grain deliveries.
May   Shakhty trial of mining personnel charged with sabotage.
May   Meets Gorky, whom Stalin wishes to persuade to repatriate and become intellectual emblem of regime.

1929
Jan–Feb   Attempts, not entirely successfully, to obtain condemnation of Bukharin by a commission of the Politburo and Presidium of Central Control Commission.
Apr   Attacks Bukharin in meeting of Central Committee and Central Control Commission.
Nov   Central Committee removes Bukharin from Politburo.
Dec   Speeches refer to 'a year of great change' and 'the liquidation of the kulaks as a class'; his fiftieth birthday receives major, if brief, fanfare.

1930
Jan   Edits decree, drafted by a commission, on the tempo of collectivization.
Mar   Publishes 'Dizzy with Success', calling for moderation of collectivization.
June–July   His reports to Sixteenth Party Congress defend programme of rapid economic transformation.

1931
Jan   Orders acceleration of construction of Magnitogorsk iron and steel plant.
June   His speech to industrial managers sets forth much-publicized 'six points'.

1932

May   At meeting of literary organizers and commission of Central
             Committee elicits artistic formula of 'socialist realism'.
8/9 Nov   Death of his wife, Nadezhda Allilueva.

1933

May   Visible beginnings of enhanced publicity concerning Stalin's greatness.
July   With Kirov and Voroshilov tours White Sea–Baltic Canal, recently
             completed by Gulag.

1934

Jan–Feb   His reports to Seventeenth Party Congress hail economic successes.
Dec   Travels to Leningrad in connection with investigation of the
             assassination of Kirov.

1935

Jan   Zinoviev and Kamenev convicted of indirect complicity in the
             assassination of Kirov.
Mar   Receives British foreign minister Eden.
Apr   Inspects Moscow Metro shortly before its opening.
May–June   Receives French and Czech foreign ministers Laval and Beneš.
June   Arranges expulsion from party of long-time friend Yenukidze.

1936

June   Plans Chkalov flight to island of Udd.
Aug   Public trial and conviction of Zinoviev, Kamenev and others.
Sept   Arranges appointment of Yezhov as head of police.
Nov   Presents new Soviet constitution, noting that the country has attained
             the stage of 'socialism' on the path to 'communism'.

1937

Jan   Public trial of Piaktakov, Radek and others.
1 Feb   Suicide of long-time friend and industrial chief Ordzhonikidze.
Feb–Mar   Central Committee hears, and evidently does not entirely approve,
             reports by Stalin, Molotov and Yezhov on the need for a purge of
             class enemies in party and state.
June   Secret trial of Tukhachevsky and top officers.
Intense level of terror within party–state élite continues through this year and into
the next.

1938

Jan   Meeting of Central Committee attempts to curb 'errors' in drive
             against 'enemies of the people'.
Mar   Public trial of Bukharin and others.
Dec   Yezhov formally replaced by Beria as head of police.

1939

Mar   In report to Eighteenth Party Congress Stalin speaks of mass purge as
             thing of the past.
Aug   Negotiates non-aggression pact and partition of eastern Europe with
             German foreign minister Ribbentrop.
Sept   Following German and Soviet invasions of Poland, renegotiates treaty
             with Ribbentrop.

Oct–Nov	Negotiates with representatives of Finland and the Baltic states, concerning their status under the conditions of the German–Soviet understanding.
Dec	Sixtieth birthday celebrated with sustained and massive display.

1940

Feb	Holds last personal negotiations with German representatives.
20 Aug	Trotsky killed in Mexico by assassin connected with Soviet police.

1941

May	Assumes post of chairman of Sovnarkom.
June	Maintains low profile following German attack on 22nd, but is named chairman of State Committee of Defence.
July	Re-emerges with radio address to populace, assumes posts of narkom of defence and commander of Stavka.
Aug	Assumes post of supreme commander of armed forces.
Nov	Delivers addresses on the anniversary of the October Revolution with Germans near the outskirts of Moscow.
Dec	Receives Eden.

1942

Jan	Orders winter offensive, which has limited success.
May	Orders spring offensive, with disastrous results.
Aug	Receives Churchill.
Sept	Orders preparation of counter-offensive at Stalingrad, which begins in November and takes city by February 1943.

1943

Mar	Assumes rank of marshal.
Aug	Pays only visit to frontline zone.
Sept	Receives Russian Orthodox Metropolitan Sergei.
Nov	Meets with Churchill and Roosevelt at Tehran.

1944

Oct	Receives Churchill.
Dec	Receives de Gaulle; establishes Soviet-sponsored committee as government of that country.
Dec	Moves Zhdanov to Moscow to play major role in party administration.

1945

Feb	Meets with Churchill and Roosevelt at Yalta.
May	Addresses populace at end of war with Germany.
June	Assumes rank of generalissimus.
Aug	Meets with Truman, Churchill and Atlee at Potsdam.
Dec	Receives foreign ministers Marshall and Bevin.

1946

Feb	Election speech to populace refers to fundamentals of Marxism–Leninism.

1947

Feb–Mar	Receives foreign ministers Byrnes and Bevin.

Dec   Currency reform, aimed at liquidating wartime accumulations of wealth and planned by Stalin.

1948
May–June   Directs letters, then Cominform resolution, to Yugoslav Communists to attempt to enforce submission.
July   Decisively throws support to Lysenko in dispute on biological sciences.
Aug   Receives American, British, French diplomats in connection with Berlin crisis.
Oct   Decrees on transformation of nature.

1949
Peak year of 'Leningrad case', involving the execution of Voznesensky and others.
Dec   Enormous festivities in honour of his seventieth birthday, including personal appearance by major foreign Communist leaders; receives Mao Zedong.

1950
Decrees announce great 'Stalinist Constructions' to advance the transformation of nature through hydraulic projects.
Feb   Attends Mao's reception in honour of Sino-Soviet treaty.
Sept(?)   Receives Zhou Enlai to discuss Chinese involvement in Korean War.

1952
Oct   Publishes 'Economic Problems of Socialism in the USSR' on the eve of the Nineteenth Party Congress, which he attends but addresses only briefly.

1953
Jan   Announcement of 'plot of Kremlin doctors' against Soviet leaders indicates more intensive anti-Jewish turn and prospect of new wave of terror.
5 Mar   Death of Stalin.

Sources and Abbreviations

To assist readers who may wish to pursue their own investigation of matters treated in this book and who do not read Russian, English translations of Russian source materials are cited when they exist. The abbreviations given are used in the notes that follow.

ABBREVIATED REFERENCES

Arkhiv	*Arkhiv A. M. Gor'kogo* (Moscow, 1964–).
BKM	'Bukharin–Kamenev Meeting, 1928', *Dissent*, winter (1979), 78–88.
BOR	*The Bolsheviks and the October Revolution: Central Committee Minutes of the Russian Social-Democratic Labour Party (Bolsheviks) August 1917–February 1918* (London, 1974).
BSE	*Bol'shaia sovetskaia entsiklopediia*, 50 vols (Moscow, 1949–58).
Corres.	*Correspondence between the Chairman of the Council of Ministers of the U.S.S.R. and the Presidents of the U.S.A. and the Prime Ministers of Great Britain during the Great Patriotic War of 1941–1945*, 2 vols (Moscow, 1957).
CSP	*Current Soviet Policies* (New York, 1953–).
CW	V. I. Lenin, *Collected Works*, 45 vols (London, 1963–70).
DGFP	*Documents on German Foreign Policy*, series D, 13 vols (Washington, 1957–64).
DKFK	*Direktivy kommandovaniia frontov Krasnoi Armii, 1917–1922 gg.*, 4 vols (Moscow, 1971–8).
DPSR	*Documents on Polish–Soviet Relations*, 2 vols (London, 1961, 1967).
FRUS	*Foreign Relations of the United States* (Washington, 1907–).
FRUS (Potsdam)	*Foreign Relations of the United States. Diplomatic Papers. The Conference of Berlin; The Potsdam Conference* (Washington, 1960).
FRUS (Tehran)	*Foreign Relations of the United States. Diplomatic Papers. The Conferences at Cairo and Tehran* (Washington, 1961).
FRUS (Yalta)	*Foreign Relations of the United States. Diplomatic Papers. The Conferences at Malta and Yalta* (Washington, 1955).
GPW	J. Stalin, *The Great Patriotic War of the Soviet Union* (New York, 1945).
Guide	R. H. McNeal (ed.), *Guide to the Decisions of the Communist Party of the Soviet Union* (Toronto, 1972).
KR	S. Talbott (ed.), *Khrushchev Remembers* (Boston, 1970).
KPSS	*Kommunisticheskaia Partiia Sovetskaia Soiuza v rezoliutsiiakh i resheniiakh s'ezdov, konferentsii, i plenumov Ts. K.*, 10 vols (Moscow, 1970–2).
KSG	B. W. Wolfe (ed.), *Khrushchev and Stalin's Ghost* (London, 1957).
Letopis'	*Letopis' zhizni i tvorchestva A. M. Gor'kogo*, 4 vols (Moscow, 1958–60).
P	*Pravda.*
PL	J. Stalin, *Problems of Leninism* (Moscow, 1953).
PSS	V. I. Lenin, *Polnoe sobranie sochinenii*, 55 vols (Moscow, 1958–65).

RDCPSU	R. H. McNeal (ed.), *Resolutions and Decisions of the Communist Party of the Soviet Union*, 5 vols (Toronto, 1974–82).
S	J. Stalin, *Sochineniia*, vols XIV–XVI, ed. by R. H. McNeal (Stanford, Calif., 1967).
SS	M. Gorky, *Sobranie Sochinenii*, 30 vols (Moscow, 1949–55).
TYP	*The Tehran, Yalta and Potsdam Conferences: Documents* (Moscow, 1969).
TP	J. M. Meijer (ed.), *The Trotsky Papers*, 2 vols (The Hague, 1965, 1971).
VILBK	*Vladimir Il'ich Lenin: Biograficheskaia khronika*, 12 vols (Moscow, 1970–82).
W	I. V. Stalin, *Works*, 13 vols (Moscow, 1952–5).

OTHER REFERENCES

Abbe, J., *I Photograph Russia* (New York, 1934).
Abramov, B. A., 'Razgrom trotsistsko-zinov'evskogo anti-partiinogo bloka', *Voprosy istorii KPSS*, no. 6 (1959), 25–47.
Abramov, B. A., 'O rabote komissii Politbiuro Ts K VKP(b) po voprose sploshnoi kollektivizatsii', *Voprosy istorii KPSS*, no. 1 (1964), 32–43.
Aleksandrov, G., 'Sovetskoe kino', *Oktiabr'*, no. 21 (1939), 112–16.
Alekseev, G., 'Kolichestvennye parametry kul'ta lichnosti', *SSSR. Vnutrenie protivorechiia* (1982) 5–9.
Allilueva, A. S., *Vospominaniia* (Moscow, 1946).
Allilueva, S., *Twenty Letters to a Friend* (New York, 1967).
Allilueva, S., *Only One Year* (New York, 1969).
Allilueva, S., *The Faraway Music* (New Delhi, 1984).
Ambrose, S. A., *Eisenhower* (New York, 1983).
Anon., 'Mandelshtam's "Ode to Stalin"', *Slavic Review*, no. 4 (1975), 683–8.
Anthology of Georgian Poetry (Tbilisi, 1958).
Antonov-Ovseenko, A., *The Time of Stalin* (New York, 1980).
Anweiler, O., *Geschichte der Schule und Pädagogik in Russland vom Ende des Zarenreiches bis zum Beginn der Stalin-ära* (Berlin, 1964).
'Arkhivnie materialy o revoliutsionnoi deiatel'nosti I. V. Stalina', *Krasnyi arkhiv*, no. 105 (1941), 3–31.
Armstrong, J. A., *The Politics of Totalitarianism* (New York, 1961).
Aronson, G., 'Stalinskaia protsess protiv Martova', *Sotsialisticheskii vestnik*, no. 7–8 (1939), 435–6.
Arsenidze, R., 'Iz vospominanii o Staline', *Novyi zhurnal*, no. 72 (1963), 218–36.
Atlas istorii SSSR, 3 vols (Moscow, 1950).
Averbakh, I., *Ot prestupleniia k trudu* (Moscow, 1936).
Avtorkhanov, A., *Stalin and the Soviet Communist Party* (New York, 1959).
Bailes, K. E., *Technology and Society under Lenin and Stalin* (Princeton, NJ, 1978).
Bajanov, B., *Avec Staline dans le Kremlin* (Paris, 1930).
Bajanov, B., *Bajanov révèle Staline* (Paris, 1979).
Barber, J., *Soviet Historians in Crisis, 1928–1932* (New York, 1981).
Barbusse, H., *Staline. Un monde nouveau vu a travers un homme* (Paris, 1935).
Barmine, A., *One Who Survived* (New York, 1945).
Batumskaia demonstratsiia 1902 goda (Moscow, 1937).

Beria, L. P., *On the History of Bolshevik Organizations in Transcaucasia* (New York, 1935).

Bialer, S., *Stalin and His Generals* (New York, 1966).

Bogdenko, L., 'For a History of the Initial Stage in the Solid Collectivization of Agriculture in the USSR', *Current Digest of the Soviet Press*, no. 36 (1963), 3–10.

Bogomazov, S., 'Deti o Staline', *Krasnaia nov'*, no. 12 (1939), 246–54.

Bohlen, C. E., *Witness to History, 1929–1969* (New York, 1973).

Boris Pasternak, 1890–1960. Colloque de Cerisy-la-Salle (Paris, 1979).

Borkenau, F., *European Communism* (New York, 1953).

Brezhnev, L. I., *Trilogy. The Little Land. Rebirth. The Virgin Lands* (New York, 1978).

Broué, P., 'Trotsky et le bloc des oppositions de 1932', *Cahiers Leon Trotsky*, no. 5 (1980), 5–37.

Browder, R. P. and Kerensky, A. F. (eds), *The Russian Provisional Government 1917*, 3 vols (Stanford, Calif., 1961).

Brown, E. J., *Mayakovsky. A Poet in the Revolution* (Princeton, NJ, 1973).

Bryant, A., *Triumph in the West* (New York, 1959).

Buber-Neumann, M., *Von Potsdam nach Moskau* (Stuttgart, 1957).

Bukhnikoshvili, G., *Gori. Istoricheskii ocherk* (Tbilisi, 1940).

Burdzhalov, E. N., 'O taktike bol'shevikov v marte–aprele 1917 g.', *Voprosy istorii*, no. 4 (1956), 35–56.

Burdzhalov, E. N., 'Eshche o taktike bol'shevikov v marte–aprele 1917 g.', *Voprosy istorii*, no. 8 (1956), 113–14.

Burdzhalov, E. N., *Vtoraia russkaia revoliutsiia. Moskva, front, periferiia* (Moscow, 1971).

Carr, E. H., *A History of Soviet Russia. The Interregnum 1923–1924* (New York, 1954).

Carr, E. H., 'Pilnyak and the Death of Frunze', *Soviet Studies*, no. 2 (1958), 162–4.

Carr, E. H., *A History of Soviet Russia. Socialism in One Country 1924–1926*, 3 vols (New York, 1958–64).

Carr, E. H., *The Twilight of the Comintern* (New York, 1982).

Carr, E. H., and Davies, R. W., *A History of Soviet Russia. The Foundations of a Planned Economy*, 3 vols (New York, 1969–78).

The Case of Leon Trotsky (New York, 1937).

The Case of V. P. Vitvitsky, V. A. Gusev, A. W. Gregory et al. (Moscow, 1933).

Chandler, A. D. (ed.), *The Papers of Dwight David Eisenhower*, 9 vols (Baltimore, 1970–).

Chelidze, A., 'Neopublikovanye materialy iz biografii Tovarishcha Stalina', *Antireligioznik*, no. 12 (1939), 17–21.

Cherkasov, N., *Zapiski sovetskogo aktera* (Moscow, 1953).

Cheternadtsatyi s'ezd Vsesoiuznoi Kommunisticheskoi Partii (b). Stenograficheskii otchet (Moscow, 1926).

Chetvertyi (ob'edinitel'nyi) s'ezd RSDRP. Protokoly (Moscow, 1959).

Churchill, W. S., *The Second World War. IV. The Hinge of Fate* (Boston, 1950).

Churchill, W. S., *The Second World War. VI. Triumph and Tragedy* (Boston, 1953).

Ciliga, A., *The Russian Enigma* (London, 1940).

Cohen, S. F., *Bukharin and the Bolshevik Revolution* (New York, 1973).

Conquest, R., *Power and Policy in the USSR* (London, 1961).

Conquest, R., *The Great Terror* (New York, 1973).

Conquest, R., *Inside Stalin's Secret Police* (Stanford, Calif., 1985).

Conquest, R., *The Harvest of Sorrow* (New York, 1986).

Coox, A. D., 'Japanese Foreknowledge of the Soviet–German War, 1941', *Soviet Studies*, no. 4 (1972), 554–72.

Daniels, R. W., *The Conscience of the Revolution* (Cambridge, Mass., 1960).

Daniels, R. W., *Red October. The Bolshevik Revolution of 1917* (New York, 1967).

Davies, R. W., *The Industrialization of Soviet Russia*, vol. 1: *The Socialist Offensive: The Collectivization of Soviet Agriculture, 1929–1930* (Cambridge, Mass., 1980).

Davies, R. W., *The Industrialization of Russia*, vol. 2: *The Soviet Collective Farm, 1929–1930* (Cambridge, Mass., 1980).

Davies, R. W., 'The Syrtsov–Lominadze Affair', *Soviet Studies*, no. 1 (1981), 29–50.

Davies, J., *Behind Soviet Power* (New York, 1946).

Dedijer, V., *The Battle Stalin Lost* (New York, 1971).

de Gaulle, C., *The Complete War Memoirs* (New York, 1964).

'Delo Martova v revoliutsionnom tribunale', *Obozrenie*, no. 15 (1985), 45–6, no. 16 (1985) 43–6.

Delon, R. S., *Stalin and Social Democracy. The Political Memoirs of David A. Sagirashvili* (Ph.D. dissertation, Georgetown University, 1974).

Deutscher, I., *The Prophet Outcast* (London, 1963).

Direktivy Glavnogo Kommandirovaniia Krasnoi Armii (Moscow, 1969).

Djilas, M., *Conversations with Stalin* (New York, 1962).

Dokumenty po istorii grazhdanskoi voiny v SSSR (Moscow, 1960).

Donskoi, V. and Ikonnikov, S., 'Razvitie leninskikh idei o partiino-gosudarstrennom Kontrole', *Kommunist*, no. 18 (1962), 30–9.

Dorokhova, G. A., *Raboche-krest'ianskaia Inspektsiia v 1920–1932 gg.* (Moscow, 1959).

Dvenadtsatyi s'ezd Rossiiskoi Kommunisticheskoi Partii (bol'shevikov): Stenograficheskii otchet (Moscow, 1923).

Dubinskii-Mukhadze, I., *Ordzhonikidze* (Moscow, 1964).

Dulles, A., *The Secret Surrender* (New York, 1966).

Dunmore, T., *Soviet Politics. 1945–1953* (London, 1984).

Eastman, M., *Since Lenin Died* (London, 1925).

Eden, A., *Facing the Dictators. The Memoirs of Anthony Eden* (Boston, 1962).

Eden, A., *The Reckoning. The Memoirs of Anthony Eden* (Boston, 1965).

Ehrenburg, I., *Eve of the War: 1933–41* (London, 1963).

Elwood, R. C., 'Lenin and *Pravda*', *Slavic Review*, no. 2 (1972), 355–80.

Elwood, R. C., *Roman Malinowsky. A Life without a Cause* (Newtonville, Mass., 1977).

Erickson, J., *The Road to Stalingrad*, vol I, *Stalin's War with Germany* (London, 1975).

Erickson, J., *The Road to Berlin*, vol II, *Stalin's War with Germany* (Boulder, Col., 1983).

Erickson, J., *The Soviet High Command* (London, 1962).

Eubank, K., *Summit at Tehran* (New York, 1985).

Evtushenko, E., *A Precocious Autobiography* (New York, 1963).

Fadeev, A. (ed.), *Vstrechi s Stalinym* (Moscow, 1939).

Fainsod, M., *Smolensk under Soviet Rule* (Cambridge, Mass., 1958).

Farnsworth, B., *William C. Bullitt and the Soviet Union* (Bloomington, Ind., 1967).

Feliks Edmundovich Dzerzhinskii. Biografiia (Moscow, 1977).

Fitzpatrick, S. (ed.), *Cultural Revolution in Russia, 1928–1931* (Bloomington, Ind., 1977).

Fitzpatrick, S., 'The Foreign Threat during the First Five-Year Plan', *Soviet Union/Union Soviétique*, no. 5 (1978), 26–35.

Flakserman, Yu., *Gleb Maksimovich Krzhizhanovskii* (Moscow, 1964).

Fotieva, L., *Pages from Lenin's Life* (Moscow, 1960).

General'nyi plan rekonstruktsii goroda Moskvy (Moscow, 1935).

Genkina, E. G., *Protokoly Sovnarkoma RSFSR kak istoricheskii istochnik* (Moscow, 1982).

Getty, J. A., 'Party and Purge in Smolensk, 1933–1937', *Slavic Review*, no. 1 (1983), 60–79.

Getty, J. A., *Origins of the Great Purges* (Cambridge, 1985).

Getty, J. A., 'Trotsky in Exile: the Founding of the Fourth International', *Soviet Studies*, no. 1 (1986), 28–9.

Ginzburg, E., *Into the Whirlwind* (London, 1967).

Goldberg, A., *Ilya Ehrenburg: Revolutionary Novelist, Poet, War Correspondent, Propagandist* (New York, 1984).

Gorbatov, A. V., *Years Off My Life* (London, 1964).

Gorky, M., *et al.*, *Belomorsko–Baltiiskii kanal imeni Stalina* (Moscow, 1934).

Gorky, M., *et al.* (eds), *Belomor* (New York, 1935).

Gorky. Materialy i issledovaniia (Moscow, 1941).

Gorodetsky, E. and Sharapov, Yu., *Sverdlov. Zhizn' i deiatel'nost'* (Moscow, 1961)

Gouré, L., and Dinerstein, H. S., *Moscow in Crisis* (Glencoe, Ill., 1955).

Graham, L. R., *Science and Philosophy in the Soviet Union* (New York, 1972).

Grossman, V., *Forever Flowing* (New York, 1972).

Gugel', Ya., 'Vospominaniia o Magnitke', *God XVIII. Al'manakh*, VI (1935), 318–49.

Guide to the Great Siberian Railway (London, 1900).

Gurvich, G. S., *Istoriia sovetskoi konstitutsii* (Moscow, 1923).

Hahn, W., *Postwar Soviet Politics* (Ithaca, NY, 1982).

Harriman, W. A. and E. Abel, *Special Envoy to Churchill and Stalin* (New York, 1975).

Haslam, J., *Soviet Foreign Policy, 1930–1933* (New York, 1983).

Heizer, J. L., The Cult of Stalin 1929–1939 (Ph.D. dissertation, University of Kentucky, 1977).

Hingley, R., *Boris Pasternak, 1890–1960* (New York, 1983).

History of the Communist Party of the Soviet Union (Moscow, 1962).

Hough, J., *How the Soviet Union Is Governed* (Cambridge, Mass., 1979).

Hoxha, E., *With Stalin* (Toronto, 1980).

Ikonnikov, S. N., *Organizatsiia deiatel'nosti RKI v 1920–1923 gg.* (Moscow, 1959).

Iosifu Vissarionovichu Stalinu. Akademiia Nauk (Moscow, 1949).

Iremaschwili, J., *Stalin und die Tragoedie Georgiens* (Berlin, 1931).

Istoricheskie mesta Tbilisi: putevoditel' po mestam sviazannym s zhizn'iu i deiatel'nost'iu I. V. Stalina (Tbilisi, 1944).

Istoriia Kommunisticheskoi Partii Sovetskogo Soiuza (Moscow, 1962).

Istoriia Kommunisticheskoi Partii Sovetskogo Soiuza v shesti tomakh, 5 vols (Moscow, 1964–70).

Istoriia Moskvy, 6 vols (Moscow, 1952–9).

Istoriia SSSR s drevneishikh vremen do nashikh dnei, 10 vols (Moscow, 1967–1973).

Istoriia Velikoi Otechestvennoi Voiny Sovetskogo Soiuza, 6 vols (Moscow, 1960–5).

Ivnitsky, N. A., 'O nachal'nom etape sploshnoi kollektivizatsii', *Voprosy istorii KPSS* no. 4 (1962), 55–71.

Ivnitsky, N. A., 'Istoriia podgotovki postanovleniia Ts K VKP(b) o tempakh kollektivizatsii sel'skogo khoziaistva ot 5 Ianvaria 1930 g.', in *Istokovedenie istorii sovetskogo obshchestva* (Moscow, 1964).

Ivnitsky, N. A., *Klassovaia bo'rba v derevene i likvidatsiia kulachestva kak klassa (1929–1932)* (Moscow, 1972).

Ivanov, L. and Shmelev, A. N., *Leninizm i ideinopoliticheskii razgrom trotskizma* (Moscow, 1970).

Iz istorii magnitogorskogo metallurgischeskogo kombinata i goroda Magnitogorska (Cheliabinsk, 1965).

Jansen, M., *A Show Trial under Lenin* (The Hague, 1982).

Jasny, N., *Soviet Industrialization 1928–1952* (Chicago, 1961).

Joravsky, D., *The Lysenko Affair* (Cambridge, Mass., 1970).

Joseph Stalin. A Short Biography (Moscow, 1940).

Kalabashkin, A. S., *Vernyi syn partii* (Kishinev, 1960).

Kamenev, L. B., *Stat'i i rechi 1905–1925*, 12 vols (Leningrad, 1925–9).

Kaminsky, V. and Vereshchagin, I., 'Detsvo i iunost' vozhdia; dokumenty, zapsiki, rasskazy', *Molodaia gvardiia*, no. 12 (1939), 22–100.

Kardelj, E., *Reminiscences* (London, 1982).

Keep, J. L. H. (ed.), *The Debate on Soviet Power* (Oxford, 1979).

Keep, J. L. H., *The Rise of Social Democracy in Russia* (Oxford, 1963).

Kelendzheridze, M., 'Stikhi iunogo Stalina', in *Rasskazy o velikom Staline* (Tbilisi, 1941).

Kennan, G. F., *Memoirs*, 2 vols (New York, 1967–72).

Kennan, G. F., 'The Historiography of the Early Political Career of Stalin', *Proceedings. American Philosophical Society*, no. 3 (1971) 165–9.

Kharmandarian, S. V., *Lenin i stanovlenie zakavkazskoi federatsii. 1921–1923* (Erivan, 1969).

Kirstein, T., 'Das Ural-Kuzneck-Kombinat (UKK) als objekt einer Entscheidungsprozessanalyse', in G. Erler and W. Süss (eds), *Stalinismus* (Frankfurt am Main, 1982) pp. 167–85.

Kolakowski, L., *Main Currents of Marxism*, 3 vols (Oxford, 1978).

Kopp, A., *Town and Revolution* (New York, 1970).

Kostiuk, H., *The Fall of Postyshev* (New York, 1954).

Krasnikov, S. V., *S. M. Kirov v Leningrade* (Leningrad, 1966).

Kravchenko, K. S., *Stalin v izobraitel'nom iskusstve* (Moscow, 1939).

Kravchenko, V., *I Chose Freedom* (New York, 1946).

Kristof, L. K. D., 'B. I. Nicolaevsky. The Formative Years', in A. and J. Rabinowitch (eds), *Revolution and Politics in Russia* (Bloomington, Ind., 1972) pp. 3–32.

Krupskaia, N. K., *O Lenine* (Moscow, 1960).

Krylenko, N. (ed.), *Ekonomischeskaia kontrrevoliutsiia v Donbasse* (Moscow, 1928).

Kuusinen, A., *The Rings of Destiny* (New York, 1974).

Kuznetsov, N. G., *Nakanune* (Moscow, 1966).

Lang, D. M., *A Modern History of Georgia* (London, 1962).

Legget, G., *The Cheka. Lenin's Secret Police* (Oxford, 1981).

Lenin, V. I., *Sochineniia*, 3rd edn, 30 vols (Moscow, 1926–32).

Lermolo, E., *The Face of a Victim* (New York, 1955).

Lerner, W., *Karl Radek. The Last Internationalist* (Stanford, Calif., 1970).

Lerner, W., 'Attempting a Revolution from without: Poland in 1920', in T. T. Hammond (ed.), *The Anatomy of Communist Takeovers* (New Haven, Conn., 1975).

Levine, I. D., *Eyewitness to History* (New York, 1973).

Levine, I. D., *Stalin's Great Secret* (New York, 1956).

Levytsky, B. (ed.), *The Stalinist Terror in the Thirties* (Stanford, Calif., 1974).

Levytsky, B., *The Uses of Terror* (London, 1971).

Loewenheim, F. L., *et al* (eds), *Roosevelt and Churchill. Their Secret Wartime Correspondence* (London, 1975).

Lyons, E., *Assignment in Utopia* (New York, 1937).

Maclean, F., *The Eastern Approaches* (London, 1966).

McNeal, R. H. (ed.), *International Relations among Communists* (Englewood Cliffs, NJ, 1967).

McNeal, R. H. (ed.), *Stalin's Works. An Annotated Bibliography* (Stanford, Calif., 1967).

McNeal, R. H., 'The Beginning of Communist Party Financial Exactions from the Soviet State', in D. A. Loeber (ed.), *Ruling Communist Parties and Their Status under Law* (Dordrecht, 1986).

Maiskii, I. M., *Vospominaniia sovetskogo diplomata 1925–1945 gg.* (Moscow, 1971).

Maiskii, I. M., 'Dni ispitanii', *Novyi mir*, no. 12 (1964), 160–94.

Mandelshtam, N., *Hope against Hope* (New York, 1970).

Mariagin, G., *Postyshev* (Moscow, 1965).

Marshal Tukhachevskii (Moscow, 1965).

Marx, K. and Engels, F., *Werke*, 39 vols (Berlin, 1956–74).

Mastny, V., 'Stalin and the Prospects of a Separate Peace in World War II', *American Historical Review*, no. 5 (1972), 1365–88.

Mastny, V., 'The Beneš–Stalin–Molotov Conversations in December 1943: New Documents', *Jahrbücher für Osteuropaischen Geschichte*, no. 20 (1972), 367–402.

Mastny, V., *Russia's Road to the Cold War* (New York, 1979).

Matthews, M., *Class and Society in Soviet Russia* (London, 1972).

Medvedev, R. A., *Let History Judge* (New York, 1971).

Medvedev, R. A., 'New Pages from the Political Biography of Stalin', in R. C. Tucker (ed.), *Stalinism. Essays in Historical Interpretation* (New York, 1977) pp. 199–238.

Medvedev, R. A., *On Stalin and Stalinism* (Oxford, 1979).

Medvedev, R. A., *Nikolay Bukharin* (New York, 1980).

Medvedev, Z. A., *The Rise and Fall of T.D. Lysenko* (New York, 1971).

Meir, G., *My Life* (London, 1975).

Meisel, J. H., and Kozera, E. S., (eds), *Materials for the Study of the Soviet System* (Ann Arbor, Mich. 1950).

Meissner, B., *Die Sowjetunion, die Baltischen Staaten und das Volkrecht* (Köln, 1956).

Menon, K. P. S., *The Flying Troika* (London, 1963).

Merkurov, S. D., 'Mysli, menia vdoknovenie', *Oktiabr'*, no. 12 (1939) 77–92.

Meyer, A. G., 'The War Scare of 1927', *Soviet Union/Union Soviétique*, no. 5 (1978) 1–25.

Mikoyan, A. I., *V nachale dvadtsatykh* (Moscow, 1975).

Miller, F., 'The Image of Stalin in Soviet Russian Folklore', *Russian Review*, no. 1 (1980) 59–67.

Miller, J., 'Soviet Planners in 1936–1937', in J. Degras and R. W. Davies (eds), *Soviet Planning* (Oxford, 1964) 116–43.

Moller, D., 'Stalin und der der "deutsche Oktober" 1923', *Jahrbücher für Geschichte Osteuropas*, XII, 212–15.

Molotov, V. M., *Voprosy vneshnei politiki* (Moscow, 1948).

Monument I. V. Stalina (Erivan, 1952).

Moskva. Entsiklopedia (Moscow, 1980).

Na mogilu Il'icha (Leningrad, 1924).

Narkiewicz, O. A., 'Stalin, War Communism and Collectivization', *Soviet Studies*, no. 1 (1961) 20–37.

Nekrich, A. M., *The Punished Peoples* (New York, 1978).

Nekrich, A. M., *Otreshis' ot strakha* (London, 1979).

Nekrich, A. M., 'Stalin i natsistskaia Germaniia', *Kontinent*, no. 24 (1980) 239–61.

Nemakov, N. I., *Kommunisticheskaia Partiia–Organizator massovogo kolkhoznogo dvizheniia 1929–1932* (Moscow, 1966).

Nove, A., *An Economic History of the U.S.S.R.* (Harmondsworth, Middx., 1972).

Orlov, A., *The Secret History of Stalin's Crimes* (New York, 1953).

Ovcharenko, A., 'Sotsialisticheskii realizm v svete mezhdunarodykh sporov', *Molodaia gvardiia* no. 9 (1973) 265–80.

Paasiviki, J. K., *Mein Moskauer Mission 1939–1941* (Hamburg, 1966).

Patolichev, N. S., *Measures of Maturity* (Oxford, 1983).

Payne, R., *The Rise and Fall of Stalin* (New York, 1965).

Perepiska Sekretariata s mestnymi partiinymi organizatsii, 8 vols (Moscow, 1957–74).

Pestkovskii, S., 'Vospominaniia o rabote v Narkomnatse', *Proletarskaia revoliutsiia*, no. 6 (1930) 124–31.

Petrov, Yu. P., *Partiinoe stroitel'stvo Sovetskoi armii i flote* (Moscow, 1964).

Piatyi (londonskii) s'ezd RSDRP. Protokoly (Moscow, 1963).

Pilnyak, B., *The Tale of the Unextinguished Moon* (New York, 1967).

Pis'ma trudiashchikhsia k V. I. Leninu (New York, 1966).

Pliushch, I., *History's Carnival* (New York, 1979).

Poretsky, E. K., *Our Own People* (London, 1969).

Proffer, E., *Mikhail Bulgakov, Life and Work* (Ann Arbor, Mich. 1984).

Rabinovich, I., 'Obraz Vozhdia v proizvedenniiakh zhivopisi i skulptury', *Arkhitektura SSSR*, no. 12 (1939) 11–21.

Rabinowitch, A., *Prelude to Revolution* (Bloomington, Ind., 1968).

Rabinowitch, A., *The Bolsheviks Come to Power* (New York, 1976).

Rapoport, V. and Alexeev, Yu., *High Treason* (Durham, NC, 1985).

Raskol'nikov, F., 'Priezd tov. Lenina Rossiiu', *Proletarskaia revoliutsiia*, no. 1 (1923).

Rasskazy starykh rabochikh o velikom Staline (Moscow, 1937).

Reck, V. T., *Boris Pil'niak. A Soviet Writer in Conflict with the State* (Montreal, 1975).

Reiman, P., *Die Geburt des Stalinismus* (Frankfurt am Main, 1979).

Report of Court Proceedings: The Trotskyite–Zinovievite Terrorist Centre (Moscow, 1936).

Report of Court Proceedings: The Anti-Soviet Trotskyite Centre (Moscow, 1937).

Report of Court Proceedings: The Anti-Soviet 'Bloc of Rights and Trotskyites' (Moscow, 1938).

Resheniia partii i pravitel'stvo po khoziaistvennym voprosam, 15 vols (Moscow, 1967–85).

Rigby, T. H., 'Party Elections in the CPSU', *Political Quarterly*, no. 4 (1964) 420–43.

Rigby, T. H., *Communist Party Membership in the U.S.S.R. 1917–1967* (Princeton, NJ, 1968).

Rigby, T. H., 'Stalinism and the Mono-organizational Society', in R. C. Tucker (ed.), *Stalinism* (New York, 1977).

Rigby, T. H., *Lenin's Government: Sovnarkom 1917–1922* (New York, 1979).

Rigby, T. H., 'Early Provincial Cliques and the Role of Stalin', *Soviet Studies*, no. 1 (1981) 3–28.

Roosevelt, E., *As He Saw It* (New York, 1945).

Rosenfeldt, N. E., *Knowledge and Power* (Copenhagen, 1978).

Royal Institute of International Affairs, *The Soviet–Yugoslav Dispute* (London, 1948).

Rustaveli, S., *The Knight in the Tiger's Skin* (New York, n.d.).

Salisbury, H. E., *Moscow Journal. The End of Stalin* (Chicago, 1961).

Salisbury, H. E., *The 900 Days. The Siege of Leningrad* (New York, 1969).

Salisbury, H. E., *A Journey for Our Time* (New York, 1983).

Saliutskii, N., 'Eshche odna versiia zvonka Stalina Pasternaku', *Pamiat'* (1979) 438–41.

Samoe dorogoe (Moscow, 1939).

Schroeder, H.-H., 'Gesellschaftliche Funktion und innere Entwicklung der bolschewisten Partei in den Jahren der NEP 1921–1928', in G. Erler and W. Süss (eds), *Stalinismus* (Frankfurt am Main, 1957) pp. 88–120.

Seaton, A., *Stalin as Warlord* (London, 1976).

Semnadtsatyi s'ezd Vsesoiuznoi Kommunisticheskoi Partii (bol'shevikov) (Moscow, 1934).

Serge, V., *Portrait de Staline* (Paris, 1940).

Shatunovskaia, L., *Zhizn' v Kremle* (New York, 1982).

Shestnadtsataia konferentsiia VKP(b), aprel'1919g. Stenograticheskii otchet (Moscow, 1962).

Shipler, D. K., *Russia. Broken Idols, Solemn Dreams* (New York, 1983).

Shliapnikov, A., *Semnadtsatyi god* (Moscow, 1925).

Shtemenko, S. M., *The Soviet General Staff at War, 1941–1945* (Moscow, 1970).

Shtemenko, S. M., *General'nyi shtab v gody voiny*, 2 vols (Moscow, 1973).

Shtemenko, S. M., *The Last Six Months* (New York, 1977).

Shturman, D., *Mertvye khvataiut zhivie* (London, 1982).

Shulman, M., *Stalin's Foreign Policy Reappraised* (Cambridge, Mass., 1963).

Shveitzer, B., *Stalin v turukhanskoi ssylke* (Moscow, 1943).

Siegelbaum, L., 'Production Collectives and Communes and the "Imperatives" of Soviet Industrialization;, *Slavic Review*, no. 1 (1986) 65–84.

Skilling, H. C., ' "People's Democracies" in Soviet Theory', *Soviet Studies*, no. 1 (1951) 16–33; no. 2 (1951) 131–49.

Simmons, R. S., *The Strained Alliance* (New York, 1975).

Slepov, L. A., and Andronov, S. A., 'Prazhskaia konferentsiia RSDRP i bor'by bol'shevikov za edinstva partii', *Voprosy istorii*, no. 2 (1965) 27–39.

Slusser, R. M., 'The Role of the Foreign Ministry', in I. J. Lederer (ed.), *Russian Foreign Policy* (New Haven, Conn., 1962).

Smith, E. E., *The Young Stalin* (London, 1968).

Smith, W. B., *My Three Years in Moscow* (New York, 1950).

Snowden, J. K., *The German Question, 1945–1973* (London, 1975).

Solomon, P. H., 'Soviet Penal Policy, 1917–1934: a Reinterpretation', *Slavic Review*, no. 2 (1980) 195–217.

Solzhenitsyn, A. I., *The Gulag Archipelago*, 3 vols (New York, 1974–8).

Sontag, J. P., 'The Soviet War Scare of 1926–27', *Russian Review*, no. 1 (1975) 66–77.

Sovetsko-frantsuzskie otnoshenie vo vremia Velikoi Otechestvennoi Voiny 1941–1945 gg. (Moscow, 1959).

Stalin, J., *O Velikom Otchestvennoi Voiny Sovetskogo Soiuza* (Moscow, 1943).

Stalin, J., *Marxism and Linguistics* (Moscow, 1951).

Stalin, J., *Economic Problems of Socialism in the U.S.S.R.* (Moscow, 1952).

Stalin. Sbornik statei k piatidesiatiletiiu so dnia rozhdeniia (Moscow, 1929).

Stalinskie sokoly (Moscow, 1937).

Stalinskii marshrut prodolzhen (Moscow, 1937).

Stalin. K shestidesiatiletiiu so dnia rozhdeniia (Moscow, Khudozhestvennaia literatura, 1940).

Stalin. K. shestidesiatiletiiu so dnia rozhdeniia (Moscow, *Pravda*, 1940).

Stalin i o Staline (Moscow, 1940).

Starr, S. F., *Melnikov: Solo Architect in a Mass Society* (Princeton, NJ, 1978).

Studitsky, A. N., 'Fly-lovers and Man-haters', *Journal of Heredity*, no. 11 (1949) 312–14.

Sukhanov, N. N., *The Russian Revolution 1917* (London, 1955).

Sumbadze, I., 'Proekt planirovki i rekonstruktsii g. Gori', *Arkhitektura SSSR* no. 12 (1939) 42–8.

Suny, R. G., 'A Journeyman for the Revolution: Stalin and the Labour Movement in Baku', *Soviet Studies*, no. 3 (1971) 372–94.

Sverdlova, K., *Yakov Sverdlov* (Moscow, 1981).

Talbott, S. (ed.), *Khrushchev Remembers. The Last Testament* (Boston, 1974).

Tertz, A., *On Socialist Realism* (New York, 1960).

Thomas, L. C., *The Linguistic Theory of N. Ja. Marr* (Berkeley, Calif., 1957).

Toranska, T., *Oni* (London, 1985).

Trevor-Roper, H. (ed.), *Hitler's Table Talk* (London, 1973).

Trotsky, L. D., *Sochineniia*, 12 vols (Moscow, 1924–7).

Trotsky, L. D., *My Life* (New York, 1930).

Trotsky, L. D., *The Suppressed Testament of Lenin* (New York, 1935).

Trotsky, L. D., *Stalin* (New York, 1941).

Trotsky, L. D., *The Permanent Revolution and Results and Prospects* (New York, 1969).

Trotsky, L. D., *The Writings of Leon Trotsky, 1937–1938* (New York, 1970).

Trotsky, L. D., *The Stalin School of Falsification* (New York, 1971).

Trotsky, L. D., *The Writings of Leon Trotsky, 1934–1935* (New York, 1974).

Trotsky, L. D., *The Challenge of the Left Opposition (1923–25)* (New York, 1975).

Trotsky, L. D., *Leon Trotsky on China* (New York, 1976).

Trotsky, L. D., *The Challenge of the Left Opposition (1926–27)* (New York, 1980).

Tsereteli, I., *Vospominiia fevral'skoi revoliutsii* (Paris, 1963).

Tucker, R. C., 'The Emergence of Stalin's Foreign Policy', *Slavic Review*, no. 4 (1977) 563–91.

Tucker, R. C., 'The Rise of Stalin's Personality Cult', *American Historical Review*, no. 2 (1979) 347–66.

Tukhachevskii, M. N., *Izbrannye proizvedeniia*, 2 vols (Moscow, 1964).

Tumarkin, N., *Lenin Lives!* (Cambridge, Mass., 1983).

Tuominen, A., *The Bells of the Kremlin* (Hanover, 1983).

Tutaev, D. (ed.), *The Alliluyev Memoirs* (London, 1968).

Tvorchestvo narodov SSSR (Moscow, 1937).

Ugolovnyi kodeks BSSR (Moscow, 1938).

Uralov, A., *The Reign of Stalin* (Moscow, 1953).

Uratadze, G. I., *Vospominaniia gruzinskogo sotsial-demokrata* (Stanford, Calif., 1968).

Vaganov, F. M., *Pravyi uklon v VKP(b) i ego razgrom* (Moscow, 1977).

Valentinov, N., *Novaia ekonomicheskaia politika i krizis partii posle smerti Lenina* (Stanford, Calif., 1971).

Van Heijenoort, J., *With Trotsky in Exile* (Cambridge, Mass., 1978).

van Rossum, L., 'A. Antonov-Ovsecenko's Book on Stalin: Is it reliable?', *Soviet Studies*, no. 3 (1984) 445–7.

Vasilevsky, A. M., *A Lifelong Cause* (Moscow, 1981).

Velikie stroiki kommunizma (Moscow, 1950).

Vesnim, V. *et al.*, 'Nezabyvaemye vstrechi', *Arkhitektura SSSR*, no. 12 (1939) 6–10.

Viola, L., The Campaign of the 25,000ers (Ph.D. dissertation, Princeton University, 1984).

Viola, L., 'Notes on the Background of Soviet Collectivization: Metal Worker Brigades in the Countryside, Autumn 1929', *Soviet Studies*, no. 2 (1984) 205–22.

Viola, L., 'The Campaign to Eliminate Kulaks as a Class', *Slavic Review*, no. 3 (1986) 503–24.

Viola, L., *The Best Sons of the Fatherland, Workers in the Vanguard of Soviet Collectivization* (New York, 1987).

Volkov, S. (ed.), *Testimony. The Memoirs of Dmitri Shostakovich* (New York, 1979).

Vosemnadtsatyi s'ezd Vsesoiuznoi Kommunisticheskoi Partii (bol'shevikov). Stenograficheskii otchet (Moscow, 1939).

Vyltsan, M. A., Ivnitsky, N. A. and Poliakov, Yu. A., 'Nekotorye problemy istorii kollektivizatsii v SSSR', *Voprosy istorii* no. 3 (1965) 3–25.

Warner, G., *Pierre Laval and the Eclipse of France* (London, 1968).

Warth, R. D., *Leon Trotsky* (Boston, 1977).

Werth, A., *Russia. The Postwar Years* (London, 1971).

Wu Xiuquan, unpublished translation of his memoirs, which appeared in Chinese in *Shije zhishi*, no. 16 (1983).

Yakovlev, A. S., *Tsel' zhizni* (Moscow, variant editions 1966, 1969, 1972).

Yakunin, G., 'Moskovskaia patriarkhiia i "kult lichnosti" Stalina', *Russkoe vozrozhdenie,* (1978) no. 1, 103–37; no. 2, 111–59.

Yaroslavskii, E., *Velikii vozhd' rabochei revoliutsii* (Moscow, 1918).

Yaroslavskii, E., *O Tovarishche Staline* (Moscow, 1939).

Yaroslavskii, E., 'Ideinaia sokroshchitnitsa partii', *Partiinoe stroitel'stvo*, no. 8 (1940) 10–15.

Yenukidze, A., *Bol'shevistskie nelegal'nie tipografii* (Moscow, 1930).

Zagoria, J. (ed.), *Power and the Soviet Elite* (New York, 1965).

Zaleski, E., *Planning for Economic Growth in the Soviet Union 1918–1932* (Chapel Hill, NC, 1971).

Zaleski, E., *Stalinist Planning for Economic Growth 1933–1952* (Chapel Hill, NC, 1980).

Zamoyski, A., *The Battle for the Marchlands* (New York, 1981).

Zelenev, T., 'Izdanie i rasprostranenie proizvedenii I. V. Stalina', *Bol'shevik*, no. 23 (1949) 85–96.

Zhukov, G. K., *The Memoirs of Marshal Zhukov* (New York, 1971).

Zhukov, Yu., 'Gori–Tbilisi', *Novyi mir*, no. 12 (1939) 142–55.

Zinoviev, G., *Sochineniia*, 16 vols (Moscow, 1924–6).

Zverev, A. G., *Zapiski ministra* (Moscow, 1973).

Notes

References are given in full at their first appearance in each chapter's notes, and are referred to thereafter by name and date. See also 'Sources and Abbreviations', pp. **324–34.**

NOTES TO CHAPTER 1   ORTHODOXY

1. Author's observation, December 1983.
2. G. Bukhnikoshvili, *Gori. Istoricheskii ocherk* (Tbilisi, 1940) 144.
3. *BSE*, xii, opposite 86.
4. Yu. Zhukov, 'Gori–Tbilisi', *Novyi mir*, no. 12 (1939) 145.
5. I. D. Levine, *Eyewitness to History* (New York, 1973) opposite 146.
6. Author's observations, December 1983.
7. Zhukov (1939) 144. The fact that only he mentions this suggests not that he erred, but that Stalin did not wish this matter to appear in the memoirs of his early life that appeared on the occasion of his sixtieth birthday. But this slipped through an imperfect system of editorial control. Two neighbours who are quoted in a different publication mention Soso's close involvement in the Charkviani family about the time he started school. V. Kaminsky and I. Vereshchagin, 'Detsvo i iunost' vozhdia; dokumenty, zapisky, rasskazy', *Molodaia gvardiia*, no. 12 (1939) 34.

    Apart from the evidence that Stalin did not live for long in the celebrated hovel, one might argue that he was not even born there. The imperial police consistently referred to him in secret reports as a peasant from Didi-Lilo, which is a town about half way between Tbilisi and Gori. See 'Arkhivnye materialy o revoliutsionnoi deiatel'nosti I. V. Stalina', *Krasnyi arkhiv* no. 105 (1939) 3–4, 12–13, 22–3, 25. There is, however, no other evidence that Stalin was born there, and it seems likely that the police were using official birth records that made him a member of the Didi-Lilo peasant commune because the terms of the serf emancipation kept families as members of communes in order to try to collect redemption dues from them, regardless of their actual place of residence. Stalin's father had been born in Didi-Lilo and in 1879 was in all likelihood still on their list of commune members.
8. *KR*, 301.
9. Kaminsky and Vereshchagin (1939) 26; *W*, i, 318; *P*, 27 October 1935, 10.
10. Kaminsky and Vereshchagin (1939) 37.
11. Zhukov (1939) 145; *P*, 27 October 1935; Kaminsky and Vereshchagin (1939) 34–5.
12. A. Chelidze, 'Neopublikovannye materialy iz biografii tovarishcha Stalina', *Antireligioznik*, no. 12 (1939) 19; *Stalin. K shestidesiatiletiiu so dnia rozhdeniia* (Moscow, Khudozhestvennaia literatura, 1940) 20.
13. *P*, 27 October 1935; Kaminsky and Vereshchagin (1939) 44; S. Allilueva, *Only One Year* (New York 1969) 360.
14. Kaminsky and Vereshchagin (1939) 44–5, which shows that Stalin was promoted to grade IV in 1893 at the beginning of the school year in which he graduated.

335

15. *P*, 27 October 1935. The year of Vissarion's death is established by a personal communication from Professor Ilya Tabagua of the Institute of History of the Academy of Sciences of Georgia, a body that has access to the archives of that nation. This is compatible with a document in the Paris archives of the Russian imperial security service, discovered at the Hoover Institution by E. E. Smith and cited in his *The Young Stalin* (London, 1967) 29. This report considers Vissarion to be alive in Tbilisi in 1909. These two sources decisively outweigh evidence that Vissarion died around 1890. This version rests mainly on the interview that the American journalist H. R. Knickerbocker had with Stalin's mother in 1930 (*New York Post*, 1 December 1930). Since the interview was conducted through an interpreter, there was room for misunderstanding Ekaterina's alleged statement that Vissarion died when Soso was eleven. The other source for this approximate dating is Joseph Iremaschwili, *Stalin und die Tragoedie Georgiens* (Berlin, 1931) 12, which refers vaguely to Vissarion's 'early death'. This memoirist must be treated with great reserve. His claim to have been acquainted with young Iosif Dzhugashvili evidently has some foundation, for a disinterested Soviet source confirms that they had some contact [Kaminsky and Vereshchagin (1939) 39, 72]. But the book's paucity of specific incidents involving Soso is but one indication that Iremaschwili greatly exaggerated the closeness of the relationship. He purports to describe Stalin's parents by sketching typical Georgian men and women and saying that Ekaterina and Vissarion were like that (10–12). He states (5) that Soso was a 'new face' in school in 1890, when in fact he started there in 1888 (*W*, ɪ, 415) and could scarcely have been a stranger in such a small community. The photograph of Stalin and his classmates definitely contradicts Iremaschwili's recollection that Soso was physically superior to the other boys (5). On the contrary, when he began school (the time to which Iremaschwili refers), he seems to have been the smallest of the lot (see plate 3). Allilueva (1967) 153, confirms the circumstances of Vissarion's death.
16. Author's notes on grade records displayed in Stalin Museum, Gori; Chelidze (1939) 17, 18, 20.
17. Allilueva (1969) 361; Chelidze (1939) 19.
18. Chelidze (1939) 18. The account that claims that the school authorities obliged the youths to attend appears in *Stalin. K shestidesiatiletiiu* (Khudozhestvennaia literatura, 1940) 20.
19. Author's observation, December 1983; *Rasskazy starykh rabochikh o velikom Staline* (Moscow 1937) 41.
20. Kaminsky and Vereshchagin (1939) 64–7; *W*, 115–16.
21. D. M. Lang, *A Modern History of Georgia* (London, 1962) 122–3.
22. Kaminsky and Vereshchagin (1939) 34.
23. Chelidze (1939) 20; author's observation of Stalin's handwriting in the Gori museum.
24. *Anthology of Georgian Poetry* (Tbilisi, 1958) 62–76.
25. M. Kelendzheridze, 'Stikhi iunogo Stalina', in *Rasskazy o velikom Staline* (Tbilisi, 1941) 67–70; Robert Payne, *The Rise and Fall of Stalin* (New York, 1965), 47–8.
26. R. S. Delon, Stalin and Social Democracy. The Political Memoirs of David A. Sagirashvili (Ph.D. dissertation, Georgetown University, 1974) 169.
27. *The Knight in the Tiger's Skin* (New York, n.d.). There were tigers in Georgia until perhaps the 1920s. The animal in question was not a panther, although one finds some references to this beast in translations.

28. Document on display in the Gori museum and also another document showing Stalin's editing of a translation into Russian of 'Tamariani'.
29. Kaminsky and Vereshchagin (1939) 71; museum in Gori, which maintains that he also read works on economics, on family and property and on 'psychophysiology'.
30. Chelidze (1939) 19.
31. *W*, XIII, 115.
32. Chelidze (1939) 17; J. Davis, *Behind Soviet Power* (New York, 1946) 14.
33. *W*, I, 416. Memoirs of Dzhugashvili's seminary days usually refer to him as 'Iosif', not as 'Koba'. Iremaschwili (1931) 18, maintains that Dzhugashvili assumed the name 'Koba' as a lad in Gori. This might be one of his embellishments, based on the common knowledge among Georgians in later years that Stalin had gone by that name in the underground. Or perhaps it was true in Stalin's school days in Gori, followed by a period in the seminary when, among a new group of people, the nickname was dropped, only to be resumed a little later. On the use of 'Koba' many years later, A. S. Yakovlev *Tsel' zhizni* (Moscow 1972) 490.
34. *W*, I, 416; document on display in the Gori museum; Kaminsky and Vereshchagin (1939) 86.

NOTES TO CHAPTER 2 UNDERGROUND

1. Exhibited in Stalin museum, Gori.
2. D. Tutaev (ed.), *The Alliluyev Memoirs* (London, 1968) 28–30.
3. *W*, I, 417–18.
4. R. S. Delon, *Stalin and Social Democracy. The Political Memoirs of David A. Sagirashvili* (Ph.D. dissertation, Georgetown University, 1974) 169; G. I. Uratadze, *Vospominaniia gruzinskogo sotsial-demokrata* (Stanford, Calif., 1968) 66.
5. Delon (1974) 170; A. Chelidze, 'Neopublikovanye materialy iz biografii Tovarishcha Staline', *Antireligioznik*, no. 12 (1939) 17, 19.
6. Uratadze (1968) 66–7, maintains that Koba was expelled from the Tbilisi organization by a 'court' of comrades on the grounds that he had intrigued against their leader, S. Dzhibladze, but official Soviet accounts claim that he was sent to Batumi by the organization. If he had been expelled, it would have been unlikely that the Batumi comrades would have accepted Koba as a leader, for the Marxist movement in Georgia was a small community and at this stage he had no credentials as an independent leader.
7. *W*, I, 26. It is difficult to authenticate Stalin's alleged works in Georgian, for, even if one could read this language, the printed texts of the originals are difficult if not impossible to obtain. There have been charges of plagiarism, for example by R. Arsenidze, 'Iz vospominanii o Staline', *Novyi zhurnal* no. 72 (1963) 225–7. On the other hand, the study of Stalin's later writings in Russian reveals various forms of editorial doctoring but not, as far as I can tell, the actual misappropriation of authorship. See R. H. McNeal (ed.), *Stalin's Works. An Annotated Bibliography* (Stanford, Calif., 1967). In the case of the document cited here, the sarcastic style suggests Stalin's authorship.
8. *Batumskaia demonstratsiia 1902 goda* (Moscow, 1937) 156–7.
9. *W*, I, 419–20.

10. *W*, I, 420–1; A. S. Yakovlev, *Tsel' zhizni* (Moscow, 1969), 508. Railway timetables show that it was quite possible to make the whole trip in five or six weeks: *Guide to the Great Siberian Railway* (London, 1900) 504–6, 509–12.

11. *RDCPSU*, I, 35.

12. *RDCPSU*, I, 42–5.

13. *CW*, V, 347–527.

14. J. L. H. Keep, *The Rise of Social Democracy in Russia* (Oxford, 1963) 117–33.

15. Chelidze (1939) 18; Arsenidze (1963) 219.

16. Arsenidze (1963) 218, 219. It may or may not have been a different meeting at about this time at which Koba 'insulted everybody in the room, calling them "petit bourgeois"', then left the meeting with two or three adherents [Delon (1974) 177].

17. *W*, I, 54–62, 395. These letters were first published only in 1946, but in 1924 Stalin apparently referred to them, back-dating them to 1903, either through an error of recollection or to lay claim to Bolshevism in the year of its inception. Here he also refers to a reply from Lenin, which he says, plausibly, he burned for security reasons (*W*, VI, 55.) A hostile memoir that establishes his Bolshevism is Arsenidze (1963) 219–20.

18. This was precisely Stalin's point in a pamphlet of 7 January 1906 (*W*, I, 205–6).

19. *CW*, IX, 15–140.

20. L. Trotsky, *The Permanent Revolution and Results and Prospects* (New York, 1969) 36–122.

21. *W*, I, 187–97.

22. Arsenidze (1963) 221–2.

23. Delon (1974) 179.

24. Arsenidze (1963) 230–1.

25. Arsenidze (1963) 221–2.

26. Delon (1974) 26.

27. Arsenidze (1963) 224.

28. G. F. Kennan, 'The Historiography of the Early Political Career of Stalin', *Proceedings. American Philosophical Society*, no. 3 (1971) 165–9; I. D. Levine, *Stalin's Great Secret* (New York, 1956); E. E. Smith, *The Young Stalin* (London, 1968).

29. Roy Medvedev, not one to defend Stalin's moral character, has published what he believes to be an authentic secret police report of 1 May 1904 which places Dzhugashvili ('from the village of Didi-Lilo') on a wanted list. 'New Pages from the Political Biography of Stalin', in R. C. Tucker (ed.), *Stalinism. Essays in Historical Interpretation* (New York, 1977) 200–1.

30. *W*, II, 438–40.

31. *W*, I, 424.

32. *Chetvertyi (ob'edinitel'nyi) s'ezd RSDRP. Protokoly* (Moscow, 1959) 78–9, 224, 311, 347, 349.

33. *Piatyi (londonskii) s'ezd RSDRP. Protokoly* (Moscow, 1963) 121, 128, 254, 349–50.

34. *FRUS (Tehran)* 513. He told Emil Ludwig approximately the same story in 1931, this time placing it in Berlin, and treating it merely as an anecdote that made the rounds (*W*, XIII, 124.) See also M. Djilas, *Conversations with Stalin* (New York, 1962) 79.

35. *Istoricheskie mesta Tbilisi: putevoditel' po mestam sviazannym s zhizn'iu i deiatel'nost'iu I. V. Stalina* (Tbilisi, 1944) 122–3, which confirms that he wrote 'Anarchism or Socialism?' while living here.

36. The dates of Ekaterina's birth and marriage are provided by Professor Ilya Tabagua of the Georgian Academy of Sciences. S. Allilueva, *Only One Year* (New York, 1969) 367, mentions the church wedding.
37. *W*, I, 297–391.
38. The robbery had to be carefully planned and directed by a leader who was familiar with the plan. Stalin returned to Tbilisi from London only 'in the first half of June' (*W*, II, 423), and the robbery took place on the 12th. Thus it is not practical to consider him the operational chief. Soviet scholars by no means cover up the event and glorify Kamo as its chief. A few blocks from the Stalin museum in Gori is a Kamo museum, for he also grew up in this town, although not a friend of the young Dzhugashvili. The museum, which the author visited in December 1983, contains a substantial body of material on the robbery, including a selection of Soviet books on the subject, but nothing to award Koba a share of the credit. In 1918 the Menshevik leader Martov accused Stalin of having been involved in some sort of robbery, but it was not the Tbilisi expropriation, but rather a murky affair in Baku (below, p. 51). As a Menshevik Martov had excellent contacts with Georgian Mensheviks who had every reasons to associate Stalin with what they considered unseemly activities, but they evidently never told Martov that Stalin had participated in the Tbilisi robbery.
39. Professor Tabagua has provided the dates of Yakov's birth and Ekaterina's death. On Stalin's security measures, *Stalin. K shestidesiatiletiiu so dnia rozhdeniia* (Moscow, *Pravda*, 1940) 271–2.
40. *W*, VIII, 183; on the Baku period in general, R. G. Suny, 'A Journeyman for the Revolution: Stalin and the Labour Movement in Baku, June 1907–May 1908', *Soviet Studies*, no. 3 (1971) 372–94.
41. *W*, II, 84–9, 90–4.
42. R. C. Elwood, Roman Malinowsky. *A Life Without a Cause* (Newtonville, Mass., 1977) 27–39.
43. For a list of Dzhugashvili's pseudonyms, Smith (1968) 453–4.
44. *W*, II, 426–8, 174–8.
45. *W*, II, 429–30.
46. 'Arkhivnie materialy o revoliutsionni deiatel'nosti I. V. Stalina', *Krasnyi s arkhiv*, no. 105 (1941) 19.
47. 'Arkhivnie materialy' (1941) 20–33; *W*, II, 431; Tutaev (1968) 132–6.
48. 'Arkhivnie materialy' (1941) 25; *W*, II, 432.
49. *RDCPSU*, I, 146–57.
50. See p. 18 above and I. Dubinskii-Mukhadze, *Ordzhonikidze* 'Moscow, 1964) 92–3.
51. *Sotsial-Demokrat*, 25 April/8 May 1912. In the days when Soviet scholars were diligently attempting to show that Stalin had been a poor Leninist, L. A. Slepov and S. A. Andronov argued that Stalin's article proved this point ['Prazhskaia konferentsiia RSDRP i bor'ba bol'shevikov za edinstva partii', *Voprosy istorii KPSS*, no. 2 (1965) 39]. But they did not quote from the article, the content of which does not sustain their argument. In the same spirit *Voprosy istorii KPSS*, no. 10 (1964) 78, published a letter from Lenin's wife Krupskaia to Ordzhonikodze, in which she states that 'Ivanovich' (Stalin) 'develops his own point of view' and is 'cut off', meaning not in full agreement with Lenin. The nature of Stalin's dissident thought was is not clear in context, but it hardly seems to have been softness on 'liquidators', which would not have led Krupskaia to write that it was 'a shame' that he could not attend the Prague Conference.
52. *W*, II, 434; L. K. D. Kristof, 'B. I. Nicolaevsky. The Formative Years', in

A. and J. Rabinowitch (eds), *Revolution and Politics in Russia* (Bloomington, Ind., 1972) 24. 24; 'Arkhivnie materialy' (1941) 26–8.
53. 'Arkhivnie materialy' (1941) 29.
54. R. C. Elwood, 'Lenin and *Pravda*, 1912–1914', *Slavic Review*, no. 2 (1972) 356–80; *W*, II, 260–72, 434–6.
55. *VILBK*, III, 52,
56. *RDCPSU*, I, 168–75; *PSS*, XLV, 122–9; *CW*, XVIII, 427–31; *W*, II, 253–61, 271–84.
57. *W*, II, 300–81, 437; McNeal, *Stalin's Works* (1967) 42–4, on some aspects of the publication history of the essay.
58. *W*, II, 344, 355,
59. *P*, 1 December 1912, not included in *W*. In addition he had used the signature 'K. St.' as early as 19 October 1912 in *P*.
60. Elwood (1977) 38; *W*, II, 438.
61. *W*, II, 438–40; A. S. Allilueva, *Vospominaniia* (Moscow 1946) 167. Stalin said that the authorities considered him too subversive to be taken into the army.
62. B. Shveitzer, *Stalin v turukhanskoi ssylke* (Moscow, 1943) 12–13; *VILBK*, III, 126; additional relevant documents on display in the Gori museum.
63. Tutaev (1968) 216–17; Allilueva (1969) 381–2.
64. *VILBK*, III, 456–7.
65. E. Gorodetsky and Iu. Sharapov, *Sverdlov. Zhizn' i deiatel'nost'* (Moscow, 1961) 84–6.

NOTES TO CHAPTER 3   PETROGRAD

1. N. N. Sukhanov, *The Russian Revolution 1917* (New York, 1955) 158; R. B. Browder and A. F. Kerensky (eds), *The Russian Provisional Government 1917. Documents* (Stanford, Calif., 1961) II, 1077–8.
2. *RDCPSU*, I, 197.
3. R. H. McNeal (ed.), *Stalin's Works. An Annotated Bibliography* (Stanford, Calif., 1967) 113, 185–6.
4. *RDCPSU*, I, 202–3; A. Shliapnikov, *Semnadtsatyi god* (Moscow, 1925) 180–2.
5. *W*, II, 4–9, 16–16; L. Trotsky, *The Stalin School of Falsification* (New York, 1971) 236–9.
6. *RDCPSU*, I, 203–4, 209–13; Trotsky (1971) 275–6.
7. *CW*, XXIV, 21–6.
8. E. N. Burdzhalov, 'O taktike Bol'shevikov v marte–aprele 1917 g.', *Voprosy istorii* no. 4 (1956) 47–50; E. N. Burdzhalov, *Vtoraia russkaia revoliutsiia. Moskva, front, periferiia* (Moscow, 1971) 376; *CW*, XXIII, 295–342; F. Raskol'nikov, 'Priezd tov. Lenina Rossiiu', *Proletarskaia revoliutsiia*, no. 1 (1923) 221.
9. Burdzhalov (1956) 51 and 'Eshche o taktike Bol'shevikov marte–aprele 1917 g.', *Voprosy istorii*, no. 8 (1956) 113–14. Burdzhalov reports that the brief statement that he quotes is the 'full text' as it appears in the record. Lenin's presence at this meeting is attested by *PSS*, XXXI, 650.
10. *W*, III, 40, 45; *CW*, XXIV, 23.
11. *W*, III, 52; *RDCPSU*, I, 217–26.
12. I. Tsereteli, *Vospominaniia fevral'skoi revoliutsii* (Paris, 1963) I, 133; Sukhanov (1955) 229–30, where he mentions Stalin as a 'grey blur'. This attests not to mediocre ability but to the role assigned him: to observe and keep the

Bolsheviks at a distance from the policies of the other parties in the Soviet. *W*, iii, 46–50.

13. *W*, iii, 101–3, 425, 444; *RDCPSU*, i, 236–9; A. Rabinowitch, *Prelude to Revolution* (Bloomington, 1968) 57, 60, 72, 86.
14. Rabinowitch (1968) 135–228; *VILBK*, iv, 287.
15. Tsereteli (1963) 266–7, 272, 333–4; McNeal, *Stalin's Works* (1967) 48–9. For the rest of Stalin's speech to the party conference: *W*, iii, 114–33.
16. *RDCPSU*, i, 249–61; *W*, iii, 121–30, 182–92; *VILBK*, iv, 304; in general on Lenin's position and the party congress, A. Rabinowitch, *The Bolsheviks Come to Power* (New York, 1976) 59–62, 83–90.
17. *BOR*, 9–13, 26, 30–2.
18. McNeal, *Stalin's Works* (1967) 51–7.
19. There were twenty-nine meetings between 4 August and 24 October, of which Stalin definitely attended sixteen and perhaps six more, the records of which do not record the names of those present. *BOR*, 9–126.
20. *BOR*, 280; *W*, iii, 449; *Perepiska Sekretariata s mestnymi partiinymi organizatsii* (Moscow, 1957) i, 378.
21. *BOR*, 57–65.
22. *CW*, xxvi, 87–136; *BOR*, 85–9.
23. *BOR*, 95–109.
24. *BOR*, 110–22; *PSS*, xxxiv, 434.
25. The Congress was scheduled to meet on the 20th, then postponed, actually opening on 25 October [R. W. Daniels, *Red October. The Bolshevik Revolution of 1917* (New York, 1967) 98].
26. *W*, iii, 417.
27. *Proletarskaia revoliutsiia*, no. 10 (1922) 92. In 1919 Stalin refuted the claim of one B. Shumiatsky that he, and not Stalin, had been the editor of *Pravda* at the time of the October revolution (*P*, 14 February, 1919).
28. *Feliks Edmundovich Dzerzhinskii. Biografiia* (Moscow, 1977) 134–5; K. Sverdlova, *Yakov Sverdlov* (Moscow, 1981) 92–3.
29. *PSS*, xxxv, 28–9; *P*, 28 October 1917.
30. R. S. Delon, *Stalin and Social Democracy. The Political Memoirs of David A. Sagirashvili* (Ph.D. Dissertation, Georgetown University, 1974) 199.
31. *BOR*, 127–40; J. L. H. Keep (ed.), *The Debate on Soviet Power* (Oxford, 1979) 92.
32. *P*, 3 November 1917; McNeal, *Stalin's Works* (1967) 57; *VILBK*, v, 26.
33. *W*, iv, 4–5.
34. *W*, iv, 457.
35. *W*, iv, 6–22, 29–30.
36. *W*, iv, 31–8.
37. *VILBK*, v, 42–3, 49. One wonders if Trotsky, as narkom for foreign affairs, really was excluded from the armistice group and the circle of persons having a pass to Lenin's quarters. It is, of course, possible that his name was expunged from the records.
38. *VILBK*, v, 169, 172, 176; *TP*, i, 6–7, 29–3.
39. *PSS*, xxxv, 332.
40. *BOR*, 173–8.
41. *BOR*, 206.
42. *VILBK*, v, 307–8; *W*, iv, 461.

NOTES TO CHAPTER 4 NARKOM

1. Stalin went to Petrograd in 1919, when it was threatened by the Whites, to finish up the extirpation of Zinoviev's machine in 1926 and to investigate the Kirov assassination in 1934. In 1933 he passed through the city on his way to tour the Baltic–White Sea Canal, but almost demonstratively avoided spending any more time in town than he had to in order to make the connections between his train and ship.
2. D. Tutaev (ed.), *The Alliluyev Memoirs* (London, 1968) 131–45, 168–75, 211–15; S. Allilueva, *Twenty Letters to a Friend* (New York, 1967) 47. The author visited the apartment, now a museum in honour of Lenin, in 1976.
3. Allilueva (1967) 47, 90–4, 105; Tutaev (1968) 214. Nadezhda's age is established by her obituary (*P*, 10 November 1932), which gives her birth date as 22 September 1901. Thus she turned sixteen just after Stalin became a lodger in her parents' apartment and was married before her next birthday.
4. Allilueva (1967) 93, states that the marriage occurred shortly after her mother wrote a particular letter, dated 'February'. The context of the letter shows that it was composed before 18 February. See also S. Allilueva, *Only One Year* (New York, 1969) 367.
5. *VILBK*, v, 309; *P*, 10 November 1932; Allilueva (1967) 93, 103.
6. *PSS*, LIV, 82–3, in which Lenin goes on at some length about Nadezhda's parents but does not mention her husband.
7. D. Shturman, *Mertvye khvataiut zhivie* (London, 1982) 23; *PSS*, LIV, 44; *VILBK*, v, 632–3; Allilueva (1967) 108.
8. *PSS*, XLV, 122, 127; *PSS*, L, 187, 338–9; *VILBK*, VIII, 366; *VILBK*, XI, 509.
9. *VILBK*, IX, 341; *PSS*, LI, 201–11, 295, 302, 429.
10. *VILBK*, IX, 498; *PSS*, LIV, 441; *DKFK*, II, 790.
11. *TP*, I, 248–51.
12. *VILBK*, VI, 390, IX, 348, 618; *VILBK*, X, 348, 566, 588, 639; *VILBK*, XI, 47, 113, 128; *W*, v, 437–8; *TP*, II, 26–9, 66–7. The only time that Stalin is known to have been incapacitated by illness during this period is in December 1921 (*VILBK*, IX, 565, 572).
13. S. Pestkovsky, 'Vospominaniia o rabote v Narkomnatse', *Proletarskaia revoliutsiia*, no. 6 (1930) 129–30.
14. 'Delo L. Martova v revoliutsionnom tribunale', *Obozrenie*, no. 15 (1985) 45–6; no. 16 (1985) 43–6; G. Aronson, 'Stalinskaia protsess protiv Martova', *Sotsialisticheskii vestnik*, no. 7–8 (1939) 435–6.
15. *W*, IV, 66–75, 87–94, 463; G. S. Gurvich, *Istoriia sovetskoi konstitutsii* (Moscow, 1923) 21–37.
16. *W*, IV, 306–16.
17. *P*, 6 November 1918; *W*, IV, 160–1, 170–3, 254–7; *W*, v, 20–2.
18. Delon (1974) 44; *PSS*, LI, 465; *PSS*, LII, 345, 347.
19. *PSS*, LI, 322; *PSS*, LII, 66, 69–70; *PSS*, LII, 345, 347, 364; *VILBK*, IX, 517, 526; *VILBK*, X, 6. This last item shows that Soviet editors have a Lenin document that they are not publishing. It states that Stalin's note of 24 January asked for a delay of several days in the Central Committee and that Lenin opposed the delay, but the document in which he states this is not provided. It is hardly likely that he wanted to oppose the Georgian operation all the sooner. When the Communists had taken Georgia Lenin's message congratulated the new regime and at the same time warned against excessive persecution of the Mensheviks, even suggesting that some might be included in the new government (*PSS*, XLII, 367). Since this message was published at the time, it is fair to say that these conciliatory ideas were included to

alleviate distress among western socialists. No Mensheviks were in fact taken into the new government.

20. *PSS*, LIII, 10, in which Lenin implies that Ordzhonikidze was responsible for calling Stalin to Tbilisi. The moderation of the Georgian Communist government of F. Makharadze was well known. *W*, v, 99, 101; Delon (1974) 126–36. Shah-Abbas had slaughtered large numbers of Georgians around 1600.
21. *W*, IV, 271.
22. *VILBK*, v, 506, 511; *PSS*, L, 127; *W*, IV, 118, 120, 465; *DKFK*, I, 289–90; *Dokumenty po istorii grazhdanskoi voiny v SSSR* (Moscow, 1960) I, 239.
23. *W*, IV, 122–3, 129, 468; *DKFK*, I, 289, 296–6, 301, 304–6, 317–20.
24. *DKFK*, I, 335, 345–8, 772; *TP*, I, 134–7, 140–41, 158–61; *W*, IV, 467–8.
25. *TP*, I, 482–3; *DKFK*, I, 773.
26. *TP*, I, 228–31; *W*, IV, 202–32 (especially 216–17), 471.
27. *PSS*, L, 325, 331, 351; *VILBK*, VII, 538; *W*, IV, 273, 277.
28. *W*, IV, 272, 279–80.
29. *W*, IV, 477–9; 284.
30. *W*, IV, 479; J. Erickson, *The Soviet High Command* (London, 1962) 65–7.
31. *DKFK*, II, 348–91 (showing forty-one orders signed or co-signed by Stalin); *W*, IV, 479–86; A. Zamoyski, *The Battle for the Marchlands* (New York, 1981) 58–9; *TP*, I, 758–62; *TP*, II, 26–9, 66–7; *PSS*, LI, 138, 409.
32. Zamoyski (1981) provides a general narrative of the war, and his map (64) indicates the military situation about the time of Stalin's arrival at front headquarters. *W*, IV, 489; *Direktivy Glavnogo Komandovaniia Krasnoi Armii* (Moscow, 1969) 693.
33. *DKFK*, III, 168–70.
34. *W*, IV, 490–1; *PSS*, LI, 248, 441.
35. W. Lerner, 'Attempting a Revolution from without: Poland in 1920', in T. T. Hammond (ed.), *The Anatomy of Communist Takeovers* (New Haven, Conn., 1975), 94–106; Zamoyski (1981) 154–60. The exchange of messages between Lenin and Stalin on 4 August 1920 shows that there was no idea that Stalin was betraying the attack on Warsaw (*DKFK*, III, 244–5). On the fate of Tukhachevsky, see below, p. 204.
36. *VILBK*, IX, 196, 235.
37. Lenin nominated Stalin as narkom of state control in a speech to the Central Committee (*VILBK*, VI, 598). *W*, IV, 221–4, 231–2, 473; G. A. Dorokhova, *Raboche-krest'ianskaia Inspektsiia v 1920–1923 gg.* (Moscow, 1959), 15–16; *PSS*, XXXVII, 541–2.
38. *W*, IV, 260, 474; *PSS*, XL, 65–6; *PSS*, LI, 426.
39. *PSS*, LIII, 441; *PSS*, XLV, 56, 531; S. N. Ikonnikov, *Organizatsiia deiatel'nosti RKI v 1920–1925 gg.* (Moscow, 1960) 72–3. Trotsky, too, thought that Lenin's proposal was Utopian (*TP*, II, 731–3.)
40. E. G. Genkina, *Protokoly Sovnarkoma RSFSR kak istoricheskii istochnik* (Moscow, 1982) 90; T. H. Rigby, *Lenin's Government: Sovnarkom 1917–1922* (New York, 1979) 36–9, 54, 76–84, 87, 184, 252. On Stalin's connection with the Revolutionary Military Council of the Republic and the Council of Labour and Defence, *W*, IV, 457, 468–70, 474, 487–8; *VILBK*, VI, 311. On the Mensheviks, *VILBK*, XI, 211, 242, 251; G. Legget, *The Cheka. Lenin's Secret Police* (Oxford, 1981) 290–1.
41. Legget (1981) 108, 112, 134, 139, 145; M. Jansen, *A Show Trial under Lenin* (The Hague, 1982) in general and especially 23, 139–40.
42. Rigby (1979) 176–89.
43. Rigby (1979) 179–80; *VILBK*, XII, 320.

44. *VILBK*, ɪx, 484, 498; *VILBK*, xɪ, 659, 673. Additional examples of Stalin's role in directing Politburo or Central Committee work may be found in *VILBK*, xɪ, 379, and *TP*, ɪɪ, 278–9. T. H. Rigby, 'Early Provincial Cliques and the Role of Stalin', *Soviet Studies*, no. 1 (1981) 24 argues that Stalin, with the support of Molotov, as 'responsible secretary' of the party, had effective control of the party as early as the Tenth Party Congress of March 1921.

45. L. D. Trotsky, *My Life* (New York, 1930) 177, and R. A. Medvedev, *Let History Judge* (New York, 1971) 17–18, attempt to absolve Lenin of responsibility for Stalin's appointment as General Secretary, but there is persuasive evidence that Lenin had entrusted Stalin with party affairs during Lenin's leave of absence (*VILBK*, xɪɪ, 140, 143, 161, 167, 173, 197, 215, 230, 237, 248) and that he proposed him as General Secretary (*PSS*, xʟv, 139; *VILBK*, xɪɪ, 267). On Stalin's office hours, *P*, 4 April 1922.

NOTES TO CHAPTER 5   DEATHWATCH

1. *VILBK*, xɪɪ, 36, 128, 217, 349.
2. *VILBK*, xɪɪ, 352.
3. *VILBK*, xɪɪ, 354; *P*, 18 June 1922.
4. *VILBK*, xɪɪ, 357–8.
5. *VILBK*, xɪɪ, 359; 363–72.
6. *VILBK*, xɪɪ, 362–3, 5–6, 76, 82, 88. On 2 September Zinoviev filled in for Stalin, who probably was on holiday (*VILBK*, xɪɪ, 370).
7. *W*, v, 136–9, written on 15 September. Ellipses noted are in the original. Lenin did discuss the show trial of the Socialist Revolutionaries (the non-Marxist radical party) with Stalin on 11 July and also asked his wife about the matter. When his health improved he wrote to Bukharin, telling him to set Maxim Gorky straight about the trials (*VILBK*, xɪɪ, 357, 373). On the trial in general, see M. Jansen, *A Show Trial under Lenin* (The Hague, 1982).
8. *VILBK*, xɪɪ, 394, 542.
9. *S*, v, 431–9.
10. V. I. Lenin, *Sochineniia* (Moscow, 1929) xxv, 624.
11. *CW*, xxx, 127.
12. *VILBK*, xɪɪ, 384.
13. Stalin's proposal is known through Lenin's critique of it (*CW*, xʟɪɪ, 421–3). *VILBK*, xɪɪ, 388. Stalin's previous visits with the recuperating Lenin had lasted only about a half an hour.
14. Among the numerous examples of Lenin using Stalin, as Gensek, to disseminate other business to the Politburo, *PSS*, xʟv, 165, 188, 194, 197, 203, 205, 220, 295.
15. L. D. Trotsky, *The Stalin School of Falsification* (New York, 1971) 66–7, which provides the document in part. The whole is in the Trotsky archives at Harvard, T755. *W*, ɪv, 72–4; *W*, v, 146, which edits the original version in *P*, 18 November 1922 to cover up Stalin's later acceptance of bicameralism.
16. *VILBK*, xɪɪ, 390; *CW*, xʟv, 582; S. V. Kharmandarin, *Lenin i stanovlenie zakvkazskoi federatsii 1921–1923* (Erivan, 1969) 351–4; *Dvenadtsatyi s'ezd Rossiiskoi Kommunisticheskoi Partii (bol'shevikov): Stenograficheskii otchet* (Moscow, 1923) 157.
17. Kharmandarian (1969) 370.
18. *VILBK*, xɪɪ, 535, 542.

19. *PSS*, xlv, 473.
20. *VILBK*, xii, 544; *VILBK*, xii, 594–5; *PSS*, xlv, 709–10.
21. *VILBK*, xii, 537. In Trotsky's suspiciously belated conclusion that Stalin murdered Lenin [L. D. Trotsky, *Stalin* (New York, 1941) 378–82] it is alleged that Lenin called Stalin to him in late February 1923 and asked to be given poison for use if his painful condition became hopeless. But it seems unlikely that such a meeting ever occurred. The Soviets have never shown any interest in Trotsky's allegation, and it is unlikely that they falsified the log of Lenin's visitors in order to deal with the charge. Nadezhda Stalina is mentioned in the log of Lenin's staff for the last time in *PSS*, xlv, 477.
22. *PSS*, xlv, 591.
23. L. Fotieva, *Pages from Lenin's Life* (Moscow, 1960) 182.
24. *PSS*, xlv, 608; *PSS*, liv, 674–5, with cuts. For full text, see *KSG*, 98–100.
25. *VILBK*, xii, 546; *PSS*, xlv, 474; *TP*, ii, 810. On Lenin's idea of appointing workers, see pp. 63–4 above.
26. *CW*, xxxvi, 594–5.
27. *CW*, xxxvi, 596–611.
28. *CW*, xxxvi, 596. Soviet scholars, who have access to the surviving documents, do not rule out the possibility that Lenin's dictation of 4 January 1923 was a reaction to Stalin's telephone call to Krupskaia. They merely conclude that he learned of this event 'not later than 5 March' (*VILBK*, xii, 590).
29. *TP*, ii, 728–37, 819, 830–3. In his response to the repeated offer Trotsky said that he would accept the job if the Central Committee ordered him to, but that this would be 'profoundly irrational' and contrary to his administrative 'plans and intentions'. This brusqueness was far from the impression of friendly relations that he described in L. D. Trotsky, *My Life* (New York, 1930) 478–9. This memoir was even more inaccurate in stating (477) that Lenin had not previously offered him the position.
30. *TP*, ii, 816–33.
31. L. Ivanov and A. N. Shmelev, *Leninizm i ideinopoliticheskii razgrom trotskizma* (Moscow, 1970) 349.
32. *CW*, xxxiii, 481–502. When a medical bulletin was published on 13 March 1923 it referred to the articles as the 'necessary link between Vladimir Il'ich and the population of the country' (*VILBK*, xii, 595). On the attempt to block publication, Trotsky (1971) 72.
33. *VILBK*, xii, 587; for his previous efforts to obtain the material, 570–1, 574, 579–80. As it turned out Lenin's health did not permit him to do anything with this hard-won material. Trotsky maintains (1930, 482) that one of Lenin's secretaries told him that Lenin was preparing a 'bomb' on the Georgian question.
34. *PSS*, xlv, 486, 608; *PSS*, liv, 329–30.
35. *VILBK*, xii, 593–5.
36. Trotsky (1930) 482–3; *PSS*, liv, 329; *PSS*, xlv, 607.
37. *KSG*, 277–9; *The Department of State Bulletin*, no. 891 (1956) 157–8; Trotsky (1971) 363.
38. *RDCPSU*, ii, 187–8; Trotsky (1971) 356.
39. *W*, v, 199–240. He borrowed the metaphor of transmission belts from Lenin (*W*, viii, 38). *RDCPSU*, ii, 189.
40. *W*, v, 241–83.
41. *W*, v, 230–1.
42. Above, p. 67.
43. Trotsky (1930) 500.
44. *Cheternadtsatyi s'ezd Vsesoiuznoi Kommunisticheskoi Partii (b).*

Stenograficheskii otchet (Moscow, 1926) 455–6. See also a different squabble between Stalin and Zinoviev in the summer of 1924 [E. H. Carr, *A History of Soviet Russia. Socialism in One Country 1924–1926* (New York, 1959) ii, 4].

45. *P*, 4 April 1922; B. Bajanov, *Bajanov révèle Staline* (Paris, 1979) 52.
46. On this subject in general, N. E. Rosenfeldt, *Knowledge and Power* (Copenhagen, 1978). Also Bajanov (1979) 51, 54–55. This memoirist established his credentials as an actual member of Stalin's staff by publishing what appears to be an authentic identification pass in his first book [*Avec Staline dans le Kremlin* (Paris, 1930)]. One hopes that the modest points mentioned above on the basis of his testimony are reliable. However, his second book (*Bajanov révèle Staline*) gravely undermines his credibility on the more pretentious assertions that he offers, which attempt to magnify his importance and ability. One major case is his claim to have drafted the first major post-revolutionary revision of the party statutes in 1922, when in fact the first such revision occurred in 1919, before he had joined either the Orgburo or Stalin's secretariat [Bajanov (1979) 20–4, 28–9; *RDCPSU*, ii, 90–8]. A second case is his claim to have proposed and prepared in 1922 the first edition of the basic collection of party decrees [Bajanov (1979) 28–9], when in fact this publication (*Spravochnik partiinogo rabotnika*) first appeared in 1921. The credibility of his second book also suffers from his willingness to make assertions concerning events that occurred in the USSR after his defection in 1928; for example, the suicide of Nadezhda Allilueva, the alleged murder of her classmates at the Industrial Academy and statements by Stalin's son Yakov to his German captors during the Second World War.
47. Bajanov (1979) 133, 75, 77. On such matters that do not involve his own importance or questions of high policy Bajanov may, perhaps, be believed.
48. Rosenfeldt (1978) 129–160.
49. *RDCPSU*, ii, 119-21 and the related resolution, 121–4.
50. L. D. Trotsky, *The Challenge of the Left Opposition (1923–25)* (New York, 1975) 50–144, especially 55, 83. According to J. Hough, *How the Soviet Union Is Governed* (Cambridge, Mass., 1979) 133, 65.3 per cent of the delegates to the party congress of 1924 were party officials and in the same year 38 per cent of the Central Committee consisted of these people.
51. A. I. Mikoyan, *V nachale dvadtsatykh* (Moscow, 1975) 140–1.
52. *RDCPSU*, ii, 11–12. The party statutes (*RDCPSU*, ii, 90–8) did not mention any system for the election of delegates to a party conference.
53. *W*, vi, 3–46, especially 3–26, 41. This was not quite Stalin's first polemic against Trotsky. There had been a short diatribe in an article of 15 December 1923 (*W*, v, 393–7).

NOTES TO CHAPTER 6   HEIRS

1. *VILBK*, xii, 595–611 on bulletins; 616 on decline. This source appears to be scrupulous in reporting Politburo or Central Committee discussions on the management of news about Lenin in this period, so in the absence of references to this after March 1922, it appears that Stalin, as the person in charge of Lenin's medical affairs, made the decision to publish or not publish bulletins.
2. L. D. Trotsky, *Stalin* (New York, 1941) 378–82; E. Lermolo, *The Face of a Victim* (New York, 1955) 135–7; L. Shatunovskaia, *Zhizn' v Kremle* (New York, 1982) 234.

3. On the autopsy, N. Tumarkin, *Lenin Lives!* (Cambridge, Mass., 1983) 169–72.
4. *W*, vi, 441–2.
5. Tumarkin (1983) 136.
6. *W*, vi, 54–66, especially 58; see p. 88 below.
7. L. D. Trotsky, *My Life* (New York, 1930) 508–9; Tumarkin (1983) 157–9.
8. Tumarkin (1983) 154–6.
9. *W*, vi, 47–53.
10. Tumarkin (1983) 166.
11. N. K. Krupskaia, *O Lenine* (Moscow, 1960) 11–12.
12. *P*, 27 January 1924.
13. Tumarkin (1983) 154; *Na mogilu Il'icha* (Leningrad, 1924).
14. Tumarkin (1983) 64–111; *Pis'ma trudiaschchikhsia k V. I. Leninu* (Moscow, 1966) 46.
15. E. Yaroslavskii, *Velikii vozhd' rabochei revoliutsii* (Moscow, 1918), source decaying, page numbers uncertain.
16. Above, footnote 14.
17. Tumarkin (1983) 182–205.
18. Tumarkin (1983) 176–9, 181–2; N. Valentinov, *Novaia ekonomicheskaia politika i krizis partii posle smerti Lenina* (Stanford, Calif., 1971) 90–2; *W*, vi, 443; on the absence of crematoria, *Moskva. Entsiklopediia* (Moscow, 1980) 385.
19. *Spravochnik partiinogo rabotnika*, vol. v (1926) 332.
20. Tumarkin (1983) 124; *P*, 25 January 1924.
21. *W*, vi, 71–196, 444. T. Zelenev, 'Izdanie i rasprostranenie proizvedenii I. V. Stalina', *Bol'shevik*, no. 23 (1949) 93, shows 16 980 000 copies of *Voprosy leninizma* published by 1949.
22. *W*, vi, 77, 137, 110–11; R. H. McNeal (ed.), *Stalin's Works. An Annotated Bibliography* (Stanford, Calif., 1967) 110–11.
23. *W*, vi, 111, 187, 177–89.
24. *W*, vi, 190–2; on Stalin's 1937 speech, see p. 197 below.
25. L. D. Trotsky, *Sochineniia* (Moscow, 1924–7); G. Zinoviev, *Sochineniia* (Moscow, 1924–6); L. B. Kamenev, *Stat'i i rechi 1905–1925* (Leningrad, 1925–9).
26. L. D. Trotsky, *The Challenge of the Left Opposition (1923–25)* (New York, 1975) 199–258.
27. *W*, vi, 338–373; 374–420, especially 365.
28. *W*, vi, 338; see pp. 16–17 above.
29. *W*, vi, 386. 387, 375–6, 415, 419, 391.
30. Cited by Stalin, *W*, vi, 388.
31. *CW*, xxxiii, 476-9.
32. *W*, iv, 167–76; 181–6; 240–4; 256–7; 405–6; *W*, v, 92–3; 119; 181–3; Dietrich Moller, 'Stalin und der "deutsche Oktober" 1923', *Jahrbücher für Geschichte Osteuropas*, xii, 212–5.
33. *W*, iv, 387–8.
34. While 'Marxism and the National Question' was not explicitly Russian nationalist, Stalin did oppose the dismemberment of the Russian Empire and the separatism of the minority nationalities (pp. 24–5 above). On the party congress of 1917, *W*, iii, 199. On the civil war, *W*, iv, 11–12, 21–2, 294–5; *P*, 14 November 1935.
35. *W*, vi, 394, 397, 373.
36. *W*, vi, 9–10,; *W*, vii, 6–10; *W*, vii, 32–3, 111–22, 205; Trotsky (1925) 304–8.
37. Trotsky (1930) 518; A. S. Kalabashkin, *Vernyi syn partii* (Kishinev, 1960)

228. This work adds that the commission included 'others', the usual method of referring to people who later were declared to be traitors, quite likely Zinoviev and/or Kamenev in this case.

38. *Cheternadtsayi s'ezd Vsesoiuznoi Kommunistichestoi Partii (b). Stenograficheskii otchet* (Moscow, 1926) 38–129, especially 38.

39. *W*, viii, 10–96, especially 73, 95, 58–9. The magic lantern slides are advertised in *P*, 2 January 26.

40. *W*, vii, 9–10; *W*, viii, 247–9, 231–2, 308, 339, 345.

41. *W*, viii, 225–310; *RDCPSU*, ii, 291–301.

42. L. D. Trotsky, *The Challenge of the Left Opposition (1926–27)* (New York, 1980) 130–64, especially 160–1.

43. *W*, vii, 269, 287–8; *W*, viii, 370.

44. *W*, ix, 1–64, and the more rambling reply to the discussion, 65–155. For Trotsky's speech, Trotsky (1980) 173–189.

45. Trotsky (1980) 301–94; 258–64; *W*, x, 4, 169–70; E. H. Carr and R. W. Davies, *A History of Soviet Russia. The Foundations of a Planned Economy* (New York, 1969–1978), vol. ii, 3–53.

46. *W*, x, 351, 84–5, 87, 92–3, 171–2, 209.

47. *W*, x, 54–7, 91, 351–2.

48. L. D. Trotsky, *Leon Trotsky on China* (New York, 1976). *W*, ix, 224–34, 243–273, 288–318; *W*, x, 10–39.

49. The party statutes governing the electoral system appear in *RDCPSU*, ii, 90–98, 178–86, 269–83; T. H. Rigby, 'Party Elections in the CPSU', *Political Quarterly*, no. 4 (1964) 420–43.

50. H.-H. Schroeder, 'Gesellschaftliche Funktion und innere Entwicklung der bolschewistischen Partei in den Jahren der NEP 1921–1928', in G. Erler and W. Süss (eds), *Stalinismus* (Frankfurt am Main, 1982) 96–7. On finance, R. H. McNeal, 'The Beginning of Communist Party Financial Exactions from the Soviet State', in D. A. Loeber (ed.), *Ruling Communist Parties and Their Status under Law* (Dordrecht, 1986) 189–94.

51. *W*, x, 193; Carr and Davies, (1969–1978) ii, 34–5.

52. *RDCPSU*, ii, 254–7. The record of voting at the congress leaves forty-one votes unaccounted for, perhaps opposition sympathizers from regions other than Leningrad.

53. *W*, viii, 150–3, 414. Only one of the two speeches that he gave in Leningrad, to the *aktiv* (the more prominent party members, including those holding substantial positions outside the party) has been published (*W*, viii, 123–56). The speech to the presumably smaller Leningrad province committee remains unpublished. This visit to Leningrad, which was Stalin's only one during Kirov's tenure there, probably is the basis for A. Antonov-Ovseenko's story [in his *The Time of Stalin* (New York, 1980) 48] of a visit by Stalin in 1927 (rather than 1926). This kind of error counteracts whatever verisimilitude Antonov-Ovseenko provides concerning the roasting of shashliks and other details.

54. *W*, ix, 153; *W*, x, 210, 356.

55. *P*, 11 August 1927.

56. V. T. Reck, *Boris Pil'niak. A Soviet Writer in Conflict with the State* (Montreal, 1975) 13–51; B. Pilnyak, *The Tale of the Unextinguished Moon* (New York, 1967); E. H. Carr, 'Pilnyak and the Death of Frunze', *Soviet Studies*, no. 2 (1958) 162–4.

57. W. Lerner, *Karl Radek. The Last Internationalist* (Stanford, Calif., 1970) 130, on Radek's expulsion.

58. *P*, 15 November 27; *Izvestiia Tsentral'nogo Komiteta*, 7 December 1927.

59. The pro-Stalin activists in various audiences appear in parenthetical interjections in most of his speeches from this period. For an example of heckling of an opponent, Trotsky (1980) 271–90, 438–48; for the allowance of more time, Trotsky (1980) 149.

60. *P*, 1 June 1924; *P*, 1 January 1926; *RDCPSU*, II, 286–8.

61. *W*, VIII, 245–310, 367–8; *W*, IX, 153; *RDCPSU*, II, 284–9.

62. Carr and Davies (1979–78), II, 32–4; P. Reiman, *Die Geburt des Stalinismus* (Frankfurt am Main, 1979) 51–2.

63. *P*, 18, 20 December 1927.

64. Rieman (1979) 65–8, 238–42, 257–61. This scholar found the original documentation for his work in German intelligence reports, available in West German archives. These are credible because they harmonize with some official Soviet publications [*W*, x, 188–93; B. A. Abramov, 'Razgrom trotsistsko-zinov'evskogo anti-partiinogo bloka', *Voprosy istorii KPSS*, no. 6 (1956) 40] and they do not seem to be the sort of thing that German intelligence, Soviet counter-intelligence or an inventive agent would have fabricated. They were not used for propaganda purposes at the time, are fragmentary in coverage and not misleading to German policy-makers. In this period Germans were well placed to engage in spying or the recruitment of spies because of the good relations that Germany and the Soviet Union enjoyed after the Treaty of Rapallo and because German Communists were active in the Comintern headquarters.

65. *W*, x, 190–1.

66. *RDCPSU*, II, 306.

67. Rieman (1979) 237–42.

68. *P*, 10 November 1927; L. Ivanov and A. N. Shmelev, *Leninizm i ideinopoliticheskii razgrom trotiskizma* (Moscow, 1970) 425.

69. *Izvestiia Tsentral'nogo Komiteta*, 15 November 1927. There was no meeting of Central Committee or Central Control Commission at this time.

70. Rieman (1979) 242–6.

71. *P*, November–December 1927. Otherwise his picture did not appear at all in the party organ in this period.

72. *W*, x, 177.

73. *W*, x, 63. He appears to have introduced the practice of referring to himself in the third person at the end of 1925 at the party congress (*W*, VII, 394). He did this increasingly in the next two years (*W*, IX, 73, 101, 121–2, 125–6, 237–8, 286, 290; *W*, x, 62, 74–5, 176, 182, 200).

74. *W*, IX, 183; *W*, x, 59; *W*, VI, 283; *W*, VII, 390, 401.

75. *W*, VII, 288–9.

76. *W*, VIII, 9, 118; *W*, x, 265.

77. *BSE*, XL, 426, 440; *W*, VIII, 414; *W*, IX, 388; *P*, 24 October 1925.

78. *P*, 24 October, 9 December 1927.

79. *W*, VII, 183. For a similar reproach to comrades from Stalin about this time, merely for asking that he send greetings to his namesake city, *KR*, 27.

80. R. H. McNeal (ed.), *Stalin's Works. An Annotated Bibliography* (Stanford, Calif., 1967) entry nos. 648, 653, 654, 658, 659, 664, 665, 673, 674, 676, 679, 685, 688, 708, 722, 726, 729, 730, 746, 747, 757, 762, 774, 776.

81. *W*, VI, 230, 245; *W*, VII, 361; *W*, x, 363.

82. *KSG*, 102, 238. An exceptionally explicit statement of this point among many is in V. Donskoi and S. Ikonnikov, 'Razvitie leninskikh idei o partiino-gosudarstvennym kontrole', *Kommunist*, no. 18 (1962) 37.

83. *KSG*, 258–9.

84. R. D. Warth, *Leon Trotsky* (Boston, 1977) 137. Trotsky probably was not

present when Stalin first read this material, but Kamenev, Trotsky's brother-in-law and, for a time, political ally probably was present. Warth discovered this in the Max Eastman archive, which shows that Trotsky wrote this to Eastman, deleting the expletive.

85. *KSG*, 258–9; B. Bajanov, *Avec Staline dans le Kremlin* (Paris, 1930) 43–5. Although one relies on Bajanov with reluctance, this account does not attempt to inflate his personal importance nor to relate some lurid tale. In general this earlier memoir seems more trustworthy than his later one. L. D. Trotsky, *The Suppressed Testament of Lenin* (New York, 1935) 13, 30.
86. *W*, x, 181.
87. M. Eastman, *Since Lenin Died* (London, 1925) 28–31; *Bol'shevik*, no. 16 (1925) 71–3.
88. Carr and Davies (1969–78), ii, 10. Krupskaia smuggled out a copy of the testament to Eastman, who published it in the *New York Times*, 18 October 1926.
89. *P*, 2 November 1927. This version omits Lenin's final sentence on the 'decisive trifle'.
90. R. A. Medvedev, *Let History Judge* (New York, 1971) 28–9, says that he saw this publication, but it was still very hard to obtain in 1983, when I could not find it listed in the catalogue of the social sciences library of the Academy of Sciences, a privileged institution. The sanitization of Stalin's speech on the subject is treated in McNeal, *Stalin's Works* (1967) 129.

NOTES TO CHAPTER 7   KULAKS

1. S. Allilueva, *Twenty Letters to a Friend* (New York, 1967) 26–7, 31.
2. *W*, vii, 237; *W*, viii, 416; *W*, ix, 391; *W*, x, 404; *W*, xi, 394–5. The official chronology of his activities for 1924, a crucial year, shows no protracted absence from Moscow (*W*, vi, 339–450). Aino Kuusinen, *The Rings of Destiny* (New York, 1974) 28–30, confirms Allilueva (1967) 33, concerning Stalin's use of a villa Matsesta near Sochi.
3. Allilueva (1967) 103; Kuusinen (1974) 29.
4. Allilueva (1967) 104, 158.
5. *BKM*, 83.
6. Western scholarship has only recently begun to perceive the importance of the radical revival from below in the late 1920s. A pioneer collective work that has cast much light on this is S. Fitzpatrick (ed.), *Cultural Revolution in Russia, 1928–1931* (Bloomington, Ind., 1977). L. Viola has contributed important studies: *The Best Sons of the Fatherland. Workers in the Vanguard of Soviet Collectivization* (New York, 1987), and 'Notes on the Background of Soviet Collectivization: Metal Worker Brigades in the Countryside, Autumn 1929', *Soviet Studies*, no. 2 (1984) 205–22; and 'The Campaign to Eliminate Kulaks as a Class', *Slavic Review*, no. 3 (1986) 503–24. L. Siegelbaum, 'Production Collectives and Communes and the "Imperatives" of Soviet Industrialization', *Slavic Review*, no. 1 (1986) 65–84 discusses another important dimension of the trend. Other aspects are mentioned in J. Barber, *Soviet Historians in Crisis, 1928–1932* (New York, 1981) 40–1 and V. Rapoport and Yu. Alexeev, *High Treason* (Durham, NC, 1985) 171.
7. *RDCPSU*, ii, 319–26.
8. *W*, x, 300–21.

9. *RDCPSU*, II, 359–61.
10. K. E. Bailes, *Technology and Society under Lenin and Stalin* (Princeton, NJ, 1978) 69–94; P. Reiman, *Die Geburt des Stalinismus* (Frankfurt am Main, 1979), 69–94; N. Krylenko (ed.), *Ekonomischeskaia kontrrevoliutsiia v Donbasse* (Moscow, 1928).
11. Reiman (1979) 237–8, 257–61, 288–91, 294. These documents contradict the assertion of A. Avtorkhanov, *Stalin and his Soviet Communist Party* (New York, 1959) 28–9, that Menzhinsky was reluctant to co-operate with Stalin in prosecuting the Shakhty case. This memoirist does not encourage confidence in his reliability by providing lengthy verbatim conversations that he could never have heard, even at second hand. The unreliability of the rumours that he relies on is demonstrated by his confusion of an actual Central Committee meeting in 1937 with a fictitious one (see p. 363 n.31 below). Menzhinsky's zeal to discover plots of the class enemy is noted in another connection, the Red Army, as early as 1927, in Abramov (1959) 40.
12. *W*, XI, 57.
13. Bailes (1978) 91; *BKM*, 83.
14. A. Nove, *An Economic History of the U.S.S.R.* (Harmondsworth, Middx., 1972) 150.
15. *W*, XI, 5–6, 389–90. N. I. Nemakov, *Kommunisticheskaia Partiia – Organizator massovogo kolkhoznogo dvizheniia 1929–1932* (Moscow, 1966) 25, concerning lists of party officials dispatched on these missions.
16. *W*, XI, 7–11.
17. *W*, XI, 12–22.
18. In general, see S. F. Cohen, *Bukharin and the Bolshevik Revolution* (New York, 1973).
19. Allilueva (1967) 31; *W*, XII, 1.
20. *BKM*, 83–5. The authenticity of this document, from the Trotsky archive, is sustained by the Soviet writer F. M. Vaganov, *Pravyi uklon v VKP(b) i ego razgrom* (Moscow, 1977) 59, 173, 224–5.
21. *W*, XI, 109, 199, 334.
22. *BKM*, 84.
23. *BKM*, 84.
24. Vaganov (1977) 59; *BKM*, 86.
25. *BKM*, 83–4, 86; Vaganov (1977) 224–5.
26. R. W. Daniels, *The Conscience of the Revolution* (Cambridge, Mass., 1960) 341–4; E. H. Carr and R. W. Davies, *A History of Soviet Russia. The Foundations of a Planned Economy* (New York, 1967–1978), II, 61–2.
27. *BKM*, 84.
28. *W*, XI, 231–48, especially 242–5, 255; 256. In July 1928 at the Sixth World Congress of the Comintern there had been talk of a Right danger in European Communism, but Stalin had not spoken at all, and the point had not been applied to internal party affairs in the Soviet Union [Daniels (1960) 334–77].
29. Carr and Davies (1969–1978) II, 82–4; *W*, XI, 327–31.
30. Vaganov (1977) 224–34. The full Central Committee did not meet at this time. *RDCPSU*. II, 349, shows that the resulting resolution of the Politburo was dated 9 February 1929. In *W*, XI, 332, there is reference to Stalin's statements at 'the end of January and beginning of February 1929'. Bukharin's statement has never been published in full, but is discussed in Cohen (1973) 305–7.
31. Vaganov (1977) 228.
32. *RDCPSU*, II, 349–57.
33. *W*, XI, 332–40, especially 340. When Stalin says 'Central Committee', a body

which was not in session at the time, he means 'Politburo'. Since the editors of *W* vaguely date this document as late January and early February, it appears to be a composite of things Stalin said at various times during the discussion of the Bukharin affair. But the concluding passage quoted must come from the final stage of the proceedings, in which the resolution was put to a vote.

34. *RDCPSU*, II, 349–57. 'Higher', which is to say larger and more representative, party assemblies on occasion ratify in blanket fashion the work of a smaller body (as in the approval of the report on Central Committee work submitted to party congresses), but this appears to be the only time a specific resolution was submitted to the larger body for ratification. Vaganov (1977) 234.

35. *W*, XII, 1–113, especially 16, 31–2, 41.

36. *W*, XII, 112–13.

37. *RDCPSU*, II, 342–9; *W*, XII, 113.

38. *RDCPSU*, II, 358; *Shestnadtsataia konferentsiia VKP(b), aprel' 1929 g.: Stenograficheskii otchet* (Moscow, 1962) 318; *W*, XII, 123, 402; R. H. McNeal (ed.), *Stalin's Works. An Annotated Bibliography* (Stanford, Calif., 1967) 136.

39. The Soviet works cited below in this chapter are relevant in this connection This scholarship was most prolific in the late years of the Khrushchev era, tapering off thereafter. O. A. Narkiewicz, 'Stalin, War Communism and Collectivization', *Soviet Studies*, no. 1 (1961) 20–37, argued that Stalin did not appear to be an active initiator of the campaign for radical transformation on the countryside, a point sustained at greater length in R. W. Davies, *The Industrialization of Russia. The Soviet Offensive: The Collectivization of Agriculture, 1929–1930* (Cambridge, Mass., 1980) I, 132–46. Viola (1986) adds weight to this interpretation.

40. *P*, 20 June 1929; N. A. Ivnitsky, *Klassovaia bor'ba v derevne i likvidatsiia kulachestva kak klassa (1929–1932)* (Moscow, 1972) 77, 298. This work is an apologia for Soviet agrarian policy as well as a serious scholarly contribution, and it may understate the extent of evictions. The relevant point here is the attribution of 10 per cent of all evictions to the year 1929, before the announcement of high-level policy on the matter. Narkiewicz (1961) 24, lists three districts that had achieved 70, 40 and 25 per cent collectivization, respectively, by September 1929. A. Fainsod, *Smolensk under Soviet Rule* (Cambridge, Mass., 1958) 180, provides another example of lower-level radical initiative.

41. *W*, XII, 131–41.

42. Among articles that assert this without any specific evidence, V. A. Abramov, 'O rabote komissii Politbiuro Ts K VKP(b) po voprose sploshnoi kollektivizatsii', *Voprosy istorii KPSS*, no. 1 (1964) 33.

43. Cohen (1973) 334; *RDCPSU*, III, 39–40.

44. Ivnitsky (1972) 87.

45. Ivnitsky (1972) 87–92; M. A. Vyltsan, N. A. Ivnitsky, Yu. A. Poliakov, 'Nekotorye problemy istorii kollektivizatsii v SSSR', *Voprosy istorii*, no. 3 (1965) 4–5; Abramov (1964) 33; N. A. Ivnitsky, 'O nachal'nom etape sposhnoi kollektivizatsii', *Voprosy istorii KPSS*, no. 4 (1962) 57–9; L. Bogdenko, 'For a History of the Initial Stage of the Solid Collectivization of Agriculture in the USSR', *Current Digest of the Soviet Press*, no. 36 (1963) 5.

46. Vyltsan *et al.* (1965) 4; Abramov (1964) 33; Bogdenko (1963) 5; Ivnitsky (1962) 59; *RDCPSU*, III, 25. On Molotov's independence, *KR*, 58. Bukharin regarded Molotov as the zealot of the left, evidently no mere mouthpiece of Stalin in this regard (*BKM*, 82–3, 85).

47. Bogdenko (1963) 5; Narkiewicz (1961) 28–30.

48. Abramov (1964) 33; Vyltsan *et al.* (1965) 5.
49. N. A. Ivnitsky, 'Istoriia podgotovki postanovleniia Ts K VKP(b) o tempakh kollektivizatsii sel'skogo khoziaistva ot 5 Ianvaria 1930 g.', in *Istokovedenie istorii sovetskogo obshchestva* (Moscow, 1964) 265–88; Bogdenko (1965) 5; Abramov (1964) 33–5, 40; *RDCPSU*, III, 40–3.
50. Abramov (1964) 34. Stalin's editing replaced the tabular presentation of targets with a condensed version that in some respects reduced the tempo set in the previous draft. For example, Stalin's version lumped the Crimea with 'other grain regions', which had the effect of postponing the target date for collectivization from spring 1930 to autumn 1931.
51. Abramov (1964) 37, 40; Bogdenko (1963) 6. Here Bogdenko argues that Stalin erred in this matter and 'the Central Committee' corrected him, a good example of the Khrushchevian policy of blaming Stalin for errors and the collective leadership of the party for correct decisions. Unfortunately for this argument, the Central Committee did not meet in this period, and the change therefore was the work of an executive body in which Stalin himself participated. The complexity of the issue of privately owned goods emerges in R. W. Davies, *The Industrialization of Russia. The Soviet Collective Farm 1929–1930* (Cambridge, Mass., 1980) 73–98. A related criticism of Stalin was Ivnitsky's charge that Stalin saw the artel merely as a transition to the commune [Ivnitsky (1964) 285]. But this is unsubstantiated and runs counter to Stalin's approval of the draft model statutes of the collective farm in March 1930.
52. Ivnitsky (1972) 167–79; *W*, XII, 147–78. The decree of 30 January was supplemented by another of 4 February [Davies, *The Socialist Offensive* (1980) 234].
53. *W*, XII, 185–9; *RDCPSU*, III, 47–50; J. Haslam, *Soviet Foreign Policy, 1930–33* (New York, 1983), 121–2.
54. Davies, *The Socialist Offensive* (1980) 203–68; Ivnitsky (1972) 217, 235; Vyltsan *et al.* (1965) 7; L. Viola, The Campaign of the 25,000ers (Ph.D. dissertation, Princeton University, 1984) 232. *W*, XII, 197–205.
55. *W*, XII, 207–34. The decree of to which Stalin referred (218) was actually dated 14 March, but was published on the 15th (*RDCPSU*, III, 47–50). In the Khrushchev era the official party history, without substantiation, claimed that the Politburo had instructed Stalin to write 'Dizzy with Success' [*Istoriia Kommunistichestoi Partii Sovetskogo Soiuza* (Moscow, 1962) 445.
56. For example, 'The Great Stalin as the Creator of the Collective Farm System', *Izvestiia*, 20 December 49.
57. Davies, *The Socialist Offensive* (1980) 319–26.
58. *W*, XII, 204–34, especially 208, 220. *P*, 6 April and 7 June 1930. The official announcement of the postponement, signed by Stalin, attributed the change to the weather.
59. Nove (1972) 179; M. Matthews, *Class and Society in Soviet Russia* (London, 1972) 53–7.
60. R. Conquest, *The Harvest of Sorrow* (New York, 1986) 215–330 (on the estimated famine deaths, p. 303).
61. *P*, 10 March 1963.

NOTES TO CHAPTER 8   BUILDER

1. L. D. Trotsky, *The Challenge of the Left Opposition (1926–27)* (New York, 1980) 222–3. Stalin also may have been influenced by the Soviet engineer Shatunovsky, who considered the project a poor investment (W, xi, 281; W, xiii, 17–19).
2. W, xi, 65, 62.
3. W, xi, 258. In conversation with Emil Ludwig Stalin denied that there was a parallel between his own rule and that of Peter the Great, but the question had been posed in terms of western culture rather than technology (W, xiii, 106–7). *KR*, 37.
4. K. E. Bailes, *Technology and Society under Lenin and Stalin* (Princeton, NJ, 1978) 69–121; A. I. Solzhenitsyn, *The Gulag Archipelago* (New York, 1974–8) i, 376–407; *The Case of N. P. Vitvitsky, V. A. Gusev, A. W. Gregory et al.* (Moscow, 1933).
5. W, xiii, 336; W, xiii, 40–1.
6. W, xi, 277; W, xii, 341, 335.
7. W, xii, 240–1; W, xiii, 47–9, 83, 105, 12, 135, 142, 145.
8. W, xiii, 145.
9. N. Jasny, *Soviet Industrialization 1928–1952* (Chicago, 1961) 51–69.
10. W, xii, 354–5.
11. W, xii, 355–6.
12. E. Zaleski, *Planning for Economic Growth in the Soviet Union 1918–1932* (Chapel Hill, NC, 1971) 117; W, xii, 323–4; *Istoriia SSSR s drevneishikh vremen do nashikh dnei* (Moscow, 1967) viii, 468.
13. W, xii, 278–9, 323, 282.
14. Solzhenitsyn (1974–8) i, 376–407.
15. L. Shatunovskaia, *Zhizn' v Kremle* (New York, 1982) 72–3. This memoirist commands respect when speaking of things that she knew from direct personal experience, though in some other matters she seems to be merely passing on the anecdotes of her set. Her reliability on matters that she knew at first hand gains credibility in that there is actually a letter from Stalin to her husband in W, xiii, 18–20, confirming her assertions that the Boss communicated with this middle-level official. An unrelated case of Stalin's arbitrary assignment of a worker to a technically demanding post appears in A. G. Zverev, *Zapiski ministra* (Moscow, 1973) 142–3.
16. Yu. Flakserman, *Gleb Maksimovich Krzizhanovskii* (Moscow, 1964) 172.
17. For example, *Iz istorii magnitogorskogo metallurgicheskogo kombinata i goroda Magnitogorsska* (Cheliabinsk, 1965) 83–5, which did not appear in *Pravda* or *Spravochnik partiinogo rabotnika*.
18. *Guide*, entry no. 300105–3.
19. *Guide*, entry nos. 290117, 290125, 290325, 290503, 290718–2, 290808, 290829, 291225–300110, 300201–2, 300305, 300306, 300410, 300514–4, 300415, 310125–2, 301121, 310426, 310430, 310615–2, 310707, 310815–2, 310929, 311025–1, 320402, 320303, 320619, 320916, 321002–2, 330408, 330521–1. Of these only 320615–2 and 320303 were actually submitted to a meeting of the Central committee.
20. *Guide*, entry no. 310125–2.
21. T. Kirstein, 'Das Ural–Kuzneck–Kombinat (UKK) als objekt einer Entscheidungsprozessanalyse' in G. Erler and W. Süss (eds), *Stalinismus* (Frankfurt am Main, 1982) 167–85; *KPSS*, iv, 398–404.
22. *Istoriia Magnitogorska* (1965) 69–75.

23. *Istoriia Magnitogorska* (1965) 83–5.
24. *Istoriia Magnitogorska* (1965) 7–8.
25. *W*, XIII, 81.
26. Ya. Gugel', 'Vospominaniia o Magnitke', *God XVIII. Al'manakh*, VI, 344.
27. J. Miller, 'Soviet Planners in 1936–1937', in J. Degras and R. W. Davies (eds), *Soviet Planning* (Oxford, 1964) 120.
28. *RDCPSU*, III, 80.
29. *W*, XIII, 161, 239, 181, 183, 185, 219.
30. *Resheniia partii i pravitel'stva po khoziaistvennym voprosam* (Moscow, 1967) II, 136–42.
31. *W*, XIII, 53–82.
32. *W*, VI, 194–6.
33. See p. 129 above; N. A. Ivnitsky, *Klassovaia bo'rba v derevene i likvidatsiia kulachestva kak klassa* (1929–1932) (Moscow, 1972) 298.
34. M. Gorky *et al.* (eds), *Belomor* (New York, 1935) 329; Solzhenitsyn (1974–8) II, 75; P. H. Solomon, 'Soviet Penal Policy, 1917–1934; a Reinterpretation', *Slavic Review*, no. 2 (1980) 195–217.
35. Gorky *et al.* (1935) 88.
36. *W*, XIII, 423–4.
37. Gorky *et al.* (1935) 305. The English translation, which was produced in Moscow, faithfully follows the Russian edition [*Belomorsko–Baltiiskii kanal imeni Stalina* (Moscow, 1924)] except for the omission of an introductory chapter entitled 'The Truth of Socialism' (Russian edition, 11–15). This was written by Gorky on 20 January 1934 (*Letopis'*, IV, 352). It was probably omitted because its praise of Stalin was considered excessive for the western reader at this time. Although the term 'American efficiency' does not appear in the book, it is clear enough that this ethos is implied.
38. I. Averbakh, *Ot prestupleniia k trudu* (Moscow, 1936).
39. Gorky *et al.* (1935) 305–6, 344.
40. *P*, 14 July 1930, 11 February 1934; P. Reiman, *Die Geburt des Stalinismus* (Frankfurt am Main, 1979) 237–46; R. W. Daniels, *The Conscience of the Revolution* (Cambridge, Mass., 1960) 376–7; S. F. Cohen, *Bukharin and the Bolshevik Revolution* (New York, 1973) 349–50.
41. See p. 121 above. R. A. Medvedev, *Let History Judge* (New York, 1971) 142. Kirov publicly stated that Syrtsov and Lominadze had been removed from their positions (*P*, 2 December 1930). R. W. Davies, 'The Syrtsov–Lominadze Affair', *Soviet Studies*, no. 1 (1981) 29–50; M. Buber-Neumann, *Von Potsdam nach Moskau* (Stuttgart, 1957) 232.
42. Davies (1981) 46; *P*, 23, 30 October 1930.
43. Nicolaevsky's assertions appeared in 'Letter of an Old Bolshevik' in the *émigré* periodical *Sotsialisticheskii vestnik*, no. 23–4 (1936) 22–33; no. 1–2 (1937) 17–24, published in English in J. D. Zagoria (ed.), *Power and the Soviet Elite* (New York, 1965), 26–65 (28–30 on Riutin). Here (p. 9) Nicolaevsky acknowledged that he used various materials, in addition to his talk with Bukharin, in composing the 'letter'. Among discussions of the credibility of Nicolaevsky's revelations, see R. M. Slusser, 'The Role of the Foreign Minister', in I. J. Lederer (ed.), *Russian Foreign Policy* (New Haven, Conn., 1962) 221–2; R. A. Medvedev, *Nikolay Bukharin* (New York, 1980) 115–18 (in which he seems to discredit the 'Letter', only to conclude that he accepts it on the whole); J. A. Getty, *Origins of the Great Purges* (Cambridge, 1985) 214–16. The present writer's confidence in the 'Letter' is undermined not only by these critiques but above all by points noted below, p. 361, nn. 42, 43.

A. Ciliga, *The Russian Enigma* (London, 1940) 278–9, maintains that he and Riutin were in the same jail, but does not claim that he actually obtained information from Riutin.

44. Ciliga (1940) 278–9; *KPSS*, v, 90. The fact that Nicolaevsky does not discuss this group detracts from its credibility as a well-informed inside source.
45. *W*, xii, 146.
46. *Stalin. Sbornik statei k piatidesiatiletiiu so dnia rozhdeniia* (Moscow, 1929) especially 167, 258–68; J. L. Heizer, The Cult of Stalin 1929–1939 (Ph.D. dissertation, University of Kentucky, 1977) 65–8, 81–98.
47. *P*, 23 February 1932; *P*, 1, 5 May, 8 August, 22 September 1932; Heizer (1977) 99–104.
48. Heizer (1977) 109; G. Alekseev, 'Kolichestvennye parametry kul'ta lichnosti', *SSSR. Vnutrenie protivorecheniia*, no. 6 (1982) 9.
49. *W*, iii, 105, 146, 264; Heizer (1977) 103–5, 111–14.
50. *Iskusstvo*, no. 1–2 (1933) 74; no. 2 (1933) 60; no. 7 (1937) 59.
51. *Letopis'*, iii, 617–23; 722–52; *w*, xii, 179–83. The idea of the essay was not Gorky's own, but was forwarded on behalf of one Kamegulov [*Arkhiv*, x (2) 256.
52. *Arkhiv*, x, kn. 1, 260–1; R. A. Medvedev, 'New Pages from the Political Biography of Stalin', in R. C. Tucker (ed.), *Stalinism. Essays in Historical Interpretation* (New York, 1977) 119.
53. *P*, 2 May 1933.
54. *P*, 6 February 1933; *P*, 2, 24 March 1933; *P*, 21 April 1933; *P*, 1, 12, 13, 17, 24, 28 May 1933.
55. Heizer (1977) 122.
56. *P*, 21 January 1934; Heizer (1977) 107.
57. *P*, 1 July 1933; Gorky *et al.* (1924) 11–15.
58. *P*, 28 June 1933; *P*, 13 August 1933; *Iskusstvo*, no. 1 (1934) 99, 112; no. 1 (1935) 7; I. Rabinovich, 'Obraz Vozhdia v proizvedenniakh zhivopisi i skulptury', *Arkhitektura SSSR*, no. 12 (1939) 11–21, which sustains the thesis that not much painting and sculpture were devoted to Stalin before 1933.
59. *P*, 3 February 1934.
60. Heizer (1977) 120–22; *P*, 1 June 1933.
61. *Guide*, 250605–1.
62. *Ugolovnyi kodeks BSSR* (Moscow, 1938) art. 67.
63. *KR*, 47.
64. *P*, 25 October 1932; *SS*, xxvi, opp. 128; *SS*, xxx, 424.
65. *RDCPSU*, iii, 115–16; Gorky's absence from the meeting of the 'organizing committee' is verified in *Letopis'*; A. Ovcharenko, 'Sotsialisticheskii realizm v svete mezhdunarodnykh sporov', *Molodaia gvardiia*, no. 9 (1973) 270–2; *P*, 20 August 1934. *Letopis'*, iv, 241. Gorky gave his blessing to 'socialist realism' in his address to the writers' congress in 1934 (*SS*, xxviii, 330).
66. *Arkhiv*, xiv, 376, 497; Zagoria, *Soviet Elite*, 32.
67. *Letopis'*, iv, 37, 126, 154, 157, 501; *Guide*, entry nos. 310730–2, 311010; *Arkhiv*, xiv, 376–7; *SS*, xxx, 424; *P*, 26 September 1932.
68. *Letopis'*, iv, 482 and *passim*; *Arkhiv*, x[2], 372–3.
69. Zagoria (1965) 45; *W*, xii, 181–2; *Arkhiv*, x, kn. 1, 206; Gorky *et al.* (1935) 337–42.
70. R. C. Tucker, 'The Rise of Stalin's Personality Cult', *American Historical Review*, no. 2 (1979) 347–66; J. Barber, *Soviet Historians in Crisis* (New York, 1981) 126–36; A. Nekrich, *Otreshis' ot strakha* (London, 1979) 17–20; L. Kolakowski, *Main Currents of Marxism* (Oxford, 1978) iii 73–6; *W*, xii, 128–34.

71. The problem as a whole is treated in O. Anweiler, *Geschichte der Schule und Pädagogik in Russland vom Ende des Zarenreiches bis zum Beginn der Stalinaera* (Berlin, 1964); for resolutions, *Guide*, entry nos. 300725–2, 310825, 320221, 340515–3; 340609; 360704. S. Allilueva, *Only One Year* (New York, 1969) 6. 'Paedology' attempted to supplant the conventional concept of education with some idea of dealing with the 'whole child'.
72. *P*, 1 January 1934.
73. S. Fitzpatrick (ed.), *Cultural Revolution in Russia 1928–1931* (Bloomington, Ind., 1977) 207–40; S. F. Starr, *Melnikov: Solo Architect in a Mass Society* (Princeton, NJ, 1978).
74. A. Fadeev (ed.), *Vstrechi s Stalinym* (Moscow, 1939) 84–93; V. A. Vesnim *et al.*, 'Nezabyvaemye vstrechi', *Arckhitektura SSSR*, no. 12 (1939) 6–10.
75. Fitzpatrick (1977) 237; A. Kopp, *Town and Revolution* (New York, 1970).
76. *KPSS*, ᴵᵛ, 544–8; *Istoriia Moskvy* (Moscow, 1957) ᵛᴵ(2), 32, 41; *Stalin. K. shestidesiatiletiiu (Khudozhestvennaia literatura)* (1940) 66–7.
77. *P*, 4 May 1935; *KR*, 68–70.
78. 'Nezabyvaemye vstrechi' (1939) 6–10. *Istoriia Moskvy* (1957) ᵛᴵ(2), 43.
79. *P*, 11 July 1935; *General'nyi plan rekonstruktsii goroda Moskvy* (Moscow, 1935); 'Nezabyvaemye vstrechi' (1939) 6–10.
80. 'Nezabyvaemye vstrechi' (1939) 6–10.

NOTES TO CHAPTER 9 MURDER

1. *W*, xᴵᴵ, 182.
2. One might argue that Stalin arranged the judicial murder of two of his own people in 1929, but in each case the circumstances are murky. Neither victim was precisely a Bolshevik, both having ties with some other faction. And it is questionable that Stalin had the primary role in ordering their conviction and execution. This is especially true of Jacob Bliumkin, an ex-Socialist Revolutionary, who had been fortunate to be allowed to turn his coat after having participated in the assassination of the German ambassador in 1918, and who later appeared to betray the confidence of the police in visiting the exiled Trotsky. See I. Deutscher, *The Prophet Outcast* (New York, 1963) 84–91. The other victim, Sultan-Galiev, an adherent of Turkic nationalism, had worked for the Soviet regime, then turned against it. See E. H. Carr, *A History of Soviet Russia. The Interregnum 1923–1924* (New York, 1954) 286–9.
3. J. E. Abbe, *I Photograph Russia* (New York, 1934) 278; E. Lermolo, *The Face of a Victim* (New York, 1955) 227–31, 227–9; A. Kuusinen, *The Rings of Destiny* (New York, 1974) 91–3; M. Vishniak in *Novoe russkoe slovo*, 21 December 1949, exemplify the different versions of the murder thesis. A more recent version comes from Shatunovskaia, *Zhizn' v Kremle* (New York, 1982) 199, who maintains that the widow of Sergo Ordzhonikidze said that she had washed Nadezhda's corpse and saw only one bullet wound, which was in the back of the skull. Shatunovskaia interprets this as evidence that Stalin shot his wife from behind. It seems equally possible, however, that this was an exit wound of the sort that temporarily confused physicians in the case of John F. Kennedy. A suicidal shot through the mouth might have created such an exit wound without leaving an obvious entry wound. Shatunovskaia (205) also considers that statements by her own interrogator in 1947 implied that she knew too much about the death of Nadezhda, and that this meant that the

officer knew that Stalin had murdered her. But it is equally possible that he meant that she knew the death was suicide, something that the public was not supposed to know.

4. S. Allilueva, *Twenty Letters to a Friend* (New York, 1967) 123–5, also 99.

5. Allilueva (1967) 122–6; Shatunovskaia (1982) 195; *KR*, 143.

6. Allilueva (1967) 95–6, 108; *Only One Year* (New York, 1969) 382; *The Faraway Music* (New Delhi, 1984) 190.

7. Allilueva (1967) 107, 152; Allilueva (1969) 385; Allilueva (1984) 117; *KR*, 301; A. Tuominen, *The Bells of the Kremlin* (Hanover, 1983) 163–6; BKM, 87; M. Djilas, *Conversations with Stalin* (New York, 1962) 109; B. Bajanov, *Avec Stalin dans le Kremlin* (Paris, 1930) 138.

8. Allilueva (1967) 54, 113, 106; Shatunovskaia (1982) 191.

9. Allilueva (1969) 400. This dates Nadezhda's final dinner party as 8 November, because Svetlana showed her mother an essay she had written about what she saw on the 7 November parade the day before. Thus this was not a large state affair on the evening of the day of the parade.

10. Allilueva (1967) 108–10.

11. Allilueva (1967) 112–13; Allilueva (1969) 149; 154; V. Serge, *Portrait de Staline* (Paris, 1940) 94–5.

12. Allilueva (1969) 381–2; Allilueva (1967) 12.

13. Allilueva (1969) 18–22; A. S. Yakovlev, *Tsel' zhizni* (Moscow, 1969) 505; author's visit to the outside of the compound, December 1983.

14. In November 1930 Stalin received an American journalist at the Central Committee building [E. Lyons, *Assignment in Utopia* (New York, 1937) 383], but in 1932 he received another American journalist in the Kremlin [Abbe (1934) 57].

15. Yakovlev (1969) 505, 584; Yakovlev (1972) 497; G. K. Zhukov, *The Memoirs of Marshal Zhukov* (New York, 1971) 280–1.

16. Yakovlev (1972) 497–500; Tuominen (1983) 164; A. Barmine, *One Who Survived* (New York, 1945) 212 (a witness to one such meeting); C. E. Bohlen, *Witness to History 1929–1969* (New York, 1973) 145; K. P. S. Menon, *The Flying Troika* (London, 1963) 29.

17. Allilueva (1967) 15, 97–9, 122; Allilueva (1969) 412; R. A. Medvedev, *Nikolay Bukharin* (New York, 1980) 110.

18. Allilueva (1967) 143–4, 96–7, 150–1; V. Kravchenko, *I Chose Freedom* (New York, 1946) 398–9.

19. Allileuva (1969) 113; Allilueva (1984) 167, 169.

20. *P*, 14 July 1930, 11 February 1934.

21. E. Zaleski, *Stalinist Planning for Economic Growth 1933–1952* (Chapel Hill, NC, 1980) 129; there was a diminishing number of published interventions by the party in industrial matters in the mid-1930s compared to the period of the First Five-Year Plan. [See *Guide*, 162–89; M. Fainsod, *Smolensk under Soviet Rule* (Cambridge, Mass., 1958) 185–7; *Istoriia KPSS v shesti tomakh* (Moscow, 1971) iv, kn. 2, 432.

22. J. A. Getty, *Origins of the Great Purges* (Cambridge, 1985) 36–57; *RDCPSU*, iii, 124–9.

23. For the case that Stalin was not behind the killing of Kirov, Getty (1985) 207–10.

24. *BSE*, xxi, 114–29.

25. *The Writings of Leon Trotsky (1934–1935)* (New York, 1974) 112–56. Nicolaevsky, who as a Menshevik also hoped for signs of worker opposition to Stalin's regime, also deceived himself on this matter and did not attribute the murder to Stalin when he wrote about it in the 1930s [J. Zagoria (ed.),

Power and the Soviet Elite (New York, 1965) 37–44]. After Stalin's death and Khrushchev's revelations he reconsidered (95–7).

26. *KSG*, 128; *CSP*, IV, 17.

27. *KSG*, 130; *CSP*, IV, 197.

28. A. Antonov-Ovseenko, *The Time of Stalin* (New York, 1980) 89; R. A. Medvedev, *Let History Judge* (New York, 1971) 158–9. In general Antonov-Ovseenko does not inspire confidence, making use of extensive imagined conversations and sometimes erring on verifiable information [L. van Rossum, 'A. Antonov-Ovseenko's Book on Stalin: Is it Reliable?', *Soviet Studies*, no. 3 (1984) 445–7; and n. 32 below]. Medvedev usually displays much more concern with the reliability of his evidence, but on this matter seems rather credulous, citing, for example, a pointless story about a friend of Kirov who supposedly was set upon on the street by two men who tried, with little success, to beat him with 'iron objects' [Medvedev (1971) 161].

29. Author's observation in Kirov Museum, Leningrad, April 1976.

30. Zagoria (1965) 30; *KR*, 61.

31. Medvedev (1971) 156; Antonov-Ovseenko (1980} 79; *History of the Communist Party of the Soviet Union* (Moscow, 1962) 486; article by L. S. Shaumian, *P*, 7 February 1964.

32. The evidence on the number of ballots cast against Stalin in the election of the Central Committee is unsatisfactory. Both Medvedev (1971, 156) and Antonov-Ovseenko (1980, 79) make reference to the testimony of a supposed member of the election commission of the Seventeenth Party Congress, V. M. Verkhovykh. At least it can be confirmed from the published record of the congress that he was a delegate and hence eligible to serve on this commission [*Semnadtsatyi s'ezd Vsesoiuznoi Kommunisticheskoi Partii (bol'shevikov)* (Moscow, 1934) 686]. Depending on which account you prefer, he said that there were either 270 or 292 votes against Stalin. But Antonov-Ovseenko elaborates on this report in such a way as to undermine the credibility of whatever source leaked information to the dissident historians. First, he maintains that Verkhovykh, in oral testimony, recalled that the correct number was not 292 but 289. Second, and more important, he claims tht Verkhovykh refused to give an official inquiry any written statement. Finally, and most unsettling, Antonov-Ovseenko describes the alleged refusal of another supposed member of the electoral commission of 1934 to acknowledge that there were more than 'two or three' votes against Stalin. Apart from these numbers, the trouble with this story is that the person in question, one Napoleon Andriasian, could not have served on the mandate commission of the congress of 1934 because, according to the record of that event, he was not a delegate.

Another version of Stalin's alleged troubles with this election maintains that he was elected only because the Central Committee was expanded at the last minute [G. Boffa, cited in B. Levytsky, *The Uses of Terror* (London, 1971) 79]. This must be incorrect, because the size of the Committee was in fact unchanged with respect to full (not candidate) members. *KR*, 49, gives his version of the election.

33. *P*, 11 February 1934; Zagoria (1965) 35; R. Conquest, *The Great Terror* (New York, 1973) 42. Nicolaevsky [Zagoria (1965) 92] suggested that Stalin had been removed as General Secretary, noting that the announcement of the new Secretariat omitted the formula of previous announcements that Stalin had been 'confirmed' in this office. In 1934 his name merely appeared first in the list of secretaries. But in 1939 when the Secretariat was reconstituted after the next party congress, when Stalin was surely in the fullness of his power,

having slaughtered all suspected opposition, the reference to confirmation
again was omitted, and this time Stalin's name appeared in its alphabetical
place in the list (*P*, 23 March 1939). Nor was the office of General Secretary
specifically mentioned after the Nineteenth Party Congress in 1952 (*P*, 17
October 1952). On the other hand, the announcement of the new Politburo in
1934 enhanced Stalin's status by placing his name first in the list (whereas it
had been alphabetical in the corresponding announcement in *P*, 14 July 1930)
and by accompanying it with a photograph of Stalin that dominated the
smaller ones of his colleagues on that body. Quite possibly Stalin thought that
the explicit reference to the confirmation of the General Secretary, alone
among all elected posts, called attention too emphatically to the power of the
Central Committee to withhold this prize.

34. *S*, xvi, 2–10.
35. *P*, 2 December 1934; S. V. Krasnikov, *S. M. Kirov v Leningrade* (Leningrad,
    1966) 196.
36. A. Orlov, *The Secret History of Stalin's Crimes* (New York, 1953) 21–2. In
    general the testimony of this police defector should be treated with reserve.
    He was out of the Soviet Union during most of the period he wrote about and
    must have relied mainly on gossip that was making the rounds in the police.
    Some of this probably was based on fact, but Orlov does not appear to have
    been able, or perhaps willing, to make a serious effort to discriminate
    between the more reliable stories and the less probable. Although he claimed
    that he took with him from Russia 'secret data' on Stalin, none of this has
    ever appeared. Rarely can his assertions be verified from other sources, but it
    is reasonably safe to describe as imaginary his assertion (44) that Stalin once
    explained to foreign 'writers' why there was no documentary evidence in the
    purge trials. In fact Stalin's few press interviews are well established, and
    none deal with any such thing. However, Orlov's assertions on the Kirov
    assassination seem more credible than most of his writing. His claims to inside
    knowledge on this subject were comparatively modest at the time he wrote
    his first memoir, and at that time he did not make the easy sensationalist case
    that Stalin arranged the killing. His testimony on this matter gains credibility
    by its assertion that Nikolaev had been taken into custody at Smolny with a
    gun in his possession, but was released by the police (17). This was
    corroborated by Khrushchev (*CSP*, iv, 197) almost twenty years after Orlov's
    book was published. Granted, this point cropped up in the trial of Bukharin
    [*Report of Court Proceedings: The Anti-Soviet 'Bloc of Rights and Trotskyites'*
    (Moscow, 1938) 572], which Orlov could have read, but he could scarcely
    have guessed that precisely this part of the lengthy fabrications at the trial
    would be confirmed in 1961.
37. *P*, 2, 6 December 1934.
38. *P*, 3–10 December 1934; I. Rabinovich 'Obraz Vozhdia v proizvedenniiakh
    zhivopisi i skulptury', *Arkhitektura SSSR*, no. 12 (1939) 16.
39. *P*, 8 December 1934; *P*, 29 November 1934 for the basic party resolution on
    which this state decree was based. *S*, xvi, 106.
40. *P*, 5 December 1934; *KSG*, 128.
41. *P*, 6 December 1934. All memoirists agree that there were many arrests in
    Leningrad [for example, Conquest (1973) 85], but there is no serious basis for
    an estimate.
42. On the first expulsion of Zinoviev and Kamenev in 1927, *RDCPSU*, 308;
    KPSS, iv, 72. On their first readmission, R. W. Daniels, *The Conscience of
    the Revolution* (Cambridge, Mass., 1960) 371. On their second expulsion in
    1932, *P*, 11 October 1932. On their second readmission in 1933 the exact

dates are uncertain, but their speeches to the Seventeenth Party Congress in January 1934 demonstrate that they had been readmitted by that time [*Semnadtsatyi s'ezd* (1934) 492–7, 516–27]. On their third expulsion, approximately coincidental with their arrest, *P*, 23 December 1934.

This reasonably well-documented record does not harmonize with Nicolaevsky's 'Letter of an Old Bolshevik' [Zagoria (1965) 46], which states that Kamenev was expelled from the party three times and three times repented, and that his last expulsion occurred in the 'winter of 1932–33'. It is hard to know what to make of these statements. Since Nicolaevsky knew that Kamenev was convicted of serious crimes in 1935 and 1936, he cannot mean that Kamenev was still a party member at that time by virtue of his third 'repentance', for it is entirely contrary to Soviet practice to allow people to remain in the party while on trial for treason. Moreover, three expulsions by the winter of 1932–3 is one more than the records indicate. Kamenev did address the party congress of January–February 1934, and Nicolaevsky states that this speech represented a 'theoretical justification' for 'personal dictatorship' (of Stalin). In fact the text of the speech had been published at the time Nicolaevsky wrote, and it does not justify this assertion. Kamenev did refer repeatedly to Stalin's wonderful leadership, which he compared with Lenin's, and he spoke of the dictatorship of the proletariat. But he did not speak of personal dictatorship.

43. *P*, 20–3 December 1934, 16, 18 January 1935; *RDCPSU*, III, 168–9; *Report of Court Proceedings: The Trotskyite–Zinovievite Terrorist Conspiracy* (Moscow, 1936) I, 174. On this matter Nicolaevsky again undermines his credibility, maintaining that the increased sentence of Kamenev occurred in the spring of 1935 and that a result of this trial was the fall of Yenukidze. In fact Yenukidze's fall was in June, well before the second trial of Kamenev (on Yenukidze, see pp. 176–80 below), so Nicolaevsky's error is not merely a question of a month or two but of alleged sequence and causality. This undermines the credibility of his allegation (57) that the second trial of Kamenev was connected to the alleged trial of some Kremlin guards who supposedly considered the assassination of Stalin. There is no reason to believe this story.

44. *P*, 24 January 1935; *KSG*, 130. Getty (1985) 113–16, shows that very few members were expelled from the party in Smolensk province despite the dispatch of a secret directive of 18 January 1935, calling for a purge of followers of Zinoviev and Kamenev.

45. *P*, 4 March, 8 June 1935.

46. *P*, 13, 16 June 1935.

47. Allilueva (1967) 33, 88, 109, 112–13., 141; *P*, 10 November 1932.

48. Allilueva (1967) 19–20, 137, 414; Allilueva (1969) 376; *P*, 17 December 1953; *KR*, 338.

49. Allilueva (1967) 19–20; *KSG*, 208; *Iskusstvo*, no. 1 (1938); *P*, 25 April 1935.

50. L. Sumbadze, 'Proekt planirovki i rekonstruktsii g. Gori', *Arkhitektura SSSR*, no. 12 (1939) 42–8; Allilueva (1967) 203–4; *P*, 7 October 1935.

51. *P*, 16 January, 4 March 1935, 20 December 1937; A. Yenukidze, *Bol'shevistskie nelegal'nie tipografii* (Moscow, 1930); L. P. Beria, *On the History of the Bolshevik Organizations in Transcaucasia* (New York, 1935).

NOTES TO CHAPTER 10 YEZHOVSHCHINA

1. S. Allilueva, *Only One Year* (New York, 1969) 358–65.
2. *KSG*, 158; *KR*, 311.
3. E. K. Poretsky, *Our Own People* (London, 1969) 182.
4. S. Allilueva, *Twenty Letters to a Friend* (New York, 1967) 166; L. D. Trotsky, *Writings of Leon Trotsky (1937–1938)* (New York, 1970) 88; L. Shatunovskaia, *Zhizn' v Kremle* (New York, 1982) 159–1.
5. J. A. Getty, *Origins of the Great Purges* (Cambridge, 1985) 48–91; T. H. Rigby, *Communist Party Membership in the U.S.S.R. 1917–1967* (Princeton, N.J. 1968) 204–9.
6. *RDCPSU*, III, 168–9, 175–6; *S*, XIV, 191–2.
7. I. Deutscher, *The Prophet Outcast* (New York, 1963) 347–9, 390–6; J. Van Heijenoort, *With Trotsky in Exile* (Cambridge, Mass., 1978) 99.
8. Getty (1985) 119–22; J. A. Getty, 'Trotsky in Exile: the Founding of the Fourth International', *Soviet Studies*, no. 1 (1986) 28–9; P. Broué, 'Trotsky et le bloc des oppositions de 1932', *Cahiers Leon Trotsky*, no. 5 (1980) 5–37. Although much of Orlov's narrative concerns the preparation of the trial of Zinoviev and Kamenev, he was unaware of this evidence, which inspires doubt about the reliability of his sources concerning the 1936 trial. I. N. Smirnov is not to be confused with A. P. Smirnov, who was connected with Tolmachev and Eismont.
9. *The Case of Leon Trotsky* (New York, 1937) in general and especially 89, where Trotsky denies having had any direct connection with Smirnov. He states that his son, L. Sedov, met Smirnov by chance on the street in Berlin, but in the light of the later correspondence this seems doubtfully fortuitous.
10. Getty (1985) 120; Getty (1986) 28; Deutscher (1978) 175.
11. See pp. 175–6 above.
12. *Report of Court Proceedings: The Trotskyite–Zinoviev Terrorist Centre* (Moscow, 1936) 24, 81, 158; *RDCPSU*, III, 170–1; Deutscher (1978) 26–7. A. Orlov, *The Secret History of Stalin's Crimes* (New York, 1953) 42–156, offers a good deal of alleged detail on the preparation of the case, which appears to reflect peripheral gossip more than the crux of the matter. He has much to say about the minor case of Anna Arkus, the ex-wife of a man implicated in the 1936 trial, but nothing about the major case of Yevdokimov.
13. *RDCPSU*, III, 168–81. This document was known only in a brief excerpt in Stalin's speech to the February–March meeting of the Central Committee (*S*, XIV, 192–3) until it turned up in the Smolensk archives. Its contents refute the assertion in Nicolaevsky [in J. Zagoria (ed.), *Power and the Soviet Elite* (New York, 1965) 63] that the trial came as a surprise to the party rank and file, the Central Committee and even some members of the Politburo. The absence of any reference to this document by Orlov also further undermines his claim to have been well informed on the preparation of the trial.
14. Smirnov confessed only on 5 August and Yevdokimov on the 10th. See *Report of Court Proceedings* (1936) 15, 17.
15. *Stalinskii marshrut prodolzhen* (Moscow, 1937) 26–7. K. E. Bailes, *Technology and Society under Lenin and Stalin* (Princeton, NJ, 1978) 382–93; *Stalinskie sokoly* (Moscow, 1937) 119–23.
16. *P*, 15 August 1936.
17. *Stalinskii marshrut prodolzhen* (1937) 27–8; *KR*, 79.
18. *P*, 21 August 1936. This translation makes no attempt to retain the rhyme and metre of the original.

19. *Report of Court Proceedings* (1936); Deutscher (1978) 335–45, 487–8; Getty (1986) 27–8.

20. *KSG*, 130; *Report of Court Proceedings* (1936) 11. Before Broué and Getty had examined the relevant material in the formerly closed section of the Trotsky archive, many writers believed that 'four years' referred to the Riutin affair, but this is no longer plausible. The Riutin affair did not figure in the scenario of the trial.

21. *Report of Court Proceedings* (1936) 55–6, 65, 115; *P*, 21 August 1936. R. A. Medvedev, *On Stalin and Stalinism* (New York, 1979) 99, relates that Tomsky's son believed that the suicide occurred just after Stalin visited Tomsky at his apartment, bearing a bottle of wine, and that a violent argument occurred between them. But it is reasonably clear that Stalin was not in Moscow at the time (*KSG*, 130), and the official report of Tomsky's death states that it occurred at his dacha in Bolshev, not in Moscow.

22. *P*, 27 September 1936.

23. *KR*, 131–2, 93; N. E. Rosenfeldt, *Knowledge and Power* (Copenhagen, 1978) 131–2; Getty (1985) 116–18.

24. *P*, 13 October 1937. Dzerzhinsky had been a candidate member of the Politburo for a short time just before his death, but he was not then in police work.

25. *KR*, 96; *P*, 23 April, 16, 28 July, 21 December 1937.

26. *P*, 6 July, 12, 13 August, 20–6 November 1936, R. A. Medvedev, *Let History Judge* (New York, 1971) 206, deals with arrests in Transcaucasia, which he attributes to Beria, not Yezhov.

27. *KSG*, 138. Medvedev (1971) identifies about 1000 individuals who became victims of the terror, but places only the merest handful of arrests before 1937. He states that there were hundreds of arrests in 1935–6, but still he calls this 'selective' and notes that the higher circles were 'scarcely touched' (166–7). The Smolensk party archives shows no wave of arrests of 'counter-revolutionaries' in 1936. See J. A. Getty, 'Party and Purge in Smolensk, 1933–1937', *Slavic Review*, no. 1 (1983) 66–73.

28. Getty (1985) 87–91.

29. R. A. Medvedev, *Nikolay Bukharin* (New York, 1980) 129–30, which also reports that Stalin called off investigators who were searching Bukharin's apartment, not a publicized step, but one that might circulate by rumour. *P*, 10 September 1936.

30. *Report of Court Proceedings: The Anti-Soviet Trotskyite Centre* (Moscow, 1937) 6. Radek was under arrest at least as early as 4 December 1936 (8). Piatakov was interrogated at least as early as 4 January 1937, but presumably not for the first time (13).

31. *RDCPSU*, ii, 121. Some writers have assumed that there was at least one session of the Central Committee in the autumn of 1936, but this is groundless. The error evidently stems from the work of A. Uralov (Avtorkhanov), *The Reign of Stalin* (London, 1953) 43–7, although it now seems that his account was a garbled version of the February–March 1937 meeting of the Committee, omitting Stalin's speech. In general, Central Committee meetings have always been major, formal events, and there is no good reason to believe that any ever were held that were not subsequently reported.

32. *P*, 29 January 1937; *Report of Court Proceedings* (1937) especially 71, 100–1, 121, 219, 229.

33. *P*, 21, 25 January, 8–14 February 1937.

34. *P*, 1, 2, 19 February 1937.

35. Bukharin did not get beyond the point of shutting himself in his room with a revolver [Medvedev (1980) 129–30]. On Kaganovich, Medvedev (1971) 310; *KR*, 47–8.
36. Molotov's speech to the February–March 1937 meeting of the Central Committee cites numerous cases of the unmasking of Trotskyite wreckers in industry. The implication is clear that all of these were recent (*P*, 21 April 1937).
37. *KR*, 84; Allilueva (1969) 262; Medvedev (1980) 134.
38. Medvedev (1971) 193–6. Medvedev turned up conflicting stories about the fate of Ordzhonikidze's brother, Papuliia. One has the police sending Sergo a falsified record of Papuliia's interrogation after the victim had been shot, while the other has Yezhov telling Sergo that his brother is alive in jail. *KR*, 85; *KSG*, 212; I. Dubinskii-Mukhadze, *Ordzhonikidze* (Moscow, 1964) 6–7; *P*, 20–22, 24 February 1937.
39. *RDCPSU*, iii, 181–7; *KSG*, 132.
40. *P*, 6 March 1937; Medvedev (1980) 135; *Izvestiia*, 17 March 1937; *KRG*, 136–8 (ellipsis in the original); H. Kostiuk, *The Fall of Postyshev* (New York, 1954) 18–24.
41. *S*, xvi, 189–247; *KSG*, 238.
42. *S*, xvi, 189, 201, 190.
43. *S*, xvi, 201, 213–18.
44. *S*, xvi, 228–47.
45. *RDCPSU*, iii, 182–4; *KSG*, 124, 132.
46. *P*, 11 February 1934, 22 March 1939 contain the lists of Central Committee members elected at those times. B. Levytsky (ed.), *The Stalinist Terror of the Thirties* (Stanford, Calif., 1974) 501–4. The four old Bolsheviks who survived were Krupskaia, Krzhizhanovsky, Badeev, Petrovsky. The symbols of special interests were Nikoaeva (women), Litvinov (western anti-Fascist opinion), Manuilsky (western Communists). The unaccountably fortunate were I. G. Makarov and G. A. Veinberg, if in fact they did survive to 1953 or died of natural causes before that year. The Politburo members who survived were Andreev, Beria, Voroshilov, Zhdanov, Kaganovich, Kalinin, Mikoyan, Molotov, Stalin, Khrushchev, Shvernik and Bulganin. Beria's dependent who survived was Bagirov. The members of Stalin's secretariat who survived were Mekhlis and Poskrebyshev.
47. The noted victims were (from the Secretariat) Bauman, Yakovlev, Knorin; (narkoms) Bubnov, Ivanov, Kosior, Liubimov, Lobov, Mezhlauk, Razumov, Rukhimovich; (federal republics) Chubar, Chuvryn, Ikramov, Kabakov, Krinitsky, Mirzoian, Ryndin, Sheboldaev; (other categories) Antipov, Kosarev, Piatnitsky, Sulimov and Lebed [Levytsky (1974) 501–4].
48. *KSG*, 146, 148; Medvedev (1980) 137–8; *KPSS*, v, 290.
49. *S*, xiv, 207–8 (final ellipses only is in the original). *P*, 6 July 1936 accused the party secretary of Dnepropetrovsk, M. M. Khataevich, a Central Committee member who later perished in the Yezhovshchina, of dragging his feet in the removal of Trotskyites. *P*, 12 August 1936 says that the Saratov province secretary protected Trotskyites. An article in *Pravda* of 22 May 1937, 'Defenders of Trotskyite–Japanese–German Spies and Diversionists', states that it was necessary for a cell to uncover these agents because the higher party authorities were not doing it. *P*, 5 June 1937 reported that the party secretary and deputy secretary of the Azov–Black Sea province protected Trotskyites. On the problem of insubordination in general, Getty (1985) 149–53.

50. R. A. Medvedev, *On Stalin and Stalinism* (Oxford, 1979) 101; Getty (1985) 168–70, 173; *S*, xvi, 231, which also mentions Vainov of Yaroslavl as a bad example.

51. T. H. Rigby, 'Stalinism and the Mono-organizational Society', in R. C. Tucker (ed.), *Stalinism* (New York, 1977) 53–76.

52. The literature on the terror as a whole is far too large to summarize here. A few works that help to illustrate the present argument are: A. I. Solzhenitsyn, *The Gulag Archipelago* (New York, 1974–8); E. Ginzburg, *Into the Whirlwind* (London, 1967); A. V. Gorbatov, *Years Off My Life* (London, 1964); I. G. Ehrenburg, *Eve of War: 1933–41* (London, 1963).

53. *P*, 8, 10, 11, 13, 17, 21, 25, 27, 28 September 1937.

54. G. Alekseev 'Kolichestvennye parametry kul'ta lichnosti', *SSSR. Vnutrenie protivorechiia* (1982) 9; J. L. Heizer, The Cult of Stalin 1929–1939 (Ph.D. dissertation, University of Kentucky, 1977) 132, 137–8, 141; R. H. McNeal (ed.), *Stalin's Works. An Annotated Bibliography* (Stanford, Calif., 1967) 165–6.

55. Allilueva (1967) 189, states that his first post-war vacation was his first since 1937.

56. *KSG*, 154.

57. *KSG*, 140–50; *P*, 18 September 1964; *KR*, 106–7; *CSP*, iv, 181.

58. Allilueva (1969) 386; *CSP*, 181. F. Maclean, *The Eastern Approaches* (London, 1966) 119–20, maintains that he saw Stalin's face at a small window high above the court-room at the trial of Bukharin, but no other visitor ever noticed such a thing.

59. See pp. 62–3 above.

60. M. N. Tukhachevsky, *Izbrannye proizvedeniia* (Moscow, 1964) i, 12–13; J. Erickson, *The Soviet High Command* (London, 1962) 411–12; *Report of Court Proceedings* (1937) 105, 146; *Marshall Tukhachevskii* (Moscow, 1965) 234.

61. Medvedev (1971) 300–1; Erickson (1962) 433–6.

62. Iu. P. Petrov, *Partiinoe stroitel'stvo Sovetskoi armii i flote* (Moscow, 1964) 299–300; *KR*, 88; *CSP*, iv, 197. The latter statement implies that neither Khrushchev nor later Soviet researchers ever saw the documents that supposedly were forged in Germany and knew of them only through the foreign press.

63. *P*, 11, 12 June 1937.

64. *P*, 12–27 June 1937.

65. Petrov (1964) 300–1 (original ellipsis); R. Conquest, *The Great Terror* (New York, 1963) 620.

66. *Report of Court Proceedings: The Anti-Soviet 'Bloc of Rights and Trotskyites'* (Moscow, 1938) especially 277, 279, 283, 284; *P*, 3 April 1937, which announced the arrest of Yagoda. (One of the extremely rare cases of publication of news of an arrest.)

67. *Report of Court Proceedings* (1938) 36, 50–5, 157–8, 383, 438–509, 553, 691.

68. *Report of Court Proceedings* (1938) 513–51, 559–60, 584–623; *P*, 26 June 1935.

69. *Report of Court Proceedings* (1938) 799–800; Medvedev (1971) 145, 200; *P*, 15–19 March 1938; *Stalin. K. shestidesiatiletiiu so dnia rozhdeniia (Khudozhestvennaia literatura)* (1940) 341–2.

NOTES TO CHAPTER 11   PEACE

1. See pp. 231–3 below; *P*, 12 December 1937.
2. *S*, XIV, 256–65.
3. *S*, XIV, 265–6; *P*, 12 February 1937.
4. *Report of Court Proceedings: The Trotskyite–Zinovievite Terrorist Centre* (Moscow, 1936) 130.
5. *RDCPSU*, III, 187–95; Yu. P. Petrov, *Partiinoe stroitel'stvo Sovetskoi armii i flote* (Moscow, 1964) 300.
6. *Report of Court Proceedings: The Anti-Soviet 'Bloc of Rights and Trotskyites'* (Moscow, 1938), R. Conquest, *The Great Terror* (New York, 1973) 604–6.
7. *KR*, 47–8, 96–7, 108; R. A. Medvedev, *Let History Judge* (New York, 1971) 310.
8. *KR*, 96, 310–11; S. Allilueva, *Twenty Letters to a Friend* (New York, 1967) 124; R. Conquest, *Inside Stalin's Secret Police* (Stanford, Calif., 1985) 71.
9. J. A. Armstrong, *The Politics of Totalitarianism* (New York, 1961) 73.
10. *Biulleten' Verkhovnogo Suda SSSR*, no. 2 (1964) 34–5; R. A. Medvedev, *On Stalin and Stalinism* (Oxford, 1979) 108, cites two resolutions concerning the reform of the procuracy and police, which he places in the autumn of 1938. *KR*, 101, confirms these but attributes them to a meeting of the Central Committee in February 1939. No formal meeting of that body occurred at that time, and there must have been so few members alive and at liberty that a full meeting would have been a strange sight. Perhaps Khrushchev's memory erred by a few months on the timing and he confused a formal meeting of the Committee with some sort of enlarged session of the Politburo or a special meeting under the aegis of the Secretariat. See also A. Antonov-Ovseenko, *The Time of Stalin* (New York, 1980) 124.
11. A. S. Yakovlev, *Tsel'zhizni* (1969) 509.
12. Yezhov was not on the list of congress delegates from Moscow, which would have been his constituency (*P*, 5 March 1939), and his name was missing from the list of delegates, in the record of the congress, which was published later that year. Thus it is impossible to give credence to the story in Medvedev (1979) 109–10, attributed to one E. Feldman, who was in fact a delegate to the congress. In this version Yezhov was humiliated by Stalin at the meeting of senior delegates to the congress that met to select nominees for the new Central Committee. But as a non-delegate Yezhov would not have been present there. Moreover the story has it that Yezhov sought to defend himself by saying that he had 'unmasked' his former aid Frinovsky, who in time was indeed purged. But at the time of the Congress Frinovsky was still in good standing and could not have been referred to as an arrested enemy. His name appeared in the list of delegates published later that year [*Vosemnadtsatyi s'ezd Vsesoiuznoi Kommunisticheskoi Partii (bol'shevikov). Stenograficheskii otchet* (Moscow, 1939) 721]. According to Admiral N. G. Kuznetsov [*Nakanune* (Moscow, 1966) 216–17], who was a delegate, it was during the congress that Frinovsky asked to be relieved of the most of narkom of the navy, to which he had been transferred from the police.
13. *KR*, 110–14; N. S. Patolichev, *Measures of Maturity* (Oxford, 1983) 66–70; *KSG*, 160.
14. Yakovlev, (1966) 264–5; A. V. Gorbatov, *Years Off My Life* (London, 1964) 147; S. Allilueva, *Only One Year* (New York, 1969) 151.
15. B. Levytsky (ed.), *The Stalinist Terror in the Thirties* (Stanford, Calif., 1974) 501–4. It is not certain that Postyshev was shot. G. Mariagin, *Postyshev*

(Moscow 1965) 298, says that his life was 'cut short' in December 1940, *CSP*, IV, 198; Allilueva (1967) 74–9.

16. Conquest (1985) 97–9; K. E. Bailes, *Technology and Society under Lenin and Stalin* (Princeton, NJ, 1978) 396–8.

17. Yakovlev (1966) 193; Patolichev (1983) 84.

18. *PL*, 746–803, especially 778, 781–2; Conquest (1973) 632; *KSG*, 124.

19. I. Deutscher, *The Prophet Outcast* (New York, 1963) 483–505.

20. *P*, 11 February 1934, 22 March 1939; *Istoriia Kommunisticheskoi Partii Sovetskogo Soiuza v shesti tomakh* (Moscow, 1964–70) v, kn. 1, 22.

21. *PL*, 790–7; *P*, 7 May 1941.

22. Allilueva (1967) 151; A. Eden, *Facing the Dictators. The Memoirs of Anthony Eden* (Boston, 1962) 171, 175; J. K. Paasiviki, *Mein Moskauer Mission 1939–1941* (Hamburg, 1966) 61; C. de Gaulle, *The Complete War Memoirs* (New York, 1964) 753.

23. Eden (1962, 171; W. S. Churchill, *The Second World War. VI. Triumph and Tragedy* (Boston, 1953) 345. Paasiviki (1966) 61.

24. *W*, vii, 283; *W*, xi, 209, xiii, 309; A. G. Meyer, 'The War Scare of 1927', *Soviet Union/Union Soviétique*, no. 5 (1978) 1–25; S. Fitzpatrick, 'The Foreign Threat during the First Five-Year Plan', *Soviet Union/Union Soviétique* no. 5 (1978) 26–35; J. P. Sontag, 'The Sovier War Scare of 1926–27', *Russian Review* no. 1 (1975) 66–77.

25. M. Buber-Neumann, *Von Potsdam nach Moskau* (Stuttgart, 1957) 284; F. Borkenau, *European Communism* (New York, 1953) 71–8.

26. *W*, xi, 307–24; *W*, xii, 261–2; E. H. Carr, *The Twilight of the Comintern* (New York, 1982) 403–4.

27. *PL*. 593.

28. Carr (1982) 150–2; Eden (1962) 170–5; G. Warner, *Pierre Laval and the Eclipse of France* (London, 1968) 81–2; *P*, 10 June 1935. On 20 November 1933 Stalin had talked with the newly arrived American ambassador, William C. Bullitt, but this was at a private dinner at Voroshilov's apartment rather than as a formal diplomatic meeting. See B. Farnsworth, *William C. Bullitt and the Soviet Union* (Bloomington, Ind., 1967) 10–11.

29. R. C. Tucker, 'The Emergence of Stalin's Foreign Policy', *Slavic Review*, no. 4 (1977) 563–91; A. M. Nekrich, 'Stalin i natsistskaia Germaniia', *Kontinent*, no. 24 (1980) 239–61.

30. *DGFP*, vii, 228; *PL*, 753–6, 759.

31. *DGFP*, vii, 62–4, 76–7, 87–90, 114, 116, 157, 168.

32. H. Trevor-Roper (ed.), *Hitler's Table Talk* (London, 1973) 267; *DGFP*, vii, 229.

33. *DGFP*, vii, 220, 223, 295–6, 356.

34. *KR*, 126–8. This is not strictly accurate, for Khrushchev states that Ribbentrop arrived in Moscow on a Sunday, when in fact he came on a Wednesday and left the following day.

35. *DGFP*, viii, 79–80, 92, 104, 130.

36. *DGFP*, viii, 159–61, 164–5.

37. *DGFP*, viii, 309–10, 320; B. Meissner, *Die Sowjetunion, die Baltischen Staaten und das Volkrecht* (Köln, 1956) 57–67.

38. *Paasiviki* (1966) 61–9, 83–6, 100–6.

39. *Kuznetsov* (1966) 214–28, 227, 257–60.

40. *DGFP*, viii, 718–22, 752–4.

41. *DGFP*, ix, 40–1, xi, 855.

42. *DGFP*, vii, 227; *KR*, 134.

43. *DGFP*, x, 207; *P*, 14 April 1941.

44. *DGFP*, xi, 317, 327–8, 353–4, 541–80.
45. *RDCPSU*, iv, 81; J. L. Heizer, The Cult of Stalin 1929–1939 (Ph.D. dissertation, University of Kentucky, 1977) 134–5, sustains this impression with a statistical study of pictures of Stalin, alone and in groups, in *Pravda*. Following 1934 the number of solo pictures increased far more than did pictures of Stalin with his associates, including Lenin.
46. *S*, vix, 274.
47. Heizer (1977) 171–3.
48. These and many other examples are in S. Bogomazov, 'Deti o Staline', *Krasnaia nov'*, no. 12 (1939) 246–54.
49. This poem, and many others like it, is in *Tvorchestvo narodov SSSR* (Moscow, 1937) 87–159.
50. *Samoe dorogoe* (Moscow, 1939) especially 27–31; F. Miller, 'The Image of Stalin in Soviet Russian Folklore', *Russian Review*, no. 1 (1980) 50–67.
51. *Tvorchestvo* (1937) frontispiece; opp. 90.
52. E. Yaroslavsky, *O Tovarishche Staline* (Moscow, 1939); H. Barbusse, *Staline. Un monde nouveau vu a travers un homme* (Paris, 1935).
53. *Teatr*, no. 11–12 (1939) 56. E. Proffer, *Mikhail Bulgakov. Life and Work* (Ann Arbor, Mich, 1984) 183–223, 322–5, 479–85, 515–23.
54. *P*, 10 March 1939.
55. Edward J. Brown, *Mayakovsky. A Poet in the Revolution* (Princeton, NJ, 1973) 370.
56. Exhibit in museum, Gori.
57. N. Mandelshtam, *Hope against Hope* (New York, 1970) 13.
58. R. Hingley, *Boris Pasternak, 1890–1960* (New York, 1983), 116–17; *Boris Pasternak, 1890–1960. Colloque de Cerisy-la-Salle* (Paris, 1979) 44; N. Saliutskii, 'Eshche odna versiia zvonka Stalina Pasternaku', *Pamiat'* (1979) 438–41. 'Mandelstam's "Ode to Stalin"', *Slavic Review*, no. 4 (1975) 683–8.
59. Hingley (1983) 127–8.
60. *Gorky. Materialy i issledovaniia* (Moscow, 1941) iii, 268–70; K. S. Kravchenko, *Salin v izobrazitel'nom iskusstve* (Moscow, 1939) especially 5, 128.
61. Rabinovich (1939) 12; S. D. Merkurov, 'Mysli, menia vdoknovenie', *Oktiabr'* no. 12 (1939) 82. Merkurov's statues at the entrance of the Volga–Don Canal and at the All-Union Agricultural Exposition (see Rabinovich, above) are examples of the immobile style.
62. *P*, 7 February 1935, 5–6 June 1936. 6 June appears to have been the inception of the usage 'Stalin Constitution'.
63. *P*, 12 June–7 August 1936.
64. *P*, 1 February 1935.
65. *PL*, 665, 679–712; J. H. Meisel and E. S. Kozera, (eds), *Materials for the Study of the Soviet System* (Ann Arbor, Mich. 1950) 242–66. In January 1934 in his report to the party congress Stalin had alluded briefly to the idea that the USSR had entered 'socialism', but the point was not stressed at the time (*W*, xiii, 5).
66. *P*, 26 November 1936, 27 January 1937.
67. *P*, 9–19 September 1938; E. Yaroslavskii, 'Ideinaia sokroishchnitsa partii', *Partiinoe stroitel'stvo*, no. 8 (1940) 11–12; *W*, i, xiv.
68. A. Tertz, *On Socialist Realism* (New York, 1960) 158; T. Zelenev 'Izdanie i rasprostranenie proizvedenii I. V. Stalina', *Bol'shevik*, no. 23 (1949) 90.
69. *P*, 21 December 1939; *Stalin. K. shestidesialiletiiu* (Moscow, one version from *Pravda* and one from *Khudozhestvennaia Litetrature* (1940); A. Fadeev (ed.), *Vstrechi s Stalinym* (Moscow, 1939); G. Aleksandrov 'Sovetskoe kino',

Oktiabr', no. 21 (1939) 112–16; *Staline i o Staline* (Moscow, 1940); K. S. Kravchenko, *Stalin v izobrazitel'nom iskusstve* (Moscow, 1939).
70. *Joseph Stalin. A Short Biography* (Moscow, 1940); *P*, 20 December 1939; *KSG*, 214–16.
71. *S*, xiv, 406; speech at Tadzhik celebration, partially exhibited at the museum in Gori. *P*, 23 April 1941 shows that Stalin attended a reception for those attending this affair and that Molotov spoke on this occasion. But Stalin's remarks were not released to the press, probably because he thought better of their gloomy impression. In his speech he uses the word *vozhd'* (leader), which by that time was applied to only one living man.

NOTES TO CHAPTER 12   WAR

1. *DGFP*, xii, 537.
2. *Istoriia Velikoi Otechestvennoi Voiny Sovetskogo Soiuza* (Moscow, 1960) i, 460; J. Erickson, *The Road to Stalingrad*, Vol. i, *Stalin's War with Germany* (London, 1975) 32; A. S. Yakovlev, *Tsel' zhizni* (Moscow, 1966) 180–1, 198–200; S. Bialer, *Stalin and His Generals* (New York, 1969) 155–6.
3. H. E. Salisbury, *The 900 Days. The Seige of Leningrad* (New York, 1970) 75; G. K. Zhukov, *The Memoirs of Marshal Zhukov* (New York, 1971) 225.
4. S. Allilueva, *Only One Year* (New York, 1969) 392; *FRUS (Teheran)*, 513; Erickson (1975) 89; A. D. Coox, 'Japanese Foreknowledge of the Soviet–German War, 1941', *Soviet Studies*, no. 2 (1972) 571.
5. Salisbury (1970) 81; Erickson (1975) 87–93; Zhukov (1971) 230, 232.
6. Zhukov (1971) 230, 232.
7. A. Seaton, *Stalin as Warlord* (London, 1976) 101–2; Zhukov (1971) 236; Erickson (1975) 124.
8. Zhukov (1971) 237–8, 255–6 (here the English translation does not seem to me to capture the meaning of the Russian original, which refers to physical condition rather than mood), 268; Bialer (1969) 210, 236–8; R. A. Medvedev, *Let History Judge* (New York, 1971) 458; Seaton (1976) 104–5. None of the three main sources for the opinion that Stalin abdicated leadership at the opening of the war were in Moscow at the time, and none reveal how they learned of his alleged abdication. They are Khrushchev (*KSG*, 176); I. M. Maisky ['Dni ispitanii', *Novyi mir*, no. 12 (1964) 163]; A. Grechko [R. A. Medvedev, *On Stalin and Stalinism* (Oxford, 1979) 123–4]. Similarly unconvincing is the assertion in *KR*, 169, that 'I'd seen him when he had been paralyzed by his fear of Hitler.' In fact Khrushchev, who was in Kiev, did not see Stalin at all in the early part of the war. In his speech of 1956 he contradicts this accusation by instead claiming that Stalin's fault early in the war was interference with military operations, hardly the same as paralysis (*KSG*, 176).
9. *P*, 23 June–2 July 1941; Zhukov (1971) 237.
10. Zhukov (1971) 237–8; *P*, 1 July 1941; *S*, xv, 203–4.
11. *KSG*, 178.
12. Maisky (1964) 165. The recorded version of Stalin's speech available at the Imperial War Museum, London, does not display the nervousness Maisky heard, presumably on a poor overseas radio transmission. On the other hand, the recorded version might not have been the one that went out on the radio.

13. *GPW*, 7–17. The general point that Stalin deliberately espoused themes of Russian nationalism is not in doubt. However, the story in Medvedev (1979) 124, that Stalin showed the draft of the speech of 3 July to the old Bolshevik Elena Stasova is hard to credit. There is no evidence that Stalin 'continued to value her opinion', and the story maintains that the speech included references to 'Suvorov and Kutuzov'. Supposedly Stasova objected to this nationalist allusion to tsarist military heroes and Stalin told her that he intended to use this kind of material because Marxism–Leninism alone would not rouse the people. But Stalin did not in fact refer to Suvorov and Kutuzov in this speech. They first appeared in his addresses on 7 November 1941 (*GPW*, 29).
14. *P*, 20 July 1941; Zhukov (1971) 279–80; *KR*, 169–70.
15. Zhukov (1971) 280–1, 282–4; Yakovlev (1969) 503.
16. Zhukov (1971) 284–5; Vasilevsky, *A Lifelong Cause* (Moscow, 1981) 449; A. Bryant, *Triumph in the West* (New York, 1959) 62.
17. Erickson (1975) 42; Bialer (1969) 352–3; *KSG*, 180.
18. Vasilevsky (1981) 451.
19. Vasilevsky (1981) 438–9; Salisbury (1970) 306; Seaton (1976) 161.
20. Bialer (1969) 451–2, 454–5; Seaton (1976) 162; Erickson (1975) 381; Salisbury (1970) 255; N. S. Patolichev, *Measures of Maturity* (Oxford, 1983) 147; Vasilevsky (1981) 424, 433; S. M. Shtemenko, *The Last Six Months* (New York, 1977) 76–7.
21. Zhukov (1971) 276–7, 287–9, 294–5, 297–300; *KR*, 171; Erickson (1975) 198–212, 210.
22. I. M. Maiskii, *Vospominaniia sovetskogo diplomata 1925–1945 gg.* (Moscow, 1971) 584–5; Zhukov (1971) 320–3, 361; Vasilevsky (1981) 117; S. Allilueva, *Twenty Letters to a Friend* (New York, 1967) 165–9; M. Djilas, *Conversations with Stalin* (New York, 1962) 38; Medvedev (1979) 129; W. A. Harriman and E. Abel, *Special Envoy to Churchill and Stalin* (New York, 1975) 107. On the Moscow scene in general, L. Gouré and H. S. Dinerstein, *Moscow in Crisis* (New York, 1955) 194–225.
23. Bialer (1969) 308–9; Zhulov (1971) 336; *GPW*, 18–46.
24. Zhukov (1971) 337, 339–40, 347–9, 352–3.
25. Seaton (1976) 145; *KR*, 184–7; *SKG*, 178–80.
26. Seaton (1976) 145, 150; Erickson (1975) 371; Vasilevsky (1981) 178–9.
27. Seaton (1976) 146–7, 156; Zhukov (1971) 376.
28. Zhukov (1971) 380–6, 404–5, 447–9; Vasilevsky (1981) 449–50.
29. *P*, 3 February–25 July 1943.
30. Seaton (1976) 181–4; Bialer (1969) 362–7; Stalin, *O Velikom Otechestvennoi Voiny Sovetskogo Soiuza* (Moscow, 1943). The first mention of the new name for the war appears to occur in *P*, 31 July 1943. From the early days of the war the expression 'patriotic war' had been used in official statements, but the full name was established only in July/August 1943.
31. Khrushchev in 1956 (*KSG*, 178) called the trip 'a short ride', which is not really descriptive of a 400-km return trip over war-torn roads. Vasilevsky (1981) 451, states that the trip took two days and included two fronts. Voronov describes part of it [Bialer (1969) 438–9].
32. *Atlas istorii SSSR* (Moscow, 1950) iii, 45; Seaton (1976) 183, 210–16, 225–6, 243.
33. Zhukov (1971) 589; Bialer (1969) 516–17; A. D. Chandler (ed.), *The Papers of Dwight David Eisenhower* (Baltimore, 1970) Vol. iv, 2583–4; S. A. Ambrose, *Eisenhower* (New York, 1983) i, 430.
34. Zhukov (1971) 621–2; Seaton (1976) 253.
35. W. S. Churchill, *The Second World War. IV. The Hinge of Fate* (Boston,

1950) 477–89; W. S. Churchill, *The Second World War. VI. Triumph and Tragedy* (Boston, 1953) 227–39; Harriman and Abel (1975) 362; *FRUS Tehran)*; *FRUS (Yalta)*; *FRUS (Potsdam)*; Corres., I, II.

36. A. Eden, *The Reckoning. The Memoirs of Anthony Eden* (Boston, 1965) 335–41; 478–82. *FRUS* (1941) I, 802–14; *FRUS* (1945) V, 299; Harriman and Abel, (1975) 296, 315, 249, 434, 502, 516, 536; *FRUS* (1942) 437.

37. *Corres.*, I, doc. nos. 36, 37, 49, 83; *Corres.*, II, doc. nos. 391, 418, 488, 494, 496, 499; *FRUS* (1942) III, 545; *FRUS* (1944) III, 1409, IV, 973, 1125; *FRUS* (1945) V, 881–2; Ambrose (1983) I, 429–30; G. F. Kennan, *Memoirs* (Boston, 1967) vol. II, 276–7; *DPSR*, I, 205–13, 231–46, 489–501; *DPSR*, II, 309–22; V. Mastny 'The Beneš–Stalin–Molotov Conversations in December 1943: New Documents', *Jahrbücher für Osteuropaischen Geschichte*, no. 20 (1972) 367–402; *FRUS* (1944) IV, 1428; C. de Gaulle, *The Complete War Memoirs* (New York, 1964) 737–57; Harriman and Abel, (1975) 494–5.

38. Mastny ('Beneš', 1972) 399; *FRUS (Potsdam)*, 250–1; *Corres.*, II, doc. nos. 17, 55, 56, 57, 83, 101, 105, 114, 127, 130, 132, 133; *Corres.*, II, doc. no. 1701.

39. K. Eubank, *Summit at Tehran* (New York, 1985) 178–9; Eden (1965) 564; C. E. Bohlen, *Witness to History, 1929–1969* (New York, 1973) 143.

40. *Corres.*, II, doc. no. 21; Churchill (1950) 493.

41. F. L. Loewenheim *et al.* (eds), *Roosevelt and Churchill. Their Secret Wartime Correspondence* (London, 1975) 196; *W*, X, 146–53; *FRUS (Yalta)*, 922–3.

42. *GPW*, 21–7; Harriman and Abel (1975) 89.

43. *GPW*, 25.

44. *Corres.*, I, doc. nos. 3, 12; *FRUS* (1942) III, 577.

45. Churchill (1950) 478–89; *Corres.*, I, doc. nos. 107, 112, 165; *Corres.*, II, doc. nos. 58, 79, 90, 92. On the naming of the war, see p. 250 above.

46. V. Mastny, *Russia's Road to the Cold War* (New York, 1979) 79–80; V. Mastny, 'Stalin and the Prospects of a Separate Peace in World War II', *American Historical Review*, no. 5 (1972) 1365–88. *FRUS* (1943) I, 687; *Corres.*, I, 232, 234.

47. *FRUS (Tehran)*, 539, 553–5; E. Roosevelt, *As He Saw It* (New York, 188–90.

48. *FRUS (Tehran)*, 510, 600–3; *FRUS (Yalta)*, 611–23, 901; *FRUS (Potsdam)*, 59, 120–1; 128. The last, referring to Stalin's challenge to his allies' honesty, is one of a number of items that western note-takers at the meetings omitted. *Corres.*, II, doc. nos. 157, 162, 169, 177.

49. *Corres.*, II, docs. no. 281, 283, 285, 286, 287, 288, 290. Allen Dulles and others met with the German General Karl Wolff on 19 March 1945, thirteen days before Roosevelt denied that there had been negotiations. See A. Dulles, *The Secret Surrender* (New York, 1966) 114–15.

50. Eden (1965) 335, 342; *DPSR*, I, 205–6, 233, 238–9.

51. *Corres.*, I, doc. nos. 150, 152, 156; *Corres.*, II, doc. no. 80.

52. *FRUS (Tehran)*, 594–9.

53. *FRUS (Tehran)*, 603–4; *Corres.*, I, doc. no. 391–2, doc. nos. 235, 236, 243, 250, 257; *Corres.*, II, doc. nos. 159, 160.

54. *Corres.*, I, doc. nos. 313, 321–3; *DPSR*, II, 313.

55. *Corres.*, I, doc. no. 381, de Gaulle (1964) 737–57; *Sovetsko-frantsuzkie otnoshenie vo vremia Velikoi Otechestvennoi Voiny 1941–1945 gg.* (Moscow, 1959) 375–82.

56. *FRUS (Yalta)*, 669–70, 853–4; *Corres.*, I, doc. nos. 416, 418, 430, 436, 439, 450, 456; *Corres.*, II, doc nos. 284, 293, 298.

57. *FRUS (Tehran)*, 503–2.

58. *FRUS (Yalta)*, 665–7; *TYP*, 86–9. The latter includes material that the western note-takers omitted.

NOTES TO CHAPTER 13 GENERALISSIMUS

1. G. K. Zhukov, *The Memoirs of Marhsal Zhukov* (New York, 1971) 652. *P*, 28 June 1945; S. M. Shtemenko, *General'nyi shtab v gody voiny* (Moscow, 1973) II, 499–500.
2. *Monument I. V. Stalina* (Erivan, 1952).
3. S. Volkov (ed.), *Testimony. The Memoirs of Dmitri Shostakovich* (New York, 1979) 256–64.
4. *Zhurnal Moskovskoi Patriarkhii*, 12 September 1943; G. Yakunin, 'Moskovskaia Patriarkhiia i "kult lichnosti" Stalina', *Russkoe vozrozhdenie*, n. 2 (1978) 110–14; *S*, XVI, 93–6. The balloon-born image was repeated on Stalin's seventieth birthday (*Ogonek*, 1949, no. 52).
5. *KR*, 289, 296–301; M. Djilas, *Conversations with Stalin* (New York, 1962) 151, 158, 161; S. Allilueva, *Only One Year* (New York, 1969) 384–6; E. Hoxha, *With Stalin* (Toronto, 1980) 147; Shtemenko (1973) 39–40; T. Toranska, *Oni* (London, 1985) 254–5.
6. S. Allilueva, *Twenty Letters to a Friend* (New York, 1967) 101, 159–63; 169, 185, 211; Allilueva (1969) 370; Zhukov (1971) 635–6. Yakov did not attend the Frunze Academy, as Svetlana recalls (1967, 157), but the Dzerzhinsky Artillery Academy, which issued him a diploma on display in the museum in Gori.
7. Allilueva (1967) 123, 133, 165, 167–8, 185, 212–15; L. Shatunovskaia, *Zhizn' v Kremle* (New York, 1982) 250; D. Bialer, *Stalin and His Generals* (New York, 1966) 455.
8. S. Allilueva, *The Faraway Music* (New Delhi, 1984) 7, 21; Allilueva (1967) 134, 154–5; Allilueva (1969) 369, 384; Djilas (1962) 110.
9. Allilueva (1967) 173–7.
10. Allilueva (1967) 177–81, 185.
11. Allilueva (1967) 68, 186–8, 193, 197–200; Allilueva (1969) 372.
12. Allilueva (1967) 37, 40–1, 50, 55–6; 60–3, 196; Allilueva (1969) 154, 162, 373; Shatunovskaia (1982) 156–8.
13. Zhukov (1971) 635; N. S. Patolichev, *Measures of Maturity* (Oxford, 1983) 284; Bialer (1966) 563; Allilueva, (1967) 188; *FRUS* (1949) V, 653; W. A. Harriman and E. Abel, *Special Envoy to Churchill and Stalin* (New York, 1975) 511–16. R. A. Medvedev, *On Stalin and Stalinism* (Oxford, 1979) 155, reflects the rumours of Stalin's illness in reporting that he was so ill in 1949 that he could not say a word at the ceremony in honour of his birthday. But the foreign Communists who saw him at just this time found him fit enough and talking. See Hoxha (1980) 127–61, and Wu Xiuquan, unpublished translation of his memoir, which appeared in Chinese in *Shijie zhishi*, no. 16 (1983).
14. *P*, 19 December 1945. In 1946 *Pravda* shows Stalin present in Moscow on 9 September and again on 21 December; in 1947 missing the ceremony in honour of Moscow's anniversary, 6 September, and signing a guest book on a cruiser on the Black Sea on 19 September, but reappearing in Moscow for the election on 21 December. In 1948 the US ambassador reported that he left Moscow shortly after 23 August [W. B. Smith, *My Three Years in Moscow* (New York, 1950) 252], and Stalin's daughter states that they returned to Moscow in November [Allilueva (1967) 194, and also 189–90, *KR*, 306].
15. Harriman (1975) 511–16; Hoxha (1980) 128; *P*, 15 October 1948; *KR*, 299; A. S. Yakovlev, *Tsel'zhizni* (1966) 448–50; Allileuva (1967) 190.
16. *BSE*, VI, 260; *KSG*, 240, 242. Khrushchev's tirade against Stalin in 1956 said

that Stalin used 'the terminology of a card player' in naming the subcommissions. But there is nothing unusual about referring to such a body by the number of its members. The Department of State translation confusingly uses the translation 'quintet', and so on, which is the terminology of a musician, not of a card player.

17. Khrushchev specifically attributed to Stalin responsibility for the deportations (*KR*, 190). In general, A. M. Nekrich, *The Punished Peoples* (New York, 1978).
18. A. Werth, *Russia. The Postwar Years* (London, 1971) 35; T. Dunmore, *Soviet Politics, 1945–1953* (London, 1984) 22–3, 28–9; T. H. Rigby, *Communist Party Membership in the U.S.S.R. 1917–1967* (Princeton, NJ, 1968) 52.
19. *BSE*, xv, 605; *KR*, 231–2. In this case Stalin did see the decree in question, but only because Malenkov and Beria wanted to discredit Khrushchev in the eyes of the Boss. Patolichev (1983) 283–7.
20. J. A. Armstrong, *The Politics of Totalitarianism* (New York, 1961) 173–87.
21. L. I. Brezhnev, *Trilogy. The Little Land. Rebirth. The Virgin Lands* (New York, 1978) 159–61; A. G. Zverev, *Zapiski Ministra* (Moscow, 231–5; *P*, 16 December 1947.
22. Allilueva (1967) 105, 209–11; Allilueva (1969) 388–9.
23. *KR*, 228–44; Zverev (1973) 244; *KPSS*, vi, 173–9; S. Talbott (ed.) *Khrushchev Remembers. The Last Testament* (Boston, 1974) 112–14.
24. *S*, xvi, 29–34.
25. J. Stalin, *Marxism and Linguistics* (New York, 1951). His editing of poetic translations from the Georgian is documented in the museum in Gori. On Albanian, Hoxha, (1980) 80–4, 120–1; on the Indian languages, K. P. S. Menon, *The Flying Troika* (London, 1963) 27–8. On Marr's theories in general, L. C. Thomas, *The Linguistic Theory of N. Ja. Marr* (Berkeley, Calif., 1957).
26. J. Stalin, *Economic Problems of Socialism in the U.S.S.R.* (Moscow, 1952).
27. D. Joravsky, *The Lysenko Affair* (Cambridge, Mass., 1970) 39–54, 295–307.
28. Joravsky (1971) 58–62, 83–130; Z. A. Medvedev, *The Rise and Fall of T. D. Lysenko* (New York, 1971) 3–99.
29. Joravsky (1971) 130–9; *P*, 21 December 1949.
30. W. Hahn, *Postwar Soviet Politics* (Ithaca, NY, 1982) 69, 78–84; L. R. Graham, *Science and Philosophy in the Soviet Union* (New York, 1972) 443–50.
31. A. A. Medvedev (1971) 109–35; A. N. Studitsky, 'Fly-lovers and Man-haters', *Journal of Heredity*, no. 11 (1949) 312–14.
32. *P*, 24 October 1948; Joravsky (1971) 130–1, 141–2, 154; *Velikie stroiki kommunizma* (Moscow, 1950); *KSG*, 224.
33. *S*, xvi, 67; *FRUS* (1947) vi, 732, 735, *P*, 27 October 20, 31 December 1945, 4, 25, 26 January, 22 February, 17, 5, 19 April, 8, 29 May, 16 June, 4 July, 22 December 1946, 17 March, 16 April 1947, 3 August 1948, 18 July, 16 August 1949.
34. *P*, 11 January, 10 April, 15 October 1947, 15 January, 10 June 1950, 6 April, 17 July, 23 August, 8 December 1952, 18 February 1953.
35. *S*, xvi, 35–43, 45–7, 53–6, 65–70, 105–7, 173–80, 183–5, 305–6, 316–17.
36. M. D. Shulman, *Stalin's Foreign Policy Reappraised* (Cambridge, Mass., 1963) 80–103, 199–237; *P*, 21 December 1939.
37. *Corres.*, ii, doc. no. 365; *FRUS* (1945) v, 883; *FRUS* (1946) vi, 736; *FRUS* (1947) ii, 343.
38. *S*, xvi, 1–4; 54, 56, 75–80, 86, 305; *FRUS* (1945) v, 882.
39. *S*, xvi, 35–43; *FRUS* (1946) vi, 734–5.

40. *S*, xvi, 56, 183–5; Djilas (1962) 153; J. Erickson, *The Road to Berlin*. Vol. ii, *Stalin's War with Germany* (Boulder, Col., 1983) 79–80; Zhukov (1971) 675; S. M. Shtemenko, *The Soviet General Staff at War, 1941–1945* (Moscow, 1970) 347–8, says that Stalin did not realize that an entirely new weapon was involved. His evidence for this is that the General Staff received no new instructions in this connection. But this discounts the probability that Stalin's agents had kept him abreast of the Manhattan project. He presumably addressed his exhortation to Kurchatov through Molotov, as a member of the State Committee of Defence, which had control of the atomic project, rather than through military, whom Stalin did not entrust with the matter.
41. A. Eden, *The Reckoning. The Memoirs of Anthony Eden* (Boston, 1965) 335; *FRUS (Tehran)*, 600; *FRUS (Yalta)*, 611–16; *S*, xv, 198. The Soviet delegation to a dismemberment commission established at Yalta lost interest in this matter as early as March 1945 [J. K. Snowden, *The German Question, 1945–1973* (London, 1975) 69].
42. *FRUS* (1947) ii, 342; *S*, xvi, 55.
43. V. M. Molotov, *Voprosy vneshnei politiki* (Moscow, 1948) 577–84. Granted, the size of military force that the Soviet Union, America, Britain and France would be permitted to retain in Germany in connection with a proposed Control Commission was not specified, so perhaps Stalin did not intend to take much chance on the question of a Soviet military presence in Germany. See *FRUS* (1947) ii, 279.
44. *FRUS* (1948) ii, 999–1006, 1065–1071; W. B. Smith, (1950) 243; *S*, xvi, 105–7, 316–17.
45. H. G. Skilling, ' "People's Democracies" in Soviet Theory', *Soviet Studies*, no. 1 (1951) 16–33; no. 2 (1951) 131–49.
46. *FRUS* (1945) ii, 752–6; E. Kardelj, *Reminiscences* (London, 1982) 40–1.
47. R. H. McNeal (ed.), *International Relations among Communists* (Englewood Cliffs, NJ, 1967) 51–3.
48. McNeal, *Relations* (1967) 54–8; Kardelj (1982) 101–2; Djilas (1962) 127–33.
49. *P*, 11, 17 April, 24, 27 May, 21, 26 July 1946, 26 February, 19 April, 12, 24 July 1947, 17 January, 4, 18 February, 17 March, 8 December 1948.
50. For example, Djilas (1962) 142–7; Hoxha (1980) 127–58, 163–216; Wu Xiuquan (1983); *KR*, 371–2.
51. Hoxha (1980) 62, 65, 76–7, 93, 163–200; Djilas (1962) 143, 154, 172–9, 181–2; 172–9, 181–2; V. Dedijer, *The Battle Stalin Lost* (New York, 1971) 31–3, 188; Kardelj (1982) 103–8, 187.
52. Royal Institute of International Affairs, *The Soviet–Yugoslav Dispute* (London, 1948) 14–15.
53. *KSG*, 200; McNeal, *Relations* (1967) 65–8; Dedijer (1971) 204; Hoxha (1980) 142.
54. Harriman and Abel, (1975) 532; *FRUS* (1945) ii, 758.
55. Wu Xiuquan (1983); R. S. Simmons, *The Strained Alliance* (New York, 1975) 59.
56. Wu Xiuquan (1983); McNeal, *Relations* (1967) 69–71.
57. Wu Xiuquan (1983).
58. *KR*, 368; *P*, 21 August 1952; *S*, xvi, 316–17.

NOTES TO CHAPTER 14 MORTALITY

1. *P*, 3, 22 December 1949.
2. *Ogonek* no. 52 (1949) 25; *Iosifu Vissarionovichu Stalinu. Akademiia Nauk* (Moscow, 1949); G. Yakunin 'Moskovskaia patriarkhiia i "kutt lichnosti" Stalina', *Russkoe vozrozhdenie*, no. 1 (1978) 104–9.
3. *P*, 21, 22 December 1949.
4. *P*, 6–20 December, 1949; *Ogonek* no. 50 (1949) 10–13, no. 51 as a whole; no. 52, 1–9; *L'Humanité*, 17, 24, December 1949.
5. *P*, 20 December 1949.
6. *KR*, 260–1, 307–10.
7. W. Hahn, *Postwar Soviet Politics* (Ithaca, NY, 1982) 101–13; *KR*, 253, 284; R. A. Medvedev, *On Stalin and Stalinism* (Oxford, 1979) 150; S. Allilueva, *Only One Year* (New York, 1969) 384–5; M. Djilas, *Conversations with Stalin* (New York, 1962) 155.
8. Hahn (1982) 122–35; *KR*, 246–58; *KSG*, 194–6; *P*, 9 September 1947, 13 March 1949.
9. *KR*, 252–7; R. Conquest, *Power and Policy in the USSR* (London, 1961) 98.
10. *KR*, 299–300; Allilueva (1969) 387–8; *Report of Court Proceedings: The Anti-Soviet 'Bloc of Rights and Trotskyites'* (Moscow, 1938) 559–60; Medvedev (1979) 151 and author's observations in the Moscow Metro.
11. *W*, II, 52 (while savouring it himself, Stalin attributed the reference to a pogrom to Alexinsky); see p. 17 above; *DPSR*, I, 241; *KR*, 263.
12. S. Allilueva, *Twenty Letters to a Friend* (New York, 1967) 196; Allilueva (1969) 153–4; V. Shatunovskaia, *Zhizn' v Kremle* (New York, 1982) 240, 250f., 308–9. *New York Times*, 14 January 1948.
13. *KR*, 260–1; Allilueva (1967) 196; G. Meir, *My Life* (New York, 1975) 206–8; A. Goldberg, *Ilya Ehrenburg: Revolutionary, Novelist, Poet, War Correspondent, Propagandist* (New York, 1984) 231–2.
14. N. Cherkasov, *Zapiski sovetskogo aktera* (Moscow, 1953) 380; *S*, XIV, 230–1.
15. *KR*, 311–12; Conquest (1961) 129–33; *New York Times*, 25 December 1954 on Ignatiev's promotion, the exact date of which remains uncertain.
16. *KR*, 276, 281, 307; *P*, 6 October 1952, 28 April 1964; *CSP*, I, 99–124, 133–9, 235–6.
17. *CSP*, I, 1–20, 133; *KR*, 271.
18. *P*, 17 October 1952. *KR*, 279–82; see p. 274 above.
19. Allilueva (1967) 205–6; *KR*, 290.
20. Allilueva (1967) 126–7; Allilueva (1969) 394; *KR*, 275.
21. Conquest (1961) 163–9; Allilueva (1967) 207; *KR*, 282–7; *KSG*, 202–4. Crankshaw's implication that Khrushchev might have been involved in the instigation of the affair (*KR*, 282) is not persuasive, considering that the affair was dangerous to Khrushchev's presumed ally Ignatiev.
22. *P*, 13 January 1953; *KR*, 286.
23. Two rather different versions of Ilya Ehrenburg's response to an alleged statement by Jewish intellectuals, favouring deportation, appear in Goldberg (1984) 281–2 and Medvedev (1979) 159–60. On other versions see Shatunovskaia (1982), who thinks that the plan was in place as early as 1948 (336–7); L. I. Pliushch, *History's Carnival* (New York, 1979) 183; V. Grossman, *Forever Flowing* (New York, 1972) 27, which reports the variant that the Jews were to be shipped to Central Asia to build a canal; A. Antonov-Ovseenko, *The Time of Stalin* (New York, 1980) 290–1, thinks that it was only the Jews of the industrial regions, and that some Jews would

be permitted to remain in Moscow and Leningrad but would have to wear
yellow stars. D. K. Shipler, in *Russia. Broken Idols, Solemn Dreams* (New
York, 1983) 135, states that 100 000 Jews actually were deported from
Moscow to the Lena River in Siberia, which is certainly not true.

24. A. M. Nekrich, *Otreshis' ot strakha* (London, 1979) 97, 106; *New York Times*, 4 September 1975.
25. Medvedev (1979) 157; Allilueva (1969) 393.
26. *P*, 4 March 53; H. E. Salisbury, *A Journey for Our Times* (New York, 1983) 436–7.
27. *KR*, 316–20 and Allilueva (1967) 5–14, provide the main basis for the present discussion, except where otherwise noted.
28. Allilueva (1967) 215–16.
29. Allilueva (1967) 23.
30. J. A. Armstrong, *The Politics of Totalitarianism* (New York, 1961) 241–9; *KSG*, 316–17.
31. Allilueva (1967) 207.
32. *P*, 4, 5 March 1953.
33. *P*, 6 March 1953; *RDCPSU*, IV, 22–4.
34. *P*, 7 March 1953; H. E. Salisbury, *Moscow Journal. The End of Stalin* (Chicago, 1961) 341; E. Evtushenko, *A Precocious Autobiography* (New York, 1963) 84–7.
35. *P*, 7, 10 March 1953.
36. *KR*, 345–53; *KSG*, 88–252; *RDCPSU*, IV, 58–72.
37. *CSP*, IV, 122, 124, 130, 168, 175, 180–2, 195–201.
38. *Istoriia SSSR s drevneishikh vremen do nashikh dnei* (Moscow, 1971) IX.
39. *P*, 3 November 1987.

NOTES TO CHAPTER 15   JUDGEMENTS

1. *KR*, 283.
2. C. E. Bohlen, *Witness to History, 1929–1969* (New York, 1973) 219.
3. K. Marx and F. Engels, *Werke* (Berlin, 1969) IV, 22.
4. *KR*, 392.
5. S. Allilueva, *Twenty Letters to a Friend* (New York, 1967) 32.
6. *KR*, 307.
7. Allilueva (1967) 204; W. A. Harriman and E. Abel, *Special Envoy to Churchill and Stalin* (New York, (1975) 362; A. Tuominen *The Bells of the Kremlin* (Hanover, 1983) 162; A. S Yakovlev, *Tsel' zhizni* (Moscow, 1969) 508.

Additional Reading

Adams, A. E., *Stalin and His Times* (New York, 1972).

Bortoli, G., *The Death of Stalin* (New York, 1975).

Daniels, R. W. (ed.), *A Documentary History of Communism* (New York, 1960).

de Jonge, A., *Stalin and the Shaping of the Soviet Union* (New York, 1986).

Deutscher, I., *Stalin. A Political Biography* (New York, 1949).

Franklin, B. (ed.), *The Essential Stalin. Major Theoretical Writings, 1905–1952* (New York, 1972).

Feis, H., *Churchill, Roosevelt, Stalin: The War They Waged and the Peace They Sought* (Princeton, NJ, 1957).

Feis, H., *Between War and Peace: The Potsdam Conference* (Princeton, NJ, 1960).

Feis, H., *From Trust to Terror: The Onset of the Cold War* (Princeton, NJ, 1970).

Fischer, L., *The Life and Death of Stalin* (New York, 1952).

Grey, I., *Stalin. Man of History* (New York, 1979).

Hingley, R., *Joseph Stalin: Man and Legend* (New York, 1974).

Hyde, H. M., *Stalin. The History of a Dictator* (New York, 1971).

Levine, I. D., *Stalin* (New York, 1931).

Ludwig, E., *Stalin* (New York, 1942).

Lyons, E., *Stalin. Tsar of all the Russias* (London, 1941).

McCagg, W., *Stalin Embattled, 1943–1948* (Detroit, 1978).

McNeal, R. H., *The Bolshevik Tradition: Lenin, Stalin, Khrushchev* (Englewood Cliffs, NJ, 1963).

Medvedev, R. A., *All Stalin's Men* (Oxford, 1983).

Souvarine, B., *Stalin. A Critical Survey of Bolshevism* (New York, 1939).

Taubman, W., *Stalin's American Policy. From Entente to Detente to Cold War* (New York, 1982).

Tolstoy, N., *Stalin's Secret War* (London, 1981).

Tucker, R. C., *Stalin as Revolutionary 1879–1929* (New York, 1973).

Ulam, A., *Stalin: The Man and His Era* (New York, 1973).

Urban, G. (ed.), *Stalinism. Its Impact on Russia and the World* (New York, 1982).

Wolfe, B. D., *Three Who Made a Revolution. A Biographical History* (New York, 1948).

Index

One Day in the Life of Ivan Denisovich, 311
Operation Bagration, 250
Orakhelashvili, M., 180
Ordzhonikidze, P., 194
Ordzhonikidze, Sergo, 8, 20, 41, 53–4, 72–3, 75, 81, 121–2, 135, 168, 186, 188, 198
Orel, 60, 249
Orgburo, *see* Communist Party
Orlemanski, Father, 253
Orlov, A., 186
Orlov, K., 228
Orthodox Church, 3–10, 87, 89, 265, 291, 314
Ostiaks, 26

Paasiviki, J., 216
painting, 148, 231
Palace of Soviets, 157–9, 224, 231
Papinin, I., 206–7
Pasternak, B., 230
Patolichev, N., 214, 243, 270, 273
Patricide, The, 10
Pavletsk, 85
Pavlov, D., 239
Pavlov, I., 246
peasants, 18, 31, 102, 113, 116, 118, 124–32, 274–5
People's Commissariat
  of Defence, 65, 204, 243
  of Justice, 65
  of Nationality Affairs, 40–2, 51–2, 67, 70
  of State Control, 63–4
  of War, 96
  Water Transport, 212
People's Democracy, 284
Pepper, C., 252
Perm, 57, 63
Pestkovsky, S., 51
Peter the Great, 59, 134
Peterson, M., 279
Petrograd, 27–30, 32, 34, 36, 39–41, 43–5, 50, 58
Philosophy of an Epoch, The' (Zinoviev), 96
Piatakov, G., 75, 108, 145, 189–94
Picasso, P., 280
Pilniak, B., 102–3
Pissa River, 221
Plekhanov, G. V., 10, 13–14, 18, 246
Poincaré, R., 134

Poland, 52, 59, 61–2, 72, 134, 193, 221–3, 284–7
  and World War II, 253, 259–62
Polish Committee of National Liberation, 261
police, Soviet, 54, 57, 105, 115, 170, 173, 176, 178, 184–6, 190–1, 194, 211–12, 299, 308
police, tsarist, 17–18, 21–2, 25–6
Politburo, *see* Communist Party
Popov, G., 295
Poskrebyshev, A., 166, 277, 301
Pospelov, P., 310
Postyshev, P., 186, 195–6, 198, 203, 213
Potsdam conference, 252, 258, 281–2
Prague, 22
Pravda, edited by S., 23–4, 28, 30, 35, 38–9
Preobrazhensky, E., 118, 121, 184
Provisional Government, 27–36, 38
Pushkin, A., 193, 201, 246
Putna, V., 203–4

Questions of Leninism, 90, 97

Rabkrin, 64, 75, 77, 80
Radek, K., 103, 120, 155–6, 184, 189, 192–3, 204
Ramadze, G. A., 4
Rapallo treaty, 217
Ratisbor, 253
Razin, 275
Red Army, 53, 55–63, 96, 105, 129, 132, 147, 203–5, 222, 224, 236–7, 239, 241–51
Redens, S., 270
Repin, I., 246
'Reply to Collective Farm Comrades', 130–1
Reston, J., 280, 290
Revolution (1905), 16–17
Revolution (1917), 27–40, 42, 48, 65, 74, 91–3, 96, 98, 105, 110, 125, 147, 156, 245
Revolutionary Military Council of the Republic, 65
Ribbentrop, J., 220–3, 225–6, 314
Riga, 59
Rigby, T., 200
Riutin, M., 145–6, 175
Roberts, F. K., 279